Kölner Schriften zum Friedenssicherungsrecht

Cologne Studies on International Peace und Security Law

Études colognaises sur le droit de la paix et de la sécurité internationales

Herausgegeben von/Edited by/Éditées par

Prof. Dr. Dr. h.c. Dr. h.c. Claus Kreß LL.M. (Cambridge)

Band/Volume 20

Fin-Jasper Langmack

Reparation in Transitional Justice

A Normative Framework

Nomos

INSTITUTE FOR
INTERNATIONAL PEACE
AND SECURITY LAW

The Deutsche Nationalbibliothek lists this publication in the Deutsche Nationalbibliografie; detailed bibliographic data are available on the Internet at http://dnb.d-nb.de

Zugl.: Köln, Univ., Diss., 2022

ISBN 978-3-7560-0526-0 (Print)
978-3-7489-3882-8 (ePDF)

British Library Cataloguing-in-Publication Data
A catalogue record for this book is available from the British Library.

ISBN 978-3-7560-0526-0 (Print)
978-3-7489-3882-8 (ePDF)

Library of Congress Cataloging-in-Publication Data

Langmack, Fin-Jasper
Reparation in Transitional Justice
A Normative Framework
Fin-Jasper Langmack
443 pp.
Includes bibliographic references.

ISBN 978-3-7560-0526-0 (Print)
978-3-7489-3882-8 (ePDF)

1st Edition 2023

Published by
Nomos Verlagsgesellschaft mbH & Co. KG
Waldseestraße 3 – 5 | 76530 Baden-Baden
www.nomos.de

Production of the printed version:
Nomos Verlagsgesellschaft mbH & Co. KG
Waldseestraße 3 – 5 | 76530 Baden-Baden

ISBN 978-3-7560-0526-0 (Print)
978-3-7489-3882-8 (ePDF)

DOI https://doi.org/10.5771/9783748938828

Onlineversion
Nomos eLibrary

To my family for their support and inspiration,
especially my parents

Preface

The number of persons that I want to thank for their contribution to this thesis far exceeds the number of words appropriate for a preface. I hope that those not named personally are nonetheless assured of my gratitude.

I am deeply indebted to my supervisor Claus Kreß. He gave me the support I needed while leaving me remarkable academic freedom. Critical parts of this study and other work reflect his insightful input and critique. To be able to rely on his guidance also beyond this project is something I greatly treasure and that I do not take for granted. His gentle and kind spirit is reflected in the "academic family" at his institute. His ability to assemble incredibly talented and kind people gave me the privilege to work in a remarkable team, many of whose members have become close friends, valued discussion partners, as well as perfect companions for many, many coffee breaks. To them and Claus Kreß: Thank you!

I also thank Angelika Nussberger for her swift secondary opinion, for giving me the opportunity to publish a German summary of this thesis in the 2021 Jahrbuch des öffentlichen Rechts, and for all the other support she extended to me over the years.

Legal knowledge and capabilities do not suffice to write a thesis; it also requires resources. Readers shall judge whether the thesis reflects the first two. The full scholarship I received from the Hamburger Stiftung zur Förderung von Wissenschaft und Kultur ensured that I at least had the last. It also ensured that this thesis would be published open access through a generous contribution to the publication costs. The Mercator Fellowship for International Affairs, which took over my financing in 2019/2020, also requires special mention for allowing me to spend a year at the International Criminal Court, the International Center for Transitional Justice, and the European Center for Constitutional and Human Rights. These stays as well as valued discussions with staff members from these institutions strongly influenced my thinking. The additional privilege to spend a year with 24 incredibly interesting and loveable Fellows adds to the gratitude I feel for this very special institution.

Many friends provided important input and support, not all of which I can thank personally here. Gabriel, Leander, Paula, and Tim: Thank you for providing critical input. Susann and Elisa were brave enough to agree to read the entire thing before knowing its scope. An especially heartfelt thank you (and sorry) goes out to them!

Of course, the case studies would not have been possible without all the interviewees that were willing to share their story and insights with me and the persons that helped me during my research stays. That group encompasses more individuals than I imagined before embarking on the research trips. The thesis would have been a very different (and worse) one had it not been for them. I cannot name all of them and not all of them would want to be named. Nevertheless, it is them whom I am most thankful for. For enabling these essential stays through their generous offer to host me at their institutions I thank Ambassador Kanu of the Sierra Leone Institute for International Law and Yesid Reyes and Nathalia Bautista of the Universidad Externado in Bogotá.

Not only per good custom but truly heartfelt do I extend my gratitude to my entire family. Their collective support, love, and reassurance contributed to this thesis probably more than anything. Each of them has been an invaluable source of resilience and inspiration. Luckily, I can say the same of the family that received me so warm-heartedly shortly before starting this project. I could lose many words on each of you but, unfortunately, the length of the foreword should not exceed that of the actual study. I cannot, however, skip two persons that stand out even among this exceptional group of kind and loving people: Heidrun and Wolfgang, your unwavering, unconditional, simply incredible support laid the foundation for everything. There are no words to thank you for that; I simply hope that you know of my deep, deep gratitude. Of course, the special mention of my parents shall not deflect from the important role all other family members played. To you too: A heartfelt thank you!

Lastly, it is a special privilege to share this process with a partner who, in addition to being ever supportive, is such a knowledgeable and talented academic that she inevitably became my most important discussion partner. It is far from ordinary that you tagged along to all the places this PhD took me. It is even more amazing that you let me accompany you on all your adventures. Thank you, and here's too many more of them!

Fin-Jasper Langmack Berlin, 26 October 2022

Overview

Table of Contents

List of Figures

Abbreviations

AC	Appeals Chamber
ACHR	American Convention on Human Rights
ACHPR	African Convention on Human and Peoples' Rights
AComHPR	African Commission on Human and Peoples' Rights
ACtHPR	African Court on Human and Peoples' Rights
AFRC	Armed Forces Revolutionary Council
AP	Additional Protocol
APC	All People's Congress
Art	Article
ASP	Assembly of States Parties
ASR	Articles on State Responsibility
AU	African Union
AUC	Autodefensas Unidas de Colombia
AVRE	Apoyo a Víctimas de Violencia Socio-Politico Recuperación Emocional
AWWA	Amputees and War Wounded Association
Basic Principles	Basic Principles and Guidelines on the Right to a Remedy and Reparation for Victims of Gross Violations of Human Rights Law and Serious Violations of International Humanitarian Law
Ca	Circa
CAJAR	Colectivo de Abogados "José Alvear Restrepo"
CARICOM	Caribbean Community and Common Market
CAT	Committee Against Torture
CCJ	Comisión Colombiana de Juristas
CDF	Civil Defence Forces
CED	Convention / Commission on Enforced Disappearances
CEDAW	Convention / Committee on the Elimination of All Forms of Discrimination Against Women
CERAC	Centro de Recursos Para el Análisis de Conflictos

CERD	Convention / Committee on the Elimination of Racial Discrimination
CESCR	Committee on Economic, Social and Cultural Rights
CEU	Council of the European Union
Cf	Confer (compare)
Ch	Chapter
CHCV	Comisión Histórica del Conflicto y sus Víctimas
CINEP	Centro de Investigación y Educación Popular
CNMH	Centro Nacional de Memoria Histórica
CODHES	Consultoria Para los Derechos Humanos y el Desplazamiento
CoE	Council of Europe
COHRE	Centre on Housing Rights and Evictions
CONPES	Consejo Nacional de Política Económica y Social
CRAV	Centros Regionales de Atención y Reparación a Víctimas
CRC	Convention / Committee on the Rights of the Child
CSMLV	Comisión de Seguimiento y Monitoreo a la Implementación de la Ley 1448 de 2011
DDR	Disarmament, Demobilization and Reintegration
DRC	Democratic Republic of the Congo
ECHR	Convention for the Protection of Human Rights and Fundamental Freedoms (European Convention on Human Rights)
ECJ	European Court of Justice
EComHR	European Commission of Human Rights
ECOSOC	Economic and Social Council
ECOWAS	Economic Community of West African States
ECSR	European Committee of Social Rights
ECtHR	European Court of Human Rights
Ed / Eds	Editor / Editors
EECC	Ehtiopia-Eritrea Claims Commission
e.g.	Exempli gratia (for example)
ELN	Ejército de Liberación Nacional
EPL	Ejército Popular de Liberación

ERE	Estratégia de Recuperación Emocional al Nivel Grupal
Esp	Especially
Et al.	Et alia (and others)
ETS	European Treaty Series
EU	European Union
f. / ff.	Folio (and the following)
FARC-EP	Fuerzas Armadas Revolucionarias de Colombia – Ejército del Pueblo
Final Agreement	Final Agreement to End the Armed Conflict and Build a Stable and Lasting Peace
Fn	Footnote
FPLC	Forces Patriotiques Pour la Liberation du Congo
FRA	Fundamental Rights Agency (European Union Agency for Fundamental Rights)
FRPI	Force de Résistance Patriotique d'Ituri
GC	General Comment
GDP	Gross Domestic Product
HIV	Human Immunodeficiency Virus
HRC	Human Rights Council
HRCom	Human Rights Committee
HRW	Human Rights Watch
IACtHR	Inter-American Court of Human Rights
IAComHR	Inter-American Commission on Human Rights
ICC	International Criminal Court
ICCPR	International Covenant on Civil and Political Rights
ICESCR	International Covenant on Economic, Social and Cultural Rights
ICJ	International Court of Justice
ICMW	International Convention on the Protection of the Rights of All Migrant Workers and Members of Their Families
IComJ	International Commission of Jurists
ICRC	International Committee of the Red Cross
ICTJ	International Center for Transitional Justice
ICSID	International Center for the Settlement of Investment Disputes

ICTR	International Criminal Tribunal for Rwanda
ICTY	International Criminal Tribunal for the Former Yugoslavia
IDMC	Internal Displacement Monitoring Centre
i.e.	Id est (that is)
ILA	International Law Association
ILC	International Law Commission
IOM	International Organization for Migration
IRIN	Integrated Regional Information Network
ITLOS	International Tribunal for the Law of the Sea
IUSCT	Iran-United States Claims Tribunal
LRV	Legal Representative for Victims
M-19	Movimiento de 19 de Abril
MAS	Muerte a Secuestradores
MPTF	Multi-Partner Trust Fund
MSEN	Multi-Sourced Equivalent Norms
NAARC	National African American Reparations Commission
NaCSA	National Commission for Social Action
NASSIT	National Social Security and Assurance Trust
NGO	Non-Governmental Organization
No	Number
NPFL	National Patriotic Front of Liberia
OHCHR	Office of the United Nations High Commissioner for Human Rights
OPCV	Office of Public Counsel for Victims
P	Page
Para	Paragraph
PAPSIVI	Programa de Atención Psicosocial y Salud Integral a Víctimas
PBF	Peacebuilding Fund
PCIJ	Permanent Court of International Justice
PHR	Physicians for Human Rights
PIRC	Plan Integral de Reparación Colectiva
PPP	Programa por la Paz

PrepCom	Preparatory Committee
PTC	Pre-Trial Chamber
PTSD	Post-Traumatic Stress Disorder
RIAA	Reports of International Arbitral Awards
RPE	Rules of Procedure and Evidence
RTDAF	Registro de Tierras Despojadas o Abandonadas Forzosamente
RUF	Revolutionary United Front
RUPTA	Registro Único de Predios y Territorios Abandonados
RUV	Registro Único de Víctimas
SCSL	Special Court for Sierra Leone
Sec	Section
Ser	Series
SIJVRNR	Sistema Integral de Justicia, Verdad, Reparación y No-Repetición
SLA	Sierra Leone Army
SLPP	Sierra Leone People's Party
SLTRC	Sierra Leone Truth and Reconciliation Commission
STD	Sexually Transmitted Disease
STI	Sexually Transmitted Infection
TC	Trial Chamber
TFV	Trust Fund for Victims
TRC	Truth and Reconciliation Commission
TWAIL	Third World Approaches to International Law
UN	United Nations
UNCC	United Nations Compensation Commission
UNDP	United Nations Development Program
UNESCO	United Nations Educational, Scientific and Cultural Organization
UNGA	United Nations General Assembly
UNHCR	United Nations High Commissioner for Refugees
UNSC	United Nations Security Council
UNTS	United Nations Treaty Series
UP	Unión Patriótica

UPC(/RP)	Union de Patriotes Congolais(/Reconciliation et Paix)
URT	Unidad de Restitución de Tierras
USAid	United States Agency for International Development
USD	United States Dollars
VCLT	Vienna Convention on the Law of Treaties
Vol	Volume
VPRS	Victims Participation and Reparations Section
WGEID	Working Group on Enforced or Involuntary Disappearances
WOLA	Washington Office on Latin America
WTO	World Trade Organization
ZDF	Zweites Deutsches Fernsehen

Introduction – The Limits of the Law

> *"Now, for myself, I have these additional things to say: Your definition of Nazi policy as a crime ('criminal guilt') strikes me as questionable. The Nazi crimes, it seems to me, explode the limits of the law; and that is precisely what constitutes their monstrousness [...] [T]his guilt, in contrast to all criminal guilt, oversteps and shatters any and all legal systems."*[1]

Like this, Hannah Arendt responded to Karl Jasper's seminal work "The Question of German Guilt", in which the German philosopher grappled with the consequences of the Shoah.[2] While the quote relates to criminal justice, Arendt had similar things to say about the topic of this book – reparative justice after atrocities:

> *"This was different. [...] Everything else somehow could have been repaired*[3]*. [...] Not this. This should never have happened [...] Something happened, with which we all cannot come to terms anymore."*[4]

Karl Jaspers and Hannah Arendt both wrestled with a complicated question, which 50 years later would come to be categorized as transitional justice: How can and must societies deal with systematic human rights violations? Both were uniquely placed to answer that question: They were not only two larger-than-life philosophers and political theorists.[5] They were also eye-witnesses and survivors of the atrocities committed in the Third Reich. The Nazi regime forced Karl Jaspers to retire from teaching at university

1 Arendt et al., *Hannah Arendt/Karl Jaspers Correspondence, 1926-1969*, 1992, 54.

2 Jaspers, *The Question of German Guilt*, 1961. Jaspers did not restrict the question of guilt to criminal guilt, but placed moral guilt, political guilt and metaphysical guilt alongside it. He assumed that only few Germans wre criminally guilty, a conclusion which did not stand the test of time, as recent findings on the criminal guilt of some of the many low-ranking participants in the crimes of the Nazi-era show. On the scandalous and winding road towards criminal accountability in Germany after the Nuremberg trials see Müller, *Furchtbare Juristen - Die Unbewältigte Vergangenheit der Deutschen Justiz*, 2014, 303 ff.

3 Arendt uses the German term "Wiedergutmachung", which literally translates to "make good again".

4 ZDF, *Günter Gaus "Zur Person" - Interview With Hannah Arendt*, 1964, minute 40 (translation by the author).

5 Arendt rejected the label philosopher and instead saw herself as a political theorist.

in 1937 and banned him from publishing in 1938.[6] Hannah Arendt – an atheist Jew – fled to France. There, the Vichy Regime interned her before she found refuge in the United States.[7] Their difficulties in finding adequate categories to even start comprehending what happened speak volumes about the complexity and inconceivability of mass atrocities. These difficulties persisted when they discussed the law's role in responding to such atrocities: Whereas Jaspers relied on it, Arendt remained skeptical of its utility.[8]

Arendt's doubts are not easily repudiated. Does the law provide adequate categories for what happened in Germany, Rwanda, the former Yugoslavia, or Syria? Or does categorizing these atrocities normalize them, cover their "monstrousness", as Hannah Arendt suggested? May law even help to sanitize atrocities when it allows societies to talk about "deportation", "push-backs", and "their sovereign prerogative to control the border" instead of facing the plain truth that they created the deadliest border in the world?[9] More practically, how does one even repair eight million registered survivors of atrocities committed in more than five decades of internal conflict in Colombia? How does one even repair a single survivor in Sierra Leone who suffered sexualized violence, forced amputation, was displaced, and lost their[10] family? Is it possible, or is it something "with which we cannot come to terms anymore"?

Many scholars follow Arendt in doubting that law can provide meaningful guidance in response to atrocities. They claim that transitional justice situations[11] are too diverse and too complex to be subjected to regulation.[12] Their arguments point to important truths and raise doubts which are difficult

6 Thornhill/Miron, *Karl Jaspers*, in: Zalta (ed.), *The Stanford Encyclopedia of Philosophy*, Online Edition 2020.

7 Young-Bruehl, *Hannah Arendt - For Love of the World*, 2nd Revised Edition 2004, 115 ff.

8 Naturally, their positions were more complex than that. See their brilliant discussion of the Eichmann trial in Arendt et al., *Hannah Arendt/Karl Jaspers Correspondence, 1926-1969*, 410 ff.

9 IOM, *Four Decades of Cross-Mediterranean Undocumented Migration to Europe - A Review of the Evidence*, 2017, 1.

10 This book uses the singular they to refer to persons of all genders. On this use of they see Merriam-Webster, *They – Pronoun*, Online Edition 2021; Merriam-Webster, *Words We're Watching - Singular "They"*.

11 For the definition see below, C. and ch. 3.

12 Falk, *Reparations, International Law, and Global Justice - A New Frontier*, in: de Greiff (ed.), *The Handbook of Reparations*, 2006, 478, 486 f.; Carrillo, *Justice in Context - The Relevance of Inter-American Human Rights Law and Practice to Repairing the Past*, in: de Greiff (ed.), *The Handbook of Reparations*, 2006, 504, 508 f.; de Greiff, *Justice and Reparations*, in: de Greiff (ed.), *Handbook of Reparations*, 2006, 451, 156.

to dissolve. However, the claim that transitional justice situations are too diverse and context-sensitive is not convincing. Human rights regulate the most politically sensitive questions societies ask themselves all over the globe. Answers to immigration, surveillance, abortion, assisted suicide, etc., vary wildly between states, as do the circumstances under which states give them. Still, the same rights apply to all of them. Diversity and complexity are not unique to transitional justice; it is a fundamental reality of human rights in general – which do not cease to apply to a situation because it is complex.[13] Advocating for the law's retreat also comes with unwanted consequences: It leaves reparation for systematic human rights violations solely to the political process. Survivors usually do not occupy a central place in domestic political discourses. Often, they are marginalized and discriminated against. Their claims can easily be framed to stand in the way of national recovery and economic progress. Leaving the question of reparation to the political discourse thus risks that survivors' legitimate claim is sacrificed on the altar of alleged greater societal goals.[14] While law alone cannot prevent that, it can play an essential role in strengthening survivors' position.

But even if that were unnecessary because of a society's genuine commitment to repair survivors, a lack of legal guidance can lead to frustration nonetheless. Everyone might agree that survivors deserve adequate reparation. Nevertheless, different actors mean different things when referring to adequacy. The state might claim that it provided adequate reparation because

13 This sentiment was echoed by several judges of the ECtHR in, ECtHR, *Georgia v. Russia (II) – Joint partly Dissenting Opinion of Juges Yudkivska, Wojtyczek and Chantura*, 38263/08 (Grand Chamber), 2021, para 9: "In our view, the role of this Court consists precisely in dealing in priority with difficult cases characterised by 'the large number of alleged victims and contested incidents, the magnitude of the evidence produced, the difficulty in establishing the relevant circumstances.'" With that they answered the questionable majority holding that the ECtHR had no jurisdiction in situations of armed conflict, ECtHR, *Georgia v. Russia (II)*, 38263/08 (Grand Chamber), 2021, para 141 ff. Since the judgment is concerned with the question whether effective control establishing jurisdiction is possible in armed conflict, it does not speak against the applicability of human rights to difficult situations. For a critique of the judgment see Duffy, *Georgia v. Russia – Jurisdiction, Chaos and Conflict at the European Court of Human Rights*, JustSecurity, 2 February 2021. Similar sentiments concerning the role of law and, relatedly, international courts in politically sensitive environments were issued by the ICJ and ICC, ICJ, ICJ, *Advisory Opinion on the Legality of the Threat or Use of Nuclear Weapons*, I.C.J. Reports 1996, 226, para 13; ICC, *Situation in the State of Palestine, Decision on the 'Prosecution Request Pursuant to Article 19(3) for a Ruling on the Court's Territorial Jurisdiction in Palestine'*, ICC-01/18-143 (PTC I), 2021, para 55 ff.

14 For details see below, ch. 4, B.

allegedly, it did the best it could do in light of society's multiple urgent needs in transitional situations. For survivors, reparation might nevertheless be inadequate because it does not even begin to repair their harm. In the end, this equivocation hinders any agreement on how to repair survivors adequately. Again, the law alone cannot solve this problem. But it can help overcome an equivocation by providing a common language in which claims for more or less or different reparation can be justified, criticized, and scrutinized. Thereby, the law can help to enable rational debate about the adequacy of reparation and, with that, a fruitful political process.

Thus, one should not prematurely abandon the law on reparation in transitional justice situations. But applying it as is to reparation in transitional justice is unfeasible. The international law on reparation is geared towards repairing isolated human rights violations through individual proceedings. It seeks to remedy all harm an individual sustained. As a result, courts frequently award amounts of reparation that, if scaled up to the number of survivors of mass atrocities, would exceed the state's abilities – leading to the absurd scenario that the state could not perform any function but to repair survivors. In addition, the sheer number of survivors would overwhelm the capacity of any ordinary judiciary. Apart from these practical concerns, disaggregating all violations into single torts and dealing with them in isolated court cases would hide the "monstrousness" of systematic human rights violations, namely their systematic and political nature. That is why most states in transitional justice situations opt to create large-scale administrative reparation programs. While much better equipped than the judiciary to handle the situation, states rarely provide sound legal justifications for the many deviations from the international law on reparation they undertake to make these programs work. Often, the perceived arbitrariness of their choices creates frustration and tension among survivors and general society, which can threaten the process of transition.

Neither Jasper's approach to use existing law nor Arendt's stance that the situation is beyond the law's capacity, therefore, provide a satisfying solution to the question of how to repair mass atrocities. So, what else is there? This book attempts to carefully adjust the existing international law on reparation to the exigencies of transitional justice. It will explore the differences between reparation under "normal" circumstances and in transitional justice. It will analyze how the international law on reparation – firmly based on the former situation – can be adapted to the latter. In the process, this study must acknowledge that reparation programs, as any transitional justice mechanism, navigate two worlds: The legal world of individual reparative justice and the political world of the transition. Since reparation is the only transitional justice mechanism directly catering to survivors, the two worlds often stand in striking contrast, forcefully pulling in opposite directions.[15] Yet, neither world can provide true justice alone, and the law must enable a balance between both.

With that in mind, this book aims to provide viable legal guidance to reparation programs in transitional justice situations. Viability presupposes that legal standards accommodate the transition's political aims, can be adapted to different contexts and can still provide meaningful guidance to achieve reparative justice. This endeavor might be naïvely optimistic. To make it less so, this introduction will continue with some remarks on the risks of relying on the law in transitional justice and the limited role law must play to mitigate those risks (A.). To further manage the reader's expectations, a delimitation of the topic fill follow (B.). Lastly, the introduction will clarify the terminology used in this study (C.) and provide an outline (D.) to prepare the reader for what is to come.

A. *The Modesty of the Law*

Legalistic approaches to transitional justice have been rightfully criticized for their narrow focus and blind spots.[16] Often emanating from human rights law, they suffer from the same defects, in that they are decidedly based in Western thought.[17] Accordingly, they tend to hegemonialize Western values and often impose them on societies of the Global South with little regard

15 Exploring these different dimensions of reparation and their relationship, Moffett, *Reparations in Transitional Justice - Justice or Political Compromise?*, 2017 Hum. Rts. Intl. Legal Discourse 11(1), 59.

16 See below, Conclusion, E. Generally on transitional justice, van der Meerwe/Moyo, *Transitional Justice for Colonial Era Abuses and Legacies - African versus European Policy Priorities*, in: Kaleck/Bergsmo/Hlaing (eds.), *Colonial Wrongs and Access to International Law*, 2020, 41, 44 ff.

17 Mutua, *Human Rights - A Political and Cultural Critique*, 2002, 39 ff.; Mutua, *Savages, Victims, and Saviors - The Metaphor of Human Rights*, 2001 Harvard Hum. Rts. J. 42(1), 201, 204 ff., 209 ff.; Mutua, *The Ideology of Human Rights*, 1995 Va. J. Intl. L. 36(3), 589, 592 ff., 604 ff.; Chimni, *Third World Approaches to International Law - A Manifesto*, 2006 Intl. Comm. L. Rev. 8(1), 3, 11, 16 f.; Rajagopal, *Counter-Hegemonic International Law - Rethinking Human Rights and Development as a Third World Strategy*, 2006 Third World Q. 27(5), 767, 769 ff.

for local fit.[18] Transitional justice is especially prone to that risk. It is a transformative project, which aims at reengineering societies towards general respect for human rights. As Mutua put it, transitional justice mechanisms "carry a definite vision of the society they seek to create."[19] To be sure, this does not render transitional justice an unjust or imperial project per se. Nevertheless, it warrants a cautious approach, reflecting whether the vision transitional justice transports in any concrete situation fits the context. Too often, the "definite vision" focuses strongly on exceptional, visible violence and responds by enforcing individual rights of bodily integrity and freedom. As a result, they snub economic, social, and cultural rights and their more substantial focus on equality and structural violence.[20] At its worst, transitional justice can even serve to legitimize structural violence by marking an exact temporal order of a "before", a "transition", and the following allegedly just state after it.[21] These blind spots often translate into a limited role of the Global North as the creator of supposedly universal standards and a financier of their global implementation. Rarely do transitional justice mechanisms examine the Global North or the International Community's role in the violence they respond to.[22] It is even rarer that transitional justice mechanisms are implemented to respond to atrocities committed by or in

18 Mutua, *What is the Future of Transitional Justice?*, 2015 Intl. J. Transitional Just. 9(1), 1, 3 ff.; Nagy, *Transitional Justice as Global Project - Critical Reflections*, 2008 Intl. J. Transitional Just. 29(2), 275, 275; Jamar, *The Crusade of Transitional Justice - Tracing the Journeys of Hegemonic Claims*, in: The British Academy (ed.), *Violence and Democracy*, 2019, 53, 54 ff.; Lundy/McGovern, *The Role of Community In Participatory Transitional Justice*, in: McEvoy/McGregor (eds.), *Transitional Justice From Below - Grassroots Activism and the Struggle for Change*, 2008, 99, 103.

19 Mutua, *What is the Future of Transitional Justice?*, 3.

20 Nagy, *Transitional Justice as Global Project*, 278; Arbour, *Economic and Social Justice for Societies in Transition*, 2007 N.Y.U. J. Intl. L. Pol. 40(1), 1, 2 ff.; van der Meerwe/Moyo, *Transitional Justice for Colonial Era Abuses and Legacies*, 52 ff. On this study's approach to economic, social and cultural rights see below, ch. 4, C.I, E.II.4.c.

21 Nagy, *Transitional Justice as Global Project*, 280; Similarly Orford, *Commissioning the Truth*, 2006 Colum. J. Gender & L. 15(3), 851, 862 f.

22 Nagy, *Transitional Justice as Global Project*, 280; Hayner, *Unspeakable Truths - Transitional Justice and the Challenge of Truth Commissions*, 2nd Edition 2011, 78 f. Similarly, Orford, *Commissioning the Truth*, 862 f. The EU transitional justice framework is a striking example, as it is understood exclusively as a foreign policy instrument, CEU, *The EU's Policy Framework on Support to Transitional Justice*, 13576/15 Annex to Annex, 2015, 10; CEU, *Council Conclusions on EU's Support to Transitional Justice*, 13576/15 Annex, 2015, para 8; van der Meerwe/Moyo, *Transitional Justice for Colonial Era Abuses and Legacies*, 59 f., 64.

the Global North, such as slavery, colonialism, or more recent aggressions.[23] Despite all these risks, the current book adopts a strictly legal approach to transitional justice nonetheless. That is mainly because it is the only thing the author feels (somewhat) qualified to write about, but also because their shortcomings do not render legalistic approaches to transitional justice useless. Acknowledging what they can and cannot do is, however, crucial to making them useful.

Correctly understood, the law itself demands the illumination of some of transitional justice's blind spots. This study will be based on the human right to reparation. This right pertains to any survivor of any violation, anywhere at any time. It pertains to violations of economic, social, and cultural rights through structural violence.[24] It also demands redress for violations committed by the Global North or the International Community through their involvement in systematic human rights violations in the Global South or atrocities committed on their territory. Fortunately, some transitional justice measures make first attempts to honor this true universality of the standards underlying transitional justice.[25]

Still, any legalistic approach to reparation would be ill-founded if it failed to account for its severe limitations. First, it presents only one of many obligations a state must fulfill towards the persons under its jurisdiction.

---

23 This fact is impressively visualized by Jamar, *The Crusade of Transitional Justice*, 55; Nagy, *Transitional Justice as Global Project*, 281 f.; Orford, *Commissioning the Truth*, 863. For reasons laid out below, B., this study is not concerned with the debate whether there is an obligation to repair and a corresponding right to receive reparation. The author is of the conviction though that even should there be no such obligation or right, transitional justice mechanisms can serve valuable purposes in addressing historical injustices.

24 See below, ch. 4, C.I.

25 Sierra Leone's Truth and Reconciliation Commission dealt in great length with the country's colonial past and the involvement of external actors in the conflict, SLTRC, *Witness to Truth - Final Report of the Truth and Reconciliation Commission*, 2004, vol. 3a, 5 ff.; vol. 3b, 57 ff. Mechanisms that dealt with atrocities committed by or in the Global North are for example, Mauritius Truth and Justice Commission, *Report of the Truth and Justice Commission Vol. 1*, 2011; CARICOM Reparations Commission, *10-Point Reparation Plan*, 2014; Canada, *Honouring the Truth, Reconciling the Future - Summary of the Final Report of the Truth and Reconciliation Commission of Canada*, 2015; Magarrell/Wesley, *Learning from Greensboro - Truth and Reconciliation in the United States*, 2008, 121 ff. It is telling that the Greensboro TRC originated from civil society and was not state-sponsored. For a critical appraisal of the broader context of Canada's transitional justice policy see Kiyani, *Avoidance Techniques – Accounting for Canada's Colonial Crimes*, in: Kaleck/Bergsmo/Hlaing (eds.), *Colonial Wrongs and Access to International Law*, 2020, 501, 510 ff.

Even though reparation can and must address structural violence, it does so in a particular form, always mediated through individually experienced harm. Its fulfillment thus does not make a just society. Accordingly, one should not burden reparation with such expectations.[26] More importantly, the nature of states' legal obligations must be correctly understood. They provide a baseline below which the state must not fall. This baseline does not prescribe the best, maybe not even a good reparation effort; it prescribes a legal reparation effort. Relatedly, the law can provide nothing more than a framework. Transitional justice situations present themselves in all shapes and forms. They range from Sierra Leone's recovery from a decade-long civil war with limited resources and a lack of vital infrastructure to Canada's response to its Indian Residential Schools.[27] There is no one-size-fits-all reparation scheme that adequately addresses legacies of all types of systematic human rights violations from the United States through Spain and Syria to Myanmar. Reparation efforts are only successful if they are tailored to the contexts they operate in.[28] Legal standards covering these vastly different situations must allow for discretion to enable viable, effective solutions. Therefore, they cannot serve as a blueprint, precisely laying out who must receive what in which way. To a degree, reparation will always remain a matter to be resolved through the political process. To paraphrase Méndez, the law must provide a framework for that process, not a straightjacket.[29] Other actors must fill this framework with creativity and ingenuity to make meaningful and effective reparation a reality in transitional justice. Law cannot prescribe these qualities. It can only open a space for other actors to develop them. Local actors, including survivors, best take up this role. They know how to address their situation best.[30]

With all that in mind, this book will yield a modest but important result: A legal baseline, below which states must not fall, which creates a space for the

26 This stands in contrast to many eminent scholars of reparation. For their proposal of so-called "transformative reparation" and this author's repudiation of their proposal see below, ch. 4, E.I.

27 Scholars debate whether Canada truly is an example of transitional justice. It will be argued below, ch. 3, A., why the author thinks that it is.

28 Fletcher et al., *Context, Timing and the Dynamics of Transitional Justice – A Historical Perspective*, 2009 Hum. Rts. Q. 31(1), 163, 208 f.; AU, *Transitional Justice Policy*, 2019, para 35 ff.

29 Méndez, *Peace, Justice and Prevention - Dilemmas and False Dilemmas*, in: Bleeker (ed.), *Dealing with the Past and Transitional Justice - Creating Conditions for Peace, Human Rights and the Rule of Law*, 2006, 15, 17.

30 See also below, Conclusion, F.

creativity and ingenuity needed to make reparation work in a wide variety of challenging circumstances.

B. Delimitation of the Topic

Naturally, one book cannot cover every aspect of such a broad topic. Delimiting the inquiry into a fascinating subject is painful but necessary; doing it explicitly is crucial. To quote Said, "there is no such thing as a merely given, or simply available, starting point: beginnings have to be made", and the act of choosing a beginning "necessarily involves an act of delimitation."[31] This choice results in aspects of the studied object remaining in the dark. This sad fact easily reproduces hegemonic narratives and research agendas.

Four limitations narrow down the focus of the present endeavor. The first was already mentioned: It employs a strictly legalistic approach, focusing on the legal baseline and nothing more. Second, the book takes a human rights approach and therefore excludes inter-state reparation.[32] Third, the book deals exclusively with state responsibility for human rights violations. It does not cover reparation for violations committed by non-state actors and, more generally, how non-state actors can be held liable. Lastly, the book focuses on what makes reparation programs adequate. It largely ignores questions about when the obligation to repair arises. The analysis hence only starts after state responsibility for human rights violations is established. That the state bears such responsibility in situations the present study could apply to is presumed. Sadly, that assumption is reasonable. Many, if not most human rights violations happening in times of conflict can be attributed to the state because state agents committed them or because the state failed to protect or fulfill the human rights of persons on its territory or under its jurisdiction.

These delimitations – legalistic approach, human rights and state focus, and presumption of an obligation to repair – reproduce a dominant transitional justice narrative. As will be further elaborated on below, transitional justice focuses on state-sponsored bodily integrity violations in the recent past.[33] This focus is a natural consequence of uncritically applied legalistic approaches to transitional justice. To take reparation as an example, surviv-

31 Said, *Orientalism*, 2019, 16.

32 For that see Günnewig, *Schadensersatz Wegen der Verletzung des Gewaltverbotes als Element Eines Ius Post Bellum*, 2019.

33 van der Meerwe/Moyo, *Transitional Justice for Colonial Era Abuses and Legacies*, 44 f.

ors' right to reparation relies on a primary violation of a human right. This fact alone lets colonial wrongs fade from view. The principle of intertemporality and other doctrines establish barriers to claim reparation that are difficult (albeit not impossible) to surmount.[34] Attention to single violations of primary rights shifts attention away from larger unjust structures as the violations' conditions of possibility. Reparation's basis in state responsibility moves attention away from the role of private actors. Although many private acts come into the purview of that basis because they are attributable to the state, it leaves uncovered private acts less directly causing human rights violations, such as economic profiteering and their interplay with the previously mentioned unjust structures.

All this is not to say that the concept of reparation should be discarded. Attention to its defects should not serve to discredit its merits. Instead, critical attention can illuminate new, constructive ways to overcome deficiencies. This study will attempt to do so where pertinent.

34 On the principle of intertemporality in colonial contexts, Kämmerer, *Colonialism,* in: Wolfrum (ed.), *Max Planck Encyclopedia of Public International Law,* 2018, para 27 f. On reparation for colonial wrongs, du Plessis, *Historical Injustice and International Law - An Exploratory Discussion of Reparation for Slavery,* 2003 Hum. Rts. Q. 25(3), 624; UNGA, *Contemporary Forms of Racism, Racial Discrimination, Xenophobia and Racial Intolerance - Note by the Secretary-General,* A/74/321, 2019, 45 ff.; Theurer/Kaleck, *Dekolonialisierung des Rechts - Ambivalenzen und Potenzial,* in: Theurer/Kaleck (eds.), *Dekoloniale Rechtskritik und Rechtspraxis,* 2020, 11, 39 ff. For an interestin proposal to loosen the principle of intertemporality in cases of historical injustices see von Arnauld, *How to Illegalize Past Injustice – Reinterpreting the Rules of Intertemporality,* 2021 Eur. J. Intl. L. 32(2), 401. For early examples of individual reparation see Musa, *Victim Reparation Under the Ius Post Bellum - An Historical and Normative Perspective,* 2018. The successor regime problem, which takes a prominent place in many debates about historic reparation, poses a surmountable problem from a legal perspective. Continuity is the norm in international law. A mere regime change, however dramatic it plays out in practice, usually does not change the state's responsibility. For a discussion of the problem see Gray, *Extraordinary Justice,* 2010 Ala. L. Rev. 62, 55, 60. On succession generally see Crawford, *Brownlie's Principles of Public International Law,* 9th Edition 2019, 409 ff. This study's findings might also be applicable to historic injustices, if the responsible states find the courage to redress them. That this book is by no means necessary to devise promising reparation proposals for historical injustices is aptly demonstrated, e.g., by the CARICOM Reparations Commission, *10-Point Reparation Plan* or NAARC, *Preliminary Reparations Program – A Document for Review, Revision and Adoption as a Platform to Guide the Struggle for Reprations for People of African Descent in the U.S.,* 2015, 3 ff.

C. Terminology

Before starting the actual inquiry, a few words on terminology and some preliminary definitions shall help orient the reader in what is to come. The international law on reparation as well as transitional justice suffer from inconsistent use of terminology. This often creates misunderstandings, lets differences appear more significant than they are and obfuscates the law's content.[35] To prevent this book from contributing to that confusion, it will clearly define its usage of terms and mention alternative terms where pertinent.

Of course, the notion of reparation is central to this book. While seldom defined explicitly, international practice and scholarship agree on its central elements. Reparation is a benefit a survivor receives from a person or entity responsible for a human rights violation. It is supposed to erase the harm the survivor incurred because of that violation and comes with an acknowledgment of responsibility of the responsible entity or person.[36] In line with these attributes and the state-centered, legalistic approach taken in this study, reparation is defined as:

Any benefit the state gives to a survivor to remedy the harm it caused by violating their human rights in acknowledgment of its responsibility for said violation.[37]

---

35 Haasdijk, *The Lack of Uniformity in the Terminology of the International Law of Remedies*, 1992 Leiden J. Intl. L. 5(2), 245; Wood, *The Rights of Victims to Reparation - The Importance of Clear Thinking*, 2018 Heidelberg J. Intl. L. 78(3), 541, 541.

36 UNGA, *Basic Principles and Guidelines on the Right to a Remedy and Reparation for Victims of Gross Violations of International Human Rights Law and Serious Violations of International Humanitarian Law*, A/RES/60/147, 2005, para 15 ff.; HRC, *Report of the Special Rapporteur on the Promotion of Truth, Justice, Reparation and Guarantees of Non-Recurrence*, A/HRC/42/45, 2019, para 29 f.; HRC, *Report of the Special Rapporteur on the Promotion of Truth, Justice, Reparation and Guarantees of Non-Recurrence, Pablo de Greiff*, A/69/518, 2014, para 11; Shelton, *Remedies in International Human Rights Law*, 3rd Edition 2015, 16 ff.; Moffett, *Justice for Victims Before the International Criminal Court*, 2014, 145; de Greiff, *Justice and Reparations*, 453; Roht-Arriaza/Orlovsky, *A Complementary Relationship - Reparations and Development*, in: de Greiff/Duthie (eds.), *Transitional Justice and Development - Making Connections*, 2009, 170, 172; Shelton, *Reparations*, in: Wolfrum (ed.), *Max Planck Encyclopedia of Public International Law*, Online Edition 2009, para 1; IACtHR, *Compendium – Truth, Justice and Reparation in Transitional Context: Inter-American Standards*, OEA/Ser.L/V/II.Doc. 121, 2021, para 165. Acknowledgment is not part of all definitions, yet it is needed to clearly distinguish reparation from other benefits a state might give individuals, see below, ch. 4, E.II.2.

37 The definition will receive further explanation and concretization in ch. 1.

The book employs the term "reparation", not "reparations", as the latter often denotes inter-state payments after an armed conflict.[38] The singular shall also draw attention to the fact that reparation is a holistic concept, not a random aggregate of reparation measures.

In contrast to reparation, there are almost as many definitions of transitional justice as scholars dedicated to the topic. For that reason, this study cannot rely on a commonly accepted definition of the term. Instead, in chapter three, the author will develop his definition of transitional justice, which relies heavily on the work of Pablo de Greiff, former Special Rapporteur of the United Nations (UN) on the topic. The definition will be derived from the consensual assumption that transitional justice addresses a legacy of systematic human rights violations. Since such systematic violations erode society's trust in a shared normative commitment to human rights, the violations question the validity of human rights as such. Transitional justice should address these consequences by aiming to restore respect for human rights and generalized trust in a shared normative commitment to human rights in society. Based on this, transitional justice is defined as:

A state's attempt to address a legacy of systematic human rights violations, which aims to transform society towards strengthened respect for human rights and generalized trust. The latter is defined as the expectation that other members of society and state institutions adhere to and support human rights.

The definition will receive more clarification and further specification later. For now, it shall only give the reader a rough idea of what the following chapters mean using the term "transitional justice". Based on the definition, the study will often use the terms "transitional justice environment", "transitional justice situation", "transitional situation", "transitional justice context", "transitional context", and "transitional society" interchangeably for:

A situation in the aftermath of systematic human rights violations, which calls for transitional justice measures that enhance respect for human rights and generalized trust.

38 Wood, *The Rights of Victims to Reparation*, 541 f. Others equate reparations with compensation, using reparation for a more holistic approach, Torpey, *Victims and Citizens – The Discourse of Reparation(s) at the Dawn of the New Millenium*, in: de Feyter et al. (eds.), *Out of the Ashes – Reparation for Victims of Gross and Systematic Human Rights Violations*, 35, 38 ff.

Since an entire chapter will be dedicated to the development and justification of these definitions, they will not receive any more explanation at this point. Interested – as well as bewildered or disgruntled – readers are invited to skip to chapter three. The definition must be followed, however, with a note of caution. The transitional justice situation will be juxtaposed frequently to the "stable situation" or "stable circumstances" – defined negatively as situations that do not fall under the abovementioned definition of transitional justice. This dichotomy underlies the project to adapt legal standards based on the "stable situation" to the transitional justice situation. Of course, though, the two situations cannot be neatly separated. Many developments in the international law on reparation – which this study treats as pertaining to the "stable situation" – even originated in transitional justice contexts. The reader is invited to regard that rough juxtaposition as a mental guide rail the author lamentably needs to develop his thoughts; a useful tool, which should guide thinking, but not blind it to the messiness of reality, which rarely corresponds to academic categories.

Lastly, instead of "victim", the book employs the term "survivor". Survivor is a more empowering term, emphasizing a survivor's journey instead of reducing them to a passive subject of a violation. The term corresponds better to the values embodied in human rights law and the vital role survivors play in transitional justice processes and other human rights mechanisms worldwide. Furthermore, the term somewhat evades a binary categorization of persons as "victims" and "perpetrators", which cannot capture the complex biographies conflicts create, in which many persons become both.[39] Since it is semantically difficult to be a survivor of a fatal human rights violation, the study still uses "victim" when referring to persons who died because of a human rights violation. For reasons of simplicity, it still uses "survivors" when referring to a group of people who suffered a human rights violation, within which only some died because of a violation.

---

39 Caswell, *Toward a Survivor-Centered Approach to Records Documenting Human Rights Abuse - Lessons From Community Archives*, 2014 Archival Sci. 14(3), 307, 308; UN Division for the Advancement of Women, *Good practices in Combating and Eliminating Violence Against Women - Report of the Expert Group Meeting*, 2005, fn. 1; UNHCR, *Sexual and Gender-Based Violence against Refugees, Returnees and Internally Displaced Persons - Guidelines for Prevention and Response*, 2003, 6; Lewis, *Systemic Silencing - Addressing Sexual Violence Against Men and Boys in Armed Conflict and its Aftermath*, in: Heathcote/Otto (eds.), *Rethinking Peacekeeping, Gender Equality and Collective Security*, 2014, 203, fn. 2; Assmann, *Der Lange Schatten der Vergangenheit – Erinnerungskultur und Geschichtspolitik*, 4th Edition 2021, 72 ff.

D. Outline

With the basic notions and some of the author's peculiar terminology explained, the inquiry will proceed as follows: Chapter one will systematize existing legal standards on reparation. Drawing from a broad range of international practice – mostly international judgments and soft law documents – the notion of full reparation emerges as a universally accepted standard for reparation under stable circumstances. All harm a human rights violation caused must be repaired through restitution, compensation, rehabilitation, satisfaction, and guarantees of non-repetition, to put the survivor in the position they would be in had the violation not occurred. With that, the chapter establishes a baseline, which the last chapter will adjust to the transitional justice context.

That adjustment cannot occur without a thorough understanding of what reparation in transitional justice is and what difficulties it faces – a task taken up by chapters two and three. Chapter two contains three in-depth case studies of six reparation programs: Sierra Leone, Colombia, and the reparation programs of the International Criminal Court (ICC) in the Lubanga, Katanga, Al Mahdi, and Ntaganda cases. The case studies are based on research and interviews conducted in Sierra Leone, Colombia, and at the ICC between 2018 and 2020. They identify points at which the exigencies of the transitional justice situation warrant deviations from the legal standards established in chapter 1. The case studies were chosen according to the logic of maximum variety sampling to reduce the risks associated with drawing general conclusions from few cases only.[40] Sierra Leone and Colombia lie at opposite ends of many relevant indicators: Colombia runs the most comprehensive reparation program in the world to date and has considerable resources to do so. Sierra Leone, in contrast, battled with resource constraints and only managed to repair survivors with minimal benefits. The study of the ICC serves a control purpose. Even though reparation at the court is not based on state responsibility and not primarily on human rights, its reparation efforts can still be compared to those of Sierra Leone and Colombia. All three take place in transitional justice settings and are therefore confronted with similar challenges. The definite differences between them can be accounted for in the analysis. Studying reparation efforts in a completely different institutional and legal context allows for weeding out deviations from the international law on reparation that are not rooted in the exigencies of

40 Patton, *Qualitative Research and Evaluation Methods*, 2015, 283.

the transitional justice situation. To further reduce the risk associated with drawing conclusions from few cases, these conclusions will be tied back to assumptions about the transitional justice situation. A cursory look at a broader range of state practices complements the in-depth studies and supports the final findings.

Chapter three provides the theoretical background to the notion of transitional justice and the role of reparation in it. It develops the definition above of transitional justice. It argues for two different roles reparation must fulfill in transitional contexts; a deontological role in providing survivors with corrective justice and an instrumental role in furthering transitional justice aims. It concludes with an account of how reparation can accomplish the latter.

Chapter four is the heart of the book, attempting to adapt the international law on reparation to the transitional justice situation. For that, it relies on established techniques of legal interpretation, directed along two guide rails. On the one hand, the legal standards for reparation in stable situations established in chapter one anchor the analysis in existing international law. On the other hand, the empirical and theoretical findings of chapters two and three guide the analysis towards the issues in transitional justice, for which the existing legal standards prove inadequate. The chapter analyses every stage of a reparation program, from determining eligibility to the intake procedure, the program's scope, content, and structure, all the way to how – and if – a reparation program can end.

With that, this book provides a viable legal baseline, below which states must not fall and which opens the space for the creativity and ingenuity necessary to make reparation work under challenging circumstances. Thereby, the book shows that reparation in transitional justice does not "explode the limits of the law", although, admittedly, it does test them.

Chapter 1 – The International Law on Reparation

Any search must start somewhere – the search for norms governing reparation in transitional justice being no exception. Since the present study is restricted to state reparation efforts towards individuals, an individual right to reparation provides a natural starting point. It conceptualizes the relationship between the decisive actors and anchors the analysis in human rights law, which is central to transitional justice.[41] Hence, the present chapter will start by tracing the existence of a human right to reparation (A.). Many decisions by international courts, tribunals, bodies, as well as numerous soft law instruments and scholarship, gave shape to this right. They converge towards a set of principles, defining how to repair survivors of human rights violations. These principles govern who (B.) receives what (C.) as reparation and place limits on the reparation to be awarded (D.). They find their philosophical basis in Aristotelian corrective justice (E.). Collectively, these principles form the international law on reparation. Subsequent chapters will show that its focus on singular human rights violations makes it a highly imperfect legal basis for reparation in transitional justice. Nevertheless, it provides a legal basis, which can be adapted to the exigencies of transitional justice. With that purpose in mind, the present chapter does not endeavor to give a comprehensive account of the detailed and complex reparation practice for human rights violations. Instead, it establishes broad principles at the heart of the international law on reparation to provide a stable basis for the subsequent analysis.

A. The Existence of a Right to Reparation

An individual right to reparation can be found primarily in human rights law (I.). Since transitional justice situations revolve around atrocity crimes and often arise out of armed conflict, the fate of reparation in international humanitarian law (II.) and international criminal law (III.) must also receive cursory treatment.

41 See below, ch. 3.

I. International Human Rights Law

No human rights treaty contains a general right to reparation. Some grant a right to reparation for specific violations only.[42] While the regional treaty systems confer the power to grant reparation upon their respective human rights courts, they do not codify a corresponding right.[43] Nevertheless, every human rights court and treaty body recognizes a right to reparation.[44] They were joined most recently by all independent experts of the Human Rights Council (HRC) special procedures in response to George Floyd's death at the hands of the US police in June 2020.[45] They base the existence of a general right to reparation on the right to an effective remedy. The right to an effective remedy is laid down in Art. 2(3) International Covenant on Civil and Political Rights (ICCPR), Art. 14 European Convention on Human Rights (ECHR), Art. 25(1) American Convention on Human Rights (ACHR). The African hu-

---

42 Art. 9(5), 14(6) ICCPR; Art. 3, 5(5) ECHR; Art. 10, 21(2) ACHR; Art. 21(2) ACHPR; Art. 6 CERD; Art. 14(1) CAT; Art. 24(4) CED; Art. 15, 16(9), 18(6), 22(5) ICMW.

43 Art. 41 ECHR; Art. 27(1) Protocol to the ACHPR on the Establishment of the ACtHPR; Art. 63(1) ACHR.

44 IACtHR, *Case of the "Street Children" (Villagrán-Morales et al.) v. Guatemala (Reparations and Costs)*, 2001, para 67; IACtHR, *Garrido and Baigorria v. Argentina (Reparations and Costs)*, 1998, para 40; ACtHPR, *Reverend Christopher R. Mtikila v. The United Republic of Tanzania (Ruling on Reparations)*, 011/2011, 2014, para 29; ACtHPR, *Beneficiaries of Late Norbert Zongo v. Burkina Faso (Judgment on Reparations)*, 013/2011, 2015, para 20; ECOWAS Court of Justice, *Djot Bayi & 14 Others v. Nigeria and 4 Others*, ECW/CCJ/JUD/01/09, 2009, para 45; IAComHR, *Principal Guidelines for a Comprehensive Reparation Policy*, OEA/Ser/L/V/II.131, 2008, para 13; AComHPR, *Noah Kazingachire, John Chitsenga, Elias Chemvura and Batanai Hadzisi (Represented by Zimbabwe Human Rights NGO Forum) v. Zimbabwe*, 295/04, 2012, para 50, 127; AComHPR, *Groupe de Travail sur les Dossiers Judiciaires Stratégiques v. Democratic Republic of Congo*, 259/2002, 2011, para 88; HRCom, *Concluding Observations of the Human Rights Committee - Central African Republic*, CCPR/C/CAF/CO/2, 2006, para 8; HRCom, *Devon Simpson v. Jamaica*, CCPR/C/73/D/695/1996, 695/1996, 2001, para 9; CAT, *E.N. v. Burundi*, CAT/C/56/D/578/2013, 578/2013, 2015, para 7.8; CERD, *V.S. v. Slovakia*, CERD/C/88/D/56/2014, 56/2014, 2015, para 7.4; CEDAW, *General Recommendation No. 28 on the Core Obligations of States Parties Under Article 2 of the Convention on the Elimination of All Forms of Discrimination Against Women*, CEDAW/C/GC/28, 2010, para 32; CRC, *General Comment No. 5 - General Measures of Implementation of the Convention on the Rights of the Child*, CRC/GC/2003/5, 2003, para 24. The ECtHR was the sole dissenting opinion for a long time, largely based on the reluctant wording of Art. 41 ECHR, ECtHR, *Sunday Times v. The United Kingdom (Article 50)*, 6538/74 (Plenary), 1980, para 15. In more recent judgments, it changed its position, ECtHR, *Naït-Liman v. Switzerland*, 51357/07 (Grand Chamber), 2018, para 97.

45 HRC, *Statement on the Protests Against Systemic Racism in the United States*, 2020.

man rights system also recognizes it.[46] It has gained the status of customary international law.[47] Unanimously, international jurisprudence argues that a remedy is not effective if it does not give survivors the possibility to obtain reparation.[48] Measuring a remedy's effectiveness against this possible outcome is in line with the object and purpose of the provision as demanded by Art. 31(1) Vienna Convention on the Law of Treaties (VCLT). Human rights would not be adequately protected if the right to an effective remedy were to encompass nothing but the right to bring a claim. On the contrary, having a violation remedied will be more important to the survivor than the procedure which reaches that outcome.

Tomuschat argues against this approach that the conventions contain explicit rights to reparation for specific violations only, showing that states had no intention to codify a general right to reparation.[49] His position could find support in the reluctant wording of the provisions in the ACHR and the ECHR, which allow the European Court of Human Rights (ECtHR) and ACtHR to award reparation only "if necessary" or "if appropriate" and – in the case of the ECtHR – only on the condition that national law does not provide the possibility to receive reparation.[50] However, the cited articles merely delineate the jurisdiction of the two courts. They have no bearing on the existence of a right to reparation. State parties' intentions, while an essential factor for treaty interpretation, do not determine its outcome. Human rights conventions are living instruments that develop with time through state and judicial practice.[51] State practice, relevant to interpretation according to

46 AComHPR, *Principles and Guidelines on the Right to a Fair Trial and Legal Assistance in Africa*, DOC/OS(XXX)247, 2003, principle C.

47 Shelton, *Human Rights, Remedies*, in: Wolfrum (ed.), *Max Planck Encyclopedia of Public International Law*, Online Edition 2006, para 5 ff., 24.

48 Roht-Arriaza, *Reparations Decisions and Dilemmas*, 2004 Hastings Intl. Comp. L. Rev. 27(2), 157, 160 ff.; HRCom, *General Comment No. 31 - The Nature of the General Legal Obligation Imposed on States Parties to the Covenant*, CCPR/C/21/Rev.1/Add.13, 2004, para 16; IACtHR, *Maria Cristina Reveron Trujillo v. Venezuela*, 2009, para 61 f.; AComHPR, *Principles and Guidelines on the Right to a Fair Trial*, DOC/OS(XXX)247, principle C(b)(ii); ECtHR, *Leander v. Sweden*, 9248/81 (Chamber), 1987, para 77(a). The French version of the judgment uses the less equivocal term "réparation" instead of "redress".

49 Tomuschat, *Reparation for Victims of Grave Human Rights Abuses*, 2002 Tulane J. Intl. Comp. L. 10, 157, 167.

50 Art. 63(1) ACHR; Art. 41 ECHR.

51 ECtHR, *Tyrer v. The United Kingdom*, 5856/72 (Chamber), 1978, para 31; ECtHR, *Magyar Helsinki Bizottság v. Hungary - Concurring Opinion of Judge Sicilianos, Joined by Judge Raimondi*, 18030/11 (Grand Chamber), 2016, para 2 ff.; IACtHR, *Case of the Gómez-Paquiyauri Brothers v. Peru*, 2004, para 165; IACtHR, *Advisory Opinion on the*

Art. 31(3)(b), 32 VCLT, supports the existence of an individual right to reparation. Many states provide comprehensive reparation for human rights violations and support resolutions acknowledging the existence of a right to reparation.[52] While many survivors, especially of large-scale violations, remain unrepaired, the international community often calls for reparation and puts pressure on the responsible states.[53] It is, therefore, on a firm basis that every human rights court, treaty body, and special mechanism recognizes a right to reparation.

With that interpretation of the right to an effective remedy, international practice and scholarship merely apply a general principle long recognized in the law on state responsibility to state responsibility for individual rights violations. The Permanent Court of International Justice (PCIJ) confirmed in its Chorzów Factory Judgment that

> *"it is a principle of international law [...] that any breach of an engagement involves an obligation to make reparation. [...] Reparation is the indispensable*

Right to Information on Consular Assistance in the Framework of the Guarantees of the Due Process of Law, OC-16/99, 1999, para 113 ff.; HRCom, *Roger Judge v. Canada*, CCPR/C/78/D/829/1998, 829/1998, 2003, para 10.3; CERD, *Stephen Hagan v. Australia*, CERD/C/62/D/26/2002, 26/2002, 2003, para 7.3.

52 UNGA, *Basic Principles*, A/RES/60/147, para 11(b); UNGA, *Adverse Consequences for the Enjoyment of Human Rights of Political, Military, Economic and Other Forms of Assistance Given to Colonial and Racist Regimes in Southern Africa*, A/RES/33/23, 1978, para 2; UNGA, *The Situation in Bosnia and Herzegovina*, A/RES/46/242, 1992, para 10; UNGA, *Situation of Human Rights in the Territory of the Former Yugoslavia*, A/RES/47/147, 1992, para 11; UNGA, *Measures to Combat Contemporary Forms of Racism and Racial Discrimination, Xenophobia and Related Intolerance*, A/RES/56/267, 2002, para 29; HRC, *Human Rights and Transitional Justice*, A/HRC/RES/21/15, 2012, para 8(b); HRC, *Human Rights, Democracy and the Rule of Law*, A/HRC/RES/19/36, 2012, para 16(vii); Henckaerts/Doswald-Beck, *Customary International Humanitarian Law Vol. I - Rules*, 2005, 541 ff.; ILA, *The Hague Conference (2010) - Reparation for Victims of Armed Conflict*, 2010, 291, 312 ff. See also the state practice cited in ch. 2 and 4.

53 UNGA, *Situation of Human Rights in the Territory of the Former Yugoslavia - Violations of Human Rights in the Republic of Bosnia and Herzegovina, the Republic of Coratia and the Federal Republic of Yugoslavia (Serbia and Montenegro)*, A/RES/48/153, 1993, para 13; UNGA, *Situation of Human Rights in the Republic of Bosnia and Herzegovina, the Republic of Croatia and the Federal Republic of Yugoslavia (Serbia and Montenegro)*, A/RES/49/196, 1994, para 13; UNGA, *Situation of Human Rights in Afghanistan*, A/RES/51/108, 1996, para 11. For condemnation as evidence for customary international law see ILC, *Draft Conclusions on Identification of Customary International Law - With Commentaries*, A/73/10, 2018, concl. 6 para 2, concl. 10 para 4.

complement of a failure to apply a convention, and there is no necessity for this to be stated in the convention itself."[54]

The ILC codified this principle in Art. 31 of the Articles on the Responsibility of States for Internationally Wrongful Acts (Articles on State Responsibility, ASR), which attained customary status.[55] While the judgment and the ASR concern obligations between states, they emphasize that *any* breach of an engagement warrants reparation.[56] The different nature of the rights holder should not be decisive. Human rights are well-established and occupy a central role in international law today.[57] There is no reason why the general principle should not apply to them. On the contrary, legal logic suggests that the holder of primary rights should benefit from secondary rights common to international law.[58] The International Court of Justice (ICJ) already broadened the obligation to repair and the corresponding right beyond the inter-state realm to include international organizations.[59] Accordingly, all

---

54 PCIJ, *The Factory at Chorzów (Claim for Indemnity) (The Merits)*, P.C.I.J. Series A 17 No. 7, 1928, para 73; See also ICSID, *Amco Asia Corporation and Others v. Republic of Indonesia, Award*, ARB/81/1, 1984, para 266 f.; IACtHR, *Aloeboetoe et al. v. Suriname (Reparation and Costs)*, 1993, para 43; Such a principle finds support in earliest works on international law, Grotius/Campbell, *The Rights of War and Peace - Including the Law of Nature and of Nations*, Autograph Édition de Luxe 1901, book 2, ch 1, para 1; de Vattel, *The Law of Nations*, 1797, book 2, ch 4, para 51.

55 ILC, *Articles on State Responsibility*, A/56/10, 2001, art. 31; ICJ, *Armed Activities on the Territory of the Congo (Democractic Republic of the Congo v. Uganda) – Reparations*, General List No. 116, 2022, para 70. While the ILC explicitly excluded the question of individual claims to reparation from the scope of the ASR, this only concerns the possibility to claim, ILC, *ASR Commentaries*, A/56/10, art. 33(2), para 4. Regarding substantive questions the ILC considers the Articles to be applicable to violations of human rights, art. 33, para 3, 5.

56 ILC, *Draft Articles on Responsibility of States for Internationally Wrongful Acts - With Commentaries*, A/56/10, 2001, Ch. 1 General Principles, para 2.

57 van Boven, *Victim's Rights to a Remedy and Reparation - The New United Nations Principles and Guidelines*, in: Ferstman / Goetz (eds.), *Reparations for Victims of Genocide War Crimes and Crimes Against Humanity - Systems in Place and Systems in the Making*, 2nd Edition 2020, 15, 23.

58 Cannizzaro, *Is There an Individual Right to Reparation? Some Thoughts on the ICJ Judgment in the Jurisdictional Immunities Case*, in: Alland et al. (eds.), *Unity and Diversity of International Law - Essays in Honour of Professor Pierre-Marie Dupuy*, 2014, 495, 502; Buyse, *Lost and Regained? Restitution as a Remedy for Human Rights Violations in the Context of International Law*, 2008 Heidelberg J. Intl. L. 68, 129, 135.

59 Buyse, *Lost and Regained?*, 134; ICJ, *Reparations for Injuries Suffered in the Service of the United Nations (Advisory Opinion)*, I.C.J. Reports 1949, 174, 179 ff.

human rights courts and the ICJ have applied the abovementioned principle to individual rights.[60]

Thus, the existence of a customary and treaty-based human right to reparation follows from the right to an effective remedy and is nothing but the logical extension of a general principle of international law.[61] Taken together with the almost uniform approval of that right in international judicial practice and the consistently supportive state practice, there can hardly be a doubt that it forms part of international human rights law today.

II. International Humanitarian Law

Contrary to human rights law, the existence of a right to reparation for violations of international humanitarian law is fiercely debated.[62] Art. 3 Hague Convention IV[63] and its almost verbatim iteration in Art. 91 First Additional Protocol to the Geneva Conventions of 1949 (AP I)[64] explicitly hold a state party liable to pay compensation for violations of the respective treaty if the case demands. Compensation is generally understood in this case to encompass not only monetary compensation but all forms of reparation.[65] According to the International Committee of the Red Cross (ICRC), the obligation to repair violations of humanitarian law is also part of customary law for

60 ICJ, *Legal Consequences of the Construction of a Wall in the Occupied Palestinian Territory (Advisory Opinion)*, I.C.J. Reports 2004, 136, para 152; ICJ, *Ahmadou Sadio Diallo (Republic of Guinea v. Democratic Republic of the Congo), Merits, Judgment*, I.C.J. Reports 2010, 639, para 161 ff.; ECtHR, *Cyprus v. Turkey*, 25781/94 (Grand Chamber), 2014, para 40 ff.; IACtHR, *Aloeboetoe v. Suriname*, para 43 f.; IACtHR, *Velasquez Rodriguez Case, Compensatory Damages*, 1990, para 25; IACtHR, *Case of the "White Van" (Paniagua-Morales et al.) v. Guatemala (Reparations and Costs)*, 2001, para 78; ACtHPR, *Mtikila v. Tanzania*, 011/2011, para 27.

61 On potential differences between these three sources and their consequences for the present study see below, ch. 4, B.

62 Evans, *The Right to Reparation in International Law for Victims of Armed Conflict*, 2012; Furuya, *The Right to Reparation for Victims of Armed Conflict - The Intertwined Development of Substantive and Procedural Aspects*, in: Peters/Marxsen (eds.), *Reparation for Victims of Armed Conflict*, 2020, 16, 28 ff.

63 Convention (IV) Respecting the Laws and Customs of War on Land.

64 Protocol Additional to the Geneva Conventions of 12 August 1949, and Relating to the Protocol of Victims of International Armed Conflict (Protocol I).

65 Pilloud et al., *Commentary on the Additional Protocols of 8 June 1977 to the Geneva Conventions of 12 August 1949*, 1987, art. 91 para 3653 f. For the distinction between different measures of reparation and their definitions see below, C.I.-V.

international and non-international armed conflicts.[66] The travaux préparatoires indicate that the drafters of the Hague Convention IV intended Art. 3 to cover reparation to states as well as to individuals. In the drafting of Art. 91 AP I reparation to individuals played no role.[67] Regardless of the drafter's intentions, state practice immediately following the respective texts' adoption clearly and almost uniformly defies the existence of a right to reparation in international humanitarian law.[68] This has changed to a certain degree.[69] Most importantly, resolutions by the UN General Assembly and the UN Security Council can be read as affirming the existence of a right to reparation in international humanitarian law.[70] However, there are still several states opposing that position.[71] A right to reparation is therefore not established in international humanitarian law.

However, even if survivors have no right to reparation under international humanitarian law, they are not necessarily without remedy.[72] Although their

66 Henckaerts/Doswald-Beck, *ICRC Customary International Law Study Vol. I*, rule 150, p. 537.

67 Kalshoven, *State Responsibility for Warlike Acts of the Armed Forces*, 1991 Intl. Comp. L. Q. 40(4), 827, 830 ff., 844 ff.; Mazzeschi, *Reparation Claims by Individuals for State Breaches of Humanitarian Law and Human Rights - An Overview*, 2003 J. Intl. Crim. Just. 1(2), 339, 341 f. Against this interpretation, even though without much reasoning, Tomuschat, *Reparation in Favour of Individual Victims of Gross Violations of Human Rights and International Humanitarian Law*, in: Kohen (ed.), *Promoting Justice, Human Rights and Conflict Resolution Through International Law - Liber Amicorum Lucius Caflisch*, 2006, 569, 576.

68 Kalshoven, *State Responsibility for Warlike Acts of the Armed Forces*, 835 ff.

69 Henckaerts/Doswald-Beck, *Customary International Humanitarian Law Vol. II - Practice Part 2*, 2005, ch. 42, para 90, 132, 140, 156, 194, 231, 318; ILA, *Reparation for Victims of Armed Conflict*, 313 ff. For a critical analysis of some of the practice mentioned as well as additional practice for and against an individual right to reparation see Correa, *Operationalising the Right of Victims of War to Reparation*, in: Peters/Marxsen (eds.), *Max Planck Trialogues on the Law of Peace and War - Vol. III: Reparations for Victims of Armed Conflict*, 2020, 95 ff.

70 UNGA, *Situation of Human Rights in Afghanistan*, A/RES/51/108, para 11; UNSC, *Resolution 827 (1993)*, S/RES/827 (1993), 1993, para 7; UNGA, *Basic Principles*, A/RES/60/147. Most importantly, in its preamble the resolution recognizes Art. 3 of the Hague Convention and Art. 91 AP I as conferring an individual right.

71 German Federal Constitutional Court, *Varvarin Case*, 2 BvR 2660/06, 2 BvR 487/07, 2013; Federal Court of Justice of Germany, *Kunduz Case*, III ZR 140/15, 2016; Henckaerts/Doswald-Beck, *ICRC Customary International Law Study Vol. II Part 2*, ch. 42, para 195 ff., 203; Stammler, *Der Anspruch von Kriegsopfern auf Schadensersatz*, 2009, 159-330.

72 This argument is inspired by and follows in large part Correa, *Operationalising the Right of Victims of War to Reparation*, 110 ff.

exact relationship to norms of international humanitarian law is disputed, human rights continue to apply in armed conflict.[73] Thus, if a violation of humanitarian law entails a violation of human rights – and it is hardly conceivable otherwise – the road to claim redress based on the human right to reparation is, in principle, open. International humanitarian law stays silent on the matter, and there is no indication that that silence was intended to preclude the application of a human right to reparation. Abrogating the human right to reparation is not necessary to meet the challenges states face in armed conflict. Reparation is a secondary right presupposing the violation of a primary right. Having to provide reparation in the aftermath of a violation hence does not reduce the courses of action a state can legally take during a conflict. The costs of reparation – which could strain a state's budget – can be avoided simply by abstaining from violating human rights, whose demands are already lowered due to the armed conflict. Accordingly, human rights courts and bodies awarded reparation to survivors of violations during an armed conflict.[74]

Still, there are some roadblocks. First, the geographical application of human rights can differ from that of international humanitarian law.[75] Consequently, some survivors of extraterritorial violations of international humanitarian law might not have a claim to reparation based on human rights law against the responsible state. Second, the perpetrating state might have derogated from the relevant human rights treaties because of a state

73 ICJ, *Wall Opinion*, para 104 ff.; ICJ, *Nuclear Weapons Advisory Opinion*, para 25; ECtHR, *Hassan v. The United Kingdom*, 29750/09 (Grand Chamber), 2014, para 102 ff.; IACtHR, *Case of the Massacres of El Mozote and Nearby Places v. El Salvador*, 2012, para 141; AComHPR, *General Comment No. 4 on the African Charter on Human and Peoples' Rights - The Right to Redress for Victims of Torture and Other Cruel, Inhuman or Degrading Punishment or Treatment (Article 5)*, 2017, para 62; AComHPR, *Democratic Republic of Congo v. Burundi, Rwanda, Uganda*, 227/99, 2003, para 79 f.; AComHPR, *Commission Nationale des Droits de l'Homme et des Libertés v. Chad*, 74/92, 1995, para 21. An overview of approaches to the question can be found at Sassòli/Nagler, *International Humanitarian Law - Rules, Controversies, and Solutions to Problems Arising in Warfare*, 2019, para 9.26 ff.

74 ECtHR, *Al Jedda v. The United Kingdom*, 27021/08 (Grand Chamber), 2011, para 107, 111 ff.; IACtHR, *Bámaca-Velásquez v. Guatemala (Merits)*, 2000, para 207 ff., 228; HRCom, *Fulmati Nyaya v. Nepal*, CCPR/C/125/D/2556/2015, 2556/2015, 2019, para 7.3, 9.

75 For an overview of this topic see Wenzel, *Human Rights, Treaties, Extraterritorial Application and Effects*, in: Wolfrum (ed.), *Max Planck Encyclopedia of International Law*, Online Edition 2008; Milanovic, *Extraterritorial Application of Human Rights Treaties - Law, Principles, and Policy*, 2011; Sassòli/Nagler, *International Humanitarian Law*, para 9.21 ff.

of emergency. The right to an effective remedy can be derogated from.[76] However, the Human Rights Committee (HRCom) specified that while a state party can adjust remedies, it cannot entirely abrogate its obligation to provide an effective remedy.[77] Any derogation from the right to a remedy must not diminish the application of non-derogable rights.[78] Since honoring the obligation to repair does not reduce a state's ability to react to the armed conflict, derogation would also likely not be "strictly required by the exigencies of the situation", as human rights treaties require for a derogation to be lawful.[79] For these reasons, abrogating the right to reparation in a state of emergency usually will not be possible. Even if that were otherwise, derogation is not the necessary consequence of the existence of an armed conflict. The state must declare it. Derogation must be limited to those areas where it is necessary.[80] These factors further diminish the importance of derogation in armed conflict.

In sum, while probably no right to reparation exists in international humanitarian law as of now, many violations will be covered by the human right to reparation.

III. International Criminal Law

Art. 75 RS introduced a right to reparation for survivors of international crimes to international criminal law. It sparked a trend followed by several hybrid tribunals established after the ICC.[81] Thus, there is a basis for asserting

76 Art. 4 ICCPR; Art. 15 ECHR. The situation is less clear for the ACHR, which declares as non-derogable "the judicial guarantees essential for the protection of such rights", Art. 27 ACHR. In a corresponding advisory opinion the IACtHR does not clarify whether reparation falls under these essential guarantees, but held that states must provide redress. Given that the opinion also clarifies that the primary function of essential judicial guarantees is to guarantee the full exercise of conventional rights, redress could primarily mean cessation, see IACtHR, *Judicial Guarantees in States of Emergency (Arts. 27(2), 25 and 8 American Convention on Human Rights)*, OC-9/87, 1987, para 20, 24. Note also that the ACHPR does not allow derogation at all.

77 HRCom, *General Comment No. 29 - Article 4: Derogations During a State of Emergency*, CCPR/C/21/Rev.1/Add.11, 2001, para 14.

78 HRCom, *General Comment No. 36 on the Right to Life*, CCPR/C/GC/36, 2018, para 67.

79 See above, fn. 76.

80 HRCom, *GC 29*, CCPR/C/21/Rev.1/Add.11, para 4.

81 Ambach, *The International Criminal Court Reparations Scheme – A Yardstick for Hybrid Tribunals?*, in: Werle/Zimmermann (eds.), *The International Criminal Court in Turbulent Times*, 2019, 131, 132 f., 137 ff.

the existence of a general right to reparation, independently of the RS, in international criminal law.[82] This right is, however, directed against individual perpetrators, not states. While the drafters of the RS debated whether Art. 75 should also cover state responsibility to provide reparation, such proposals did not find sufficient support.[83] Given that the present inquiry is limited to state responsibility, the right to reparation in international criminal law cannot serve as a basis for the normative framework to be erected.[84]

B. *Beneficiaries of the Right to Reparation*

Only survivors have a right to reparation. The definition of "survivor" is therefore crucial to understand the international law on reparation. Many questions revolve around that definition, leading one author to conclude that there are "almost as many definitions as categories of [survivors] envisaged by international norms."[85] There are, however, certain elements most definitions have in common. Among them is the distinction between direct (I.) and indirect (II.) survivors.

I. Direct Survivors

International practice defines three requirements a direct survivor must meet: First, they must have suffered a violation of their rights. Second, they must have suffered harm. Third, the violation must have caused that harm.[86]

82 An excellent examination of the origins and development of a right to reparation in international criminal law is provided by Evans, *The Right to Reparation in International Law for Victims of Armed Conflict*, 87 ff.

83 PrepCom, *Report of the Preparatory Committee on the Establishment of an International Criminal Court*, A/Conf.183/2/Add.1, 1998, 117; PrepCom, *Article 66 - Reparations to Victims: Rolling Text*, UD/A/AC-249/1998/WG-4/IP, 1998; Muttukumaru, *Reparation to Victims*, in: Lee (ed.), *The International Criminal Court - The Making of the Rome Statute: Issues, Negotiations, Results*, 1999, 262, 267 ff.

84 The practice of the ICC is still relevant to the inquiry, since the court relies on the human right to reparation when devising its reparation principles and programs. For details see below, ch. 2, D.I.

85 de Casadevante Romani, *International Law of Victims*, 2010 Max Planck Y.B. U. Nations L. 14, 219, 237.

86 Shelton, *Remedies in International Human Rights Law*, 241 f.; Moffett, *Justice for Victims Before the ICC*, 17 ff.; UNGA, *Declaration of Basic Principles of Justice for Victims of Crime and Abuse of Power*, A/RES/40/34, 1985, para 1; UNGA, *Basic Principles*, A/RES/60/147,

This study presumes the violation of a primary right, making fuller exploration of the first requirement unnecessary. The notion of harm is understood widely.[87] It encompasses material and non-material harm. The former denotes losses with a directly equivalent market value such as damages to or loss of property, loss of earnings, and costs incurred, e.g., for legal, medical, or psychological assistance. Non-material harm features damages to the well-being of a person, which has no direct equivalent market value. Examples are pain suffered, mental and bodily harm, grievance, and humiliation.[88] Given this broad spectrum of recognized harms, only a few disadvantages do not warrant reparation, for example, general concerns or impaired general interests.[89]

The requirement of causation limits the right to reparation. It must not be equated with a mere sine qua non test. As the Inter-American Court of Human Rights (IACtHR) put it: "To compel the perpetrator of an illicit act to erase all the consequences produced by his action is completely impossible since that action caused effects that multiplied to a degree that cannot be measured."[90] Instead, the causal connection between the violation and the damage must be sufficiently close to warrant reparation. Criteria to assess this requirement are "direct causation", "certainty", "immediate effect", "foreseeability" or "proximity" and may vary with the type of violation and the circumstances of the case.[91]

---

para 8; CoE, *Eradicating Impunity for Serious Human Rights Violations - Guidelines Adopted by the Committee of Ministers on 30 March 2011 at the 1110th Meeting of the Ministers' Deputies,* H/Inf (2011) 7, 2011, sec. II, para 5; AU, *Transitional Justice Policy,* 2019, para 21; ACtHPR, *Comparative Study on the Law and Practice of Reparations for Human Rights Violations,* 2019, 16 f. The terms "harm" and "damage" will be used interchangeably throughout this study. Other terms frequently used to denote the same are "injury", "prejudice" and "loss". On some differences between these terms see Wittich, *Non-Material Damage and Monetary Reparation in International Law,* 2005 Finnish Y.B. Intl. L., 321, 323 f.

87 The European Court of Justice (ECJ) determined that the meaning of harm is "common to all international law-subsystems", ECJ, *Axel Walz v. Clickair SA,* C-63/09, 2010, para 27.

88 See below for further detail ch. 2, B.II., C.II., D.III.2.a., D.III.3.a. D.III.4.a., and IComJ, *The Right to Remedy and Reparation for Gross Human Rights Violations - A Practitioners' Guide,* 2nd Revised Edition 2018, 189 ff.

89 ILC, *ASR Commentaries,* A/56/10, art 31, para 5.

90 IACtHR, *Aloeboetoe v. Suriname,* para 48.

91 ILC, *Third Report on State Responsibility by Mr. James Crawford, Special Rapporteur,* A/CN.4/507, 2000, para 28 f.; Shelton, *Remedies in International Human Rights Law,* 40 f.; Wittich, *Compensation,* in: Wolfrum (ed.), *Max Planck Encyclopedia of Public International Law,* Online Edition 2008, para 17; IACtHR, *Aloeboetoe v. Suriname,* para

International practice increasingly recognizes collectives as potential survivors.[92] Courts and treaty bodies awarded reparation to indigenous communities, groups of persons residing in the same area, and society as a whole.[93] Details surrounding the notion of collective reparation, such as the exact scope and nature of eligible collectives, are unclear. International practice has provided little clarification on these issues.[94] Nevertheless, since collectives can be right holders and certain violations cause collective harm, there is no reason why, in principle, they should not be regarded as survivors under international law.[95]

Aggregating the abovementioned elements, a direct survivor in international law can be defined as every person or collective that suffered harm as a direct result of a violation of their right.

49; ECtHR, *İpek v. Turkey*, 25760/94 (Second Section), 2004, para 223; ICJ, *Certain Activities Carried Out by Nicaragua in the Border Area (Costa Rica v. Nicaragua)*, I.C.J. Reports 2018, 15, para 32; ICJ, *Armed Activities Reparations*, para 94, 382.

92 ICC, *The Prosecutor v. Thomas Lubanga Dyilo, Decision Establishing the Principles and Procedures to be Applied to Reparations*, ICC-01/04-01/06-2904 (TC I), 2012, para 219 ff.; IACtHR, *Case of the Mayagna (Sumo) Awas Tingni Community v. Nicaragua (Merits, Reparations and Costs)*, 2001, para 164 ff.; UNGA, *Basic Principles*, A/RES/60/147, para 8; Peru TRC, *Final Report*, 2003, vol. IX, ch. 2.2.2.2.2.2; SLTRC, *Witness to Truth*, vol. 2, ch. 4; Rosenfeld, *Collective Reparation for Victims of Armed Conflict*, 2010 Rev. Red Cross 92(879), 731, 739 ff. While not entirely clear on this issue, the AComHPR held that the Ogoni society was damaged as a whole. This at least suggests that some reparation measures – especially the clean-up of degraded land – is meant to remedy collective harm, AComHPR, *Social and Economic Rights Action Center (SERAC) and Center for Economic and Social Rights (CESR) v. Nigeria*, 155/96, 2001, para 68 and holding.

93 IACtHR, *The Kaliña and Lokono Peoples v. Suriname*, 2015, para 273; AComHPR, *SERAC and CESR v. Nigeria*, 155/96, para 68 and holding; ACtHPR, *AComHPR v. Republic of Kenya – Judgment on Reparations*, 006/2012, 2022, 4; ICC, *The Prosecutor v. Ahmad Al Faqi Al Mahdi, Reparations Order*, ICC-01/12-01/15-236 (TC VII), 2017, para 51 ff. Rosenfeld argues that only collectives holding collective rights are collective survivors, Rosenfeld, *Collective Reparation for Victims of Armed Conflict*, 732. This is not supported by international practice.

94 Odier Contreras-Garduno, *Collective Reparations - Tensions and Dilemmas Between Collective Reparations With the Individual Right to Receive Reparations*, 2018, 320.

95 For more details on collective reparation see below, C.VII.

II. Indirect Survivors

International law recognizes three groups of persons as indirect survivors: the direct survivor's close family members, dependents, and persons who suffered harm while trying to assist the direct survivor or prevent the violation.[96] They all have in common that the original violation was not aimed at but still harmed them. Who counts as a close family member differs from case to case, also depending on cultural differences.[97]

Indirect survivors' own rights can be violated due to the suffering caused by the original violation of the direct survivor's rights. For example, the pain and anguish suffered by a close relative of a disappeared person, coupled with the authorities' inaction and denial of justice, can violate the relative's rights not to be subjected to inhumane treatment.[98] In this constellation, the term indirect survivor is misleading, as the survivor is violated in their own right, albeit through a slightly longer chain of causation.[99] There is hence no principled distinction between indirect and direct survivors in this case.[100]

---

96 AComHPR, *GC 4*, para 17; ECtHR, *Colozza v. Italy*, 9024/80 (Chamber), 1985, para 38; IACtHR, *Case of the Gómez-Paquiyauri Brothers v. Peru*, para 118; UNGA, *Basic Principles for Victims of Crime and Abuse of Power*, A/RES/40/34, para 2; UNGA, *Basic Principles*, A/RES/60/147, para 2; CAT, *General Comment No. 3 of the Committee Against Torture - Implementation of Article 14 by States Parties*, CAT/C/GC/3, 2012, para 3; CEDAW, *R.P.B. v. The Philippines*, CEDAW/C/57/D/34/2011, 34/2011, 2014, para 9; ACtHPR, *Beneficiaries of Late Norbert Zongo v. Burkina Faso (Judgment on Reparations)*, 013/2011, para 46 ff.; HRCom, *Quinteros v. Uruguay*, CCPR/C/OP/2, 107/1981, 1983, para 14; ICC, *Lubanga Reparations Decision*, ICC-01/04-01/06-2904, para 195 f.; ICC, *The Prosecutor v. Thomas Lubanga Dyilo, Redacted Version of "Decision on 'Indirect Victims'"*, ICC-01/04-01/06-1813 (TC I), 2009, para 40 ff., 51; Art. 2(b) European Convention on the Compensation of Victims of Violent Crimes.

97 ICC, *Lubanga Reparations Decision*, ICC-01/04-01/06-2904, para 195; IACtHR, *Aloeboetoe v. Suriname*, para 62.

98 IACtHR, *Myrna Mack Chang v. Guatemala*, 2003, para 232; ECtHR, *Kurt v. Turkey*, 24276/94 (Chamber), 1998, para 130 ff., 175. It must be noted however, that the ECtHR does not apply the concept consistently, often denying reparation to indirect surivors, Rubio-Marín et al., *Repairing Family Members - Gross Human Rights Violations and Communities of Harm*, in: Rubio-Marin (ed.), *The Gender of Reparations - Unsettling Sexual Hierarchies While Redressing Human Rights Violations*, 2009, 215, 232 ff.

99 Accordingly, the Working Group on Enforced or Involuntary Disappearances (WGEID) rejects the distinction between direct and indirect survivors and draws particular attention to its possible gendered impact, WGEID, *General Comment on Women Affected by Enforced Disappearances*, A/HRC/WGEID/98/2, 2013, para 38.

100 IACtHR, *Case of Bámaca-Velásquez v. Guatemala (Merits) - Separate Concurring Opinion of Judge Sergio García Ramírez*, 2000, para 5.

The IACtHR and ECtHR also award reparation to persons whose own rights were not violated but who suffered harm because of the violation of the direct survivor's rights. This practice is based on a differentiation between survivors and injured parties in the ECHR and ACHR.[101] Since that distinction is peculiar to these two treaties, it cannot be taken to amend the survivor-definition in the international law on reparation. Hence, the notion of an indirect survivor does not add anything to the survivor definition. It merely draws attention to groups of survivors who suffered harm because of a violation of their rights through a longer chain of causation than direct survivors. The notion of indirect survivor must not be confused with reparation family members of deceased direct survivors receive as heirs. [102]

III. Survivors of Violations Committed by Non-State Actors

As a secondary right, the right to reparation arises from violations of primary human rights. Since traditionally, these rights bind states, no right to reparation follows from violations that non-state actors[103] commit. Especially in transitional justice situations, however, non-state actors commit many, if not most human rights violations.[104] Excluding survivors of these violations from

101 Art. 63 ACHR; Art. 41 ECHR; ECtHR, *Aktas v. Turkey*, 24351/94 (Third Section), 2003, para 364; ECtHR, *Cakici v. Turkey*, 23657/94 (Grand Chamber), 1999, para 130; IACtHR, *Loayza-Tamayo v. Peru (Reparations and Costs)*, 1998, para 88 ff.; IACtHR, *Myrna Mack Chang v. Guatemala - Reasoned Concurring Opinion of Judge Sergio García-Ramírez*, 2003, para 57.

102 For an analysis of international jurisprudence on this matter see Rubio-Marín et al., *Repairing Family Members*, 225 ff.; Wühler, *Reparations and Legal Succession – What Happens When the Victims Are Gone?*, 2018 Heidelberg J. Intl. L. 78(3), 597.

103 The term non-state actors covers a broad range of actors, Clapham, *Non-State Actors*, in: Binder et al. (eds.), *Elgar Encyclopedia of Human Rights*, Online Edition 2022, para 1 ff. This section will not narrow it down further, as it should not be decisive at the outset which non-state entity violates a person's human rights. In many cases, non-state armed groups will be the most visible non-state actor violating human rights. But often, that is as much a reflection of the focus of attention as of the quantity and quality of the violations committed. The violations of economic actors, e.g., tend not to be at the center of attention of transitional justice processes.

104 To give examples from the case studies below, Sierra Leone's Truth and Reconciliation Commission found that the Revolutionary United Front (RUF), a non-state actor, committed most violations, Ch. 2 B.II. In Colombia, non-state actors are responsible for a wide array of violations. Paramilitary forces predominantly committed the infamous massacres. While they were closely affiliated with state forces, an attribution of their actions to the state seems at least complicated, Ch. 2 C.I, II. The International

reparation seems intuitively unfair and detrimental to transitional justice processes. The question hence is whether direct and indirect survivors of human rights violations by non-state actors also have a right to reparation. Such a right can be established against the state if it bears responsibility for the actions of non-state actors through omission or attribution. Beyond that, survivors could have an independent right to reparation directed against non-state actors.

Within human rights doctrine, states are responsible for violations by non-state actors if they fail to discharge their positive obligations to protect and fulfill human rights. These dimensions oblige states to protect individuals against specific threats by private actors and to create conditions under which individuals can enjoy their human rights.[105] The scope of these obligations is contingent on the protection feasible in the given situation. The state only has to do what can reasonably and proportionately be expected under the circumstances.[106]

These standards open two avenues of establishing the responsibility of states for human rights violations by non-state actors based on omission: First, if the state had the possibility to protect individuals against concrete violations with proportionate means it violated its obligation to protect their human rights. Second, if the state failed to prevent or contributed to the situation that gave rise to systematic human rights violations, it failed to fulfill the human rights of those subsequently victimized.[107]

Establishing the state's responsibility for its failure to protect human rights will often fail in situations of systematic human rights violations due to the impossibility to prevent concrete violations. In both Sierra Leone

---

Criminal Court so far only ordered reparation against members of non-state actors, Ch. 2 D.2.a, 3.a., 4.a, 5.a.

105 Mégret, *Nature of Obligations*, 103; de Schutter, *International Human Rights Law*, 461; Lavrysen, *Positive Obligations in the Jurisprudence of the Inter-American Court of Human Rights*, 2014 Inter-Am. Eur. Hum. Rts. J. 7, 94, 110; Schabas, *ECHR Commentary*, 90 f.; HRCom, *GC 31*, CCPR/C/21/Rev.1/Add.13, para 7 f.; ECOSOC, *Updated Study on the Right to Food, Submitted by Mr. Asbjorn Eide*, E/CN.4/Sub.2/1999/12, 1999, para 52; ECtHR, *Budayeva and Others v. Russia*, 15339/02 (20 March 2008, First Section), para 128 ff.; ECtHR, *Özel and Others v. Turkey*, 14350/05 (17 November 2015, Second Section), para 170 f.

106 HRCom, *GC 31*, CCPR/C/21/Rev.1/Add.13, para 8; ECtHR, *Budayeva and Others v. Russia*, 15339/02 (20 March 2008, First Section), para 128 ff.; ECtHR, *Özel and Others v. Turkey*, 14350/05 (17 November 2015, Second Section), para 170 f.

107 Cf. HRCom, *GC 36*, CCPR/C/GC/36, para 69; HRCom, *General Comment No. 6 - Article 6 (Right to Life)*, HRI/GEN/1/Rev.1, 1982, para 2.

and Colombia, for example, the states lost control over wide areas of their territories for a significant time.[108] In that situation, they had no proportionate means at their disposal to prevent non-state actors from committing violations in these areas. Further, as a practical problem, this basis to attribute responsibility would require an examination of every single violation and the state's ability to prevent it; which will quickly prove impractical in situations of mass victimization.

In response to the same problem under the law of occupation, the ICJ reversed the burden of proof. In light of the occupying power's obligation to prevent violations of human rights law and international humanitarian law on the occupied territory, the court held that the state must establish that any violation that occurred was *not* due to its failure to take protective measures.[109] It is, however, unclear whether that reversal of the burden of proof can be extended to violations occurring on the territory of the state in question. While one could argue that a state usually has a greater degree of control over its own territory than territory it occupies, the occupation subject to the dispute before the ICJ was itself the result of a wrongful act.[110] Hence, the ICJ could also have based the reversal of the burden of proof on the illegality of the situation. In other cases, the ICJ did not extend the same reversal to violations on the territory of a state.[111] It did not apply it to other positive obligations either.[112] The reversal also drew strong criticism from the bench and – to the knowledge of the author – finds no direct equivalent in human rights jurisprudence.[113] Hence, it remains doubtful whether reversing the burden of proof can circumvent the difficulty to establish the ability of a state to prevent concrete violations in contexts of mass victimization.

108 See below, Ch. 2, B.I., C.I.

109 ICJ, *Armed Activities Reparations,* para 78, 95, 118, 149, 161, 257.

110 ICJ, *Armed Activities,* para 345(1). On the legality of belligerent occupation as such see Benvenisti, *Occupation, Belligerent,* in: Wolfrum (ed.), *Max Planck Encylopedia of International Law,* Online Edition 2009, para 20 f.

111 ICJ, *Corfu Channel Case (Merits)*, I.C.J. Reports 1949, 4, 18, concerning inter alia the positive obligations to not allow one's territory to be used for unlawful acts. For an analysis of the Diallo judgment to the same effect see ICJ, *Armed Activities on the Territory of the Congo (Democratic Republic of the Congo v. Uganda), Reparations – Separate Opinion of Judge Yusuf,* para 14.

112 ICJ, *Case Concerning the Application of the Convention on the Prevention and Punishment of the Crime of Genocide,* I.C.J. Reports 2007, 43, para 462. The ICJ took care, however, to emphasize that that jurisprudence did not purport to establish standards for all positive obligations either, but only for the obligation to prevent genocide, para 492 and ICJ, *Armed Activities Reparations,* para 96.

113 ICJ, *Armed Activities Reparations – Separate Opinion of Judge Yusuf,* para 6 ff.

Relying on a state's failure to fulfill human rights avoids this complication. This obligation does not concern the state's ability to prevent single incidents. Instead, the state is responsible for contributing or failing to prevent the mass victimization as a whole. At the outset, this avenue seems promising: Most systematic human rights violations arise out of unjust situations to which the state contributed, for example through an authoritarian government style or oppression of minorities. At least, states often will have failed to act decisively against factors contributing to conflict, such as pervasive inequality. Based on such failures, the Peruvian and Sierra Leonean Truth and Reconciliation Commissions (TRCs) assumed their respective states' responsibility for all violations of international law during the armed conflict they investigated.[114] With that, they followed the Special Rapporteur on reparation for gross violations of human rights.[115] This, however, seems contrary to the requirement of causation in the international law on reparation: Reparation is only owed for consequences that are sufficiently close to the illegal act.[116] The ICJ and the EECC held that a state is not responsible for every harm that occurred during a conflict it caused.[117] Especially when the wrongful act is not deliberately causing a conflict, but merely contributing to or failing to prevent it, many ensuing injuries will not be sufficiently close to that original violation to warrant reparation.[118] Furthermore, many harms of a conflict will be caused more immediately by wrongful conduct of another party to the conflict. While

114 Peruvian Truth and Reconciliation Commission, *Final Report,* 143. On Sierra Leone see below, Ch. 2 B.IV.1.a. On the conflict more generally see below, Ch. 2 B.I., II.

115 Commission on Human Rights, *Study Concerning the Right to Restitution, Compensation and Rehabilitation for Victims of Gross Violations of Human Rights and Fundamental Freedoms – Final Report Submitted by Mr. Theo van Boven, Special Rapporteur,* E/CN.4/Sub.2/1993/8, 1993, para 41.

116 See above, I.

117 ICJ, *Armed Activities Reparations,* para 161, 250, 382; The EECC emphasized though, that its standard does encompass unplanned evolutions of conflicts, even if based on actions of the opposing party, Ethiopian-Eritrea Claims Commission, *Final Award – Ethiopia's Damages Claims,* RIAA XXVI 631, 2009, para 284, 289 f. For further discussion of this topic see the overview in Pobije, *Victims of the Crime of Aggression,* in: Kress / Barriga (eds.), *The Crime of Aggression – A Commentary,* 2017, 816, 834 ff. The EECC emphasized though, that its standard does encompass unplanned evolutions of conflicts, even if based on actions of the opposing party, EECC, *Final Award,* para 298 f., 303, 305.

118 The EECC established a lower threshold for causation for deliberate attacks based on the criterion of foreseeability. Given that states must carefully weigh their decision to deliberately embark upon conflict, they are bound to duly consider all possible consequences. Hence, more consequences can be held to be foreseeable, EECC, *Final Award,* para 290, 297.

such a concurrent responsibility – be it of a state or non-state actor – does not exclude an obligation to repair of the state causing the conflict, it does bear on the assessment whether the resulting harm is sufficiently close to that original wrongful act.[119] Given these complications, relying on positive human rights obligations to establish an obligation to repair acts of non-state actors will leave accountability gaps.[120]

States can also violate their obligation to respect human rights if the actions of non-state actors are attributable to them. The law on state responsibility provides four avenues to do that. Most importantly, if a state instructs, directs, or controls the conduct of a non-state actor, that conduct is attributed to the state.[121] The high threshold of this mode of attribution makes it hard to apply, though.[122] Exceptionally, non-state actors might assume governmental authority in circumstances that call for such assumption, triggering attribution of their actions under Art. 9 ASR. However, even if of customary status, this article applies to situations of leveé en masse rather than the more common situation of an armed insurrection and will hence be applicable only in exceptional situations.[123] Lastly, non-state actors' "success" can result in attributability, namely if the actor establishes a de facto government, replaces the old government, or forms a new state on part of the old state's territory.[124]

One of these six ways[125] will often establish state responsibility for human rights violations by non-state actors. In that case, the state cannot evade its obligation by pointing to the responsibility of the non-state actor. Generally, the responsibility of a non-state actor does not relieve the state from its re-

---

119 ICJ, *Armed Activities Reparations*, para 94, 97; EECC, *Final Award*, para 289.

120 Given that this study assumes state responsibility, see above Introduction, B., it will not dive deeper into this complicated topic.

121 Art. 8 ASR.

122 See ICJ, *Military and Paramilitary Activities in and Against Nicaragua (Nicaragua v. United States of America), Merits*, I.C.J. Reports 1986, 14, para 109 ff. The ICTY established a lower, but still demanding threshold of overall control, ICTY, *Prosecutor v. Duško Tadič, Judgment*, IT-94-1-A (AC), 1999, para 145.

123 ILC, *ASR Commentaries*, A/56/10, art. 9, para 2, 6. Of course that distinction is very difficult to draw and usually depends heavily on the viewpoint. Nevertheless, also given the provision's exceptional character, it wil rarely be applicable.

124 Art. 10 ASR. On its customary status, ILC, *ASR Commentaries*, A/56/10, art. 9, para 4; art. 10, para 3.

125 A violation of the obligation to protect (1) or fulfill (2); the attribution of non-state actors' actions through instruction, direction, or control (3); the assumption of governmental authority (4); formation of a de facto government (5); or establishment of a new government (6).

sponsibility for the entire harm the survivor sustained.[126] The state, therefore, remains accountable to provide full reparation to the survivor even if a private individual contributed to the human rights violation or committed it.[127]

However, there are scenarios in which none of the six ways serves to establish state responsibility.[128] An ironclad guarantee that all survivors have a right to reparation can thus only be achieved if non-state actors had an independent obligation to repair survivors of their unlawful acts.[129]

Such a right could be the corollary to international obligations non-state actors incur. After all, the PCIJ held that the obligation to repair follows from any breach of an international obligation.[130] Accordingly, that obligation has been extended to international organizations and individuals.[131] However, while non-state actors have international obligations, their scope is unclear. Whether they encompass an obligation to repair remains particularly con-

---

126 ILC, *ASR Commentaries*, A/56/10, art. 31, para 12 f.; *D. Earnshaw and Others (Great Britain) v. United States (Zafiro Case)*, R.I.A.A. VI, 1925, 160, 164 f. In case of co-responsibility of a plurality of states, the law is less clear. Here it depends on the situation, whether one actor owes reparation for the entire harm or whether the responsibility is allocated, ILC, *ASR Commentaries*, A/56/10, art. 31 para 12 f., art. 47 para 4 ff. The ICJ left that question open in ICJ, *Certain Phosphate Lands in Nauru (Nauru v. Australia), Preliminary Objections, Judgment*, I.C.J. Reports 1992, 240, para 48, 56. It chose the first alternative in the Corfu Channel Case, ICJ, *Corfu Channel*, para 22 f. In the Armed Activities reparation proceedings it opted for the latter alternative, since two armies acted independently, ICJ, *Armed Activities Reparations*, para 98, 221, 253. As this situation concerned two state actors which beared independent responsibility it cannot be applied without qualification to situations of concurrent responsibility or causation of a state and a non-state actor. The latter will often not bear responsibility under international law. Even if it does, it probably does not incur an obligation to repair, see below in this section.

127 IACtHR, *Ximenes-Lopes v. Brazil*, 2006, para 232; The IACtHR, ECtHR, and HRC award full reparation also for violations of positive obligations, IACtHR, *Case of the Workers of the Fireworks Factory in Santo Antônio de Jesus and Their Families v. Brazil*, 2020, 115 ff., 257 f.; HRC, *Martínez et al. v. Colombia*, 3076/2017, CCPR/C/128/D/3076/2017, 2020, para 11; ECtHR, *Berkman v. Russia*, 46712/15 (Third Section), 2020, operative para 7, in which the court awards the 10.000 € claimed by the applicant regardless of the contributions of private actors to the violation.

128 See for example ICJ, *Armed Activities Reparations*, para 82.

129 I am indebted to Olivia Herman for providing me with a copy of her thesis on the topic in advance of publication. The following argument in large part follows her excellent analysis. Interested readers are referred for more detail to Herman, *Righting Wrongs – Non-State Armed Groups and Reparations for Victims of Armed Conflict, With a Case Study of Colombia*, 2021 (on file with the author).

130 PCIJ, *Chorzów Factory Case*, para 73.

131 ILC, *Draft Articles on the Responsibility of International Organizations*, A/66/10, 2011, art. 31; Art. 75 RS.

troversial.[132] In international humanitarian law, AP II, which is applicable to non-international armed conflict, does not contain a provision on reparation akin to Art. 91 AP I. In any case, as established above, international humanitarian law does not (yet) provide survivors with a right to reparation.[133]

Some scholars argue that at least those non-state actors exercising territorial control assume some obligations under human rights law. Again, though, the extent of these obligations is subject to strong debate.[134] Specifically for reparation, state practice provides little support for the extension of such an obligation to non-state actors[135]:

While in some instances, states obliged non-state actors to provide reparation under the law of belligerency and insurgency,[136] little contemporary practice builds on these attempts.[137] Soft law documents are inconclusive. The Basic Principles and Guidelines on the Right to a Remedy and Reparation (Basic Principles) state that a person, legal person or other entity should repair survivors if found liable.[138] The responsible

132 ICRC, *Commentary on the Third Geneva Convention,* 2020, para 931; Henckaerts/Doswald-Beck, *ICRC Customary International Law Study Vol. I,* rule 150, p. 536, 550; Herman, *Beyond the State of Play – Establishing a Duty of Non-State Armed Groups to Provide Reparations,* 2020 Int. Rev. Red Cross 102(915), 1033, 1037 f.; Heffes/Frenkel, *The International Responsibilityx of Non-State Armed Groups – In Search of the Applicable Rules,* 2017 Goettingen J. Intl. L. 8(1), 39, 65 ff.

133 See above, A.II.

134 The vibrant discussion on the application of human rights law generally to non-state actors is outside the scope of the present study. See as a starting point, Clapham, *Non-State Actors,* in: Moeckli/Shah/Sivakumaran, *International Human Rights Law,* 2nd Ed. 2014, 531, 543 ff.; Clapham, *Human Rights Obligations of Non-State Actors in Conflict Situations,* 2006 Intl. Rev. Red Cross 88(863), 491 ff.; Rodenhäuser, *Organizing Rebellion – Non-State Armed Groups Under International Humanitarian Law, Human Rights Law, and International Criminal Law,* 2018, 121 ff.; Murray, *Human Rights Obligations of Non-State Armed Groups,* 2016, 160 ff. Berkes, *International Human Rights Law Beyond State Territorial Control,* 2021, 176 ff.; Clapham, *Non-State Actors,* para 18.

135 Moffett, *Beyond Attribution – Responsibility of Armed Non-State Actors for Reparations in Northern Ireland, Colombia and Uganda,* in: Gal-Or/Ryngaert/Noortman (eds.), *Responsibilities of the Non-State Actor in Armed Conflict and the Market Place - Theoretical Considerations and Empirical Finding,* 2015, 323, 328 f.; Iñigo, *Towards a Regime of Responsibility of Armed Groups in International Law,* 2020, 173 f.; Herman, *Righting Wrongs,* 66 f.

136 Herman, *Beyond the State of Play,* 1041.

137 Henckaerts/Doswald-Beck, *ICRC Customary International Law Study Vol. I,* rule 150, p. 549 f.; Herman, *Righting Wrongs,* 86 ff.; Clapham, *Non-State Actors,* para 12 f.; Gillard, *Reparation for Violations of International Humanitarian Law,* 2003 Intl. Rev. Red Cross 85(851), 529, 534 f.

138 UNGA, *Basic Principles,* A/RES/60/147, para 15.

Special Rapporteur felt that this principle introduced the responsibility and liability of non-state actors.[139] However, the use of the word "should" in the decisive paragraph indicates the lack of a legally binding rule.[140] In contrast to paragraphs establishing state responsibility for reparation,[141] the paragraph on non-state actors fails to mention any basis of liability, leaving the possibility that they are found responsible solely under domestic law. Other UN-documents consistently emphasize the importance of reparation provided for by non-state actors without indicating an international legal obligation to that end.[142]

Taken together, this sparse and unclear practice cannot sustain an international obligation of non-state actors to repair survivors of violations they committed – much less a right of these survivors to claim reparation from non-state actors. If at all, such a concept is only in statu nascendi.[143]

The absence of an independent obligation to provide reparation need not keep states from forcing such an obligation on non-state actors, though. They can do so through domestic law or peace agreements. Several ways exist to involve non-state actors in reparation programs. A prime example is the

139 van Boven, *The United Nations Basic Principles and Guidelines on the Right to a Remedy and Reparation for Victims of Gross Violations of International Human Rights Law and Serious Violations of Intenrational Humanitarian Law,* United Nations Audiovisual Library, 2010, 1, 3.

140 ECOSOC, *The Right to Restitution, Compensation and Rehabilitation for Victims of Gross Violations of Human Rights and Fundamental Freedoms – Final Report of Special Rapporteur, Mr. M. Cherif Bassiouni, Submitted in Accordance With Commission Resolution 1999/33,* E/CN.4/2000/62, 2000, para 8.

141 See e.g. UNGA, *Basic Principles,* A/RES/60/147, para 3, 11, 15.

142 UN Commission of Human Rights, *Situation of Human Rights in Afghanistan,* E/CN.4/1998/70, 1998, para 5d; UNGA, *Situation of Human Rights in Afghanistan,* A/RES/53/165, 1999, para 10c; OHCHR, *Situation of Human Rights in Libya, Including the Impilementation of Technical Assistasnce and Capacity-Building and Efforts to Prevent and Ensure Accountability for Violations and Abuses of Human Rights,* A/HRC/40/46, 2019, para 79c; HRC, *Report on Domestic Reparation Programs,* A/HRC/42/45, 2019, para 95. Remarks of the UN Secretary-General are ambiguous, e.g. in UNSC, *Report of the Secretary-General on the Protection of Civilians in Armed Conflict,* S/2009/277, 2009, para 68. While he refers to the responsibility of parties to an armed conflict to comply with international humanitarian law and human rights, he only mentions "the duty to make reparations", without specifying the actors carrying the obligation. The sole exception might be the International Commission of Inquiry on Darfur, *Report of the International Commission of Inquiry on Darfur to the United Nations Secretary-General,* 2005, para 175.

143 See Herman, *Righting Wrongs,* 107 f. and Herman, *Beyond the State of Play,* 1042, coming to that conclusion after a much more comprehensive practice review.

involvement of the FARC-EP in reparation efforts through the Colombian Peace Agreement from 2016.[144] The guerilla had to hand over an inventory of its asset, which were then used to finance reparation.[145] It committed to contribute to reparation measures, such as infrastructure rebuilding, mine clearance, and the search for disappeared persons.[146] The Special Jurisdiction for Peace (SJP), a special criminal court within Colombia's transitional justice system, can sanction criminally responsible individuals to contribute to reparation efforts as part of the "special sanctions" regime.[147]

The telos of reparation in transitional situations strongly speaks in favor of such a solution, whether state responsibility for the violations can be established or not.[148]

In sum, states bear responsibility for many violations non-state actors commit, either on the basis of their positive obligations to respect and fulfill human rights or through attribution, e.g. when a non-state actor forms a de facto government or fully assumes power. For the remaining cases, international law does not endow survivors with the right to claim reparation from the responsible non-state actor. However, states can and do change that by integrating non-state actors into their reparation programs; be it de facto, based on domestic law or a peace agreement. Thus, in practice, survivors rarely remain without a remedy simply because a non-state actor violated their human rights.

---

144 *Final Agreement to End the Armed Conflict and Build a Stable and Lasting Peace*, 2016, e.g. Ch. 5.1.3.2. On details see Herman, *Righting Wrongs*, 246 ff. Regarding the context see below Ch. 2 C. For a similar attempt see *Agreement on Accountability and Reconciliation Between the Government of the Republic of Uganda and the Lord's Resistance Army/Movement*, 2007 para 6.4.

145 Wilson, *FARC During the Peace Process*, Perry Center Occasional Paper, 2020, 18; Bernal et al., *2018 Global Review of Constitutional Law: Colombia*, 2019 Intl. J. Const. L. 17(2), 671, 676. For further ways to involve non-state actors in the financing of reparation programs see below, Ch. 4 E.II.2.a.

146 *Final Agreement*, 5.1.3.2. On problems with mine clearing see Bermúdez Liévano, *Will Colombia's FARC be Allowed to Clear Mines to Repair Their Victims?*, Justiceinfo.net 2020.

147 *Final Agreement*, 5.1.2.III.; Levy, *Can Colombia's Special Jurisdiction for Peace be Considered Slow? A Preliminary Comparative Study of Trials of International Crimes*, Justice in Conflict 2021.

148 Since that telos will only be established in Ch. 3, the author kindly asks readers to simply believe him at this point, acknowledging the breach of scientific standards this entails. Suffice it to say that the telos of reparation is to send the message that human rights are valid, applicable, enforceable and important again. This message is seriously undermined if non-state actors seem excepted from that rule and many survivors do not receive reparation at all.

C. Content of the Right to Reparation

International practice abounds on how to repair direct and indirect survivors of human rights violations. While the standards employed differ in detail,[149] they arise out of the same fundamental principle and therefore tend to converge around a limited set of the same fundamental rules. These rules detail which forms of reparation are adequate for which situation. The differences in detail are not decisive for adapting the human right to reparation to the transitional justice situation. The present study, therefore, does not embark upon a detailed review of international reparation practice.[150] Instead, it provides an overview of principles common to all international reparation endeavors, which can be condensed to an international law on reparation. At the heart of this international law on reparation lies the principle of full reparation, first and most famously articulated by the PCIJ in its Chorzów Factory Case[151]:

> *"The essential principle contained in the actual notion of an illegal act – a principle which seems to be established by international practice and in particular by the decisions of arbitral tribunals – is that reparation must, as far as possible, wipe out all the consequences of the illegal act and re-establish*

149 A strong divergence in terminology lets these differences often appear greater than they actually are in substance. On this general problem see Haasdijk, *The Lack of Uniformity in the Terminology of the International Law of Remedies.*

150 Such a review is provided by IComJ, *Practitioners' Guide.*

151 It is by no means clear that the content of the human right to reparation can be determined by looking at general international law. Especially with regard to the ILC ASR this seems questionable, since the ILC explicitly excluded the question of individual claims to reparation from the scope of the ASR, ILC, *ASR Commentaries*, A/56/10, art. 33(2), para 4. This however only concerns the possibility to claim. Regarding substantive questions the ILC considers the Articles to be applicable to violations of human rights, art. 33, para 3, 5. The ILC cites human rights bodies to establish and explain certain obligations, art. 33, para 3; art. 36, para 19. Vice versa, various international bodies, including human rights courts invoke the ARS when determining human rights obligations, IACtHR, *Case of Ruano Torres et al. v. El Salvador,* 2015, para 160; ECtHR, *Big Brother Watch v. The United Kingdom,* 58170/13, 2018, para 420; ACtHPR, *Tanganyika Law Society, the Legal and Human Rights Centre and Reverend Christopher R. Mtikila v. The United Republic of Tanzania*, 009&011/2011, 2013, para 108. For more practice see Duffy, *Articles on Responsibility of States for Internationally Wrongful Acts and Human Rights* Practice, EJIL:Talk!, 2021. Lastly, since the principle of full reparation governs both reparation in general international law and in human rights law, it is plausible that any inferences from this principle are valid for both areas of law.

> *the situation which would, in all probability, have existed if that act had not been committed."*[152]

Since then, the ICJ, the ECtHR, the IACtHR, and the African Court of Human and Peoples' Rights (ACtHPR) cited this judgment as a basis for their reparation jurisprudence.[153] The International Law Commission (ILC) modeled Art. 31 of its Articles on State Responsibility (ASR) on it.[154] Several treaty bodies base their reparation awards on the obligation to provide full reparation.[155]

Full reparation is provided through different forms of reparation. In inter-state disputes, the standard forms are restitution (I.), compensation (II.), and satisfaction (III.).[156] In the field of human rights, rehabilitation (IV.) and guarantees of non-repetition (V.) complement those measures.[157] While general international law also recognizes guarantees of non-repetition as a form of satisfaction and – more importantly – as an independent obligation related to the cessation of an unlawful act,[158] rehabilitation is specific to human rights. The following section provides details on each form of reparation before specifying their relationship (VI.) and turning to the concept of collective reparation (VII.).

I. Restitution

Restitution is most commonly defined as the reestablishment of the situation that had existed before the human rights violation has been committed.[159] Restitution hence addresses harm that can be reversed directly. It can also be

---

152 PCIJ, *Chorzów Factory Case*, para 125.

153 ICJ, *Armed Activities, Reparations,* para 100; ICJ, *Armed Activities on the Territory of the Congo (Democratic Republic of the Congo v. Uganda), Judgment*, I.C.J. Reports 2005, 168, para 259; ICJ, *Wall Opinion*, para 152; ECtHR, *Cyprus v. Turkey*, 25781/94, para 41 ff.; IACtHR, *Aloeboetoe v. Suriname*, para 43 f.; ACtHPR, *Mtikila v. Tanzania*, 011/2011, para 27.

154 ILC, *ASR Commentaries*, A/56/10, art. 31, para 2 f.; ICJ, *Armed Activities, Reparation,* para 101.

155 HRCom, *Bakar Japalali and Carmen Baloyo-Japalali v. Philippines*, CCPR/C/125/D/2536/2015, 2536/2015, 2019, para 7.6; CAT, *Saadia Ali v. Tunisia*, CAT/C/41/D/291/2006, 291/2006, 2008, para 15.8.

156 ILC, *ASR*, A/56/10, 2001, art. 31 ff.

157 UNGA, *Basic Principles*, A/RES/60/147, para 18.

158 ILC, *ASR*, A/56/10, art 30; ILC, *ASR Commentaries*, A/56/10, art. 30, para 11.

159 IACtHR, *Annual Report 2011*, 2011, 19; UNGA, *Basic Principles*, A/RES/60/147, para 19; CAT, *GC 3*, CAT/C/GC/3, para 8; AComHPR, *GC 4*, para 36.

defined as the establishment of the situation that would exist had the breach not been committed. But since that is the goal of full reparation generally, this definition conflates restitution with reparation as such.[160] Typical restitution measures are the return of property, release from detention and return to one's place of residence.[161] Most forms of harm caused by human rights violations do not lend themselves to restitution. It is impossible to restore a survivor to a status quo ante, e.g., before suffering a mental or physical injury. Therefore, restitution is rarely performed in human rights practice. Even if it is, it must usually be accompanied by other forms of reparation.[162]

Restitution raises two conceptual problems: First, it is often difficult to distinguish from cessation. States must cease unlawful acts according to Art. 30 ASR. This often requires the same action as restitution, for example, the release of an unlawfully detained person. Still, both obligations have an independent scope of application. On the one hand, cessation is more limited, as it only concerns ongoing violations. On the other hand, restitution is not required if it involves a burden out of all proportion for the state concerned, while cessation must be performed without exception.[163] The concepts can be distinguished in two steps. First, the violation in question must be ongoing because otherwise, cessation does not apply. This depends on the nature of the violated right and cannot be determined in the abstract.[164] If the violation is ongoing, cessation concerns the violation as such, whereas restitution addresses its consequences. The critical distinguishing question is: Would the survivor continue to suffer harm that can be reversed directly if the responsible state starts to abide by its obligation from now on? If that is the case, restitution is in order. If not, cessation suffices.

The second conceptual problem arises if a lawful state of affairs never existed. Then, the reestablishment of the status quo ante is impossible.[165] This case might occur, for example, if a person is lawfully detained but from day

160 ILC, *ASR Commentaries*, A/56/10, art. 35, para 2.

161 UNGA, *Basic Principles*, A/RES/60/147, para 19; ACtHPR, *Comparative Study on the Law and Practice of Reparations for Human Rights Violations,* 2019, 46 ff. Instructive, IACtHR, *Case of the Indigenous Communities of the Lhaka Honhat (Our Land) Association v. Argentina*, 2020, para 319 ff.

162 Odier Contreras-Garduno, *Collective Reparations*, 118; Antkowiak, *A Dark Side of Virtue*, 47; IACtHR, *Case of Bámaca-Velásquez v. Guatemala (Reparations and Costs) – Concurring Opinion of Judge Sergio García Ramírez*, 2002, 1 f.

163 ILC, *ASR Commentaries*, A/56/10, art. 30, para 7.

164 ILC, *ASR Commentaries*, A/56/10, art. 30, para 8.

165 A variant of this difficulty gives rise to the call for transformative reparation in transitional justice, which will be discussed below, ch. 4, E.I.

one in inhuman and degrading circumstances. While the obligation to cede violations will often cover such situations, they can also serve to refine the definition of restitution. Rather than demanding the restoration of the actual situation that existed before the violation was committed, restitution should require establishing an ideal normative conception of the status quo ante.[166]

II. Compensation

Compensation denotes a material benefit equivalent to the value of the harm suffered.[167] It usually takes the form of money but can also consist of other goods.[168] Compensation addresses financially assessable harm, whether material or non-material.[169] Material harm denotes the loss or impairment of a good with direct market value, including a person's ability to work, lost profits, and costs and expenses.[170] Non-material harm refers to "any damage, which is not damage to a person's assets, wealth or income."[171] In more detail, it refers to "mental suffering, injury to (the victim's) feelings, humiliation, shame, degradation, loss of social position or injury to his credit or reputation."[172]

This comprehensive notion of harm can complicate the assessment of the amount of compensation owed to a survivor. The task is straightforward in principle for material harm, even though many practical difficulties occur: The directly equivalent economic value can be calculated and reimbursed. The valuation methods differ with the kind of good lost or impaired and with the violation.[173] Non-material harm cannot be treated the same because

166 The concept will not be further developed here. Suffice it to say that the normative ideal will often be obvious when measured against human rights standards.

167 UNGA, *Basic Principles*, A/RES/60/147, para 20; PCIJ, *Chorzów Factory Case*, para 125; AComHPR, *GC 4*, para 38; IComJ, *Practitioners' Guide*, xiii f.

168 ILC, *ASR Commentaries*, A/56/10, art 36 para 4; IACtHR, *Goiburú et al. v. Paraguay*, 2006, para 156.

169 Material and non-material damage is often referred to as pecuniary and non-pecuniary damage. Non-material damage is also termed moral damage.

170 UNGA, *Basic Principles*, A/RES/60/147, para 20; CAT, *GC 3*, CAT/C/GC/3, para 9 f.; AComHPR, *GC 4*, para 37 ff.; PCIJ, *Chorzów Factory Case*, para 125; ILC, *ASR Commentaries*, A/56/10, art. 36, para 16.

171 Wittich, *Non-Material Damage and Monetary Reparation in International Law*, 329.

172 United States - German Mixed Claims Commission, *Lusitania Case*, R.I.A.A. VII, 1923, 32, 40. See above, fn. 170.

173 For different valuation methods see ILC, *ASR Commentaries*, A/56/10, art. 36, para 21 ff.; Marboe, *Compensation and Damages in International Law - The Limits of Fair*

it has no direct equivalent economic value. Instead, international courts and treaty bodies award compensation based on equity, considering all the circumstances of the case at hand.[174] The most important basis for that determination is the gravity of the violation and of the harm suffered.[175] Beyond that, international jurisprudence considers many factors related to the violation, the responsible state, the survivor, and the prevailing circumstances. Regarding the violation, courts, tribunals, and treaty bodies take into account the duration of the suffering[176], the importance of the right violated[177], a denial of justice after the violation[178], the amount of time passed since the violation occurred[179] , and the treatment of the survivor after the violation occurred.[180] Intent on behalf of the responsible state usually leads to higher amounts of compensation.[181] The IACtHR lowers the amount of

---

Market Value, 2006 J. World Investment Trade 7(5), 723, 735 ff.; ICJ, *Armed Activities Reparations;* ACtHPR, *Comparative Study on the Law and Practice of Reparations for Human Rights Violations*, 2019, 78 ff.

174 ACtHPR, *Beneficiaries of Late Norbert Zongo v. Burkina Faso (Judgment on Reparations)*, 013/2011, para 61; ECtHR, *Varnava and Others v. Turkey*, 16064/90 (Grand Chamber), 2009, para 224; ECtHR, *Practice Directions - Just Satisfaction Claims*, 2007, para 14; IACtHR, *Velásquez-Rodríguez v. Honduras (Reparations and Costs)*, 1989, para 27; IACtHR, *El Amparo v. Venezuela (Reparations and Costs)*, 1996, para 37; ICJ, *Armed Activities Reparations*, para 164; ICJ, *Case Concerning Ahmadou Sadio Diallo (Republic of Guinea v. Democratic Republic of the Congo), Compensation, Judgment*, I.C.J. Reports 2012, 324, para 24; ECtHR, *Al Jedda v. The United Kingdom*, 27021/08, para 114; *Affaire Campbell (Royaume-Uni Contre Portugal)*, R.I.A.A. II, 1931, 1145, 1158. For a valuation method based on economic considerations see Geistfeld, *Placing a Price on Pain and Suffering - A Method for Helping Juries Determine Tort Damages for Nonmonetary Injuries*, 1995 Cal. L. Rev. 83(3), 773, 818 ff.

175 HRCom, *Wilson v. The Philippines*, CCPR/C/79/D/868/1999, 868/1999, 2003, para 9; ECtHR, *Mentes and Others v. Turkey*, 23186/94 (Grand Chamber), 1998, para 20; CEDAW, *Inga Abramova v. Belarus*, CEDAW/C/49/D/23/2009, 23/2009, 2011, para 7.9; CEDAW, *R.P.B. v. The Philippines*, 34/2011, para 9; see also: UNGA, *Basic Principles*, A/RES/60/147, para 20.

176 ACtHPR, *Beneficiaries of Late Norbert Zongo v. Burkina Faso (Judgment on Reparations)*, 013/2011, para 62; ECtHR, *Price v. The United Kingdom*, 33394/96 (Third Section), 2001, para 34.

177 Peters et al., *Measuring Violations of Human Rights - An Empirical Analysis of Awards in Respect of Non-Pecuniary Damage Under the European Convention on Human Rights*, 2016 Heidelberg J. Intl. L. 76(1), 1, 18 f.

178 IACtHR, *Fernández Ortega et al. v Mexico*, 2010, para 293; ECtHR, *Varnava and Others v. Turkey*, 16064/90, para 224.

179 IACtHR, *Fernández Ortega et al. v Mexico*, para 293.

180 IACtHR, *Fernández Ortega et al. v Mexico*, para 293.

181 ECtHR, *Price v. The United Kingdom*, 33394/96, para 34.

compensation when the state accepts its responsibility.[182] Factors related to the survivor are their age[183], a subsequent change of living conditions[184], and contribution to the damage.[185] In the case of indirect survivors, the closeness of their relationship to the direct survivor plays a role.[186] Other than that, the general economic situation at the place the violation occurred is factored in.[187] The ECtHR refrained from awarding compensation to homeless persons and terrorists based on the morality of their previous lifestyle.[188] Needless to say, this practice cannot be justified because reparation addresses harm and does not reward or punish personal traits arbitrarily perceived as moral or immoral by the ECtHR. Lastly, in inter-state cases, the ICJ and the Ethiopia-Eritrea Claims Commission (EECC) held that because in situations of mass violations a reduced evidentiary standard applies[189] the resulting uncertainties allows reducing the level of compensation.[190]

To a certain extent, the lack of a directly equivalent economic value necessarily makes the determination of the amount of compensation for non-material damage arbitrary.[191] Courts and treaty bodies have devised different strategies to deal with this problem. Many refrain from determining com-

182 Pasqualucci, *Victim Reparations in the Inter-American Human Rights System - A Critical Assessment of Current Practice and Procedure*, 1996 Mich. J. Intl. L. 18(1), 1, 35.

183 IACtHR, *Caracazo v. Venezuela (Reparations and Costs)*, 2002, para 102; ECtHR, *Kostovska v. the Former Yugoslav Republic of Macedonia*, 44353/02 (Fifth Section), 2006, para 60.

184 IACtHR, *Fernández Ortega et al. v Mexico*, para 293.

185 ECtHR, *Practice Directions - Just Satisfaction Claims*, para 2.

186 Rubio-Marín et al., *Repairing Family Members*, 240 f.

187 ECtHR, *Practice Directions - Just Satisfaction Claims*, para 2.

188 Ichim, *Just Satisfaction Under the European Convention on Human Rights*, 2014, 168 ff. Correa sees a similar tendency in a recent judgment of the IACtHR, although the court did not provide an explicit reasoning for limiting reparation, Correa, *Inter-American Court's Dangerous Precedent in Limiting Insurgents' Right to Reparations*, JusticeInfo.net, 2 September 2015.

189 See below, Ch. 4 D.II.

190 ICJ, *Armed Activities Reparations*, para 107; EECC, *Final Award*, para 38. The EECC relies on practice of the UNCC and others.

191 The internal criticism that the ICJ drew with its fixation of global sums in the Armed Activities case shows that this is especially salient in cases of mass violations, given that then a scarcity of evidence often compounds the problem: ICJ, *Armed Activities on the Territory of the Congo (Democratic Republic of the Congo v. Uganda), Reparations – Declaration of Judge Tomka*, para 8 ff.; ICJ, *Armed Activities Reparations – Separate Opinion of Judge Yusuf*, para 24, 35 f.; ICJ, *Armed Activities on the Territory of the Congo (Democratic Republic of the Congo v. Uganda), Reparations – Separate Opinion of Judge Robinson*, para 4 ff.

pensation amounts completely and leave this either to negotiations between the parties or national court systems.[192] This delegation does not make international law indifferent to the amount of compensation. Compensation must still be "fair", "proportionate", "just", or "adequate", indicating that international law establishes a corridor of adequate compensation within which the parties or national courts can determine the exact amount due.[193] The ECtHR uses tables indicating a medium amount of compensation for particular harms suffered, which can be tailored to the circumstances of the case.[194] Previous case law often orients the courts or treaty bodies.[195] These approaches cannot erase the fundamental arbitrariness of determining the value of non-material harm; they can merely ensure that "the arbitrariness [is] at least uniform."[196] Given that this problem lies in the highly subjective nature of non-material harm, it probably does not lend itself to more precise calculation.

Another aspect of compensation rarely receives attention: International jurisprudence has established a gravity threshold non-material financially assessable harm must reach to warrant compensation. All international courts and tribunals frequently hold that a judicial finding of a violation – a form of satisfaction – constitutes sufficient reparation for less severe violations.[197] Thus, even though survivors suffered non-material but financially assessable damage, they do not receive compensation if that damage remains below a certain threshold.

---

192 AComHPR, *Groupe de Travail sur les Dossiers Judiciaires Stratégiques v. Democratic Republic of Congo*, 259/2002, para 88; HRCom, *Guidelines on Measures of Reparation Under the Optional Protocol to the International Covenant on Civil and Political Rights,* CCPR/C/158, 2016, para 9.

193 HRCom, *Sterling v. Jamaica*, CCPR/C/57/D/598/1994, 598/1994, 1996, para 10; CAT, *Hajrizi Dzemajl et al. v. Yugoslavia*, CAT/C/29/D/161/2000, 161/2000, 2002, para 11.

194 Ichim, *Just Satisfaction Under the ECHR*, 121.

195 ECtHR, *Practice Directions - Just Satisfaction Claims*, para 14; IACtHR, *Suárez-Rosero v. Ecuador (Reparations and Costs)*, 1999, para 67.

196 Plant, *Damages for Pain and Suffering Symposium - Personal Injury Litigation*, 1958 Ohio St. L. J. 19(2), 211. A more detailed critique of the approaches listed above can be found in Geistfeld, *Placing a Price on Pain and Suffering.*

197 ECtHR, *Öcalan v. Turkey*, 46221/99 (Grand Chamber), 2005, para 212; ECtHR, *Golder v. United Kingdom,* 4451/70 (Grand Chamber), 1975, para 50; ECtHR, *Varnava and Others v. Turkey,* 16064/90 (Grand Chamber), 2009, para 224; IACtHR, *Case of "The Last Temptation of Christ" (Omedo-Bustis et al.) v. Chile,* 5 February 2001, para 99; ICJ, *Armed Activities Reparations,* para 387; ACtHPR, *AComHPR v. The Republic of Kenya – Judgment on Reparations,* 006/2012, 2022, 7. On declaratory judgments as satisfaction see below, III.

In sum, states must compensate all financially assessable damage by giving the survivor a benefit equal to the value of the harm suffered – usually money. The amount of compensation for material damage can be calculated. Compensation for non-material damage is based on equity considering all factors of the case. If non-material damage remains below a certain gravity threshold, satisfaction suffices.

III. Satisfaction

There is no agreed-upon definition of satisfaction in international law. It usually refers to the performance of a symbolic act to remedy damage that is not financially assessable.[198] The main question is hence which damage is not financially assessable. Most often, satisfaction remedies damage to dignity, honor, or reputation.[199] Some authors further contend that "an injury [...] is necessarily inherent in every violation of a [...] right [...]" and that this alleged "legal damage" lends itself to satisfaction.[200] The concept of legal damage, however, erases the distinction between the violation of a primary obligation and the secondary obligation to repair. This does not concord with international practice, which still requires the positive determination that survivors suffered harm to be eligible for reparation.[201] Consequently, legal damage has only found sporadic use in international jurisprudence[202] and does not form part of the international law on reparation.[203]

---

198 ILC, *ASR Commentaries*, A/56/10, art. 37, para 3.

199 Wyler/Papaux, *The Different Forms of Reparation - Satisfaction*, in: Crawford et al. (eds.), *The Law of International Responsibility*, 2010, 623, 625; ILC, *Second Report on State Responsibility, by Mr. Gaetano Arangio-Ruiz, Special Rapporteur*, A/CN.4/425, 1989, para 13; *Rainbow Warrior* R.I.A.A. XX, 1990, 215, para 122, citing the second report on state responsibility by Arangio-Ruiz. Ramírez, *La Jurisprudencia de la Corte Interamericana de Derechos Humanos en Materia de Reparaciones*, in: Inter-American Court of Human Rights (ed.), *La Corte Interamericana de Derechos Humanos - Un Cuarto de Siglo: 1979-2004*, 2005, 1, 80.

200 ILC, *Third Report on State Responsibility, by Mr. Roberto Ago, Special Rapporteur*, A/CN.4/246, 1971, para 74; ILC, *Second Report on State Responsibility by Special Rapporteur Arangio-Ruiz*, A/CN.4/425; Hoss, *Satisfaction*, in: Wolfrum (ed.), *Max Planck Encyclopedia of Public International Law*, Online Edition 2011, para 9 ff.

201 See above, Introduction, C.

202 *Rainbow Warrior Case*, para 122.

203 Wittich, *Non-Material Damage and Monetary Reparation in International Law*, 348 ff.; McIntyre, *Declaratory Judgments of the International Court of Justice*, in: Kok/Lavranos (eds.), *Hague Yearbook of International Law*, 2013, 107, 149 ff.

Satisfaction takes a wide variety of forms. The most common ones are official apologies and the acknowledgment of wrongdoing.[204] Other forms include the naming of streets, plazas, and schools after survivors, monuments, radio broadcasts, and the publication of a judgment finding a violation.[205] International practice gives little guidance on what forms of satisfaction are adequate in which case. It depends on the nature and the consequences of the violation. The resulting flexibility of this instrument allows judicial bodies to tailor satisfaction to the needs of survivors, redressing their harm as effectively as possible.

Four forms of satisfaction warrant further discussion: Declaratory judgments, truth, prosecution, and punishment. A judgment declaring the conduct in question to be unlawful belongs to the most common forms of satisfaction.[206] Yet, it does not fit into the general concept of reparation without difficulty since a neutral entity performs it, not the state responsible. This conceptual difference evinces a punitive function of satisfaction.[207] Declaratory judgments facilitate a reparatory transaction. They punish the responsible state through a loss of reputation, from which the survivor receives satisfaction.

Truth, prosecution, and punishment are a form of satisfaction and independent obligations under human rights law.[208] Even if prosecution and

204 UNGA, *Basic Principles*, A/RES/60/147, para 22(e); HRCom, *Reparation Guidelines*, CCPR/C/158, para 11(e); IACtHR, *Rosendo Cantú et al. v. Mexico*, 2010, para 226; ILC, *ASR*, A/56/10, art. 37(2).

205 Correa, *Artículo 63,* in: Christian Steiner et al. (eds.), *Convención Americana Sobre Derechos Humanos - Comentario,* 2nd Edition 2019, 1019, 1057; Correa, *Artículo 63*, in: Steiner/Uribe (eds.), *Convención Americana Sobre Derechos Humanos - Comentario,* 2014, 817, 850.

206 Amerasinghe, *Jurisdiction of International Tribunals*, 2003, 419 ff.; ECtHR, *Öcalan v. Turkey*, 46221/99 (Grand Chamber), 2005, para 212; IACtHR, *Victor Neira-Alegría et al. v. Peru (Reparations and Costs)*, 1996, para 56; IACtHR, *Ríos et al. v. Venezuela*, 2009, para 403; IACtHR, *Perozo et al. v. Venzuela*, 2009, para 413; UNGA, *Basic Principles*, A/RES/60/147, para 22(d). A well-founded critique of this measure of satisfaction is provided by McIntyre, *Declaratory Judgments of the International Court of Justice*.

207 Wyler/Papaux, *The Different Forms of Reparation - Satisfaction*, 623 ff.; McIntyre, *Declaratory Judgments of the International Court of Justice*, 153 ff.

208 ILC, *ASR Commentaries*, A/56/10, art. 37, para 5; ICJ, *Armed Activities Reparations,* para 389 f.; UNGA, *Basic Principles*, A/RES/60/147, para 22(b), (f); AComHPR, *GC 4*, para 44; HRCom, *GC 31*, CCPR/C/21/Rev.1/Add.13, para 16; HRCom, *Reparation Guidelines*, CCPR/C/158, para 11(b); IACtHR, *Myrna Mack Chang v. Guatemala*, para 274; IACtHR, *Radilla-Pacheco v. Mexico*, 2009, para 336. But see also the Court's indication to the contrary in IACtHR, *Case of the "Street Children" (Villagrán-Morales*

punishment were also individual rights[209], any individual's responsibility would first have to be determined through a trial compatible with international standards. Prosecution and punishment remain within the hands of the state. Survivors can merely demand that it be carried out thoroughly.[210]

IV. Rehabilitation

Rehabilitation is a form of reparation specific to human rights law. The concept was introduced in the 1985 Declaration of Basic Principles of Justice for Victims of Crime and Abuse of Power[211] and is now widely used by different human rights courts and treaty bodies. It addresses harm to an individual's independence and integration into society by helping them restore or acquire skills.[212] Understood narrowly, rehabilitation means the provision of medical and psychological care.[213] The more extensive notion which most international courts and tribunals follow, at least in practice, also includes legal and social care, including vocational training and education.[214] Rehabilitation bears some resemblance to restitution since it encompasses

---

et al.) v. Guatemala (Reparations and Costs), para 99. A perfect example of the unclear status of prosecution and punishment is provided by the IACtHR, which frequently puts the obligation to prosecute and punish under the heading of "Other Forms of Reparation", but gives the impression in the respective text of the judgment that the obligation is not connected to reparation. See as an example IACtHR, *Case of the Miguel Castro-Castro Prison v. Peru (Merits, Reparations and Costs)*, 2006, para 436. On truth see OHCHR, *Study on the Right to Truth*, E/CN.4/2006/91, 2006, 112 ff.; Shelton, *Remedies in International Human Rights Law*, 107 ff.

209 The HRCom denies survivors such a right, while the ECtHR and IACtHR grant it, HRCom, *Mohamed Rabbae, A.B.S. and N.A. v. The Netherlands*, CCPR/C/117/D/2124/2011, 2124/2011, 2017, para 10.3; HRCom, *H.C.M.A. v. The Netherlands*, CCPR/C/35/D/213/1986, 213/1986, 1989, para 11.6; ECtHR, *Aksoy v. Turkey*, 21987/93 (Chamber), 1996, para 98; IACtHR, *Trujillo-Oroza v. Bolivia (Reparations and Costs)*, 2002, para 100.

210 IACtHR, *Case of the "White Van" (Paniagua-Morales et al.) v. Guatemala (Merits)*, 1998, para 178; HRCom, *Rodger Chongwe v. Zambia*, CCPR/C/70/D/821/1998, 821/1998, 2000, para 7; ECtHR, *Gül v. Turkey*, 22676/93 (Fourth Section), 2000, para 88.

211 UNGA, *Basic Principles for Victims of Crime and Abuse of Power*, A/RES/40/34, para 14 ff. The Principles use the term assistance. The term rehabilitation was introduced by Art. 14 CAT.

212 Redress, *Rehabilitation as a Form of Reparation Under International Law*, 2009, 8 ff.; CAT, *GC 3*, CAT/C/GC/3, para 11; AComHPR, *GC 4*, para 40 f.

213 IACtHR, *Annual Report 2011*, 19; HRCom, *Reparation Guidelines*, CCPR/C/158, para 8.

214 UNGA, *Basic Principles*, A/RES/60/147, para 21; CAT, *GC 3*, CAT/C/GC/3, para 11; AComHPR, *GC 4*, para 41; Correa, *Art. 63*, 1068.

measures that directly reverse harm. However, while the two coincide, rehabilitation has a broader approach to redress: It seeks to empower the survivor through medical, psychological, and social means. For example, providing a disabled survivor with a wheelchair or crutches does not directly reverse the violation's consequences, but it does restore their independence and thus mitigates the violation's consequences.

Sometimes the state pays money dedicated to cover the costs of medical or psychological assistance.[215] For conceptual clarity, this form of reparation should only be considered rehabilitation if the payment is made upfront and restricted to enable the survivor to get the services they need. If the payment reimburses the survivor for costs of services they already incurred or if the survivor can freely decide how to spend the money, it is better considered compensation for material damage.

V. Guarantees of Non-Repetition

Guarantees of non-repetition aim at preventing future violations. They often address underlying structural causes for a violation.[216] They take many different forms, including institutional and legislative reform, training of public officials, and the elaboration of codes of conduct.[217] Because of their strong preventive dimension, guarantees of non-repetition cannot easily be categorized as reparation. While providing reassurance to survivors, guarantees of non-repetition are mostly directed at society as a whole or hypothetical future survivors. They are predicated on the risk of repetition of the violation, not on damage arising from it.[218] Consequently, their categorization is far

---

215 IACtHR, *Loayza-Tamayo v. Peru (Reparations and Costs)*, para 129(b), (d); ECtHR, *Z and Others v. The United Kingdom*, 29392/95 (Grand Chamber), 2001, para 127.

216 IACtHR, *Annual Report 2011*, 20; IACtHR, *Atala Riffo and Daughters v. Chile*, 2012, para 267; AComHPR, *Malawi African Association and Others v. Mauritania*, 54/91, 2000, operative para 5; CAT, *GC 3*, CAT/C/GC/3, para 18; AComHPR, *GC 4*, para 45.

217 UNGA, *Basic Principles*, A/RES/60/147, para 23.

218 Sullivan, *Changing the Premise of International Legal Remedies - The Unfounded Adoption of Assurances and Guarantees of Non-Repetition*, 2002 UCLA J. Intl. L. Foreign Aff. 7, 265, 269; Colandrea, *On the Power of the European Court of Human Rights to Order Specific Non-Monetary Measures - Some Remarks in Light of the Assanidze, Broniowski and Sejdovic Cases*, 2007 Hum. Rts. L. Rev. 7(2), 396, 409; Tigroudja, *La Satisfaction et les Garanties de Non-Repetition de l'Illicite*, in: Société de Législation Comparée - Unité Mixte de Recherche de Droit Comparé de Paris (ed.), *Réparer les Violations Graves et Massives des Droits de l'Homme - La Cour*

from uniform: The African Commission on Human and Peoples' Rights (AComHPR), the International Tribunal on the Law of the Sea (ITLOS), Art. 24(5) Convention on the Elimination of All Forms of Discrimination (CERD) and the Basic Principles treat them exclusively as a form of reparation.[219] The ICJ and the ACtHPR do not specify their legal basis.[220] While the HRCom and the Committee on the Elimination of All Forms of Discrimination Against Women (CEDAW) generally categorize guarantees of non-repetition as reparation, they usually separate them from orders of reparation in their communications, treating them as an independent obligation.[221] The IACtHR, the Committee Against Torture (CAT), and the ILC expressly follow this approach. The former two base guarantees of non-repetition on the obligation to repair and the obligation to prevent violations.[222] The ILC primarily sees them as an independent obligation but also affirms that they can serve as satisfaction.[223]

Based on this ambiguous practice, guarantees of non-repetition seem to have a dual nature: They do form part of the international law on reparation

---

Interaméricaine, Pionnière et Modèle?, 2010, 69; HRC, *Report of the Special Rapporteur on the Promotion of Truth, Justice, Reparation and Guarantees of Non-Recurrence, Pablo de Greiff*, A/HRC/30/42, 2015, para 26.

219 AComHPR, *Kazingachire et al. v. Zimbabwe*, 295/04, para 130; ITLOS, *The M/V "Saiga" (No.2) Case (Saint Vincent and the Grenadines v. Guinea)*, ITLOS Reports 1999, 10, para 171; UNGA, *Basic Principles*, A/RES/60/147, para 23; ILC, *Second Report on State Responsibility by Special Rapporteur Arangio-Ruiz*, A/CN.4/425, 148 ff.

220 ICJ, *LaGrand (Germany v. United States of America)*, I.C.J. Reports 2001, 466, para 124; ICJ, *Case Concerning Avena and Other Mexican Nationals (Mexico v. United States of America)*, I.C.J. Reports 2004, 12, para 149 ff. The ACtHPR included guarantees of non-repetition in its ruling on reparations in the case concerning Reverend Mtikila. However, it merely reiterated an order it made in the judgment on the merits in which it explicitly found that it could not decide on reparation, since the applicant did not claim any reparation at that stage of the proceedings, ACtHPR, *Mtikila v. Tanzania*, 011/2011, para 42 f.; ACtHPR, *Tanganyika Law Society, the Legal and Human Rights Centre and Reverend Christopher R. Mtikila v. The United Republic of Tanzania*, 009&011/2011, 2013, para 124, 126.

221 HRCom, *GC 31*, CCPR/C/21/Rev.1/Add.13, para 16; HRCom, *Reparation Guidelines*, CCPR/C/158, para 2; HRCom, *Guillermo Ignacio Dermit Barbato et al. v. Uruguay*, CCPR/C/OP/2, 84/1981, 1990, para 11; HRCom, *Beatriz Weismann Lanza and Alcides Lanza Perdomo v. Uruguay*, CCPR/C/9/D/8/1977, 8/1977, 1980, para 17; HRCom, *William Torres Ramirez v. Uruguay*, CCPR/C/10/D/4/1977, 4/1977, 1980, para 19; CEDAW, *General Recommendation 28*, CEDAW/C/GC/28, para 32.

222 CAT, *GC 3*, CAT/C/GC/3, para 2, 18; Schönsteiner, *Dissuasive Measures and the Society as a Whole - A Working Theory of Reparations in the Inter-American Court of Human Rights*, 2007 Am. U. Intl. L. Rev. 23(1), 127, 145 ff.

223 ILC, *ASR Commentaries*, A/56/10, art. 30, para 11.

and at the same time exist as an independent legal obligation. However, international practice is unclear under which circumstances they may be ordered as reparation and to which kind of damage they respond.[224]

VI. The Relation Between the Different Forms of Reparation

The five forms of reparation are not neatly separate. They overlap, and in practice, some reparation measures cannot be categorized clearly as one or the other. Since the concepts differ nonetheless, the question of their relationship arises. Restitution takes primacy over other forms of reparation because it comes closest to the overall goal of full reparation to erase all consequences of the violation. Other forms of reparation only come into play if or insofar as restitution is impossible or inadequate.[225] The relation between the remaining forms of reparation is unclear. The ILC submits that compensation takes precedence over satisfaction.[226] However, according to the definitions sketched out above, the two forms address different harms. They are, therefore, complementary rather than placed in a hierarchical order.[227] The same holds for guarantees of non-repetition. Rehabilitation can address the same harm as compensation. Here, the question of relationship turns into the question of who gets to choose adequate forms of reparation.

The ILC assumes that the survivor has – in principle – a right to choose their preferred mode of reparation, regardless of what is objectively required to mitigate the harm suffered.[228] It finds limited support in the jurisprudence of the ICJ,[229] but not in international human rights practice. On the contrary, the ECtHR held that „if restitutio in integrum is in practice impossible the respondent States are free to choose the means whereby they will comply

224 An exploration of the practice is provided by El-Zein/Langmack, *Conceptualizing Guarantees of Non-Repetition - Chances and Risks for Human Rights Jurisprudence*, presented at: AHRI Conference 2018 (Edinburgh) (on file with the author).

225 Shelton, *Remedies in International Human Rights Law*, 298; IACtHR, *Compendium*, OEA/Ser.L/V/II.Doc. 121, para 167; ACtHPR, *Comparative Study on the Law and Practice of Reparations for Human Rights Violations*, 2019, 50.

226 ILC, *ASR*, A/56/10, art. 37(1).

227 Kerbrat, *Interaction Between the Forms of Reparation*, in: Crawford et al. (eds.), *The Law of International Responsibility*, 2010, 573, 581; IACtHR, *Compendium*, OEA/Ser.L/V/II.Doc. 121, para 167.

228 ILC, *ASR Commentaries*, A/56/10, art. 34, para 4.

229 ICJ, *Jurisdictional Immunities of the State (Germany v. Italy: Greece Intervening)*, I.C.J. Reports 2012, 99, para 137.

with a judgment [...], and the Court will not make consequential orders or declaratory statements in this regard."[230] According to the court, a state's freedom to choose between adequate reparation measures is the necessary corollary of the freedom to choose how to comply with the primary obligations under the convention.[231] This freedom does not apply to restitution and monetary compensation, which the court frequently orders without leaving the state any room to choose. Hence, in the ECtHR practice, the state is only free to choose between different forms of rehabilitation, satisfaction, and guarantees of non-repetition. This finds some support in further international practice.[232] The majority of human rights courts and treaty bodies neither leaves the survivor nor the state any explicit room to choose. Instead, they determine adequate reparation measures based on both parties' arguments, which must be implemented regardless of either party's preferences.[233] There is often some automatic leeway in implementing reparation awards, which the states enjoy as the implementing agent.[234] But international practice grants a right to choose neither to the survivor nor the state responsible. Rather, the adequate forms of reparation are determined on an objective basis. According to the principle of effectiveness, they must be chosen to overcome the harm suffered as effectively as possible.[235]

VII. Collective Reparation

Corresponding to the rise of collectives as potential survivors, collective reparation is now firmly entrenched in the law on reparation.[236] Rather than being a particular form of reparation, the term designates reparation to collectives, reparation through collective goods, as well as a mode of distribution of individual reparation.[237] It can encompass restitution, compensation,

230 ECtHR, *Papamichalopoulos and Others v. Greece (Article 50)*, 14556/89 (Chamber), 1995, para 34.

231 ECtHR, *Papamichalopoulos v. Greece*, 14556/89, para 34.

232 HRCom, *Bariza Zaier v. Algeria - Individual Opinion of Gerald L. Neumann (Concurring)*, CCPR/C/112/D/2026/2011, 2026/2011, 2014, para 6.

233 Contreras-Garduno, *Collective Reparations*, 145.

234 This aspect will receive further treatment below, ch. 4, B.III.

235 On that see below, ch. 4, E.II.3.

236 See above, B.I.

237 HRC, *Report of the Special Rapporteur on Transitional Justice on Reparation*, A/69/518, para 38.

rehabilitation, satisfaction as well as guarantees of non-repetition.[238] As with the exact scope of collective beneficiaries of reparation, the exact content of the concept and its relation to the international law on reparation is unclear.[239] These challenges are complex and have received detailed treatment elsewhere.[240] For this study, it suffices to establish that the international law on reparation obliges states to repair collective harm and enables them, where appropriate, to distribute individual reparation collectively and to repair through collective goods.

D. Limits of the Right to Reparation

Reparation is only adequate if it is proportionate to the gravity of the harm and the violations suffered.[241] The proportionality requirement is best conceived of as an overarching principle placing different limits on the obligation to provide reparation. Under certain circumstances, it allows awarding less reparation than the damage incurred.[242] Beyond that, proportionality limits certain forms of reparation. According to Art. 35(b) ASR, restitution must not be performed if it places a disproportionate burden on the state. While this is not reflected overtly in human rights practice, the IACtHR held that restitution is not always appropriate, even though it did not elaborate under which

238 Odier Contreras-Garduno, *Collective Reparations*, 138 ff.; HRC, *Report of the Special Rapporteur on Transitional Justice on Reparation*, A/69/518, para 38 ff.

239 Odier Contreras-Garduno, *Collective Reparations*, 320.

240 A further examination of collective reparation is outside the scope of the present study. For that see Odier Contreras-Garduno, *Collective Reparations*; Rosenfeld, *Collective Reparation for Victims of Armed Conflict*; Mégret, *The Case for Collective Reparations Before the International Criminal Court*, in: Wemmers (ed.), *Reparation for Victims of Crimes Against Humanity*, 2014, 171; Brodney, *Implementing International Criminal Court-Ordered Collective Reparations - Unpacking Present Debates*, 2016 J. Oxford Centre Socio-L. Stud., 1; ACtHPR, *Comparative Study on the Law and Practice of Reparations for Human Rights Violations*, 2019, 69 ff.

241 CEDAW, *R.P.B. v. The Philippines*, 34/2011, para 9; CEDAW, *Inga Abramova v. Belarus*, 23/2009, para 7.9; AComHPR, *GC 4*, para 34; UNGA, *Basic Principles*, A/RES/60/147, para 15; ECSR, *Syndicat de Défense des Fonctionnaires v. France (Merits)*, 73/2011, 2012, para 59; CAT, *GC 3*, CAT/C/GC/3, para 6; IACtHR, *Castillo-Paéz v. Peru (Reparations and Costs)*, 27 November 1998, para 51.

242 Gray, *Remedies*, in: Cesare et al. (eds.), *Oxford Handbook of International Adjudication*, 2013, 871, 891. See also below, ch. 4, E.II.4.b.

circumstances it is not.[243] Proportionality plays an obvious role in the equitable assessment of compensation for immaterial damage. It limits compensation to the reimbursement of actual losses, excluding, e.g., punitive compensation.[244] The requirement of proportionality also excludes remote damage from reparation.[245] It would place a disproportionate burden on the responsible state if it had to repair all the damage the unlawful act caused. Third, it plays a role in assessing the scope of reparation in cases of concomitant causes and contributory negligence.[246] The rights of third parties also limit reparation. Reparation easily conflicts with third-party rights, for example, if land is to be restituted to an original owner even though the current owner acquired the land lawfully. Such conflicts will be treated at length below.[247] Suffice it to say for now that the international law on reparation leaves enough room for solutions tailored to the specific circumstances of the case.

E. The Theoretical Foundation of the International Law on Reparation

The theoretical foundation of reparation in transitional justice, which will be discussed below,[248] is best understood compared to the theoretical foundation of reparation in non-transitional contexts. The international law on reparation rests on the theory of corrective justice Aristotle developed in his Nicomachean Ethics: Corrective justice serves to reverse unjust transactions. Unjust transactions deviate from the state of equality, in which each party possesses what they are morally entitled to.[249] Corrective justice requires the restoration of the state of equality by using the perpetrator's unjust gain to

---

243 IACtHR, *Aloeboetoe v. Suriname*, para 49; Pasqualucci, *The Practice and Procedure of the Inter-American Court of Human Rights*, 2nd Edition 2013, 192.

244 IACtHR, *Velásquez-Rodríguez v. Honduras (Reparations and Costs)*, para 37 f.; ECtHR, *Mentes and Others v. Turkey*, 23186/94, para 21; ICJ, *Armed Activities Reparations*, para 102.

245 See above, B.I.

246 This function is beyond the scope of this chapter. For more detail see ILC, *Second Report on State Responsibility by Special Rapporteur Arangio-Ruiz*, A/CN.4/425, para 44, 89. See also below, ch. 4, E.II.2.a.

247 See below, ch. 4, B.II.2, E.II.4.

248 See below, ch. 3.

249 Weinrib, *Corrective Justice in a Nutshell*, 2002 U. Toronto L. J. 52(1), 349, 349, 354. For a broader understanding of corrective justice see Polansky, *Giving Justice its Due*, in: Polansky (ed.), *The Cambridge Companion to Aristotle's Nicomachean Ethics*, 2014, 151, 161.

restore the survivor to the situation that would exist had the violation not been committed.[250] Aristotle compares this operation to a set of lines. If one of the lines exceeds the other's length, the judge has to transfer half of the exceeding length to the shorter line so that both are equally long.[251] Corrective justice is thus an arithmetic operation that takes an unjust gain away from the perpetrator to remedy the unjust loss the survivor of an unjust transaction suffered. Notably, the terms "transaction", "gain", and "loss" do not only refer to economic goods. According to Aristotle, "gain" and "loss" are merely the terms used to estimate damage, no matter whether material or immaterial. "Gain" should not be interpreted literally as an addition to the perpetrator's assets. It merely denotes the amount of reparation the perpetrator owes the survivor.[252] Corrective justice is therefore not only applicable to economic injustices but also assaults, murders, etc.[253] While corrective justice is usually taken as the basis for tort law and other private law constellations, the international law on reparation for human rights violations also developed from its principles.[254] In addition to this primary purpose of corrective justice, reparation also serves condemnation and deterrence.[255]

F. Summary: The International Law on Reparation

Even though many details remain unresolved, international practice converges towards an international law on reparation based on the principle of full reparation. Individuals have a customary and treaty-based human right to reparation, which, in principle, is also applicable in international and non-international armed conflicts. The right is a logical extension of a recognized general principle of international law and finds a basis in the right to an effective remedy. It places an obligation of result on the state to

250 Miller, *Justice*, in: Zalta (ed.), *Stanford Encyclopedia of Philosophy*, Online Edition 2017, 2.2.

251 Aristotle/Rackham, *Nicomachean Ethics*, 2014, 277 f.

252 Aristotle/Rackham, *Nicomachean Ethics*, 275.

253 Weinrib, *The Gains and Losses of Corrective Justice*, 1994 Duke L. J. 44(2), 277, 282 ff.

254 Shelton, *Remedies in International Human Rights Law*, 19 f.; Buti, *Reparations, Justice Theories and Stolen Generations*, 2008 U. W. Australia L. Rev. 34(1), 168, 171 f. This overlap is no coincidence, since the international law on reparation developed from private law principles, IACtHR, *Loayza-Tamayo v. Peru (Reparations and Costs) - Joint Concurring Opinion of Judges A.A. Cançado Trindade and A. Abreu-Burelli*, 1998, para 6.

255 Shelton, *Remedies in International Human Rights Law*, 20 ff.

achieve full reparation: erasing all consequences of the illegal act by putting the survivor in the position they would be in had the violation not occurred. The state owes this obligation to every person who suffered harm due to a violation of their rights, be it directly, indirectly, individually, or collectively, as long as the harm is not caused too remotely. In many cases, the state will also owe reparation to survivors of violations by non-state actors based on its positive human rights obligations or on the attribution of the actions of the non-state actor to the state.

How to achieve full reparation depends on the damage the survivor suffered. Different forms of reparation are adequate for different types of damages. Directly reversible damage must be repaired through restitution – the act of restoring the survivor to the position they were in before the violation was committed. Insofar as that is impossible or inadequate, the state must resort to compensation, satisfaction, rehabilitation, and guarantees of non-repetition. Compensation is a material benefit – most often money – which addresses financially assessable damage of material and non-material nature. Material damage must be compensated according to its economic value, non-material damage that crosses a certain gravity threshold based on equity. Satisfaction repairs damage that is not financially assessable, as well as financially assessable damage below said gravity threshold. International law equips states with a laundry list of mostly symbolic measures to accomplish that task. Rehabilitation denotes the provision of medical and psychological care as well as legal and social assistance to repair impairments to the survivor's independence and integration in society. Guarantees of non-repetition address the risk that the violation recurs. Again, a laundry list of measures is available to states for that aim.

The principle of proportionality limits reparation. Principally, reparation must be proportionate to the violation, and the harm suffered. This requirement limits reparation to the damage incurred and excludes remote damage.

This short chapter cannot and does not pretend to reflect all details of reparation in international law. It established basic principles according to which states need to repair survivors of human rights violations. These principles demand a lot. Assessing, calculating, and erasing all the damage caused by human rights violations can require a tremendous amount of time and resources. Only a few entry points exist in the law on reparation to alleviate this heavy burden. In principle, that is warranted: The state voluntarily violated the survivor's human rights. It, not the survivor, needs to bear the consequences of that action. However, as the following chapter will evince, the rigor of the international law on reparation makes it difficult to accommodate the unique challenges reparation faces in the transitional justice situation.

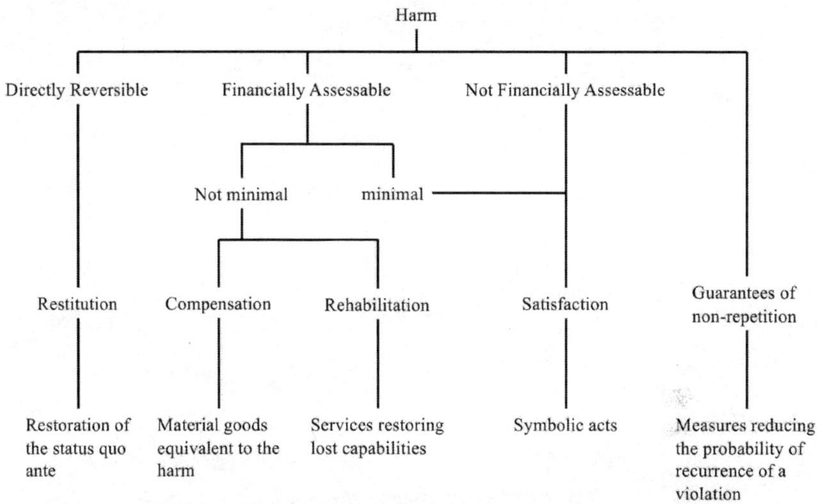

Figure 1: The International Law on Reparation – Overview (created by the author)

Chapter 2 – Case Studies

At the core of this project lies the assumption of a disconnect between the international law on reparation and transitional justice practice. This disconnect is not due to states' unwillingness to repair survivors – although the frequent lack of political will does not exactly aid the cause. The international law on reparation is built to respond to individual, not systematic, violations. It, therefore, cannot accommodate the unique challenges the transitional justice situation brings with it.

With the preceding chapter clarifying that disconnect's legal side, its practical side now warrants closer attention. Three in-depth case studies of six transitional justice reparation programs will demonstrate that transitional justice practice deviates in significant ways from international legal standards. It will be shown that these deviations are reasonable responses to the challenges of the transitional justice situation. The identified differences will – together with theoretical considerations laid out in chapter three – serve as guide rails for this project's central endeavor: Bridging the disconnect between law and practice by adapting the international law on reparation to the transitional justice context.

A. Introduction

I. Case Selection

The cases surveyed are Sierra Leone's reparation program operating since 2008 in response to the country's internal armed conflict (B.), Colombia's efforts, starting in 2011, to repair survivors of its internal armed conflict (C.) and the reparation programs created under the auspices of the ICC in the Lubanga, Katanga, Al Mahdi and Ntaganda cases in the Democratic Republic of the Congo (DRC) and Mali (D.). All surveyed programs are transitional justice reparation programs. To recall, this study defines transitional justice as a state's attempt to address a legacy of systematic human rights violations, which aims to transform society towards a strengthened respect for human rights and generalized trust. The latter is defined as the expectation that other members of society and state institutions adhere to and support human rights. A transitional justice situation is consequently defined as a situation in the aftermath of systematic human rights violations, which calls for measures to enhance respect for human rights and generalized trust.[256] The reparation programs this chapter examines all respond to systematic human rights violations and aim at societal transformation.[257] While not all of them conceptualize this transformation as enhanced respect for human rights and generalized trust, their broader transformational aims come close enough. As will be further explained in chapter three, this study's definition of transitional justice is vague and only one of several possible conceptualizations of transitional justice. Some deviations in the aims pursued hence do not let reparation programs fall outside the definition.

The reparation programs were selected according to the logic of maximum variety sampling.[258] They represent opposite ends of important geographical, institutional, political, legal, economic, and other factors. This choice mitigates the risks associated with drawing comparative conclusions from a small sample. Of course, there can be too much variety in case studies, making them not comparable. Readers might think that that is precisely the case with the author's counterintuitive choice to conduct a case study on reparation at the ICC. ICC reparation programs are not state-run; they are not based on state responsibility and are primarily subject to the RS, not the human right to reparation. They hence differ from the reparation programs of Sierra Leone and Colombia and the topic of this study.[259] Exactly those differences make the ICC reparation programs perfect objects of study. They are transitional justice reparation programs. By definition, the ICC deals with systematic human rights abuses – the main feature of transitional justice situations.[260] ICC reparation programs pursue goals often attributed to transitional justice, like

256 See above, Introduction and below, ch. 3, A. Note that this study uses the terms "transitional justice situation", "transitional situation", "transitional justice environment", "transitional justice context", "transitional context", and "transitional society" interchangeably.

257 For this study's definition of transitional justice see above, Introduction, C. and for further detail below, ch. 3.

258 See above, Introduction, D. and Patton, *Qualitative Research and Evaluation Methods*, 283.

259 See above, Introduction, B.

260 See above, Introduction, C. and for further detail below, ch. 3, A.I. See also ICC, *The Prosecutor v. Thomas Lubanga Dyilo, Judgment on the Appeals Against Trial Chamber II's 'Decision Setting the Size of the Reparations Award for Which Thomas Lubanga Dyilo is Liable - Separate Opinion of Judge Luz del Carmen Ibáñez Carranza,* ICC-01/04-01/06-3466-AnxII (AC), 2019, para 42 ff.

societal transformation and reconciliation.[261] No wonder that ICC reparation orders and implementation plans rely on and draw inspiration from transitional justice considerations.[262] Conversely, the ICC is often perceived to play a part in transitional justice efforts.[263] The similarities extend to the legal basis of the programs. While the formal basis for reparation at the ICC is Art. 75 RS, the human right to reparation is of crucial relevance. Protecting human rights is a fundamental value of international criminal law.[264] Art. 21(3) RS obliges the ICC to consider human rights in the interpretation of the RS. Accordingly, the reparation orders and implementation plans make frequent reference to human rights jurisprudence and cite the right to reparation as inspiration.[265] As the right to reparation, the guiding principle

---

261 ICC, *The Prosecutor v. Germain Katanga, Order for Reparations Pursuant to Article 75 of the Statute*, ICC-01/04-01/07-3728 (TC II), 2017, para 268, 289, 317; ICC, *Al Mahdi Reparations Order*, ICC-01/12-01/15-236, para 28, 140; ICC, *Lubanga Reparations Decision*, ICC-01/04-01/06-2904, para 192 f., 222, 236. For details on these goals in transitional justice see below, ch. 3, A.II, B.

262 ICC, *Lubanga Reparations Decision*, ICC-01/04-01/06-2904, para 185, fn. 376; ICC, *Case of the Prosecutor v. Thomas Lubanga Dyilo, Judgment on the Appeals Against the "Decision Establishing Principles and Procedures to be Applied to Reparations"*, ICC-01/04-01/06-3129 (AC), 2015, para 196; ICC, *Katanga Reparations Order*, ICC-01/04-01/07-3728, para 48, 57, 61, 284.

263 UN Secretary General, *Guidance Note of the Secretary-General on the United Nations Approach to Transitional Justice*, 2010, 8; CEU, *Council Conclusions on EU's Support to Transitional Justice*, 13576/15 Annex, 2015, para 6; ICC, *The Role of the ICC in the Transitional Justice Process in Colombia - Speech by James Stewart, Deputy Prosecutor of the International Criminal Court*, 2018, para 44 ff.; Gallen, *The International Criminal Court - In the Interests of Transitional Justice?*, in: Lawther et al. (eds.), *Research Handbook on Transitional Justice*, 2017, 305, 314 ff.

264 Kress, *International Criminal Law*, in: Wolfrum (ed.), *Max Planck Encyclopedia of Public International Law*, Online Edition 2009, para 10.

265 Consider for example, ICC, *Katanga Reparations Order*, ICC-01/04-01/07-3728, para 57, 127 f., 230 f., 283; ICC, *Al Mahdi Reparations Order*, ICC-01/12-01/15-236, fn. 134; ICC, *Lubanga Reparations Decision*, ICC-01/04-01/06-2904, para 185 f., 229, fn. 434. The Appeals Chamber (AC) in the Lubanga Case was more sceptical in this regard, ICC, *Lubanga Reparations Order (Appeals Decision)*, ICC-01/04-01/06-3129 para 127 f., 154. However, it remains that the subsequent court practice gave great weight to human rights jurisprudence. See generally, ICC, *The Prosecutor v. Thomas Lubanga Dyilo, Judgment on the Appeals Against Trial Chamber II's 'Decision Setting the Size of the Reparations Award for Which Thomas Lubanga Dyilo is Liable - Separate Opinion of Judge Luz del Carmen Ibáñez Carranza*, ICC-01/04-01/06-3466-AnxII (AC), 2019, para 49 ff.

for reparation at the ICC is that of full reparation.[266] Obviously, the analysis of the ICC reparation programs must and will account for relevant differences to the other case studies.[267] But since ICC reparation programs are transitional justice reparation programs and share a similar normative basis with state-run programs, they can, in principle, be compared with the reparation efforts of Sierra Leone and Colombia. Doing so allows assessing transitional justice reparation programs in a wholly different legal and institutional context. This is crucial for identifying strategies commonly employed to overcome the unique challenges of the transitional justice situation. If the ICC uses similar strategies as Sierra Leone and Colombia, it can be assumed that this choice is based on nothing but these challenges – one of the few features ICC reparation programs have in common with their counterparts in Sierra Leone and Colombia. This last case study, therefore, serves a control purpose.

To further corroborate the assumption that common strategies respond to unique challenges in transitional justice, the chapter will conclude with some reasoned speculation that ties back the differences identified to features of the transitional justice situation (E.). A more cursory analysis of a wider variety of state practice in chapter four will complement the in-depth studies and support the final normative framework.

The case studies on Sierra Leone and Colombia are based mainly on research stays in the second half of 2018. The study on the ICC was concluded in the second half of 2019. While later developments are included up until October 2022, they could not be treated in the same depth.

II. Methodological Reflections

The studies detail the benefits offered, the process by which survivors receive reparation, and the challenges and criticism each program faces. They will concentrate on the reparation programs, mostly ignoring connections to other transitional justice mechanisms and their reparative dimensions. The case studies are based on research in Sierra Leone and Colombia in 2018. A stay at the ICC in 2019 and 2020 informed the third case study, although the

266 ICC, *Case of the Prosecutor v. Thomas Lubanga Dyilo, Judgment on the Appeals Against Trial Chamber II's 'Decision Setting the Size of the Reparations Award for Which Thomas Lubanga Dyilo is Liable'*, ICC-01/04-01/06-3466-Red (AC), 2019, para 36.

267 For details on that see below, D.I.

findings do not rely in the same manner on the research done in place. What is commonly denoted as "field research"[268] always comes with epistemological and ethical problems. These problems cannot be entirely avoided or solved. They can be somewhat mitigated by critically reflecting the research process and the researcher's place in it. Such reflexivity accounts for the finding's epistemological limits and their ethical implications.[269] Reflection does not solve those challenges, but it can constructively deal with them.[270]

The author conducted interviews in Sierra Leone from June until August 2018 and in Colombia from September until November 2018. Further interviews were conducted in Germany in preparation. The studies cite interviews with a dozen individuals. Interviews with several other individuals informed the author's research, both consciously and unconsciously, but are not relied upon directly. The interviewees were government officials working for the respective reparation programs, survivors, or civil society representatives. They were semi-structured and – mostly upon request of the interviewees – not recorded. For the most part, they are hence cited based on notes the author made during the interview.

Every research conducted in the Global South "carries legal and ethical concerns every step of the way."[271] Research, theories, and methodologies have always been implicated in and furthered imperialism and colonialism – international law being no exception.[272] Researchers often engage in

268 The term "field" is problematic in itself, as it often denotes any place outside the Global North, evokes images of otherness and exoticism, and is often problematically embedded in mechanisms for career advancement. The term is for the most part avoided here. If it is used, it denotes any place in which the studied object, in this case reparation programs, unfolds. It thus includes the ICC. On this use of the term see Nouwen, *As You Set Out for Ithaka - Practical, Epistemological, Ethical, and Existential Questions About Socio-Legal Empirical Research in Conflict*, 2014 Leiden J. Intl. L. 27(1), 227, 257.

269 Nouwen, *As You Set Out for Ithaka*, 233 ff.; Sultana, *Reflexivity, Positionality and Participatory Ethics - Negotiating Fieldwork Dilemmas in International Research*, 2007 ACME 6(3), 374, 375 ff.

270 Nouwen, *As You Set Out for Ithaka*, 250 ff. This is not to "reflect away" the fact that this type of research remains problematic, 257 f.

271 Johan et al., *Navigating the Terrain of Methods and Ethics in Conflict Research*, in: Johan et al. (eds.), *Researching Violence in Africa - Ethical and Methodological Challenges*, 2011, 1, 2.

272 Said, *Orientalism*, 31 ff.; Smith, *Decolonizing Methodologies - Research and Indigenous Peoples*, 1999, 37 ff., 43 ff., 80 ff.; Mutua/Anghie, *What Is TWAIL?*, 2000 Proceedings of the ASIL Annual Meeting 94, 33 f. For international law in general see Anghie, *Imperialism, Sovereignty and the Making of International Law*, 2005. For human rights law specifically see Badaru, *Examining the Utility of Third World Approaches to Interna-*

parasitic research, advancing their career on the back of the societies from which they take information without reciprocating.[273] These concerns are especially salient for a researcher from a former colonial power, whose response to this past is beyond shameful.[274] During field research in Sierra Leone and Colombia, the author experienced various instances in which these concerns materialized. Especially in Sierra Leone, he had access to high-level government officials, which probably would not have answered to inquiries of non-Western researchers. Several situations materialized in the messiness of intercultural interactions, in which the author cannot guarantee to have behaved appropriately. The author turned the research into several publications and presentations, from which the interviewees did not benefit directly.

While the discipline of law is relatively new to these concerns, other disciplines, especially anthropology, went to great lengths to grapple with these "conundrums that have haunted the discipline from its inception."[275] Still, they did not come up with clear-cut ways to deal with them. It is not a solution to refrain from research in place altogether. Bringing in an outsider perspective can result in a different course of the research, local researchers would not necessarily embark on. It can yield results, which otherwise would not have come about. Being an outsider can also give independence local researchers might not have.[276] Of course, these benefits accrue regardless

---

tional Law for International Human Rights Law, 2008 Intl. Com. L. Rev. 10(4), 379, 383 ff.; Mutua, *Human Rights*.

273 Ross, *Impact on Research of Security-Seeking Behaviour*, in: Sriram et al. (eds.), *Surviving Field Research - Working in Violent and Difficult Situations*, 2009, 177, 183 f.

274 Boehme, *Reactive Remembrance - The Political Struggle Over Apologies and Reparations Between Germany and Namibia for the Herero Genocide*, 2020 J. Hum. Rts. 19(1), 1; Terkessidis, *Wessen Erinnerung Zählt? Koloniale Vergangenheit und Rassismus Heute*, 2019; Grill, *Wir Herrenmenschen - Unser Rassistisches Erbe: Eine Reise in die Deutsche Kolonialgeschichte*, 2019.

275 Sharon, *Uncertain Ethics - Researching Civil War In Sudan*, in: Johan et al. (eds.), *Researching Violence in Africa - Ethical and Methodological Challenges*, 2011, 79, 80.

276 Ukoha, *Hidden Agendas In Conflict Research - Informants' Interests And Research Objectivity In The Niger Delta*, in: Johan et al. (eds.), *Researching Violence in Africa - Ethical and Methodological Challenges*, 2011, 137, 144 ff.; Baines, *Gender Research in Violently Divided Societies - Methods and Ethics of "International" Researchers in Rwanda*, in: Porter (ed.), *Researching Conflict in Africa - Insights and Experiences*, 2005, 140, 147; Smith, *Decolonizing Methodologies*, 10. On the influence of being an insider or outsider, and the many grey areas between the two extremes, Jones et al., *Producing Knowledge on and for Transitional Justice - Reflections on a Collaborative Research Project*, in: Jones/Lühe (eds.), *Knowledge for Peace - Transitional Justice and the Politics of Knowledge in Theory and Practice*, 2021, 49, 57 ff. Rohlin argues that "opening a community

of the researcher's origin and the society they research. It not only applies to researchers from the Global North researching in the Global South. It is high time that the Global North benefits from and actively seeks other perspectives on its transitional processes.[277] While complete abstention from research in the Global South is not the solution, the concerns evince a divide in transitional justice and international law more generally.[278]

The author had and has no satisfying solution to avoid all these ethical pitfalls during his research. All he can offer is some critical reflection. On the issue of parasitic research, the author tried to reciprocate in some ways, albeit much less than warranted for the time and effort interviewees spend for him. Interviewees often asked the author to "tell their story", which the present chapter does to an extent. However, telling someone else's story after a 30- to 60-minute interview is less than ideal. It can only be the author's

---

to wider participation as well as to outside criticism increases the likelihood that some default assumptions are challenged in appropriate ways. The more diversity there is in a scientific community, the more likely it is that its default assumptions are challenged, and consequently either defended, modified, or abandoned", Rohlin, *The Bias Paradox in Feminist Standpoint Epistemology,* 2006 Episteme 3(1-2), 125, 135. More generally, standpoint theory provided great insights on the connection between knowledge generation and "experiences, social practices, social values and the ways in which perception and knowledge production are socially organized", Stoetzler/Yuval-Davis, *Standpoint Theory, Situated Knowledge and the Situation Imagination,* 2002 Feminist Theory 3(3), 315, 316. For an overview see Intemann, *25 Years of Feminist Empiricism and Standpoint Theory – Where are we now?,* 2010 Hypatia 25(4), 778, 783 ff. Specifically for the field of peace studies, closely related to transitional justice, Halistoprak, *Knowledge Production and its Politicization Within International Relations and Peace Studies,* in: Jones/Lühe (eds.), *Knowledge for Peace - Transitional Justice and the Politics of Knowledge in Theory and Practice,* 2021, 21, 24 ff. Of course, this is not to suggest that the perspective of a male researcher from the Global North is desperately needed. To the contrary, Haraway showed that it is the hegemonic perspective of science and that rather there is a danger of "romanticizing and/or appropriating the vision of the less powerful while claiming to see from their position", Haraway, *Situated Knowledges – The Science Question in Feminism and the Privilege of Partial Perspective,* 1988 Feminist Studies 14(3), 575, 575 ff., 584. This paragraph hopes to evade that risk by reflecting on the author's own standpoint. On that process again see Intemann, *25 Years of Feminist Empiricism and Standpoint Theory,* 785.

277 Only then can what Haraway called "shared conversations in epistemology" be realized, Haraway, *Situated Knowledges,* 584, which are "approximating the truth as part of a dialogical relationship among subjects who are differentially situated", Stoetzler/Yuval-Davis, *Standpoint Theory,* 315. Of course, opening the scientific community, as demanded by the authors cited in this and the preceding footnote is much more urgent in this direction than in the direction the author represents.

278 On that see also below, Conclusion, E.

interpretation of the story, much rather than the interview partner's version of it.[279] For these reasons, the author tried to take a middle ground. He does not quote from the interviews conducted to not misrepresent someone else's story and guard against dramatizing it. At the same time, he does not anonymize the interview partners, honoring their explicit requests not to do so. On the North-South-divide, which the author's mere presence in Sierra Leone and Colombia evinced, perspective is critical: The author considered it necessary to research in the Global South because states of the Global South implement the most wide-ranging and innovative reparation programs worldwide. The Global North either refrains from creating such programs altogether or conceived its programs long ago, never updating them to accommodate new developments in law and practice. By no means is that an outcome of the impeccable morality and legality of the Global North's recent international conduct. It is rather a striking testament to inequalities in international relations.[280] The author sincerely hopes that his research does not reproduce such inequalities to a more considerable degree than necessary. Instead, he hopes that the present case studies can modestly contribute to a genuine interest in transitional justice innovations in the countries studied. There is great potential to learn from Sierra Leone and Colombia's reparation efforts and private initiatives created around them.[281]

Luckily, the epistemological problems encountered during research in Sierra Leone and Colombia can be dealt with more satisfactorily than the ethical ones. In Sierra Leone and Colombia, the author was an outsider with little previous knowledge of the cultural, political, historical, and further context. While that can play out as an advantage and disadvantage simultaneously, it will have affected the way information was gathered and interpreted.[282] That both research stays were singular, short-term, and restricted to the respective states' capitals and their surrounding area will have exacerbated the outsider

279 Clark, *Fieldwork and its Ethical Challenges - Reflections from Research in Bosnia*, 2012 Hum. Rts. Q. 34(3), 823, 836 f.; Zahar, *Fieldwork, Objectivity, and the Academic Enterprise*, in: Sriram et al. (eds.), *Surviving Field Research - Working in Violent and Difficult Situations,* 2009, 191, 206.

280 See also below, Conclusion, E.

281 Especially the amazing work of the Sierra Leonean NGO Fambul Tok (www.fambultok.org) and the Colombian artist Juan Manuel Echavarría (www.jmechavarria.com) warrants mentioning as impressive examples of grassroots transitional justice activism. See further below, Conclusion, F.

282 Ukoha, *Hidden Agendas in Conflict Research*, 144 ff.; Baines, *Gender Research in Violently Divided Societies*, 147; Smith, *Decolonizing Methodologies*, 10.

phenomenon.[283] Furthermore, the author had little experience in interview techniques when embarking on the research.

Due to a dearth of written information, the Sierra Leone study relies chiefly on interviews conducted in Freetown and its surroundings. Some information was impossible to verify through an independent second or even third source. For completeness, such information is still included but marked in the text and/or footnote. The interviews in Sierra Leone were scheduled mainly through a snowball system, as is common in difficult research environments.[284] The method carries the inherent danger of a selection bias in the persons interviewed since professional or personal relationships connect the interviewees.[285] Survivor organizations organized most interviews with survivors. Those gatekeepers, as well as interviewees, probably took the research project as an opportunity to advance their agenda.[286] Survivors and representatives of survivor organizations likely saw the research project as an opportunity to voice their demands for more reparation and draw attention to their present situation. Given that Sierra Leone's reparation program was supposed to end soon after the research stay, government officials interviewed probably saw the research project as an opportunity to work on the program's legacy. Survivors often spoke Krio, for which the author required translation. While a trusted translator was available for some interviews, a survivor organization's representative translated others. During some interviews, that representative started asking questions himself, taking increasing control of the interview.[287] His neutrality at that point is doubtful, to say the least. While the author tried his best, he cannot guarantee that he fully accounted for these challenges.[288]

283 On the problem of restricted geographical reach see Zahar, *Fieldwork, Objectivity, and the Academic Enterprise*, 194.

284 Cohen/Arieli, *Field Research in Conflict Environments - Methodological Challenges and Snowball Sampling*, 2011 J. Peace Research 48(4), 423, 426 f.

285 Cohen/Arieli, *Field Research in Conflict Environments*, 428 f.

286 It would be problematic to assume otherwise, thereby denying agency to the interviewees. On the challenge see Russell, *Interviewing Vulnerable Old People - Ethical and Methodological Implications of Imagining our Subjects*, 1999 J. Aging Stud. 13(4), 403, 408 ff.; Ukoha, *Hidden Agendas in Conflict Research*, 137 f., 146 f., 151 f. On the gatekeeper problem see 149 f.; Zahar, *Fieldwork, Objectivity, and the Academic Enterprise*, 206.

287 These interviews are not cited in the study. Since they did inform the author's further research, consciously and unconsciously, the challenge is still mentioned.

288 On challenges to objectivity in general Clark, *Fieldwork and its Ethical Challenges*, 826 ff.

The case studies of Colombia and the ICC suffer from similar problems – snowball sampling of interviewees, cultural gaps, and interviewees' agendas – with the difference that the author did not require translation. Both studies rely mainly on written sources and use interviews only sparingly to complement them. The challenges encountered will therefore distort the studies less, and the reader will be in a much better position to ascertain their reliability.

Acknowledging these ethical and epistemological challenges, the author abstained, for the most part, from evaluating the reparation programs. He also refrains from speculation about causes or consequences of the conflicts preceding the reparation programs or the programs themselves. There are exceptions at points at which the author felt that not drawing the readers' attention to specific issues would be mistaking neutrality for complicity. The author cannot guarantee that he made the right call and hopes for readers' leniency in that regard.

For the abovementioned reasons, none of the case studies should be taken as a complete history, neither of the reparation programs nor their context. The accounts of the history of the conflicts only contain the minimum information necessary to understand the reparation programs' background. In the case of Sierra Leone and the ICC, they rely mainly on the sources that also provided the basis for the reparation programs, namely the final report of the SLTRC and the judgments, respectively. The resulting histories are deliberately devoid of any attempts at explaining their root causes.[289] To make a long story short, the reader should be mindful that the following case studies present a mere snapshot out of a highly imperfect angle.[290]

B. Sierra Leone

After a decade-long civil war, Sierra Leone had to cater to numerous severely harmed survivors. Years after the end of the conflict, it started a reparation program that faced many hurdles. The following section will first recount

289 Such a selection and history writing is again not neutral and has often been intertwined with imperialism and colonialism. For that see Smith, *Decolonizing Methodologies*, 29 ff. For the example of the Rwandan Genocide see, Andrews, *The New Age of Empire - How Racism and Colonialism Still Rule the World*, 2021, 49 ff. The author's socialization in the Global North alone makes it likely that the bits of history recalled in this chapter represent a colonial angle. The author hopes to have kept that at a minimum.

290 Johan et al., *Navigating the Terrain*, 8.

the history of Sierra Leone's conflict (I.) and the harms it caused (II.), before placing Sierra Leone's reparation efforts within its transitional justice process (III.) and analyzing them (IV.)

I. The History of Sierra Leone's Internal Conflict

Sierra Leone gained independence from British colonial rule in 1961. Colonial occupation left it with significant economic and ideological rifts between the peninsula on which its capital Freetown lies and the rest of the country. It destabilized traditional authorities and laid the ground for poor governance.[291] After independence, Sierra Leone became more and more autocratic, culminating in a change of constitution in 1978, which established a one-party rule under the All People's Congress (APC).[292] Rampant mismanagement and corruption led to growing frustration and social tensions in the 1970s. When student protests erupted in 1977 at Freetown's Fourah Bay College, the government responded violently and forced some protesters into exile. In Libya, some of them were trained to be insurgents.[293] Two critical figures met in such a training camp: Foday Sankoh, later leader of the insurgency and Charles Taylor, later president of Liberia. When Taylor began his attempt to overthrow Liberia's government, Sankoh supported him. Since international troops used Sierra Leone as an airbase to fight Taylor's National Patriotic Front of Liberia (NPFL), Taylor wanted to ensue chaos in the neighboring country. He allowed Sankoh to recruit from Sierra Leonean captives of the NPFL and pushed him to start an insurgency in Sierra Leone.[294] Sankoh's newly formed Revolutionary United Front (RUF) launched its first attack on the border town of Bomaru on 23 March 1991, marking the official start of the conflict. It received massive support from the NPFL – some estimate that over 80 % of the RUF's initial fighting force relied on Taylor's fighters.[295] The attack formed part of a two-front incursion, which caught the Sierra Leone Army (SLA) by surprise. Being ill-equipped and badly trained,

291 SLTRC, *Witness to Truth*, vol. 3a, 5 ff. The account of the history of Sierra Leone's internal conflict follows in large part the final report of the SLTRC, because the report also served as the basis for Sierra Leone's reparation program.

292 Cook, *Conflict Dynamics - Civil Wars, Armed Actors, and Their Tactics*, 2017, 36, 39.

293 SLTRC, *Witness to Truth*, vol. 3a, 91 ff.

294 Keen, *Conflict and Collusion in Sierra Leone*, 2005, 37; Fuchs-Kaminski, *Der Beitrag des Sondergerichtshof für Sierra Leone zum Völkerstrafrecht*, 2015, 42.

295 SLTRC, *Witness to Truth*, vol. 3a, 120.

the SLA had little to challenge the RUF. Additionally, Sierra Leone's government failed to take the threat seriously at first.[296] Frustrated by the slow course of action, a group of young militaries around Captain Valentin Strasser staged a coup d'etat on 29 April 1992. They tripled the number of recruits in the SLA. The recruits had an even lower level of training, and many persons of dubious background enlisted. As a result, the SLA became more violent towards civilians.[297] Still, the measures brought the RUF to the brink of defeat in 1993. In response, the RUF changed its approach to a guerilla tactic, allowing it to regain strength.[298] In this dangerous situation, a new actor came to the fore: The Civil Defence Forces (CDF). Rather than a homogenous fighting force, communities founded local civil defense groups for their protection. The largest and most infamous one, the Kamajor Society, developed out of a hunter society. Their increasing resistance against the RUF became a significant factor in the war.[299] In 1996 Brigadier General Julius Maada Bio overthrew Strasser's government. He quickly held democratic elections, which gave the presidency to Ahmad Tejan Kabbah of the Sierra Leone People's Party (SLPP). Kabbah did not hold on to power for long, though. Yet another coup d'etat forced him into exile on 25 May 1997 and brought Johnny Paul Koroma and the Armed Forces Revolutionary Council (AFRC) into power. The AFRC invited the RUF to join a national unity government – a call the rebels answered willingly.[300] Meanwhile, Kabbah's government in exile in Guinea mobilized international support. In early 1998, troops of the Monitoring Group of the Economic Community of West African States (ECOWAS) ousted the AFRC and the RUF from Freetown with the help of CDF, enabling Kabbah's triumphant return on 10 March.[301] The triumph did not last. In January 1999, marking the beginning of the war's final, devastating act, the RUF and AFRC launched an attack on Freetown. For two weeks, they occupied large parts of the capital and wreaked havoc.[302] After being driven out,

296 Hazen, *What Rebels Want - Resources and Supply Networks in Wartime*, 2013, 76 f.

297 Keen, *Conflict and Collusion in Sierra Leone*, 97 ff.

298 Peters, *War and the Crisis of Youth in Sierra Leone*, 2011, 66 f.; Cook, *Conflict Dynamics*, 42.

299 Hoffman, *The Meaning of a Militia - Understanding the Civil Defence Forces of Sierra Leone*, 2007 Afr. Aff. 106(425), 639, 641 ff.

300 Cook, *Conflict Dynamics*, 43 f.; Fuchs-Kaminski, *Der Beitrag des Sondergerichtshofs für Sierra Leone zum Völkerstrafrecht,* 44 ff.

301 SLTRC, *Witness to Truth*, vol. 3a, 248 ff., 288 ff.

302 UNSC, *Fifth Report of the Secretary-General on the United Nations Observer Mission in Sierra Leone,* S/1999/237, 1999, para 20 ff.

national and international pressure for a peaceful solution prompted the government and the RUF to conclude a peace agreement in Togo`s capital Lomé four months later. Both sides continuously violated its terms in the months to come. The government did not abide by the agreed-upon power-sharing system, and the RUF continued to attack UN peacekeepers and government troops. A series of hostage-takings of UN peacekeepers eventually escalated the situation. A large peace rally gathered in Freetown, just outside Foday Sankoh's residence. After it turned violent, Sankoh fled the premises and was captured several days later. Other members of the RUF were also detained or killed, marking the end of its political arm. The still existing military arm was defeated in the weeks to come, first by the SLA and, after the remaining rebels fled to Guinea, by the Guinean army.[303] The RUF and the government agreed on a ceasefire on 10 November 2000, and the RUF succumbed to a process of disarmament, demobilization, and reintegration (DDR) on 2 May 2001. After the process was finalized on 18 January 2002, all parties met at Lungi Airport to ceremonially burn the weapons collected from the RUF. This day marks the official end of ten years of devastating conflict.[304]

II. Human Rights Violations and Harms in the Conflict

Sierra Leone's civil war is infamous for the brutality and the disregard for civilian life and suffering all parties displayed. While the RUF was responsible for most atrocities, all parties to the conflict committed numerous violations of human rights and international humanitarian law. Obviously, an exhaustive treatment of all violations committed in a complicated ten-year war is impossible. Nevertheless, since reparation erases harm caused by human rights violations, an initial, rough idea of the violations and harms the conflict caused is vital for understanding Sierra Leone's reparation program. To facilitate such an understanding, the following account will provide a panorama of typical violations suffered by the five survivor groups eligible for

303 Evans, *The Right to Reparation in International Law for Victims of Armed Conflict*, 166 ff.; SLTRC, *Witness to Truth*, vol. 3a, 348 ff., 356 ff., 405 ff., 457 ff. Guinea and Sierra Leone worked together from the beginning to counter the insurgency. On that see Fuchs-Kaminski, *Der Beitrag des Sondergerichtshofs für Sierra Leone für das Völkerstrafrecht*, 42.

304 SLTRC, *Witness to Truth*, vol. 3a, 461 f.

Sierra Leone's reparation program – amputees, war-wounded, survivors of sexualized violence, war widows, and children.[305]

From the outset, the RUF built its numerical strength upon forced conscription and abduction, primarily affecting many child survivors. Other factions did the same, albeit to a lesser degree. Thus, a large portion of the fighting forces consisted of children. Some suggest that they made up 50 % of rebel forces.[306] Amputees evoked the most vivid pictures from the Sierra Leonean conflict. Mostly the RUF cut off arms, legs, hands, fingers, ears, noses, and sexual organs. During the "Operation Stop Election" in 1996, the RUF deliberately cut off persons' hands to either stop them from voting or punish them for having voted.[307] Other prevalent violations suffered by the mentioned survivor groups were torture, assault, arbitrary detention, looting, and property destruction. Often, fighters burnt whole villages to the ground.[308] The conflict displaced approximately 2.6 million Sierra Leoneans.[309]

All these violations caused severe harm to survivors. It is even more problematic to provide an account of typical harm than generalize the violations committed. Harm is often highly subjective and contingent on the circumstances of the individual survivor. Still, since reparation is harm-centered, it is crucial to understand the kind of harm a reparation program aims to mitigate. Therefore, a necessarily under-complex overview of typical harms survivors suffered must be attempted at this point. Its broad brush should not paint over the fact that every survivor experienced harm differently and that survivors do not just passively endure harm. Instead, many find remarkable, creative ways to deal with their plight and build resilience, which would merit much more scholarly attention.

Most survivors suffered more than one violation. These violations often created a complex web of intertwined harms on an individual, family, and community level. Paired with the devastating macrosocial and economic

305 With that the chapter reproduces severe blindspots of transitional justice, which too often focuses on violations of life and bodily integrity at the expense of economic, social and cultural rights, see Carranza, *Plunder and Pain - Should Transitional Justice Engage With Corruption and Economic Crimes?*, 2008 Intl. J. Transitional Just. 2(3), 310, and below, Conclusion, E.

306 Mazurana/Carlson, *From Combat to Community - Women and Girls of Sierra Leone*, 2004, 3.

307 SLTRC, *Witness to Truth*, vol. 3a, 472 ff.

308 COHRE, *Housing Rights in West Africa - Report of Four Fact-Finding Missions*, 2004, 103; SLTRC, *Witness to Truth*, vol. 3a, 489 f.

309 UNDP, *Evaluation of UNDP Assistance to Conflict-Affected Countries - Case Study Sierra Leone*, 2006, 4.

effects of the war, many survivors were and still are caught in that web with little chance to escape it.

A type of harm that spanned all categories of survivors and indeed the country as a whole was the rupture in Sierra Leone's social fabric. Apart from the fact that many communities were physically torn apart by displacement and destruction of their community spaces, the fighting factions ensured that their actions had a lasting effect on community relations. Mostly the RUF deliberately destroyed social ties and culture by strategically overstepping cultural boundaries and social taboos. Often, they tortured, humiliated, and killed figures of authority.[310] They strategically destroyed family bonds by forcing persons to kill, mutilate or rape family members. When abductees were forced to commit such acts, it kept them from returning to their original community, even after the war ceded.[311] The fighting factions employed sexualized violence as an especially effective tool to destroy social taboos, and with them, community bonds: Rape in public, by several perpetrators, of pregnant or lactating persons and forced incest were frequent and violated deeply-rooted fundamental social norms.[312] After the war, the social fabric in many communities was thus profoundly shattered. This harmed society, added another layer to the harm survivors experienced, and took away support networks that could have helped them cope with their experiences.

Amputees were the most visible survivors in Sierra Leone's conflict. Many probably died of their wounds either immediately or during the war. For those who survived, amputation often caused further medical issues, such as phantom pain and infections as well as severe psychological problems. It often led to a dramatic reduction in earning capacity and accordingly to impoverishment or a heightened if not complete dependence on others. Such dependence further affected amputees' psychological well-being. Some amputees also reported that their communities stigmatized and discriminated against them.[313] Sexualized violence created a multitude of complex, intertwined harms. First, there were medical consequences, mostly in the form of recto-vaginal and vesico-vaginal fistulas.[314] This condition is not only

310 SLTRC, *Witness to Truth*, vol. 3a, 509 ff.

311 SLTRC, *Witness to Truth*, vol. 3a, 498 ff.

312 HRW, *"We'll Kill You if You Cry" - Sexual Violence in the Sierra Leone Conflict*, 2003, 35 ff.

313 Berghs, *War and Embodied Memory - Becoming Disabled in Sierra Leone*, 2012, 114 f., 132 f., 140 ff.

314 Fistulas are tears in tissue, which in case of survivors of sexualized violence can occur e.g. between the vagina and rectum (rectovaginal fistula) or between the vagina and

painful but can lead to infertility and incontinence. Sexually Transmitted Infections and Diseases (STIs / STDs), as well as HIV, were common ailments in the survivor population, some of which also led to infertility. Psychological consequences were manifold and severe, often amounting to depression and Post-Traumatic Stress Disorder.[315] In addition, many survivors of sexualized violence faced severe social consequences. Survivors were stigmatized and often ostracized by their partners, families, and communities. Ingrained gender roles exacerbated the stigma if survivors became infertile or had difficulties engaging in relationships. If armed forces had abducted them, they were often perceived as part of the warring factions. Many persons became pregnant after being raped and carried the child to full term. "Rebel children" faced similar stigmatization and ostracism. The combined social, psychological, and physical effects marginalized survivors and thus diminished their opportunities in life.[316] War widows not only suffered the emotional and psychological pain that losing a spouse entails. Their partner often was the primary breadwinner of the household. In that case, war widows found themselves deprived of their livelihood.[317] Children experienced many different forms of victimization. Often, they were abducted and forced to fight. In that case, they witnessed traumatic events and had to engage in traumatic action. They were abused and, in the aftermath, often suffered severe psychological problems.[318] Forced drugging was rampant so that many children developed severe drug addictions.[319] Upon return to their communities, they were met with suspicion, ostracism, and stigma. Often, this prevented former child soldiers from returning to their community.[320]

---

the bladder (vesicovaginal fistula), Noack-Lundberg, *Impacts of Sexual Violence on Women's Sexual Health*, in: Ussher et al. (eds.), *Routledge International Handbook of Women's Sexual and Reproductive Health,* 2019, 468, 470 f.; Onsrud et al., *Sexual Violence-Related Fistulas in the Democratic Republic of Congo*, 2008 Intl. J. Gynecology Obstetrics 103(3), 265.

315 HRW, *"We'll Kill You if You Cry"*, 50 ff.; SLTRC, *Witness to Truth*, vol. 3b, 207 ff.

316 Coulter, *Bush Wives and Girl Soldiers – Women's Lives Through War and Peace in Sierra Leone*, 2009, 132, 208 ff.; HRW, *"We'll Kill You if You Cry"*, 52 f.; SLTRC, *Witness to Truth*, vol. 3b, 197 ff.

317 SLTRC, *Witness to Truth*, vol. 2, 244.

318 Betancourt et al., *Sierra Leone's Child Soldiers - War Exposures and Mental Health Problems by Gender*, 2011 J. Adolescent Health 49(1), 21, 21.

319 SLTRC, *Witness to Truth*, vol. 3a, 479 ff.

320 Denov, *Coping With the Trauma of War - Former Child Soldiers in Post-Conflict Sierra Leone*, 2010 Intl. Soc. Work 53(6), 791, 798 f.; Denov, *Child Soldiers in Sierra Leone - Experiences, Implications and Strategies for Rehabilitation and Community Reintegration*, 2005.

Many children had their parents or one parent killed and suffered the involved psychological and social consequences. The breakdown of the education system in large parts of the country kept many children from enjoying an education.[321] In sum, the experience of war fundamentally altered the trajectory of many children's life.

III. Sierra Leone's Transitional Justice Effort

To deal with this complex web of violations and harms, Sierra Leone's transitional justice process consisted of three main parts. The Sierra Leone Truth and Reconciliation Commission (SLTRC) and the Special Court for Sierra Leone (SCSL) were created right after the civil war.[322] The SLTRC handed in a comprehensive report on the conflict, its causes, and consequences in 2004, after taking numerous testimonies from survivors, perpetrators, and other stakeholders.[323] The SCSL conducted several notable trials, including against Charles Taylor. Foday Sankoh's trial could not commence since he died in custody of natural causes.[324] The reparation program started its work in 2008, complementing the efforts at truth and punishment.

IV. Sierra Leone's Reparation Effort

The convoluted way reparation entered the Sierra Leone peace process already cast a shadow on the state's future handling of its responsibility towards survivors. The Lomé Agreement did not contain an explicit obligation to repair the survivors of the conflict. It merely obliged Sierra Leone to establish a rehabilitation program.[325] The SLTRC gave the decisive impetus

---

321 Denov, *Coping With the Trauma of War*, 799 f.

322 On the SLTRC see Hayner, *Unspeakable Truths*, 58 ff.; Dougherty, *Searching for Answers - Sierra Leone's Truth and Reconciliation Commission*, 2004 Afr. Stud. Q. 8(1), 39. On both institutions and their relationship see Schabas, *Conjoined Twins of Transitional Justice - The Sierra Leone Truth and Reconciliation Commission and the Special Court*, 2004 J. Intl. Crim. Just. 2(4), 1082. On the SCSL see Fuchs-Kaminski, *Der Beitrag des Sondergerichtshofs für Sierra Leone zum Völkerstrafrecht.*

323 SLTRC, *Witness to Truth.*

324 Bassiouni, *Introduction to International Criminal Law*, 2nd Revised Edition 2013, 739 ff.

325 Art. XXIX Peace Agreement Between the Government of Sierra Leone and the Revolutionary United Front (Lomé Peace Agreement).

to Sierra Leone's reparation program by dedicating an entire chapter of its final report to reparation recommendations. In doing so, the Commission stretched its mandate, which just vaguely tasked it to respond to survivors' needs, restore their dignity, and foster healing and reconciliation.[326] With a delay of eight months, Sierra Leone's government reluctantly accepted the SLTRC recommendations "in principle", but conditioned their implementation on the availability of resources and external support.[327] More than 15 years later, few of the recommendations have been implemented.

1. The Recommendations of the Sierra Leone Truth and Reconciliation Commission

a. Framework

The SLTRC held the state responsible for repairing all survivors, relying on the state's positive obligation to prevent human rights violations and notions of equality, justice, and fairness.[328] While employing the broad survivor definition of the Basic Principles, it restricted reparation to the most vulnerable survivors: amputees, severely war-wounded, survivors of sexualized violence, war widows, and children. Arguing that repairing every survivor would be an impossible burden on the state, it limited reparation for everyone else to symbolic measures.[329] Reparation was supposed to further reconciliation, the restoration of civic trust and solidarity. To achieve that, reparation was to signal the government's and society's interest in survivors and relationships of equality with them. Concretely, the SLTRC wanted to restore survivors' dignity by improving their quality of life and facilitating their independence and reintegration into their communities.[330] Symbolic reparations were supposed to show respect for survivors, recognize

326 § 6 Truth and Reconciliation Commission Act 2000; Schabas, *Reparation Pratices in Sierra Leone and the Truth and Reconciliation Commission,* in: de Feyter et al. (eds.), *Out of the Ashes – Reparation for Victims of Gross and Systematic Human Rights Violations,* 289, 293.

327 Government of Sierra Leone, *White Paper on the Truth and Reconciliation Report,* 2005, 16.

328 SLTRC, *Witness to Truth,* vol. 2, 231 f.

329 SLTRC, *Witness to Truth,* vol. 2, 234, 242. The survivor definition of the Basic Principles coincides with the one established above, ch. 1, B.

330 SLTRC, *Witness to Truth,* vol. 2, 236 f., 239 ff., 247.

their harm, preserve the memory of what happened and show the shared determination of society never to let these violations happen again.[331]

The SLTRC departed from the international law on reparation by arguing that there is no proportionate reparation for the crimes committed. Instead, the Commission balanced survivors' needs, the state's capacities, and development agenda. As a result, the Commission emphasized services and symbolic measures over cash payments. This choice corresponded with the needs and preferences survivors expressed before it. Services were also deemed more sustainable as they enhanced the country's infrastructure and lessened social tensions because whole communities, not only survivors, benefitted from them.[332]

Three principles guided the SLTRC in designing its recommendations: No harm, accessibility, and participation. The first mandated avoiding additional stigma and social divisions through reparation. The second justified creating an administrative, not a court-based reparation program because the latter would have heavily overburdened the judicial system. It also warranted removing potential barriers for survivors during the registration and disbursement process. The last principle tasked the SLTRC to allow for the broad participation of survivors in all stages of the process.[333]

b. Reparation Recommendations

As mentioned above, the SLTRC recommended confining reparation to amputees, war-wounded, survivors of sexualized violence, children, and war widows. Survivors were considered amputees if they lost upper or lower limbs. All those who sustained other injuries were designated as war-wounded. These survivors could only benefit from reparation if their injuries – either singly or collectively – reduced their earning capacity by at least 50 %. The reduction was to be determined either by a list appended to Sierra Leone's workers compensation act or – if the injury sustained was not listed – by a medical professional. Survivors of sexualized violence were defined as any person subject to acts such as rape, sexual slavery, mutilation of genitals or breasts, and forced marriage. The 50 % reduction in earning capacity threshold did not apply to them. The SLTRC determined that their reduction

331 SLTRC, *Witness to Truth*, vol. 2, 232, 234 f.

332 SLTRC, *Witness to Truth*, vol. 2, 232, 234 f., 244 ff.

333 SLTRC, *Witness to Truth*, vol. 2, 229, 232, 245 ff.

in earning capacity did not result chiefly from their injury but stigma. The SLTRC granted war widows reparation because it assumed that they had depended on their husbands. It did not apply the assumption vice versa, thereby excluding widowers from the program. Children were considered survivors if they were under 18 by 1 March 2002 and sustained physical or psychological harm, if their parents were killed, or if they were born out of sexualized violence and raised by a single mother.[334]

The SLTRC recommended reparation in the areas of physical and mental health, education, finances, and symbolic reparation. It demanded free health care for war-related injuries for amputees, war-wounded survivors of sexualized violence, and children. Amputees were to benefit their entire life, the other three groups as long as necessary. Spouses and minor children of survivors were supposed to access free health care as long as the direct survivor could. Healthcare should encompass specialized services different groups of survivors needed, e.g., assistive and orthotic devices for amputees, specialized surgery for survivors of sexualized violence, and physiotherapy for war-wounded. In addition to these individual measures, the SLTRC advocated for systemic changes to overcome structural shortcomings in Sierra Leone's health sector. It recommended strengthening the referral system so that survivors could receive care from specialized professionals. It tasked the government with establishing more medical facilities, training medical professionals, and incentivizing foreign specialists to come to the country.[335] In mental health, the SLTRC demanded free counseling and psychosocial support for all survivors and their dependents. On a systemic level, the government should recruit and train counselors, include mental health in the curriculum of nursing and medical schools, and install trauma counseling services at all rehabilitation centers and at all facilities, which treated women.[336] As regards education, child survivors were to receive a free education until senior secondary school level. The government should assist teacher training programs and provide incentives for teachers to work in remote areas.[337]

334 SLTRC, *Witness to Truth*, Vol. 2, 248 ff.

335 The shortcomings at that time were dramatic. In 2004 only 250-300 doctors catered to the needs of a population of ca. 5 million people. Half of them practised in Freetown. Three years after the conflict had ended, still only one psychiatrist practiced in Sierra Leone, SLTRC, *Witness to Truth*, vol. 2, 251 ff.; vol. 3b, 208.

336 SLTRC, *Witness to Truth*, vol. 2, 258 f.

337 SLTRC, *Witness to Truth*, vol. 2, 261.

Adult amputees, war-wounded, and survivors of sexualized violence were to receive pensions. The amount depended on the reduction in earning capacity suffered. All survivors should receive skill training, including courses on running small-scale businesses. Upon completion of these courses, survivors should be eligible to receive a micro-credit or micro-project.[338]

As symbolic reparation, the government should apologize "for all actions and inactions since 1961", the year of independence. Further, all responsible individuals, groups, and organizations were asked to apologize for their role in the conflict. A national war memorial in Freetown and several memorials in other parts of the country were to be built after consultation with survivors and affected communities. The government should organize commemoration ceremonies by traditional and religious leaders, including symbolic reburials. Some of these were to be held on a designated National Reconciliation Day. Actual reburials were to be facilitated if survivors so wished.[339] For the communities most affected by the war, the government was to provide financial and technical assistance for the reconstruction and consolidation of their institutions. These processes were to be held in close consultation with the communities concerned especially considering women and youth.[340] Lastly, the SLTRC made recommendations for the registration process. It should be easily accessible also in remote areas; local leaders and civil society organizations should support survivors' identification and registration. It was deemed crucial to maintain the privacy of individuals, especially of survivors of sexualized violence. The SLTRC emphasized the importance of sensitization programs before a reparation program started.[341]

2. Implementation

Eight months after the SLTRC handed in its report, the government accepted its recommendations "in principle", but conditioned their implementation on the availability of resources and outside support.[342] The half-hearted acceptance already hinted at a familiar pattern over the following years: Reparation has been delivered in a piece-meal fashion, mostly dependent on external funding.

338 SLTRC, *Witness to Truth*, vol. 2, 259, 262 f.
339 SLTRC, *Witness to Truth*, vol. 2, 264.
340 SLTRC, *Witness to Truth*, vol. 2, 265.
341 SLTRC, *Witness to Truth*, vol. 2, 270.
342 Government of Sierra Leone, *White Paper*, 16.

Three phases of the program can be identified. The initial phase comprised the registration of survivors (a.), an "interim-relief-payment", and educational support (b.). It lasted from 2008 until 2010. In the other two phases, Sierra Leone distributed rehabilitation grants to amputees and war-wounded between 2011 and 2015 and to war widows and survivors of sexualized violence from 2016 until at least 2019 (c.). These grants constituted the core of the program. Other measures complemented them, mostly funded and implemented by external actors (d.).

a. Initiation and Registration

The reparation program was created in 2008 after the United Nations Peacebuilding Fund (PBF) granted three million US-Dollars (USD) to start it. The government complemented the effort with 246.000 USD, mostly consisting of office space and personnel.[343] The International Organization for Migration (IOM) helped set up a reparation unit within the National Commission for Social Action (NaCSA), which the SLTRC designated to lead the reparation efforts. A National Steering Committee was created, in which representatives of NaCSA, the government, the UN, civil society, and survivor organizations were supposed to advise on the implementation.[344] The program started registering survivors in 2008. NaCSA held stakeholder meetings and broadcasted information over TV and radio in a sensitization and awareness campaign. In two phases, 33.863 survivors registered – twice as many as the IOM project proposal expected, but only half the number NaCSA estimated in its five-year strategic plan.[345] To register, survivors had to give a detailed account of their victimization to a NaCSA official. The account was

343 PBF, *NaCSA/IOM Reparations Project Proposal,* PBF/SLE/A-4, 2008, 11; PBF, *Final Programme Narrative Report,* PBF/SLE/A-4, 2010, 1.

344 For the complete allocation of the seats in the committee see PBF, *Project Proposal,* PBF/SLE/A-4, 11. Amnesty International bemoaned that no Women NGO was represented in the committee, Amnesty International, *Sierra Leone - Getting Reparations Right for Survivors of Sexual Violence,* AFR 51/005/2007, 2007, 23. The steering committee stopped meeting in 2011, Ottendörfer, *Translating Victims' "Right to Reparations" Into Practice - A Framework for Assessing the Implementation of Reparations Programs From a Bottom-Up Perspective,* 2018 Hum. Rts. Q. 40(4), 905, 922.

345 MPTF, *Enhancing Social Protection and Rehabilitation fo War Victims Through Reparations, Project Document,* 2013, 3; PBF, *Final Report,* PBF/SLE/A-4, 3; NaCSA, *Statistical Overview of Administered Reparations,* 2018, on file with the author; Ottendörfer, *Translating Victims' "Right to Reparations" Into Practice,* 920.

verified either by cross-referencing the survivor's name with lists provided by the SLTRC and designated civil society organizations or by a local authority's confirmation of the account, e.g., a chief or religious leader.[346] The rules attached to the grant of the PBF proved detrimental to the registration process. 75 % of the funds had to benefit survivors directly, and the project had to be finalized within a year.[347] Due to the scarcity of funds and the strict timeframe, the sensitization and awareness campaign had limited reach, and the initial registration phase only lasted two months. Given the obvious shortcomings, a second phase with better outreach followed. Still, many survivors probably failed to register. Some simply did not know about the possibility. Others, especially survivors of sexualized violence, did not register out of shame or fearing stigma.[348] As a result, registration remained open and closed for good only in 2010.[349]

b. Interim-Relief

The institutional rules of the PBF also hindered the effective design of reparation measures. The project proposal foresaw pensions, free education and healthcare, skills training, micro-credits, community reparations, and psychosocial support. Funding needed beyond the initial three million USD was to be sourced from taxes, former fighters' assets, and debt-relief-for-reparation-schemes, among others.[350] These sources were never uncovered. Faced with limited time and resources and the increasing agitation of survivors, those responsible abandoned the initial plan and limited the

---

346 Ottendörfer, *The Fortunate Ones and the Ones Still Waiting - Reparations for War Victims in Sierra Leone*, 2014, 15. "Chiefs" are part of Sierra Leone's administrative structure and lead one of the 149 "Chiefdoms", Sierra Leones lowest administrative entity. The system has its origins in British colonial rule, Jackson, *Reshuffling an old Deck of Cards? The Politics of Local Government Reform in Sierra Leone,* 2007 Afr. Aff. 106(422), 95, 95 ff. More generally on the role of chiefs in British colonial rule, Reinhard, *Die Unterwerfung der Welt*, 2016, 992 f.

347 ICTJ, *Report and Proposals for the Implementation of Reparations in Sierra Leone*, 2009, 1 f.

348 ICTJ, *Reparations in Sierra Leone* 4 f.; Williams/Opdam, *The Unrealised Potential for Transformative Reparations for Sexual and Gender-Based Violence in Sierra Leone*, 2017 Intl. J. Hum. Rts. 21(9), 1281, 1291 f.

349 Interview with *Amadu Bangura* (Program Manager Sierra Leone Reparation Program), Freetown, 8 August 2018.

350 PBF, *Project Proposal*, PBF/SLE/A-4, 4, 13; ICTJ, *Reparations in Sierra Leone*, 6.

program to an interim-relief payment of approximately 100 USD[351] for every survivor.[352] Children received the same amount as an educational grant paid directly to their school to cover school fees, material, etc.[353] Additionally, 49 survivors in urgent need of medical attention received medical care, e.g., surgical removal of bullets. 235 survivors of sexualized violence underwent examination and received financial assistance to treat STIs. Some underwent surgery, e.g., to repair vaginal fistulas.[354] Those who received medical care received another 100 USD for the costs incurred.[355] Few survivors received psychological support.[356]

Survivors collected their interim-relief payment from central disbursement places in Freetown and other large cities upon presenting the ID they received after registration. NaCSA ensured that survivors of sexualized violence could not be identified as such during the disbursement process.[357] Before receiving the money, every survivor attended a workshop on using the grant for an income-generating activity to ensure some sustainability.[358] In the end, 20.107 of the 21.700 eligible survivors received the payment.[359] Those who did not receive the grant in 2009 were attended to in 2011 when the PBF provided funding for that purpose.[360]

Symbolic reparation was disbursed equally among 40 out of 149 chiefdoms to avoid creating social tensions.[361] It comprised ceremonies and memorials. Local and religious leaders symbolically cleansed the community of the atrocities committed. Vigils, consecrations, and symbolic reburials were

---

351 If the sources state monetary values in Leones, the author calculated the equivalent in USD based on the then-applicable exchange rate, as taken from https://www.exchangerates.org.uk/SLL-USD-exchange-rate-history-full.html.

352 Ottendörfer, *The Fortunate Ones and the Ones Still Waiting*, 14; Interview with *Bangura*, 8 August 2018.

353 Interview with *Bangura*, 8 August 2018.

354 PBF, *Final Report*, PBF/SLE/A-4, 7.

355 ICTJ, *Reparations in Sierra Leone*, 10.

356 PBF, *Final Report*, PBF/SLE/A-4, 7.

357 ICTJ, *Reparations in Sierra Leone*, 7.

358 Interview with *Bangura*, 8 August 2018.

359 ICTJ, *Reparations in Sierra Leone*, 8; Ottendörfer, *Translating Victims' "Right to Reparations" Into Practice*, 921. Of those, 6.984 persons received the amount as educational support, PBF, *Final Report*, PBF/SLE/A-4, 7.

360 MPTF, *Reparation Project Document*, 4.

361 Interview with *Bangura*, 8 August 2018. On the concepts of chiefdoms see above, B.IV.2.a.

performed. Peace trees were planted. Survivors and perpetrators told their stories, and survivors had the opportunity to forgive perpetrators.[362]

c. Rehabilitation Grants

After this initial relief effort, the government decided to concentrate on rehabilitation grants coupled with workshops on financial literacy to foster survivors' independence.[363] Since there was not enough funding to pay rehabilitation grants to all survivors at once, the government decided to sequence reparation based on survivors' vulnerability. Because it measured vulnerability as survivor's physical ability to generate income, amputees and war-wounded were prioritized over war widows and survivors of sexualized violence. Children did not receive any reparation after the initial education grants.[364]

In 2011, the first amputees received 200 USD with funding from the PBF. Two years later, a grant of the Multi-Partner Trust Fund (MPTF) worth 2,5 million USD enabled NaCSA to give rehabilitation grants of 1.400 USD to 1138 amputees and 162 especially vulnerable war-wounded.[365] In 2014 and 2015, another 2.608 war-wounded received 600 USD, concluding the reparation process for the first two categories of survivors.[366] After the Ebola crisis stalled NaCSA's work in 2015, the agency spent much of 2016 updating the survivor register. Seven years after the initial registration, much of the information was outdated. The reverification paused in 2017 because government funding did not arrive until December. NaCSA completed it in 2018.[367] In mid-2018, the government approved funding for NaCSA to cater to the reverified war widows and survivors of sexualized violence. NaCSA started distributing

362 NaCSA, *Sierra Leone Reparations Programme Newsletter*, 2016, 5; HOPE - Sierra Leone, *Report of Symbolic Reparations (Memorials and Reburials) - Bomaru, Kailahun District, 21st - 23rd March 2009*, 2009, 4 ff.

363 NaCSA, *Annual Report 2015*, 2015, 24; Interview with *Bangura*, 8 August 2018.

364 Interview with *Bangura*, 8 August 2018.

365 MPTF, *Updated Consolidated Report on Projects Implemented Under the Sierra Leone Multi-Donor Trust Fund*, 2015, 65.

366 NaCSA, *Statistical Overview*, on file with the author.

367 Interview with *Bangura*, 8 August 2018.

rehabilitation grants in the second half of 2019. Once that process concludes, the program will close.[368]

d. Additional Measures

Beyond the core-prong of providing rehabilitation grants, outside funding enabled several projects for specific survivor groups. The Norwegian Refugee Council and later the Norwegian Friends for Sierra Leone built 888 houses to shelter survivors. The government provided land for some of them, and NaCSA assisted in the coordination of the project.[369] In 2009, then president Koroma inaugurated the War Victims Trust Fund, which was supposed to receive donations from private individuals, companies, and organizations to support the reparation efforts. The 50.000 USD it collected – significantly less than initially pledged by different actors – were used for interim-relief payments to 330 survivors and emergency medical relief for 14 survivors.[370] The grant of the MPTF provided 26 further survivors with medical support.[371] On international women's day 2010, Koroma apologized to the women of Sierra Leone.[372] A joint funding effort of UNWomen and the PBF enabled further reparation for survivors of sexualized violence. It provided 650 women with three to six months of skill training. They received a monthly stipend of 60 USD during the training. Afterward, they received a 500 USD grant and a starter kit containing tools, training manuals, and other equipment. Further, according to government statements, 16.500 persons received psychosocial counseling until 2016, when funding for the program ran out.[373]

---

368 Interview with *Bangura*, 8 August 2018; NaCSA, *NaCSA Pays 2,250 Female War Victims Nationwide*, 2019.

369 NaCSA, *Reparations Newsletter*, 9; Schanke, *Housing and Reintegration of Amputees and War-Wounded in Sierra Leone*, 2004 Forced Migration 21, 60; COHRE, *Housing Rights in West Africa*, 110; Schabas, *Reparation Practices in Sierra Leone*, 297.

370 NaCSA, *Reparations Newsletter*, 8; PBF, *Final Report*, PBF/SLE/A-4, 6.

371 MPTF, *Updated Consolidated Report*, 65.

372 CEDAW, *Consideration of Sixth Periodic Reports of States Parties - Sierra Leone*, CEDAW/C/SLE/6, 2012, para 85. For the full text of the apology see, *President Koroma Apologizes to Sierra Leonean Women*, Sierra Express Media, 29 March 2010.

373 CEDAW, *List of Issues and Questions in Relation to the Sixth Periodic Report of Sierra Leone - Replies of Sierra Leone*, CEDAW/C/SLE/Q/6/Add.1, 2014, para 9; NaCSA, *Reparations Newsletter*, 9; Interview with *Bangura*, 8 August 2018.

NaCSA also tried to negotiate free health care and education for survivors, but the competent ministries denied its requests.[374] Freetown's Connaugh Hospital provided some medical assistance. Lastly, NaCSA secured university scholarships for ten survivors.[375]

3. Challenges and Criticism

Sierra Leone's reparation program did not manage to fulfill the expectations the SLTRC created. It offered much fewer benefits in a piece-meal fashion depending on the funds available at any given moment. Severe delay pervaded the entire program. It started only four years after the government accepted the SLTRC reparation recommendations. Most survivors waited several more years before they received their grant. Survivors of sexualized violence and war widows found themselves at the end of a long queue. They waited 14 years from the point the SLTRC promised them reparation until they finally received them. The delay coupled with almost no survivor participation and a non-transparent process sent a fatal signal of neglect to survivors.[376] While the government related the delay and the piece-meal implementation to a lack of funds, the short-term nature of international donations and competing demands in the country,[377] civil society, and survivors saw a lack of political will as the actual reason for most problems the program faced.[378]

Given that the government provided less than half of the program's resources, one could doubt whether it actually discharged its obligation to repair. During the first half of the program's existence, the bulk of its budget came from external sources, whereas the second half was primarily paid for by the state.[379]

374 ICTJ, *Reparations in Sierra Leone* 10 f.

375 Interview with *Bangura*, 8 August 2018; NaCSA, *Annual Report 2014*, 2014, 22.

376 Interview with *John Caulker* (President of Fambul Tok), Freetown, 19 July 2018; Berghs, *Local and Global Phantoms - Reparations National Memory and Sacrifice in Sierra Leone*, in: Devlieger et al. (eds.), *Rethinking Disability - World Perspectives in Culture and Society*, 2016, 275, 284 f.

377 NaCSA, *Annual Report 2014*, 23; IOM, *What Hope of Reparations for Sierra Leone's War Victims?*, 2009; Interview with *Bangura*, 8 August 2018.

378 Interview with *John Caulker*, 19 July 2018; Interview with *Tommy Ibrahim* (Director of the Center for Accountability and the Rule of Law), Freetown, 27 July 2018.

379 ICTJ, *Reparations in Sierra Leone* 13; Interview with *Bangura*, 8 August 2018; Interview with *John Caulker*, 19 July 2018; Interview with *Tommy Ibrahim* 27 July 2018.

Specific critique pertains to the registration and disbursement phase. It is safe to say that a large number of survivors were unable to register for the program. Many did not receive information about its existence owed to the short-lived and limited sensitization and awareness campaign. Other survivors lived far away from registration centers, travel and accommodation costs deterred them.[380] Accordingly, the regional distribution of registered survivors does not concur with the distribution of wartime violations.[381] Especially, but not solely, survivors of sexualized violence often refrained from registering out of shame or fear of stigma.[382] NaCSA tried to counter these problems by employing more female staff and cooperating with experienced non-governmental organizations (NGOs) to reach survivors via persons they trusted.[383] Despite these efforts, comparing estimates with the number of registered survivors of sexualized violence speaks volumes: Physicians for Human Rights (PHR) estimated in 2002 that 50.000 to 64.000 internally displaced women alone were survivors of sexualized violence – almost twice the number of *all* registered survivors.[384]

Much criticism pertained to the content of the reparation program. Many survivors felt that the reparation they received was inadequate. The rehabilitation grants were deemed too low to have a transformative effect. Often, survivors used them to cater to primary needs. The lack of a safety net for survivors amplified this effect.[385] As a result, many survivors emphasized the importance of service-based reparation in addition to rehabilitation grants. They wished for pensions, free healthcare, including psychosocial care and education to count on a safety net for them and their children.[386] On the

---

380 Ottendörfer, *Translating Victims' "Right to Reparations" Into Practice*, 922 f.

381 ICTJ, *Reparations in Sierra Leone* 4 f.

382 Berghs/Conteh, *'Mi At Don Poil' - A Report on Reparations in Sierra Leone for Amputee and War-Wounded People*, 2014, 7, 24; Ottendörfer, *The Fortunate Ones and the Ones Still Waiting*, 20, 22; ICTJ, *Reparations in Sierra Leone* 4 f.

383 Interview with *Bangura*, 8 August 2018.

384 PHR, *War-Related Sexual Violence in Sierra Leone - A Population-Based Assessment*, 2002, 3 f.

385 Berghs/Conteh, *'Mi At Don Poil'*, 7, 15 f.; Ottendörfer, *The Fortunate Ones and the Ones Still Waiting*, 27.

386 Interview with *Edward Conteh* (Survivor, President of AWWA), Freetown, 17 July 2018; Interview with *Tommy Ibrahim* 27 July 2018; Interview with Lahai Sia-Bintu (Survivor), 26 July 2018, Freetown, 26 July 2018; Interview with *Osman Kamara* (Survivor), Grafton, 26 July 2018; Interview with *Eiah M'Bayoh* (Survivor), Grafton, 26 July 2018. The lack of psychosocial services also concerned the HRCom, *Concluding Observations on the Initial Report of Sierra Leone*, CCPR/C/SLE/CO/1, 2014, para 8.

other hand, the government claimed that many survivors demanded a lump-sum payment instead of pensions and that the competent National Social Security and Assurance Trust (NASSIT) lacked the expertise and funding to implement pensions.[387] When compensation was paid, it sometimes created social tensions. First, survivors envied ex-combatants. Sierra Leone was quick to set up a DDR-program so that ex-combatants received more extensive and swifter benefits than survivors did.[388] Second, tensions arose within communities because some survivors did not enter the program. Third, tensions arose between registered survivors because of the stark and arbitrary differences in their waiting periods. Also, NaCSA often failed to explain why some groups received more than others. Lastly, compensation sometimes led to tensions within families. Some survivors' relatives relinquished support once they learned about the payment and demanded a share.[389] Some husbands demanded control over their wives' grants in line with traditional views of gender and marital roles.[390]

Survivors judged the housing project as necessary but criticized the location of the houses. There was no fertile farming land nearby, and their distance to urban centers deprived survivors of access to health care facilities.[391]

Symbolic reparation was deemed to be of little effect.[392] While survivors welcomed the effort, they emphasized that symbolic reparation is of little use if they still suffer materially.[393] Many survivors did not understand why commemoration ceremonies were held. The local population at times did not understand what the memorials were supposed to commemorate. Where

387 Interview with *Bangura*, 8 August 2018.

388 Schabas, *Reparation Practices in Sierra Leone*, 302. On the DDR-program in general, Bradley et al., *Sierra Leone - Disarmament, Demobilization and Reintegration (DDR)*, 2002 World Bank Africa Region Findings & Good Practice Infobriefs No. 81; ICTJ, *Transitional Justice and DDR - The Case of Sierra Leone*, 2009. On the gendered impact of the early focus on the DDR-program and the program's shortcomings in that regard see Williams/Opdam, *Unrealised Potential*, 1292 f.

389 Berghs/Conteh, *'Mi At Don Poil'*, 6, 10, 20 ff., 27; Berghs, *Local and Global Phantoms*, 285; Ottendörfer, *The Fortunate Ones and the Ones Still Waiting*, 25 f.

390 Berghs, *War and Embodied Memory*, 123; Interview with *Sanusi Savage* (Head of IOM Freetown Mission), Freetown, 11 July 2018.

391 Berghs/Conteh, *'Mi At Don Poil'*, 16, 19; Asiedu/Berghs, *Limitations of Individualistic Peacebuilding in Postwar Sierra Leone*, 2012 Afr. Conflict Peacebuilding Rev. 2(1), 136, 146; Berghs, *War and Embodied Memory*, 112 ff.

392 Interview with *Edward Conteh*, 17 July 2018.

393 Asiedu/Berghs, *Limitations of Individualistic Peacebuilding in Postwar Sierra Leone*, 148; Interview with *Edward Conteh*, 17 July 2018; Interview with *Tommy Ibrahim* 27 July 2018.

that was clear, survivors signaled incomprehension as to why memorials were built in city centers and not at the sites of massacres.[394] Survivors bemoaned the lack of a comprehensive governmental apology.[395]

As a result of these inadequacies and problems, survivors interviewed for this study often felt forgotten, abandoned, or neglected by the government.[396] The large discrepancy between the SLTRC recommendations and the actual reparation program led them to accuse the government of breaking its promises.[397] They explained the inadequacy of reparation by a perceived wish of the government and society to forget the war and its survivors.[398] A study on survivors' perception of the reparation program corroborates these findings and reaches the damning conclusion that reparation had a "minimally positive effect on the living conditions of very few war victims [...], it did not have any positive effect on the beneficiaries' perceptions of the state or their position as citizens [...]."[399] The state failed to communicate that reparation was a right, and instead, a narrative of being fortunate to receive reparation came into being.[400] According to the largest survivor organization, the Amputees and War-Wounded Association (AWWA), the message that survivors did not deserve reparation as of right trickled down to society and led to discrimination.[401]

C. Colombia

In stark contrast to Sierra Leone's modest reparation program, Colombia created one of, if not the most comprehensive and complex transitional justice reparation program in the world. It provides a wide range of measures to more than 9 million survivors of Colombia's internal conflict. The following section will detail those measures (IV.) and the transitional justice process surrounding them (III.) after recounting the history of the Colombian conflict (I.) and the human rights violations and harms accompanying it (II.).

---

394 Ottendörfer, *The Fortunate Ones and the Ones Still Waiting*, 23 f.
395 IRIN News, *Lack of Aid Funds for Amputees, Rape Survivors, War Widows*, 2009.
396 Interview with *Edward Conteh*, 17 July 2018; Interview with *Lahai Sia-Bintu*, 26 July 2018.
397 Interview with *Edward Conteh*, 17 July 2018.
398 Interview with *Edward Conteh*, 17 July 2018; Interview with *Tommy Ibrahim* 27 July 2018.
399 Ottendörfer, *The Fortunate Ones and the Ones Still Waiting*, 28.
400 Ottendörfer, *The Fortunate Ones and the Ones Still Waiting*, 23.
401 Berghs/Conteh, *'Mi At Don Poil'*, 23.

I. The History of the Colombian Conflict

The Colombian conflict was the longest-running conflict in the western hemisphere.[402] It dates back to the 1960s. Colombia had come out of a ten-year civil war between its liberal and conservative party in 1958. To end the violence, both parties formed a national front, in which they divided up key governmental positions and agreed that the presidency would alternate between them for 16 years.[403] While successful at ending violence on a national level, the national front did not manage to overcome the structural inequalities, which pervaded Colombia. Communist political forces felt excluded from legal avenues to voice their ideas.[404] Frustration about the political situation rose. When the military attacked self-proclaimed independent republics in the country's south, it was the straw that broke the camel's back. In the mid-1960s, Manuel Maranda and others founded the orthodox communist Fuerzas Armadas Revolucionarias de Colombia – Ejército del Pueblo (FARC-EP)[405] out of pre-existing peasant self-defense forces. Around the same time, the Ejército de Liberación Nacional (ELN)[406] emerged out of student protests in Bogotá, looking to Castro's Cuba for inspiration. Lastly, the Ejército Popular de Liberación (EPL)[407] started fighting for a Maoist revolution. Some years later, the urban communist guerilla Movimiento de 19 de Abril (M-19)[408] was founded in reaction to alleged electoral fraud, which supposedly prevented their left-leaning candidate from assuming the presidency.[409] Despite these manifold actors, the conflict was of low intensity

402 ICTJ, *An Overview of Conflict in Colombia*, 2009, 1.

403 Hristov, *Paramilitarism and Neoliberalism - Violent Systems of Capital Accumulation in Colombia and Beyond*, 2014, 76 ff.

404 CNMH, *¡Basta Ya! Colombia - Memorias de Guerra y Dignindad*, 2014, 117; CHCV, *Contribución al Entendimiento del Conflicto Armado en Colombia*, 2015, 26 ff., 34 ff.

405 Armed Revolutionary Forces of Colombia – People's Army. The guerilla added "-EP" to its name only in 1982, when it officially turned into an offensive guerilla, Olaya, *Férrea Pero Consciente - Disciplina y Lazo Identitario en las Organizaciones Clandestinas de las Fuerzas Armadas Revolucionarias de Colombia-Ejército del Pueblo (FARC-EP)*, 2020 Izquierdas 49, 540, 546 f. The full name is used throughout the text to prevent confusion.

406 National Liberation Army.

407 Popular Liberation Army.

408 Movement of the 19th of April.

409 Metelits, *Inside insurgency - Violence, Civilians, and Revolutionary Group Behavior*, 2010, 90; CNMH, *¡Basta Ya!*, 117; Buitrago, *Armed Actors in the Colombian Conflict*, in: Koonings/Kruijt (eds.), *Armed Actors - Organised Violence and State Failure in Latin America*, 2004, 87, 88.

and did not reach a national scale in its first decades.[410] This changed towards the end of the 1970s when the economy slowed down, social inequalities deepened, and drug trafficking became rampant in the country.[411] In the 1980s, guerilla groups increasingly kidnapped members of Colombia's elite to finance their operations. In response, drug lords, together with economic and political elites, founded Muerte a Secuestradores (MAS)[412] to defend themselves against kidnappings by guerillas. While the group itself was short-lived, MAS served as a model for future right-wing paramilitary groups, which became a central factor in the conflict's further trajectory.[413] With the conflict gaining pace, then-president Betancur searched for a political solution from 1982 onwards. The government and the FARC-EP agreed to transform the guerilla into a political party, the Unión Patriótica (UP)[414]. Colombia's military, political and economic elites soon began to torpedo the process. Scared by the UP's first electoral successes, they started an assassination campaign against party members. It cost the lives of around 4.000 persons, among them two presidential candidates, several senators, members of Congress, and mayors, and eventually led to the party's factual disappearance. The FARC-EP also undermined the peace process by declaring itself an offensive guerilla in 1982 and increasing its military capacity and operations.[415] In parallel, the number of paramilitary groups increased. The indigenous guerilla Movimiento Armado Quintín Lame started fighting for indigenous interests and defended indigenous communities.[416] In this already difficult climate, M-19 launched an attack on Colombia's highest court in 1985, taking several judges and staff hostage. The recapture by the military led to a bloodbath and struck the final blow to the already fragile peace talks.[417] In contrast, the 1990s started hopefully. Peace talks with M-19 and the EPL led to their disarmament and demobilization. A new constitution fundamentally altered the Colombian state and strengthened its democratic structures. Finally, in the first half

---

410 CHCV, *Contribución al Entendimiento del Conflicto Armado* 31 f.

411 CNMH, *¡Basta Ya!*, 130 ff.

412 Death to Kidnappers.

413 CNMH, *¡Basta Ya!*, 134 f.; CHCV, *Contribución al Entendimiento del Conflicto Armado* 49.

414 Patriotic Union.

415 Metelits, *Inside Insurgency*, 98 f.; CNMH, *¡Basta Ya!*, 135 f.

416 Suárez Flórez/Wilches Sierra, *El Movimiento Armado Quintín Lame y su Proceso de Paz - Una Lección de Dignidad y Resistencia*, 2016, 28 ff.

417 IACtHR, *Rodríguez Vera et al. (The Disappeared From the Palace of Justice) v. Colombia*, 2014, para 89 ff.

of the decade, Colombia managed to dismantle the largest drug cartels operating in the country. Ironically, successes in fighting organized crime strengthened the guerillas and paramilitaries and exacerbated the conflict. Armed groups filled the void cartels left, turning Colombia into the largest coca producer, the raw ingredient of cocaine, from 1997 onwards. Among other factors, a new law legalizing certain paramilitary groups led to a sharp increase in such groups in 1994. Many paramilitary groups organized and fused their operations in 1997 in Autodefensas Unidas de Colombia (AUC)[418]. These dramatic developments turned the conflict from aggregated localized violence to a national struggle.[419] Under these circumstances, a new attempt at peace negotiations in 1999 was fraught from the start. While negotiating, the government ramped up its military capacities with the help of the United States. The FARC-EP continued military operations. When it kidnapped the Senate peace commission president in 2002, it was thus rather the trigger than a reason for the government to end the process.[420] The failed peace process coupled with a slowing economy led to the rise of Alvaro Uribe. He took the presidency with huge popular support in 2002 when the conflict had reached its peak geographical extension.[421] He campaigned on the promise to defeat the guerillas militarily and denied the existence of a conflict by reducing them to "narcoterrorists". Undeniably, he delivered on his promises. Under Uribe's "Democratic Security" doctrine, military action escalated and struck decisive blows against the guerillas. By 2008 the FARC-EP found itself in a profound crisis. A significant portion of its leadership was dead, and its military capacity was lower than it had been in decades. At the same time, Uribe's government started a disarmament and demobilization process with paramilitaries in 2005. As a result, the conflict's geographical reach was heavily diminished.[422] However, Uribe's successes came at a high cost. The military progress was bought with severe violations of human rights and

418 United Colombian Self-Defence Groups.

419 CNMH, *¡Basta Ya!*, 146 ff., 158 ff.; Buitrago, *Armed Actors in the Colombian Conflict*, 94 ff.

420 Buitrago, *Armed Actors in the Colombian Conflict*, 100 f.; Echavarria, *In/security in Colombia - Writing Political Identities in the Democratic Security Policy*, 2010, 87 ff.

421 CNMH, *¡Basta Ya!*, 176.

422 Echavarria, *In/security in Colombia*, 33, 85 f., 197 ff.; Pachon, *Colombia 2008 - Éxitos, Peligros y Desaciertos de la Política de Seguridad Democrática de la Administración Uribe*, 2009 Rev. Cienc. Polít. (Santiago) 29(2), 327, 329 ff.

international humanitarian law.[423] The disarmament of the paramilitaries was at best partially successful. Many groups rearmed and only became more volatile and detached from the state.[424] Still, Uribe's popularity remained high until the end of his second term, when his former defense minister, Juan Manuel Santos, won the presidency. To the surprise of many – and contrary to his previous positions – Santos did not continue Uribe's hardline politics. From 2012 he engaged in peace negotiations with the FARC-EP, culminating in the 2016 Final Agreement to End the Armed Conflict and Build a Stable and Lasting Peace (Final Agreement). The process hung by a thread when a slim majority defeated the agreement in a referendum, also owed to Uribe's vocal campaign against it. Since a popular vote was not necessary under the Colombian Constitution, Santos renegotiated the agreement, refrained from scheduling a second referendum, and merely sought approval by the legislature. The revised agreement entered into force in November 2016 after it passed the Senate and the House of Representatives.[425] The FARC-EP disarmed and demobilized as planned and newly established transitional justice mechanisms slowly took up their work in 2017 and 2018.[426] A change of government in 2018 put a protégé of Uribe in office, Ivan Duque. The first moves of the new government raised serious concern about its agenda for the transitional justice process.[427] They led some former FARC-EP fighters to take up arms again – a move widely condemned, including by most former

423 WOLA, *Colombia - Don't Call it a Model*, 2010; Eleanor, *Crimes of the Powerful in Conflict-Affected Environments - False Positives, Transitional Justice and the Prospects for Peace in Colombia*, 2017 State Crime J. 6(1), 132, 137; Aranguren Romero et al., *Inhabiting Mourning - Spectral Figures in Cases of Extrajudicial Executions (False Positives) in Colombia*, 2021 Bull. Lat. Am. Res. 40(1), 6, 6 f.; HRC, *Statement by Professor Philip Alston, UN Special Rapporteur on Extrajudicial Executions - Mission to Colombia 8-18 June 2009*, 2009. See also below on false positives, C.II.

424 CNMH, *¡Basta Ya!*, 179.

425 Alto Comisionado Para La Paz/Presidencia De La Republica, *Biblioteca Del Proceso de Paz con las FARC-EP - Tomo VIII*, 2018, 30 ff.

426 The implementation of the peace process is monitored and documented by the International Verification Commission (www.cinep.org.co) and in the KROC institute (www.kroc.nd.edu).

427 Ambos, *Transitional Justice Without Truth?*, EJIL:Talk!, 27 August 2018; Ambos, *Another Challenge for Colombia's Transitional Justice Process - Aggravated Differential Treatment between Armed Forces and FARC*, EJIL:Talk!, 19 October 2018; Langmack, *Reforming Land Restitution – A Concerted Effort to Derail Colombia's Transitional Justice System?*, EJIL:Talk!, 2 November 2018.

FARC-EP leadership.[428] Since the agreement's ratification, many human rights defenders and community leaders were killed by armed groups and organized crime, further putting the peace process in jeopardy.[429]

II. Human Rights Violations and Harms in the Conflict

All actors in the conflict committed severe violations of human rights and international humanitarian law. Of course, this study cannot exhaustively describe all violations and harms suffered by the nine million registered survivors of the Colombian conflict. Just as in the previous case study, it will describe typical patterns in a necessarily under complex panorama of the violations and harms survivors endured.

Forced displacement was by far the most prevalent violation in the Colombian conflict. In 2019, the United Nations High Commissioner for Refugees (UNHCR) counted 7.5 million internally displaced, a figure only outmatched at the time by Syria.[430] All actors contributed to this humanitarian catastrophe. Assassinations, threats, and other violations forced survivors to leave their land. More often, though, the parties to the conflict created an atmosphere of terror through prominent attacks and threats in a calculated attempt to displace entire populations. Armed actors thereby gained control over territory and, with it, sources of income.[431]

As in most conflicts, death, injury, and sexualized violence were rampant. The Colombian conflict is infamous for targeted killings and massacres, which were used primarily by paramilitaries to consolidate control over

428 UNSC, *United Nations Verification Mission in Colombia - Report of the Secretary-General,* S/2019/780, 2019, para 3 f.

429 CCJ et al., *Panorama de Violaciones al Derecho a la Vida, Libertad e Integridad de Líderes Sociales y Defensores de Derechos Humanos en 2016 y Primer Semestre de 2017,* 2017; CSMLV, *Sexto Informe de Seguimiento al Congreso de la República 2018-2019,* 2019, 51 ff.; HRC, *Annual Report of the United Nations High Commissioner for Human Rights on the Situation of Human Rights in Colombia,* A/HRC/37/3/Add.3, 2018, para 8 ff.; McVeigh, *2017 was the Deadliest Year on Record for Colombian Human Rights Defenders,* The Guardian, 1 May 2018.

430 UNHCR, *Global Focus Colombia,* 2020, People of Concern; IDMC, *Global Report on Internal Displacement,* 2020, 11; Sánchez León / Sandoval-Villalba, *Go Big or Go Home? Lessons Learned From the Colombian Victims' Reparation Program,* in: Ferstman / Goetz (eds.), *Reparations for Victims of Genocide War Crimes and Crimes Against Humanity - Systems in Place and Systems in the Making,* 2nd Edition 2020, 547, 568.

431 Ibañez, *Forced Displacement in Colombia - Magnitude and Causes,* 2009 Econ. Peace Sec. J. 4(1), 48, 50 ff.; CNMH, *¡Basta Ya!,* 71 ff., 104 ff.

territory and population. Targeted killings were often aimed at community leaders and public figures. Coupled with highly visible massacres, these violations instilled fear and terror in the population.[432] Under the infamous "false positives"-policy, the Colombian armed forces killed civilians and masqueraded them as guerilla fighters to improve their statistics.[433] Guerillas were mostly responsible for death and injury by antipersonnel mines and improvised explosive devices, which they used strategically to offset military disadvantages.[434] All sides engaged in sexualized violence, albeit on different scales, with different aims and ways. Survivors endured rape, sexual slavery, forced prostitution, forced pregnancy, forced sterilization, forced abortion, and forced labor.[435] Paramilitaries used rape and other forms of sexualized violence to destroy community bonds and control a population. For that, they often attacked female community leaders and perceived collaborators. They also used sexualized violence as a punishment for transgressions of the "good order" they created in communities under their control.[436] The FARC-EP employed a significant portion of female fighters. They had to take contraceptives and undergo forced abortions, regardless of when the pregnancy was discovered. Although on a lesser scale than the paramilitaries, the FARC-EP and the armed forces also violated civilians' sexual and reproductive rights.[437]

Armed actors further committed numerous enforced disappearances and kidnappings. Enforced disappearance harrowingly shows the absolute power an armed actor exercises over a person. It thus effectively complemented the paramilitaries strategy to control communities through spreading a climate of fear and terror. The armed forces used the covert nature of this crime to evade

---

432 CNMH, *¡Basta Ya!*, 43 ff., 47 ff.; CHCV, *Contribución al Entendimiento del Conflicto Armado* 75, 81.

433 HRC, *Report of the Special Rapporteur on Extrajudicial, Summary or Arbitrary Executions, Philip Alston - Mission to Colombia,* A/HRC/14/24/Add.2, 2010, para 10 ff.; IACtHR, *Villamizar-Durán y Otros v. Colombia,* 2018, para 58 ff. The SJP opened an entire so-called macro-case on the false positives, SJP, *Ruling No. 033 of 2021,* 2021. It informs the public about the case in a shining example for judicial communication in transitional justice at: https://www.jep.gov.co/especiales1/macrocasos/03.html.

434 CNMH, *¡Basta Ya!*, 92 ff.

435 Casa de la Mujer, *Primera Encuesta de Prevalencia - Violencia Sexual en Contra de las Mujeres en el Contexto del Conflicto Armado Colombiano 2001-2009*, 2011, 15 ff.

436 CNMH, *¡Basta Ya!*, 77 ff.; CNMH, *La Guerra Inscrita en el Cuerpo*, 2017, 48 ff., 54 ff., 94 ff.

437 Fajardo Arturo/Valoyes Valoyes, *Violencia Sexual Como Crimen Internacional Perpetrado por las FARC*, 2015, 37; Casa de la Mujer, *Violencia en el Conflicto Armado*, 15 ff.

accountability.[438] While the guerillas were less engaged in disappearances, they committed the clear majority of kidnappings. They used ransom as a source of income and kidnapped high-profile members of the Colombian elite for propagandistic purposes and to destabilize the state and its elites. At times, guerillas used kidnappings to increase their leverage in peace processes. Many abductees did not return alive.[439] Lastly, irregular armed groups, mostly the FARC-EP, frequently enlisted or forcibly recruited children.[440]

These violations caused multitudes of harm, which again can only be described in an under complex panorama. To repeat, survivors experience harm differently. They do not only passively endure it but develop resilience and find astonishing, creative ways to deal with it. Nonetheless, violations caused typical complex, intertwined harms on an individual, family, and community level.

Individuals suffered severe physical and psychological injuries, often with long-term effects. Violations ruptured their existing relationships and hurt their capacity to engage in new ones. Many survivors carry a stigma because people believe that perpetrators "had their reason" to victimize them.[441] Violations often altered family roles, for example, when a family needed to replace a dead, incapacitated, or disappeared breadwinner. Such changes and other sources of internal conflict often tore families apart.[442] Communities lost spaces, central figures, and, with them, knowledge, rituals, and traditions. Armed groups and the general violent environment inhibited the performance of rituals and traditions and sowed distrust among community members. Many communities disintegrated or were torn apart by displacement.[443] Harms on all three levels often reinforced each other by destroying support structures and ways to cope with what happened.[444]

About harm specific to typical violations, displacement fundamentally ruptured the life of persons, families, and communities and threw them into deep insecurity. It destroyed families and communities by physically tearing them

438 CNMH, *¡Basta Ya!*, 57 ff.

439 CNMH, *¡Basta Ya!*, 64 ff.; CHCV, *Contribución al Entendimiento del Conflicto Armado* 78.

440 CNMH, *¡Basta Ya!*, 84 ff.

441 AVRE, *Aspectos Psicosociales de la Reparación Integral*, 2006, 7, 10 ff., 15, 35 f.; CNMH, *¡Basta Ya!*, 261 ff.

442 AVRE, *Aspectos Psicosociales*, 7, 12; PPP, *La Viga en el Ojo*, 2003, 29.

443 AVRE, *Aspectos Psicosociales*, 7, 21 f.; PPP, *La Viga en el Ojo*, 28 f., 49 f., 79 ff.; CNMH, *¡Basta Ya!*, 266, 272 ff., 289 f.

444 AVRE, *Aspectos Psicosociales*, 23.

apart.[445] In addition to the psychological effects of that insecurity and the loss of most social relations, displacement also had severe economic effects. Individuals often lacked the labor skills required in their new environment, especially if they fled from rural to urban settings. They had to abandon their belongings and means of subsistence. Survivors' new community often discriminated against them, stigmatized, and ostracized them.[446]

Enforced disappearance had brutal effects on the family and community of the disappeared. It left them in excruciating insecurity about the whereabouts and possible suffering of a loved one, with no possibility of closure. The experiences of relatives and other persons close to the survivor often amounted to psychological torture.[447] If the disappeared was a breadwinner or if they spent considerable sums on searching for them, families experienced economic pressure.[448] The general climate of terror and fear caused by enforced disappearance often deteriorated community relations. Additionally, armed groups often disappeared leaders or other persons with essential roles in the community.[449] Kidnapping similarly exposed those left behind to a fundamental uncertainty about a loved one's fate, significantly altered family relations, and could cause significant conflict within families and communities. Ransom could ruin survivors' families just as the absence of a breadwinner could. The experience of being at the complete mercy of the perpetrators, a constant fear of death, and a total loss of privacy often left the abducted scarred for life.[450]

Survivors of anti-personal mines report that beyond severe physical injuries, their reintegration into society is hampered by impediments to their ability to work, especially in rural settings, where much of the work is

445 CNMH, *Una Nación Desplazada - Informe Nacional del Desplazamiento Forzado en Colombia*, 2015, 443 ff.

446 CHCV, *Contribución al Entendimiento del Conflicto Armado*, 76; CNMH, *¡Basta Ya!*, 268; Weber, *Trapped Between Promise and Reality in Colombia's Victims' Law - Reflections on Reparations, Development and Social Justice*, 2020 Bulletin Latin Am. Research 39(1), 5, 8 ff.

447 CNMH, *Entre la Incertidumbre y el Dolor - Impactos Psicosociales de la Desaparición Forzada*, 2014, 55 ff.

448 CNMH, *¡Basta Ya!*, 293.

449 CNMH, *Entre la Incertidumbre y el Dolor*, 73 f.

450 CNMH, *¡Basta Ya!*, 299 ff.; PPP, *La Viga en el Ojo*, 31 f.; CHCV, *Contribución al Entendimiento del Conflicto Armado* 78.

physical.[451] Survivors of sexualized violence faced manifold consequences. Aside from the psychological and physical effects detailed in the Sierra Leone case study, survivors also suffered from stigma, discrimination, and ostracism by their partner, family, and community.[452] Forced and unwanted pregnancies exacerbated their social, psychological, and economic marginalization.[453] Lastly, child soldiers experienced a traumatic conflict that fundamentally altered their lives' trajectory. Most lost all ties to their family and community, educational opportunities, and, in sum, a normal childhood.[454]

III. Colombia's Transitional Justice Effort

In response to 50 years of conflict and the multiple human rights violations and harms that came with it, the 2016 Final Agreement between the FARC-EP and the Colombian government foresaw a comprehensive transitional justice effort, the Sistema Integral de Justicia, Verdad, Reparación y No-Repetición (SIJVRNR)[455]. It comprises three main institutions: the Special Jurisdiction for Peace for the prosecution and punishment of the most responsible perpetrators, a truth commission, and the Search Unit for Disappeared Persons.[456] Reparation measures constitute the fourth element of the system. It predates the Final Agreement, which only modified it. The components of

451 Sanchez/Rudling, *Reparations in Colombia - Where to? Mapping the Colombian Landscape of Reparations for Victims of the Internal Armed Conflict*, 2019, 19. See generally, Case-Maslen/Vestner, *A Guide to International Disarmament Law,* 2019, 156 f.

452 CINEP/PPP, *Reparación Psicosocial*, 2011; CNMH, *La Guerra Inscrita en el Cuerpo*, 338 ff., 362 ff., 376 ff. See above, B.II.

453 CNMH, *La Guerra Inscrita en el Cuerpo*, 349 ff.

454 Villanueva O'Driscoll et al., *Children Disengaged From Armed Groups in Colombia - Integration Processes in Context*, 2013, 110 ff. See above, B.II.

455 Integral System of Justice, Truth, Reparation and Non-Repetition.

456 An introduction to the Special Jurisdiction for Peace can be found here, Ambos/Aboueldahab, *The Colombian Peace Process and the Special Jurisdiction for Peace*, 2018 Diritto Penale Contemporaneo 4, 255. Information on the Truth Commission and the Search unit can be found on their homepages: https://comisiondelaverdad.co; https://www.ubpdbusquedadesaparecidos.co. The Truth Commission published its final report in 2022, see Comisión para el Esclarecimieto de la Verdad, la Convivencia y la No Repetición, *Hay Futuro si hay Verdad,* 2022.

the SIJVRNR are interconnected and slowly took up their work mostly in 2017 and 2018.[457]

IV. Colombia's Reparation Effort

Colombia started several early attempts at repairing the survivors of the armed conflict. Unfortunately, all efforts had fatal defects. While Law 418 of 1997 provided survivors with benefits to mitigate their harm, it was initially conceived as humanitarian assistance. Only retroactively did Colombia flag it as reparation.[458] The Justice and Peace Law of 2005 provided the normative framework for the demobilization of the paramilitaries. It emphasized prosecution and only enabled individual reparation proceedings against convicted perpetrators or their armed group. Conditioning reparation upon individual convictions made the reparation provisions de-facto inoperative: After five years, only two survivors had benefitted from the regime.[459] In reaction to this failure, Decree 1290 of 2008 created an administrative reparation program. However, it only repaired violations committed by illegal armed groups and denied state responsibility. Accordingly, the government based it on the principle of solidarity rather than responsibility.[460]

Colombia's current administrative reparation program is based on the 2011 Law on Victims and Land Restitution (Victims Law).[461] The 2016 Final Agreement modified details of the law. Most importantly, the Colombian government recognized Colombia's responsibility for the violations as a basis for reparation. Just as Decree 1290 of 2008, the original Victims Law had evaded this question.[462]

457 A comprehensive and updated assessment can be found in the Trimestral Reports of the International Verification Commission (www.cinep.org.co) and in the reports by the KROC institute (www.kroc.nd.edu).

458 ICTJ, *From Principles to Practice - Challenges of Implementing Reparations for Massive Violations in Colombia*, 2015, 13.

459 Evans, *The Right to Reparation in International Law for Victims of Armed Conflict*, 213 f.

460 Art. 2 f. Decreto 1290 de 2008 por el Cual se Crea el Programa de Reparación Individual por vía Administrativa Para las Víctimas de los Grupos Armados Organizados al Margen de la Ley.

461 Ley de Víctimas y Restitución de Tierras, officially Ley 1448 de 2011 Por la Cual se Dictan Medidas de Atención, Asistencia y Reparación Integral a las Víctimas del Conflicto Armado Interno y se Dictan Otras Disposiciones, in the following "Victims Law" or "Ley 1448 de 2011".

462 Final Agreement, Introduction to Chapter 5, 5.1; ICTJ, *From Principles to Practice*, 25.

Colombia's reparation program provides individual and collective restitution, compensation, rehabilitation, satisfaction, and guarantees of non-repetition. At the moment of writing, it caters to more than nine million individual survivors and 754 collectives.[463] The numbers continue to grow, albeit at a much slower pace than in the first years of the program's existence. Throughout the reparation process, the program ensures a differential treatment of Colombia's minorities, ethnicities, and women.[464] It further emphasizes survivor participation.[465] The massive universe of survivors and the variety of reparation measures make the Colombian program probably the most comprehensive and complex administrative reparation program globally.[466]

1. Eligibility

Art. 3 of the Victims Law defines an individual survivor as any person who suffered harm because of a violation of international humanitarian law or because of a grave and manifest breach of their human rights. The violation must have happened after 1 January 1985 and must be related to the armed

463 The exact number of individual survivors can be seen here, https://www.unidadvictimas.gov.co/es/registro-unico-de-victimas-ruv/37394 (data from 15 October 2022). The number of collectives can be seen at Unidad de Víctimas, *Boletín Fichas Estadísticas Nacional*, 2022 (data from 15 October 2022).

464 Measures ensuring differential treatment pervade every stage of the program and are present in most reparation measures. For reasons of space and clarity and because the normative framework in ch. 4 does not focus on differential treatment, they are for the most part left out in the present account. For an overview see de la Hoz del Villar et al., *El Enfoque de Género Dentro del Sistema Integral de Verdad, Justicia, Reparación y No Repetición*, 2019 Justicia 24(36), 1, 9 ff., 12 f.; Ministerio del Interior de Colombia, *El Enfoque Diferencial y Étnico en la Política Pública de Víctimas del Conflicto Armado*, 2015; Unidad de Víctimas, *ABC del Modelo de Operación con Enfoque Diferencial y de Género*, 2017; Unidad de Víctimas, *Guía Operativa Para la Implementación de Acciones de Enfoque Diferencial y de Género en los Procesos de Asistencia y Reparación a las Víctimas*, 2017.

465 Survivor participation is regulated in Art. 261 ff. Decreto 4800 de 2011 por el Cual se Reglamenta la Ley 1448 de 2011 y se Dictan Otras Disposiciones. Examples of participation are listed in Procuraduría General, *Primer Informe al Congreso Sobre el Estado de Avance de la Implementación del Acuerdo de Paz 2016 – 2019*, 2019, 267. A comprehensive analysis of survivors participation is provided by de Waardt/Weber, *Beyond Victims' Mere Presence - An Empirical Analysis of Victim Participation in Transitional Justice in Colombia*, 2019 J. Hum. Rts. Prac. 11(1), 209.

466 Sikkink et al., *Evaluation of Integral Reparations Measures in Colombia - Executive Summary*, 2015, 3; Sánchez León / Sandoval-Villalba, *Go Big or Go Home?*, 565

conflict. Survivors of violations committed before 1985 have access to symbolic reparation, truth, and guarantees of non-repetition.[467] Relatives and companions of dead or disappeared survivors and persons, which suffered harm while trying to assist the survivor or prevent victimization qualify as indirect individual survivors. The Colombian Constitutional Court understands the required nexus between the violation and the armed conflict broadly. It covers acts of criminal groups, which surged because of the conflict.[468] The Victims Law excluded adult combatants of illegal armed groups from survivor status while explicitly including members of the armed forces. In the Final Agreement, the parties agreed to abolish this distinction. Victimized members of the FARC-EP and the Public Forces were to be repaired through different programs. To date, the provision was not implemented.[469] In a landmark case, Colombia's Constitutional Court held the exclusion of an ex-combatant and survivor of sexualized violence from the Victims Law to be unconstitutional. While it emphasized that this holding was valid for the concrete case only, it could have wider repercussions on ex-combatants' eligibility.[470] A point of contention between the government and civil society was how else the Final Agreement modified the individual survivor definition. Some organizations contended that the agreement established a "principle of

467 Art. 69(3) Ley 1448 de 2011.

468 Corte Constitucional de Colombia, *Sentencia C-280 de 2013*, C-280/13, 2013; Corte Constitucional de Colombia, *Auto 119 de 2013*, 2013; ICTJ, *From Principles to Practice*, 3.

469 Members of the FARC-EP receive reparation from the DDR-program, members of the Armed Forces from the Ministry of the Interior, Final Agreement, 5.1.3.7. To date, the provision has not been implemented, Secretaría Técnica et al., *Segundo Informe de Verificación de la Implementación del Acuerdo Final de Paz en Colombia Para los Verificadores Internacionales Felipe González y José Mujica*, 2018, 159; Secretaría Técnica et al., *Tercer Informe de Verificación del Primer Año de Implementación del Acuerdo Final de Paz en Colombia Para los Verificadores Internacionales Felipe González y José Mujica*, 2018, 190; Rivera, *Opinión - ¿Pueden los/las ex FARC ser Considerados Víctimas?*, 2020 ICON-S Colombia. For a critique of this distinction see Aguirre-Aguirre, *Victimario - La Víctima Desconocida del Conflicto Armado Colombiano: Análisis de su Reparación en Torno al Principio de Igualdad*, 2019 Revista Derecho del Estado 43, 291.

470 Corte Constitucional de Colombia, *Sentencia SU-599 de 2019*, SU-599/19, 2019; Rivera, *¿Pueden los/las ex FARC ser Considerados Víctimas*; de Vos, *Colombia's Constitutional Court Issues Landmark Decision Recognising Victims of Reproductive Violence in Conflict*, IntLawGrrls, 11 January 2020.

universality" at odds with the cut-off date of 1985 and other limiting provisions. The government denied the necessity of any further changes.[471]

Collective reparation is open to communities, organizations, and other groups, which suffered collective harm. A collective must demonstrate shared practices, organizational structures, relations between its members, a collective project, and some form of self-recognition or recognition by third parties. These attributes must have existed before the violation occurred. The collective suffered collective harm if a violation of its collective rights or individual rights of its members affected these collective attributes. Violations of individual member's rights must be of relevance to the collective, either because of their scale or because they affected important community figures.[472]

2. Registration

To start their reparation processes, all individual and collective survivors must request to be registered in the Registro Único de Víctimas (RUV)[473]. They must do so within two years after the violation.[474] Survivors can present their claim in Centros Regionales de Atención y Reparación a Víctimas (CRAV)[475] or at offices of other state entities. The CRAV are supposed to be attended by all government agencies relevant to the reparation program. They shall thereby ensure that survivors can access centralized, uniform information. In practice, only some departments have CRAVs. Not all relevant government entities are present in them, and they suffer from deteriorating infrastructure.[476] The registration starts with an interview conducted by a

471 Secretaría Técnica et al., *Primer Informe de Verificación del Primer Año de Implementación del Acuerdo Final de Paz en Colombia Para los Verificadores Internacionales Felipe González y José Mujica*, 2018, 163; CODHES/USAid, *13 Propuestas Para la Adecuación Participativa de la Normativa Sobre Víctimas al Acuerdo Final de Paz Entre las FARC-EP y el Gobierno de Colombia - Aportes Para la Implementación del Subpunto 5.1.3.7*, 2017, 13 ff., 17 f., 20.

472 Art. 152 Ley 1448 de 2011; Art. 2.2.7.8.2 Decreto 1084 de 2015 por Medio del Cual se Expide el Decreto Único Reglamentario del Sector de Inclusión Social y Reconciliación; Unidad de Víctimas, *Modelo de Reparación Colectiva*, 2018, 25 ff., 50 ff., 54 ff.

473 Unified Victims Register.

474 Meza/Escalante, *Transformative Procedural Law in the Reparation of the new Victims of the Armed Conflict in Colombia - Challenges for the State Liability Proceedings*, 2019 Rev. Chilena Derecho 46(1), 129, 132.

475 Regional Centers for the Care and Reparation of Victims.

476 CSMLV, *Sexto Informe*, 65, 72 ff.; CSMLV, *Quinto Informe de Seguimiento al Congreso de la República 2017-2018*, 2018, 59 ff.

state official. The interview covers a range of questions on the violation, the personal data, and the socio-economic situation of the survivor and their family.[477] The survivor must substantiate their claim. To facilitate this task, their good faith is presumed, and only summarical evidence is required.[478] While this does not imply a lower standard of proof, it prohibits the Victims Unit[479] – the central state entity running the reparation program – from challenging the evidence provided.[480] The Victims Unit can ask a variety of state entities for information to corroborate the survivor's claim.[481] It has 60 days to decide on the survivor's request to be registered. Survivors can appeal an adverse decision at the Victims Unit.[482] Once the survivor entered the register, they start the individual (3.) or collective reparation route (4.).

3. The Individual Route

The individual reparation route begins with an interview between the survivor and an official from the Victims Unit. The official presents the program and what it offers and assesses the survivor's socio-economic situation and the harm they suffered. On that basis, the official and the survivor devise an individual reparation plan, which defines adequate measures of restitution (a.), compensation (b.), rehabilitation (c.), satisfaction (d.), and guarantees of non-repetition (e.). After the interview, the official stays on the case and serves as a survivor's contact person.[483] Because survivors of forced displacement have access to special humanitarian assistance, they only proceed to the initial interview in two cases: Either their basic needs in terms of housing, nutrition, and health are met, or they are extremely vulnerable because no household member can generate income. If they do not fulfill either requirement,

477 Art. 31 No. 6 Decreto 4800 de 2011; ICTJ, *Estudio Sobre la Implementación del Programa de Reparación Individual en Colombia*, 2015, 19.

478 Art. 5 Ley 1448 de 2011; Unidad de Víctimas, *Manual de Criterios de Valoración V2*, 2017, 25.

479 Unidad de Víctimas.

480 Corte Constitucional de Colombia, *Sentencia C-523 de 2009*, C-523/09, 2009; Unidad de Víctimas, *Manual de Criterios de Valoración V2*, 167; DeJusticia, *La Buena Fe en la Restitución de Tierras - Sistematización de Jurisprudencia*, 2017, 19.

481 Art. 37 Decreto 4800 de 2011.

482 Art. 156 f. Ley 1448 de 2011.

483 ICTJ, *Implementación de Reparación Individual en Colombia*, 25 ff.

they qualify for special humanitarian assistance and are relegated to the relevant entities.[484]

a. Restitution

Given that 15 % of Colombia's population and 89 % of all registered survivors were displaced, the focus of restitution – if not of the whole reparation program – lies on land restitution.[485] According to Art. 75 of the Victims Law, every survivor of forced displacement can reclaim the land they legally owned, possessed, or occupied after 1 January 1991.[486] The reparation program tackles this massive task through a specialized entity, the Unidad de Restitución de Tierras (URT)[487], and a three-stage administrative and judicial restitution process.

In the first, administrative stage, the survivor requests the URT to enter a plot of land into the Registro de Tierras Despojadas o Abandonadas Forzosamente (RTDAF)[488]. A URT official records the survivor's account of the violation, the alleged perpetrator, personal data, the survivor's relation to the land, and other information. Survivors can initiate the process collectively if the land in question is adjacent and the same violation caused the displacement.[489] Given the continuously difficult security situation in many parts of

484 Unidad de Victimas, *Esta es mi Ruta*, available at: https://www.unidadvictimas.gov.co/es/esta-es-mi-ruta/8948.

485 UNHCR, *Global Focus Colombia*, People of Concern 2018.

486 The rigid cut-off date was set on the basis that by that year, armed groups started to use forced displacement as an important strategy. The constitutional court upheld it, also relying on valid fiscal reasons for the choice, Baade, *Post-Conflict Land Restitution - The German Experience in Relation to Colombian Law 1448 of 2011,* 2021 W. Comp. L. 54, 1, 11.

487 Land Restitution Unit.

488 Register of Evacuated or Forcibly Abandoned Land. Another database, the Registro Único de Predios y Territorios Abandonados, RUPTA, is based on an earlier law on land restitution and also covers plots of land outside of microfocalized zones (on that process see below, fn. 490), CSMLV, *Quinto Informe*, 10. RUPTA displays a slow progress, URT, *RUPTA - Registro Único de Predios y Territorios Abandonados*, 2017, 132 f.

489 Art. 8 Decreto 4829 de 2011 por el Cual se Reglamenta el Capítulo III del Título IV de la Ley 1448 de 2011 en Relación con la Restitución de Tierras; URT, *Memorias de la Restitución - Lecciones Aprendidas y Metodologias Para Restituir Tierras y Terrotorios en Colombia*, 2018, 74 f.; Delgado Mariño, *Segundos Ocupantes en el Marco de la Ley 1448 de 2011 - Un Debate Abierto*, in: del Pilar García Pachón (ed.), *Lecturas Sobre Derecho de Tierras - Tomo II,* 2018, 193, 205.

Colombia, the URT first verifies whether the conditions in the area of the reclaimed land allow for the process to proceed.[490] If that is not the case, it suspends the request until conditions in the area improve. If it is the case, the official examines within ten days whether the survivor is eligible for land restitution according to their account, whether there are reasons to prioritize the case and whether third parties currently occupy the land. Afterward, the URT has 60-90 days to decide the request.[491] Here again, the survivor must corroborate their claim through evidence. Evidentiary rules in the Victims Law greatly facilitate the task. Once the survivor summarily[492] proved their survivor status and legal relation to the land, the burden of proof is reversed. Several norms presume the nullity of contracts over land in a conflict-affected zone because of a lack of consent. Also, the URT helps to gather evidence.[493]

---

490 Art. 1, 2 Decreto 1167 de 2018 por el Cual se Modifica el Artículo 2.15.1.1.16 del Decreto 1071 de 2015, Decreto Único Reglamentario del Sector Administrativo Agropecuario, Pesquero y de Desarrollo Rural, Relacionado con las Zonas Microfocalizadas. The URT officially designated certain zones as ready for restitution processes through a process of macro- and microfocalization, which it carried out together with other entities. First, the ministry of defence evaluated the security situation in large areas, e.g. provinces or departments – the macrofocalization. The URT then entered secure areas and evaluated municipalities or even smaller zones, looking at the density of displacement, security conditions and whether basic state services are available – the microfocalization. Only if the latter two conditions were fulfilled did the URT open the zone up for restitution processes. The density of displacement served as a criteria for the prioritization of certain zones in the process. In 2016 the whole Colombian territory was macrofocalized. At the time of writing, almost the whole territory was microfocalized, URT, *Memorias de la Restitución,* 75, 97 ff. The introduction of an end-date to present claims relating to focalized zones and a three months limit to present claims beginning with the date on which new zones become focalized was criticized by civil society, Dejusticia, *Coadyuvancia a Solicitud de Suspensión Provisional de los Efectos del Decreto 1167 de 2018, por el Cual se Modifica el Artículo 2.15.1.1.16 del Decreto 1071 de 2015,* 2018; CCJ, *Radiografía de la Restitución de Tierras en Colombia - Informe Presentado Ante la Comisión Interamericana de Derechos Humanos por Incumplimiento de Reparación a las Víctimas Despojadas de Tierras en Colombia,* 2019, 5 f. 15 f.

491 Art. 79 Ley 1448 de 2011; Art. 9 ff., 14 ff. Decreto 4829 de 2011; URT, *Memorias de la Restitución,* 78 f., 248.

492 For the concept of summary evidence see above, Fn. (480).

493 Art. 77 Ley 1448 de 2011; Art. 2(4) Decreto 4829 de 2011; del Llano Toro, *El Desequilibrio Procesal y Probatorio del "Opositor Víctima o Sujeto Vulnerable" en el Proceso de Restitución de Tierras,* 2016, 91; URT, *ABC Para Jueces en Materia de Restitución de Tierras,* 2012, 45 ff.; URT, *Memorias de la Restitución,* 209 f., 228 ff.

Once the survivor entered the RTDAF, the second, judicial, phase begins. Specialized judges decide the case in an expedited and simplified process.[494] The survivor can be represented by the URT or by a lawyer of their choice. In both cases, the URT covers the legal costs.[495] The same reversal of the burden of proof and presumptions as in the administrative proceedings favor the survivor.[496] The judge communicates the initiation of proceedings to possible third parties with a legal interest in the case, which have 15 days to respond. In the following 30 days, the judge takes evidence from both sides. Once convinced, the judge can decide the case without entertaining outstanding requests for evidence by either party.[497] A decision in favor of the survivor can order one of three main measures: Primarily, the judge is supposed to restitute the reclaimed land. If that is impossible due to security issues or if the land became uninhabitable, the judge can compensate the survivor with a similar land plot. In both cases, the judgment is a title to the land and overrides any contrary register entries, administrative or judicial decisions. If both options are unavailable, the survivor can receive monetary compensation.[498] The judge can order a range of additional measures to facilitate a safe and sustainable return. Among them are prioritized access to housing subsidies, debt restructuring or repayment, and even infrastructure projects.[499] Only under limited circumstances can a party appeal such a judgment.[500]

Once the judgment is issued, the survivor enters the third, post-judgment, phase. The specialized judge remains seized of the case and can order further measures to facilitate the return if the need arises. The URT implements the judgment. Depending on what is ordered, the URT negotiates with private

494 Art. 82 f., 94 Ley 1448 de 2011; Ramírez et al., *El Amparo de Tierras - La Acción,el Proceso y el Juez de Restitución*, 2015, 75 f.

495 URT, *Memorias de la Restitución,* 83, 275 ff., 434 f.

496 Art. 77 f. Ley 1448 de 2011.

497 Art. 87 ff. Ley 1448 de 2011; Ramírez et al., *El Amparo de Tierras,* 81.

498 Art. 97 f. Ley 1448 de 2011; Art. 38 Decreto 4829 de 2011; URT, *Memorias de la Restitución,* 84.

499 URT, *Memorias de la Restitución,* 85; Sabogal Urrego, *Los Mecanismos de la Acción de Restitución de Tierras - Garantías Para las Víctimas y la Reconciliación*, in: del Pilar García Pachón (ed.), *Lecturas Sobre Derecho de Tierras - Tomo II,* 2018, 167, 177; Ramírez et al., *El Amparo de Tierras*, 59. These again correspond to elaborate reparation schemes, which for reason of space will not be detailed here. For a review of some of them see CSMLV, *Quinto Informe*, 133 ff., 155 ff. The resulting judgments are quite complex. They usually encompass 60-80 pages, García-Godos/Wiig, *Ideals and Realities of Restitution - The Colombian Land Restitution Programme*, 2018 J. Hum. Rts. Prac. 10(1), 40.

500 Ramírez et al., *El Amparo de Tierras*, 84; URT, *ABC Para Jueces*, 39 ff.

creditors for debt restructuring, repays the debt, brings state entities to waive outstanding tax debt, or facilitates the survivor's entry into the state housing subsidies program.[501]

Independently of the judgment, the URT and the Victims Unit offer displaced persons two programs to accompany their return. The URT and the survivor can create a so-called Plan de Vida Productiva[502] in which they devise an income-generating project tailored to the survivor's situation. The URT gives up to 55 monthly minimum salaries[503] in support and provides technical assistance.[504] Under the second program, the Victims Unit facilitates the survivor's decision to return by providing information on the security situation and the availability of essential state services in the area of return. Once survivors decide to return, the Victims Unit covers transportation costs. It also obliges all municipalities to which survivors return or relocate to elaborate a Plan of Return or Relocation. These serve to coordinate all state entities involved in the process and ensure that they provide essential services and infrastructure to survivors. The program also offers to assist and fund projects for survivors' socio-economic stabilization for up to two years. Examples are building or strengthening community infrastructure or giving computers, sports equipment, or other goods to the community.[505] For survivors of other violations than forced displacement, the reparation program offers mainly debt restructuring, special credit lines, and services as restitution.[506]

While showing promising results, the land restitution process faces two key challenges: the scarcity of evidence and the treatment of secondary occupants. Colombia has a history of informal land holdings and transactions. In 2016, 28 % of its territory was not featured in any register. In the most conflict-affected areas, this number jumped to 79 %. 63,9 % of the registered land was

501 Art. 102 Ley 1448 de 2011; DeJusticia, *Restitución de Tierras, Política de Vivienda y Proyectos Productivos,* 2017, 30; URT, *Memorias de la Restitución,* 85, 430 ff.

502 Plan for a Productive Life.

503 The amount of compensation is determined on the basis of the monthly minimum salary, which in 2021 was around 260 $. The current value of the monthly minimum salary can be seen at http://www.salariominimocolombia.net.

504 URT, *Programa Proyectos Productivos Para Población Beneficiaria de Restitución de Tierras,* 33 ff., 43 ff. In practice, such programs are of very limited reach and rarely tailored to the situation of the displaced population, CSMLV, *Quinto Informe,* 187.

505 Unidad de Víctimas, *Proceso de Acompañamiento al Retorno, Reubicación o Integración Local,* 2015, 5 ff., 11; Unidad de Víctimas, *Retornos y Reubicaciones - Hacia la Reparación Integral a Víctimas del Desplazamiento Forzado,* 2015, 25 f., 32, 47 ff.

506 Art. 128 f. Ley 1448 de 2011; Art. 140, 143 f. Decreto 4800 de 2011.

entered with outdated information so that different registers contradicted each other. Land transactions usually relied on the spoken word leading to a scarcity of evidence for such transactions.[507] The URT devised creative methods to overcome this massive evidentiary problem. It draws maps and timelines of land holdings and violations based on interviews with displaced populations. It also researches the general history of displacement in an area to create contextual information.[508] Still, evidence remains a massive challenge in the proceedings, which is particularly threatening for persons who currently occupy a reclaimed plot of land. These so-called secondary occupants often had nothing to do with the act of displacement. While some of them profited from the situation, many took the land out of necessity. They are themselves survivors of displacement or other violations and rely on the land to sustain themselves.[509] The evidentiary rules heavily tilt the administrative as well as the judicial restitution process against them. Coupled with the scarcity of evidence, secondary occupants are highly unlikely to win a restitution case and keep the land they occupy. They have a right to compensation if they prove an aggravated form of good faith, buena fe exenta de culpa[510]. For that, secondary occupants must show that they were convinced that the land acquisition was legal and took steps to verify their conviction.[511] Primarily since specialized judges treat the existence of a conflict in many areas as a notorious fact, many secondary occupants cannot meet this demanding standard.[512] More importantly, the standard does not correspond to the situation on the ground. As mentioned, many secondary occupants took the land out of necessity, often fully aware of what happened before. As a result, the land restitution process threatens to throw them off the land without compensation and stripping them of their means of subsistence.[513] In reaction to this dilemma, the URT devised a support program for secondary occupants, with measures similar to those provided for returning

507 CONPES, *Política Para la Adopción e Implementación de un Catastro Multipropósito Rural-Urbano (CONPES 3859)*, 2016, 3; CSMLV, *Cuarto Informe al Congreso de la República Sobre la Implementación de la Ley de Víctimas y Restitución de Tierras*, 2017, 190; DeJusticia, *Restitución de Tierras* 31, 33 ff.; URT, *Memorias de la Restitución*, 203 f.

508 URT, *Memorias de la Restitución*, 209 f., 228 ff.

509 Delgado Mariño, *Segundos Ocupantes*, 206.

510 Literally: good faith without guilt.

511 Art. 98 Ley 1448 de 2011; DeJusticia, *La Buena Fe en la Restitución de Tierras*, 30 f.

512 DeJusticia, *La Buena Fe en la Restitución de Tierras*, 58 ff.

513 Delgado Mariño, *Segundos Ocupantes*, 206; del Llano Toro, *El Desequilibrio Procesal y Probatorio*, 83 f.

survivors, including awarding secondary occupants land and productive projects.[514] The Constitutional Court ordered the specialized judges to treat the buena fe exenta de culpa-requirement with flexibility or even disregard it in cases of vulnerable secondary occupants who were not involved in the survivor's displacement.[515] Thus, vulnerable secondary occupants must show a lower standard of good faith or even no good faith at all to access compensation and the support program of the URT.[516]

b. Compensation

The Colombian reparation program awards compensation to survivors of forced displacement, homicide, enforced disappearance, kidnapping, torture, inhuman or degrading treatment, forced recruitment, sexualized violence, children born out of acts of sexualized violence, and survivors who sustained physical or psychological injuries, which caused a permanent or temporal disability.[517] The survivor requests compensation by filling out a form together with an official of the Victims Unit. Based on this information, the Unit determines their eligibility and recognizes possible reasons for their prioritization.[518] If eligible, the survivor enters either the prioritized or the regular route.[519] The prioritized route is open to survivors over the age of 74, displaced households in a state of extreme vulnerability[520], and survivors whose income-generating capacity was reduced by more than 40 % due to a disability or illness. In both routes, the Victims Unit has 120 days to decide on the request.[521] Afterward, it ranks all eligible survivors to determine the order in

514 Art. 1 Acuerdo 33 de 2016; Delgado Mariño, *Segundos Ocupantes*, 213 ff.; URT, *Memorias de la Restitución*, 424.

515 Corte Constitucional de Colombia, *Sentencia C-330 de 2016*, C-330/16 (Sala Plena), 2016, para 112.2.

516 Delgado Mariño, *Segundos Ocupantes*, 215 ff.; DeJusticia, *La Buena Fe en la Restitución de Tierras*, 66 ff.

517 Art. 149 Decreto 4800 de 2011; Unidad de Víctimas, Resolución 00848 de 30 Diciembre 2014, Art. 5 f.

518 Unidad de Víctimas, Resolución 01958 de 6 Junio 2018, Art. 9; CSMLV, *Cuarto Informe*, 145.

519 A third route is available for persons, who requested compensation under previous reparation programs, the so-called transitional route.

520 For the definition see above, C.IV.3.

521 Unidad de Víctimas, Resolución 01958 de 6 Junio 2018, Art. 7 f., 13, 15. Raising the age for prioritization to 74 was criticized by survivor organizations, Secretaría Técnica et al., *Sexto Informe de Verificación de la Implementación del Acuerdo Final de Paz en*

which they receive compensation. Those in the prioritized route enter at the top of the order. All others are ranked based on an individual assessment of demographic and socio-economic variables and the harm suffered.[522] The number of compensation requests by far surpasses the annual budget available for compensation, so that the exercise is crucial. Still, prioritization is not always implemented uniformly, and the process suffers from structural deficiencies.[523] Survivors entering the lower end of the ranking often wait for several years until they receive compensation.[524]

The amount of compensation is determined based on the severity of the harm suffered. Compensation for each violation is capped at between 17 and 40 minimum monthly salaries. If a survivor suffered multiple violations, the amounts are added, but the total can never exceed 40 minimum monthly salaries.[525]

Groups of 100-200 survivors receive the compensation in a half-day "dignifying event", which culminates in the delivery of the compensation together with a dignifying letter.[526] At the event, survivors can attend a support program, which offers financial literacy training on saving, investing, and financial planning. Survivors can choose between additional specialized training on investment in housing, business, or education. Lastly, investment opportunities are presented at fairs, and the Victims Unit tries to create such opportunities itself.[527]

Colombia Para los Verificadores Internacionales Felipe González y José Mujica, 2019, 218.

522 Unidad de Víctimas, Resolución 01958 de 6 Junio 2018, Art. 4, 13; Art. 2.2.4.7.4 Decreto 1084 de 2015. This system replaced one based on fixed criteria for prioritization, enumerated in Unidad de Víctimas, Resolución 00090 de 17 Febrero 2015, Art. 4, because that system suffered from structural and practical problems, CSMLV, *Quinto Informe*, 200 f.

523 CSMLV, *Quinto Informe*, 198, 200 f.

524 ICTJ, *Implementación de Reparación Individual en Colombia*, 43.

525 Art. 148 f. Decreto 4800 de 2011. The value of 40 minimum monthly salaries is explained above, fn. 503.

526 ICTJ, *Implementación de Reparación Individual en Colombia*, 42, 45 f. The dignifying letter is a measure of satisfaction described below, C.IV.3.d.

527 Unidad de Víctimas, *Programa de Acompañamiento*, available at: https://www.unidadvictimas.gov.co/es/ruta-integral-individual/programa-de-acompanamiento/8931.

c. Rehabilitation

The rehabilitation component of the reparation program consists of three prongs. Its core is the Programa de Atención Psicosocial y Salud Integral a Víctimas (PAPSIVI)[528], which offers individualized psychological and medical support based on an initial interview with each survivor.[529] Specialized psychological treatment on an individual, family, and community level seeks to mitigate and repair psychological damages and alleviate the emotional suffering of the survivor, their family, and community. The physical health component offers prioritized access to free, individualized, and specialized healthcare. It encompasses biomechanic, physiological, psychiatric, and neuropsychological care as well as prevention and rehabilitation measures for two years. The program also covers limited ambulant or stationary group and individual therapy. The goal of the health component is to enhance the survivor's corporal, personal and social autonomy.[530]

Because the Ministry of Health delayed the creation of PAPSIVI, the Victims Unit devised the Estratégia de Recuperación Emocional al Nivel Grupal (ERE)[531], which provides survivors with nine two-hour group sessions, in which they share their experiences, coping strategies, and feelings.[532] Importantly, these programs only complement the health care already available to survivors as assistance. Lastly, the whole reparation program seeks to incorporate a psychosocial approach. Survivors receive psychosocial accompaniment in the CRAVs.[533] The staff tries to prevent revictimization and incorporates psychosocial care in every interaction with survivors.[534]

Apart from psychosocial and health measures, the program offers preferential access to formal and informal education, which lasts from a couple of months to three years. A special education credit line for survivors existed but

528 Program of Psychosocial and Health Attention for Victims.

529 Oficina de Promoción Social, *Programa de Atención Psicosocial y Salud Integral a Víctimas en el Marco de la Ley 1448 de 2011 - Versión 2 Justada*, 2012, 41 f., 80 f.

530 Oficina de Promoción Social, *PAPSIVI - Versión 2 Justada*, 42 ff., 58 ff., 63 ff., 74 ff.; Oficina de Promoción Social, *Programa de Atención Psicosocial y Salud Integral a Víctimas del Conflicto Armado - Documento Marco*, 2017, 18; CSMLV, *Cuarto Informe*, 125.

531 Strategy for Emotional Recuperation on a Group Level.

532 CSMLV, *Cuarto Informe*, 126 f.

533 CSMLV, *Sexto Informe*, 72 f.

534 Unidad de Víctimas, *Elementos Para la Incorporación del Enfoque Psicosocial en la Atención, Asistencia y Reparación a las Víctimas*, 2014.

only had minimal reach. In general, the education sector of the reparation program suffers severe difficulties.[535]

d. Satisfaction

The program's satisfaction measures aim to reestablish the survivors' dignity, enhance their well-being and mitigate the pain. On a societal level, they serve to establish and disburse the truth about the violation.[536] All measures must be carried out with survivors' involvement to meet their expectations and wishes.[537] The Victims Law contains a non-exhaustive list of satisfaction measures, to which the Final Agreement added some more. It encompasses memorials, a memorial day for survivors, public acts of commemoration and acknowledgment of responsibility on the part of the government and the FARC-EP, official apologies, and exemption from military service.[538] The dignifying letter, which survivors receive together with their compensation, acknowledges the victimization and aims to restore the survivor's honor. However, it does not contain an acknowledgment of state responsibility.[539]

e. Guarantees of Non-Repetition

Finally, the Victims Law and the Final Agreement provide a laundry list of guarantees of non-repetition. Among them are changes in state policies, legal reform, awareness campaigns, and changes in school curriculums.[540]

---

535 Art. 130 f. Ley 1448 de 2011; ICTJ, *Implementación de Reparación Individual en Colombia*, 33 f.; CSMLV, *Sexto Informe*, 158 ff.; CSMLV, *Quinto Informe*, 167 ff.

536 Art. 139 ff. Ley 1448 de 2011.

537 Subcomité Técnico de Medidas de Satisfacción, *Guía de Medidas de Satisfacción*, 19, 25.

538 Final Agreement, 5.1.3.1. f.; Subcomité Técnico de Medidas de Satisfacción, *Guía de Medidas de Satisfacción*, 8 ff.; Procuraduría General, *Primer Informe*, 266. Many survivors reported difficulties in securing the exemption from military service. Until 2017, the measure was interpreted in a way that only survivors of forced displacement received it without incurring costs. Other survivors were subjected to certain fees, CSMLV, *Quinto Informe*, 206 f., 209.

539 ICTJ, *Implementación de Reparación Individual en Colombia*, 56 f.; ICTJ, *From Principles to Practice*, 21.

540 Art. 149 Ley 1448 de 2011; Final Agreement, 5.1.4.

Additionally, Colombia has started a human rights education program in schools and human rights training for militaries and other state officials.[541]

4. The Collective Route

The collective route can be initiated on request of eligible collectives or by the Victims Unit, which can approach collectives propio motu.[542] The route proceeds in five phases. First, the Victims Unit creates a preliminary description of the collective and the harm it suffered. Second, the Victims Unit meets with the collective and other stakeholders to prepare them for the reparation process. The Unit informs them about possible benefits and the upcoming process. It helps the collective create structures to communicate with the Unit and support the reparation process. In a third step, the Victims Unit and the collective engage in an in-depth analysis of the collective, the harm it suffered, causes for its victimization, its coping strategies, and socio-economic situation. On that basis, the collective and the Victims Unit create the Plan Integral de Reparación Colectiva (PIRC)[543]. It contains the envisaged outcome of the reparation process, the necessary measures, and a timeframe. In the fifth phase, the PIRC gets implemented within three years.[544]

All five forms of reparation are available to collectives. Restitution concentrates on the reconstruction of community spaces, infrastructure, and organizational capacities. The Victims Unit can give goods or between 242 and 394 monthly minimum salaries[545] as compensation. As collective rehabilitation, the Victims Unit devised a psychosocial recovery program, the Entrelazando-Strategy. It centers on community reflection, memory activities, acknowledgment of the harm suffered, and creating and strengthening collective coping strategies. The collective can choose whether to implement the strategy or other rehabilitation measures of a similar kind. All rehabilitation measures seek to enhance the collective's social fabric as well as its internal and external relations. Collective satisfaction consists of activities reconstructing collective

541 CSMLV, *Segundo Informe de Seguimiento y Monitoreo a la Implementación de la Ley de Víctimas y Restitución de Tierras 2012-2013*, 2013, 554 f.

542 Art. 227 Decreto 4800 de 2011. On eligibility for collective reparation see above, C.IV.1.

543 Collective Integral Reparation Plan.

544 Unidad de Víctimas, *Modelo de Reparación Colectiva*, 73 ff., 102; Unidad de Víctimas, Resolución 03143 de 23 Julio 2018 Capítulo I.

545 See above, C.IV.3.a.

memory and the creation of memory spaces. Symbolic measures, such as commemoration acts, serve to dignify survivors and restore their good name. Satisfaction measures help to recover lost practices and traditions of the collective. Lastly, just as the individual route, the collective route offers a laundry list of guarantees of non-repetition, among them human rights education, education against gender-based violence, technical assistance in establishing methods of alternative conflict resolution, capacity training for social leaders, and support to local reconciliation initiatives.[546]

5. Challenges and Criticism

Colombia conceived and implemented an impressively comprehensive, complete, and complex program. It devised innovative procedures regarding access to the program, differential treatment, etc. That makes the program a potential role model to many reparation programs worldwide. Still, naturally, such a complex and comprehensive program meets a wide array of challenges and critiques. These will not be recounted here in all detail. Some more considerable structural challenges and critiques will be pointed out in the following.

Most importantly, while the program provides an ambitious range of benefits on paper, its implementation has been slow and its coverage limited. Partially, this is because the government wildly underestimated the number of survivors.[547] Additionally, many trace the problem back to a lack of political will.[548] The individual and collective routes are significantly underfunded, suffer from staff shortage, and proceed at a pace at which they will take much

546 Unidad de Víctimas, *Modelo de Reparación Colectiva*, 62, 78 ff., 86 ff., 95 ff.; CSMLV, *Cuarto Informe*, 166; Sánchez León / Sandoval Villalba, *Go Big or Go Home?*, 558 f.

547 ICTJ, *From Principles to Practice*, 8 f.; Montes Alba, *El Reclamo de las Víctimas al Gobierno por Demoras en las Indemnizaciones*, El Espectador, 21 February 2018. This was also due to the fact that the Constitutional Court later held the many survivors of internal displacement to be eligible for compensation as well, which increased the potential beneficiaries of that measure manifold, Sánchez León / Sandoval-Villalba, *Go Big or Go Home?*, 555.

548 Group Interview with *Efraín Villamíl* (Confederación Nacional de Juntas de Acción Communal), *Guillermo Cardona Monreno* (Confederación Comunal Nacional, Collective Reparation Subject), *Jorge Marín Rivela* (Survivor, Confederación de Acción Comunal), *Jairo Alberto Delgado Beltran* (Universidad Pedagógica y Tecnológica de Colombia, Facultad de Derecho), and *Gloria Inés González Bravo* (Agro Comunal), Bogotá, 8 October 2018.

longer to complete than expected.[549] This led the international verification commission for the 2016 Final Agreement to conclude in 2018 that the implementation of the envisaged reparation showed so little progress that compliance with the agreement in this area was impossible to verify.[550] While the commission noted few advancements in later reports, it still lamented delays and partial non-compliance.[551]

Regarding single measures, the Victims Law's monitoring commission sees the judicial stage of the land restitution process as ill-equipped to handle the expected caseload. Proceedings are slow due to evidentiary problems, a lack of resources, and the continuing dire security situation in many parts of the country. In addition, requests for security and other post-judgment measures distract the specialized judges from the core restitution cases, over which they take priority. Cooperation with other state entities, for example, those administrating housing subsidies, is slow and difficult.[552] Often, parts of the judicial orders are not complied with.[553] While the administrative stage complies more or less with its caseload, a suspicious number of negative decisions sparks doubts about possible false negatives.[554] Survivors are sometimes barred from accessing the land restitution program because of the continuingly insecure situation in some parts of the country. Also, the government started to close restitution processes in zones, which have a low density of cases or show substantial progress.[555] The return assistance faces grave difficulties, mainly due to the dire security situation in some parts of the country,

549 CSMLV, *Cuarto Informe*, 137 f., 158, 176 f., 196 ff.; CSMLV, *Quinto Informe*, 46; CSMLV, *Sexto Informe*, 48 f.; KROC Institute, *Tercer Informe Sobre el Estado de Implementación del Acuerdo de Paz de Colombia*, 2019, 152; Secretaría Técnica et al., *Segundo Informe*, 159; Montes Alba, *El Reclamo de las Víctimas*, El Espectador 2018.

550 Secretaría Técnica et al., *Segundo Informe*, 156.

551 Secretaría Técnica/CINEP/PPP-CERAC, *Cuarto Informe de Verificación de la Implementación del Acuerdo Final de Paz en Colombia Para los Verificadores Internacionales Felipe González y José Mujica*, 2019, 215; Secretaría Técnica et al., *Sexto Informe*, 220; Secretaría Técnica et al., *Quinto Informe de Verificación de la Implementación del Acuerdo Final de Paz en Colombia Para los Verificadores Internacionales Felipe González y José Mujica*, 2019, 193.

552 CSMLV, *Cuarto Informe*, 195 ff.; CSMLV, *Sexto Informe*, 134 ff., 138 ff. 143 f., 154 f.; CSMLV, *Quinto Informe*, 127; Procuraduría General, *Primer Informe*, 264; DeJusticia, *Restitución de Tierras* 38 ff., 65 ff.; García-Godos/Wiig, *Ideals and Realities of Restitution*.

553 CSMLV, *Sexto Informe*, 138 f.

554 CSMLV, *Sexto Informe*, 137; CSMLV, *Quinto Informe*, 126 ff.

555 CSMLV, *Sexto Informe*, 136; CSMLV, *Quinto Informe*, 127; García-Godos/Wiig, *Ideals and Realities of Restitution*.

the deterioration of land due to abandonment, and the lack of infrastructure and economic opportunity.[556] As regards compensation, survivors can wait years for their turn. By 2019 only 13 % of eligible survivors were compensated.[557] The lack of resources also affects the support program, which is supposed to facilitate the sustainable investment of compensation. In 2016, it covered only 12 % of eligible survivors.[558] The same problem affects the rehabilitation program PAPSIVI, which by 2019 had only covered 13 % of survivors in need of the program.[559] The collective reparation route cannot meet the demand either. Only a few collectives have moved beyond the planning stage. Collective rehabilitation is not available in all regions. Infrastructure projects are often not implemented, partially because they were not planned in cooperation with actors necessary for their implementation.[560] In light of the delay and limited coverage, civil society and other actors mounted pressure on the government to extend the Victims Law beyond its originally envisaged cut-off date in 2021. Shortly before the Constitutional Court decided in their favor[561], Colombia's government announced that it would prolong the reparation program for another ten years.[562]

Not only the limited coverage of many measures but also their quality has received criticism. Survivor organizations criticized new changes implemented by Ivan Duque's government as a turn towards minimalist reparation, centered on individual monetary benefits.[563] The effort to provide land restitution beneficiaries with productive projects is often thwarted by an unfavorable macroeconomic climate and poor socio-economic conditions at the place of return.[564] Compensation is deemed too low to have a life-changing

556 Weber, *Trapped Between Promise and Reality*, 11; Guzman-Rodriguez, *Dignity Takings and Dignity Restoration - A Case Study of the Colombian Land Restitution Program*, 2017 Chi.-Kent L. Rev. 92(3), 871, 893 f. On some of the structural causes for these problems imbedded in the Victims Law see Attansio/Sánchez, *Return Within the Bounds of the Pinheiro Principles - The Colombian Land Restitution Experience*, 2012 Wash. U. Global Stud. L. Rev. 11(1), 1, 45 ff.

557 CSMLV, *Sexto Informe*, 191 ff.

558 CSMLV, *Cuarto Informe*, 156.

559 CSMLV, *Sexto Informe*, 113. Until 2018, it only covered 800.000 persons, CSMLV, *Cuarto Informe*, 127 f.

560 CSMLV, *Sexto Informe*, 215 ff., 222, 226 f.; CSMLV, *Quinto Informe*, 214, 219, 227.

561 Corte Constitucional, *C-588 de 2019*, C-588/19 (Sala Plena), 2019.

562 UNSC, *Verification Mission Report*, S/2019/780, para 10; Liévano, *More Time to Redress Colombia's Victims - The Question is How*, JusticeInfo.net, 24 October 2019; *Corte Constitucional Amplió la Vigencia de la Ley de Víctimas*, El Espectador, 5 December 2019.

563 Secretaría Técnica et al., *Quinto Informe*, 199.

564 DeJusticia, *Restitución de Tierras* 78.

effect. The accompanying seminars and productive projects are criticized for not being tailored to survivors' needs, capabilities, and situations.[565] The rehabilitation program varies in its quality depending on the region.[566] In contrast to what has been promised, it rarely offers specialized health care for survivors. Complicated cases are often remitted to the regular health care system, whose professionals lack training on dealing with survivors. Even the supposedly specialized health professionals in the reparation program sometimes lack previous experience with survivors. Also, putting a deadline on psychosocial support measures misconceives the nature of most of the psychological issues survivors have. Especially trauma-related problems tend to occur cyclically so that lifelong psychosocial support would be necessary.[567] An evaluation of both PAPSIVI and ERE showed little measurable effect, even though most participants said they benefitted from both programs.[568]

A third large problem concerns access. Many survivors are in a dire economic situation and live in remote areas. For them, receiving reparation or presenting a claim can require many resources, such as time and money for transport and accommodation. Some survivors cannot attend measures that require their prolonged presence, e.g., education, because the program does not offer childcare. These factors dissuade some survivors from claiming their rights.[569] Organizations also criticize legal barriers to claim reparation, such as the strict and somewhat arbitrary cut-off dates for eligibility and the deadlines to present claims.[570] Crucial information about the program does not reach all survivors. The Victims Unit officials, which are supposed to guide survivors through the process and disseminate information, are heavily overburdened and thus difficult to reach after the initial interview.[571]

---

565 CSMLV, *Sexto Informe*, 201; ICTJ, *Implementación de Reparación Individual en Colombia*, 44.

566 CSMLV, *Sexto Informe*, 122 f.; CSMLV, *Quinto Informe*, 114 f., 117.

567 CSMLV, *Cuarto Informe*, 127; ICTJ, *Implementación de Reparación Individual en Colombia*, 50; ICTJ, *From Principles to Practice*, 17.

568 CSMLV, *Cuarto Informe*, 130 ff., 135 ff., 139 f.

569 ICTJ, *Implementación de Reparación Individual en Colombia*, 33 f.; CSMLV, *Cuarto Informe*, 134.

570 CODHES/USAid, *13 Propuestas*, 19 ff.; CAJAR et al., *Organizaciones y Víctimas Exigimos Mayor Compromiso del Congreso con el Acuerdo de Paz*, 2017; Luna Escalante, *Tierras Despojadas, ¿Derechos Restituidos? - Encuentros Acerca del Problema de la Tierra en Colombia en un Escenario de "Justicia Transicional"*, 2013, 67.

571 ICTJ, *Implementación de Reparación Individual en Colombia*, 23, 25 ff.; DeJusticia, *Restitución de Tierras* 35 f.; CSMLV, *Cuarto Informe*, 134.

Lastly, Colombia's reparation program often confuses social policy and the fulfillment of social, economic, and cultural rights with reparation.[572] This is most obvious for rehabilitation. Under this heading, the Victims Law offers a wide range of measures. In a seemingly arbitrary manner, it denotes some as reparation, some as assistance.[573] As mentioned, Colombia retroactively labeled assistance given under previous regimes as reparation.[574] Some collective reparation projects generate confusion about whether the state is fulfilling an obligation to repair or its obligation to provide essential services.[575] All these problems frustrate survivors. Many feel that the state did not live up to its promises. This led to a significant loss of trust in the state and its institutions.[576]

D. *The International Criminal Court*

The ICC is the first international criminal court or tribunal equipped with a reparation mechanism.[577] Four cases have reached this last stage of the process: those against Thomas Lubanga Dyilo, Germain Katanga, Ahmad Al Faqi Al Mahdi, and Bosco Ntaganda. Each process culminated in a unique and independent reparation program. A study of 622 survivors in four situation countries found that reparation is a primary motivation for survivors to

572 ICTJ, *Implementación de Reparación Individual en Colombia*, 7, 10 ff., 14; ICTJ, *From Principles to Practice*, 7, 10 ff.; DeJusticia, *Restitución de Tierras* 70, 90 ff.; Vargas Valencia, *Antecedentes Normativos y Jurisprudenciales Sobre Justicia Restaurativa en Colombia - A Propósito de la Reparación de Víctimas en el Acuerdo Final de Paz*, in: del Pilar García Pachón (ed.), *Lecturas Sobre Derecho de Tierras - Tomo II*, 2018, 135, 156. This is especially obvious in Art. 25(1) Ley 1448 de 2011.

573 see Art. 49 ff., 135 ff. Ley 1448 de 2011, respectively.

574 See above, C.IV.

575 CSMLV, *Cuarto Informe*, 179.

576 ICTJ, *From Principles to Practice*, 12 f.; ICTJ, *Implementación de Reparación Individual en Colombia*, 27 f.; Secretaría Técnica et al., *Segundo Informe*, 158 f.; Weber, *Trapped Between Promise and Reality*, 14 f.; Montes Alba, *El Reclamo de las Víctimas*, El Espectador; Group Interview with *Efraín Villamíl, Guillermo Cardona Monreno, Jorge Marín Rivela, Jairo Alberto Delgado Beltran, and Gloria Inés González Bravo, Bogotá*, 8 October 2018.

577 Ambach, *The International Criminal Court Reparations Scheme – A Yardstick for Hybrid Tribunals?*, 132 f.

participate in ICC proceedings. It is fundamental for their positive perception of the ICC and the feeling that justice has been rendered.[578]

I. Comparability and Methodology

The rationale behind examining ICC reparation programs was explained above.[579] To quickly recall, these programs differ from those of Sierra Leone and Colombia because they are not rooted in state responsibility, are not state-run, and do not rest principally on the human right to reparation. Nevertheless, ICC reparation programs are transitional justice reparation programs. They respond to systematic human rights violations and pursue broader transformational aims. They draw inspiration from transitional justice reparation programs, and the international law on reparation plays a crucial role in their setup. This makes them comparable to the reparation efforts of Sierra Leone and Colombia. The undeniable differences make ICC reparation programs perfect for control purposes. Strategies common to Sierra Leone, Colombia, and the ICC in all likelihood serve to overcome challenges unique to the transitional situation – one of the few things all case studies have in common.

To effectively serve control purposes, the analysis must acknowledge differences between ICC reparation programs and those of Sierra Leone and Colombia nonetheless. As was already mentioned, the Rules of Procedure and Evidence (RPE) and the Regulations of the Trust Fund for Victims (TFV) create a unique normative regime for reparation. The international law on reparation is a key factor in that regime, but not the only one. The ICC orders reparation against an individual with rights.[580] Its reparation programs are therefore of a much more adversarial nature than the two state-run programs considered before. The financial limitations of ICC reparation programs are often stronger and political considerations fewer or at least distinct. Lastly,

578 Berkeley Human Rights Center, *The Victims' Court? A Study of 622 Victim Participants at the International Criminal Court*, 2015, 36 f., 45 f., 58; Balta et al., *Trial and (Potential) Error - Conflicting Visions on Reparations Within the ICC System*, 2019 Intl. Crim. Just. Rev. 29(3), 221, 224.

579 See above, A.I.

580 For a critical take on the rights of the accused and the defence in reparation proceedings see Dijkstal, *Destruction of Cultural Heritage Before the ICC – The Influence of Human Rights on Reparations Proceedings for Victims and the Accused,* 209 J. Intl. Crim. Just. 17(2), 369, 401 ff., 408 ff.

the ICC faces different constraints in working in the target state than a state, which operates a reparation program on its own territory. While these differences do not make a comparison between ICC reparation programs and those of Sierra Leone and Colombia impossible, they warrant consideration. The analysis must disregard features of the ICC reparation programs, which are likely to be a consequence of these differences and not of the transitional justice situation's particular exigencies. Where that is the case, it will be pointed out below.[581]

Two final caveats apply to methodology: First, the study relies exclusively on the facts and harms established in the respective reparation orders. Historical accounts mainly derived from one source will necessarily have blind spots. But since the reparation programs are based exclusively on that source, the author deliberately confined the historical accounts to the chambers' findings, with anything but a claim to comprehensiveness. The short summaries of the history, violations, and harms at the basis of the reparation programs must hence be taken with more than a grain of salt.[582] Second, the study is confined, for the most part, to the reparation decisions and implementation plans. There are rarely details available on the actual state of implementation of the reparation programs. The reports of the TFV are either unavailable publicly or heavily redacted. The case studies on Sierra Leone and Colombia evinced that implementation can differ starkly from plans made at the outset. The reader should hence be mindful that the following sections recite plans, not necessarily practice. Still, these ideals can inform the study, as they display strategies to deal with transitional situations' special exigencies.

II. The Reparation System of the International Criminal Court

Art. 75 RS introduces independent reparation proceedings following the conviction of a perpetrator. Based on its wording, the court needs to establish reparation principles in each case propio motu. Only the more detailed decisions on concrete reparation measures and the extent of harm can be

581 Of course the distinction between features based on such decisive differences and features based on other factors is not obvious to draw. The author will explain his choices and leave a more reasoned judgment of his decisions to the reader.

582 For similar considerations see above, A.II.

instigated upon application of survivors or by the court, if it so chooses.[583] It seems rather futile for the court to establish reparation principles, if no survivor applies for reparation. This odd constellation probably is the result of the drafters' vision that there would be one set of overarching reparation principles, whereas the court later chose a case-by-case approach.[584] In all likelihood, the odd relationship between the potentially mandatory reparation principles and the non-mandatory nature of reparation proceedings will remain theoretical though. So far, in all four reparation proceedings survivors applied for reparation, relieving the court of the decision whether it needs to establish reparation principles absent survivors' request.[585] Also, the chamber is not bound by the applications and can order reparation to further survivors yet to be identified.[586]

After hearing the parties[587], the court issues a reparation order, specifying the reparation modalities for the case at hand. At the Rome Conference, delegates recognized that reparation would be complex and hard to deliver for a criminal court. They decided to establish a TFV to support the court's reparation efforts in Art. 79 RS.[588] The Fund has two mandates. Under it's

---

583 Donat-Catin, *Article 75*, in: Ambos (ed.), *Rome Statute of the International Criminal Court - A Commentary*, 4th Edition 2022, para 10, 20.

584 Cf. Carayon/O'Donohue, *The International Criminal Court's Strategies in Relation to Victims*, 2017 J. Intl. Crim. Just. 15(3), 567, 581 f.; Pérez-León-Acevedo, *Reparation Principles at the International Criminal Court*, in: Andenas et al. (eds.), *General Principles and the Coherence of International Law*, 2019, 328, 339 ff. Hence, Dwertmann opines that the entire proceedings are not mandatory, Dwertmann, *The Reparation System of the International Criminal Court - Its Implementation, Possibilities and Limitations*, 2010, 195.

585 ICC, *The Prosecutor v. Thomas Lubanga Dyilo, First Report to the Trial Chamber on Applications for Reparations, ICC01-/04-01/06-2847* (Registry), 2012; ICC, *The Prosecutor v. Germain Katanga, Transmission de Demandes en Réparation,* ICC-01/04-01/07-3614 (Registry), 2015; ICC, *The Prosecutor v. Ahmad al Faqi al Mahdi, First Transmission and Report on Applications for Reparations,* ICC-01/12-01/15-200 (Registry), 2016. Unclear, but likely that survivors requested reparation: ICC, *The Prosecutor v. Bosco Ntaganda, Joint Response of the Legal Representatives of Victims to the Registry's Observations on Reparations,* ICC-01/04-02/06-2430 (Office of Public Counsel for Victims), 2019, para 32 ff.

586 See e.g. ICC, *Ntaganda Reparations Order*, ICC-01/04-02/06-2659, para 105.

587 More detail on survivor participation in the proceedings is provided by Safferling/Petrossian, *Victims Before the International Criminal Court,* 286 ff.

588 Moffett, *Reparations for Victims at the International Criminal Court - A New Way Forward?*, 2017 Intl. J. Hum. Rts. 21(9), 1204, 1205. The TFV was never intended to operationalize and implement the reparation awards though, Moffett/Sandoval, *Tilting at Windmills,* 762. However, that it eventually assumed this function might reflect its greater ability to handle the complex issues involved in setting up large-scale re-

assistance mandate, the TFV conceives and supports projects that benefit survivors in situation countries, independently of any proceeding or judgment. Here, the Trust Fund basically acts as a development agency specifically for the benefit of survivors of potential crimes within the court's jurisdiction.[589] The TFV's reparation mandate is more relevant to the present study. The court usually relies on the TFV to administer reparation following Art. 75(2) RS. In that case, the Fund helps with the conception and implementation of the reparation program based on the court's reparation order. The relationship between the Fund and the ICC is still in an embryonic phase, with many details unsettled. Generally speaking, the chamber lays down broad parameters of reparation, based on which the Fund drafts a concrete implementation plan. The chamber must approve that plan and supervise its implementation by the Trust Fund.[590] The TFV receives the money for reparation from the convicted person, Rule 98 RPE. The Fund can complement reparation efforts with its resources, Rule 98(5) RPE. So far, it chose to do so in the Lubanga, Katanga, and Al Mahdi cases in light of the defendants'

paration programs, de Greiff/Wierda, *The Trust Fund for Victims of the International Criminal Court,* in: de Feyter et al. (eds), *Out of the Ashes – Reparation for Victims of Gross and Systematic Human Rights Violations,* 225, 228, 239 ff. On the TFV's operational structure, Safferling/Petrossian, *Victims Before the International Criminal Court,* 300 f.

589 For an overview and analysis of the assistance mandate and the work carried out under it see Dutton/Ní Aoláin, *Between Reparations and Repair - Assessing the Work of the ICC Trust Fund for Victims Under its Assistance Mandate,* 2019 Chicago J. Intl. L. 19(2), 490.

590 ASP, Regulations of the Trust Fund for Victims, regulations 54, 57; Capone, *An Appraisal of the Al Mahdi Order on Reparations and its Innovative Elements - Redress for Victims of Crimes Against Cultural Heritage,* 2018 J. Intl. Crim. Just. 16(3), 645, 655 f. The intricacies of this relationship are still subject to quarrels between the court and the TFV. For an overview see Balta et al., *Trial and (Potential) Error,* 231 ff. Apart from the TFV, some aspects of the implementation of reparation require the cooperation of states parties. For that dimension see Kress/Broomhall, *Implementing Cooperation Duties Under the Rome Statute - A Comparative Synthesis,* in: Kress et al. (eds.), *The Rome Statute and Domestic Legal Orders - Vol. II: Constitutional Issues, Cooperation and Enforcement,* 2005, 515, 538 ff.; ICC, *Ntaganda Reparations Order,* ICC-01/04-02/06-2659, para 102.

indigence.[591] It has been asked to do the same in the Ntaganda case.[592] For these situations, as well as its activities under the assistance mandate, the TFV receives funds from the Assembly of States Parties (ASP) and voluntary donations. The court can also transfer seized assets and collected fines to the TFV, according to Art. 79(2) RS.[593]

III. The Reparation Programs of the International Criminal Court

Other than initially planned, the ICC did not create one set of overarching reparation principles, e.g., at the plenary session of judges.[594] Instead, the court opted to develop them case by case. At the time of writing, four chambers issued reparation orders. Since, naturally, no chamber reinvented the wheel, the orders show strong similarities and introduce first strategies in the ICC reparation practice.[595] They gave rise to overarching reparation principles (1.),

---

591 ICC, *The Prosecutor v. Thomas Lubanga Dyilo, Notification d'un Complément Additionnel en Vertu de la Règle 56 du Règlement du Fonds au Profit des Victimes*, ICC-01/04-01/06-3432 (TC II), 2018; ICC, *The Prosecutor v. Thomas Lubanga Dyilo, Notification of the Board of Directors' Decision on the Trial Chamber's Supplementary Complement Request Pursuant to Regulation 56 of the Regulation 5 of the Regulations of the Trust Fund for Victims*, ICC-01/04-01/06-3422 (TC II), 2018; ICC, *The Prosecutor v. Germain Katanga, Notification Pursuant to Regulation 56 of the TFV Regulations Regarding the Trust Fund Board of Director's Decision Relevant to Complementing the Payment of the Individual and Collective Reparations Awards as Requested by Trial Chamber II in its 24 March 2017 Order for Reparations*, ICC-01/04-01/07-3740 (TC II), 2017; ICC, *The Prosecutor v. Ahmad Al Faqi Al Mahdi, Public Redacted Version of "Monthly Update Report on the Implementation Plan, Including Notification of the Board of Directors' Decision on the Trial Chamber's Complement Request Pursuant to Regulation 56 of the Regulations of the Trust Fund for Victims"*, ICC-01/12-01/15-277-Red (TFV), 2018, para 14 ff..

592 ICC, *The Prosecutor v. Bosco Ntaganda, Reparations Order*, ICC-01/04-02/06-2659 (TC VI), 2021, para 257.

593 ASP, TFV Regulations, regulation 21. On the practical difficulties see Moffett/Sandoval, *Tilting at Windmills Reparations and the International Criminal Court*, 2021 Leiden J. Intl. L. 34, 749, 753 f.; Safferling/Petrossian, *Victims Before the International Criminal Court*, 301 ff.

594 Carayon/O'Donohue, *The International Criminal Court's Strategies in Relation to Victims*, 2017 J. Intl. Crim. Just. 15(3), 567, 581 f.; Pérez-León-Acevedo, *Reparation Principles at the International Criminal Court*, in: Andenas et al. (eds.), *General Principles and the Coherence of International Law*, 2019, 328, 339 ff.

595 Subsequent reparation orders referred to the first reparation order of the court: ICC, *Katanga Reparations Order*, ICC-01/04-01/07-3728, para 30; ICC, *Al Mahdi Reparations Order*, ICC-01/12-01/15-236, para 26; ICC, *Ntaganda Reparations Order*,

which underlie the four reparation programs in the Lubanga (2.), Katanga (3.) Al Mahdi (4.), and Ntaganda (5.) cases.

1. General Principles

The Appeals Chamber in Lubanga held that any reparation order must make at least five determinations: (1) The chamber must issue the order against the convicted person; (2) it must identify survivors or set out criteria for identifying them; (3) it must define the harm caused by the crime; (4) it must determine the scope of liability of the convicted person and (5) it must specify the type of reparation ordered, especially whether it shall be individual, collective or both.[596] Chambers in the Katanga, Al Mahdi, and Ntaganda cases confirmed these elements.[597] Only points two, three, and five are relevant to the present study. Points one and four are rooted in the particularities of international criminal law. According to the reparation orders so far, the principal purpose of reparation is to remedy the harm suffered.[598] In addition, reparation shall contribute to reconciliation between the convicted person and survivors.[599]

Art. 75(1) RS foresees restitution, compensation, and rehabilitation as possible forms of reparation. Since that list is not exhaustive, the court can also order satisfaction and guarantees of non-repetition.[600] The court's definitions

ICC-01/04-02/06-2659, para 29. See also Safferling/Petrossian, *Victims Before the International Criminal Court – Definition, Participation, Reparation*, 2021, 270.

596 ICC, *Lubanga Reparations Order (Appeals Decision)*, ICC-01/04-01/06-3129, para 1.

597 ICC, *Katanga Reparations Order*, ICC-01/04-01/07-3728, para 31; ICC, *Al Mahdi Reparations Order*, ICC-01/12-01/15-236, para 38; ICC, *Ntaganda Reparations Order*, ICC-01/04-02/06-2659, para 23.

598 ICC, *Lubanga Reparations Decision*, ICC-01/04-01/06-2904, para 179; ICC, *Katanga Reparations Order*, ICC-01/04-01/07-3728, para 267; ICC, *Al Mahdi Reparations Order*, ICC-01/12-01/15-236, para 27 f.

599 ICC, *Lubanga Reparations Decision*, ICC-01/04-01/06-2904, para 179, 193, 244; ICC, *Lubanga Reparations Order (Appeals Decision)*, ICC-01/04-01/06-3129, para 202 f.; ICC, *Katanga Reparations Order*, ICC-01/04-01/07-3728, para 268; Brodney, *Implementing International Criminal Court-Ordered Collective Reparations - Unpacking Present Debates*, 2016 J. Oxford Centre Socio-Legal Stud. 2(1), 19.

600 ICC, *Lubanga Reparations Decision*, ICC-01/04-01/06-2904, para 222, 237; ICC, *Lubanga Reparations Order (Appeals Decision)*, ICC-01/04-01/06-3129, para 202 f.; ICC, *Katanga Reparations Order*, ICC-01/04-01/07-3728, para 297; ICC, *Al Mahdi Reparations Order*, ICC-01/12-01/15-236, para 46, 67; Moffett, *Justice for Victims Before the ICC*, 176 f.

of these categories match those employed in general international law.[601] The court can order individual, collective, or both kinds of reparation. Possible factors for making that decision are the number of survivors as well as the scope and extent of the damage.[602] Collective reparation is often more appropriate for collective harm or large numbers of eligible survivors since it maximizes the programs' speed and efficiency.[603] In case the chamber orders only collective reparation, there is no need to examine individual applications for reparation. Still, collective reparation measures must benefit eligible individuals.[604]

Eligibility is determined based on the survivor definition in Rule 85 RPE. It resembles the survivor definition in general international law identified above[605]: A survivor is any natural and certain legal persons specified in Rule 85(2) RPE, who suffered harm due to the commission of any crime within the court's jurisdiction. The definition covers direct and indirect survivors. The latter category encompasses persons with a close relationship with the direct survivor or persons who suffered harm while intervening to prevent the violation or help the direct survivor. What constitutes a close relationship depends on the cultural context. It usually covers immediate family members.[606] The court determines causality through a but/for- coupled with a proximate cause test.[607] In conformity with general international law, the ICC employs a broad

601 ICC, *Lubanga Reparations Decision*, ICC-01/04-01/06-2904, para 223 f., 226, 230, 243. For the definitions see above, ch. 1, C.I-V.

602 Rule 97 (1), 98 (2) RPE; ICC, *Katanga Reparations Order*, ICC-01/04-01/07-3728, para 271 ff.; ICC, *Al Mahdi Reparations Order*, ICC-01/12-01/15-236, para 67.

603 ICC, *Katanga Reparations Order*, ICC-01/04-01/07-3728, para 272 ff.; ICC, *Al Mahdi Reparations Order*, ICC-01/12-01/15-236, para 67, 76; ICC, *Ntaganda Reparations Order*, ICC-01/04-01/07-3728, para 186 ff.; Dwertmann, *The Reparation System of the International Criminal Court*, 121 f.; McCarthy, *Reparations and Victim Support in the International Criminal Court*, 2012, 254 ff.

604 ICC, *Lubanga Reparations Order (Appeals Decision)*, ICC-01/04-01/06-3129, para 152 ff., 214.

605 See above, ch. 1, B.

606 ICC, *Lubanga Reparations Decision*, ICC-01/04-01/06-2904, para 194 ff.; ICC, *Ntaganda Reparations Order*, ICC-01/04-02/06-2659, para 37.

607 ICC, *Lubanga Reparations Decision*, ICC-01/04-01/06-2904, para 249 f.; ICC, *Lubanga Reparations Order (Appeals Decision)*, ICC-01/04-01/06-3129, para 120, 129; ICC, *Katanga Reparations Order*, ICC-01/04-01/07-3728, para 162; ICC, *The Prosecutor v. Germain Katanga, Judgment on the Appeals Against the Order of Trial Chamber II of 24 March 2017 Entitled "Order for Reparations Pursuant to Article 75 of the Statute"*, ICC-01/04-01/07-3778 (AC), 2018, para 49; ICC, *Al Mahdi Reparations Order*, ICC-01/12-01/15-236, para 44; ICC, *Ntaganda Reparations Order*, ICC-01/04-02/06-2659, para 132 f.

understanding of harm.[608] Under the subcategories of damage, loss, and injury, established by Rule 97(1) RPE, it recognized, among others, physical and psychological suffering, financial loss, as well as a loss of reputation, rights, and opportunities.[609]

The form and the general process to identify survivors varies subject to the circumstances of each case.[610] Survivors need to prove their eligibility for reparation on a balance of probabilities.[611] The standard of evidence is lower than in criminal proceedings but the highest standard the court exacts in all survivor participation modes.[612] Evidentiary questions are treated flexibly to take into account the difficulties survivors face in procuring evidence.[613]

---

608 ICC, *Lubanga Reparations Decision*, ICC-01/04-01/06-2904, para 229 f.; ICC, *Katanga Reparations Order*, ICC-01/04-01/07-3728, para 74 ff.; ICC, *Al Mahdi Reparations Order*, ICC-01/12-01/15-236, para 42 ff; ICC, *Ntaganda Reparations Order*, ICC-01/04-02/06-2659, para 68 ff. For the notion of harm in international law generally see above, ch. 1, B.

609 ICC, *Situation in the Democratic Republic of the Congo, Decision on the Applications for Participation in the Proceedings of VPRS 1, VPRS 2, VPRS 3, VPRS 4, VPRS 5 and VPRS 6 (Public Redacted Version)*, ICC-01/04-101-tEN-Corr (PTC I), 2006, para 116, 147; ICC, *Lubanga Reparations Decision*, ICC-01/04-01/06-2904, para 230; ICC, *Lubanga Reparations Order (Appeals Decision)*, ICC-01/04-01/06-3129, para 191; Dwertmann, *The Reparation System of the ICC*, 83; ICC, *The Prosecutor v. Thomas Lubanga Dyilo, Judgment on the Appeals Against Trial Chamber II's 'Decision Setting the Size of the Reparations Award for Which Thomas Lubanga Dyilo is Liable - Separate Opinion of Judge Luz del Carmen Ibáñez Carranza*, ICC-01/04-01/06-3466-AnxII (AC), 2019, para 96 ff.

610 ICC, *The Prosecutor v. Ahmad Al Faqi Al Mahdi, Public Redacted Version of "Trust Fund for Victims' Submission of Draft Application Form"*, ICC-01/12-01/15-289 (TFV), 2018, para 10; Contreras-Garduno/Fraser, *The Identification of Victims Before the Inter-American Court of Human Rights and the International Criminal Court and its Impact on Participation and Reparation - A Domino Effect*, 2014 Inter-Am. Eur. Hum. Rts. J. 7(1), 174, 187 f., in relation to the participation process, which can influence the reparation application process. See also the studies on specific cases below, D.III.2.b.aa., 3.b.cc, 4.b.aa.

611 ICC, *Lubanga Reparations Decision*, ICC-01/04-01/06-2904, para 252 f.; ICC, *Katanga Reparations Order*, ICC-01/04-01/07-3728, para 46 ff.; ICC, *Al Mahdi Reparations Order*, ICC-01/12-01/15-236, para 44; ICC, *Katanga Reparations Order (Appeals Judgment)*, ICC-01/04-01/07-3778, para 42; ICC, *Ntaganda Reparations Order*, ICC-01/04-02/06-2659, para 136; Benzing, *Das Beweisrecht vor Internationalen Gerichten und Schiedsgerichten in Zwischenstaatlichen Streitigkeiten*, 2010, 508.

612 Delagrange, *The Path Towards Greater Efficiency and Effectiveness in the Victim Application Processes of the International Criminal Court*, 2018 Intl. Crim. L. Rev. 18(3), 540, 547 f.

613 ICC, *Lubanga Reparations Decision*, ICC-01/04-01/06-2904, para 198; ICC, *Al Mahdi Reparations Order*, ICC-01/12-01/15-236, para 58; ICC, *Katanga Reparations Order*,

To apply for reparation, survivors need to fill out an application form in conformity with Rule 94 RPE, which requires establishing a survivor's identity and address; injury, loss or harm; location and date of the incident, and – if possible – the identity of perpetrators. Furthermore, survivors shall describe lost assets, property, or other items, if they seek restitution and include claims for compensation, rehabilitation, or other forms of remedy, as well as supporting documentation to the extent possible.

Reparation must respect several principles: It must be appropriate, adequate, and prompt.[614] Reparation must respect survivors' dignity and rights, avoid further discrimination or stigmatization, and address previously existing discriminatory structures. The principle of non-discrimination also obliges the court to proactively facilitate access to reparation for all survivors, especially the most vulnerable ones.[615] Survivors shall participate in the process, and the court must take measures to ensure their safety, physical and emotional well-being, and privacy.[616] Particularly vulnerable survivors may be prioritized over others.[617] Lastly, if possible, reparation should contribute to self-sustaining programs.[618]

ICC-01/04-01/07-3728, para 47, 53, 57 ff., 185; ICC, *The Prosecutor v. Thomas Lubanga Dyilo, Judgment on the Appeals Against Trial Chamber II's 'Decision Setting the Size of the Reparations Award for Which Thomas Lubanga Dyilo is Liable - Separate Opinion of Judge Luz del Carmen Ibáñez Carranza,* ICC-01/04-01/06-3466-AnxII (AC), 2019, para 161 ff.

614 With that the court, as many other sources on reparation, echoes the Hull formula, controversially used for determining compensation for expropriation, see Antkowiak, *A Dark Side of Virtue – The Inter-American Court and Reparations for Indigenous Peoples,* 2014 Duke J. Comp. Intl. L. 25(1), 1, 69. On the formula see Kriebaum/Reinisch, *Property, Right to, International Protection,* in: Peters/Wolfrum, *Max Planck Encyclopedia of International Law,* Online Edition 2019, para 24; Dickerson, *Minimum Standards,* in: Peters/Wolfrum, *Max Planck Encyclopedia of International Law,* Online Edition 2010, para 14 ff.

615 ICC, *Lubanga Reparations Decision*, ICC-01/04-01/06-2904, para 188 f., 227; ICC, *Katanga Reparations Order*, ICC-01/04-01/07-3728, para 30, 267 f.; ICC, *Al Mahdi Reparations Order*, ICC-01/12-01/15-236, para 29 ff., 105; ICC, *Ntaganda Reparations Order*, ICC-01/04-02/06-2659, para 41 ff., 89 ff.

616 ICC, *Lubanga Reparations Decision*, ICC-01/04-01/06-2904, para 190, 202 ff.; ICC, *Katanga Reparations Order*, ICC-01/04-01/07-3728, para 30; ICC, *Al Mahdi Reparations Order*, ICC-01/12-01/15-236, para 32; ICC, *Ntaganda Reparations Order*, ICC-01/04-02/06-2659, para 46 f.

617 ICC, *Lubanga Reparations Decision*, ICC-01/04-01/06-2904, para 200; ICC, *Al Mahdi Reparations Order*, ICC-01/12-01/15-236, para 140; ICC, *Ntaganda Reparations Order*, ICC-01/04-02/06-2659, para 92 f.

618 ICC, *Katanga Reparations Order*, ICC-01/04-01/07-3728, para 268; ICC, *Al Mahdi Reparations Order*, ICC-01/12-01/15-236, para 35.

Based on these principles, the ICC currently runs four distinct yet similar reparation programs. They address the harms caused by Thomas Lubanga Dyilo (2.), Germain Katanga (3.), Ahmad Al Faqi Al Mahdi (4.), and Bosco Ntaganda (5.).

2. The Lubanga Reparation Program

Thomas Lubanga Dyilo was the first defendant at the ICC. Accordingly, he was also the first person the court ordered to repair survivors. The trial began on 26 January 2009.[619] On 14 March 2012, Lubanga was convicted of enlisting and conscripting child soldiers under the age of 15 and using them to participate actively in hostilities pursuant to Art. 8(2)(e)(vii) and 25(3)(a) RS.[620] The reparation order was handed down on 7 August 2012.[621] As the first reparation proceeding before the court, the Lubanga case was a "pioneer case, associated with judicial and administrative challenges" warranting implementation "in a complex security- and health-context."[622] The detailed amendment of the reparation order, which the Appeals Chamber issued with considerable delay on 3 March 2015, further evinced the challenges.[623] Implementation suffered severe delays and became increasingly difficult because of the Covid-19 pandemic and a worsening security situation in Ituri.[624]

a. Case and Harm

The ICC convicted Thomas Lubanga Dyilo for enlisting, conscribing, and using child soldiers during the Ituri Conflict in the DRC between early

619 ICC, *Launch of the Information Campaign on the Opening of the Trial of Thomas Lubanga Dyilo in Ituri*, 2009.

620 ICC, *The Prosecutor v. Thomas Lubanga Dyilo, Judgment Pursuant to Article 74*, ICC-01/04-01/06 (TC I), 2012.

621 ICC, *Lubanga Reparations Decision*, ICC-01/04-01/06-2904.

622 ICC, *The Prosecutor v. Thomas Lubanga Dyilo, Décision Faisant Droit à la Requête du Fonds au Profit des Victimes du 21 Septembre 2020 et Approuvant la Mise en Œuvre des Réparations Collectives Prenant la Forme de Prestations de Services*, ICC-01/04-01-06-3495 (TC II), 2021, para 114, translation by the author.

623 ICC, *Lubanga Reparations Order (Appeals Decision)*, ICC-01/04-01/06-3129.

624 ICC, *Décision Faisant Droit à la Requête du Fonds au Profit des Victimes du 21 Septembre 2020*, ICC-01/04-01-06-3495, para 1 ff., 26 f., 39, 41, 109; ICC, *The Prosecutor v. Bosco Ntaganda, Trust Fund for Victims' Observations on the Impact of Covid-19 on Operational Capacity*, ICC-01/04-02/06-2517 (TFV), 2020, para 11 ff., 21.

September 2002 and 13 August 2003. The conflict between the Hema and Lendu in the eastern province of the DRC had an ethnic dimension and was fought over political power and resources.[625] Himself a former child soldier, Lubanga presided over the Union des Patriotes Congolais (UPC, later Union de Patriotes Congolais/Reconciliation et Paix, UPC/RP) and was the Commander-in-Chief of its military wing, the Forces Patriotiques pour la Liberation du Congo (FPLC).[626] The ICC found that Lubanga, together with other senior UPC and FPLC officials, devised and carried out the plan to seek military and political control over Ituri. This plan led to the enlistment and conscription of child soldiers below the age of 15 and their use in combat and as bodyguards.[627] Lubanga played an active role in massive recruitment campaigns and used child soldiers as his bodyguards.[628]

Against this background, the court recognized as survivors the children enlisted, conscribed, and used for hostilities as well as their families and other persons with a close relationship to them.[629] The Appeals Chamber determined that the survivors suffered "with respect to direct [survivors]:

i. Physical injury and trauma;
ii. Psychological trauma and the development of psychological disorders, such as, inter alia, suicidal tendencies, depression, and dissociative behavior;
iii. Interruption and loss of schooling;
iv. Separation from families;
v. Exposure to an environment of violence and fear;
vi. Difficulties socializing within their families and communities;
vii. Difficulties in controlling aggressive impulses; and
viii. The non-development of 'civilian life skills' resulting in the victim being at a disadvantage, particularly as regards employment.

With respect to indirect [survivors]:

i. Psychological suffering experienced as a result of the sudden loss of a family member;
ii. Material deprivation that accompanies the loss of the family members' contributions;

625 ICC, *Lubanga Verdict*, ICC-01/04-01/06-2842, para 67, 72 ff.
626 ICC, *Lubanga Verdict*, ICC-01/04-01/06-2842, para 81, 1115.
627 ICC, *Lubanga Verdict*, ICC-01/04-01/06-2842, para 1126 ff., 1351 ff.
628 ICC, *Lubanga Verdict*, ICC-01/04-01/06-2842, para 911, 915, 1356.
629 For details on the definition of survivor in the Lubanga case see below, D.III.2.b.aa.

iii. Loss, injury or damage suffered by the intervening person from attempting to prevent the child from being further harmed as a result of a relevant crime; and
iv. Psychological and/or material sufferings as a result of aggressiveness on the part of former child soldiers relocated to their families and communities."[630]

b. Reparation Efforts

Because of the widespread nature of the crime, the large number of potential survivors, and the contrasting limited number of individual applicants, the chamber decided only to award collective reparation.[631] The reparation order focused on rehabilitation, namely medical services, healthcare, psychological, psychiatric, and social assistance. Reparation should help reintegrate former child soldiers and therefore included education, vocational training, and sustainable work opportunities. Further, the chamber ordered symbolic reparation, including commemorations, tributes, and the wide publication of the ICC's verdict.[632]

Reparation must be appropriate for survivors of sexualized violence, and consider the age-related and gendered harm child soldiers experienced.[633] Survivors who received reparation from a different source remained eligible, but the court could deduct the amount of reparation already received.[634]

Based on these principles, the TFV filed its initial Draft Implementation Plan in 2015, which the Trial Chamber rejected as too vague. The TFV then filed separate implementation plans for symbolic and service-based collective reparations, which the chamber approved in October 2016 and April 2017, respectively.[635] Due to significant rises in the expected number of

630 ICC, *Lubanga Reparations Order (Appeals Decision)*, ICC-01/04-01/06-3129, para 191.
631 ICC, *Lubanga Reparations Order (Appeals Decision)*, ICC-01/04-01/06-3129, para 140, 153.
632 ICC, *Lubanga Reparations Decision*, ICC-01/04-01/06-2904, para 233 ff.
633 ICC, *Lubanga Reparations Decision*, ICC-01/04-01/06-2904, para 207, 210.
634 ICC, *Lubanga Reparations Decision*, ICC-01/04-01/06-2904, para 201.
635 ICC, *The Prosecutor v. Thomas Lubanga Dyilo, Order Approving the Proposed Plan of the Trust Fund for Victims in Relation to Symbolic Collective Reparation*, ICC/01/04-01/06-3251 (TC II), 2016; ICC, *The Prosecutor v. Thomas Lubanga Dyilo, Order Approving the Proposed Programmatic Framework for Collective Service-Based Reparations Submitted by the Trust Fund for Victims*, ICC-01/04-01/06-3289 (TC II), 2017.

eligible survivors, the plans may still be subject to change.[636] The complicated process resulted in a complex reparation program. Its assessment is further complicated by the fact that parts of the relevant documents are redacted. The chamber and the TFV devised a detailed and controversial process to enter the program (aa.). The program comprised symbolic (bb.) and service-based reparation (cc.)

aa. Program Entry

To start the program, the TFV conducted outreach activities to identify potential survivor populations beyond those who participated in the trial. To that end, it consulted with relevant stakeholders, including local governments, community leaders, and civil society.[637] The TFV took a proactive approach to enable marginalized survivors, especially women, to enter the reparation program.[638] Identified potential survivors were subject to an eligibility-screening interview. Survivors could establish their identity through official or unofficial identification documents, other documents, or a statement signed by two credible witnesses. They could prove their status as a former child soldier through records of the DDR-program, knowledge about the armed group the survivor allegedly had fought for, or military effects, among others.[639] The Victims Participation and Reparations Section (VPRS) conducted a preliminary examination of all applications. It transmitted dossiers of complete applications to the TFV, whose Board of Directors determined each applicant's eligibility. Its decisions were transmitted to the

636 ICC, *The Prosecutor v. Thomas Lubanga Dyilo, Observations in Relation to the Victim Identification and Screening Process Pursuant to the Trial Chamber's Order of 25 January 2018*, ICC-01/04-01/06-3398 (TFV), 2018, para 33 ff. See below, D.II.2.b.bb.

637 ICC, *Lubanga Reparations Decision*, ICC-01/04-01/06-2904, para 200, 205; ICC, *The Prosecutor v. Thomas Lubanga Dyilo, Draft Implementation Plan for Collective Reparations to Victims*, ICC-01/04-01/06-3177-AnxA (TFV), 2015, para 42 f.; ICC, *The Prosecutor v. Thomas Lubanga Dyilo, Thirteenth Progress Report on the Implementation of Collective Reparations*, ICC_01/04-01/06-3512-Red (TFV), 2021, para 32; ICC, *The Prosecutor v. Thomas Lubanga Dyilo, Fifteenth Progress Report on the Implementation of Collective Reparations*, ICC-01/04-01/06-3524 (TFV), 2021, para 24.

638 ICC, *Lubanga Reparations Decision*, ICC-01/04-01/06-2904, para 198; ICC, *Lubanga Draft Implementation Plan*, ICC-01/04-01/06-3177-AnxA, para 45 ff.

639 ICC, *Lubanga Draft Implementation Plan*, ICC-01/04-01/06-3177-AnxA, para 45 ff.

chamber and the Legal Representative for Victims (LRV).[640] Survivors had judicial recourse to the Trial Chamber if the Board denied their eligibility.[641] During the screening process, the TFV also identified vulnerable survivors and those who require urgent assistance for prioritization. Reasons for prioritization were the presence of injuries or harm, requiring an immediate response; the lack of assistance or rehabilitation so far; as well as being a woman, young mother, widow or widower, an orphan, elderly, disabled person, or a single parent head of household.[642] The TFV proposed a deadline for applying to the reparation program six months before the program ended because a later entry was impossible to process. The Trial Chamber followed that suggestion with the exact cut-off date being redacted.[643]

The eligibility screening procedure was subject to a hard-fought controversy. In the beginning, the Trial Chamber demanded that the TFV compiled much more detailed dossiers of potential survivors to assess the scope of Lubanga's liability.[644] The TFV strongly rejected that approach, especially after employing it in one field mission. According to the TFV, the level of detail the chamber required made the process slow, costly, and cumbersome for survivors. An interview took 4-5 hours, sometimes even more than a day. Since many survivors incurred travel costs and could not earn a living during the interview, the process placed a tremendous burden on them. Accordingly, some potential survivors did not conclude the process. The interview attained

640 ICC, *The Prosecutor v. Thomas Lubanga Dyilo, Annexe A au Sixième Rapport sur le Progrès de la Mise en Œuvre des Réparations Collectives Conformément aux Ordonnances de la Chambre de Première Instance II des 21 Octobre 2016 (ICC-01/04-01/06-3251) et 6 Avril 2017 (ICC-01/04-01/06-3289) et la Décision du 7 Février 2019 (ICC-01/04-01/06-3440-Red)*, ICC-01/04-01/06-3467-AnxA-Red (TFV), 2019, para 44 f.

641 ICC, *Observations on the Victim Identification and Screening Process*, ICC-01/04-01/06-3398, para 16; ICC, *The Prosecutor v. Thomas Lubanga Dyilo, Decision Approving the Proposals of the Trust Fund for Victims on the Process for Locating New Applicants and Determining Their Eligibility for Reparations*, ICC-01/04-01/06-3440-Red-tENG (TC II), 2019, para 34 ff.

642 ICC, *Lubanga Reparations Decision*, ICC-01/04-01/06-2904, para 200; ICC, *Lubanga Draft Implementation Plan*, ICC-01/04-01/06-3177-AnxA, para 29 ff., 56 f.; ICC, *The Prosecutor v. Thomas Lubanga Dyilo, Eighteenth Progress Report on the Implementation of Collective Reparations*, ICC-01/04-01/06-3537-Red (TFV), 2022, para 39(i), (ii).

643 ICC, *Observations on the Victim Identification and Screening Process*, ICC-01/04-01/06-3398, para 23 ff.; ICC, *Decision Approving the Process for Locating New Applicants*, ICC-01/04-01/06-3440-Red-tENG, para 41 f.

644 ICC, *Order to Supplement Lubanga Draft Implementation Plan*, ICC-01/04-01/06-3198, para 17; Brodney, *Implementing International Criminal Court-Ordered Collective Reparations*, 24 ff.

an adversarial dynamic, and the detailed questions retraumatized many interviewees. The slow pace and high costs put a strain on the TFV's limited resources and further delayed the start of the reparation program.[645] These complications exacerbated existing challenges. The trauma experienced by many survivors impeded their ability to describe their harm, express needs, and emotions. Many survivors voiced security concerns. Some communities exerted pressure on survivors not to come forward because they still supported Lubanga. Shame and stigma kept more survivors from accessing the program. These concerns and the pressure affected female survivors in particular. They made it hard, if not impossible, to go through with the detailed and comprehensive determination of eligibility the chamber demanded. The procedure likely negatively affected survivors and the reparation program as a whole. Despite these concerns, the chamber stood by its order and only allowed for the less strict procedure described above after setting Lubanga's liability.[646] In practice, the survivor identification process became increasingly difficult due to the worsening security situation in Ituri.[647] Even though the Covid-19 pandemic and local containment measures had halted the process for a while,[648] the Trial Chamber ordered that the last reparation applications should be transmitted to the VPRS on 31 December 2020.[649] It since twice extended the deadline for identifying potential survivors until it was reached on 1 October 2021.[650]

Once deemed eligible – be it through the original demanding or the later simplified procedure – each survivor automatically began the reparation process with a local counselor. In their first session, the counselor oriented

645 ICC, *First Submission of Victim Dossiers*, ICC-01/04-01/06-3208, para 16, 39 ff., 46, 60 ff., 78 ff.

646 ICC, *Order on Request of OPCV*, ICC-01/04-01/06-3252, para 11 ff.; ICC, *Decision Approving the Process for Locating New Applicants*, ICC-01/04-01/06-3440-Red-tENG, para 19.

647 ICC, *The Prosecutor v. Thomas Lubanga Dyilo, Further Information on the Reparations Proceedings in Compliance With the Trial Chamber's Order of 16 March 2018*, ICC-01/04-01/06-3399-Red (TC II), 2018, para 18 ff. and above, fn. 624.

648 ICC, *TFV Observations on the Impact of Covid-19,* ICC-01/04-02/06-2517 (TFV), 2020, para 16.

649 ICC, *Décision Faisant Droit à la Requête du Fonds au Profit des Victimes du 21 Septembre 2020,* ICC-01/04-01-06-3495, para 36.

650 ICC, *The Prosecutor v. Thomas Lubanga Dyilo, Decision on the Submissions by the Legal Representative of Victims V01 in its Response to the Twelfth Report of the Trust Fund for Victims on the Implementation of Collective Reparations,* ICC-01/04-01/06-3508 (TC II), 2021, para 15 ff. and operative paragraphs; ICC, *Lubanga, Fifteenth Progress Report,* ICC-01/04-01/06-3524, para 10 ff.

the survivor in the reparation process. The survivor and the counselor discussed the reparation process and the measures available, collected basic information about the survivor, their experiences, and coping strategies. In further sessions over several months, the counselor gained a deeper understanding of the survivor's harm. As a result, the program counted with the necessary information. The survivor, on the other hand, enjoyed enhanced mental health, better thought, and coping capacity, as well as tools to manage stress. Without such preparation, the TFV feared that highly traumatized survivors could not take full advantage of service-based reparation measures, which followed the counseling.[651] The staff involved in the process had to behave in a way to prevent further stigmatization, victimization, and re-traumatization.[652] Beyond counseling upon entry into the program, the TFV's implementation plan foresaw a range of collective symbolic (bb.) and service-based reparation measures (cc.).

bb. Symbolic Reparation

The symbolic collective measures served to raise awareness about the consequences of recruiting child soldiers, enabling their reintegration and rehabilitation. The measures encompassed three fixed and five mobile community centers.[653] The former were supposed to be a space for dialogue about Lubanga's crimes, the harm they caused, and survivors' reintegration. The communities should actively shape the spaces themselves. The Fund envisioned that the centers would host exhibitions and other artistic events relating to the crimes. The communities were to choose certain design features of the buildings. The centers should be built preferably by local builders and masons, especially those which employed former child soldiers. The TFV chose the fix centers' location based on the views survivors expressed, the hosting communities' connection to the crime, their size, and their importance.[654]

651 ICC, *The Prosecutor v. Thomas Lubanga Dyilo, Information Regarding Collective Reparation,* ICC-01/04-01/06-3273 (TFV), 2017, para 92 ff.

652 ICC, *Lubanga Draft Implementation Plan,* ICC-01/04-01/06-3177-AnxA, para 87; ICC, *Information Regarding Collective Reparation,* ICC-01/04-01/06-3273, para 89.

653 ICC, *Filing Regarding Symbolic Collective Reparations,* ICC-01/04-01/06-3223, para 29.

654 ICC, *Filing Regarding Symbolic Collective Reparations,* ICC-01/04-01/06-3223, para 31 ff.

The mobile community centers should cover communities outside the reach of the fix centers. They, too, should host awareness-raising events, the highlight of which would be a yearly commemoration week. In preparation for that event, the TFV would train local leaders, including young people, in memorialization and reconciliation activities, children's rights, the harms suffered by former child soldiers, and mediation techniques. Leading up to the event, local leaders and experts, e.g., psychologists, would conduct radio broadcasts. They would discuss the harm child soldiers experienced and how to reintegrate them into the communities. During the commemoration week, other radio programs would be broadcasted, artistic events organized, and the communities would hold open debates about the crimes and how they had affected them.[655]

Symbolic reparation measures served to create an enabling climate for the service-based reparation measures that should follow them. By increasing awareness about former child soldiers' suffering and their challenges, symbolic reparation should reduce stigma, discrimination, and resentment. Without these measures, the TFV feared that a hostile and discriminatory environment for former child soldiers could undermine the success of the subsequent therapeutic and socio-economic reparation measures.[656]

The worsening security situation in Ituri challenged the implementation of symbolic reparation measures. The TFV wanted to halt its call for tender for symbolic reparation in April 2018. It evaluated the possibility of reopening it in October 2018. By then, however, three years had passed since survivors had been consulted. Given the worsened security situation and Lubanga's release from prison, they now objected to the planned symbolic reparation measures, especially the commemoration centers. Hence, the TFV planned to consult the affected communities anew and restart identifying implementing partners.[657] It did so in 2022 and formed committees of survivors, civil society, and authorities of the relevant community to monitor the construction of the centers and the implementation of symbolic reparation measures. Constructions are currently set to begin in March 2023.[658]

655 ICC, *Filing Regarding Symbolic Collective Reparations*, ICC-01/04-01/06-3223, para 38 ff.

656 ICC, *Filing Regarding Symbolic Collective Reparations*, ICC-01/04-01/06-3223, para 13.

657 ICC, *Décision Faisant Droit à la Requête du Fonds au Profit des Victimes du 21 Septembre 2020,* ICC-01/04-01-06-3495, para 27, 109.

658 ICC, *The Prosecutor v. Thomas Lubanga Dyilo, Seventeenth Progress Report on the Implementation of Collective Reparations,* ICC-01/04-01/06-3533-Red (TFV), 2022,

cc. Service-Based Reparation

Service-based reparation measures should enhance survivors' psychological and physical health and rebuild their socio-economic opportunities.[659] The TFV operated on the presumption that all eligible survivors suffered psychosocial harm, making potentially damaging in-depth inquiries into their mental health unnecessary.[660] To remedy this harm, the Fund wanted to offer the psychological counseling described above to all survivors who entered the program.[661] In response to the enormous caseload, a limited number of health care professionals would train local non-professional counselors. The counselors should be recruited with an eye to gender parity. They received two weeks of intensive training on the psychosocial impacts of the crimes, how to carry out interventions and psychosocial assessments as well as gender sensitivity training.[662] In a so-called life skill program for all survivors, the counselors met weekly with groups of ten survivors for roughly three months. After a one-on-one psychosocial assessment, they counseled them on coping with their traumatic experiences, communicating effectively, managing daily life, and dealing with interpersonal conflicts, among others. Survivors with more severe psychological ailments should receive additional weekly counseling of approximately three months in groups of eight to ten people. Here, the group focused on coping strategies, tackling traumatic experiences, coping with the loss of loved ones, and other interventions.[663] After the life skill program and group counseling had ended, the counselors would mentor the participants and provide follow-up.[664] In addition, survivors was provided with a phone number after the intake

---

para 28 ff.; ICC, *Lubanga Eighteenth Progress Report,* ICC-01/04-01/06-3537-Red, para 43 ff.

659 ICC, *Information Regarding Collective Reparation,* ICC-01/04-01/06-3273, para 81.

660 ICC, *Information Regarding Collective Reparation*, ICC-01/04-01/06-3273, para 86; ICC, *Lubanga Draft Implementation Plan (General Part)*, ICC-01/04-01/06-3177, para 271; ICC, *Lubanga Draft Implementation Plan*, ICC-01/04-01/06-3177-AnxA, para 71, 80.

661 ICC, *Information Regarding Collective Reparation,* ICC-01/04-01/06-3273, para 85 ff. See above, D.III.2.b.aa.

662 ICC, *Information Regarding Collective Reparation,* ICC-01/04-01/06-3273, para 98; ICC, *Lubanga Draft Implementation Plan,* ICC-01/04-01/06-3177-AnxA, para 116 ff.

663 ICC, *Lubanga Draft Implementation Plan*, ICC-01/04-01/06-3177-AnxA, para 125, 138 ff.

664 ICC, *Lubanga Draft Implementation Plan*, ICC-01/04-01/06-3177-AnxA, para 125, 130 ff., 147 ff.

procedure they could reach in case they needed to reach a psychologists.[665] All psychological interventions were to be adapted to the survivors' beliefs.[666]

To remedy the bodily harm survivors endured, the TFV would provide subsidized access to health care based on contracts with local doctors and hospitals. The implementing partner should discuss a treatment plan with the survivor and adjust it to their needs and employment obligations.[667] The TFV helped with admittance, attaining treatment, managing bills, transport costs, counseling during treatment, and follow-up. It supported survivors with physiotherapy and assistive mobility devices such as wheelchairs and crutches.[668]

Educational and material benefits would even out socio-economic harm. The TFV would develop training courses based on a local market analysis it would conduct together with survivors. The courses would include accelerated literacy and numeracy classes. These would enable survivors to fully benefit from more advanced training afterward, such as masonry or carpentry. To offer the courses, the TFV planned to conclude memoranda of understanding with local accredited vocational schools and institutes. Every survivor would have an individual consultation with a social worker to choose the best available training option based on their education level, experience, interests, and other factors. The training schedules would be flexible to allow survivors to meet other commitments. Survivors would also receive payments for their training duration to ensure that they could meet other obligations. The program would facilitate transport and admittance of survivors, manage bills, provide follow-up and mentoring after the training had concluded.[669] In addition, the Fund would offer training on improved agricultural techniques. It would help select suitable and profitable crops based on market analysis, facilitate access to markets and provide pricing data. Home visits ensured follow-up.[670] After conducting studies and in-depth need assessments, the TFV started implementing the vocational training at the end of 2021. Survivors

665 ICC, *Lubanga Eighteenth Progress Report,* ICC-01/04-01/06-3537-Red, para 23
666 ICC, *Décision Faisant Droit à la Requête du Fonds au Profit des Victimes du 21 Septembre 2020,* ICC-01/04-01-06-3495, para 150 ff.
667 ICC, *Information Regarding Collective Reparation,* ICC-01/04-01/06-3273, para 102 ff.
668 ICC, *Information Regarding Collective Reparation*, ICC-01/04-01/06-3273, para 103.
669 ICC, *Information Regarding Collective Reparation,* ICC-01/04-01/06-3273, para 111 ff.; ICC, *Lubanga Draft Implementation Plan*, ICC-01/04-01/06-3177-AnxA, para 160 ff.; ICC, *Décision Faisant Droit à la Requête du Fonds au Profit des Victimes du 21 Septembre 2020,* ICC-01/04-01-06-3495, para 141 f., 144 f.
670 ICC, *Information Regarding Collective Reparation*, ICC-01/04-01/06-3273, para 118 ff.

were trained, inter alia for setting up taxi-services, selling food, or being a mechanic.[671] The TFV wanted to help create savings and loan associations. In these, 20-30 survivors pooled their savings to give microcredits to each other in turn. To obtain a loan, applicants must present a business plan, which the group subsequently voted on.[672] Later, the TFV also planned to give pensions to certain vulnerable survivors.[673] Lastly, based on wishes survivors relayed to the Office of the Public Counsel for the Victims (OPCV), the TFV planned a project for the localization and identification of missing child soldiers. However, until the date of writing, the TFV was unable to identify an organization or individuals suitable to deliver such a project in Ituri.[674]

The TFV deemed it vital to build upon existing infrastructure when delivering service-based reparation.[675] A potential problem was the geographical reach of the measures. The TFV demanded that potential implementing partners suggested how they could include survivors living in more isolated locations.[676]

Implementation of service-based reparation seemed to progress faster than the collective reparation projects. Still, it was not without detours. Newly identified survivors changed what the TFV perceived as survivors' expectations and wishes for service-based reparation measures. They also came up with their own ideas for reparation measures, which the TFV wanted to support. Accordingly, the TFV adapted its search for implementing partners and the projects it defined together with them.[677] In January 2021, the TFV identified implementing partners and evaluated four proposals for service-based collective reparation projects. The Trial Chamber approved the project

---

671 ICC, *The Prosecutor v. Thomas Lubanga Dyilo, Information Provided Pursuant to Regulation 28 of the Regulations of the Court in Relation to the Trust Fund's "Fifteenth Progress Report on the Implementation of Collective Reparations"*, ICC-01/04-01/06-3527 (TFV), 2021, para 10; ICC, *The Prosecutor v. Thomas Lubanga Dyilo, Sixteenth Progress Report on the Implementation of Collective Reparations,* ICC-01/04-01/06-3530-Red (TFV), 2022, para 20.

672 ICC, *Information Regarding Collective Reparation,* ICC-01/04-01/06-3273, para 123 ff.

673 ICC, *Décision Faisant Droit à la Requête du Fonds au Profit des Victimes du 21 Septembre 2020,* ICC-01/04-01-06-3495, para 143, 146.

674 ICC, *Lubanga Information on Fifteenth Progress Report,* ICC-01/04-01/06-3527, para 17.

675 ICC, *Information Regarding Collective Reparation,* ICC-01/04-01/06-3273, para 54.

676 ICC, *Information Regarding Collective Reparation,* ICC-01/04-01/06-3273, para 36.

677 ICC, *Further Information on the Reparations Proceedings,* ICC-01/04-01/06-3399-Red, para 23 ff.

proposals in March 2021 with some minor modifications.[678] Roughly 30 % of the direct project costs were allocated to psychological support, 15 % to physical rehabilitation, and 55 % to socio-economic measures. These measures were supposed to be implemented in parallel.[679]

Generally the difficult security situation in Ituri and the Covid-19 pandemic continued to hinder the effective implementation of the reparation program.[680] Because of that and the long time that passed since the beginning of the survivor identification process, the TFV encountered great problems reaching eligible survivors.[681] Additionally, the TFV had problems coming up with the envisaged funds.[682]

3. The Katanga Reparation Program

The ICC's second reparation program redressed the harm Germain Katanga had caused by committing crimes against humanity and war crimes pursuant to Art. 7(1)(a), 8(2)(c)(i), (e)(i), (e)(v), (e)(xii), 25(3)(d) RS.[683] His trial began on 24 November 2009.[684] He was convicted on 7 March 2014. Trial Chamber II handed down the reparation order on 24 March 2017.[685] As in the Lubanga case, implementation likely became more difficult in 2020 due to Covid-19 and a worsening security situation in Ituri.[686]

---

678 ICC, *Décision Faisant Droit à la Requête du Fonds au Profit des Victimes du 21 Septembre 2020,* ICC-01/04-01-06-3495, para 38, 87, 122 ff.

679 ICC, *Décision Faisant Droit à la Requête du Fonds au Profit des Victimes du 21 Septembre 2020,* ICC-01/04-01-06-3495, para 88, 135.

680 ICC, *Lubanga Thirteenth Progress Report,* ICC-01/04-01/06-3512-Red, para 11 ff., 32; ICC, *The Prosecutor v. Thomas Lubanga Dyilo, Fourteenth Progress Report on the Implementation of Collective Reparations,* ICC-01/04-01/06-3519-Red (TFV), 2021, para 17 ff.; ICC, *Lubanga Sixteenth Progress Report,* ICC-01/04-01/06-3530-Red, para 9 f.; ICC, *Lubanga Eigteenth Progress Report,* ICC-01/04-01/06-3537-Red, para 8 ff.

681 ICC, *Lubanga, Fifteenth Progress Report,* ICC-01/04-01/06-3524, para 19; ICC, *Lubanga Sixteenth Progress Report,* ICC-01/04-01/06-3530-Red, para 21.

682 ICC, *Lubanga Eigteenth Progress Report,* ICC-01/04-01/06-3537-Red, para 39.

683 ICC, *The Prosecutor v. Germain Katanga, Judgment Pursuant to Article 74 of the Statute,* ICC-01/04-01/07-3436, 2014.

684 ICC, *Opening of the Trial in the Case of Germain Katanga and Mathieu Ngudjolo Chui on 24 November, 2009*, 2009.

685 ICC, *Katanga Reparations Order*, ICC-01/04-01/07-3728.

686 ICC, *TFV' Observations on the Impact of Covid-19,* ICC-01/04-02/06-2517 (TFV), 2020, para 11 ff., 21.

a. Case and Harm

Germain Katanga led the Force de Résistance Patriotique d'Ituri (FRPI),[687] a Ngiti militia in the abovementioned Ituri conflict – the Ngiti being a subgroup of the Lendu.[688] Katanga's trial concentrated on his responsibility for the attack on the village of Bogoro on 24 February 2003. During the attack, the Ngiti militia – which gradually adopted the name FRPI – committed a series of crimes against humanity and war crimes. Among those were indiscriminate killings mostly of the Hema, sexualized violence, destruction of civilian buildings, and pillaging. Furthermore, the FRPI used child soldiers under the age of 15 in the attack.[689] Katanga was convicted pursuant to Art. 25(3)(d) RS for having provided logistical support to the attack.[690] The chamber acquitted him of responsibility for sexualized violence and the use of child soldiers.[691]

In the reparation proceedings, the chamber found that the attack on Bogoro caused significant economic and moral harm. Different property categories were destroyed or pillaged, including housing, personal effects, livestock, and houseware.[692] Survivors experienced psychological harm from witnessing the attack and especially from the deaths of relatives. They suffered losses of opportunity, standard of living, and forced departure.[693]

b. Reparation Efforts

The Trial Chamber deemed 297 survivors of the attack on Bogoro eligible for reparation. Considering the manageable caseload, it awarded both individual and collective reparation.[694] Individual reparation consisted of 250 USD for each survivor as a symbolic acknowledgment of their suffering.[695] The

---

687 Patriotic Resistance Force in Ituri.

688 ICC, *The Prosecutor v. Germain Katanga, Judgment Pursuant to Article 74 of the Statute*, ICC-01/04-01/07-3436 (TC II), 2014, para 702, 1360 ff. On the Ituri conflict see also above, D.III.2.a.

689 ICC, *Katanga Verdict*, ICC-01/04-01/07-3436, para 817, 824, 828, 833, 849, 924, 932, 1032, 1084.

690 ICC, *Katanga Verdict*, ICC-01/04-01/07-3436, para 1360 ff., 1671 ff.

691 ICC, *Katanga Verdict*, ICC-01/04-01/07-3436, para 1085, 1664.

692 ICC, *Katanga Reparations Order*, ICC-01/04-01/07-3728, para 77, 87,95 ff.

693 ICC, *Katanga Reparations Order*, ICC-01/04-01/07-3728, para 122, 129, 139.

694 ICC, *Katanga Reparations Order*, ICC-01/04-01/07-3728, para 168, 281 ff., 287.

695 ICC, *Katanga Reparations Order*, ICC-01/04-01/07-3728, para 300. For a critique see Moffett/Sandoval, *Tilting at Windmills*, 759.

chamber ordered collective reparation measures in housing, income generation, education, and psychological support. Within these areas, the reparation measures should provide some flexibility to accommodate different needs.[696] The chamber allowed prioritizing some survivors based on their vulnerability or urgent need for care.[697] The Appeals Chamber largely confirmed the order.[698] Based on the chamber's determination, the TFV drafted an implementation plan, which contained the ICC's most complex reparation program to date.[699] For survivors who proved their eligibility following a special procedure (aa.), it offered complex reparation measures (bb.), which made a special intake procedure necessary (cc.)

aa. Eligibility

The 297 survivors had to prove their eligibility on a balance of probabilities. Recognizing the passage of time, the ample destruction, and unavailability of evidence, the chamber allowed circumstantial evidence. It established far-reaching presumptions in favor of the applicants. For example, based on general information about Bogoro and the attack, the chamber presumed that anyone who lived in Bogoro at the time in question suffered pillaging. It also presumed a minimum amount of harm of pillaging of livestock based on the per capita consumption of that good in Bogoro at the time the crime was committed.[700]

bb. Reparation Measures

Survivors should choose whether they received their individual compensation of 250 USD in installments or as a lump sum payment. They were guaranteed a "timely, confidential and discrete transfer," which could include assistance with setting up a bank account. The TFV had to account for gender

696 ICC, *Katanga Reparations Order*, ICC-01/04-01/07-3728, para 301 ff.
697 ICC, *Katanga Reparations Order*, ICC-01/04-01/07-3728, para 310.
698 ICC, *Katanga Reparations Order (Appeals Judgment)*, ICC-01/04-01/07-3778.
699 ICC, *Katanga Draft Implementation Plan*, ICC-01/04-01/07-3751, para 113.
700 ICC, *Katanga Reparations Order*, ICC-01/04-01/07-3728, para 45 ff., 68 ff., 76 ff.

and power dynamics when meting out individual compensation.[701] The TFV implemented this measures fairly quickly.[702]

The Fund proposed measures for each of the four collective reparation areas targeted at different needs within the survivor population. In housing assistance, the TFV wanted to aid with purchasing or constructing and furnishing a new home, expanding an existing home, buying land, or paying rent. In education, the Fund planned to award two years of school fees on a primary or secondary level for two children or minor dependents of survivors, as well as a school material kit. As an income-generating activity, the TFV sought to offer vocational training, e.g., in animal husbandry, small business, and agriculture, as well as training on developing business plans and budgets. It would provide business kits – e.g., a sewing machine and material to make clothes – or livestock and veterinary kits. The TFV wanted to assist survivors seeking higher education with the payment of university fees and enrolment. Assistance with creating savings and loans associations[703] should facilitate small business opportunities. In the last area of psychological support, the TFV wanted to offer individual and group therapy and a referral procedure for individuals requiring specialized intensive treatment.[704] Since psychological services were unavailable in the region, the TFV liaised with a local psychologist who identified persons well-placed to receive training on managing PTSD. These could counsel survivors under the psychologist's supervision. The TFV further educated survivors and other members of the community on how to recognize PTSD through a pamphlet and other measures.[705]

While this collective reparation program should benefit the survivors who continued to live in the DRC, a second, similar program should aim at those who had fled to Uganda. It could differ slightly because of legal limitations related to survivors' refugee status. Several survivors participated in resettlement programs to Europe or the US. Because a comparable collective reparation program for them would exceed budgetary capacities,

701 ICC, *Katanga Draft Implementation Plan*, ICC-01/04-01/07-3751, para 115.

702 ICC, *The Prosecutor v. Germain Katanga, Report on the Trust Fund's Execution of the Payment of the Individual Reparations Awards,* ICC-01/04-01/07-3772 (TFV), 2017, para 28.

703 These associations were described above, D.III.2.a.cc.

704 ICC, *Katanga Draft Implementation Plan*, ICC-01/04-01/07-3751, para 105 f., 124 ff.

705 ICC, *The Prosecutor v. Germain Katanga, Public Redacted Version of the Fifth Quarterly Update Report,* ICC-01/01-04/07-3885-Red (TFV), 2021, para 44 ff.; ICC, *The Prosecutor v. Germain Katanga, Third Quarterly Update Report,* ICC-01/04-01/07-3870-Red2 (TFV), 2021, para 34 ff.

they would receive another symbolic monetary award. Publicly available documents did not specify its amount.[706] In the implementation phase, the TFV learned that implementing the planned reparation program in refugee settlements in Uganda would present too many obstacles and that some survivors there were in the process of resettlement. For these reasons, it decided to treat the survivors in Uganda as those in other countries, providing them with compensation.[707]

Not all survivors were to receive all collective reparation measures. The TFV categorized survivors based on harm. The five survivor categories were eligible for different reparation packages[708]:

Survivor Category	**Reparation Package**
(1) Loss of home and livestock	– Housing – Education – Income-generating activity (one cow and a veterinary kit, plus additional activities chosen by the survivor. Details were redacted) – Psychological rehabilitation
(2) Loss of home or equivalent material loss	– Housing – Education – Income-generating activity – Psychological rehabilitation
(3) Loss of immediate family member	– Housing *or* – Education *and* – Income-generating activities (one cow and a veterinary kit) *and* – Psychological rehabilitation
(4) Loss of personal affairs and minor material loss	– Housing *or* – Education *or* – Income-generating activities *and* – Psychological rehabilitation
(5) Moral Harm only partially covered by the individual award	– Psychological rehabilitation

Figure 2: Katanga Reparation Measures (created by the author)

706 ICC, *Katanga Draft Implementation Plan*, ICC-01/04-01/07-3751, para 60 ff.

707 ICC, *The Prosecutor v. Germain Katanga, Information Relevant to the Modalities of Implementation of Collective Reparations*, ICC-01/04-01/07-3811 (TFV), 2018, para 9 v.

708 Based on ICC, *Katanga Draft Implementation Plan*, ICC-01/04-01/07-3751, para 99.

Categories one, two, four, and five contained two subcategories for survivors who lost one family member or several family members in addition to the harm in the respective main category. They should receive augmented reparation packages containing one and two additional cows and veterinary kits, respectively.[709] A third subcategory encompassed survivors who lost a family home. It covered cases where a family, not individual survivors, suffered the harm grouped in main category one or two.[710] Survivors in this subcategory were to receive additional reparation based on the size of the home lost. Details were redacted.[711] The program also gave survivors a degree of flexibility. They could forgo the benefit of one category to increase the benefits received under another. For example, a childless survivor could substitute their education assistance with more housing assistance or an additional cow under the income-generating activity category. Survivors could also designate their individual award of 250 USD to top up collective awards. They could, for example, build additional rooms in the housing category, receive additional livestock or school fees for additional children.[712]

During implementation, the TFV frequently had to adjust the program. Survivors chose the purchase motorcycles, produce and the opening of small restaurants and bakeries as income-generating-activity.[713] The TFV chose an approach to allow maximum survivor participation in choosing the products for purchase.[714] As reaction to supply chain problems and price increases, the TFV allowed survivors to shift from originally chosen motorcycles to other options or cheaper models.[715] When procuring housing proved difficult, some survivors also shifted to other reparation modalities.[716] When the government announced in 2019 that basic education would be

709 ICC, *Katanga Draft Implementation Plan*, ICC-01/04-01/07-3751, para 96 f.

710 ICC, *Katanga Draft Implementation Plan*, ICC-01/04-01/07-3751, para 81 ff.

711 ICC, *Katanga Draft Implementation Plan*, ICC-01/04-01/07-3751, para 99 f.

712 ICC, *Katanga Draft Implementation Plan*, ICC-01/04-01/07-3751, para 100 ff.

713 ICC, *The Prosecutor v. Germain Katanga, Update Report on the Implementation of the Collective Reparations Awards*, ICC-01/04-01/07-3836-Red, 2019 (TFV), para 35; ICC, *The Prosecutor v. Germain Katanga, Second Quarterly Update Report*, ICC-01/04-01/07-3865-Red (TFV), para 11 ff.

714 ICC, *Katanga Update Report July 2019*, ICC-01/04-01/07-3836-Red, para 26, 28.

715 ICC, *Katanga Second Quarterly Update Report*, ICC-01/04-01/07-3865-Red, para 26 f.; ICC, *The Prosecutor v. Germain Katanga, Update Report on the Implementation of the Collective Reparations Awards*, ICC-01/04-01/07-3857-Red (TFV), 2020, para 50 ff.

716 ICC, *The Prosecutor v. Germain Katanga, Fourth Quarterly Update Report*, ICC-01/04-01/07-3878-Red (TFV), 2021, para 15 ff.

free, the education component of the reparation program lost much of its value. Therefore, the TFV allowed survivors to shift that reparation modality towards an income-generating-activity.[717] Generally, the dwindling security situation in Ituri coupled with the Ebola- and Covid-19-outbreak impeded implementation.[718]

cc. Intake

Given the complexity of awards and options provided, the TFV suggested a particular intake procedure for eligible survivors. They should meet, among other things, with TFV staff and the implementing partner, a financial advisor, and a counselor. First, the survivor and the financial advisor should discuss the transfer of the money and whether it should be paid in installments or as a lump sum. They should explore possible uses of the individual award, including coupling it with collective reparation measures. Those survivors who received education assistance should devise a plan with the financial advisor to ensure that survivors could cover school fees beyond the two years supported by the reparation program. Then, the survivor could select the measures suitable to their situation and confirm them with the TFV and implementing partner staff. Lastly, the survivor would meet with the counselor to discuss available therapy options. They were to assess the survivor's needs and – if warranted and wanted – could schedule individual or group therapy sessions. The counselor should further inform the survivor that they could access therapy at any point during the reparation program. The TFV planned to take special measures to meet the needs of women and girl survivors and mitigate the challenges they faced when accessing reparation measures.[719] The TFV and LRV conducted this process in the beginning of 2018.[720]

---

717 ICC, *Katanga Update Report July 2020,* ICC-01/04-01/07-3857-Red, para 39 ff.; ICC, *Katanga Second Quarterly Update Report,* ICC-01/04-01/07-3865-Red, para 8 ff.

718 ICC, *The Prosecutor v. Germain Katanga, Update Report on the Implementation of the Collective Reparations Awards,* ICC-01/04-01/07-3836-Red (TFV), 2019, para 15 ff.; ICC, *Katanga Update Report July 2020,* ICC-01/04-01/07-3857-Red, para 18 ff.; ICC, *Katanga Fourth Quarterly Update Report,* ICC-01/04-01/07-3878-Red, para 11, 26.

719 ICC, *Katanga Draft Implementation Plan,* ICC-01/04-01/07-3751, para 114 ff.

720 ICC, *Katanga Information Relevant to the Modalities of Implementation of Collective Reparations,* ICC-01/0401/07-3811, para 12 ff.

4. The Al Mahdi Reparation Program

The ICC's third reparation program followed the trial against Ahmad Al Faqi Al Mahdi, which began on 22 August 2016.[721] Due to Al Mahdi's admission of guilt, it was the shortest trial before the ICC to date, the verdict and sentence being rendered on 27 September 2016.[722] The reparation order was issued on 17 August 2017 and was largely confirmed by the Appeals Chamber on 8 March 2018. [723]

a. Case and Harm

Ahmad Al Faqi Al Mahdi played crucial roles in the insurgent government in northern Mali in 2012 of the radical islamist groups Ansar Dine and Al-Qaeda in the Islamic Maghreb. The groups had established a strict administration over the area following their interpretation of sharia law. Al Mahdi was deemed an expert in religious matters. The newly established "Islamic Tribunal" consulted him frequently, and he headed the morality brigade "Hesbah", which regulated the people's morality.[724] In mid-2012, the "governor" of northern Mali ordered Al Mahdi to destroy religious buildings in Timbuktu because the local population used them for prayer and pilgrimage. Nine mausoleums and the door of one mosque were destroyed under Al Mahdi's control and supervision. The United Nations Educational, Scientific and Cultural Organization (UNESCO) listed all sites except for one mausoleum as world heritage.[725] Al Mahdi bought and distributed tools for their destruction, gave moral support, and participated in five of the ten attacks. He explained and justified the attacks to journalists.[726] On 27 September 2016, Al Mahdi was sentenced to nine years in prison as a co-perpetrator of the war crime of attacking historic and religious buildings and monuments pursuant to Art. 8 (2)(e)(iv) and 25 (3)(a) RS.[727]

---

721 ICC, *The Prosecutor v. Ahmad Al Faqi Al Mahdi, Judgment and Sentence*, ICC-01/12-01/15-171 (TC VII), 2016, para 7.

722 ICC, *Al Mahdi Judgment and Sentence*, ICC-01/12-01/15-171.

723 ICC, *Al Mahdi Reparations Order*, ICC-01/12-01/15-236; ICC, *The Prosecutor v. Ahmad Al Faqi Al Mahdi, Public Redacted Judgment on the Appeal of the Victims Against the "Reparations Order"*, ICC-01/12-01/15-259-Red2 (AC), 2018.

724 ICC, *Al Mahdi Judgment and Sentence*, ICC-01/12-01/15-171, para 31 ff.

725 ICC, *Al Mahdi Judgment and Sentence*, ICC-01/12-01/15-171, para 39.

726 ICC, *Al Mahdi Judgment and Sentence*, ICC-01/12-01/15-171, para 34 ff.

727 ICC, *Al Mahdi Judgment and Sentence*, ICC-01/12-01/15-171, para 46, 62 f., 109.

In the reparation proceedings, the Trial Chamber found that these crimes caused, first and foremost, the destruction and damage to property.[728] The chamber also recognized individual economic harm suffered by those whose livelihood depended on the destroyed monuments and the moral injury of those whose ancestors' graves were destroyed.[729] The chamber acknowledged that the destruction caused collective moral suffering to the Timbuktu community in the form of mental pain and anguish, disruption of culture, and a sense of insecurity since the community believed that the mausoleums offered protection.[730] Further, the Timbuktu community suffered collective economic loss due to loss of tourism and hindrance of other economic activity.[731] Persons who fled as a result of the crime experienced loss of childhood, opportunities, and relationships.[732]

b. Reparation Efforts

The Trial Chamber faced the challenge to devise a reparation order for the destruction of world heritage – a first in the history of the court.[733] In response, the chamber designated the people of Timbuktu, Malians, and the international community as survivors of Al Mahdi's crimes. Immediately scaling back its bold determination, it held that reparation measures aimed at the former also adequately repaired the latter two.[734]

The Trial Chamber ordered individual and collective reparation. It recognized that the harm was mostly collective and would not be adequately reflected by simply aggregating all personal damage. Hence, collective reparation was deemed the primary avenue of redress. However, those survivors, whose livelihood depended exclusively on the monuments and the descendants of the saints buried in the destroyed monuments, suffered exceptional and more acute economic and moral losses. Hence, the chamber awarded them

728 That UNESCO restored them in the meantime was deemed irrelevant, ICC, *Al Mahdi Reparations Order*, ICC-01/12-01/15-236, para 60 ff.
729 ICC, *Al Mahdi Reparations Order*, ICC-01/12-01/15-236, para 57 ff., 72 ff., 84 ff.
730 ICC, *Al Mahdi Reparations Order*, ICC-01/12-01/15-236, para 85 ff., 90.
731 ICC, *Al Mahdi Reparations Order*, ICC-01/12-01/15-236, para 73, 76, 81.
732 ICC, *Al Mahdi Reparations Order*, ICC-01/12-01/15-236, para 85.
733 Dijkstal, *Destruction of Cultural Heritage Before the ICC*, 369.
734 ICC, *Al Mahdi Reparations Order*, ICC-01/12-01/15-236, para 51 ff.

individual compensation.[735] Due to the more significant harm these survivors suffered, it ordered the TFV to prioritize individual awards.[736]

All reparation measures had to be implemented with due regard to local conditions and after consultation with all stakeholders.[737] The TFV must conduct an outreach campaign to enable all survivors to participate.[738] While survivors must prove their eligibility on a balance of probabilities, the chamber recognized that the dire security situation and lack of official records in Timbuktu greatly complicated that task. It hence allowed for flexible evidentiary standards.[739]

From these principles, the TFV drafted an implementation plan. After a rather chilling response from the chamber, it devised an updated implementation plan based on a consultative process with relevant stakeholders. The implementation plans detailed the intake procedure (aa.) and the administration of individual reparation (bb.). The also contained nine collective reparation projects (cc.). The updated plan was approved on 4 March 2019.[740]

aa. Intake

To facilitate proof of eligibility, the TFV and LRV created attestation templates.[741] Given the scarcity of official documentation, the TFV concocted an elaborate attestation system.[742] To be considered for individual reparation for economic harm, survivors had to fill out an *attestation d'activité et de*

735 ICC, *Al Mahdi Reparations Order*, ICC-01/12-01/15-236, para 67, 76, 81 ff., 88 ff. This led to uncertainty whether as of yet unborn descendants of the saints could also become eligible for reparation. The TFV ultimately decided against that, Lostal, *Implementing Reparations in the Al Mahdi Case – A Story of Monumental Challenges in Timbuktu,* 2021 J. Intl. Crim. Just. 19(4), 831, 845 ff.

736 ICC, *Al Mahdi Reparations Order*, ICC-01/12-01/15-236, para 140; Capone, *An Appraisal of the Al Mahdi Order on Reparations,* 645 ff.

737 ICC, *Al Mahdi Reparations Order*, ICC-01/12-01/15-236, para 148.

738 ICC, *Al Mahdi Reparations Order*, ICC-01/12-01/15-236, para 148.

739 ICC, *Al Mahdi Reparations Order*, ICC-01/12-01/15-236, para 58.

740 ICC, *Decision on Al Mahdi Updated Implementation Plan*, ICC-01/12-01/15-324.

741 ICC, *Al Mahdi Draft Application Form*, ICC-01/12-01/15-289, para 45; ICC, *Decision on Al Mahdi Implementation Plan*, ICC-01/12-01/15-273-Red, para 168; ICC, *The Prosecutor v. Ahmad al Faqi Al Mahdi, Monthly Update Report on the Implementation Plan With Two Confidential Annexes,* ICC-01/12-01/15-283-Red (TFV), 2019, para 15 ff.

742 ICC, *The Prosecutor v. Ahmad al Faqi al Mahdi, Public Redacted Version of "Trust Fund for Victims' Submission of Draft Application Form"*, ICC-01/12-01/15-289-Red (TFV), 2018, para 45.

revenue detailing that their revenue drastically declined after the destruction of the mausoleums. To proof their eligibility for enhanced awards when harm derived from the destruction of more than one building, survivors had to submit an *attestation de famille* detailing their involvement in the maintenance of the buildings. The latter questionnaire had to be signed by a witness able to establish their identity and how they know the veracity of the information.[743] The former questionnaire needed to be signed by an authority recognized by the TFV based on their knowledge of the social fabric around the mausoleums and place in the community. The TFV trained the authorities on their role in the attestation process and the eligibility criteria for reparation.[744] Receiving individual compensation for moral harm as a descendant of a buried saint required survivors to fill out an *attestation de filiation*. The TFV identified "prominent families" which are commonly known descendants of the saints by asking persons to generate lists of such families independently from each other and cross-checking the results.[745] An application by a member of such a family must be signed by an official authority or traditional leader recognized as such by the TFV. These needed to attest to survivors' identity and how they know the truthfulness of the information provided. An applicant not belonging to a prominent family must submit the questionnaire signed by a member of a prominent family or must supply documents proving direct descendancy.[746] The TFV also mapped the social fabric around the mausoleums itself to obtain additional information on potentially eligible survivors.[747] If deemed ineligible based on

743 ICC, *The Prosecutor v. Ahmad al Faqi al Mahdi, Public Redacted Version of "Fourth Monthly Update Report on the Updated Implementation Plan"*, ICC-01/12-01/15-299-Red2 (TFV), 2018, para 13 f.

744 ICC, *The Prosecutor v. Ahmad al Faqi al Mahdi, Public Redacted Version of "Tenth Update Report on the Implementation Plan"*, ICC-01/12/01-15-335-Red2 (TFV), 2019, para 17 ff.; ICC, *The Prosecutor v. Ahmad al Faqi al Mahdi, Public Redacted Version of "Eleventh Update Report on the Implementation Plan"*, ICC-01/12/01-15-336-Red2 (TFV), 2019, para 11 ff.

745 ICC, *The Prosecutor v. Ahmad al Faqi al Mahdi, Public Redacted Version of "Eighth Update Report on the Updated Implementation Plan*, ICC-01/12-01/15-331-Red (TFV), 2019, para 21 ff.

746 ICC, *Al Mahdi Fourth Update Report*, ICC-01/12-01/15-299-Red2, para 18.

747 ICC, *The Prosecutor v. Ahmad al Faqi al Mahdi, Public Redacted Version of "Thirteenth Update Report on the Updated Implementation Plan"*, ICC-01/12-01/15-346-Red2 (TFV), para 23; ICC, *The Prosecutor v. Ahmad al Faqi al Mahdi, Trust Funds's Submission on the Amendment of the Screening Process*, ICC-01/12-01/15-372-Conf (TFV), 2020, para 13.

that information survivors could appeal the unfavorable decision before the Trial Chamber.[748]

The TFV and LRV jointly and separately collected applications.[749] To facilitate filling out the attestations and collecting them, the TFV selected and trained intermediaries it identified through contacts in Mali.[750] It also conducted outreach in Mali and other countries and maintained continuous contact with relevant families.[751] Once the majority of applications was collected did the TFV stop the active process and only passively accepted new applications.[752] The TFV ensured that women and girls were not discouraged from applying. To that end, it included a gender dimension in its staff guidelines and train relevant staff on gender issues.[753] It placed special emphasis on women in its outreach.[754] The TFV wanted to ensure that eligibility criteria would not reproduce discriminatory practices present in the Timbuktu community. For example, when determining individual compensation eligibility for descendants of a saint buried in a mausoleum, the Fund considered male- and female-based lineage, even though Malian law did not recognize the latter. It implemented such approaches in close cooperation with the relevant families.[755] When the list of authorities contained only men

---

748 ICC, *Al Mahdi Implementation Plan*, ICC-01/12-01/15-265, para 169 ff.; ICC, *Decision on Al Mahdi Implementation Plan*, ICC-01/12-01/15-273-Red, para 35 ff.

749 For details on that process see ICC, *Al Mahdi Thirteenth Update Report*, ICC-01/12-01/15-346-Red2, para 21 ff.

750 ICC, *Al Mahdi Eighth Update Report*, ICC-01/12-01/15-331-Red, para 14 ff.

751 ICC, *Al Mahdi Eleventh Update Report*, ICC-01/12-01/15-336-Red2, para 31; ICC, *Al Mahdi Thirteenth Update Report*, ICC-01/12-01/15-346-Red2, para 19; ICC, *The Prosecutor v. Ahmad al Faqi al Mahdi, Public Redacted Version of "Eighteenth Update Report on the Updated Implementation Plan"*, ICC-01/12-01/15-377-Red (TFV), 2020, para 23 f.

752 ICC, *The Prosecutor v. Ahmad al Faqi al Mahdi, Public Redacted Version of "Nineteenth Update Report on the Updated Implementation Plan"*, ICC-01/12-01/15-381-Red (TFV), 2021, para 17; ICC, *The Prosecutor v. Ahmad al Faqi al Mahdi, Public Redacted Version of "Twenty-First Update Report on the Updated Implementation Plan"*, ICC-01/12-01/15-405-Red (TFV), 2021, para 10.

753 ICC, *Al Mahdi Draft Application Form*, ICC-01/12-01/15-289, para 17.

754 ICC, *The Prosecutor v. Ahmad al Faqi al Mahdi, Public Redacted Version of "Twenty-Third Update Report on the Updated Implementation Plan"*, ICC-01/12-01/15-438-Red (TFV), 2022, para 36 f.

755 ICC, *Al Mahdi Draft Application Form*, ICC-01/12-01/15-289, para 38; ICC, *Al Mahdi Updated Implementation Plan*, ICC-01/12-01/15-291, para 54; ICC, *Al Mahdi Implementation Plan*, ICC-01/12-01/15-265, para 144 f.; Lostal, *Implementing Reparations in the Al Mahdi Case*, 847 ff.

at first, the TFV set out to remedy that imbalance.[756] To further facilitate access to reparation, the TFV recommended not to impose any deadline for applications. It is unclear whether the chamber followed that proposal since it redacted the relevant parts of its decision.[757] Lastly, the TFV would prioritize survivors who demonstrated an urgent need for individual compensation.[758]

bb. Individual Reparation

The amount of compensation survivors received was redacted. The TFV calculated the amount of compensation for economic harm based on salary statistics and the cost of living in Timbuktu. The TFV relied on statistics on men's salaries for both genders to not reproduce a gender pay gap. The amount of compensation for economic harm seemed to differ based on the different revenues the destroyed buildings had created. At the same time, the TFV stressed the need to avoid tension in the Timbuktu community because of the varying amounts of compensation.[759]

To assess the amount of compensation for moral harm, the TFV took a fine from the Malian Cultural Heritage Act as a baseline and multiplied it to ensure that the amount provided survivors some relief and reflected the international dimension of the crime, its symbolic and emotional features as well as the religious discriminatory intent. The resulting sum was not supposed to remedy all harm incurred. Instead, it should be proportionate to the harm considering the circumstances of the case, Al Mahdi's limited liability, and the availability of funds.[760] While the exact amounts were redacted, in a discussion about comparable human rights jurisprudence, the TFV remarked that 1.000 – 50.000 USD "would grossly overstate the amount that would be

756 ICC, *The Prosecutor v. Ahmad al Faqi al Mahdi, Public Redacted Version of "Third Monthly Update Report on the Updated Implementation Plan"*, ICC-01/12-01/15-288-Red2 (TFV), 2018, para 26.

757 ICC, *Al Mahdi Implementation Plan*, ICC-01/12-01/15-265, para 161; ICC, *Decision on Al Mahdi Implementation Plan*, ICC-01/12-01/15-273-Red, para 34; ICC, *Decision on Al Mahdi Updated Implementation Plan*, ICC-01/12-01/15-324, para 33 ff.

758 ICC, *Al Mahdi Updated Implementation Plan*, ICC-01/12-01/15-291, para 83.

759 ICC, *Al Mahdi Updated Implementation Plan*, ICC-01/12-01/15-291, para 61 ff., 67 ff.

760 ICC, *Al Mahdi Updated Implementation Plan*, ICC-01/12-01/15-291, para 44, 50 ff.

appropriate to set in the present case."[761] It reserved 500.000 USD in total for individual compensation.[762]

For security reasons, TFV staff disbursed the money via mobile banking apps after a detailed agreeing with each recipient on safe and convenient modalities for disbursement and explaining the reparation award in a phone call. The TFV chose such individual notifications to avoid survivors being pressured into sharing their award.[763] Women got special attention during the process to ensure that they were free to use their award as they saw fit.[764] The recipients were prioritized based on age and vulnerability.[765] Also, the first recipients were chosen to represent a gender-balanced selection of all eligible families to avoid tensions. The TFV chose leaders from those families as first recipients as they were best-placed to spread information on the process.[766]

cc. Collective Reparation

The chamber concentrated its collective reparation efforts at the protected sites and the community of Timbuktu. Since UNESCO had already rebuilt the sites, the chamber ordered measures for their protection, maintenance, rehabilitation, and – a first in the ICC reparation jurisprudence – guarantees of non-repetition.[767] To rehabilitate the Timbuktu community, it ordered education and awareness campaigns, return and resettlement programs, and a microcredit system to help the population generate income.[768] The chamber deemed symbolic measures adequate to relieve the collective emotional distress. It proposed a memorial, or commemoration and forgiveness ceremonies.[769] Lastly, Al Mahdi's apology should be translated into Timbuktu's primary languages, distributed via the court's website, and – if requested by individual survivors – in paper. The chamber also ordered the TFV

---

761 ICC, *Al Mahdi Updated Implementation Plan*, ICC-01/12-01/15-291, fn 52.

762 ICC, *Lesser Redacted Version of Al Mahdi Updated Implementation Plan*, ICC-01/12-01/15-291-Red3, para 76.

763 ICC, *Al Mahdi Nineteenth Update Report*, ICC-01/12-01/15-381-Red, para 35 ff.; ICC, *Al Mahdi Thirteenth Update Report*, ICC-01/12-01/15-346-Red2, para 62.

764 ICC, *Al Mahdi Eighteenth Update Report*, ICC-01/12-01/15-377-Red, para 55.

765 ICC, *The Prosecutor v. Ahmad al Faqi al Mahdi, "Twentieth Update Report on the Updated Implementation Plan"*, ICC-01/12-01/15-386-Red (TFV), 2021, para 31.

766 ICC, *Al Mahdi Nineteenth Update Report*, ICC-01/12-01/15-381-Red, para 39.

767 ICC, *Al Mahdi Reparations Order*, ICC-01/12-01/15-236, para 67.

768 ICC, *Al Mahdi Reparations Order*, ICC-01/12-01/15-236, para 83.

769 ICC, *Al Mahdi Reparations Order*, ICC-01/12-01/15-236, para 90.

to explore further possibilities to utilize the apology.[770] However, after survivors expressed reservations against or outright rejected the apology in consultations with the TFV, the chamber and the Fund agreed that they must respect the survivors' wishes in this regard.[771] Apart from these main measures, the chamber awarded one symbolic Euro each to the Malian State and UNESCO in lieu of the international community.[772]

Based on this order, the TFV proposed four projects to restore and protect the rebuilt sites and five projects aimed at rehabilitating the Timbuktu community. The TFV wanted to renovate the cemetery walls surrounding the rebuilt sites to protect them from the elements and unwanted human or animal access.[773] The TFV also proposed planting trees around the locations to shield them from desertification, winds, and sand.[774] Lighting should increase visibility, security, and surveillance. This project also had a community dimension because it should increase pride in the Timbuktu community, enhancing its resilience.[775] An unnamed organization should receive two motorbikes and 50 plastic chairs. The former should increase its capacity to monitor the sites periodically and rapidly respond to dangers. The plastic chairs were supposed to provide infrastructure for community training.[776] As the last rehabilitation project, the TFV wanted to create measures for the sites' maintenance. These included creating a fund that supported traditional community-based forms of maintenance impeded by the crimes.[777] The TFV partnered with UNESCO for the rehabilitation and maintenance measures, whose proposals were developed together with representatives from the Malian government and survivor representatives.[778]

770 ICC, *Al Mahdi Reparations Order*, ICC-01/12-01/15-236, para 71.
771 ICC, *Al Mahdi Updated Implementation Plan*, ICC-01/12-01/15-291, para 167; ICC, *The Prosecutor v. Ahmad Al Faqi Al Mahdi, Decision on the Updated Implementation Plan From the Trust Fund for Victims*, ICC-01/12-01/15-324 (TC VIII), 2019, para 98 f.
772 ICC, *Al Mahdi Reparations Order*, ICC-01/12-01/15-236, para 106 f.
773 ICC, *Al Mahdi Updated Implementation Plan*, ICC-01/12-01/15-291, para 89.
774 ICC, *Al Mahdi Updated Implementation Plan*, ICC-01/12-01/15-291, para 97.
775 ICC, *Al Mahdi Updated Implementation Plan*, ICC-01/12-01/15-291, para 100 ff.
776 ICC, *Al Mahdi Updated Implementation Plan*, ICC-01/12-01/15-291, para 103 f.; ICC, *Decision on Al Mahdi Updated Implementation Plan*, ICC-01/12-01/15-324, para 75.
777 ICC, *Lesser Redacted Version of Al Mahdi Updated Implementation Plan*, ICC-01/12-01/15-291-Red3, para 108 ff.
778 ICC, *Al Mahdi Tenth Update Report*, ICC-01/12-01/15-335-Red2, para 28 f.; ICC, *Ahmad al Faqi al Mahdi, Public Redacted Version of "Twelfth Update Report on the Updated Implementation Plan"*, ICC-01/12-01/15-340-Red (TFV), 2019, para 22 ff.

The remaining five projects aimed at rehabilitating the Timbuktu community. To counter its moral harm, the TFV would offer workshops and a psychological support program. The latter seemed to include a referral process to existing specialized services and regular training and capacity-building for staff. A second program explicitly aimed at women and girls. It would create safe spaces for group therapy, which featured discussions on cultural heritage.[779] Lastly, the Fund would rebuild one mausoleum, which fell outside UNESCO's competence and was therefore not rebuilt by the organization.[780]

Two projects sought to redress collective economic harm. First, the TFV wanted to create an Economic Resilience Facility, which offered financial support and advisory services to local economic initiatives. The advisory services were to encompass support for crop and livestock farming, handicraft, and activities contributing to the preservation of Timbuktu's cultural heritage. The facility should offer basic accounting and administrative training as well as training on drafting business plans, investment, and management strategies. Lastly, the facility should lend support in business registration and tax issues. If possible, members of the Timbuktu business community should conduct all training. In addition, the Economic Resilience Facility should help farmers around the sites and thereby increase social surveillance. It was supposed to support activities that maintain the traditional architecture and celebratory cultural activities related to the sites' maintenance. To ensure that all activities of the facility met local needs, the TFV would conduct a baseline market study.[781] The last proposed collective reparation project should facilitate the return of displaced survivors. Within a timeframe of two and a half years, it would cover their transportation costs and provide funds to facilitate their proper and permanent return. Further details of the project were redacted.[782] The TFV would prioritize elderly survivors and

779 ICC, *Al Mahdi Updated Implementation Plan*, ICC-01/12-01/15-291, para 106, 142 f., 148 ff.

780 ICC, *Lesser Redacted Version of Al Mahdi Updated Implementation Plan*, ICC-01/12-01/15-291-Red3, 113 ff.

781 ICC, *Al Mahdi Updated Implementation Plan*, ICC-01/12-01/15-291, para 120 ff.; ICC, *Al Mahdi Twenty-Third Update Report*, ICC-01/12-01/15-438-Red, para 31 f.

782 ICC, *Lesser Redacted Version of Al Mahdi Updated Implementation Plan*, ICC-01/12-01/15-291-Red3, 117 ff.; ICC, *Decision on Al Mahdi Updated Implementation Plan*, ICC-01/12-01/15-324, para 79 f.; ICC, *Al Mahdi Eighth Update Report*, ICC-01/12-01/15-331-Red, para 48.

women for these collective reparation projects due to their dire financial circumstances.[783]

The ceremony to award symbolic euros to the Malian State and UNESCO took place on 30 March 2021. The Chair of the TFV Board of Directors handed one Euro framed together with abstracts from the preamble of the Rome Statute to the Malian President of the Transition and the Deputy General Director of UNESCO each. The Prosecutor, members of the Timbuktu community, and government and diplomatic representatives attended. This was accompanied, among others, by speeches and the screening of films the TFV produced that summarized the case and illustrated the importance of the mausoleums for the community. The ceremony was live-streamed. Parallel activities included side events on topics of international justice, the inauguration of a memorial stone, and a work of art commemorating survivors.[784] The ceremony only proceeded after other reparation measures had commenced avoiding offending survivors.[785] Afterwards, the TFV conducted further outreach and follow-up activities to maximize the ceremony's impact. This included the wider screening of the two movies.[786] Before the ceremony, some persons raised the issue that one Euro would not evoke much symbolic value, since it was foreign currency and money had little symbolic value in Mali.[787] It is unclear whether or how the TFV reacted to that. As another symbolic reparation measure, the TFV would support a memorialization project. Since survivors did not have a uniform opinion about how to memorialize best what happened, the TFV developed a strategy based on the concept of "restorative agency" that let the local community steer all memorialization efforts according to local customs, rules, and practices. It would form committees of young adult men, young adult women, elderly men, elderly women, and children. Each would develop their own suggestion on memorialization. A joint committee consisting of one representative of each group would determine whether some proposals could be joined. If not, they would be implemented separately. That way, the TFV ensured the inclusion of marginalized groups in the process.[788] This resulted in four

783 ICC, *Al Mahdi Implementation Plan*, ICC-01/12-01/15-265, para 245.

784 ICC, *Al Mahdi Twentieth Update Report*, ICC-01/12-01/15-386-Red, para 44 ff.

785 ICC, *Al Mahdi Updated Implementation Plan*, ICC-01/12-01/15-291, para 157 ff.

786 ICC, *Al Mahdi Twenty-Third Update Report*, ICC-01/12-01/15-438-Red, para 39.

787 ICC, *Al Mahdi Eighteenth Update Report*, ICC-01/12-01/15-388-Red, para 61.

788 ICC, *Lesser Redacted Version of Al Mahdi Updated Implementation Plan*, ICC-01/12-01/15-291-Red3, para 160 ff.; ICC, *Decision on Al Mahdi Updated Imple-*

committees being established in Timbuktu and one in Bamako.[789] Generally, the deteriorating security situation and Covid-19 impeded implementation of the reparation program on many levels.[790]

5. The Ntaganda Reparation Program

The latest ICC reparation program followed the conviction of Bosco Ntaganda as a direct and indirect perpetrator of multiple crimes against humanity and war crimes.[791] Ntaganda was convicted on 8 July 2019 and sentenced on 7 November 2019.[792]

a. Case and Harm

Ntaganda was the third defendant tried for his role in the Ituri conflict.[793] He was first Deputy and then interim Chief of Staff in charge of Operations and Organisation of the FPLC.[794] Together with other members of the armed group, he devised a plan to take control of Ituri.[795] The plan led to the targeting of civilians and their property, rape, sexualized violence, and displacement.[796] In his role within the FPLC, Ntaganda devised the tactic behind an attack and fulfilled other essential functions. He gave orders to target and kill civilians and supported child recruitment. He also took part in attacks and killed persons himself. [797]

The chamber recognized as direct survivors of these crimes those who suffered harm from the attacks, child soldiers, children born out of rape

---

mentation Plan, ICC-01/12-01/15-324, para 97; Lostal, *Implementing Reparations in the Al Mahdi Case*, 849 ff.

789 ICC, *Twenty-Third Update Report*, ICC-01/12-01/15-438-Red, para 34 f.; ICC, *Al Mahdi Twenty-First Update Report*, ICC-01/12-01/15-405-Red, para 30.

790 See e.g., ICC, *Al Mahdi Tenth Update Report*, ICC-01/12-01/15-335-Red2, para 10 ff.

791 ICC, *The Prosecutor v. Bosco Ntaganda, Judgment*, ICC-01/04-02/06-2359 (TC VI), 2019, disposition.

792 ICC, *Ntaganda Judgment*, ICC-01/04-02/06-2359; ICC, *The Prosecutor v. Bosco Ntaganda, Sentencing Judgment*, ICC-01/04-02/06-2442 (TC VI), 2019.

793 See above, D.III.2.a., 3.a.

794 ICC, *Ntaganda Judgment*, ICC-01/04-02/06-2359, para 321 ff.

795 ICC, *Ntaganda Judgment*, ICC-01/04-02/06-2359, para 787.

796 ICC, *Ntaganda Judgment*, ICC-01/04-02/06-2359, para 493 ff.

797 ICC, *Ntaganda Judgment*, ICC-01/04-02/06-2359, para 830 ff.

and sexual slavery.[798] When identifying categories of indirect survivors, the chamber oriented itself at the Lubanga case. Based on the broader notion of family in the DRC, it included extended family members of direct survivors in its definition. The principle of non-discrimination led it to include further unmarried partners and children born out of wedlock. If they suffered the requisite harm, persons in whose lives a direct survivor had significant importance, and persons who witnessed the crimes could also qualify as indirect survivors.[799] Apparently, the chamber also recognized persons intervening to prevent harm to direct survivors as indirect survivors. Confusingly, the chamber determined such a situation to be a kind of harm instead of a distinct survivor category.[800]

The chamber listed in detail different types of harm suffered by four categories of survivors: One, direct survivors of the attacks; two, child soldiers; three, direct survivors of rape or sexual slavery and children born out of rape or sexual slavery; and four, indirect survivors. Each suffered different kinds of psychological, physical, and material harm. Direct survivors of the attack and child soldiers sustained a loss of childhood, life plans, educational opportunities, productive capacity, socio-economic opportunities, and a reduced standard of living, among others. The Trial Chamber recognized that direct survivors of the attack also suffered damage to a health center and the consequent loss of healthcare provision. The chamber also recognized transgenerational harm of indirect survivors – a type of harm the Katanga Trial Chamber had rejected before based on doubts about the causality of the violation.[801] These last two determinations were quashed by the Appeals Chamber. It held that the Trial Chamber did not assess whether the concept of transgenerational harm was established to the requisite degree of scientific certainty. It ordered the Trial Chamber to make that assessment and, if it

798 ICC, *Ntaganda Reparations Order*, ICC-01/04-02/06-2659, para 109 ff.

799 ICC, *Ntaganda Reparations Order*, ICC-01/04-02/06-2659, para 124 ff. The AC upheld that persons to whom a direct survivor had significant importance could qualify as indirect survivors but cautioned that more guidance needed to be given to the TFV in administering the criteria of importance, ICC, *The Prosecutor v. Bosco Ntaganda, Judgment on the Appeals Against the Decision of Trial Chamber VI of 8 March 2021 Entitled "Reparations Order"*, ICC-01/04-02/06-2782 (AC), 2022, para 625 ff.

800 ICC, *Ntaganda Reparations Order*, ICC-01/04-02/06-2659, para 183.

801 ICC, *Ntaganda Reparations Order*, ICC-01/04-02/06-2659, para 183; ICC, *The Prosecutor v. Germain Katanga, Public Redacted Version of Decision on the Matter of the Transgenerational Harm Alleged by Some Applicants for Reparations Remanded by the Appeals Chamber in its Judgment of 8 March 2018*, ICC-01/04-01/07-3804-Red (TC II), 2018, para 141.

found that such certainty existed, to give more guidance to the TFV on how to assess this kind of harm in the eligibility determination. It also deemed the damage to the health center insufficiently proven.[802]

b. Reparation Efforts

The Ntaganda reparation effort is still very much in flux. At the time of writing, the Appeals Chamber had just released its judgment on the appeal against the reparation order, tasking the Trial Chamber to reconsider several parts of its decision.[803] It is not clear yet, how this will change the program that is partially already being planned and implemented.

The Trial Chamber ordered collective reparation with individualized components.[804] It held that such measures would be collective but focused on individual members of the group and resulted in personal benefits.[805] The chamber deemed them more cost-effective, quicker, and better to deliver in the volatile security situation in Ituri. Collective measures also reduced community tensions and the risk that reparation would expose survivors of rape and sexual slavery or child soldiers and subject them to further discrimination. The individualized component paid tribute to survivors' preferences for individual financial measures.[806] The reparation measures should be sensitive to the unique needs of survivors who were victimized as children and employ a gender-sensitive, intersectional lens. They should have transformative value by addressing "the cultural meaning of violence" and structural violence.[807] The Trial Chamber concentrated on rehabilitation and satisfaction. It deemed restitution impossible and left it to the TFV to determine whether compensation would be feasible and adequate.[808]

802 ICC, *Ntaganda Reparations Appeal*, ICC-01/04-02/06-2782, para 439 ff., 535 ff. It hence remains to be seen, whether the TFV's proposals to deal with transgenerational harm will be implementend. See, ICC, *Ntaganda Draft Implementation Plan*, ICC-01/04-02/06-2750-AnxA-Red-Corr, para 215 ff. On the reparation plans for the Sayo Health Center see below, bb.

803 ICC, *Ntaganda, Reparations Appeal*, ICC-01/04-02/06-2782.

804 ICC, *Ntaganda Reparations Order*, ICC-01/04-02/06-2659, para 186 ff., 191 f.

805 ICC, *Ntaganda Reparations Order*, ICC-01/04-02/06-2659, para 81.

806 ICC, *Ntaganda Reparations Order*, ICC-01/04-02/06-2659, para 191 ff.

807 ICC, *Ntaganda Reparations Order*, ICC-01/04-02/06-2659, para 53 ff., 60 ff., 209.

808 ICC, *Ntaganda Reparations Order*, ICC-01/04-02/06-2659, para 201 f.

As a novelty in ICC reparation proceedings, the Chamber ordered the TFV to hand in an initial implementation plan to be implemented before the main reparation program for priority survivors in a particularly vulnerable situation. Among those were survivors who require immediate physical or psychological care, survivors with disabilities, elderly or homeless survivors, and survivors experiencing financial hardship. Survivors of sexual or gender-based violence, child soldiers, and children born out of rape and sexual slavery should also receive prioritized care.[809]

The TFV handed in its initial implementation plan for prioritized survivors on 8 June 2021, which the Trial Chamber approved on 23 July 2021. The Draft Implementaion Plan plan followed in April 2022.[810] The initial implementation plan covered the time until the Draft Implementation Plan would be approved.[811] Survivors would stay in the initial reparation program until the main program can offer them the same level of benefits.[812]

aa. Intake

The Trial Chamber significantly eased the burden of proof for survivors. Any official or unofficial document or other means sufficed to establish their identity. Absent documentation, they could provide a statement signed by two credible witnesses. With that, the chamber tried to offset the frequent loss of documents during pillaging. The chamber employed a "gender-inclusive and sensitive approach" to evidence. It acknowledged that survivors of rape

809 ICC, *Ntaganda Reparations Order*, ICC-01/04-02/06-2659, para 214, 252. Further details on prioritiziation are provided in ICC, *The Prosecutor v. Bosco Ntaganda, Annex A to the Public Redacted Version of "Report on Trust Fund's Preparation for Draft Implementation Plan"*, ICC-01/04-02/06-2676-AnxA-Corr-Red (TFV), 2021, para 77.

810 ICC, *The Prosecutor v. Bosco Ntaganda, Corrigendum of Public Redacted Version of Annex 1 to the Trust Fund for Victims' Second Submission of Draft Implementation Plan,* ICC-01/04-02/06-2750-AnxA-Red-Corr (TFV), 2022.

811 ICC, *Ntaganda Initial Draft Implementation Plan,* ICC-01/04-02/06-2676-AnxA-Corr-Red, para 2b; ICC, *The Prosecutor v. Bosco Ntaganda, Decision on the TFV's Initial Draft Implementation Plan With a Focus on Priority Victims,* ICC-01/04-02/06-2696 (TC II), 2021.

812 ICC, *Ntaganda Draft Implementation Plan,* ICC-01/04-02/06-2750-AnxA-Red-Corr, para 250 ff.

and/or sexual slavery faced challenges procuring evidence. Hence, their coherent and credible account should be sufficient to establish their eligibility.[813]

The chamber established far-reaching presumptions of harm. It presumed psychological, physical, and material harm of former child soldiers, direct survivors of rape or sexual slavery, and their family members living in the same household. Direct survivors of attempted murder and crimes committed during the attacks who personally experienced the attacks were presumed to have suffered psychological harm. Lastly, psychological harm was presumed for survivors who lost their home or important assets and close family members of murder victims.[814] The Appeals Chamber sacked another presumption of physical harm for survivors of the attacks the Trial Chamber established due to insufficient reasoning.[815]

The TFV suggested several eligibility determination processes for different groups covered by the initial implementation plan for priority survivors and the general reparation program under the later implementation plan. The details are not of relevance to this study.[816] Determination of eligibility for the priority program was based on a special questionnaire survivors filled out with the help of implementing partners which received special training to that effect.[817] The eligibility determination was envisaged as a purely administrative one without involvement of the Trial Chamber in decision-making. The Appeals Chamber found that to be erroneous.[818] The

813 ICC, *Ntaganda Reparations Order*, ICC-01/04-02/06-2659, para 137 ff. The AC upheld these changes to the evidentiary standards, it emphasized that survivors still needed to meet the balance of probabilities test, ICC, *Ntaganda Reparations Appeal,* ICC-01/04-02/06-2782, para 511 ff.

814 ICC, *Ntaganda Reparations Order*, ICC-01/04-02/06-2659, para 143 ff.

815 ICC, *Ntaganda Reparations Appeal,* ICC-01/04-02/06-2782, para 701 ff.

816 ICC, *Ntaganda Draft Implementation Plan,* ICC-01/04-02/06-2750-AnxA-Red-Corr, para 327 ff.; ICC, *Ntaganda Draft Initial Implementation Plan,* ICC-01/04-02/06-2676-AnxA-Corr-Red, para 58, 84 ff.; ICC, *Ntaganda Decision on Draft Initial Implementation Plan,* ICC-01/04-02/06-2696, para 23 ff.; ICC, *The Prosecutor v. Bosco Ntaganda, Public Redacted Version of "Trust Fund First Progress Report on the Implementation of the Initial Draft Implementation Plan",* ICC-01/04-02/06-2710-Red (TFV), 2021, para 44 ff.

817 ICC, *Ntaganda Third Update Report,* ICC-01/04-02/06-2741-Red, para 15 ff.; ICC, *The Prosecutor v. Bosco Ntaganda, Public Redacted Version of Trust Fund for Victims' Sixth Update Report on the Implementation of the Initial Draft Implementation Plan,* ICC-01/04-02/06-2775-Red (TFV), 2022, para 27.

818 ICC, *Ntaganda Decision on Draft Initial Implementation Plan,* ICC-01/04-02/06-2696, para 382 f.; ICC, *The Prosecutor v. Bosco Ntaganda, Public Redacted Version of Decision on the TFV's First Progress Report on the Implementation of the Initial Draft Imple-*

processes should be complemented by outreach campaigns throughout the life cycle of the reparation programs.[819] Given that, as will be detailed below, the plan for priority survivors foresees that they receive benefits through an existing assistance program of the TFV, the outreach for that part of the reparation program should focus especially on the fact that survivors receive access to that program as part of their right to reparation, not as assistance and on explaining why only certain survivors receive reparation at that point in time.[820]

bb. Reparation Measures

The chamber suggested several inter-disciplinary rehabilitation measures aimed at survivors, their families, and communities. These included psychological, psychiatric, psychosocial, and medical services, with particular attention given to addiction and trauma. Psychological support should be integrated into the program from the beginning. Housing assistance should also be part of the program. Rehabilitation should reintegrate survivors, address the shame some of them feel, help prevent future conflicts, and raise awareness that their "effective reintegration [...] requires eradicating their victimization, discrimination, and stigmatisation." [821]

The TFV proposed to ensure rehabilitation of priority survivors through two programs, one for former child soldiers, one for survivors of the two attacks. The latter were to be incorporated into an existing project under the TFV's assistance limb in Ituri that provided physical and psychosocial rehabilitation through, inter alia, an assessment of the survivors' psychological state, group and individual therapy, psychoeducational sessions for families, and training of community leaders on psychotherapy. The program

---

mentation Plan, ICC-01-/04-02/06-2718 (TC II), 2021, para 17; ICC, *Ntaganda Reparations Appeal,* ICC-01/04-02/06-2782, para 387.

819 ICC, *Ntaganda Draft Implementation Plan,* ICC-01/04-02/06-2750-AnxA-Red-Corr, para 338 ff.; ICC, *Ntaganda Draft Initial Implementation Plan,* ICC-01/04-02/06-2676-AnxA-Corr-Red, para 93.

820 ICC, *Ntaganda Decision on Draft Initial Implementation Plan,* ICC-01/04-02/06-2696, para 26; ICC, *Ntaganda Draft Initial Implementation Plan,* ICC-01/04-02/06-2676-AnxA-Corr-Red, para 26 ff., 80 ff.; ICC, *Ntaganda First Progress Report,* ICC-01/04-02/06-2710-Red, para 55 ff.; ICC, *Ntaganda Second Update Report,* ICC-01/04-02/06-2723-Red, para 34 ff.

821 ICC, *Ntaganda Reparations Order*, ICC-01/04-02/06-2659, para 203 ff.

should achieve socio-economic reintegration through vocational and other training based on a study on economic opportunities in areas in which survivors lived, as well as microfinance associations.[822] The adequate priority reparation of the former group was subject to a longer dispute between the TFV and the Trial Chamber.[823] In the end, former child soldiers that were subject to sexualized and gender-based violence could enter a project under the assistance limb. That project referred girl-mothers and other vulnerable female beneficiaries to health screenings and provided psychosocial care also on a family level. The project supported social reintegration through community centers and economic reintegration through microcredits, kits and vocational training for income-generating-activity, literacy and school recovery courses, sensitization courses inter alia on early marriage, peace education, and conflict management. For children of beneficiaries it provided school referrals and temporary nurseries to enable attendance of classes.[824] Other former child soldiers were provided with similar services through another service provider.[825]

822 ICC, *Ntaganda Draft Initial Implementation Plan,* ICC-01/04-02/06-2676-AnxA-Corr-Red, para 91; ICC, *Ntaganda First Progress Report,* ICC-01/04-02/06-2710-Red, para 29 ff.

823 The TFV proposed their incorporation into the Lubanga collective service-based and symbolic reparation program that it would extend to cover survivors' specific needs and further relevant geographical areas, ICC, *Ntaganda, Draft Initial Implementation Plan,* ICC-01/04-02/06-2676-AnxA-Corr-Red, para 4, 21 ff., 31 ff., 41, 47 ff., 67 ff.; ICC, *The Prosecutor v. Bosco Ntaganda, Public Redacted Version of "Trust Fund's Second Update Report on the Implementation of the Initial Draft Implementation Plan",* ICC-01/04-02/06-2723-Red (TFV), 2021, para 29 f. The TC rejected that approach ICC, *Ntaganda Decision on Draft Initial Implementation Plan,* ICC-01/04-02/06-2696, para 22; ICC, *The Prosecutor v. Bosco Ntaganda, Decision on the TFV's Second Progress Report on the Implementation of the Initial Draft Implementation Plan,* ICC-01/04-02/06-2730-Conf (TC II), 2021, para 14 ff.; ICC, *The Prosecutor v. Bosco Ntaganda, Public Redacted Version of "Trust Fund for Victims' Third Update Report on the Implementation of the Initial Draft Implementation Plan",* ICC-01/04-02/06-2741-Red (TFV), 2022, para 26 ff.

824 ICC, *Ntaganda First Progress Report,* ICC-01/04-02/06-2710-Red, para 16 ff.

825 ICC, *The Prosecutor v. Bosco Ntaganda, Public Redacted Version of „Trust Fund for Victims' Fourth Update Report on the Implementation of the Initial Draft Implementation Plan",* ICC-01/04-02/06-2751-Red (TFV), 2022, para 30 ff. This decision came after some back and forth about whether these survivors could also be included in the aforementioned program, ICC, *Ntaganda Decision on First Progress Report,* ICC-01-/04-02/06-2718, para 10(i); ICC, *Ntaganda Second Update Report,* ICC-01/04-02/06-2723-Red, para 29 f.; ICC, *The Prosecutor v. Bosco Ntaganda, Decision on the TFV's Fourth Update Report on the Implementation of the Initial Draft Implementation Plan,* ICC-01/04-02/06-2761-Conf (TC II), 2022, para 9.

The chamber proposed for satisfaction, inter alia, campaigns to improve survivors' position and reduce the stigmatization and marginalization of survivors of rape and sexual slavery, children born out of rape, and child soldiers. Measures raising awareness about the crimes and their consequences should aid survivors' rehabilitation and reintegration and reduce stigma.[826]

The main program should enable survivors through different rehabilitation services to overcome their harm and achieve resilience in three areas: mental health and social functioning; physical health and mobility; socio-economic status, and outlook.[827] Survivors should choose between an array of available measures. Additional measures should be directed at the community to raise awareness and understanding for certain behaviors of survivors.[828] Early on in the program, possibly at the intake, survivors would receive a modest starter sum in cash to cover the most basic needs, put them in the mental space to benefit from further measures, and develop trust in the TFV and the court after waiting for reparation for a long time. If they wished, they could receive advise on how to invest the money.[829]

For mental health and social functioning, the TFV planned to couple the intake process with an assessment of psychological needs of the survivors and their family. Ideally slightly before other interventions, survivors could avail themselves of group or family sessions, discussion groups and support networks to exchange trauma and recovery experience, and, in case of need, intensive group or individual therapy or psychosomatic treatment.[830] Measures for physical health and mobility should primarily consist of medical interventions and referrals coupled with assistance with transport and admission. Individual discussions on treatment options and modalities should precede the interventions, also to ensure that the treatment would collide as little as possible with other obligations.[831] To enhance survivors' socio-economic status and outlook, the TFV planned to first assess their

826 ICC, *Ntaganda Reparations Order*, ICC-01/04-02/06-2659, para 207.

827 ICC, *Ntaganda Draft Implementation Plan,* ICC-01/04-02/06-2750-AnxA-Red-Corr, para 136 f.

828 ICC, *Ntaganda Draft Implementation Plan,* ICC-01/04-02/06-2750-AnxA-Red-Corr, para 158.

829 ICC, *Ntaganda Draft Implementation Plan,* ICC-01/04-02/06-2750-AnxA-Red-Corr, para 182 ff.

830 ICC, *Ntaganda Draft Implementation Plan,* ICC-01/04-02/06-2750-AnxA-Red-Corr, para 162 ff.

831 ICC, *Ntaganda Draft Implementation Plan,* ICC-01/04-02/06-2750-AnxA-Red-Corr, para 172 ff.

priorities and develop an individual response plan.[832] They should then have access to social counsellors helping to reintegrate into society,[833] as well as educational measures and income-generating activities. Depending on their educational level to be assessed in the beginning of the component, survivors could receive a refresher training enabling them to get professional training, university scholarships, or English or French language courses. They could also receive school kits and a fix budget covering school fees of dependants of their choice from 1st to 6th grade.[834] As income-generating activities, survivors would be eligible to receive vocational training coupled with a kit containing necessary supplies, financial assistance during the training, and a starter kit with basic materials necessary to set up the chosen business. Advisors should stand ready to help survivors choose their preferred vocational path. The TFV would further assist with setting up cooperatives and saving and credit associations among survivors.[835]

In implementing the program, the TFV plans to uphold the distinction between reparation programs for former child soldiers and the survivors of the two attacks.[836] Former child soldiers should receive the mentioned services through the already existing Lubanga reparation program.[837] That program would be amended to train employees specifically on treatment methods for and approaching survivors of sexualized and gender-based violence. The TFV would ensure that such survivors have life-long access to treatment beyond the existence of the reparation program. It would also lay a particular focus on the creation of support network groups.[838] The program for the attack victims would still need to be created. This raised the problem that former child soldiers would likely receive reparation much earlier given that the structures to implement reparation for them already existed. The TFV

832 ICC, *Ntaganda Draft Implementation Plan,* ICC-01/04-02/06-2750-AnxA-Red-Corr, para 179.

833 ICC, *Ntaganda Draft Implementation Plan,* ICC-01/04-02/06-2750-AnxA-Red-Corr, para 197.

834 ICC, *Ntaganda Draft Implementation Plan,* ICC-01/04-02/06-2750-AnxA-Red-Corr, para 188 ff.

835 ICC, *Ntaganda Draft Implementation Plan,* ICC-01/04-02/06-2750-AnxA-Red-Corr, para 133 ff.

836 ICC, *Ntaganda Draft Implementation Plan,* ICC-01/04-02/06-2750-AnxA-Red-Corr, para 143.

837 ICC, *Ntaganda Draft Implementation Plan,* ICC-01/04-02/06-2750-AnxA-Red-Corr, para 206 ff. On the Lubanga program see above, 2.

838 ICC, *Ntaganda Draft Implementation Plan,* ICC-01/04-02/06-2750-AnxA-Red-Corr, para 211 ff.

planned to counter this through a strong outreach campaign explaining the reasons for the different timelines.[839] In addition to these two programs, the TFV opted to award survivors living outside Ituri a lump sum payment with the possibility to get advise on how to invest it, since offering them the services foreseen for the other programs would produce disproportionate costs.[840]

In addition to the rehabilitation component, the TFV proposed several satisfaction measures. Former child soldiers should benefit from the community centers to be built through the Lubanga program.[841] Direct survivors of sexualized and gender-based violence and children born out of rape or sexualized violence should receive a symbolic sum of money. The TFV would advocate for lacking identification and other legal documents to facilitate reintegration into society. Immediate family members and community workers should receive training in gender sensitivity, ethical standards and other topics.[842] The TFV also wanted to hire a consultant to search for missing persons.[843]

In addition, the Trial Chamber suggested several symbolic measures tailored to two high-profile violations. Following survivors' preferences, it sought to ensure that such symbolic measures served a practical purpose.[844] As in previous reparation orders, the chamber suggested that a voluntary apology by Ntaganda to individual or groups of survivors after their consultation could contribute to the reparation process.[845] A newly constructed community center could be named after Abbé Bwanalonga, an influential priest whom Ntganda killed.[846] After consultations with the clergy and local authorities, the TFV confirmed that to be a viable reparation measure. The adequate placement of the center and other details were still subject to further

839 ICC, *Ntaganda Draft Implementation Plan,* ICC-01/04-02/06-2750-AnxA-Red-Corr, para 218, 143.

840 ICC, *Ntaganda Draft Implementation Plan,* ICC-01/04-02/06-2750-AnxA-Red-Corr, para 154, 198 ff.

841 See above, 2.b.bb.

842 ICC, *Ntaganda Draft Implementation Plan,* ICC-01/04-02/06-2750-AnxA-Red-Corr, para 135, 238 ff.

843 ICC, *Ntaganda Draft Implementation Plan,* ICC-01/04-02/06-2750-AnxA-Red-Corr, para 241. On the problems with that see above, 2.b.cc.

844 ICC, *Ntaganda Judgment,* ICC-01/04-02/06-2359, para 506.

845 ICC, *Ntaganda Reparations Order,* ICC-01/04-02/06-2659, para 210; ICC, *Ntaganda Draft Implementation Plan,* ICC-01/04-02/06-2750-AnxA-Red-Corr, para 244 ff.

846 ICC, *Ntaganda Reparations Order,* ICC-01/04-02/06-2659, para 208; ICC, *Ntaganda Judgment,* ICC-01/04-02/06-2359, para 737 ff.

consultations.[847] Lastly, it proposed to attach a plaque to the Sayo health center, damaged in an attack, indicating that the building enjoys special protection under international humanitarian law.[848] The TFV proposed to implement that after consultations with the local community through a ceremony.[849] However, given the appeals judgment's doubts about the harm to the health center, it remains to be seen, whether that reparation measure can remain in the program.[850] As in the other programs, the security situation in Ituri and the Covid-19 pandemic posed severe problems in the implementation of the program.[851]

IV. Critique and Challenges

The ICC's institutional and legal structure makes the implementation of reparation programs extremely challenging. As Moffett noted, reparation proceedings are "copy-and-pasted onto the end of the trial,"[852] resulting in

847 ICC, *Ntaganda Draft Implementation Plan,* ICC-01/04-02/06-2750-AnxA-Red-Corr, para 228 ff.

848 ICC, *Ntaganda Judgment,* ICC-01/04-02/06-2359, para 506.

849 ICC, *Ntaganda Draft Implementation Plan,* ICC-01/04-02/06-2750-AnxA-Red-Corr, para 232 ff.

850 See above, a.

851 ICC, *Ntaganda Second Update Report,* ICC-01/04-02/06-2723-Red, para 7 ff.; ICC, *Ntaganda Third Update Report,* ICC-01/04-02/06-2741-Red, para 8 ff.; ICC, *Ntaganda Initial Draft Implementation Plan,* ICC-01/04-02/06-2676-AnxA-Corr-Red, para 32 ff., 43.

852 Moffett, *Reparations for Victims at the ICC,* 1204.

853 Carayon/O'Donohue, *The ICC's Strategies in Relation to Victims,* 582 f.; Berkeley Human Rights Center, *The Victims' Court?,* 4 f., 44; ASP, *Independent Expert Review of the International Criminal Court and the Rome Statute System – Final Report,* ICC-ASP/19/16, 2020, para 879 ff. For a potential solution delinking the reparation procedure from the criminal procedure and coupling it with measures at other levels see Moffett/Sandoval, *Tilting at Windmills,* 765 f. While complementing ICC-efforts at other levels, especially on the national level pursuant to reparative complementarity certainly is a promising avenue and many other of the authors' suggestions to improve the ICC reparation regime are promising, "delinking" reparation from criminal proceedings could lead to the ICC determining reparation for crimes it then finds the perpetrator before it not guilty of. This would turn the ICC more into a general forum to seek reparation, something it was never intended to and that could overburden it even more with expectations and proceedings. Also, it must be doubted whether such a stand-alone reparation order would really bring the benefits Moffett and Sandoval suggest of being able to claim reparation before domestic fora and raising funds through the TFV. The TFV does not really enjoy an abundance of funds to take on

several difficulties. First, the process is too time-consuming. Even after a trial started, survivors wait for years until reparation programs get off the ground. In the Lubanga case, they waited for more than a decade. This on top of the often considerable time survivors wait until a suspect is apprehended and put on trial. Such delay causes uncertainty, disappointment, resentment, and distrust towards the court.[853] Second, because the reparation process is confined to the crimes a person is convicted for, the court's reparation programs often exclude survivors. Especially in cases of narrow charging, survivors of other crimes the perpetrator likely committed are not eligible for reparation.[854] In the Lubanga case, the decision not to charge sexualized violence excluded survivors of those crimes from reparation.[855] Relatedly, the perpetrators selected, or the sequence in which they appear before the court, can impact delicate post-conflict situations.[856] In the Lubanga case, survivors were predominantly Hema since the UPC mostly recruited child soldiers from its side of the conflict. The TFV feared that the resulting imbalance of the reparation program would exacerbate tensions between the two ethnicities.[857]

Regarding the TFV's structure, its double assistance and reparation mandate can create confusion. Especially collective reparation measures run the danger of being confused with projects under the Fund's assistance

---

this additional tasks. Arguably, domestic reparation proceedings rarely fail because damage cannot be proven, but rather because the forum is lacking to begin with or individuals cannot access it. A safer way is to let sentencing and appellate proceedings run in parallel, ASP, *Independent Expert Review,* para 899 ff., although this of course shortens the proceedings much less than Moffett's and Sandoval's.

854 Balta et al., *Trial and (Potential) Error*, 227 ff.; ASP, *Independent Expert Review,* para 885; Owiso, *The International Criminal Court and Reparations – Judicial Innovation or Judicialisation of a Political Process?,* 2019 Intl. Crim. L. Rev. 19, 505, 515.

855 Chappell, *The Gender Injustice Cascade - 'Transformative' Reparations for Victims of Sexual and Gender-Based Crimes in the Lubanga Case at the International Criminal Court,* 2017 Intl. J. Hum. Rts. 21(9), 1223, 1228 ff.

856 Mégret, *Reparations Before the ICC - The Need for Pragmatism and Creativity,* in: Steinberg (ed.), *Contemporary Issues Facing the International Criminal Court,* 2016, 252, 256; Mégret, *Of Shrines, Memorials and Museums - Using the International Criminal Court's Victim Reparation and Assistance Regime to Promote Transitional Justice,* 2010 Buff. Hum. Rts. L. Rev. 16, 1, 14 f., 20 f.; Stahn, *Reparative Justice After the Lubanga Appeal Judgment - New Prospects for Expressivism and Participatory Justice or 'Juridified Victimhood' by Other Means?,* 2015 J. Intl. Crim. Just. 13(4), 801, 812; van den Wyngaert, *Victims Before International Criminal Courts - Some Views and Concerns of an ICC Trial Judge,* 2011 Case W. Res. J. Intl. L. 44(1 and 2), 475, 492; Berkeley Human Rights Center, *The Victims' Court?,* 55, 58.

857 ICC, *Lubanga Draft Implementation Plan,* ICC-01/04-01/06-3177-AnxA, para 21; Moffett, *Justice for Victims Before the ICC,* 161.

mandate.[858] The scarcity of funds creates further problems. So far, the TFV covered the first three reparation programs' costs because all defendants were indigent. The same is likely to occur in the Ntaganda case.[859] Apart from the problem that reparation is then not actually paid for by the liable person, the TFV's budget is not up to the task.[860] Ironically, the ICC itself can create that situation since defendants must pay enormous legal fees and other expenses to conduct their trial. While this problem has not been relevant so far, because all defendants arrived indigently at the court, it is only a matter of time until that changes.[861] Furthermore, the TFV has been criticized as inefficient compared to other reparation implementation bodies.[862]

Conditions in the situation countries further complicated reparation efforts. Security concerns often hamper access to survivor populations. An issue often exacerbated by the ICC's remoteness to the crime sites.[863] For the same reason, survivors often lack access to information about the ICC or fear engaging with the court.[864] Too few resources are available to meaningfully connect to survivor populations, adequately explain to them the court's inner workings, manage their expectations, and ensure their safety. Accordingly, survivors' expectations are often disappointed, which creates distrust towards

858 Mégret, *Of Shrines, Memorials and Museums*, 13 ff., 20 f.; Moffett/Sandoval, *Tilting at Windmills*, 762 f.

859 See above, II.

860 ASP, *Independent Expert Review*, para 888 ff.; Moffett, *Reparations for Victims at the ICC*, 1207 ff.; Moffett, *Justice for Victims Before the ICC*, 183 ff.; Moffet/Sandoval, *Tilting at Windmills*, 767 f.; van den Wyngaert, *Victims Before International Criminal Courts*, 490; de Greiff/Wierda, *The Trust Fund for Victims of the International Criminal Court, 228;* Berkeley Human Rights Center, *The Victims' Court?*, 5. However, the Berkeley study also provides the counterexample of Cote D'Ivoire, where apparently, survivors' expectations were managed well, preventing disappointment, 68 f.

861 Mégret, *Reparations Before the ICC*, 254; Stahn, *Reparative Justice After the Lubanga Appeal Judgment*, 812; van den Wyngaert, *Victims Before International Criminal Courts*, 490. It would probably have changed with the Bemba case, had it arrived at the reparation phase, Owiso, *The International Criminal Court and Reparations*, 527.

862 ASP, *Independent Expert Review*, para 942 ff.; Moffett/Sandoval, *Tilting at Windmills*, 762. It must be doubted though, whether the authors' comparison of the TFV with the 9/11 fund and German forced labour compensations is fair, given that the TFV operates in a entirely different institutional context and must operate several different reparation programs in different countries far removed from its headquarters.

863 Moffett, *Reparations at the ICC - Can it Really Serve as a Model?*, 2019, 1209; Case in point is the fact that the TFV refrained from implementing certain reparation measures because of the dire security situation in northern Mali, ICC, *Al Mahdi Updated Implementation Plan*, ICC-01/12-01/15-291, para 140 f.

864 Berkeley Human Rights Center, *The Victims' Court?*, 4, 21, 45, 56 f., 67 f.

the court.[865] Other issues the court faces are language barriers, which, together with illiteracy, can already pose a significant challenge in filling out survivor application forms.[866]

When it comes to concrete reparation programs, the court's focus on collective reparation seems contrary to many survivors' interests. Survivors expressed fear that collective reparation projects would foster corruption and benefit perpetrators. In general, survivors voiced concern that the court treated communities unequally, giving more reparation to some while ignoring others. This sentiment creates another danger of disappointment.[867] Lastly, few instances of corruption on the part of the court's intermediaries were reported, which, e.g., demanded bribes for filling out the application forms.[868] All this led the Independent Expert Review of the ICC to conclude that the system "has not delivered fair, adequate, effective and prompt reparations to victims of crimes under the jurisdiction of the Court."[869]

E. Summary: Common Differences

After examining six transitional justice reparation programs in Sierra Leone, Colombia, and at the ICC, their stark differences are most notable. But once one steps back from looking at trees and appreciates the woods, the broader perspective reveals commonalities. All programs followed a transformative[870]-collectivistic logic, which influences their goals (I.), structure (II.), intake procedure (III.), and content (IV.). This logic contrasts with the conservative-individualistic nature of the international law on reparation laid out in chapter one. The following section argues that the resulting deviations from the international law on reparation are reasonable because they respond

865 Berkeley Human Rights Center, *The Victims' Court?*, 24, 44.

866 Berkeley Human Rights Center, *The Victims' Court?*, 24.

867 Berkeley Human Rights Center, *The Victims' Court?*, 45, 55, 58, 68; Moffett, *Reparations for Victims at the ICC*, 1213; Stahn, *Reparative Justice After the Lubanga Appeal Judgment*, 811. On the danger of intra-community distinction in collective reparation measures Owiso, *The International Criminal Court and Reparations*, 524.

868 Berkeley Human Rights Center, *The Victims' Court?*, 24.

869 ASP, *Independent Expert Review*, para 887.

870 This should not lead to the conclusion that the principle of full reparation needs to be replaced by the often-proposed principle of "transformative reparation". The present section is descriptive, not normative. It will be argued below, why the principle of full reparation suffices to accommodate the transformative logic identified here, see below, ch. 4, E.I.

to defining characteristics of transitional justice situations – namely the large number of survivors, the challenging societal environment, and the transformative aim of transitional justice.[871]

I. A Different Goal

The international law on reparation seeks to erase all harm an individual suffered as far as possible and place them in the situation they would be in had the violation not occurred. This principal, conservative goal concurs with the private law roots of the international law on reparation.[872] It played no role in the Sierra Leone program and only a subsidiary part in Colombia and at the ICC. Instead, the explicit goal of all programs was to transform survivors' lives and society in general. They expressed this transformative aim as reconciliation, trust, healing, etc. Reparation measures differing from those usually ordered under the corrective justice logic served to realize the transformation. Individual advice, training, and counseling ensured that survivors received the measures best suited for their needs and potential and that they could put their material reparation to its best possible use. The reparation programs worked with communities to reduce stigma and discrimination and ensured that survivors lived in a welcoming environment. Educational campaigns, memorial days, etc., aimed at transforming the entire society. As the subsequent chapter will show, this differing approach has its basis in the very nature of transitional justice as a transformative project and reparation's communicative function within it.[873]

II. A Different Structure

The international law on reparation is individualistic as it concentrates on individual cases. Usually, judicial or quasi-judicial bodies conduct separate proceedings to verify each survivor's status and assess their complete harm. This allows them to devise reparation measures that erase all the damage

871 Shelton, *Remedies in International Human Rights Law*, 121. These defining characteristics will receive more detailed treatment in the next chapter, A.II.

872 IACtHR, *Loayza-Tamayo v. Peru (Reparations and Costs) - Joint Concurring Opinion of Judges A.A. Cançado Trindade and A. Abreu-Burelli*, para 6.

873 See below, ch. 3.

an individual suffered as far as possible.[874] Sierra Leone, Colombia, and the ICC chose a collectivistic approach over this individualistic one. They created administrative reparation programs instead of relying on the judiciary (1.) and categorized survivors and generalized their harm (2.).

1. Administrative vs. Judicial Reparation

Sierra Leone, Colombia, and the ICC created special administrative mechanisms to repair survivors. The ordinary judicial system played – if at all – only a subsidiary role. In Colombia, only the land restitution process relied decisively on courts. Beyond that, they only served as an instance of appeal for certain decisions. In Sierra Leone, courts played no role at all.[875] Even at the ICC, the TFV conceived and administered the bulk of each program. The Trial Chamber again played a supervisory role and acted as an instance of appeal for decisions to the detriment of survivors. Since no continuously existing judiciary repaired survivors, the special mechanisms often instated cut-off dates for application and sometimes end-dates for their termination.

2. Categorization and Generalization

The administrative reparation programs generalized different types of harms and categorized survivors on that basis. These categories determined their eligibility, the structure of the reparation program, and the measures it provided.[876] This made individual proceedings and harm assessments either unnecessary or less exacting. Colombia's and the ICC's more elaborate

874 Malamud-Goti/Grosman, *Reparations and Civil Litigation - Compensation for Human Rights Violations in Transitional Democracies*, in: de Greiff (ed.), *The Handbook of Reparations*, 2006, 539, 542.

875 The Lomé Peace Agreement barred any court action against any combatant from any side, Article IX(3) Lomé Peace Agreement; Schabas, *Reparation Practices in Sierra Leone*, 296. While this did not bar actions against the state, to the knowledge of the author, no such action was pursued in Sierra Leonean courts. Even though they were not accorded a prominent role in most parts of the reparation program Colombian Courts still left a decisive imprint on the program through parallel and appellate proceedings, Sánchez León / Sandoval-Villalba, *Go Big or Go Home?*, 567.

876 Malamud-Goti/Grosman, *Reparations and Civil Litigation*, 541; Falk, *Reparations, International Law, and Global Justice*, 495 f.; ICTJ, *Reparations in Theory and Practice*, 2007, 3 f., 7.; IAComHR, *Compendium*, OEA/Ser.L/V/II.Doc. 121, para 177.

reparation efforts countered this high level of generalization by providing survivor participation opportunities and an array of measures within each category from which survivors could choose. This collective nature of the examined reparation programs is exemplified best by the Sierra Leone and Katanga programs. In Sierra Leone, the SLTRC devised five highly abstract categories of eligible survivors and tied specific reparation measures to them. The war widow category illustrates their level of generality. It excluded men altogether based on the assumption that widowers did not depend on their deceased partner.[877] In the Katanga reparation program, the TFV devised five categories of survivors and created appropriate reparation measures for these categories. It somewhat countered the generalization by offering various measures among which the survivor chose the most appropriate.

The sheer number of survivors usually present in transitional situations explains the collectivistic approach of using administrative mechanisms that categorize and generalize survivors and their harm. Individual judicial processes would overburden any judiciary. Generalization and categorization make them unnecessary or less exacting. An administrative mechanism can also meet other difficulties of the transitional situation more efficiently, such as scarce evidence or a volatile security situation. Specific cut-off and end dates of such mechanisms are an attractive tool to ensure budget and planning security in light of limited resources and an unknown number of survivors. Furthermore, reparation programs allow a more holistic approach to reparation. They do not split up survivors of systematic human rights violations into individual torts, which is more conducive to transitional justice's transformative aim.[878]

III. Intake

The transformative-collectivistic approach resulted in a different intake process. Categorization served the state-run programs to restrict survivor eligibility (1.). In return for the resulting programs' limited scope, eligible survivors received support when accessing reparation (2.).

877 SLTRC, *Witness to Truth*, vol. 2, 244.

878 Malamud-Goti/Grosman, *Reparations and Civil Litigation*, 542 ff.; de Greiff, *Justice and Reparations*, 458 f.; ICTJ, *Reparations in Theory and Practice*, 3, 5; McLeod, *Envisioning Abolition Democracy*, 2019 Harv. L. Rev. 132, 1613, 1645 f.

1. Eligibility

To manage the high caseload and the limited resources available, the examined state-run programs restricted eligibility to a limited number of survivor categories. In Sierra Leone, only survivors of sexualized violence, war widows, war-wounded, children, and amputees had access to reparation. With that, the program disregarded, for example, survivors of forced displacement or property destruction. Colombia only comprehensively redressed grave and manifest human rights violations after 1985, even though the conflict started in the 1960s. Neither program redressed violations, e.g., of the right to freedom of expression or economic, social, and cultural rights. At the ICC, all survivors of the crimes a defendant was convicted for have a right to redress. However, survivor eligibility is restricted at earlier stages of the process. Only some systematic human rights violations amount to international crimes, and of those, only some are charged and finally adjudicated upon. The specificities of the ICC reparation system, therefore, eliminate the need for formal limits on eligibility.

These substantial restrictions do not bode well with the international law on reparation, which in principle gives every survivor of any human rights violation a right to reparation.

2. Access

All programs – except the Katanga reparation program – were created without knowledge of the exact number and location of survivors. In light of the large caseload and the volatile environment in which they operated, the programs could not count on each eligible survivor to present their claim without assistance. Hence, all examined programs took great care to reach all eligible survivors and allow them to access reparation. First, this required comprehensive outreach activities to inform the survivor population about the existence of the respective programs, eligibility requirements, and modes of access. Second, intake procedures and evidentiary standards were designed to facilitate access. Beyond intake, questions of access permeated all stages of the reparation programs. Sierra Leone ensured that survivors of sexualized violence did not have to identify as such when they received reparation. The TFV offered basic literacy and numeracy courses to allow survivors to access more advanced education measures. Colombia's program provided differential treatment to women, distinct ethnicities, and minorities at all stages of the program, also to facilitate access.

IV. Different Content

The high caseload and limited resources available also made it impossible for the programs to award full reparation through restitution, compensation, satisfaction, rehabilitation, and guarantees of non-repetition, as foreseen by the international law on reparation. Instead, in a collectivistic spirit, the examined reparation programs determined adequate reparation measures by balancing each survivor category's needs and harms with the state's (or Fund's) capacity and the broader society's needs.[879] As a result, survivors received much less than what full reparation would have demanded.[880]

In keeping with the transformative-collectivistic approach, reparation programs emphasized collective reparations, services, and symbolic measures over individual monetary awards. These measures required fewer resources, produced synergy effects with general development, and better served the program's transformative aim. For similar reasons, the programs often rely on existing infrastructure, projects, and partners to implement reparation measures. Examples abound. To provide the most poignant ones, the Katanga Appeals Chamber and the SLTRC explicitly recommended devising reparation measures based on the harms found in the survivor population in general instead of assessing individual damage.[881] The SLTRC balanced multiple factors to develop its reparation recommendations. The resulting Sierra Leone reparation program was largely funded and administered with outside help and relied heavily on existing projects. Colombia remitted survivors to the general health care system for specialized care and granted them prioritized access to pre-existing government housing subsidies. The TFV emphasized the necessity to use existing infrastructure in the Lubanga reparation program and used local partners, existing projects, and NGOs for many, if not most, of its reparation measures.

879 See OHCHR, *Rule of Law Tools for Post-Conflict States - Reparation Programs*, 2008, 28 f. Only some reparation programs engage in an individual harm assessment at a later stage to choose the reparation measures appropriate for the individual case among all measures offered.

880 This point is difficult to generalize though, mostly because the monetary value of reparation in international law differs to a large degree. Thus, while the difference in monetary value is striking when compared to awards made by the IACtHR, it is less noteworthy, albeit still existent, when the ECtHR is taken as benchmark. Furthermore, one needs to consider difficulties in valuing services, symbolic and collective measures, which at least the ECtHR rarely provides.

881 ICC, *Katanga Reparations Order (Appeals Judgment)*, ICC-01/04-01/07-3778, para 69 ff.

F. Conclusion

A holistic look at the reparation programs of Sierra Leone, Colombia, and the ICC evinces that transitional justice reparation programs differ fundamentally from the international law on reparation. They employ a transformative-collectivist approach. To that end, special administrative mechanisms administer reparation. These generalize the harm suffered by the survivor population and devise survivor categories on that basis. These categories are the fundamental building blocks of the programs. To manage the high caseload, eligibility for the reparation program is usually restricted to some survivor categories. Eligible survivors then receive support to overcome barriers to access reparation, often present in the transitional justice situation. The appropriate forms of reparation are determined in a broad balancing exercise encompassing each survivor category's needs and harms, the state's capacity, and the needs of society. This exercise results in limited reparation awards. Reparation programs emphasize collective, symbolic, and service-based reparation measures. These are less resource-intensive, produce synergy effects with the general society's needs, and serve the program's transformative aim more efficiently. To further maximize resource efficiency, existing infrastructure is often used to administer reparation.

This approach stands in stark contrast to the individualized and conservative one foreseen by the international law on reparation as laid out in chapter one. Of course, the reality is not as black and white as this raw juxtaposition conveys. Most transitional justice reparation programs and individual proceedings based on the international law on reparation will lie somewhere between the conservative-individualistic and the transformative-collectivistic extremes. However, this chapter still showed that transitional justice reparation programs are difficult to reconcile with the international law on reparation. Changing the transitional justice practice to align with the international law on reparation is not a viable option. The strategies exemplified by the case studies respond to pressing challenges of the transitional justice situation. They are a necessary response to an enormous caseload, volatile environment, and limited resources. Under these circumstances, it is probably impossible to adhere fully to the international law on reparation. At the very least, it would produce unjust results. Without accounting for barriers to access, many marginalized survivors would be unable to obtain reparation. The amounts states had to pay under the international law on reparation would exceed their capacity, just as the caseload would overwhelm their judiciary. Also, disaggregating reparation into individual cases would shift focus away from collective harm systematic human rights violations produce, thereby hindering the fulfillment of transitional justice's transformative aim.

The danger behind these facts is then not that deviation from the international law on reparation occurs. The fundamental threat is that states could be right in deviating. The international law on reparation was not conceived for transitional justice situations. It risks losing the capacity to provide normative guidance in transitional justice and, with that, its legitimacy. Answering this challenge by abandoning the international law on reparation in transitional justice situation is no option. As argued in the introduction, there is no legal basis to do so, and it would leave reparation to the goodwill of the responsible state. Given that survivors are often not the strongest political actor, they could then easily come away empty-handed.[882] The present study argues that the most promising road is to carefully adjust the international law on reparation to the particular difficulties of the transitional justice situation. But such an endeavor requires a clearer picture of the challenges transitional justice situations pose to reparation efforts. Therefore, the next chapter will elaborate on the purpose of reparation in transitional justice. The theoretical inquiry, together with this chapter's empirical insights, will create guide rails. Along these, chapter four will eventually adjust the international law on reparation to the particular exigencies of transitional justice.

882 For further detail see above, Introduction and below, Conclusion, C.

Chapter 3 – Theoretical Framework

The preceding chapter evinced that reparation practice in transitional justice does not reflect the normative approach and rules identified in chapter one. Isolated incidents of such disparity could be brushed off as mere violations of the international law on reparation. However, the deviation is standard and responds to challenges inherent in the transitional justice situation – suggesting that not the practice but the norms are inadequate. To further substantiate that premise, this chapter will examine the question: *What is the purpose of reparation in transitional justice?*

The answer will provide a deeper understanding of how and why reparation in transitional justice differs from the international law on reparation. It will also enable teleological reasoning. Together with the practical insights of chapter two, this chapter will thereby constitute a further guide rail along which chapter four can adapt the international law on reparation to the unique challenges of transitional justice. Unfortunately, posing the question is more straightforward than answering it. Transitional justice is a rapidly growing field; it confronts scholars who want to engage with its fascinating enigmas with an unmanageable number of debates, perspectives, and opinions. The tremendous growth rate of transitional justice scholarship, its interdisciplinary nature, and the prevalence of descriptive, case-study-centered approaches makes it even harder to orient oneself. Anachronistically, de Greiff's lament that transitional justice is "tremendously undertheorized"[883] holds nonetheless. The wealth of scholarship does neither converge towards an accepted definition of transitional justice nor agree on its goals or the inner workings of its measures. Even whether it is an independent field of study remains open for debate.[884] The dearth of agreement on the theoretical foundations of transitional justice forecloses any appeal to authority, mandating that this study explicates and justifies its assumptions about the purpose of reparation in transitional justice. This first requires a vague definition of

883 de Greiff, *Theorizing Transitional Justice*, in: Williams et al. (eds.), *Transitional Justice*, 2012, 27, 31 f. Specifically for reparation with the same sentiment Posner/Vermeule, *Reparations for Slavery and Other Historical Injustices*, 2003 Col. L. Rev. 103, 689, 689 f.

884 Bell, *Transitional Justice, Interdisciplinarity and the State of the 'Field' or 'Non-Field'*, 2009 Intl. J. Transit. Just. 3(1), 5.

transitional justice (A.) before the role(s) of reparation in transitional justice can be examined (B. and C.).

To prevent the argument from becoming entangled in countless tangential controversies, it will be restricted to what is necessary for answering this chapter's central question. For that, the argument concentrates on the purpose of *reparation*. It will not pursue implications for other transitional justice measures or transitional justice in general. Since this chapter aims to enable *legal* reasoning, the study takes a legalistic perspective. From that perspective, positive law must be followed without requiring further justification. The comfort of this perspective comes at a cost. The dominance of legalistic approaches in transitional justice has been rightfully criticized. They tend to overemphasize the law's effect and fail to capture the influence of non-state actors and non-legal mechanisms adequately.[885] The following account must plead guilty to the same charge. It ignores the contributions of these actors and mechanisms. It does so not for their lack of importance – they might be the true pillar upon which successful transitions rest[886] – but because the relevant body of law, human rights law, as of now centers on states.[887] The resulting blind spots call for "legal humility"[888]: Law is not the most effective, most advisable, or most important lens through which transitional justice can be viewed. Successful transitional justice processes require creativity and ingenuity, which the law cannot mandate. For that reason, the law cannot ensure the success of transitional justice processes. Nevertheless, concrete, shared, verifiable legal obligations can facilitate the implementation of justice under challenging circumstances. Within these limits, the law has

885 McEvoy, *Beyond Legalism - Towards a Thicker Understanding of Transitional Justice*, 2007 J. L. Soc. 34(4), 411; McEvoy, *Letting Go of Legalism - Developing a 'Thicker' Version of Transitional Justice*, in: McEvoy/McGregor (eds.), *Transitional Justice From Below - Grassroots Activism and the Struggle for Change*, 2008, 47; Nagy, *Transitional Justice as Global Project*, 276 f., 278 f., 284 ff.; Sriram, *Beyond Transitional Justice - Peace, Governance, and Rule of Law*, 2017 Intl. Stud. Rev. 19(1), 53, 56, 64; Gready, *Analysis - Reconceptualising Transitional Justice - Embedded and Distanced Justice*, 2005 Conflict Sec. Dev. 5(1), 3.

886 The author had the privilege to witness the important work of non-state actors in transitional justice processes in Sierra Leone and Colombia especially through extensive interviews with John Caulker from Fambul Tok (Sierra Leone) and Yolanda Sierra León from the Universidad Externado (Colombia) and is extremely grateful for these inspiring discussions. For details see further below, Conclusion, F.

887 On the connection between non-state actors and state responsibility see above, Ch. 1 B.III.

888 McEvoy, *Beyond Legalism*, 425 ff.

an important role to play, regardless of its relative importance to other perspectives and methods.[889]

A. Defining Transitional Justice

Discerning the purpose of reparation in transitional justice requires an understanding of what transitional justice is. While the Introduction above already introduced this study's understanding of the term, it only sketched the explanation and justification of that understanding.[890] As mentioned above, since no shared understanding of the concept of transitional justice exists, this does not suffice. Hence, the following section will justify why this study defines transitional justice as:

A state's attempt to address a legacy of systematic human rights violations, which aims to transform society towards strengthened respect for human rights and generalized trust. The latter is defined as the expectation that other members of society and state institutions adhere to and support human rights.

Transitional justice refers to a political practice, the scientific field studying that practice, and a body of law governing it.[891] The variety of political practices covered by the term grew by leaps and bounds throughout its short history.[892] Transitional justice started narrowly, defined solely as the transition from autocratic to democratic regimes. It soon evolved to cover the shift from conflict to peace. Lately, it was also applied to describe stable

889 On legal humility see also above, Introduction, A. and below Conclusion, D.

890 See above, Introduction.

891 Eisikovits, *Transitional Justice*, in: Zalta (ed.), *Stanford Encyclopedia of Philosophy*, Online Edition 2016. An example of that legal approach is provided by Bell, *The "New Law" of Transitional Justice*, in: Ambos et al. (eds.), *Building a Future on Peace and Justice - Studies on Transitional Justice, Peace and Development*, 2009, 105.

892 Of course, it is difficult to pinpoint the origin of transitional justice. One possibility is to credit a 1979 conference on how emerging democracies reckon with past authoritarian regimes with starting the discourse, Zunino, *Justice Framed – A Genealogy of Transitional Justice*, 2019, 59 ff. Neil Kritz's three-volume study on the topic certainly was a milestone, Kritz, *Transitional Justice – How Emerging Democracies Reckon With Former Regimes*, 1995. For the development of the field generally see Mihr, *An Introduction to Transitional Justice*, in: Simić (ed.), *An Introduction to Transitional Justice*, 2021, 1, 7 ff. and, more detailed, Reiter, *The Development of Transitional Justice*, in: Simić (ed.), An Introduction to Transitional Justice, 2021, 29 ff.

democracies' attempts to deal with a violent past. Colombia contributed an example of transitional justice during an ongoing conflict to the field.[893] As a result of this expansion of potential transitional justice situations, the field's boundaries became ambiguous. Fortunately, an answer to the core question of the purpose of reparation in transitional justice does not warrant a complete definition of the term. Presumably, teleological reasoning will become the more precise, the better the definition is. But even a vague definition will give an idea of the goal of reparation, enabling solid – albeit not perfect – teleological reasoning.[894] Naturally, the subsequent attempt at defining transitional justice is not the first of its kind. On the contrary, the number of transitional justice definitions probably approaches that of transitional justice scholars worldwide. Hence, the definition presented here is nothing but a modified version of existing accounts.[895]

I. Justice

There is virtual unanimity in scholarship and practice about what links transitional justice to justice: The field searches for ways to provide justice in the face of a legacy of systematic human rights violations.[896] This rare

893 Hansen, *The Vertical and Horizontal Expansion of Transitional Justice - Explanations and Implications for a Contested Field*, in: Buckley-Zistel (ed.), *Transitional Justice Theories*, 2014, 105, 109; Weiffen, *Transitional Justice - Eine Konzeptionelle Auseinandersetzung*, in: Mihr et al. (eds.), *Handbuch Transitional Justice*, 2015, 1, 7 ff.; Arthur, *How Transitions Reshaped Human Rights - A Conceptual History of Transitional Justice*, 2009 Hum. Rts. Q. 31(2), 321, 334 ff.; Huhle, *Transitional Justice*, in: Binder et al. (eds.), *Elgar Encyclopedia of Human Rights*, Online Edition 2022, para 18 ff, 23.

894 A vague definition tolerates borderline cases, which neither fall within nor outside its ambit, Sorensen, *Vagueness*, in: Zalta (ed.), *The Stanford Encyclopedia of Philosophy*, Online Edition 2018.

895 The present account was heavily influenced by de Greiff, *Theorizing Transitional Justice*; de Greiff, *A Normative Conception of Transitional Justice*, 2010 Politorbis 50(3), 17.

896 UN Secretary General, *The Rule of Law and Transitional Justice in Conflict and Post-Conflict Societies - Report of the Secretary-General*, S/2004/616, 2004, para 8; ICTJ, *What is Transitional Justice?*, 2009, 1; AU, *Transitional Justice Policy*, 2019, para 19; CEU, *The EU's Policy Framework on Support to Transitional Justice*, 13576/15 Annex to Annex, 2015, 7; Teitel, *Transitional Justice Genealogy*, 2003 Harv. Hum. Rts. J. 16, 69, 69; Seibert-Fohr, *Transitional Justice in Post-Conflict Situations*, in: Wolfrum (ed.), *Max Planck Encyclopedia of Public International Law*, Online Edition 2015, para 1; Eisikovits, *Transitional Justice*, subsec. 1. In line with the legalistic perspective, "justice" will not be further defined. It is assumed that the fulfillment of international legal obligations towards survivors and society in general constitutes justice.

occasion of harmony in the contested transitional justice world provides a safe foundation for a more detailed definition. To make it truly reliable, the term "systematic" requires some clarification. As will be argued below, transitional justice reacts to the specific consequences of systematic human rights violations.[897] Systematic norm transgression undermines the trust members of societies have in the validity of basic norms. This erodes and ultimately destroys those norms.[898] These consequences occur when human rights transgressions become normalized in society. It must attain such a probability that it influences large parts of the quotidian life of members of society.[899] The exact determination of this threshold is of limited relevance here. Suffice it to say that the quantity and quality of human rights violations are relevant for its determination. Since the erosion of trust relates to a subjective state of mind, not only the objective occurrence of such violations matters but also how members of society perceive their quantity and quality.[900] It suffices that norm transgression becomes normalized for a defined subset of the population, as trust can erode within such subsets. In the past, transitional justice hence responded to systematic violations, which only affected minorities, specific geographical areas, etc.[901]

II. Transition

Transitional justice starts with a legacy of systematic human rights violations: It should be employed when systematic human rights violations occurred. That only denotes the situation in which transitional justice should start; but where lies the finish line? What does it mean to "address" a legacy of systematic human rights violations? In contrast to the unanimity encountered before, this question is highly controversial. Some evade it by employing a "toolbox approach" to transitional justice. They define a set of transitional justice measures – usually prosecutions, truth-seeking, reparations, and others –

897 See below, A.II.

898 See below, A.II.1.

899 Murphy, *The Conceptual Foundations of Transitional Justice*, 2017, 55 f.

900 For the latter point see Shelton, *Remedies in International Human Rights Law*, 121.

901 Examples of such limited transitional justice efforts are the Greensboro Truth Commission and Canada's Truth and Reconciliation Commission, Magarrell/Wesley, *Learning from Greensboro - Truth and Reconciliation in the United States*; TRC Canada, *Summary of the Final Report.*

and concentrate on making them work under challenging circumstances.[902] While essential for transitional justice practice, such an approach is not suitable for this study. Teleological reasoning requires a normative account. Such accounts take transitional justice to be a transformative project, which responds to systematic human rights violations by seeking societal change. This begs the question of what that change entails. From a legalistic perspective, one goal of society's transition is evident. If states must adhere to their legal obligations, the change required after systematic human rights violations is cessation and non-repetition: Society must change towards general respect for human rights.[903] Of course, that goal in no way differs from the goal of human rights law generally. What makes transitional justice distinct is the societal situation it operates in. The societal effects of systematic human rights violations differ from those of isolated violations. As the following sections will detail, systematic human rights violations undermine and ultimately destroy the validity of human rights in society (1.). The usual tools to deal with human rights violations are inept at responding to this effect. They are geared to mitigate the individual consequences of isolated violations – e.g., through individual prosecutions, arithmetic reparation, etc. Hence, they cannot adequately respond to the challenge that systematic violations pose to the validity of norms.[904] In the transitional situation, the goal of respect for human rights is therefore too far removed from reality to provide guidance. A mediate goal to bridge that gap is needed (2.) – and a more thorough understanding of the effects of systematic human rights violations provides the key to find it.

1. The Erosion of Trust

Systematic human rights violations erode trust. Trust materializes in societal relations. For analytical purposes, these relations will be grouped into

902 Naturally, such an approach is dominant – even though not exclusive – in more practically oriented publications on the subject, such as UN Secretary General, *The Rule of Law and Transitional Justice*, S/2004/616, para 8; Viane/Brems, *Transitional Justice and Cultural Contexts - Learning from the Universality Debate*, 2010 Neth. Q. Hum. Rts. 28(2), 199, 200; Sharp, *Addressing Dilemmas of the Global and the Local in Transitional Justice*, 2014 Emory Intl. L. Rev. 29(1), 71, 75 ff.

903 De Greiff seems to hint at this goal when stating that transitional justice should give "force to human rights norms that were systematically violated", de Greiff, *Theorizing Transitional Justice*, 40.

904 de Greiff, *Justice and Reparations*, in: Miller/Kumar (eds.), *Reparations - Interdisciplinary Inquiries*, 2007, 153, 156 f.

relations between members of society on the one hand (horizontal relations, a.) and between members of society and state institutions on the other (vertical relations, b.).

a. Horizontal Trust

Trust finds its primary and paradigmatic application as horizontal trust in interpersonal relationships. In this realm, it denotes a three-way relationship, in which person A trusts person B with a thing or issue C. B has some discretionary power over C, which A trusts that B will use as A expects them to. This trust makes A vulnerable because B could disappoint their expectation.[905] The mere expectation of behavior is not sufficient to define trust. If B always smiles at A, A might expect B to continue to do so. If one day B does not smile because they have a bad day, A could hardly lament that they misplaced trust in B. In that case, A merely relied on B; they did not trust B.[906] The difference between reliance and trust lies in the reason for which A expects B to use their discretion over C in a certain way. Whereas reliance rests on the consistency of behavior over time, trust relies on normative expectations. A trusts B to behave in a certain way with C because B *should* behave that way for normative reasons. A can trust B not to take their wallet (C) because A expects B to adhere to the social and legal norm that one should not steal. Trust thus denotes reliance on the fact that another person will conform to normative expectations regarding a thing or issue over which they have discretionary power.[907]

In interpersonal relationships, trust can arise because a person proved trustworthy in the past. This mode of creating trust cannot be scaled up to a societal level because it relies on gaining information about a person's past

905 Baier, *Trust and Antitrust*, 1986 Ethics 96(2), 231, 235, 237; Baier, *Trust - The Tanner Lectures on Human Values*, 1991, 117.

906 On the distinction see Goldberg, *Trust and Reliance*, in: Simon (ed.), *The Routledge Handbook of Trust and Philosophy*, 2020, 97, 97 ff.

907 Jones, *Trust and Terror*, in: Desautels/Walker (eds.), *Moral Psychology - Feminist Ethics and Social Theory*, 2004, 3, 6; Frost-Arnold, *Imposters, Tricksters, and Trustworthiness as an Epistemic Virtue*, 2014 Hypatia 29(4), 790, 796; Walker, *Moral Repair - Reconstructing Moral Relations After Wrongdoing*, 2006, 79 f. With that, this account follows a normative expectation approach to trust. For an overview of criticism of that approach and alternatives see McLeod, *Trust*, in: Zalta (ed.), *Stanford Encyclopedia of Philosophy*, Online Edition 2020.

behavior. Societal trust does not rely on interpersonal information but shared societal normative expectations.[908] These, in turn, often rely on social roles.[909] The most crucial role in the present context is that of Member of Society.[910] Each member of society expects from other members of society that they adhere to basic norms. To give an example, probably all societies around the globe expect their members in principle not to kill or otherwise harm fellow members of society. Since one knows any given individual to have the role of Member of Society, one can expect every individual to adhere to such basic social norms. Put else, one can trust them to do so.[911] Horizontal societal trust thus hinges on the existence of basic social norms.

These norms exist if enough persons within a reference group prefer to follow the norm because they have the empirical expectation that other persons in the reference group will do the same and the normative expectation that other persons expect them to do what the norm demands. This can be illustrated in a slightly simplified way by the following formula:

$$R \rightarrow P' \in P = ee + ne$$

where R is a social norm, P' a sufficiently large subset (∈) of reference network P, ee empirical expectations and ne normative expectations.[912] To give an example, if A observes that from all inhabitants of his village (reference

908 Walker, *Moral Repair*, 75 ff.; de Greiff, *Theorizing Transitional Justice*, 45.

909 Jones, *Trust and Terror*, 7; Jones, *Trustworthiness*, 2012 Ethics 123(1), 61, 68; Walker, *Moral Repair*, 73, 81. Social role is defined with Dahrendorf as the bundle of expectations towards the behavior of someone in a certain social position. Such expectations exist in any human group, Dahrendorf, *Homo Sociologicus - Ein Versuch zur Geschichte, Bedeutung und Kritik der Kategorie der Sozialen Rolle*, 16th Edition 2006, 37, 39, 53.

910 Contrary to lamentable developments in national and international politics around the globe, Member of Society is used here to designate all persons, who take part in the daily life of a society. This includes refugees, persons without a legal status, minorities etc.

911 de Greiff, *Theorizing Transitional Justice*, 44 f. The notion of a social role of Member of Society was introduced into the argument by the author. Individuals must have a reason to expect exactly the person they interact with to adhere to basic norms. Such an expectation towards a concrete person must be based on information. That other persons are members of society is the only information, an individual has about virtually any person they interact with, which can justify the expectation of adherence to basic norms. Similarly on the role of "citizen", Hardimon, *Role Obligations*, 1994 J. Phil. 91(7), 333, 342 ff. For a complementary theory of similar conventional roles as relvant for this account see below, C.I.

912 Bicchieri, *Norms in the Wild*, 2017, 36; Bicchieri, *The Grammar of Society*, 2006, ch. 1.

network, P), a large number goes to church on Sundays, he expects them to do the same in the future (empirical expectation, ee). Suppose A also thinks that the other inhabitants of his village expect him to go to church on Sundays (normative expectation, ne). In that case, he will believe that a corresponding social norm exists. If enough village inhabitants (subset of reference network P, P') form the same empirical and normative expectations as A, such a social norm (R) will form within that village.[913] For now, it is assumed that most societies have basic social norms, with which they expect all members of society to comply, and which correspond to a degree with some human rights.[914] There are, for example, social norms not to kill, not to treat persons inhumanely, etc. To emphasize, it is only claimed that basic social norms *correspond* to *some* human rights *to a degree.* First, it is not claimed that human rights cause social norms or vice versa. Second, not all human rights have a corresponding social norm everywhere. Lastly, the content of the corresponding norms is not necessarily congruent. This already follows from the fact that they have different addressees. Whereas social norms address members of society, human rights address the state. They might also differ materially. There might be a social norm not to discriminate and not to treat persons inhumanely. Contrary to the corresponding human rights norm, in some communities, that social norm seems reconcilable with gross abuse of certain groups, e.g., people of color or refugees.[915] Still, the material content of human rights and basic social norms can correspond to a degree. As a result of this overlap, systematic human rights violations will often violate not only legal but also social norms:

913 For the purpose of this study, it is immaterial, how this process of norm formation starts. For different possibilities see Brennan et al., *Explaining Norms*, 2013, 96 ff.

914 This description resembles Rawls' "well-ordered society", Rawls, *A Theory of Justice*, Revised Edition 1999, 4 ff. It will be argued below, in this section, that this empirical requirement is not necessary.

915 Amnesty International, *Living Insecurity - How Germany is Failing Victims of Racist Violence*, 2016, 41 ff.; HRC, *Report of the Working Group of Experts on People of African Descent on its Mission to Germany*, A/HRC/36/60/Add.2, 2017, para 30 ff., 42 ff., 52.

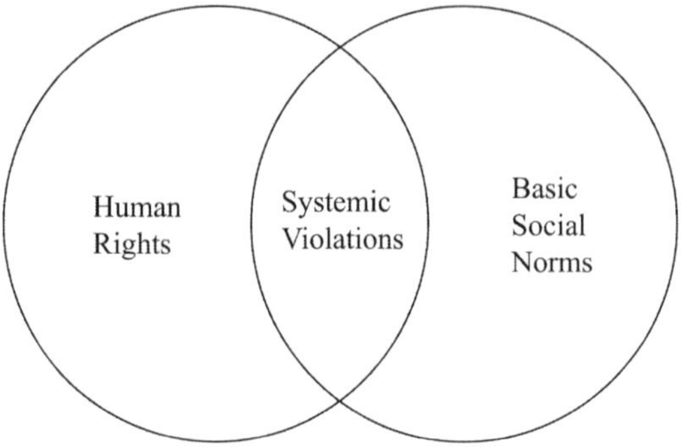

Figure 3: Human Rights and Social Norms (created by the author)

Since social norms rely on the empirical observation that a sufficiently large number of persons adhere to them, their systematic violation weakens and ultimately destroys them.[916] If that happens, any given person can no longer expect members of society to adhere to basic social norms, undermining the basis of generalized horizontal trust. Hence, systematic human rights violations weaken and ultimately destroy generalized horizontal trust.[917]

b. Vertical Trust

A similar process occurs for the vertical relationship between members of society and state institutions. The conceptualization of vertical trust needs to be adjusted, though, because state institutions are abstract entities that cannot commit to social norms. They have, however, an ethos or culture, which all members of the institution are expected to follow.[918] Based on this,

---

916 Brennan et al., *Explaining Norms*, 106 ff.; Bicchieri, *Norms in the Wild*, 109 f., 124 f., 137 ff.; Bicchieri, *The Grammar of Society*, 26 ff.

917 As indicated above, A.I., this can either happen in general society or in subsets of society affected by systematic human rights violations. For empirical studies supporting this assumption see Cassar et al., *Legacies of Violence - Trust and Market Development*, 2013 J. Econ. Growth 18(3), 285, 286 f.; Rohner et al., *Seeds of Distrust - Conflict in Uganda*, 2013 J. Econ. Growth 18(3), 217, 230 f.; de Luca/Verpoorten, *From Vice to Virtue? Civil War and Social Capital in Uganda - LICOS Discussion Paper Series 298/2011*, 2011, 19 f.

918 Miller, *The Moral Foundations of Social Institutions - A Philosophical Study*, 2009, 49 f.; Offe, *How can we Trust our Fellow Citizens?*, in: Warren (ed.), *Democracy and Trust*, 1999, 42, 70; Miller, *Social Institutions*, in: Zalta (ed.), *The Stanford Encyclopedia*

state institutions can embody basic *institutional* norms. Generalized trust in state institutions then denotes the expectation that the persons running those institutions adhere to basic institutional norms, and that a sufficiently large subset of society supports these norms, guaranteeing the institutions' continued existence.[919]

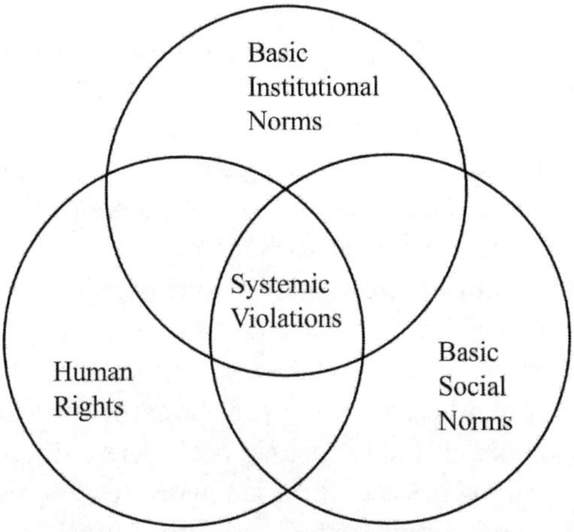

Figure 4: Human Rights, Social Norms, and Institutional Norms (created by the author)

If institutional norms are constantly violated, there is no reason to expect institutions and other members of society to uphold them, destroying the basis for generalized trust in state institutions.[920] Subject to the same caveats as above, it can be assumed that some basic institutional norms correspond to a degree to some human rights and some basic social norms. Hence, systematic human rights violations also violate social and institutional norms:

In sum, systematic human rights violations also violate basic social and institutional norms. Empirical and normative expectations uphold both so

of Philosophy, Online Edition 2014; Bahdi/Kassis, *Institutional Trustworthiness, Transformative Judicial Education and Transitional Justice - A Palestinian Experience,* in: El-Masri et al. (eds.), *Transitional Justice in Comparative Perspective,* 2020, 185, 189; Rawls, *A Theory of Justice,* 47 ff.; Hartmann, *Vertrauen - Die Unsichtbare Macht,* 2020, 126 ff.; Walker, *Moral Repair,* 83 f.

919 de Greiff, *Theorizing Transitional Justice,* 45 f.; Offe, *How can we Trust our Fellow Citizens?,* 70 f.

920 For an empirical study to the same effect see Hutchison/Johnson, *Capacity to Trust? Institutional Capacity, Conflict, and Political Trust in Africa, 2000–2005,* 2011 J. Peace Res. 48(6), 737, 749.

that systematic norm violation weakens and ultimately destroys both. Since basic social and institutional norms form the basis of generalized trust in horizontal and vertical societal relationships, systematic human rights violations ultimately destroy generalized trust in society.

2. Restoring Trust

Above, transitional justice was partially defined as a state's attempt to address systematic human rights violations. This suggests that transitional justice must deal with the consequences of systematic human rights violations. Therefore, transitional justice should restore generalized horizontal and vertical trust. Beyond its connection to the consequences of systematic human rights violations, restoring trust is also intrinsically and instrumentally connected to transitional justice's ultimate goal – strengthening respect for human rights. Human agency lies at the core of human rights.[921] Generalized trust strengthens agency because it allows persons to form stable expectations about the behavior and attitude of members of society and state institutions. Such stability enables persons to form life plans. It frees resources to carry them out, which would otherwise be needed to control one's environment. As Luhmann put it, trust allows persons to get up in the morning.[922] To give an example, a constant fear of getting killed forces a person to invest mental and economic resources in their protection, which they cannot employ for other goals. Investing in long-term plans becomes less appealing because the person fears that premature death will deprive them of the benefits. Loss of generalized trust thus greatly diminishes agency.

921 For one account of autonomy being the core value of human rights see Griffin, *On Human Rights*, 2010, mainly ch. 2. For assessments of the role of agency within the larger discourse on the foundations of human rights see, Biletzki, *The Philosophy of Human Rights*, 2020, 77 ff.; O'Byrne, *Human Rights - An Introduction*, 2013, 49 ff.; Cruft et al., *The Philosophical Foundations of Human Rights - An Overview*, in: Cruft et al. (eds.), *Philosophical Foundations of Human Rights*, 2015, 1, 11 ff.

922 Luhmann/Poggi, *Trust and Power*, 2017, 5, 27 f. On this function of norms see Brennan et al., *Explaining Norms*, 106 f. Walker describes a similar phenomenon under the notion of default trust, Walker, *Moral Repair*, 83 ff. Baier writes that "we inhabit a climate of trust as we inhabit an atmosphere and notice it as we notice air, only when it becomes scarce or polluted", Baier, *Trust and Antitrust*, 234. Of course, trust can also impair agency, if it pertains to normative expectations, which prohibit certain behavior. However, as will be argued below, in this section, transitional justice aims at creating social norms, which correspond to human rights, so that they too have agency at their core.

Several instrumental reasons also connect generalized trust to strengthen human rights. If social and institutional norms correspond to a legal norm, they make compliance with the latter more likely. People internalize social and institutional norms, obtaining an intrinsic motivation to follow them.[923] Reinforcing legal with social norms brings social means of enforcement into play: Society and state institutions usually incentivize compliance with social and institutional norms, whereas they sanction deviance through stigma, ostracism, and other means.[924] Since formal law enforcement is weak in many transitional justice situations, social enforcement mechanisms become essential. Even formal norm enforcement relies on generalized trust. People are more likely to cooperate with law enforcement institutions if they trust them. Without such cooperation, norm enforcement often becomes impossible.[925] Beyond these more obvious connections, it will further be argued below that the concept of restoring trust also provides a way to understand more generally how transitional justice mechanisms can restore respect for human rights in society. Therefore, the concept can bridge the gap mentioned above between that ordinary goal of human rights law and the inability of ordinary means to reach it when dealing with systematic violations.

With that, two independent reasons justify assuming the restoration of trust as a goal of the transition: its connection to the consequences of systematic human rights violations and its connections to the ultimate goal of transitional justice, strengthening respect for human rights. The independence of the latter justification from the former has an important implication. The argument that generalized trust addresses the consequences of systematic human rights violations requires that such consequences actually occurred. That, in turn, requires that basic social and institutional norms corresponding to human rights had existed before systematic human rights violations weakened and destroyed them. In most societies, that assumption will hold. Yet, societies might exist without such basic social and institutional

923 Elster, *The Cement of Society*, 1989, 99 f., 130 ff.; Bicchieri, *Norms in the Wild*, 118 f.

924 Elster, *The Cement of Society*, 99 f., 130 ff.; Bicchieri, *Norms in the Wild*, 118 f.; Coleman, *Foundations of Social Theory*, 1990, 278 ff., 310 f.

925 de Greiff, *Theorizing Transitional Justice*, 47 f.; de Greiff, *Justice and Reparations*, 462 f.; Hartmann, *Vertrauen*, 126 f. Some empirical support for this argument can be derived from, Levi et al., *Conceptualizing Legitimacy, Measuring Legitimating Beliefs*, 2009 Am. Behavioral Scientist 53(3), 354, 356 ff., 363 ff. The researchers found significant correlation between inter alia the relationship between perceptions of trustworthiness and procedural fairness of the government and cooperation. Both indicators overlap to a degree with the notion of generalized vertical trust employed here.

norms. Because of the intrinsic and instrumental connections between generalized trust and the transition's ultimate goal of strengthening human rights, the mediate goal of generalized trust can still apply to such societies. Transitional justice can then aim at strengthening respect for human rights by creating trust in new basic social and institutional norms, which correspond to human rights.

III. Conclusion: A Vague Definition of Transitional Justice

Based on the preceding argument, transitional justice can be defined as follows:

> *Transitional justice addresses a legacy of systematic human rights violations. It aims to transform society towards respect for human rights and generalized trust. Generalized trust means that a person can expect other members of society and state institutions to adhere to and support basic social and institutional norms, which correspond to human rights.*

A definition of the often-mentioned transitional justice situation[926] can be derived from this definition of transitional justice. A transitional justice situation is every situation in which systematic human rights violations occurred and which therefore calls for the employment of transitional justice to restore respect for human rights and generalized trust.

IV. Challenges

Three challenges can be brought against the preceding definition of transitional justice. It could be over-inclusive, under-inclusive, or incapable of adequately capturing the great variety of situations it supposedly applies to. The first two challenges become less pressing when one recalls that this study's aim only requires a vague definition of transitional justice. Even if it turns out that the definition lacks conditions or includes unnecessary ones, it can still help adapt legal standards to the transitional justice situation.

926 Note that this study uses the terms "transitional justice environment", "transitional justice situation", "transitional situation", "transitional justice context", "transitional context" and "transitional society" interchangeably with the term transitional justice situation.

Regarding the challenge of over-inclusiveness, many definitions of transitional justice are stricter because they encompass more goals of the transition or more attributes of the transitional justice situation. Many scholars assume that transitional justice aims at reconciliation, the rule of law, or democracy.[927] Others name structural inequality as a necessary attribute of the transitional justice situation.[928] Naturally, a complete rebuttal of such arguments is only possible against concrete proposals. Since academic discussion abounds with such proposals, this section cannot comprehensively refute the challenge of over-inclusiveness. Instead, some general remarks must suffice as an imperfect defense of the preceding argument. As a preliminary point, the narrow legalistic perspective makes the challenge of over-inclusiveness less pressing. The goal to adapt universal legal standards warrants the concentration on necessary conditions of the transitional justice situation. Nothing keeps a state from making the political decision to include further goals in its transitional justice process. For other types of research, other possible attributes of the transitional justice situation might provide valuable insights. Likely, such added goals and attributes would not change the interpretation of the international law on reparation much. Beyond that, two general points can defend the assumption of only two features of the transitional justice situation. First, transitional justice addresses the distinct societal effects of systematic human rights violations. As soon as such effects exist, the route to employ transitional justice should be open. If a definition includes requirements unrelated to the consequences of systematic human rights violations, it might foreclose applying transitional justice measures when they would be an adequate response. Second, the definition proposed here serves to identify cases, which warrant a transformation of legal standards. To guard against extralegal considerations justifying the

927 An account which comprises all three goals is proposed by de Greiff, *Theorizing Transitional Justice*. His account strongly influenced the present one. Thus, his definition of reconciliation is close to what has been termed here "generalized trust". Other accounts comprising further goals of the transition are for example, Winter, *Towards a Unified Theory of Transitional Justice*, 2013 Intl. J. Transitional Just. 7(2), 235 ff.; Sharp, *Emancipating Transitional Justice From the Bonds of the Paradigmatic Transition*, 2015 Intl. J. Transitional Just. 9(1); Hansen, *Transitional Justice - Toward a Differentiated Theory*, 2011 Oregon Rev. Intl. L. 13(1), 1, 47 ff.; Fletcher/Weinstein, *Violence and Social Repair - Rethinking the Contribution of Justice to Reconciliation*, 2002 Hum. Rts. Q. 24(3), 573, 624 ff.; Crocker, *Reckoning With Past Wrongs - A Normative Framework*, 2012 Ethics Intl. Aff. 13, 43.

928 Murphy, *The Conceptual Foundations of Transitional Justice*, 43 ff.

curtailment of rights, the definition's attributes should be searched solely within the notion of systematic human rights violations.

The opposite view that the account is under-inclusive could argue that transitional justice should not prescribe any goals. Instead, it can be a toolbox for societies to achieve the transitional goals they set for themselves. Here again, the legalistic perspective does not inhibit a state from choosing additional goals. It excludes further goals only for its narrow legalistic purpose. That exclusivity is in order because adapting legal standards to an extraordinary situation must make them more flexible. Assuming respect for human rights and generalized trust as the only necessary goals of the transition ensures that states only enjoy the benefit of more flexible legal standards to safeguard human rights under extraordinary circumstances. A broader notion of transitional justice risks making human rights obligations flexible to a degree that significantly weakens the human rights regime.

The account could also be under-inclusive because it assumes a transition as a necessary goal of transitional justice. Examples of transitional justice processes in stable democracies or during ongoing conflict led some scholars to argue that transitional justice emancipated from the need to pursue a transition.[929] New Zealand accounted for human rights violations against its native population, and Canada dealt with its residential school system through transitional justice measures. Upon closer analysis of New Zealand, Canada, the United States, and Australia, Winter convincingly concluded that transitional justice processes in stable democracies still seek to alter the fundamental norms governing state authority.[930] The same holds for the paradigmatic example of transitional justice during an ongoing conflict, Colombia. In all these cases, systematic human rights violations questioned the validity of fundamental norms governing the relations between the state and society or the affected subset of society. While the respective societies and state institutions remained more or less stable, they still showed their systematic disregard for the human rights of subsections of society. These subsections hence lost their generalized trust. Consequently, these processes do not only aim at individual justice, but also at "healing", "reconciliation",

929 Sharp, *Emancipating Transitional Justice*, 156. Such a position risks nurturing the narrative that the Global North, with which many definitions of "stable democracies" coincide, is not implicated in transitional justice. For a critique of that position see below, Conclusion, E.

930 Winter, *Towards a Unified Theory of Transitional Justice*; Winter, *Transitional Justice in Established Democracies - A Political Theory*, esp. ch. 3 and 5.

etc.[931] By encompassing broader societal change, the notion of transition captures the necessary response to these broader consequences.[932]

Lastly, one could doubt whether a unitary definition is even feasible given the extreme contextual varieties transitional justice situations exhibit. As the present chapter attempts to create a unitary definition, it attempts to refute that challenge. Undeniably, transitional justice situations vary greatly on numerous levels. In response, both goals of the transition – respect for human rights and generalized trust – are sufficiently flexible to be adapted to different contexts. Human rights are inherently flexible and count with different tools to be adapted to different circumstances.[933] Since social and institutional norms arise through societal processes and only correspond to a degree to human rights, the concept allows for flexibility. Thus, even though the aims of the transition should always be to restore respect for human rights and generalized trust, the concrete shape of the two goals will vary with the context they operate in. Ultimately though, in light of the author's heavy natural bias in favor of his own attempt to provide a unitary yet flexible definition of transitional justice, it must be left to the reader to judge its success. As a substitute, the legalistic perspective can justify not the feasibility but the necessity of a unitary definition of transitional justice. From a legalistic perspective, transitional justice is based on universally applicable law, which needs to be adapted to the transitional justice situation.[934] Accordingly, a universal standard should tell norm-addressees, under which circumstances those norms are transformed.

931 TRC Canada, *Summary of the Final Report*, 183 ff.; Art. 7.01 ff. Indian Residential Schools Settlement Agreement. An example from New Zealand is the apology by the government in accordance with the Deed of Settlement of the Historical Claims of Ngati Tuwharetoa (Bay of Plenty), 48. An overview of some reconciliation efforts in New Zealand can be found in Sullivan, *The Politics of Reconciliation in New Zealand*, 2016 Pol. Sci. 68(2), 124. For Colombia see Final Agreement, e.g. point 2.2.4.

932 See above, ch. 2, E.II.

933 Consider for example the margin of appreciation in the European human rights system. For further details see below, ch. 4, B.III and Brems, *Human Rights - Universality and Diversity*, 2001, 341 ff.

934 This is no statement on the debate about the universality of human rights. The comfortable legalistic perspective can simply rely on the fact that at least the human rights commonly of concern to transitional justice form universal customary international law. For a comprehensive introduction to the debate see, Brems, *Human Rights - Universality and Diversity*. An important contribution to this debate was made by, Mutua, *Human Rights*.

B. The Role(s) of Reparation in Transitional Justice

Through defining transitional justice, the present chapter established two goals of the transitional justice process. While an essential stepping-stone, these goals need not equal the purpose(s) of reparation in transitional justice. The following two sections will detail the relationship between the ordinary aim of reparation to provide corrective justice and the transition's objectives.

I. The Deontological and Instrumental Role of Reparation

Since reparation is a transitional justice measure, it seems intuitive that it should further the aims of the transition; for how should transitional justice achieve its goals if not through its measures? The question is whether these aims replace reparation's ordinary aim to provide corrective justice or whether the different aims coexist.[935] The answer depends on one's conception of the nature of transitional justice. Roughly, three positions shape that debate. For the first, transitional justice is a special form of justice with unique features and challenges. Within this framework, transitional justice measures fully serve the goals of the transition. Ordinary justice conceptions are inapplicable.[936] The opposite view disputes the supposedly exceptional character of transitional justice. According to its proponents, all allegedly unique transitional justice features are present in stable democracies as well. Rather than as unique political situations, transitional justice and stable democracies are regarded as opposite ends on a continuum.[937] Accordingly, transitional justice efforts are measured solely against the demands of ordinary justice. That the particular challenges in transitional situations can make it impossible to fulfill those demands completely must be acknowledged and accepted.[938] The third opinion occupies a middle ground between the previously mentioned extremes. Its proponents conceptualize transitional justice as ordinary justice applied in a principled manner to

935 On corrective justice as the ordinary aim of reparation see above, ch. 1, E.

936 Examples are cited in de Greiff, *Theorizing Transitional Justice*, 40, fn. 71. A particularly apt example of this kind of reasoning is Murphy, *The Conceptual Foundations of Transitional Justice*. For examples in the realm of reparation see below, ch. 4, E.I.

937 Posner/Vermeule, *Transitional Justice as Ordinary Justice*, 2004 Harv. L. Rev. 117(3), 761.

938 Ohlin, *On the Very Idea of Transitional Justice*, 2007 Whitehead J. Dipl. Intl. Rel. 8, 51, 60.

extraordinary circumstances. With that, they anchor transitional justice in ordinary justice while acknowledging that the situation requires modifying it through principled reasoning to fit the extraordinary circumstances of transitional justice.[939]

This last approach provides the most attractive conceptualization of transitional justice. Seeing transitional justice as nothing but ordinary justice, because all phenomena associated with it are also present in stable democracies, misses the essential point. It is not the presence of certain phenomena, which makes transitional justice distinct; it is the extent to which they are present. While instability and norm violations exist in stable democracies, they become normalized in transitional justice situations, fundamentally altering basic norms governing society and eroding generalized trust. The same applies to transitional justice measures. While stable democracies regularly apply some transitional justice measures, e.g., replacing civil servants and unsettling property rights, they do not use them as tools to alter society's norms.[940] They follow ordinary, individualistic justice conceptions, such as corrective justice, and hence cannot appreciate the broader societal effects of systematic norm transgression. Simply put, ordinary justice conceptions leave no room for the transformation necessary in transitional justice situations.[941]

Still, the ordinary justice view should make transitional justice scholars cautious of excessive exceptionalism. Proponents of the special justice view convincingly show why transitional justice has extraordinary demands. They fail to demonstrate why these extraordinary demands render ordinary justice inapplicable. Dismissing ordinary conceptions of justice creates a normative gap. In the contentious political settings of transitions, such a gap risks being filled by unnecessarily low standards or by an extreme form of contextualism, which denies the applicability of general standards altogether. Special justice accounts also easily succumb to a full instrumentalist view of transitional justice measures, seeing them as mere means to achieve societal transformation. Salient demands for individual justice are then in peril of being sacrificed too readily for society's greater good.[942]

939 de Greiff, *Theorizing Transitional Justice*, 59.

940 Posner/Vermeule, *Transitional Justice as Ordinary Justice*, 777 ff., 783 ff., use these examples to illustrate similarities between transitional and stable situations. A similar argument is made by Teitel, *Transitional Justice Genealogy*, 92 f.

941 Murphy, *The Conceptual Foundations of Transitional Justice*, 96 ff.

942 Ohlin, *On the Very Idea of Transitional Justice*, 54. See also below on extraordinary conceptions of reparation in transitional justice, ch. 4, E.I.

The middle ground view, which conceptualizes transitional justice as ordinary justice applied in a principled manner to extraordinary circumstances, guards against both its competitors' perils. On the one hand, it firmly anchors transitional justice in ordinary justice, countering contextualism, pure instrumentalism, and the arbitrariness of new standards. On the other hand, it allows modifying ordinary standards to accommodate the societal effects of systematic norm transgression. But what exactly does it mean to apply ordinary justice in a principled manner to extraordinary circumstances? Ordinary conceptions of justice still apply. In addition, de Greiff apodictically concludes that transitional justice measures must support restructuring society.[943] Above, it was shown that such restructuring should lead to strengthened respect for human rights and enhanced generalized trust.[944] With that, transitional justice measures attain the dual role of achieving ordinary justice and furthering the transition. That dual role is necessary to provide true justice under the extraordinary circumstances of the transition:

Reparation could hardly achieve corrective justice in transitional situations absent broader societal restructuring.[945] The case studies in chapter two and the previous section evinced that systematic human rights violations cause a distinct form of societal harm. They destroy societal relationships and sow distrust. This harm reverberates back on individuals, deepens their harm, and takes away possible coping mechanisms. Survivors of sexualized violence in Sierra Leone, who had to stay with the RUF, did not only suffer from the violations' immediate physical and psychological effects. Once they returned to their communities, they also encountered discrimination and ostracism, inter alia, because they were perceived to belong to rebel forces. Coupled with weak infrastructure and an almost complete lack of economic opportunities after the conflict, many survivors found themselves entangled in a web of overlapping harms, escape from which was extremely difficult. Sierra Leone's example shows that, if left unmitigated, harms on a communal and societal level can undermine any attempt to repair individuals.[946] Under these circumstances, reparation can hardly erase all harm without societal restructuring.

943 de Greiff, *Theorizing Transitional Justice*, 64.

944 See above, A.II.

945 See also below, ch. 4, E.I.

946 See above, ch. 2, II. For further examples see the case studies on Sierra Leone, Colombia and the ICC and the sources listed there, ch. 2, B.-D.

Vice versa, it is also doubtful whether macrosocial reconstruction is possible without addressing the damages to individuals and their relationships.[947]

Applying corrective justice in transitional situations uncritically, without considering its transitional-justice-specific goals, can also produce unjust results. Systematic human rights violations rarely occur out of a void. They usually are the consequence of preexisting injustices, such as structural inequality, discrimination, etc.[948] Corrective justice restores survivors to the status quo ante. When employed uncritically, it thus risks returning individuals to such previous, unjust states. Tasking reparation with furthering the transition can mitigate that risk.[949]

Additional pragmatic reasons justify opening reparation to the transitional-justice-specific goal of societal restructuring. Societal restructuring is an arduous task with an unclear outcome. Each policy employed to that end has its weaknesses, and all available policies must be combined to increase the chance of success.[950] Further, reparation in transitional justice is often a high-profile policy in times of normative uncertainty. As such, it will have some effect on society. The very least a state can do is trying to steer this effect in a preferable direction.

---

947 On different aspects of the micro- and macrosocial processes at play in transitional justice generally and reparation specifically see, Sveaass/Lavik, *Psychological Aspects of Human Rights Violations - The Importance of Justice and Reconciliation*, 2000 Nordic J. Intl. L. 69(1), 35, 43 f.; Hamber, *Narrowing the Micro and Macro - A Psychological Perspective on Reparations in Societies in Transition*, in: de Greiff (ed.), *The Handbook on Reparations,* 2006, 560, 563 f.; Lykes/Mersky, *Reparations and Mental Health - Psychosocial Interventions Towards Healing, Human Agency and Rethreading Social Realities*, in: de Greiff (ed.), *The Handbook of Reparations,* 2006, 589, 592 f.

948 This was researched particularly comprehensively regarding sexualized violence, CEDAW, *General Recommendation No. 30 on Women in Conflict Prevention, Conflict and Post-Conflict Situations,* CEDAW/C/GC/30, 2013, para 34; *Nairobi Declaration on Women's and Girls' Right to a Remedy and Reparation*, 2007, Preamble; HRC, *Report of the Special Rapporteur on Violence Against Women, its Causes and Consequences, Rashida Manjoo*, A/HRC/14/22, 2014, para 24, 31; Rubio-Marín, *The Gender of Reparations in Transitional Societies*, in: Rubio-Marin (ed.), *The Gender of Reparations - Unsettling Sexual Hierarchies While Redressing Human Rights Violations,* 2009, 63, 85; Duggan/Abusharaf, *Reparation of Sexual Violence in Democratic Transitions - The Search for Gender Justice*, in: de Greiff (ed.), The Handbook of Reparations, 2006, 623, 624, 627. More generally see the sources in the following footnote.

949 Yepes, *Transformative Reparations of Massive Gross Human Rights Violations - Between Corrective and Distributive Justice* 2009 Neth. Q. Hum. Rts. 27(4), 625, 633 f.; Rubio-Marín/de Greiff, *Women and Reparations*, 2007 Intl. J. Transitional Just. 1(3), 318, 325. Still, it is not necessary to abandon corective justice. For details on that debate and the limits of the related transformative reparation discourse see below, ch. 4, E.I.

950 de Greiff, *A Normative Conception of Transitional Justice*, 19.

In sum, transitional justice should be conceptualized as ordinary justice applied in a principled manner to extraordinary circumstances. This characterization provides the answer to this chapter's core question: All transitional justice measures play a dual role. They continue to fulfill the demands of ordinary justice while they also support the goals of the transition. Therefore, the purpose of reparation in transitional justice is to provide corrective justice and to strengthen respect for human rights and generalized trust in society. The former demand can be called reparation's "deontological role" because corrective justice demands reparation regardless of its broader consequences.[951] The latter demand is fulfilled by reparation's "instrumental role" because, in this role, reparation serves the instrumental purpose of bringing about the transition.[952]

II. The Relationship Between the Roles

Assuming a dual role of reparation creates a challenge of priority in case the two roles conflict. Since both fulfill justice demands, and neither provides full justice on its own, no role takes evident priority over the other. A lexical priority is therefore inadequate.[953] Instead, both demands for justice should be maximized. Reparation must therefore search for a Pareto-optimum[954] in the fulfillment of its dual roles. Since individual rights give rise to both roles, one cannot be wholly sacrificed for the other's sake. Reparation must hence aim to achieve a subclass of Pareto-optimums, in which it fulfills both

951 cf. Alexander/Moore, *Deontological Ethics*, in: Zalta (ed.), *Stanford Encyclopedia of Philosophy*, Online Edition 2016.

952 For a similar distinction between the instrumental and inherent value of transitional justice mechanisms see Duthie, *Introduction*, in: Duthie/Seils (eds.), *Justice Mosaics - How Context Shapes Transitional Justice in Fractured Societies*, 2017, 8, 10; Méndez, *Accountability for Past Abuses*, 1997 Hum. Rts. Q. 19(2), 255, 271 f. Famously, Zalaquett analysed the transitional situation in somewhat similar terms, albeit on a different level, referring to Weberian ethics of responsibility and conviction, Zalaquett, *Balancing Ethical Imperatives and Political Constraints - The Dilemma of new Democracies Confronting Past Human Rights Violations*, 1992 Hastings L. J. 43(6), 1425, 1430 ff.

953 On the problem of priority and lexical orders see Rawls, *A Theory of Justice*, 36 ff.

954 A pareto-optimum is a condition, in which it is impossible to increase one preference criterion, without making another one worse off, Mock, *Pareto Optimality*, in: Chatterjee (ed.), *Encyclopedia of Global Justice*, 2011, 808.Translated to the realm of conflicting roles of transitional justice measures, it means that one cannot increase the fulfillment of one role, without decreasing the fulfillment of the other.

roles to an adequate degree.[955] The far ends of the Pareto-optimum-curve are thus out of bounds. The identification of possible Pareto-optimums must consider that the repairing agent has no complete control over the success of reparation's instrumental role.[956] Reparation can merely induce people to trust and respect human rights with a certain probability. In contrast, the repairing agent can fulfill the demands of corrective justice at will. The following graphic illustrates the preceding considerations:

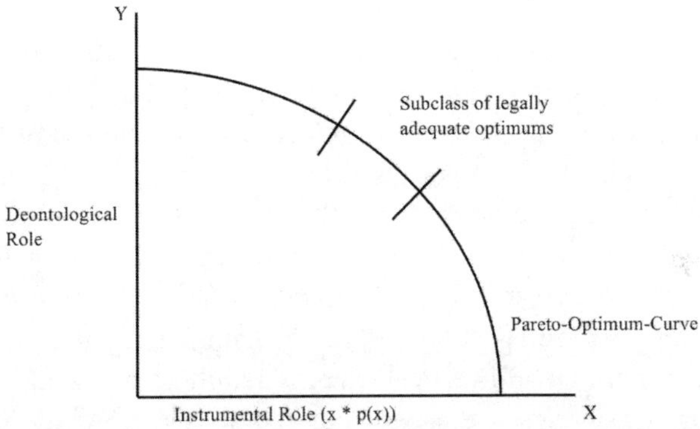

Figure 5: The Relationship Between the Roles of Reparation in Transitional Justice (created by the author)

To give a simplified example, imagine a situation in which individual compensation payments had no effect on furthering respect for human rights and generalized trust but were necessary to overcome survivors' harm. Conversely, a memorial contributed little to overcoming individual harm but was necessary to enhance respect for human rights and generalized trust. The state's resources did not suffice to implement both measures to the full extent. Since both measures were necessary to achieve the deontological and instrumental role reparation, the state could not fully implement one measure

955 In the strongest form of the doctrine, only one Pareto-optimum is legally adequate: The one in which both roles are fulfilled to an equal degree. However, it is implausible that this optimum is practically identifiable. For reasons of practicality, a subclass of optimums, in which both roles are fulfilled to an adequate degree, but one role is fulfilled more than the other, is deemed permissible. The size of this subclass will depend on the situation at hand. This concept resembles Rawls' expanded notion of Pareto-optimality coupled with a principle that can justify selecting certain points on the Pareto-curve over others, Rawls, *A Theory of Justice*, 59 f.

956 de Greiff, *Theorizing Transitional Justice*, 52.

at the other's expense. That course of action would correspond to the far ends of the Pareto-optimum-curve. Instead, the state would need to limit both measures' costs, implementing them to a degree with the maximum amount of resources it can spare. Only then is a Pareto-optimum within the legally adequate range achieved.

III. Summary: The Purposes of Reparation in Transitional Justice

Considering the goals and nature of transitional justice leads to a dual purpose of reparation in transitional justice. Reparation still aims to fulfill the demands of corrective justice. In this deontological role, reparation aims to erase all harm human rights violations caused to an individual. Fulfilling this role alone would, however, not lead to full justice in the transitional justice situation. As every transitional justice measure, reparation must also mitigate the societal effects of systematic human rights violations by furthering the goals of the transition: general respect for human rights in society and generalized horizontal and vertical trust. When these two goals conflict, an adequate balance between the two must be struck, realizing both to the maximum degree, without entirely disregarding either one.

C. The Instrumental Role of Reparation

In contrast to its deontological role, reparation fulfills its instrumental role only indirectly. Whereas each benefit given to a survivor as reparation brings them closer to the state of affairs demanded by corrective justice, it does not automatically create respect for human rights and generalized horizontal and vertical trust. Therefore, a complete understanding of reparation's instrumental role warrants an account of how reparation can support the aims of transitional justice. This section will attempt to create such an account based on the theory of symbolic interactionism.[957] Before diving into that attempt, some notes of caution are in order. The account does not pretend to provide a complete explanation of how reparation programs contribute to respect for human rights and generalized trust in practice. It is incomplete because it analyses a highly-idealized situation with a theory that might not fully capture the processes at play. The account would need to be amended with complic-

957 On the origins and content of that theory see below, C.I.

ating factors and processes to describe any actual situation. The account is also incomplete because symbolic interactionism is not the only approach to explain the instrumental role. The author chose the theory because it provides a convincing conceptualization of reparation's instrumental role, offering entry points for further legal inquiry. Other approaches will yield different results, probably not farther from the truth. Nevertheless, this incomplete account can have explanatory force. In Hempel's terminology, it resembles a potential explanation of the instrumental role of reparation – whose truth cannot be guaranteed because its component laws and assumptions are not necessarily valid.[958] Such an explanation can be defective because it relies on incomplete or false assumptions or laws or because another process than the one described caused the explained phenomenon.[959] Fact- or law-defectiveness need not be fatal. False factual assumptions or laws can be sufficiently close to the truth to yield explanations with explanatory power.[960] If assumptions or laws are missing from the explanation, its value can lie in a partial explanation, only concerning certain aspects of the phenomenon studied. It might also be possible to add known complicating factors to the explanation if need be.[961] If another process caused the phenomenon, the described process might still contribute to understanding if it is coherent and could have caused the phenomenon or if it is close to the actual process.[962]

Obviously, estimating how close the laws, facts, and processes at the basis of the account are to the truth requires knowledge of that truth[963] – which

958 Hempel, *Aspects of Scientific Explanation and Other Essays in the Philosophy of Science*, 1965, 338; Nozick, *Anarchy, State, and Utopia*, 2013, 7 f.

959 The first case is described by Nelson, *Explanation and Justification in Political Philosophy*, 1986 Ethics 97(1), 154, 165 f. as a missing component process explanation. The other cases are termed by Nozick, *Anarchy, State, and Utopia*, 7 f. as fact-defective, law-defective and process-defective explanations.

960 Nelson, *Explanation and Justification*, 161 ff. Nelson specifies what the author sloppily termed "close to the truth" in the case of laws as the reduceability of the law employed to the correct law. On the notion of reduction see Schaffner, *Approaches to Reduction*, 1967 Phil. Sci. 34(2), 137.

961 Nelson, *Explanation and Justification*, 162, 165 ff.; Woodward, *Explanation in Social Theory - Comments on Alan Nelson*, 1986 Ethics 97(1), 187, 193.

962 Nozick, *Anarchy, State and Utopia*, 7 f.; Nelson, *Explanation and Justification*, 165 ff.

963 Woodward, *Explanation in Social Theory*, 189 f. Woodward suggests some criteria to replace the "approximation to truth"-criterion, 190 ff. Since they are geared towards the natural sciences, this author will not rely on them. They might however provide inspiration for analoguous criteria for the social sciences. Especially the criterion of robustness and continuity, meaning that variations in assumptions or even their replacement does not lead to fundamentally different results, proves useful in this regard.

the author cannot pretend to have. Still, he hopes that the coherence and plausibility of the account indicate sufficient proximity. Furthermore, the account is open for amendment with complicating factors arising in any concrete transitional situation. Explanations derived from other approaches can supplement it. Lastly, this author is comforted by the fact that the following account is merely a building-block for a stepping-stone based on which teleological reasoning can transpire. The telos of reparation stands independently of the following account of how reparation could further that telos. So even if the real road towards the goal ends up being different, a slightly misled attempt to find that road can still illuminate how the international law on reparation should be interpreted so that it travels in the direction of its telos. The following sections will search for the road by introducing symbolic interactionism (I.). On that basis, they will examine the state's role in that theoretical framework (II.) before turning to the role of reparation (III.).

I. The Theoretical Basis: Symbolic Interactionism

Respect for norms and trust are individual attitudes, which rely on and find expression in human behavior. An account of how reparation can induce a change in individual attitudes and behavior can rely on H.G. Mead's symbolic interactionism. The theory rests on the assumption that individuals construct a social world by interpreting the physical world around them.[964] Interpretation turns objects into social objects endowed with meaning to the individual. Social objects are anything that persons can refer to: other persons, abstract ideas, oneself, past events, future events, hopes, wishes, etc.[965] Individuals arrive at their interpretation of social objects primarily through interaction with other persons.[966] This interaction happens through symbols, usually in speech, writings, gestures, or body language. People understand symbols through interpretation so that symbols are social objects too.[967] If

---

This author hopes that the following account will exhibit this kind of robustness and continuity.

964 Charon, *Symbolic Interactionism - An Introduction, an Interpretation, an Integration*, 10th Edition 2010, 43 f.

965 Blumer/Morrione, *George Herbert Mead and Human Conduct*, 2004, 36. For a list of examples see Charon, *Symbolic Interactionism*, 47.

966 Mead et al., *Mind, Self, and Society*, 2015, 77 f.; Shibutani, *Society and Personality - An Interactionist Approach to Social Psychology*, 1961, 480 ff.

967 Charon, *Symbolic Interactionism*, 48 ff.

people interact in a group over an extended period, their interpretations often converge and attain stability within that group.[968] To give an example: A sees a wooden object. She interprets it as a chair because she heard her parents call it that and saw them use it. Maybe her parents reprimanded her when she stood on the chair and told her how to use it properly. Thus, through interaction with her parents, A arrived at a specific interpretation of the wooden object before her. It is safe to assume that A's society developed a similar, stable definition of "chair" and upholds it through constant interaction at meetings, parties, cafés, etc.

Not all social objects are inanimate. They can include concrete or generalized persons, such as a friend, neighbors, the book club, or the ruling party. In contrast to inanimate social objects, these concrete and generalized persons have views, attitudes, and feelings. To interact with them, a person must attempt to interpret these subjective states of mind correctly. For that, the interpreter must take the other person's role and imagine how they will perceive and react to the interpreter.[969] Conventional roles facilitate both individual and generalized role-taking. Groups, e.g., a society, form stable conventions around specific roles. These roles determine how lawyers, police officers, parents, etc., should act and feel in certain situations; not because of their personality, but because society expects them to fulfill their conventional role.[970] To come back to the example: If A's mother reprimands her daughter because she stands on the chair, she must take her daughter's role. That allows her to imagine which words A understands and how A will react to the reprimand. A's mother might take roles of generalized others to imagine how, for example, society reacts to the situation. If the scene happens in the presence of guests the mother does not know personally, she can rely on the conventional role of "guest" to imagine how they will react.

How do this interpretation and role-taking influence attitudes and behavior? When faced with a situation, an individual interprets every social object of relevance to it.[971] This situation definition includes possible actions a person can take in response to the situation. When contemplating such actions, a person interprets how social objects will relate to the action. The person takes

968 Shibutani, *Society and Personality*, 115 ff., 127 ff.; Blumer, *Symbolic Interactionism - Perspective and Method*, 1969, 71 f.; Blumer/Morrione, *Mead and Human Conduct*, 40.
969 Charon, *Symbolic Interactionism*, 105 ff., 158 f.; Mead et al., *Mind, Self, and Society*, 154 ff.; Shibutani, *Society and Personality*, 142 ff.
970 Shibutani, *Society and Personality*, 46 ff.
971 Blumer/Morrione, *Mead and Human Conduct*, 36 f.

the role of other persons and generalized others to interpret how they react to the contemplated act. A person also regards themselves as a social object and imagines how the act will reflect on their self. This all-encompassing situation definition shapes a person's attitude towards a situation and the social objects in it. It also influences how they interpret a particular act and, thereby, whether they engage in that act.[972]

To return one last time to the example, when the mother defines the situation that her daughter stands on a chair, A, the guests, and kitchen objects become relevant social objects. She takes the role of the unknown guests and society and imagines their disapproval of the situation. She interprets the candles on the table as a potential danger to the child and arrives at a protective attitude. Through interaction with the child and others, A's mother has come to interpret her child as rebellious and stubborn, making persuading A to come down from the chair an unfeasible course of action. Consequently, she contemplates fetching A of the chair. When taking A's role, she imagines a negative reaction. She considers her wish to have a good relationship with her daughter in the future as a social object and interprets that her contemplated action would negatively influence that social object. She also interprets how the act will reflect on her self. She considers herself an anarchist, opposed to society's norms. So, after taking the guests' and society's role, imagining their approval of fetching the child of the chair, she decides that not doing so is better in line with her self-perception. She removes the candles to avert the danger and lets A play on the chair, silently enjoying the guests' indignation.

In sum, how a person interprets all social objects relevant to any given situation shapes their attitude and behavior. Their interaction with others, role-taking, and conventional roles influence their interpretation. Certainly, a parent's reaction to their child standing on a chair bears little resemblance to a society repairing systematic human rights violations. So how does symbolic interactionism work in that situation?

---

972 Blumer/Morrione, *Mead and Human Conduct*, 63 ff.; Charon, *Symbolic Interactionism*, 118 f.; Shibutani, *Society and Personality*, 91 f., 195 ff., 260 f., 277; Mead et al., *Mind, Self, and Society*, 141.

II. The Role of the State in the Symbolic Interactionist Framework

Reparation is state action.[973] As such, it is a symbol through which the state communicates. This communication influences the situation definition of individuals and, with that, their attitudes and behavior. Uncovering how a communicative act by the state influences individuals' situation definitions requires to discern first, the interpretation of which social objects state action influences (1.) and second, how it influences them (2.).

1. Objects of State Communication

State action can influence the interpretation of three critical social objects: the State, Society, and Member of Society. First and most directly, it communicates the stance of the state on specific issues. Put differently, state action enables individuals to take the state's role, imagining its interpretation of and reaction to any given situation. Taking the role of the state can be of vital importance to many situation definitions. Interpretations of behavior as "lawful", "unlawful", or "rebellious" depend on how the state conceptualizes an action. Many definitions of the self develop by contrast with the state's stance: "law-abiding", "good citizen", "rebel", "terrorist", etc. Individuals must also know the state's stance to interpret the consequences of many acts, most obviously potentially criminal acts.[974]

Communicative action by the state can also influence the interpretation of the social object Society. The state is a powerful communicative actor in most societies. It permeates society on many levels. State and society are thus not two separate and independent spheres but interact and influence each other.[975] The relationship runs deeper, considering that states ensure

973 State action is understood widely as action by state officials and institutions as well as legislation. This section oversimplifies in large parts by reducing communication between the state and society to the communication between two unitary actors. Of course, in reality, different state institutions communicate differently with different sectors of society, Sellers, *State-Society Relations*, in: Bevir (ed.), *The SAGE Handbook of Governance*, 2011, 124, 125.

974 The importance of these interpretations of course varies with the presence the state has in the lives of the relevant individuals.

975 Bank, *Societal Dynamics and Fragility - Engaging Societies in Responding to Fragile Situations*, 2013, 26 ff.; Weakliem, *Public Opinion, Political Attitudes and Ideology*, in: Janoski et al. (eds.), *The Handbook of Political Sociology - States, Civil Societies and Globalization*, 2005, 227, 241 ff.; Migdal, *State in Society - Studying how States and Societies Transform and Constitute one Another*, 2001, 49 ff.; Migdal, *Strong Societies*

their legitimacy by claiming to represent their citizens' will. While this applies to democracies by definition, even authoritarian regimes cannot survive without some form of public support. They often claim to represent their constituents through mock democratic procedures and discourse.[976] Given these links between state and society, state communication is likely to influence how individuals interpret society's values and expectations. Of course, state communication's influence on the interpretation of Society varies with the state-society relationship in any given scenario. As Migdal put it, in every society, a mélange of actors struggles over the power to determine societal rules. The state is but one of them, and its relative power varies from society to society.[977] Still, to varying degrees, the state can influence individuals' interpretation of Society. This interpretation is vital for many situation definitions. Whether attitudes and actions are "leftist",

---

and Weak States - State-Society Relations and State Capabilities in the Third World, 1988, 24 ff. This assumption is central to certain liberal theories of international relations, see Schieder, *Neuer Liberalismus*, in: Schieder/Spindler (eds.), *Theorien der Internationalen Beziehungen*, 2010, 187, 195; Moravcsik, *Taking Preferences Seriously - A Liberal Theory of International Politics*, 2003 Intl. Org. 51(4), 513, 518.

976 That authoritarian regimes need some kind of popular support was shown by Hannah Arendt in her essay On Violence, printed in Arendt, *Crises of the Republic*, 1972, 140; Geddes, *What do we Know About Democratization After Twenty Years?*, 1999 Ann. Rev. Pol. Sci. 2(1), 115, 125; von Haldenwang, *The Relevance of Legitimation – A new Framework for Analysis*, 2017 Contemp. Pol. 23(3), 269, 271. Nowadays, authoritarian regimes increasingly resort to claims that they represent the will of the governed through democractic procedures, Dukalskis/Gerschewski, *What Autocracies Say (and What Citizens Hear) - Proposing Four Mechanisms of Autocratic Legitimation*, 2017 Contemp. Pol. 23(3), 251, 257 f.; von Soest/Grauvogel, *Identity, Procedures and Performance - How Authoritarian Regimes Legitimize Their Rule*, 2017 Contemp. Pol. 23(3), 287, 296. For special forms of these claims see Mayer, *Strategies of Justification in Authoritarian Ideology*, 2001 J. Pol. Ideologies 6(2), 147, 161 ff. Further examples, including on how the claims might differ with their target audience are given by Omelicheva, *Authoritarian Legitimation - Assessing Discourses of Legitimacy in Kazakhstan and Uzbekistan*, 2016 Cent. Asian Surv. 35(4), 481, 488, 493; Edel/Josua, *How Authoritarian Rulers Seek to Legitimize Repression - Framing Mass Killings in Egypt and Uzbekistan*, 2018 Democratization 25(5), 882, 885, 893 f.

977 Migdal, *State in Society*, 49 ff.; Migdal, *Strong Societies and Weak States*, 24 f., 32. As regards questions of legitimacy, the legitimation claims by the government and corresponding demands by the population must be distinguished from the level of popular endorsement of those claims and the degree to which the state can fulfill the demand for legitimation, von Haldenwang, *The Relevance of Legitimation*, 273 ff.; Dukalskis/Gerschewski, *What Autocracies Say*, 260. For different degrees of sucess in legitimation in Uzbekistan and Kazakhstan see, Omelicheva, *Authoritarian Legitimation*, 489 ff., 494.

"right-wing", "normal", "deviant", etc. depends to a degree on society's judgment. Interpretations of Society can influence social norms. Social norms exist when individuals form empirical and normative expectations towards other persons.[978] Interpretations of Society can support such expectations. If a person interprets Society as Christian, for example, they can assume a greater chance that people visit the church on Sundays.

Relatedly, the state can influence the definition of the conventional role of Member of Society. Members of society are generally expected to follow legal and certain social norms.[979] The state decides upon and upholds the content of legal norms. Since it represents society to a degree, it also influences social norms. Its actions thereby shape the expectations towards members of society. The importance of the role of Member of Society cannot be underestimated. Member of Society is the only role an individual knows every other person to fit into. In most quotidian situations, it is the only role that individuals know the persons they interact with to have. Thus, the interpretation of Member of Society is crucial to many situation definitions.

2. Content of State Communication

The state can communicate many things about the three social objects State, Society, and Member of Society. Four potential messages are particularly relevant for reparation. First, state action can affirm values.[980] The prohibition of manslaughter, for example, does not only prohibit an act. It also communicates that life should be valued.[981] Beyond value affirmation, legislation

978 See above, A.II.1.

979 See above, A.II.1.

980 Kindermann, *Symbolische Gesetzgebung*, in: Grimm/Maihofer (eds.), *Gesetzgebungstheorie und Rechtspolitik*, 1988, 222, 230 f.

981 Some state actions carry less symbolic value, some more and some are almost exclusively symbolic. Art. 22 of the German Constitution determines that the flag of the Federal Republic of Germany shall be black, red and gold. This prominent determination is a belated decision in the flag controversy, which engulfed the Weimar Republic. During Germany's first and highly contested democratic phase, monarchists campaigned for a red, white and black flag, whereas democrats insisted upon a black, red and gold flag – the colors of early German democratic movements. By opting prominently for the latter, the drafters of the 1949 constitution firmly placed the new Federal Republic of Germany in the family of democratic states and in a historic lineage to the earliest champions of democracy in Germany. Fundamentally, Art. 22 of the German Constitution therefore serves as a symbolic statement that the Federal Republic of Germany cherishes democratic values. The example is a more detailed ac-

designates what should be considered legally deviant behavior. Since the state claims to represent society, it can also, to a degree, designate socially deviant behavior.[982] In the simplest case, the state legally prescribes or proscribes behavior, marking non-abidance as deviant. Beyond that, the state counts on numerous other forms to condemn or applaud behavior, e.g., public speeches, acts of parliament, awards, etc. Third, state action can communicate the valuation or devaluation of groups in society. Apart from doing so directly, the state can value or devalue norms, principles, behavior, etc., which are closely associated with a group. If the state prescribes behavior associated with one group, it enhances that group's standing in society. Vice versa, proscribing such behavior decreases the group's standing.[983] Through this mechanism, the state demonstrates that it considers a group's views when devising policies. It can also decide group struggles over status in society. Both measures are especially significant if there is doubt about the relative

---

count of Noll, *Symbolische Gesetzgebung*, 1981 Zeitschrift für schweizerisches Recht 100, 347, 350.

982 Gusfield, *On Legislating Morals - The Symbolic Process of Designating Deviance*, 1968 Cal. L. Rev. 56(1), 54, 54 ff.; Sunstein, *On the Expressive Function of Law*, 1996 U. Pennsylvania L. Rev. 144(5), 2021, 2031 f.

983 Gusfield, *Symbolic Crusade - Status Politics and the American Temperance Movement*, 1963, 173. Gusfield famously analyzed the prohibition of alcohol in the United States in these terms. By outlawing the sale of alcohol, the United States delegitimized the newly arrived immigrants from Ireland and Germany, who were associated with drinking. At the same time the prohibition law legitimized the temperance movement, which mostly consisted of rural, evangelical US-Americans, who immigrated several generations before, and reassured its members of their status in society. A summary can be found on p. 5 ff. Gusfield's analysis is criticized mainly on the assumption that his example, not his theory, is wrong Noll, *Symbolische Gesetzgebung*, 350; Friedman, *The Legal System - A Social Science Perspective*, 1975, 51. A more contemporary example could be European bans on religious symbols in public. These more or less thinly veiled attempts to ban muslim symbolism from public life rest on essentializing, for example, headscarves as symbols for a supposedly "politicized" religion, incompatible with "Western" values. By banning such symbols from public life, the state takes a stance on whom gets to be part of society, and the status of muslim minorities. See Vrielink, *Symptomatic Symbolism - Banning the Face Veil 'as a Symbol'*, in: Brems (ed.), *The Experience of Face Veil Wearers in Europe and the Law*, 2014, 184, 190 f.; Fadil, *Asserting State Sovereignty - The Face-Veil Ban in Belgium*, in: Brems (ed.), *The Experience of Face Veil Wearers in Europe and the Law*, 2014, 251, 254 ff. and the excellent analysis of the German debate by Barskanmaz, *Das Kopftuch als das Andere - Eine Notwendige Postkoloniale Kritik des Deutschen Rechtsdiskurses*, in: Berghahn/Rostock (eds.), *Der Stoff aus dem Konflikte Sind – Debatten um das Kopftuch in Deutschland, Österreich und der Schweiz*, 361, 361, 372 ff.

power of groups in society.[984] Lastly, state action can carry future-oriented messages. While that is clear, e.g., for government programs, legislation also fulfills such a function.[985] Norms create a counterfactual image of society and mark that state as desirable. Legislation thereby allows the state to distance itself from society's current situation and pledge to work for a positive vision of the future.[986]

III. The Role of Reparation in the Symbolic Interactionist Framework

To recall, state action can affirm abstract values, designate deviant behavior, value and devalue societal groups and designate goals towards which the state pledges to work. State action can thereby influence how individuals see the state, society, and their fellow members of society. It remains to be seen how reparation can use these social objects and messages to further respect for human rights, vertical and horizontal generalized trust.[987]

Reparation is state action. As such, it communicates with its direct addressees – survivors – and society at large.[988] The following section will

---

984 Gusfield, *Symbolic Crusade*, 172 ff., 177, 189 ff.; Edelman, *The Symbolic Uses of Politics*, 1964, 189.

985 The following part is based on Möllers, *Die Möglichkeit der Normen*, 2015. It must be noted at the outset that Möllers does not intend to provide an account on how law can influence society. Rather, he tries to define the term normativity. The application of his theory to the present question is thus not within the ambit of Möllers' work, but solely a doing of the author.

986 Möllers, *Die Möglichkeit der Normen*, 13 ff., 127, 131 ff.

987 The following account focuses exclusively on these societal aims of reparation. Of course, beyond mere corrective justice, reparation can also pursue further individual goals. Many commentators identify recognition as such a further individual goal, see e.g. de Greiff, *Theorizing Transitional Justice*, 42 ff. The author readily subscribe to the importance of recognition and the great potential the concept has in transitional justice. It plays no role in this chapter because it has little relevance for the chapter's limited aim. Excellent discussions of the concept are provided by Honneth, *The Struggle for Recognition*, 1996, and, especially concerning the relationship between recognition and remembrance, Assmann, *Der Lange Schatten der Vergangenheit*, 74 ff.

988 This communicative function of reparation bears resemblance to Günther Jakobs' theory of punishment, Kreß, *Einleitung*, in: Kindhäusier/Kreß et al. (eds.), *Strafrecht und Gesellschaft – Ein Kritischer Kommentar zum Werk von Günther Jakobs*, 1, 21 f. Given that prosecution and punishment are a central element of transitional justice processes and that the theory developed can be transferred to such other elements, the author draws some comfort from the fact that it offers points of connection to existing, recognized theories for one of the most sensitive transitional justice measures

decipher possible messages of reparation to survivors and society (1.) and analyze how they influence individuals in furtherance of the transitional justice goals (2.). Both steps are, at the same time, too basic and too ideal. They are too basic because the following account does not look at any concrete reparation program. It will analyze the messages of reparation's essence – a benefit the responsible state gives a survivor of a human rights violation to erase the resulting harm in acknowledgment of wrongdoing. This approach makes the account too ideal because it aggregates the state and society into two coherent and completely distinct actors. It describes how one-sided communication from the state to society influences the latter without disturbance by other factors. The clinical nature of this account should be apparent. Metaphorically speaking, it looks at the source of a river to determine what happens in its delta. A complex web of circumstances influences the actual communicative content and consequences of any real reparation program. As any ideal, the following account should be considered an unreachable goal, which can orient real efforts. Complicating factors presenting themselves in any concrete transitional justice situation can be factored into the account so that its ideal character is not fatal to its explanatory power.[989]

1. Reparation's Message

Reparation's message can be split fourfold. First, a necessary precondition for reparation is to acknowledge that human rights are valid. If they were not, they could not be violated and could not produce a valid claim to reparation. Second, reparation redresses the harm a concrete action by a specific actor caused to a specific survivor. Thereby, reparation brings human rights down from the realm of lofty goals and proves that they can provide normative guidance in the messy reality of daily life. In a word, reparation shows the applicability of human rights to quotidian life. Third, reparation is a form of human rights enforcement. It communicates that survivors can turn to the state to enforce their rights. Fourth, the state makes considerable material and immaterial efforts to administer reparation on a large scale. It thereby communicates that it values human rights as important. Lastly, when states embark upon comprehensive reparation efforts, they create a vision

---

that require greatest justification. I thank Claus Kreß for this comforting and thought-provoking reference.

989 See the discussion above, C.

of a society that settles legitimate claims and upholds human rights. This future-oriented message of reparation cuts across all previously mentioned ones and lends them stability.[990]

2. Reparation's Influence

How can the message of present and future validity, applicability, enforceability, and importance of human rights change individual attitudes and behavior towards strengthened respect for human rights and generalized trust? Answering that question warrants a closer analysis of the sender and the receiver of the message. As established above, the state communicates for two actors: itself and – to a degree – society. The state, in turn, is always represented by its institutions. Reparation, therefore, communicates that state institutions and society deem human rights valid, applicable, important, and enforceable. Concretizing the receiver(s) of that message takes the analysis directly to the question of how the message can generate trust.

As discerned above, generalized trust in human rights relies on the normative and empirical expectations that state institutions and members of society adhere to human rights in their societal relationships. Trust in state institutions was termed vertical trust, trust in members of society horizontal trust.[991] Reparation's fourfold message directly implicates vertical trust. When the state communicates the validity, applicability, importance, and enforceability of human rights, it communicates that state institutions will apply, attach importance to, and enforce human rights in their vertical relationships. Since the state also communicates partially on behalf of society, the fourfold message also suggests that society supports and demands human rights compliant state institutions. This gives individuals reasons to form the normative expectation that state institutions adhere to human rights and that the state and society will hold them to account if they do not.

Reparation has a more challenging time to influence horizontal trust. It must give individuals reasons to form the normative expectation that members of society will adhere to human rights in their horizontal relationships. Member of Society was defined above as a conventional role entailing adherence to legal and social norms.[992] In principle, what the state

990 These are of course not the only messages attributable to reparation. Other examples can be found in Hamber, *Narrowing the Micro and the Macro*, 568.

991 See above, A.II.1.

992 See above, A.II.1.a.

communicates about its institutional norms says nothing about the norms governing personal relationships. However, when reparation communicates that state and society expect adherence to human rights from state institutions, individuals can reasonably assume that similar expectations apply to members of society. This would be a coherent position valuing individual rights, regardless of the actor that endangers them. Reparation says as much when it repairs violations committed by private individuals, based on the state's failure to protect or fulfill human rights. Such reparation presupposes that members of society must adhere to human rights in their horizontal relationships. Especially if implemented for violations of human rights in personal relationships, reparation therefore also communicates that the state and – to a degree – society deem human rights valid, applicable, important, and enforceable in horizontal relationships.

Reparation's fourfold message thus gives individuals reason to form the normative expectation that state institutions and members of society will adhere to human rights in their societal relations. This can change the interpretation of the social objects State, Society and Member of Society and make them trustworthy. Reparation's future-oriented message lends stability to these new interpretations, as it does not only signal the current validity, importance, enforceability, and applicability of human rights. It also signals the state's commitment to upholding human rights in the future. As detailed above, normative expectations are necessary but not sufficient to form trust. They must be coupled with congruent empirical expectations, meaning that state institutions and members of society must actually adhere to human rights for trust to arise. A critical mass of persons needs to form these normative and empirical expectations for horizontal and vertical trust in human rights to take hold.[993] This can only happen incrementally, and reparation is but one factor influencing this delicate process.

If successful, the process also contributes to strengthened respect for human rights as the ultimate transitional justice goal. The fourfold message changes the importance of the social object Human Rights for individuals' situation definition. When systematic human rights violations erode the trust that other members of society and state institutions adhere to human rights,[994] Human Rights cease to be relevant for individuals' situation definitions. Communicating the validity, applicability, enforceability, and importance of human rights raises their relevance. It communicates that

993 See above, A.II.1.
994 See above, A.II.1.

human rights guide the state, society, and members of society. When taking these roles to define their situation, individuals must therefore pay attention to human rights. If individuals contemplate violating human rights, they must consider that the state and society mark such behavior as deviant and threaten legal and social enforcement action.

IV. Summary

In sum, reparation fulfills its instrumental role in transitional justice by acting as a symbol communicated by the state, which changes individuals' interpretation of four important social objects: Human Rights, the State, Society, and Members of Society. Affirming the validity, applicability, enforceability, and importance of human rights increases their relevance in individuals' situation definitions. State institutions become trustworthier because reparation shows that the state and society demand human rights compliance on their part.[995] Other members of society become trustworthier because reparation signals that the state and society expect them to adhere to human rights and threaten negative consequences if they do not. The future-oriented message of reparation lends stability to these interpretations. Naturally, this account is idealistic and will not be realized in the purity described here. It rather functions as an ideal that real reparation programs can thrive to achieve.

V. Challenges

The account of reparation in transitional justice suffers from a critical problem: It relies on the state's power to influence people through communication. Such an influence depends on the state reaching people who are ready to hear the message. The first issue is problematic when the state is of little importance to parts of society, e.g., in regions where state services and institutions only have a limited reach. If that is so, the preceding account of the state's communicative action is not necessarily wrong, but the circumstances might strip it of any effect. Again, this calls for legal humility. If the law is insignificant to people, there is little it can influence. Other measures and perspectives are then more effective.

995 For an empirical approach to communication as a trust-building measure see Wong, *How can Political Trust be Built After Civil Wars? Evidence From Post-Conflict Sierra Leone*, 2016 J. Peace Res. 53(6), 772, 775.

Even if people listen to the state's message, it is fair to speculate that after witnessing and suffering massive state wrongdoing, a major part of the population will not be inclined to embrace the state's or society's new-found passion for human rights. There is a good chance that the state's persuasive force is the lowest when it is needed the most. Some features of reparation put it in a unique position to mitigate this challenge. It is the only transitional justice measure that directly addresses those whose trust in state institutions and other society members suffered the most: survivors. Reparation requires the state to take sides, allowing it to send a strong message of group valuation. For better or for worse[996], reparation categorizes people into "survivors" and "perpetrators". By giving the former benefits in response to the latter's unlawful actions, the state sides radically with survivors. It values them over perpetrators. It also demonstrates its ability to take the perspective of survivors and govern for them. Several factors further underline the sincerity of reparation's message. Reparation is resource-intensive, requiring visible effort from the state. It entails an unequivocal acknowledgment of wrongdoing. Reparation thus enables the state to distance itself from and devalue the past regime. Reparation efforts take time and entail lasting objects such as letters of apology, monuments, etc. The state continuously renews its commitment to human rights and builds trust incrementally over time. This longevity can also sustain faith in the profoundly idealistic vision reparation creates. According to Möllers, a failure to realize norms' future-oriented claims within an adequate time delegitimizes them. The further removed the norm's stated ideal is from current reality, the harder it is to immunize the norm from delegitimization.[997] Publicly visible reparation acts over a long period can continuously affirm reparation's vision, bridging its aspirational gap.[998] Lastly, the message that the state will enforce human rights decreases the costs of misplaced trust. Individuals can treat the state as insurance against the costs of having their rights violated.

Beyond these factors, the circumstances of transitional justice might help to achieve the instrumental role of reparation. While the communicator might be far from ideally placed to convey the messages discerned above, their content might fall on fruitful soil. Crises bring norms, values, and perspectives

996 It is too rarely acknowledged that transitional justice measures tend to label persons strictly as survivors or perpetrators. Often, too little space is given for the biographical grey areas conflict inevitably produces. See below, ch. 4, C.II.1.

997 Möllers, *Die Möglichkeit der Normen*, 322 ff.

998 cf. Möllers, *Die Möglichkeit der Normen*, 328 ff.

in flux because they shatter old ones without establishing new ones. In that scenario, people might be particularly perceptible to reparation's new messages.[999] Still, the instrumental role of reparation faces an uphill battle in the complex reality of transitional situations.

Beyond the challenge that the state might not be in a position to communicate successfully, a similar challenge to the one against the unified definition of transitional justice given above presents itself: Can one set of messages capture the functioning of reparation across a broad spectrum of contexts?[1000] Unsurprisingly, the answer is similar – and may be similarly unsatisfying – to the one given above. The messages discerned provide a framework. Their concrete form depends on the context. The kind of monument a state erects, the form an apology takes, the kind and amount of material benefits given may vary significantly from context to context. The exact messages these actions send may also vary. Still, at their core, they can provide a message of present and future validity, applicability, enforceability, and importance of human rights.

D. *Summary: The Purposes of Reparation in Transitional Justice*

A veritable tour de force across some of the most controversial questions currently debated in transitional justice led to an account of the goals of reparation in transitional justice and how it might achieve them. Naturally, covering such a broad spectrum of controversies within such limited space makes an argument fragile. It relies on many laws and assumptions, each of which can be challenged. However, even if the argument is defeated at one point or the other, it may still give a general idea about the functioning of reparation in transitional justice. Even a partially defeated account might provide guide rails, which are sufficiently close to the "correct" road – if there is one – to enable the transformation of legal standards through teleological reasoning.

The account started by defining transitional justice as a state's attempt to address a legacy of systematic human rights violations, which aims to transform society towards strengthened respect for human rights and generalized trust. The latter was defined as the expectation that other members

999 Shibutani, *Society and Personality*, 300; Blumer/Morrione, *Mead and Human Conduct*, 40.
1000 See above, A.IV.

of society and state institutions adhere to and support basic social and institutional norms, which correspond to human rights. Since transitional justice is ordinary justice applied in a principled manner to extraordinary circumstances, reparation – as any transitional justice measure – serves a dual purpose. In its deontological role, reparation fulfills the demands of corrective justice. However, under the extraordinary circumstances of the transition, corrective justice alone does not suffice to achieve complete justice. Reparation must fulfill an additional instrumental role: furthering the goal of the transitional process. The answer to this chapter's core question – what is the purpose of reparation in transitional justice? – thus is:

> *Reparation in transitional justice serves two goals. First, it must render corrective justice by erasing all harm a survivor endured as far as possible. Second, it must further the goals of the transition by strengthening respect for human rights as well as generalized horizontal and vertical trust in society.*

In case the two roles collide, the state must seek to establish a Pareto-optimum, which fulfills both roles to a sufficient degree. Reparation does not fulfill its instrumental role automatically. Its communicative content can merely induce people to respect human rights and trust that other members of society and state institutions will do the same. Reparation sends the message of present and future validity, applicability, enforceability, and importance of human rights. Doing so strengthens respect for human rights by increasing the importance and influence of the social object "human rights" in individuals' situation definitions. It also makes state institutions and members of society trustworthy by providing different reasons to believe that they will uphold human rights in their societal relationships.

These messages will not take the same form in any two situations. Their effectiveness depends on how adequately they are tailored to the context they operate in. Even then, success is far from guaranteed. On the contrary, reparation's effect may be limited. On the one hand, this provides a reason to approach transitional justice holistically, employing all possible measures to increase success. On the other hand, the argument comes full circle by reverting to legal humility: Law is but one avenue to success and probably not the most effective one. Still, it is grounded in ordinary justice and valid legal obligations. Hence, there are intrinsic demands of justice to take that avenue, regardless of whether it leads to the noble goals, which are – maybe naïvely – sought at its end.

Chapter 4 – A Normative Framework for Reparation in Transitional Justice

Chapters two and three evinced that the international law on reparation, as established in chapter one, does not fit the transitional justice situation. Not only does it fail to respond to unique factual challenges. It cannot adequately capture the transformative aim of reparation in transitional justice – namely to (re)establish respect for human rights and generalized horizontal and vertical trust in society. Based on these differences, some argue that the international law on reparation does not apply in transitional contexts. As has been shown before, that position has no legal basis and produces unjust results.[1001] So what remains to be done instead?

A. *Introduction: What Tool to Use?*

Three ways exist to approach the problem: First, one can distill new rules for reparation in transitional justice from international practice (I.).[1002] Second, one can employ legal concepts, which allow to modify obligations under challenging circumstances, namely the declaration of emergency and necessity (II.). Third, one can adapt existing standards – namely the right to reparation and other relevant human rights – from within through interpretation (III.).

I. Seeking New Standards

The first approach could rely on occasional international practice. The IACtHR postulated principles according to which it would judge domestic reparation programs.[1003] However, the court did not provide a legal basis for these principles. It failed to concretize or even apply them to the cases

1001 See above, Introduction.

1002 For such an approach to transitional justice generally see Bell, *The "New Law" of Transitional Justice.*

1003 IACtHR, *García Lucero et al. v. Chile*, 2013, para 189; IACtHR, *Gomes Lund et al. ("Guerrilha Do Araguaia") v. Brazil*, 2010, para 303; IACtHR, *Manuel Cepeda Vargas v. Colombia*, 2010, para 246.

cited. It switched to different criteria in subsequent cases.[1004] Other human rights bodies do not follow the approach of the IACtHR. Hence, it is difficult to generate any valid independent norms to guide reparation in transitional justice from this jurisprudence. Relying on state practice proves equally difficult. For independent norms governing reparation in transitional justice to arise from state practice, they would need to take the form of customary international law, backed by settled practice and opinio juris.[1005] Regarding some aspects of reparation in transitional justice, state practice is far from uniform. A case in point is the relationship between special reparation mechanisms and the ordinary judiciary, which differs starkly across transitional justice reparation programs.[1006] While state practice does converge in other areas, states do not provide any normative criteria for their behavior. In some cases, this makes it impossible to distill norms from state practice. Almost all states engage in outreach efforts to inform survivors of the reparation program. But the way they do it and the degree to which they embark on the effort differs starkly. States do not justify these different degrees of outreach. Hence, practice does not provide any normative criteria to measure the degree to which states should conduct outreach.[1007] Even where states give normative criteria for their behavior, they fail to legally justify it, raising doubts whether they act out of a sense of a legal obligation.[1008] For example, states almost uniformly restrict eligibility for reparation to the gravest violations that occurred. But they do not justify why international law permits them to limit the right to reparation of survivors that drastically. By and large, state practice seems neither conclusive nor sufficiently backed by opinio juris to distill adequate independent norms on reparation in transitional justice. Admittedly, the author has not conducted an in-depth review of all transitional justice reparation efforts, precluding him from drawing this conclusion with finality. Additionally, that none or only

1004 Sandoval, *Two Steps Forward, One Step Back - Reflections on the Jurisprudential Turn of the Inter-American Court of Human Rights on Domestic Reparation Programmes*, 2018 Intl. J. Hum. Rts. 22(9), 1192, 1201 f.

1005 ICJ, *Jurisdictional Immunities*, para 55. The Basic Principles are often cited as a strong instance of state practice in support for norms pertaining to domestic reparation programs. However, only once do they explicitly mention such programs in relation to repairing violations of non-state actors. Other than that, they focus on judicial redress, UNGA, *Basic Principles*, A/RES/60/147, para 16.

1006 See below, G.

1007 See below, D.I.

1008 See below, C.V.

a few independent rules on reparation in transitional justice can be distilled from practice need not be fatal to the approach. It could simply mean that international law leaves states considerable freedom in that realm. But that is not true. The international law on reparation regulates states' behavior, and there is no normative basis not to apply it in transitional justice. As argued above, the mere fact that the situation presents an enormous challenge to an application is no reason.[1009] Thus, where practice does not provide independent legal standards, the problem persists that the international law on reparation applies to a situation it does not fit. Where independent standards might be discerned, their relationship to the international law on reparation is unclear. This last issue points to a deeper problem with the approach. Independent norms on reparation in transitional justice would need to be a customary lex specialis derogating from the international law on reparation. Because the international law on reparation is largely treaty-based, such derogation would be highly unusual. Customary international law rarely is lex specialis to treaty law.[1010] It is even more difficult to imagine a customary lex specialis derogating from human rights standards to provide less protection. Human rights law does not impose reciprocal but integral obligations on states. States do not owe compliance to individual treaty parties but individual persons and the collectivity of state parties.[1011] This makes it harder for states to derogate from those obligations, as the prohibition of inter se agreements and the modified reservations system for human rights law evince.[1012] Thus, it is doubtful whether state practice alone could

1009 See above, Introduction.

1010 ICJ, *Military and Paramilitary Activities in and Against Nicaragua (Nicaragua v. United States of America), Merits,* para 274; IUSCT, *Amoco International Finance Corporation v. Iran*, IRAN-U.S. C.T.R. 15, Case No. 56, 1987, 189, para 112; ILC, *Fragmentation of International Law - Difficulties Arising From the Diversification and Expansion of International Law,* A/CN.4/L.682, 2006, 79 ff.

1011 Pauwelyn, *Conflict of Norms in Public International Law - How WTO Law Relates to Other Rules of International Law*, 2003, 56 ff.; IACtHR, *Advisory Opinion on the Effect of Reservations on the Entry Into Force of the American Convention on Human Rights (Arts. 74 and 75)*, OC-2/82, 1982, para 29 ff.; IACtHR, *Opinión Consultative Sobre la Denuncia de la Convención Americana Sobre Derechos Humanos y de la Carta de la Organización de los Estados Americanos y sus Efectos Sobre las Obligaciones Estatales en Materia de Derechos Humanos,* OC-26/20, 2020, para 51 ff.; EComHR, *Austria v. Italy*, 788/60, 1961, para 19.

1012 ICJ, *Reservations to the Convention on Genocide - Advisory Opinion*, I.C.J. Reports 1951, 15, 23 f.; ILC, *Report on Fragmentation of International Law*, A/CN.4/L.682, para 311 ff.

result in a new norm derogating from an established human rights norm.[1013] At the very least, because of the prohibition of inter se agreements, state practice would need to establish consent between all parties to the respective human rights conventions.[1014] Practice on reparation in transitional justice is far removed from that unanimity. Therefore, distilling independent norms on reparation in transitional justice from state practice seems inadequate for the situation at hand. Instead, human rights jurisprudence considers state practice as a means of interpretation[1015] – which concords with this study's approach. A broad review of state practice guides the interpretation of the international law on reparation forwarded in this chapter, led by the in-depth review of the six reparation programs examined in chapter two and complemented by a more cursory review of other transitional justice reparation programs worldwide.[1016]

II. Necessity and State of Emergency

Before this interpretation proceeds, one competitor to that approach remains: The reliance on doctrines that modify international obligations, namely necessity or the declaration of a state of emergency. This approach cannot

1013 ILC, *Report on Fragmentation of International Law*, A/CN.4/L.682, para 109; Orakhelashvili, *Restrictive Interpretation of Human Rights Treaties in the Recent Jurisprudence of the European Court of Human Rights*, 2003 Eur. J. Intl. L. 14(3), 529, 536; Killander, *Interpreting Regional Human Rights Treaties*, 2010 Sur - Intl. J. Hum. Rts. 7(13), 145, 149.

1014 Pauwelyn, *Conflict of Norms in Public International Law*, 306; ECtHR, *Öcalan v. Turkey*, 46221/99 para 162 ff.

1015 ECtHR, *Demir and Baykara v. Turkey*, 34503/97 (GC), 2008, para 76; ECtHR, *Soering v. The United Kingdom*, 14038/88 (Plenary), 1989, para 102; Schlütter, *Aspects of Human Rights Interpretation by the UN Treaty Bodies*, in: Ulfstein/Keller (eds.), *UN Human Rights Treaty Bodies - Law and Legitimacy, Studies on Human Rights Conventions*, 2012, 261, 292 ff.

1016 The programs cursorily surveyed here were implemented in Argentina, Chile, Timor Leste, Brazil, Malawi, Morocco, Guatemala, Nepal, Peru, Kosovo, South Africa, El Salvador, Northern Ireland, Uganda, Philippines, Bolivia, Mexico, Paraguay, Uruguay, Nicaragua, and Switzerland. In addition, the UNCC and the Trust Fund for Victims of Hissène Habré's Crimes were included in the analysis. It must be noted however that the analysis of some of these programs, e.g. of the TFV of Hissène Habrés Crimes, only rests on their founding legal documents. Sadly, practice shows that implementation is often not as inspiring as the promises made in legislative form. The TFV of Hissène Habré's Crimes is an unfortunate example thereof, HRW, *African Union - No Reparations for Ex-Chad President's Victims*, 2021.

sufficiently accommodate the exigencies of the transitional justice situation. First, it is disputed whether states can invoke necessity in the realm of human rights. Most human rights treaties allow states to derogate from human rights obligations in a state of emergency, which could preclude necessity pursuant to Art. 25(2)(a) ASR.[1017] Second, even if the necessity defense applied, it would be difficult to meet its requirements.[1018] Art. 25(1)(a) ASR demands that the envisaged measure is "the only way to safeguard an essential interest against a grave and imminent peril." The mere lack of resources to pay reparation will rarely cross that threshold, as the various instances of failed economic necessity claims in international arbitration suggest.[1019] Instead, the state could claim that paying reparation would result in civil unrest, risking a return to the era of systematic human rights violations. However, that claim relies on such an unpredictably complicated causal chain that it will rarely suffice to establish an imminent peril, which can be averted only by forgoing reparation. Third, Art. 25(2)(b) ASR will exclude the defense in most cases because the state contributed to the situation of necessity. The state caused its obligation to repair by violating a primary right, and it usually also contributed to bringing about the transitional justice situation. These three legal obstacles to invoking necessity will often be insurmountable. But more importantly, the application of necessity does not bring about the legal consequences needed in transitional justice situations. If applicable, it does not alter the obligation as such. It only excuses a state's non-performance as long as the circumstances of necessity persist. Afterward, the state must comply with the obligation again.[1020] Art. 27(a) ASR allows for gradual compliance if the situation betters. From this angle, reparation is an optimization problem and must be performed fully as soon as circumstances permit. Necessity thus only allows delaying full reparation. Yet, chapter three evinced that reparation in transitional justice assumes an additional instrumental role of furthering the goals of the transition, namely creating trust and respect for human rights. The standards of chapter one cannot capture this transformative dimension

1017 ICJ, *Wall Opinion*, para 140; Kretzmer, *Emergency, State of*, in: Wolfrum (ed.), *Max Planck Encyclopedia of International Law,* Online Edition 2008, 3 ff.; Ryngaert, *State Responsibility, Necessity and Human Rights,* 2010 Nth. Ybk. Intl. L. 41, 79.

1018 The ILC states on that topic: "[...] necessity will only rarely be available to excuse non-performance on an obligation and [...] is subject to strict limitations to safeguard against possible abuse", ILC, *ASR Commentary,* A/56/10, 2001, art. 31 para 2.

1019 Waibel, *Sovereign Defaults Before International Courts and Tribunals*, 2011, 88 ff.

1020 ICJ, *Case Concerning the Gabčíkovo-Nagymaros Project (Hungary/Slovakia),* I.C.J. Reports 1997, 7, para 101; Paparinskis, *A Case Against Crippling Compensation in International Law of State Responsibility,* 2020 Modern L. Rev. 83(6), 1246, 1272.

warranted by the transitional situation and therefore need to be adapted. Necessity does not leave room for that.

Derogation in a state of emergency does not allow an adequate approach to reparation in transitional justice either. Chapter one already discussed why a state of emergency would likely not permit substantial derogation from the right to reparation for violations committed during the state of emergency.[1021] A state might derogate from the right to reparation once the obligation to repair has arisen and is of such an extent that it imperils the state's functioning. This might be the case in certain transitional justice situations. It is, however, a dangerous road to refer states to. Declarations of emergency can have a "catastrophic effect" on human rights.[1022] Especially in the volatile circumstances of transitional justice, they can come with dangerous side-effects.[1023] Also, as with necessity, declaring a state of emergency reduces the problem to optimization and does not allow adapting standards to the transitional justice logic of transformation.

III. The Limits of Interpretation

Since new standards cannot satisfactorily be distilled or brought into relationship with the existing international law on reparation and neither necessity nor the declaration of a state of emergency provides adequate solutions, normative standards for reparation in transitional justice should be sought through interpretation. That path runs the opposite risk than the one previously considered. Whereas necessity and the declaration of a state of emergency only allow binary solutions, too coarse for the intricacies of reparation in transitional justice, interpretation can easily lead to over-determination. Pellet cautioned against human-rightism and the related confusion of wishful thinking and legal standards.[1024] The chance of falling

1021 See above, ch. 1, A.II.

1022 Mégret, *Nature of Obligations*, in: Moeckli et al. (eds.), *International Human Rights Law*, 2nd Edition 2014, 96, 114.

1023 For a differentiated analysis of the effects on transitions in different states of the executive assuming emergency powers in response to the Covid-19 pandemic, Mollay et al., *Emergency Law Responses and Conflict-Affected States in Transition*, Verfassungsblog, 13 March 2021.

1024 Pellet, *"Human Rightism" and International Law - Gilberto Amado Memorial Lecture*, 2000, 4 f. For the use of the state of emergency in the colonial context see Reynolds, *Empire, Emergency and International Law*, 2017, esp. 111 ff.

prey to these fallacies is exceptionally high when interpreting a right that has received no authoritative written restatement. Yet, over-determination would be fatal to the present endeavor. As chapter two evinced, transitional justice situations vary widely on numerous levels. Reparation efforts are highly politically and culturally sensitive and contingent on an incalculable number of factors. It is for this reason that the present chapter is entitled normative framework. In complex transitional justice situations, the law can only play a limited role. It can establish a normative baseline, below which states must not fall. Fulfillment of this baseline does not guarantee a good reparation program. Effective reparation in transitional justice requires creativity, ingenuity, and context-sensitivity.[1025] Law cannot prescribe these virtues. It can provide a framework that is for the relevant actors to fill. If the law over determines their choices, it will inhibit instead of enabling the qualities needed to make reparation work effectively in a complex situation. To resist the urge of over-determination, the following chapter will first elaborate on how transitional justice affects the interpretation of the international law on reparation (B.). It will then attempt to adapt the international law on reparation so that it can provide normative guidance to different aspects of reparation programs (C.-H.). The process will be based on the normative standards established in chapter one. The empirical and theoretical findings of chapters two and three provide guide rails along which the adaptation proceeds.

B. Interpretation and Transitional Justice: Methodological Aspects

Adapting the international law on reparation to the transitional justice context does not require a transitional-justice-specific interpretation approach. Nevertheless, some thoughts on how interpretation can and should incorporate the unique features of transitional justice facilitate the endeavor and guard against over-determination.

First, the object of interpretation warrants clarification. As shown in chapter one, the right to reparation is treaty-based, customary international law, and a general principle of international law. To simplify, the following

1025 On the latter see as a particularly well-researched example among many, Fletcher et al., *Context, Timing and the Dynamics of Transitional Justice – A Historical Perspective*, 2009 Hum. Rts. Q. 31(1), 163, 208 f. See also AU, *Transitional Justice Policy*, 2019, para 35 ff.

normative framework will concentrate on the former two sources. General principles of international law rarely receive detailed treatment in international jurisprudence and scholarship, so that the rules pertaining to their interpretation are all but clear. Furthermore, their role in international law is to fill gaps and provide guidance for interpreting other sources, rather than being the focal point of analysis.[1026] As Lauterpacht put it: "the main function of 'general principles of law' has been that of a safety-valve to be kept in reserve rather than a source of law of frequent application."[1027]

The remaining two sources of the right to reparation – treaty law and customary international law – are, in essence, subject to the same rules of interpretation: Based on its text, the norm must be interpreted in light of its context, object, and purpose.[1028] Since the right to reparation has not received an authoritative written restatement, it is difficult to take its text as a basis for interpretation. Instead, formulations by different entities will substitute an official text. Since no single restatement is authoritative, the interpretation must rely on the restatements' common essence.[1029] There is no indication

1026 Bassiouni, *A Functional Approach to General Principles of International Law*, 1989 Michigan J. Intl. L. 11(3), 768, 775 ff., 791 ff.; Gaja, *General Principles of Law*, in: Wolfrum (ed.), *Max Planck Encyclopedia of International Law,* Online Edition 2013, para 21; ICJ, *Case Concerning the Right of Passage Over Indian Territory (Merits)*, I.C.J. Reports 1960, 6, 43.

1027 Lauterpacht, *The Development of International Law by the International Court*, 1958, 166.

1028 For treaty law see art. 31 VCLT. For customary international law see Bleckmann, *Zur Feststellung und Auslegung von Völkergewohnheitsrecht*, 1977 Heidelberg J. Intl. L. 37, 504, 525 ff.; Orakhelashvili, *The Interpretation of Acts and Rules in Public International Law*, 2008, 496 ff.; Ammann, *On the Interpretability of Customary International Law – A Response to Nina Mileva and Marina Fortuna,* OpinioJuris, 2019; ICJ, *Fisheries Case (United Kingdom v. Norway) - Seperate Opinion of Judge Hsu Mo*, I.C.J. Reports 1951, 42, 42 f.; ICJ, *North Sea Continental Shelf Case - Dissenting Opinion of Judge Tanaka*, I.C.J. Reports 1969, 172, 182; Merkouris, *Article 31(3)(c) VCLT and the Principle of Systemic Integration - Normative Shadows in Plato's Cave*, 2015, 264 ff.; Merkouris, *Interpreting the Customary Rules on Interpretation*, 2017 Intl. Commun. L. Rev. 19(1), 126, 139 ff. For the opposing position and rebuttals of their main arguments see 137 f. The ILC is at least open to deductive approaches to customary international law, ILC, *Commentary on the Identification of Customary International Law*, A/73/10, concl. 2, para 5.

1029 For that, these restatements need not necessarily have the same wording, Bleckmann, *Zur Feststellung und Auslegung von Völkergewohnheitsrecht*, 524 f., 526; Orakhelashvili, *The Interpretation of Acts and Rules in Public International Law*, 496 f.; Merkouris, *Article 31(3)(c) VCLT and the Principle of Systemic Integration*, 264 f. Similarly, Ammann, *On the Interpretability of Customary International*, OpinioJuris, 2019.

that the treaty-based and customary right to reparation differ decisively in scope.[1030] Consequently, this chapter will not distinguish between the two.

I. Object and Purpose: The Transformative Goal of Reparation

Interpretation must consider the object and purpose of a norm and the body of law it pertains to.[1031] This means of interpretation is closely connected to the principle of effectiveness, which favors an interpretation that effectively fulfills the object and purpose of a norm and its body of law.[1032] The principle plays a dominant role in the interpretation of human rights.[1033]

1030 This probably places the right to reparation into the category of multi-sourced equivalent norms (MENS). While experience with MENS shows that the norms are rarely fully congruent, the differences might not make much practical difference. In the following what has been termed a "cumulative approach" will be employed, treating the different norms as cumulatively applicable. For details see Broude/Shany, *The International Law and Policy of Multi-Sourced Equivalent Norms*, in: Broude/Shany (eds.), *Multi-Sourced Equivalent Norms in International Law*, 2011, 1, 8 f., 13 f. ; Michaels/Pauwelyn, *Conflict of Norms or Conflict of Laws - Different Techniques in the Fragmentation of Public International Law*, 2011 Duke J. Comp. & Intl. L. 22(3), 349, 372 ff.

1031 Art 31(1) VCLT; Dörr, *Article 31 - General Rule of Interpretation*, in: Dörr/Schmalenbach (eds.), *Vienna Convention on the Law of Treaties - A Commentary*, 2nd Edition 2018, 559, para 53; Gardiner, *Treaty Interpretation*, 2nd Edition 2015, 220 f.; Bleckmann, *Zur Feststellung und Auslegung von Völkergewohnheitsrecht*, 528; Orakhelashvili, *The Interpretation of Acts and Rules in Public International Law*, 498 f.; Merkouris, *Article 31(3)(c) VCLT and the Principle of Systemic Integration*, 264 ff.; ICJ, *North Sea Continental Shelf Case - Dissenting Opinion of Judge Tanaka*, 181.

1032 Fitzmaurice, *Law and Procedure of the International Court of Justice - Treaty Interpretation and Certain Other Treaty Points*, 1951 Brit. Y.B. Intl. L. 28, 18 f.; Gardiner, *Treaty Interpretation*, 221 f.; Dörr, *Art. 31*, para 52; PCIJ, *The Mavrommatis Palestine Concessions Case (Greece v. The United Kingdom)*, P.C.I.J. (ser. B) No. 3, 1924, 7, 34; ICJ, *Corfu Channel*, 24.

1033 ILC, *Report on Fragmentation of International Law*, A/CN.4/L.682, para 428; ECtHR, *Stoll v. Switzerland*, 69698/01 (GC), 2007, para 128; IACtHR, *Advisory Opnion on the Right to Information on Consular Assistance in the Framework of the Guarantees of the Due Process of Law*, OC-16/99, 1999, para 58; Rietiker, *The Principle of "Effectiveness" in the Recent Jurisprudence of the European Court of Human Rights - Its Different Dimensions and its Consistency With Public International Law: No Need for the Concept of Treaty Sui Generis*, 2010 Nordic J. Hum. Rts. 79(2), 245, 255 ff.; Jayawickrama, *The Judicial Application of Human Rights Law*, 2nd Edition 2017, 161.

Primarily, the right to reparation aims to provide corrective justice, that is, to erase the harm the survivor suffered as far as possible.[1034] In that context, the principle of effectiveness invites a pragmatic approach to interpretation, allowing the delivery of meaningful reparation in the demanding transitional justice environment.[1035] Chapter three evinced that reparation in transitional justice also serves transitional justice's transformative aim. Hence, strengthening respect for human rights and generalized trust must be considered a further object and purpose of reparation in transitional justice. As shown above, interpretation must seek to optimize the realization of both goals as far as possible.[1036]

II. Normative Environment

Transitional justice reparation programs have more notable effects on other rights and interests than individual reparation awards. Partially, this is intended in light of reparation programs' transformative aim. Other effects are simply a result of the programs' much larger scale. Whatever the reason, one must consider the effects of an interpretation of the international law on reparation on other rights and interests – which in sum can be termed the normative environment of the international law on reparation.[1037]

1. Systemic Integration

The principle of systemic integration encapsulates consideration of a norm's environment. It demands that the interpreter considers how the interpreta-

1034 Commonly accepted secondary purposes of reparation are also the condemnation of the violation, retribution and deterrence Shelton, *Remedies in International Human Rights Law*, 19 ff.

1035 Similarly, IAComHR, *Compendium*, OEA/Ser.L/V/II.Doc. 121, para 169.

1036 See above, ch. 3, B.II.

1037 Fitzmaurice, *Law and Procedure of the ICJ*, 18; Fitzmaurice, *The Law and Procedure of the International Court of Justice 1951-4 - Treaty Interpretation and Other Treaty Points*, 1957 Brit. Y.B. Intl. L. 33, 203, 220; ILC, *Report on Fragmentation of International Law*, A/CN.4/L.682, para 413; McLachlan, *The Principle of Systemic Integration and Article 31(3)(C) of the Vienna Convention*, 2005 Intl. Comp. L. Q. 54(2), 279; Pauwelyn, *Conflict of Norms in Public International Law*, 247, 253 f.; Merkouris, *Article 31(3)(c) VCLT and the Principle of Systemic Integration*, 266 f.

tion of one norm affects the operation of other norms.[1038] The principle is embodied both in Art. 31(1) VCLT, speaking of the context of a norm, and Art. 31(1)(c) VCLT, referring to norms outside of the treaty under consideration. It plays a prominent role in human rights interpretation.[1039] Behind the principle of systemic integration lies the basic assumption that international law forms a system in which normative conflict should be avoided.[1040] Therefore, separate provisions should be treated as "aspects of an overall aggregate of the rights and obligations of states."[1041] Since this requires establishing a shared systemic objective behind a set of rules and prioritizing concerns in that light, systemic integration is bound up closely with teleological interpretation.[1042]

2. Resolving Normative Conflict

Considering the context of a human rights norm often gives rise to the problem of normative conflict. Narrowly defined, conflict means incompatibility: following one norm necessarily leads to a breach of another norm.[1043] Such situations call for conflict resolution rules, which prioritize one norm over the other, such as rules of hierarchy, lex posterior, lex specialis, etc.[1044] In most circumstances, such rules do not apply to competing human rights. While several propositions for a hierarchy between human rights exist, the predominant approach upholds their indivisibility and consequently rejects any notion of hierarchy.[1045] The ius cogens nature of some human rights

1038 ICJ, *Dispute Regarding Navigational and Relational Rights (Costa Rica v. Nicaragua)*, I.C.J. Reports 2009, 213, para 77 ff.; ECtHR, *Klass and Others v. Germany*, 5029/71 (Plenary), 1978, para 68.

1039 Corten, *The Vienna Conventions on the Law of Treaties - Vol. I*, 2011, art. 31 para 41; ECtHR, *Saadi v. The United Kingdom*, 13229/03 (GC), 2008, para 62.

1040 Corten, *VCLT - Vol. I*, art. 31 para 41; McLachlan, *The Principle of Systemic Integration*, 318; ECtHR, *Saadi v. The United Kingdom*, 13229/03, para 62.

1041 ILC, *Report of the International Law Commissions - Fifty-Seventh Session (2 May - 3 June and 11 July - 5 August 2005)*, A/60/10, 2005, para 467.

1042 ILC, *Report on Fragmentation of International Law*, A/CN.4/L.682, para 412, 419.

1043 ILC, *Report on Fragmentation of International Law*, A/CN.4/L.682, para 24; Pauwelyn, *Conflict of Norms in Public International Law*, 175 f. The author also gives an overview over other definitions, 166 ff.

1044 ILC, *Report on Fragmentation of International Law*, A/CN.4/L.682, para 412; Milanovic, *Norm Conflict in International Law - Whither Human Rights*, 2009 Duke J. Comp. Intl. L. 20(1), 69, 73.

1045 de Schutter/Tulkens, *Rights in Conflict - The European Court of Human Rights as a Pragmatic Institution*, in: Brems (ed.), *Conflicts Between Fundamental Rights*, 2008,

provides the only generally accepted exception to that stance. Since the boundaries of that category are intensely disputed, it has not had much practical effect.[1046] The right to reparation does not have ius cogens status. Even if it redeems the violation of a primary ius cogens norm, that primary norm's status does not extend to the secondary norm. Given that the right to reparation has its independent basis in the right to an effective remedy, the violation that gave rise to it is not its source but rather a condition of applicability.[1047] Put differently, if the right to reparation arises from the violation of a ius cogens obligation, it does not share its ius cogens status.[1048] Solving normative conflict between the right to reparation and other human rights based on an a priori hierarchy will thus rarely be possible. Lex specialis or lex posterior rules are of limited help, too, as different human rights are

169, 179 ff.; Cariolou, *The Search for an Equilibrium by the European Court of Human Rights*, in: Brems (ed.), *Conflicts Between Fundamental Rights*, 2008, 249, 259 ff.; Donnelly/Whelan, *International Human Rights*, 5th Edition 2018, 68 ff.; de Schutter, *International Human Rights Law - Cases, Materials, Commentary*, 2010, 446 f.; Meron, *On a Hierarchy of International Human Rights*, 1986 Am. J. Intl. L. 80(1), 1; Koji, *Emerging Hierarchy in International Human Rights and Beyond - From the Perspective of Non-Derogable Rights*, 2001 Eur. J. Intl. L. 12(5), 917; ICC, *The Prosecutor v. Thomas Lubanga Dyilo, Judgment on the Appeals Against Trial Chamber II's 'Decision Setting the Size of the Reparations Award for Which Thomas Lubanga Dyilo is Liable - Separate Opinion of Judge Luz del Carmen Ibáñez Carranza*, ICC-01/04-01/06-3466-AnxII (AC), 2019, para 71 ff.; van Boven, *Categories of Rights*, in: Moeckli et al. (eds.), *International Human Rights Law*, 2nd Edition 2014, 143, 147 ff. While van Boven stipulates a hierarchy in the sense that some human rights are "more fundamental or basic", it is doubtful that that leads him to a lexical priority of those rights over others in all circumstances. Further problems with the notion of hierarchy are summarized by Arosemena, *Conflicts of Rights in International Human Rights - A Meta-Rule Analysis*, 2013 Global Constitutionalism 2(1), 6, 15 ff., 31 f.

1046 Bianchi, *Human Rights and the Magic of Jus Cogens*, 2008 Eur. J. Intl. L. 19(3), 491, 499 ff.; Meron, *On a Hierarchy of International Human Rights*, 14 ff.; de Schutter, *International Human Rights Law*, 64 ff.; de Wet, *Jus Cogens and Obligations Erga Omnes*, in: Shelton (ed.), *The Oxford Handbook of International Human Rights Law*, 2013, 541; Shelton, *Normative Hierarchy in International Law*, 2006 Am. J. Intl. L. 100(2), 291, 279 ff.; Milanovic, *Norm Conflict in International Law*, 71 f.

1047 Even if that were otherwise, Waldron convincingly argued that different obligations flowing from the same right can have different statuses, Waldron, *Rights in Conflict*, 1989 Ethics 99(3), 503, 515. On the relationship between the rights to a reparation and the right to an effective remedy see above, ch. 1, A.I.

1048 ILC, *ASR Commentaries*, A/56/10, art. 55 para 2. To the knowledge of the author, there is no international practice suggesting that the right to reparation is of a ius cogens nature, if the primary obligation violated is of ius cogens nature.

complementary rather than in a specialty relationship, and later created rights were not intended to abrogate earlier rights.[1049]

Instead, as in general international law, genuine normative conflicts should be avoided as far as possible through harmonizing interpretation.[1050] Then, not incompatibility, but a conflict of norms in a broader sense exists. Different norms might frustrate each other's objectives because they apply to the same situation but pursue different aims. Such is often the case when the law on immunity and human rights law apply to the same situation.[1051] In human rights law, such conflicts in the broader sense are resolved on two levels. First, the scope of protection a right offers is interpreted in a way to avoid normative conflict.[1052] This technique can only be examined in light of concrete situations. It will therefore receive further treatment below, where pertinent. Second, normative conflict is resolved by way of restricting a right for a legitimate aim.

a. Limiting the Right to Reparation

This technique is without problems for so-called two-stage rights, which expressly lay down conditions under which they can be limited.[1053] Neither the right to reparation nor the right to an effective remedy does the interpreter this favor. Still, the right to reparation can be restricted. The ACHR and

1049 For the role of party intent in the application of the lex posterior maxim see, ILC, *Report on Fragmentation of International Law*, A/CN.4/L.682, para 229 f., 243, 272. For the special difficulties in norm regimes erected by successive multilateral treaties, para 235.

1050 ILC, *Report on Fragmentation of International Law*, A/CN.4/L.682, para 37 ff.; Pauwelyn, *Conflict of Norms in Public International Law*, 240 f.; Milanovic, *Norm Conflict in International Law*, 73; ECtHR, *N.D. and N.T. v. Spain*, 8675/15 (Grand Chamber), 2020, para 172.

1051 ILC, *Report on Fragmentation of International Law*, A/CN.4/L.682, para 24 f.

1052 This technique is used especially for rights considered "absolute", that is, not subject to restrictions, Sottiaux, *Terrorism and the Limitation of Rights - The ECHR and the US Constitution*, 2008, 40 f., 47 f.; Battjes, *In Search of a Fair Balance - The Absolute Character of the Prohibition of Refoulement Under Article 3 ECHR Reassessed*, 2009 Leiden J. Intl. L. 22(3), 583, 595 ff., 614 ff., 620 f.; Addo/Grief, *Does Article 3 of the European Convention on Human Rights Enshrine Absolute Rights?*, 1998 Eur. J. Intl. L. 9(3), 510, 522 f.; van der Schyff, *Cutting to the Core of Conflicting Rights - The Question of Inalienable Cores in Comparative Perspective*, in: Brems (ed.), *Conflicts Between Fundamental Rights*, 2008, 131, 139.

1053 van der Schyff, *Cutting to the Core of Conflicting Rights*, 139 ff.

the African Convention on Human and Peoples' Rights (ACHPR) contain general limitation clauses applicable to all rights.[1054] While the ECHR and the ICCPR lack such a clause, the ECtHR and the HRC held that the right to an effective remedy is subject to implied limitations.[1055] By extension, these should apply to the right to reparation as part of the right to an effective remedy.[1056] The opposite view would be implausible. Disallowing restrictions means that the respective right cannot be lawfully interfered with.[1057] It trumps other rights in case of conflict. Only the most fundamental human rights, such as the prohibition of torture, are firmly placed in that category of absolute rights.[1058] The right to reparation does not protect equally important values, which would justify putting it above all other possible interests. Accordingly, it can be derogated from in situations of emergency.[1059] Other indicators of absolute rights – such as a rigorous duty to investigate – are absent in the case of the right to reparation.[1060] Considering that

1054 Art. 32(2) ACHR contains a general clause according to which "[t]he rights of each person are limited by the rights of others, by the security of all, and by the just demands of the general welfare, in a democratic society." This provision is applicable especially to rights, whose legitimate restrictions are not specified, IACtHR, *Advisory Opinion on the Compulsory Membership in an Association Prescribed by Law for the Practice of Journalism*, OC-5/85, 1985, para 65. Similarly, ch. II of the ACHPR contains duties, which serve as a limitation of every right. Esp. art. 27(2) ACHR demands that "[t]he rights and freedoms of each individual shall be exercised with due regard to the rights of others, collective security, morality and common interest."

1055 ECtHR, *Kudla v. Poland*, 30210/96 (Grand Chamber), 2000, para 151 f.; HRCom, *Sechremelis et al v. Greece*, CCPR/C/100/D/1507/2006/Rev.1, 1507/2006, 2011, para 10.4 f.

1056 The ECtHR held that implied limitations are especially pertinent, if the right is not mentioned expressly in the convention, ECtHR, *Golder v. The United Kingdom*, 4451/70 (Plenary), 1975, para 38.

1057 Gewirth, *Are There any Absolute Rights?*, 1981 Phil. Q. 31(122), 1, 2; Addo/Grief, *Does Article 3 ECHR Enshrine Absolute Rights?*, 516.

1058 Even the few rights considered absolute are interpreted in a way that they can accommodate proportionate restrictions with a view to other competing rights and interests, Sottiaux, *Terrorism and the Limitation of Rights* 40 f., 47 f.; Battjes, *In Search of a Fair Balance*, 595 ff., 614 ff., 620 f.; Addo/Grief, *Does Article 3 ECHR Enshrine Absolute Rights?*, 516, 522 f.; van der Schyff, *Cutting to the Core of Conflicting Rights*, 139.

1059 It still holds true as argued above, A.II., that such a derogation will rarely be necessary. For non-derogability being a necessary condition to consider a right absolute, Mavronicola, *What is an 'Absolute Right'? Deciphering Absoluteness in the Context of Article 3 of the European Convention on Human Rights*, 2012 Hum. Rts. L. Rev. 12(4), 723, 729 ff.

1060 cf. Addo/Grief, *Does Article 3 ECHR Enshrine Absolute Rights?*, 516.

reparation does not protect paramount values but can touch other vital interests, allowing to limit reparation better serves the effective protection of all human rights.[1061]

Human rights bodies unanimously hold that where restrictions are allowed, they must pursue a legitimate aim, be necessary and proportionate.[1062] A restriction is necessary if no other equally effective means to reach the legitimate aim exists.[1063] It is proportionate if a fair balance between the opposing rights and interests is struck.[1064]

For the most part, the necessity requirement can be judged only in light of concrete situations and possible alternative courses of action. It will thus be discussed below in relation to concrete problems. It has one crucial general consequence, though. States cannot simply assume the existence of a conflict. Before sacrificing part of the protection a right offers for the sake of other legitimate aims, the state must evaluate whether the conflict can be avoided.

1061 Rombouts et al., *The Right to Reparation for Victims of Gross and Systematic Violations of Human Rights*, in: de Feyter et al. (eds.), *Out of the Ashes - Reparation for Victims of Gross and Systematic Human Rights Violations*, 2005, 345, 452 f.

1062 ECtHR, *Ashingdane v. The United Kingdom*, 8225/78 (Chamber), 1985, para 57; ECtHR, *A. v. The United Kingdom*, 35373/97 (Second Section), 2002, para 74 ff.; HRCom, *GC 31*, CCPR/C/21/Rev.1/Add.13, para 6; IACtHR, *Kimel v Argentina (Merits, Reparations and Costs)*, 2008, para 54, 81; IACtHR, *Claude-Reyes et al. v. Chile (Merits, Reparations and Costs)*, 2006, para 90 ff.; IACtHR, *Advisory Opinion OC-5/85*, OC-5/85, para 46, 67; AComHPR, *Centre for Minority Rights Development (Kenya) and Minority Rights Group International on Behalf of Endorois Welfare Council v. Kenya*, 276/2003, 2010, para 214; AComHPR, *Sudan Human Rights Organisation & Centre on Housing Rights and Evictions (COHRE) v. Sudan*, 279/03-296/05, 2009, para 188; Ducoulombier, *Conflicts Between Fundamental Rights and the European Court of Human Rights - An Overview*, in: Brems (ed.), *Conflicts Between Fundamental Rights*, 2008, 217, 228; Khosla, *Proportionality - An Assault on Human Rights? A Reply*, 2010 Intl. J. Const. L. 8(2), 298, 299 f.; Mac-Gregor/Möller, *Artículo 32*, in: Steiner/Uribe (eds.), *Convención Americana Sobre Derechos Humanos - Comentario*, 2014, 722, 732 f.

1063 IACtHR, *Chaparro Álvarez and Lapo Íñiguez v. Ecuador*, 2007, para 93; HRCom, *General Comment No. 34 - Article 19: Freedoms of Opinion and Expression*, CCPR/C/GC/34, 2011, para 34; HRCom, *General Comment No. 27 - Article 12 (Freedom of Movement)*, CCPR/C/21/Rev.1/Add.9, 1999, para 14; CESCR, *General Comment No. 14 - The Right to the Highest Attainable Standard of Health*, E/C.12/2000/4, 2000, para 29; AComHPR, *Zimbabwe Lawyers for Human Rights v. Zimbabwe*, 294/04, 2009, para 176; Gerards, *How to Improve the Necessity Test of the European Court of Human Rights*, 2013 Intl. J. Const. L. 11(2), 466, 481 ff.

1064 IACtHR, *Kimel v Argentina (Merits, Reparations and Costs)*, para 54, 84; ECtHR, *Jahn and Others v. Germany*, 46720/99 (Grand Chamber), 2005, para 93; Ducoulombier, *Conflicts Between Fundamental Rights*, 228 f.; Khosla, *Proportionality*, 299 f.

If the state can dissolve the conflict by changing background circumstances, infringing one right to safeguard another is unnecessary.[1065]

b. The Role of Balancing

The balancing exercise that determines the proportionality of a restriction is the core of resolving normative conflicts in human rights law. It also is subject to intense criticism. The most pertinent one is that balancing is little more than a metaphor, whose lack of guiding principles opens the door for judicial arbitrariness.[1066] In the search for a remedy to that problem, scholars have resorted to practical concordance doctrine, stemming originally from German constitutional law.[1067] While it has not found explicit application in international human rights jurisprudence, some judges of international tribunals at least allude to the idea in their writings and individual opinions.[1068] The author chooses to rely on it because it is a highly compelling method.[1069] It introduces principles, which concretize the unqualified balancing metaphor to the degree that it becomes more than an opening for arbitrary, subjective standards. It also operationalizes the idea that no hierarchy between rights exists and all merit as full a protection as possible.[1070]

1065 de Schutter/Tulkens, *Rights in Conflict*, 206 ff.

1066 de Schutter/Tulkens, *Rights in Conflict*, 191 f., 197; Cariolou, *The Search for an Equilibrium by the ECtHR*, 266 f.; Arosemena, *Conflicts of Rights in International Human Rights*, 19 f., 32 f.; Habermas, *Between Facts and Norms - Contributions to a Discourse Theory of Law and Democracy*, 1997, 253 ff., specifically 259 stating that "because there are no rational standards for [bringing values into a transitive order], weighing takes place either arbitrarily or unreflectively, according to customary standards and hierarchies."

1067 Hailbronner/Martini, *The German Federal Constitutional Court*, in: Jakab et al. (eds.), *Comparative Constitutional Reasoning*, 2017, 356, 373.

1068 ECtHR, *Fretté v. France - Joint Partly Dissenting Opinion of Judge Sir Nicolas Bratza and Judges Fuhrmann and Tulkens*, 36515/97, 2002; de Schutter/Tulkens, *Rights in Conflict*, 203.

1069 Admittedly, that the author received a German legal education might explain just as well as the actual merits of the theory why he thinks of practical concordance as a compelling method. However, the former is a scientifically much more dubious reason to choose a theory and, hence, acknowledged but banished to the footnotes.

1070 Brems, *Conflicting Human Rights: An Exploration in the Context of the Right to a Fair Trial in the European Convention for the Protection of Human Rights and Fundamental Freedoms*, 2005 Hum. Rts. Q. 27(1), 294, 303.

Practical concordance requires striking a balance between competing rights and/or interests, giving maximal effect to them all.[1071] Alexy developed one of the most elaborate operationalizations of that idea. According to him, balancing is a three-step procedure. When right A is restricted to safeguard another right B, one must first establish the detriment caused to a right A – that is, the *interference* with right A. Interference can result from a limited fulfillment of a right's positive dimension (non-satisfaction) or a failure to respect its negative dimension. Second, one must establish the *importance* of the competing right B – the degree of interference if, hypothetically, right A would not be interfered with. In the third step, one must weigh the importance of right B against the interference with right A.[1072] Alexy enables this last step with his "Weight Formula". It determines each competing right's weight with three factors: Each right's abstract weight, concrete importance[1073], and the probability with which the interference materializes.

Although human rights are indivisible and non-hierarchical, different rights have different abstract weights, determined by the values they protect and their overall importance for the human rights system.[1074] In case the competing rights have the same abstract weight, the factor becomes

1071 Marauhn/Ruppel, *Balancing Conflicting Human Rights - Konrad Hesse's Notion of "Praktische Konkordanz" and the German Federal Constitutional Court*, in: Brems (ed.), *Conflicts Between Fundamental Rights,* 2008, 273, 179 ff.; de Schutter/Tulkens, *Rights in Conflict*, 203 ff.; Arosemena, *Conflicts of Rights in International Human Rights*, 20 ff.; For an overview of similar "maximization accounts of balancing" and the most relevant critique see Urbina, *A Critique of Proportionality and Balancing*, 2017, ch. 2-3. For a similar theoretical issue see above ch. 3, B.II.

1072 Alexy, *On Balancing and Subsumption - A Structural Comparison*, 2003 Ratio Juris 16(4), 433, 436 f.

1073 Alexy uses the terms "degrees of interference" for right A and "concrete importance" for right B. For reasons of simplicity, both will be referred to as "concrete importance" in the following.

1074 cf. Alexy, *On Balancing and Subsumption*, 440. See for example the right to life, which the AComHPR describes as "the fulcrum of all other rights" and "foundational", AComHPR, *General Comment No. 3 on the African Charter on Human and Peoples' Rights - The Right to Life (Article 4)*, 2015, para 1, 5. The IACtHR emphasizes "the fundamental role the Convention assigns to this right", IACtHR, *Case of the Sawhoyamaxa Indigenous Community v. Paraguay*, 2006, para 151. The ECtHR ranks the right to life "as one of the most fundamental provisions in the Convention", ECtHR, *McCann and Others v. United Kingdom*, 18984/91, 1995, para 147; ECtHR, *Giuliani and Gaggio v. Italy*, 23458/02, 2011, para 174 ff.; ECtHR, *Karatas v. Turkey - Joint Partly Dissenting Opinion of Judges Wildhaber, Pastor Ridruejo, Costa and Baka*, 23168/94, 1999.

irrelevant.[1075] As a secondary right, the right to reparation will not have the same abstract weight as absolute rights, e.g., the right to be free from torture. It also has less abstract weight than rights protecting fundamental individual positions, such as the right to life. The right to reparation's abstract weight is probably similar to other secondary rights, such as prosecution and investigation. [1076]

The concrete importance of the rights in conflict depends on the degree of interference. Since right B is not actually interfered with, its concrete importance is determined by considering the degree of interference if, hypothetically, right A would not be interfered with.[1077]

Lastly, determining the concrete importance of both rights rests on assumptions because it relies on hypothetical scenarios of interference and non-interference. Hence, the probability with which these scenarios materialize must be considered. The less likely a scenario of interference is, the lower is the weight attached to it in the balancing exercise. [1078]

From these three factors on each side of the equation arises the Weight Formula:

$$WA, B = \frac{IA \times WA \times RA}{IB \times WB \times RB}$$

Where I_A is the abstract weight of right A, I_B the abstract weight of right B, $W_{A,}$ and W_B the concrete importance of right A and B respectively, and R_A and R_B the probability with which the interferences with both rights materialize. The result, $W_{A, B}$, is the concrete weight of right A under the circumstances of the case under consideration.[1079]

1075 Alexy, *On Balancing and Subsumption*, 440. Assigning abstract weights to rights does not create a hierarchy understood as a lexical order of rights, one taking precedence over the other. The abstract weight of a right stems from positions it protects, which can be weightier or less weighty. Its high abstract weight is a factor to be taken into account when assessing the situation at hand. The concrete importance and the probability assessment can still tilt the scales in favor of the right with less abstract weight.

1076 Even though these might stem from fundamental or absolute rights, Waldron showed that different obligations arising from the same right need not have the same abstract weight, Waldron, *Rights in Conflict*, 515.

1077 Alexy, *On Balancing and Subsumption*, 441.

1078 Alexy, *On Balancing and Subsumption*, 446 f.

1079 Alexy, *On Balancing and Subsumption*, 440 ff., 446.

To enable the insertion of values into the formula, Alexy introduces a triadic scale. A cardinal scale cannot be employed since interferences with rights rarely lend themselves to concrete quantification. Instead, Alexy proposes an ordinal scale with three values: l, m, and s.[1080] It is possible to determine whether any given interference is light (l), moderate (m), or serious (s), whether the abstract weight is light (l), medium (m), or strong (s), and whether the probability of the scenarios is low (l), medium (m), or strong (s). Numbers can represent l, m, and s, e.g., 1, 2, and 4 for abstract weight and concrete importance and 1, ½, and ¼ for reliability. If the subsequent calculation results in a value higher than 1, balancing weights in favor of right A. If it is below 1, B comes out on top.[1081] Suppose a state forbids a newspaper to publish the name of an undercover agent in a prominent criminal case because there is a slim chance that the suspects might kill the agent.[1082] Here, the right to freedom of the press conflicts with the right to life. The abstract weight of the right to life is high, whereas the freedom of the right to press shall be defined to be of a medium weight.[1083] The concrete importance of the right to life is again high because the purported interference would result in its complete negation, death. It will be assumed that freedom of the press enjoys high concrete importance. The criminal case might be of public interest, and the undercover agent's name relevant because of their known unreliability.[1084] The weight formula for this case would yield the following result, with the upper part of the formula representing the agent's right to life and the lower part of the formula representing the freedom of the press:

$$0{,}5 = \frac{4 \times 4 \times 1/4}{2 \times 4 \times 1}$$

1080 On the differences and usages of cardinal and ordinal scales see Peterson, *An Introduction to Decision Theory*, 2nd Edition 2017, 24 ff., 297 ff. On the impossibility of a cardinal scale in the present context see Alexy, *Die Gewichtsformel*, in: Jickeli et al. (eds.), *Gedächtnisschrift für Jürgen Sonnenschein,* 2003, 771, 783.

1081 Alexy, *On Balancing and Subsumption*, 440 ff., 444 ff. A slightly finer scale – e.g. a six-step or nine-step model – could also be used. Beyond that, classification becomes increasingly difficult, 440, 443 f.

1082 To keep the example simple, it is assumed that the unlikeliness of the agent being killed is established. Also, only the detriment to the right to life will be considered, not any state interests in continuing the investigation. One could assume, e.g. that the agent already secured all the evidence needed.

1083 This abstract weight is of course debatable. It is assumed here for the sake of argument.

1084 Naturally, a real assessment of the right's concrete importance would need to rely on much more information.

Thus, even though the right to life has a higher abstract weight than freedom of the press (4 vs. 2) and the concrete importance of the two cancel each other out (4 vs. 4), freedom of the press prevails because of its certain infringement in contrast to the agent's unlikely death (1 vs. 1/4). An outcome below 1 (0,5) reflects that result.

c. Inviolable Cores?

The Weight Formula also allows addressing the notion of inviolable cores of human rights. Such a core is sometimes said not to be subject to balancing.[1085] Yet, what constitutes the core of a right must be assessed in relation to the right's context. Law cannot demand the impossible from the state. Abstractly defining impenetrable boundaries risks being deaf to exceptional circumstances.[1086] Also, since human rights operate in a system, it risks elevating a right's core above all other interests, which in the situation at hand might be weightier. For that reason, a right's inviolable core is better conceived of as the product of a balancing exercise than a limit on it. Interference with a core of a right should be conceived as very strong, giving the right in question a very high concrete importance – up until the point at which it is almost impossible to justify the interference under normal circumstances.[1087]

d. Summary

In sum, normative conflicts between human rights and between human rights and state interests can be resolved by interpreting their scope with regard to potentially conflicting norms and restricting them. Restrictions must pursue

1085 ECtHR, *Ashingdane v. The United Kingdom*, 8225/78, para 57; *The Siracusa Principles on the Limitation and Derogation Provisions in the International Covenant on Civil and Political Rights*, 1985 Hum. Rts. Q. 7(1), 3, 4, principle I.A.2.

1086 See below for examples, E.II.4.c.bb.

1087 van der Schyff, *Cutting to the Core of Conflicting Rights*, 133 ff.; Klatt/Meister, *Proportionality - A Benefit to Human Rights? Remarks on the I·CON Controversy*, 2012 Intl. J. Const. L. 10(3), 687, 691 f.; Brems, *Conflicting Human Rights*, 303 f.; Alexy, *Constitutional Rights, Balancing, and Rationality*, 2003 Ratio Juris 16(2), 131, 139 f.; An application of this principle can be seen in ECtHR, *A. v. The United Kingdom*, 35373/97, para 78.

a legitimate aim, be necessary and – most importantly – strike a fair balance between all rights and interests involved. While the last step is criticized as arbitrary, it remains the approach taken by human rights practice.[1088] The practical concordance doctrine, operationalized by Alexy's Weight Formula, can somewhat mitigate the arbitrariness of balancing. What factors into the balancing exercise can only be determined concerning concrete situations.[1089] Therefore, the technique will be concretized below in relation to concrete challenges of reparation programs.

III. Discretion and Deference

A last methodological point pertains to the law's limits in the complex transitional situation. Reparation in transitional justice operates in highly complex, politically sensitive environments. Implementing the right to reparation is contingent on many factors, including the history, culture, norms, practices, and traditions at play. It is therefore commonplace to demand that reparation be context-sensitive. Much speaks to the fact that otherwise, it will lose its effectiveness.[1090] As argued before, a normative framework for reparation in transitional justice must therefore leave states enough flexibility to tailor reparation to the situation at hand.[1091] This flexibility is not alien to international human rights law. Arguably, it constitutes a "structural principle" of the field.[1092] The convoluted discussion unfolding around keywords such as subsidiarity, deference, discretion, the margin of

1088 ECtHR, *Hatton and Others v. The United Kingdom*, 36022/97 (Grand Chamber), 2003, para 98, 125; IACtHR, *Fontevecchia y D'Amico v. Argentina*, 2011, para 50; HRCom, *Siobhán Whelan v. Ireland*, CCPR/C/119/D/2425/2014, 2425/2014, 2017, para 7.9; AComHPR, *Zimbabwe Lawyers for Human Rights & Associated Newspapers of Zimbabwe v. Republic of Zimbabwe*, 284/03, 2003, para 176.

1089 Some relevant factors are listed e.g. by Brems, *Conflicting Human Rights*, 303 ff.

1090 UN Secretary General, *The Rule of Law and Transitional Justice*, S/2004/616, 1; Duthie, *Introduction*, 29; Waldorf, *Institutional Gardening in Unsettled Times - Transitional Justice and Institutional Contexts*, in: Duthie/Seils (eds.), *Justice Mosaics - How Context Shapes Transitional Justice in Fractured Societies*, 2017, 40, 61; Vinjamuri/Snyder, *Law and Politics in Transitional Justice*, 2015 Ann. Rev. Pol. Sci. 18, 303, 320; Fletcher et al., *Context, Timing and the Dynamics of Transitional Justice*, 208 f.

1091 Kress/Grover, *International Criminal Law Restraints in Peace Talks to End Armed Conflicts of a Non-International Character*, in: Bergsmo/Kalmanovitz (eds.), *Law in Peace Negotiations*, 2009, 29, 32.

1092 Carozza, *Subsidiarity as a Structural Principle of International Human Rights Law*, 2003 Am. J. Intl. L. 97(1), 38, 56 ff.

appreciation, and many others is far outside the present study's scope. A few clarifying remarks without any claim to comprehensiveness shall still serve to sustain attention to the issue.

To a degree, there is inherent flexibility to the implementation of human rights. Human rights are abstract principles, which rarely regulate any specific situation in detail. They must be specified to apply to concrete situations. This automatically gives the actor implementing human rights – usually states – some flexibility. There are usually several equivalent options for specification – or at least options about whose equivalency there can be reasonable disagreement.[1093] The right to reparation is no exception to that rule. Its basic premise of full reparation and the different forms of reparation remain abstract and must be specified to the situation at hand.[1094] This form of flexibility is necessary and therefore uncontroversial. It can be advantageous for human rights protection because it allows human rights to cover and be effective under wildly different circumstances.[1095]

A different question is the level of scrutiny international institutions should employ when reviewing how states used their inherent discretion in implementing human rights. International jurisprudence differs whether and to what degree it should defer to states' choices in implementing human rights. While deference plays a vital role in the ECtHR's jurisprudence[1096], other international bodies are less enthusiastic about the idea. Some only hesitantly grant a margin of appreciation. Others reject it.[1097] This heterogeneity also

---

1093 Besson, *Subsidiarity in International Human Rights Law - What is Subsidiary About Human Rights?*, 2016 Am. J. Juris. 61(1), 69, 84; Etinson, *Human Rights, Claimability and the Uses of Abstraction*, 2013 Utilitas 25(4), 463, 480, 485 ff.; Letsas, *The Margin of Appreciation Revisited - A Response to Follesdal*, in: Etinson (ed.), *Human Rights - Moral or Political?*, 2018, 294, 296 ff.; Follesdal, *Appreciating the Margin of Appreciation*, in: Etinson (ed.), *Human Rights - Moral or Political?*, 2018, 269, 277 f.; Çalı, *Specialized Rules of Treaty Interpretation - Human Rights*, in: Hollis (ed.), *The Oxford Guide to Treaties*, 2012, 525, 531.

1094 Rombouts et al., *The Right to Reparation for Victims of Gross and Systematic Violations of Human Rights*, 451 f., 455.

1095 Etinson, *Human Rights, Claimability and the Uses of Abstraction*, 485 ff.

1096 Spielmann, *Allowing the Right Margin - The European Court of Human Rights and The National Margin of Appreciation Doctrine: Waiver or Subsidiarity of European Review?*, 2017 Cambridge Y.B. Eur. L. Stud. 14, 381, 386 ff. For an analysis on colonial aspects of the doctrine in its connections to the state of emergency see Reynolds, *Empire, Emergency and International Law*, 170.

1097 The doctrine was used e.g. bei the IACtHR, the AComHPR and the CESCR, Contreras, *National Discretion and International Deference in the Restriction of Human Rights - A Comparison Between the Jurisprudence of the European and the Inter-*

extends to the deference paid to states in the choice between remedial measures.[1098] There is some evidence that international bodies pay greater deference to states' choices in the implementation of reparation for systematic human rights violations.[1099] Much speaks in favor of that approach. The right to reparation is an obligation of result. That states achieve the demanded result is more important than the way they achieve it. The right itself remains abstract and, therefore, often provides little guidance for states in concrete situations. To then subject their actions to close scrutiny would place a heavy burden on them. This holds especially true in transitional contexts, which require complicated choices contingent on many political, societal, economic, and other factors. States are often in a better position to assess and evaluate these factors than supervisory bodies.[1100] As will be further elaborated below, international or national supervisory bodies might not even have the epistemic abilities to assess a state's choice fully.[1101]

Thus, there are good arguments for paying deference to states' decisions regarding transitional justice reparation programs. International standards for domestic reparation programs in transitional justice should consequently not over-determine states' obligations to truly leave them the flexibility needed to devise context-specific and therefore effective reparation measures.

American Court of Human Rights, 2012 Nw. J. Intl. Hum. Rts. 11(1), 28, 57 ff.; AComHPR, *Gurreth Anver Prince v. South Africa*, 255/02, 2004, para 50 ff.; CESCR, *An Evaluation of the Obligation to Take Steps to the "Maximum of Available Resources" Under an Optional Protocol to the Covenant*, E/C.12/2007/1, 2007, para 11. The HRC has expressed scpeticism, HRCom, *GC 34*, CCPR/C/GC/34, para 36.

1098 Besson, *Subsidiarity in International Human Rights Law*, 82 f.; Neumann, *Subsidiarity*, in: Shelton (ed.), *The Oxford Handbook of International Human Rights Law*, 2013, 360, 371 ff.; ICJ, *Case Concerning Avena and Other Mexican Nationals (Mexico v. United States of America)*, para 131; ICJ, *LaGrand (Germany v. United States of America)*, para 125.

1099 Sandoval, *Two Steps Forward, One Step Back*, 4, 7 f., 10 ff.; Oette, *Bringing Justice to Victims? Responses of Regional and International Human Rights Courts and Treaty Bodies to Mass Violations*, in: Ferstman et al. (eds.), *Reparations for Victims of Genocide, War Crimes and Crimes Against Humanity - Systems in Place and Systems in the Making*, 2009, 217, 238; IACtHR, *Yarce et al v. Colombia*, 2016, para 326.

1100 This epistemological justification for deference is frequently raised in scholarship, see for example Besson, *Subsidiarity in International Human Rights Law*, 84; Letsas, *The Margin of Appreciation Revisited*, 303; Legg, *The Margin of Appreciation in International Human Rights Law - Deference and Proportionality*, 2012, 145 ff. Follesdal draws attention to the fact that this epistemic argument only applies to some factors that need to be assessed, Follesdal, *Appreciating the Margin of Appreciation*, 275 f.

1101 See below, G.I., II.2.

IV. Summary: A Tripartite Approach

This section did not argue for a new, somehow transitional-justice-specific approach to interpretation. It raised specific points, which are of heightened importance for the subsequent analysis. The interpretation of the right to reparation in transitional justice should emphasize the object and purpose of reparation and the transitional justice considerations entering through that door. Due regard should be paid to pragmatic approaches that make reparation and human rights protection effective under the difficult circumstances of transitional justice. Interpretation should be approached holistically, considering other rights and interests affected by reparation programs. Wherever possible, these should be harmonized. If that proves impossible, one can resolve norm conflicts by proportionally restricting the right concerned and striking a balance between legitimate positions. Lastly, the nature of human rights as abstract principles, coupled with the heightened difficulties of implementing reparation programs in transitional justice situations, requires that states be allowed some discretion and deference when implementing reparation in transitional justice.

Backed by these methodological clarifications, the chapter will proceed by tackling the common differences identified in chapter two, which deviate from the international law on reparation. The chapter proceeds in loosely chronological order, starting with the law behind eligibility criteria for reparation programs (C.) and the intake procedure (D.), proceeding to various considerations related to the content of reparation programs (E.). It will then take up procedural and structural considerations (F. and G.) before finishing with the circumstances under which transitional justice reparation programs can end (H.).

C. Survivor Eligibility

A hallmark of successful reparation programs is their comprehensiveness, that is, that they cover as many survivors as possible.[1102] Yet, no program to date achieved or even attempted to achieve full comprehensiveness.[1103]

1102 HRC, *Report of the Special Rapporteur on Transitional Justice on Reparation*, A/69/518, para 26; IACtHR, *Yarce et al v. Colombia*, para 325.

1103 HRC, *Report of the Special Rapporteur on Transitional Justice on Reparation*, A/69/518, para 26.

Restricting the eligibility for a reparation program to certain categories of survivors is the main bottleneck through which states try to limit the resources they must spend on reparation. That is no problem if excluded survivors have other means of obtaining redress. In Colombia, survivors who also perpetrated human rights violations (survivor-perpetrators) could not obtain benefits under the Victims Law but could seek redress through the ordinary justice system.[1104] As long as all mechanisms available to survivors adhere to international standards as elaborated in this chapter and the distinction does not lead to discriminatory treatment, this approach is acceptable, albeit not always recommendable. However, usually states restrict eligibility for reparations as such, effectively denying reparation to those outside of the scope of reparation programs. Most authors display little problem with that, simply assuming that it is necessary to do so.[1105] On a factual level, this position is intuitive. Times of systematic human rights violations see a plethora of violations committed – not only the prominent violations of bodily integrity but also less visible or "minor" violations, e.g., of freedom of expression. The field of violations becomes even broader if one considers economic, social, and cultural rights. Still, the passing-by legitimization of restricted eligibility does not do justice to this decision's fundamentality. It not only shapes the program's content and success.[1106] It also denies many survivors their rights. What is more, excluding certain groups of survivors from reparation programs can frustrate the object and purpose of reparation in transitional justice. Reparation is supposed to send the message that human rights are valid, applicable, enforceable, and important. Excluding certain groups of

1104 Tribunal Superior de Medellín, *Olimpo de Jesús Sánchez Caro y Otros, Sentencia*, 2015, 230 f.; Other states implemented successive reparation programs for different survivor groups, see for example Lira, *The Reparations Policy for Human Rights Violations in Chile*, in: de Greiff (ed.), *Handbook of Reparations*, 2006, 55, 95 ff.; Guembe, *Economic Reparations for Grave Human Rights Violations - The Argentinean Experience*, in: de Greiff (ed.), *Handbook of Reparations*, 2006, 21, 21 ff.

1105 HRC, *Report of the Special Rapporteur on Transitional Justice*, A/HRC/30/42, para 26; HRC, *Report on Domestic Reparation Programs*, A/HRC/42/45, para 78; OHCHR, *Reparation Programmes*, 18 ff.; Moffett, *Transitional Justice and Reparations - Remedying the Past?*, in: Lawther et al. (eds.), *Research Handbook on Transitional Justice*, 2017, 377, 383 ff.; Peté/du Plessis, *Reparations for Gross Human Rights Violations in Context*, in: Peté/Du Plessis (eds.), *Repairing the Past? International Perspectives on Reparations for Gross Human Rights Abuses*, 2007, 3, 17; AComHPR, *Study on Transitional Justice in Africa*, 2019, para 55.

1106 Restrictions on eligibility often result in ignorance towards violations and phenomena not included, e.g. structural violence expressing itself in the violation of economic, social, and cultural rights.

survivors from reparation undermines that message. It might even suggest that certain human rights violations are not condemned. While this does not provide sufficient reason to dismiss the possibility of excluding groups of survivors from reparation programs, it raises the demands for justifying such a policy.

The following sections scrutinize different types of restrictions on eligibility and their possible justifications, namely the restriction of eligibility to violations of certain rights (I.), the exclusion of certain persons (II.), and the imposition of cut-off-dates (III.). After analyzing these special justifications, the last section examines the general justifications that restrictions on eligibility are simply necessary because there are not enough resources to redress all survivors (IV.) and that state practice justifies restrictions (V.).

I. Excluding Rights

The most prevalent restriction of eligibility is that reparation programs repair violations of some rights only, usually the most fundamental civil and political rights protecting bodily integrity. Sierra Leone only redressed survivors of five types of violations of bodily integrity.[1107] Many other reparation programs placed similar limits on eligibility.[1108] No legally sound justification backs this

1107 These were amputees, severely war-wounded, survivors of sexualized violence, war widows and children, see above, ch. 2, B.IV.1.b.

1108 Guembe, *The Argentinean Experience*, 26 f., 30 ff., 34 ff., 43 ff.; Lira, *The Reparations Policy for Human Rights Violations in Chile*, 95 ff.; Cammack, *Reparations in Malawi*, in: de Greiff (ed.), *Handbook of Reparations,* 2006, 215, 223, 224, 231; Cano/Ferreira, *The Reparations Program in Brazil*, in: de Greiff (ed.), *Handbook of Reparations,* 2006, 102, 102, 116, 138, 146; Houtte et al., *The United Nations Compensation Commission*, in: de Greiff (ed.), *Handbook of Reparations,* 2006, 321, 336 ff.; ICTJ, *Dealing With the 2006 Internal Displacement Crisis in Timor-Leste - Between Reparations and Humanitarian Policymaking*, 2012, 17; Slyomovics, *Reparations in Morocco - The Symbolic Dirham*, in: Johnston/Slyomovics (eds.), *Waging War, Making Peace - Reparations and Human Rights,* 2009, 95, 105; ICTJ, *Transitional Justice in Morocco - A Progress Report*, 2005, 10, 11; Burt, *Transitional Justice in the Aftermath of Civil Conflict - Lessons from Peru, Guatemala and El Salvador*, 2018, 30; Martínez/Gómez, *A Promise to be Fulfilled - Reparations for Victims of the Armed Conflict in Guatemala*, 2019, 17; Sharma et al., *From Relief to Redress - Reparations in Post-Conflict Nepal*, 2019, 25, 38; Guillerot, *Reparations in Peru - 15 Years of Delivering Redress*, 2019, 17 f.; Congreso Nacional de Bolivia, Ley de Resarcimiento a Víctimas de la Violencia Politica, art. 4; Cámara de Diputados de Paraguay, Ley No. 838 que Indemniza a Victimas de Violaciones de Derechos Humanos Durante la Dictadura de 1954 a 1989, art. 1 f.; Asamblea General de Uruguay, Actuación Ilegítima del Estado

practice – indeed, states usually do not provide any reason whatsoever for their choice of violations eligible for reparation.[1109]

This practice runs counter to the international law on reparation. The right to reparation attaches to the violation of any human right, which causes harm.[1110] The exclusion of certain violations creates hierarchies between survivors, can exacerbate tensions, and send the message that only some violations are worth redressing. This undermines the message that all and everyone's human rights are valid, applicable, enforceable, and important. The universality and object and purpose of the right to reparation thus prohibit excluding violations of certain rights from reparation programs. Accordingly, the IACtHR awarded reparation to survivors for violations for which a domestic reparation program did not provide redress.[1111]

II. Excluding Persons

Many reparation programs exclude certain persons. This happens mostly on two grounds: the person also perpetrated human rights violations (1.) or is an indirect survivor remotely connected to the direct survivor (2.).

Entre el 13 de Junio de 1968 y el 28 de Febrero de 1985 - Reconocimiento y Reparación a las Víctimas, art. 4 f.

1109 de Greiff, *DDR and Reparations - Establishing Links Between Peace and Justice Instruments*, in: Ambos/Wierda (eds.), *Building a Future on Peace and Justice,* 2009, 321, 338.

1110 In light of the debate about the justiciability of economic, social, and cultural rights, one could doubt whether survivors of violations of these rights have a right to reparation. However, that debate is now more or less settled. Indivisibility and lack of hierarchy between human rights prevail, making that position implausible. Therefore, the CESCR rightfully assumes that violations of economic, social and cultural rights give rise to an obligation to repair, which some reparation programs also attempted to discharge. For the stance of the CESCR see CESCR, *GC 14*, E/C.12/2000/4, para 59; CESCR, *Evaluation of the Obligation to Take Steps to the "Maximum Available Resources"*, E/C.12/2007/1, para 13(a). For a discussion of reparation programs, which arguably addressed violations of economic, social and cultural rights see, Arbour, *Economic and Social Justice for Societies in Transition*, 17 f.; Roht-Arriaza, *Reparations and Economic, Social and Cultural Rights*, in: Sharp (ed.), *Justice and Economic Violence in Transition,* 2014, 109, 121 ff. Generally on economic issues and transitional justice see Carranza, *Plunder and Pain.*

1111 IACtHR, *Omar Humberto Maldonado Vargas et al. v. Chile*, 2015, para 175; IACtHR, *Yarce et al. v. Colombia (Interpretation of the Judgment on Preliminary Objections, Merits, Reparations and Costs)*, 2017, para 41.

1. Survivor-Perpetrators

In most transitional contexts, individuals rarely fit neatly into the dual scheme of survivor or perpetrator. Instead, complicated biographies prevail, with people turning into both at different points.[1112] Such survivor-perpetrators can create a political problem.[1113] Survivors are often equated in public perception with innocence, in contrast to the "wicked" perpetrator.[1114] Granting reparation to survivor-perpetrators, who do not fit the public perception and putting them on an equal level with "deserving" ones, often causes political and social backlash.[1115] When the IACtHR ordered reparation for survivors of a brutally crushed prison riot in Peru, public outcry followed. The survivors were primarily members of the guerilla Sendero Luminoso[1116]. Accordingly, Peru's president vowed not to pay them a single Sol, and the monument that was supposed to honor those killed was vandalized.[1117] To avoid such contentious scenarios, states, e.g., Colombia, often exclude survivor-perpetrators

1112 Schotsmans, *Victims' Expectations, Needs and Perspectives After Gross and Systematic Human Rights Violations*, in: de Feyter et al. (eds.), *Out of the Ashes - Reparation for Victims of Gross and Systematic Human Rights Violations*, 2005, 105, 107; Borer, *A Taxonomy of Victims and Perpetrators - Human Rights and Reconciliation in South Africa*, 2003 Hum. Rts. Q. 25(4), 1088. Child soldiers are a prime example, Steinl, *Child Soldiers as Agents of War and Peace - A Restorative Transitional Justice Approach to Accountability for Crimes Under International Law*, 2017, 9 ff., on different prevailing images of child soldiers and passim for their treatment in transitional justice. For an illuminating autobiographic account of the complicated histories of child soldiers see Beah, *A Long Way Gone - Memoirs of a Boy Soldier*, 2007.

1113 Humphrey, *The Politics of Atrocity and Reconciliation - From Terror to Trauma*, 2013, 113 captures the problem and cynicism behind it perfectly: "The ambiguity of the 'survivor' is highlighted in the problem of social reparation for the living, as opposed to dead victims. While the dead can be unambiguously made casualties of state repression (war), living victims carry both the scars of repression and the shadow that they too were implicated in or contaminated by violence. Dead victims can be politically appropriated much more easily than living victims (...)." Examples from state practice can be found in Evans, *The Right to Reparation in International Law for Victims of Armed Conflict*, 157; Sharma et al., *From Relief to Redress*, 32, 40.

1114 Moffett, *Reparations for "Guilty Victims" - Navigating Complex Identities of Victim-Perpetrators in Reparation Mechanisms* 2016 Intl. J. Transitional Just. 10(1), 146, 148 f.; McEvoy/McConnachie, *Victimology in Transitional Justice - Victimhood, Innocence and Hierarchy*, 2012 Eur. J. Crimonology 9(5), 527, 531 f.

1115 Moffett, *Reparations for "Guilty Victims"*, 151, 153 ff.

1116 Shining Path.

1117 Moraña, *El Ojo que Llora - Biopolítica, Nudos de la Memoria y Arte Público en el Perú de Hoy*, 2012 Latinoamérica 54, 183, 204 ff.; *Humala Sobre Chavín de Huántar - No voy a Dar ni un Sol a los Terroristas*, RPP Noticias, 26 June 2015; Burt, *Transitional Justice in the Aftermath of Civil Conflict*, 21 f. See also below, E.IV.4.

from reparation programs.[1118] On the one hand, this avoids tension and protects the reparation program, if not the whole transitional justice process, from becoming delegitimized in the public's eyes. On the other hand, excluding survivor-perpetrators sends a deeply troubling message. It gives the impression that the applicability of human rights depends on righteous conduct. The hierarchy created between "problematic" and "unproblematic" survivors goes against human rights' inalienable nature. Persons enjoy them regardless of some notion of moral worthiness. Thus, the object and purpose of the right to reparation in transitional justice lend some force to both sides.

A thorough analysis of survivor-perpetrators' exclusion must distinguish between two scenarios: First, states exclude this category of survivors solely because of their "problematic" status.[1119] Second, they could be excluded because they receive benefits through a DDR-program.

The first reason for exclusion could find some support in the ECtHR's jurisprudence in McCann. The court held that "having regard to the fact that the three terrorist suspects who were killed had been intending to plant a bomb in Gibraltar, the Court does not consider it appropriate to make an award" for pecuniary or non-pecuniary damage.[1120] This jurisprudence is deeply flawed, as it effectively amounts to a forfeiture of human rights based on previous actions. Such a notion similar to the clean hands doctrine does not exist in international human rights law, as the ECtHR noted in Hirst.[1121] Accordingly, the court's holding is subject to severe criticism, not followed by any other international human rights court or treaty body, and

---

1118 See above, ch. 2, C.IV.1.

1119 Burt, *Transitional Justice in the Aftermath of Civil Conflict*, 9; Guillerot, *Reparations in Peru*, 20; Secretary of State of Northern Ireland, Victims' Payments Regulations 2020, art. 6(2); Cammack, *Reparations in Malawi*, 231, 237. Some states have separate reparation programs for survivor-perpetrators, see e.g. Sharma et al., *From Relief to Redress*, 32; Martínez/Gómez, *A Promise to be Fulfilled*, 18. Moffett makes different suggestions on how to repair survivor-perpetrators while maintaining a difference to survivors, who did not victimize others, Moffett, *Reparations for "Guilty Victims"*, 162 ff.

1120 ECtHR, *McCann and Others v. United Kingdom*, 18984/91, para 219.

1121 ECtHR, *Hirst v. United Kingdom (No. 2)*, 74025/01 (Grand Chamber), 2005, explicitly saying that "[t]here is no question, therefore, that a prisoner forfeits his Convention rights merely because of his status as a person detained following conviction. Nor is there any place under the Convention system, where tolerance and broadmindedness are the acknowledged hallmarks of democratic society, for automatic disenfranchisement based purely on what might offend public opinion", para 84; Laplante, *The Law of Remedies and the Clean Hands Doctrine - Exclusionary Reparation Policies in Peru's Political Transition*, 2009 Am. U. Intl. L. Rev. 23(1), 51, 64 ff.

apparently given up by the ECtHR itself.[1122] Instead, (partially) losing a right due to previous conduct is treated as a limitation of said right,[1123] which will be discussed below.[1124]

Regarding the second scenario, states sometimes argue that perpetrators already benefit from DDR-programs, making them ineligible for further reparation. This argument is valid if the benefits received under the DDR-program constituted reparation.[1125] As stated above, states are free to create an independent reparation program for survivor-perpetrators. Usually, though, they do not. Benefits distributed in DDR-programs usually serve the sole purpose of reintegrating perpetrators into society and lack an acknowledgment of wrongdoing and responsibility. In that case, DDR-programs do not discharge the obligation to repair because the benefits do not constitute reparation.[1126] Awarding survivor-perpetrators reparation in addition to those benefits is then not foreclosed by the prohibition of enrichment of survivors.[1127]

1122 Ichim, *Just Satisfaction Under the ECHR*, 169 f.; Moffett, *Reparations for "Guilty Victims"*, 160 ff.; Shelton, *Remedies in International Human Rights Law*, 151 f. A recent judgment of the ECtHR raises doubts, whether the court's renunciation of such jurisprudence still stands. The court held that asylum seekers "illegally" entering Spanish territory could be turned away without having access to individual proceedings, because they failed to avail themselves of supposedly available legal possibilities of entry, ECtHR, *N.D. and N.T. v. Spain*, para 206 ff. Again the court suggests the deeply flawed and dangerous notion that states can take courses of action that would violate human rights, if the individuals concerned did not act illegally before. Critique of the judgment has hence rightfully been damning, Ciliberto, *A Brand-New Exclusionary Clause to the Prohibition of Collective Expulsion of Aliens - The Applicant's Own Conduct in N.D. and N.T. v Spain*, 2021 Hum. Rts. L. Rev. 21(1), 203; Raimondo, *N.D. and N.T. v Spain - A Slippery Slope for the Protection of Irregular Migrants*, Border Criminologies, 20 April 2020; Markard, *A Hole of Unclear Dimensions – Reading ND and NT v. Spain*, EU Immigration and Asylum Law and Policy, 1 April 2020. Whether the court was right in its assessment that legal procedures for entry were available to the applicants must be doubted, Forensic Architecture, *Pushbacks in Melilla – ND and NT v. Spain*, 2020.

1123 ECtHR, *Hirst v. United Kingdom (No. 2)*, 74025/01 para 71.

1124 See E.II.4. There are circumstances however, in which the human rights of perpetrators are not violated by conduct, which would violate the human rights of non-perpetrators, e.g. when members of non-state armed forces are injured due to legitimate use of force under international humanitarian law. Since this study presupposes the existences of legitimate claims for reparation and only analyses the output such claims necessitate, the scenario will not be further discussed.

1125 This was supposed to be the case in Colombia, see above, ch. 2, C.IV.1.

1126 See above, Introduction, C.

1127 cf. IACtHR, *La Cantuta v. Peru*, 2006, para 202 and IACtHR, *Goiburú et al. v. Paraguay,* 22 September 2006, para 143, stating that reparation measures may not

Survivor-perpetrators do not receive double reparation but reparation and a voluntary benefit.

Excluding participants in DDR-programs from reparation programs even though they do not receive reparation in the DDR-program could be justified by claiming that they waived their right to reparation upon entering the DDR-program. In principle, individuals can waive their human rights if the right concerned protects the individual sphere, making it less critical for society.[1128] Such is the case with the right to reparation, as its primary objective is to overcome individual harm.[1129] Even though the additional transitional justice goals to establish respect for human rights and generalized trust are relevant to society, they do not suffer from waivers. Voluntary waivers do not undermine the message of validity, applicability, enforceability, and importance of human rights. Yet, waivers must be free, unequivocal, and informed.[1130] While procedural safeguards in DDR-programs can secure the last two requirements, the first is problematic. A waiver is only free if it is concluded without any form of coercion, neither direct nor through circumstance.[1131] Given that waivers strongly affect the individual and may

---

enrich survivors. See also above, ch. 1, D., on the role of proportionality in limiting reparation to the actual loss incurred.

1128 de Schutter, *Waiver of Rights and State Paternalism Under the European Convention on Human Rights*, 2000 N. Ireland L. Q. 51(3), 481, 482; Aall, *Waiver of Human Rights - Setting the Scene (Part I/III)*, 2010 Nordic J. Hum. Rts. 28(3), 300, 357 ff.; Caflisch, *Waivers in International and European Human Rights Law*, in: Arsanjani et al. (eds.), *Looking to the Future - Essays on International Law in Honor of W. Michael Reisman*, 2011, 407, 422, 424; ECtHR, *Neumeister v. Austria (Article 50)*, 1936/63 (Chamber), 1974, para 36; IACtHR, *Kimel v Argentina (Merits, Reparations and Costs)*, para 26, 36, operative para 4; IAComHR, *Annual Report of the Inter-American Commission on Human Rights 2012*, 2012, 122. The HRC expressed scepticism about waiving access to judicial overview of reparation programs, but did not specify on which grounds, HRCom, *Report on Follow-Up to the Concluding Observations of the Human Rights Committee*, CCPR/C/119/2, 2017, 10, 12 ff. It did not reject the possibility of a waiver outright, as it did e.g. concerning certain rights pertaining to the right to vote, HRCom, *General Comment No. 25 - Article 25 (Participation in Public Affairs and the Right to Vote)*, CCPR/C/21/Rev.1/Add.7, 1996, para 20. The IACtHR held that a waiver of the right to access to justice and truth in exchange for financial support is not compatible with the convention without specifying the reasons for this holding, IACtHR, *González et al. ("Cotton Field") v. Mexico*, 2009, para 558.

1129 The IACtHR considered the waiver of the right to reparation possible, IACtHR, *Case of the Rio Negro Massacre v. Guatemala*, 2012, para 253.

1130 An overview of conditions for the validity of waiver in the european system is given by de Schutter, *Waiver of Rights*, 489 ff.; Aall, *Waiver of Human Rights (I)*, 324 ff.

1131 Aall, *Waiver of Human Rights (I)*, 339 f.

jeopardize human rights protection, the threshold for assuming coercion is low. Coercive circumstances can already exist if the benefits obtained through waiving a right are markedly disproportionate to the disadvantages of a refusal to waive.[1132] This problem is especially salient if the decision concerns essential goods, such as the possibility to earn a living.[1133]

A waiver of the right to reparation as a requirement to enter a DDR-program can hardly meet these standards. Often, DDR-programs are individuals' best or even only chance to start a successful civilian life and reintegrate into society. Sometimes they even are the only option to leave an armed faction. Reparation is no substitute for that. It is often not offered when a person enters a DDR-program and does not focus on reintegration into society from a former combatant's perspective.[1134] Under these circumstances, the waiver's benefits and the disadvantages of a refusal to waive will often be out of all proportion. Accordingly, most waivers of the right to reparation would be void. In addition, waiving their right to reparation would require survivor-perpetrators to fully and visibly embrace the assigned role as perpetrator only, further invisibilizing their identity as a survivor. Apart from the societal and political effects described at the beginning of the present section, this could be an additional source of revictimization.[1135]

Therefore, if states want to exclude survivor-perpetrators from reparation programs because they receive benefits through a DDR-program, these benefits must constitute reparation. Only then does the state discharge its obligation to repair. In that scenario, DDR-programs must adhere to the standards discerned in this chapter. The benefits received through the program must have an adequate relation to the harm suffered and be given in acknowledgment of the state's wrongdoing and responsibility towards survivor-perpetrators.

1132 ECtHR, *Deweer v. Belgium*, 6903/75 (Chamber), 1980, para 51, 54. In the case, a Belgian butcher paid 10.000 Belgian Francs by way of friendly settlement, in order to avert the closure of his shop due to violations of limits on pricing. The settlement barred him from taking any legal action. The Court found that the prospect of having to close the shop as his only means of income for the duration of proceedings against the order before national courts – possibly several months – were "by far a lesser evil" than paying 10.000 Francs. This "flagrant disproportion" exerted pressure on the applicant to a degree that his waiver was not free. See also de Schutter, *Waiver of Rights*, 489 ff.; Aall, *Waiver of Human Rights (I)*, 337 ff.

1133 Aall, *Waiver of Human Rights (I)*, 340.

1134 de Greiff, *DDR and Reparations*, 344 ff.

1135 I am indebted to Tim Schneider for drawing my attention to this aspect of the use of waivers.

2. Indirect Survivors

Chapter one distinguished between indirect survivors whose own rights were violated and those who only suffered harm because of the violation of the direct survivor's rights.[1136] Regarding the former, there is no justification for excluding them if no violation can be excluded. The mere fact that a primary violation gave rise to a secondary violation does not change the fact that there has been a violation of the indirect survivor's rights. Furthermore, there is no general assumption that indirect survivors suffer less than direct survivors. Accordingly, the IACtHR ordered reparation for indirect survivors, who received only inadequate redress from a domestic reparation mechanism.[1137] States retain some flexibility, though, when defining indirect survivors. The Basic Principles carefully demand the reparation of indirect survivors only "where appropriate and in accordance with domestic law."[1138] The exact scope of persons included in the notion varies greatly in international practice.[1139] International jurisprudence acknowledges that the definition of indirect survivors varies with cultural circumstances.[1140]

Regarding persons who did not suffer a violation of their rights, only the IACtHR and the ECtHR award them reparation. Their jurisprudence relies on the wordings of their respective conventions, enabling them to provide reparation to an "injured party".[1141] Other treaties or soft law documents do not recreate such a distinction between a survivor and an injured person. Hence, the jurisprudence seems specific to the two regional human rights courts, based on Art. 41 ECHR and Art. 63(1) ACHR respectively. Accordingly,

1136 For details on that distinction see above, ch. 1, B.

1137 IACtHR, *Gomes Lund v. Brazil*, para 309 ff.

1138 UNGA, *Basic Principles*, A/RES/60/147, para 8. The value of the Basic Principles in the determination of the law on reparation in transitional justice is unclear. They only mention administrative reparation programs in para 16 as a way to redress survivors of violations by non-state actors, if these actors do not repair the survivor themselves. Other than that, the principles seem to give primacy to judicial proceedings. Still, they are regularly taken as a basis for administrative programs as well.

1139 Cano/Ferreira, *The Reparations Program in Brazil*, 115, 126; Guembe, *The Argentinean Experience*, 26; Lira, *The Reparations Policy for Human Rights Violations in Chile*, 63, 80; Sharma et al., *From Relief to Redress*, 37; Cámara de Diputados de Paraguay, Ley No. 838, art. 6 ; Asamblea General de Uruguay, Ley No 18.596, art. 11.

1140 See above ch. 1, B.II.

1141 See above, ch. 1, B.II.

such persons do not constitute survivors for the purpose of the right to reparation and need not be repaired.[1142]

III. Excluding Dates

Lastly, some reparation programs only redress violations before or after a specific date. Again, this is a legitimate consideration if it only aims at giving the reparation program a clear scope and purpose and if other survivors retain different avenues to claim redress. In contrast, Colombia only redresses survivors who suffered violations from the year 1985 onwards. Such cut-off dates are often born out of concern for evidentiary difficulties. That, however, is no legitimate consideration on the level of eligibility. The difficulties in obtaining evidence rarely go to the disadvantage of the state. The survivor bears the initial burden of proof and usually faces much more significant evidentiary obstacles.[1143] Therefore, it is the survivor's decision whether to embark upon the task to prove a violation.

Extinctive prescription could justify a general cut-off date.[1144] However, it is doubtful whether that principle exists and applies to claims arising from human rights.[1145] To the knowledge of the author, no state has relied on prescription with regard to reparation. Human rights jurisprudence has given reparation to survivors long after the events in question occurred.[1146] Even if it did apply, the conditions of prescription will usually not be met. Extinctive

1142 They can of course be the heirs of the direct survivor's claim to reparation. On that topic see Wühler, *Reparations and Legal Succession.*

1143 See below, D.II.

1144 Importantly, this does not concern the complex question of reparation for historic injustices. Here, the main legal question is not prescription, but whether a claim exists in the first place given the principle of intertemporality. This question can of course also play a role in transitional justice reparation programs, if they concern violations happening before the rise of an individual right to reparation. However, since the existence of a claim is presumed throughout this study, this question will not be examined. On details see above, Introduction, B.

1145 To the knowledge of the author, it has never been applied to claims arising out of the violation of a human right. Against its application altogether in relation to compensation in international law, Ronzitti, *Access to Justice and Compensation for Violations of the Law of War*, in: Francioni (ed.), *Access to Justice as a Human Right*, 2007, 95, 114.

1146 Consider IACtHR, *Case of the Massacres of El Mozote and Nearby Places v. El Salvador*, in which the court ordered the state to identify survivors of the massacer concerned in order to repair them more than thirty years after the events, para 310.

prescription applies only if the claimant presents the claim with unreasonable delay. If there were valid reasons to delay the claim – e.g., conflict or fear – it does not apply.[1147] Most survivors encounter significant obstacles to present their claim in transitional justice settings.[1148] Under these circumstances, only isolated cases could fulfill the prescription criteria, making the concept inept at justifying a general cut-off date.

Instead of relying on international law, states could apply domestic statutes of limitation to claims arising from human rights violations. In principle, the obligation to provide an effective remedy allows the application of statutes of limitation.[1149] Some international practice holds that domestic statutes of limitations are inapplicable to reparation claims, especially concerning human rights violations amounting to international crimes.[1150] It is argued that since the prosecution of these crimes cannot be subject to statutes of limitation, neither should claims for damages resulting from such crimes.[1151]

1147 Wouters/Verhoeven, *Prescription*, in: Wolfrum (ed.), *Max Planck Encyclopedia of International Law,* Online Edition 2008, para 6, 10.

1148 See below, D.

1149 Shelton, *Remedies in International Human Rights Law*, 97; ECtHR, *Guzzardi v. Italy*, 7367/76 (Plenary), 1980, para 72; ECtHR, *Cardot v. France (Preliminary Objections)*, 11069/84 (Chamber), 1991, para 34; IACtHR, *Velásquez-Rodríguez v. Honduras (Merits)*, 1988, para 67. Here the court speaks only of the possibility that claims are not presented in a timely manner, not specifying whether that relates to prescription or to a procedural requirement to present a claim within a certain timeframe. All cited judgments are concerned with the procedural requirements of the exhaustion of local remedies. Since in the jurisprudence of the respective courts, only effective remedies must be exhausted, it can be assumed that the jurisprudence is transferrable to the substantive requirements under the obligation to provide an effective remedy. On that see Schabas, *The European Convention on Human Rights - A Commentary*, 2017, 765; IACtHR, *Advisory Opinion on the Exceptions to the Exhaustion of Domestic Remedies*, OC-11/90, 1990, para 21 ff.

1150 ECOSOC, *Updated Set of Principles for the Protection and Promotion of Human Rights Through Action to Combat Impunity,* E/CN.4/2005/102/Add.1, 2005, principle 23; CAT, *GC 3*, CAT/C/GC/3, para 40; OHCHR, *Preliminary Observations from the Official Visit to Bosnia and Herzegovina by the Special Rapporteur on the Promotion of Truth, Justice, Reparation and Guarantees of Non-Recurrence, Mr. Fabián Salvioli (2-10 December 2021),* 2021; IACtHR, *Ordenes Guerra and Others v. Chile,* 2018, para 86 ff.; IAComHR, *Ordenes Guerra and Others v. Chile, Merits Report,* 52/16, 2016, para 118.

1151 IACtHR, *Ordenes Guerra and Others v. Chile,* 2018, para 86 ff.; IAComHR, *Ordenes Guerra and Others v. Chile, Merits Report,* 52/16, 2016, para 118; Ronzitti, *Access to Justice*, 113 f., although explicitly arguing de lege ferenda. The position finds support in IACtHR, *Case of Barrios Altos v. Peru (Merits)*, 2001, para 41 ff. Although mostly concerned with barriers to prosecution, the court states that laws erecting such

However, the parallelism between prosecution and reparation is a mere assertion. Each is a separate obligation, subject to different conditions.[1152] Several states apply statutes of limitation to reparation for grave human rights violations, depriving the practice of the necessary uniformity to support such an independent exception.[1153]

The CAT relies on a continuous effect theory to disallow the application of domestic statutes of limitation, asserting that claims should not be time-barred since the damage persists.[1154] The IACtHR displayed an inclination

barriers, including prescription laws, prevent survivors from receiving reparation. While the customary nature of the prohibition to subject international crimes to statutes of limitation is not unchallenged, the majority of state practice and scholarship supports that character, Pinzauti, *Principle 23*, in: Haldemann/Unger (eds.), *The United Nations Principles to Combat Impunity - A Commentary*, 2018, 250, 252 ff.

1152 van den Herik, *Addressing "Colonial Crimes" Through Reparations? Adjudicating Dutch Atrocities Committed in Indonesia*, 2012 J. Intl. Crim. Just. 10(3), 693, 699. Van den Herik does however cite a Dutch ruling casting aside statutory limitations for reparation claims.

1153 Hessbruegge, *Justice Delayed, not Denied - Statutory Limitations and Human Rights Crimes*, 2011 Geo. J. Intl. L. 43(4), 335, 373 ff. Even most of the few supporting incidents Hessbruegge cites are not as clear as may seem. The pronunciations of UN treaty bodies on Aboriginal lost generations and comfort women either relate solely to the inapplicability of statutes of limitations to prosecution or do not elaborate why they deem reparation still to be an obligation. As will be explained below, instead of the inapplicability of statutes of limitations, it could also be argued that they cannot be applied because no effective remedy was available to survivors before. Hessbruegge's citation from the Basic Principles could also just relate to prosecution, given that the preceding paragraph relates solely to prosecution and only the following paragraph states that statutes of limitation for civil claims "should not be unduly restrictive". Some practice in favour of a general inapplicability of statutes of limitations to reparation claims is cited in Kok, *Statutory Limitations in International Criminal Law*, 2007, 46, 48, 70 ff. In Malawi, the National Compensation Tribunal could waive the statute of limitation for individual cases, showing that, in principle, the statute applied, Cammack, *Reparations in Malawi*, 228. In Argentina, the statute of limitation applied, but only began to run after democracy was restored, because before, survivors had no effective remedy. Some courts did not apply the statute of limitation at all, Guembe, *The Argentinean Experience*, 28 ff. In Chile, courts differed on whether the statute of limitation should apply. The Supreme Court decided that it applied, whereas single lower courts found it inapplicable, Lira, *The Reparations Policy for Human Rights Violations in Chile*, 89 f.

1154 CAT, *A v. Bosnia and Herzegovina*, CAT/C/67/D/854/2017, 854/2017, 2019, para 7.5; CAT, *GC 3*, CAT/C/GC/3, para 40. See also Commission on Human Rights, *Final Report Submitted by Mr. Theo van Boven*, E/CN.4/Sub.2/1993/8, para 135. The IAComHR made similar statements, but in the end assessed the proportionality of statutes of limitations, as suggested here, although leaving little room to apply proportionate statutes of limitation to reparation claims for crimes against humanity,

towards that view but did not rely on it when determining the inapplicability of statutes of limitations to reparation claims for crimes against humanity on another occasion.[1155] International practice supporting the inapplicability of statutes of limitation to continuing violations relies on the continuous commission, not persistent damages.[1156] In the latter case, international practice allowed statutes of limitation to apply, undermining this position.[1157]

Hessbruegge claims that national statutes of limitation cannot bar international claims because national law cannot justify non-compliance with international law.[1158] This argument misconstrues the problem. It is not argued that domestic statutory limitations in and of themselves can bar international claims. Instead, the question is whether the right to an effective remedy gives states the freedom to apply domestic statutes of limitation as a legitimate restriction, which, as shown, it does.

Still, as any restriction of a right, statutes of limitation must be necessary and proportionate. They must hence not be unduly short.[1159] Furthermore, it would be disproportionate to apply statutes of limitation to individuals who

IAComHR, *Compendium,* OEA/Ser.L//V/II.Doc. 121, para 183; IAComHR, *Ordenes Guerra and Others v. Chile, Merits Report,* 52/16, 2016, para 118, 129; IAComHR, *Ordenes Guerra y Otros v. Chile, Merits Report,* 52/16, 2016, para 130 ff. (inexplicably, the Spanish and English versions of the report differ).

1155 The court noted that although Chile's statute of limitation covered grave human rights violations in principle, some domestic courts did not apply it to such cases. It further stated that the previously cited CAT, *GC 3*, CAT/C/GC/3, para 40 and other documents with a similar line of argument should be taken into account, IACtHR, *García Lucero et al. v. Chile,* para 204. In Ordenes Guerra, the court deemed Chile's statute of limitation inapplicable but did not repeat the argument of continuous effects, even though the commission mentioned it in its report on the case, IACtHR, *Ordenes Guerra and Others v. Chile,* 2018, para 86 ff.; IAComHR, *Ordenes Guerra and Others v. Chile, Merits Report,* 52/16, 2016, para 118.

1156 Kok, *Statutory Limitations*, para 41, 114. On the difference, Neuner, *The Notion of Continuous or Continuing Crimes in International Criminal Law,* in: Kaleck/Bergsmo/Hlaing (eds.), *Colonial Wrongs and Access to International Law,* 2020, 123, 129. The ICTR held that the commission of an act must be differentiated from its effects, ICTR, *Nahimana, Barayagwiza and Ngeze v. The Prosecutor, Judgment,* ICTR-99-52-A (AC), 2007, para 723.

1157 It is reasonable to assume that grave human rights violations cause persistent damage. Hence, the practice review in fn. 1153 also applies to this question.

1158 Hessbruegge, *Justice Delayed, not Denied*, 373.

1159 ECtHR, *Stubbings and Others v. The United Kingdom*, 22083/93, 1996, para 53; UNGA, *Basic Principles*, A/RES/60/147, para 7; HRCom, *GC 31*, CCPR/C/21/Rev.1/Add.13, para 18, although concerned with prosecution rather than reparation.

were unable to access a remedy for no fault of their own.[1160] Otherwise, states would profit from an illegal situation they helped create. They are obligated to provide effective access to justice, including a general environment that makes remedies accessible.[1161] Benefitting from the contrary situation by having claims time-barred would contravene the principle ex iniuria ius non oritur.[1162] It would give states an incentive to evade their obligation to repair by preventing survivors from accessing the justice system.

Thus, in principle, states can introduce a cut-off date for reparation based on domestic statutes of limitation. These statutes must not be unduly restrictive and do not apply if it was impossible or too onerous for survivors to make their claims on time. Given the circumstances prevailing in times of systematic human rights violations, the last-mentioned exception will usually apply.[1163] In practice, a general cut-off date is therefore not likely to conform to international standards.

1160 ECtHR, *Howald Moor v. Switzerland*, 52067/10, 2014, para 74 ff.; ECtHR, *Eşim v. Turkey*, 59601/09 (Second Section), 2013, para 19 ff. The HRCom held that a remedy was ineffective because the applicant was unable to avail herself of it within the short timeframe until statutes of limitations applied. She was first detained and then social stigma and a lack of information precluded her from accessing the remedy, HRCom, *Nyaya v. Nepal*, 2556/2015, para 6.4; *Cayuga Indians (Great Britain) v. United States*, R.I.A.A. VI, 1926, 173, 189. Japanese and Argentinean courts applied the same standards, Bong, *Compensation for Victims of Wartime Atrocities - Recent Developments in Japan's Case Law*, 2005 J. Intl. Crim. Just. 3(1), 187, 199 f.; Guembe, *The Argentinean Experience*, 28 ff. See further, US Court of Appeals, *Arce v. Garcia*, 2006, para 18 ff.; Kok, *Statutory Limitations*, 201; UNGA, *Declaration on the Protection of All Persons From Enforced Disappearance*, A/RES/47/133, 1992, art. 17(2).

1161 See below, D.

1162 "Law does not arise from injustice". On the applicability of the doctrine see ICJ, *Gabčíkovo-Nagymaros Case*, para 132; CERD, *Dragan Durmic v. Serbia and Montenegro*, CERD/C/68/D/29/2003, 29/2003, 2006, para 9.4; IACtHR, *Cotton Field Case*, para 558. A detailed treatment can be found at Fitzmaurice, *The General Principles of International Law Considered From the Standpoint of the Rule of Law*, 1957 Collected Courses of the Hague Academy of International Law 92, 1, 117 ff.

1163 Medina Quiroga, *The American Convention on Human Rights - Crucial Rights and Their Theory and Practice*, 2nd Edition 2016, 361; Ibañez Rivas, *Artículo 25*, in: Steiner/Uribe (eds.), *Convención Americana Sobre Derechos Humanos - Comentario*, 2014, 606, 616.

IV. A Necessary Restriction?

From what has been examined so far, only in very exceptional circumstances can states limit eligibility for reparation programs, as long as they do not provide the remaining survivors with other adequate avenues for redress. The exceptional nature of these circumstances makes general restrictions on eligibility unlikely to be legal. Thus, full comprehensiveness of reparation programs is not only a lofty goal. With few exceptions, it is an obligation. Teleological considerations support this position. Full comprehensiveness communicates that all human rights are valid, applicable, enforceable, and important, not just for certain people under certain circumstances. While this position is noble, it means that reparation programs need to accommodate much more survivors than they currently do – up to the point at which the majority of a state's population could be eligible. Such a bold position necessarily raises strong objections: First, in most cases, it will be impossible to fulfill. Second, even if possible, the benefits awarded would need to be diluted to a degree that makes them meaningless. Third, if most of the population is considered survivors, the status itself becomes meaningless.[1164]

The last objection is a mere assertion about the subjective perception of a status by the general population. It is unclear why the survivor status would become meaningless because many persons suffered from violations, especially since a distinction between grave and less grave violations remains possible.[1165] Also, following the objection would mean denying survivors their right to make the status more meaningful to others. It would mean glossing over the fact that systematic human rights violations occur on many levels, not only concerning bodily integrity but also economic inequality, widespread structural violence, etc.

The other two objections come down to the argument that restrictions on eligibility are simply a necessary restriction of the right to reparation. As a testimony to their strength, they can only be countered thoroughly below once other essential considerations are established. For now, a brief

1164 de Greiff, *Articulating the Links Between Transitional Justice and Development - Justice and Social Integration*, in: de Greiff/Duthie (eds.), *Transitional Justice and Development - Making Connections*, 2009, 28, 40; Rombouts et al., *The Right to Reparation for Victims of Gross and Systematic Violations of Human Rights*, 468 f.; Duthie, *Toward a Development-Sensitive Approach to Transitional Justice*, 2008 Intl. J. Transitional Just. 2(3), 292, 307.

1165 See below, E.IV.2.b.

anticipation of the complete argument must suffice.[1166] It will be argued that the state must strike a fair balance between survivors' right to reparation and all other legitimate claims against its resources. That allows the state to lower the amount of reparation awarded to the degree necessary and proportionate to fulfill its other obligations. Per definition, this enables the state to repair all survivors with the resources it has at the given moment. Of course, this makes the dilution objection all the more pressing. In response, it will be argued that purely symbolic reparation can repair less grave harm. That way, most survivors receive less costly but still meaningful symbolic measures, freeing enough resources to award meaningful material reparation to those who suffered the most significant harm. Broadly balancing the relevant positions and repairing most survivors through symbolic means is a less intrusive measure to make reparation work in transitional justice. Far-reaching restrictions on eligibility are hence not necessary. What sounds much like wishful thinking now will hopefully be conclusively argued later. For now, one last challenge remains: The proposal contradicts most contemporary state practice – relevant to interpretation according to Art. 31(b), 32 VCLT.

V. A Restriction Based on State Practice?

The Special Rapporteur on Transitional Justice rightfully noted that no reparation program had achieved full comprehensiveness.[1167] It might be added that no program even tried. This seemingly unanimous practice in favor of restricting eligibility could justify interpreting the right to reparation to allow such restrictions. However, states rarely provide any reason for limiting eligibility, making it hard to read the practice as support for any concrete rule that excludes specific survivors. Furthermore, states regularly amended their reparation programs as a reaction to protest from previously excluded survivors or court rulings.[1168] In the same vein, international courts and treaty bodies regularly ordered reparation for individuals outside the scope of

1166 Impatient readers are invited to skip directly to the full argument below, esp. E.II.4, III., IV.2.

1167 HRC, *Report of the Special Rapporteur on Transitional Justice on Reparation*, A/69/518, para 26.

1168 Cano/Ferreira, *The Reparations Program in Brazil*, 106, 124, 141; Guembe, *The Argentinean Experience*, 33 f., 43 f.; Lira, *The Reparations Policy for Human Rights Violations in Chile*, 67, 79; Sharma et al., *From Relief to Redress*, 28; ICTJ, *Reparations in Peru - From Recommendations to Implementation*, 2013, 19 f.

national reparation programs.[1169] The IACtHR even held that survivors who already received reparation through a program had to be repaired again for violations not covered by the first award.[1170] Thus, often, the initial exclusion did not hold up in court or against political realities.

Beyond the inconclusiveness of international practice, it is doubtful whether even consistent practice could justify the large-scale exclusion of survivors from reparation programs. As seen above, the right to reparation leaves no room for such exclusion when defining its scope of protection, and as a limitation, it will rarely be necessary.[1171] Accordingly, allowing large-scale exclusion of survivors might be beyond the reach of interpretation and warrant an amendment of the respective norms.

VI. Conclusion: An Illegal Bottleneck

Neither the specific nor general justifications for restricting eligibility hold up against scrutiny. Only restrictions based on waiver and statutes of limitations can apply to isolated cases under narrow circumstances. It follows that with very few exceptions, all survivors must receive reparation. The enormous challenge this restrictive position on limiting eligibility poses to the content of reparation programs will be taken up below. First, the analysis will proceed chronologically: Full comprehensiveness must turn into completeness – that is, every survivor must become a beneficiary of the respective reparation program.[1172] This is only possible if every survivor is identified as such and manages to enter the program. For that, a successful intake procedure is crucial.

D. Intake

The case studies showed that instead of relying on survivors to initiate reparation claims, states proactively encourage them to enter reparation

1169 Moffett, *Reparations in Transitional Justice - Justice or Political Compromise?*, 2017 Hum. Rts. Intl. Legal Discourse 11(1), 59, 63; IAComHR, *Rufino Jorge Almeida v. Argentina, Merits Report,* 147/18, 2018, para 55 ff.

1170 IACtHR, *Vargas et al. v. Chile,* para 175; IACtHR, *Yarce et al. v. Colombia (Interpretation of the Judgment on Preliminary Objections, Merits, Reparations and Costs),* para 41.

1171 See above, C.I-IV.

1172 OHCHR, *Reparation Programmes,* 15.

programs. For that, each survivor must know about the program, present themselves, and must be able to prove their status. This intake procedure is decisive to achieve the completeness of the program.

States' obligations in this realm derive from the right to access justice. Access to domestic justice was already part of the standard of treatment of aliens. In modern times, the obligation is based on the human right to an effective remedy and fair trial and has achieved customary status.[1173] It obliges states to organize their institutions so that all individuals have a real and practical opportunity to access a remedy.[1174] Access has a normative and an empirical dimension. On the normative side, remedies must not be limited too strictly by procedural or substantive rules, e.g., statutes of limitation. On the empirical side, accessing remedies must not place a disproportionate burden on potential claimants, e.g., because remedies are too far removed from their place of residence or because of too onerous costs.[1175] Furthermore, states must take care to provide equal access to justice, considering the special vulnerabilities of certain potential claimants.[1176]

1173 Importantly, this only holds true for the right to access domestic justice mechanisms, not necessarily international ones, Francioni, *The Rights of Access to Justice Under Customary International Law*, in: Francioni (ed.), *Access to Justice as a Human Right*, 2007, 1, 10 ff., 41; Schmitt, *Access to Justice and International Organizations - The Case of Individual Victims of Human Rights Violations*, 2017, 97 ff.

1174 Shelton, *Remedies in International Human Rights Law*, 96; UNGA, *Basic Principles*, A/RES/60/147, para 3(c), 11(a), 12 ff.; HRCom, *GC 31*, CCPR/C/21/Rev.1/Add.13, para 15; IAComHR, *Access to Justice as a Guarantee of Economic, Social, and Cultural Rights - A Review of the Standards Adopted by the Inter-American System of Human Rights*, OEA/Ser.L/V/II.129, 2007, para 245 ff.; AComHPR, *Principles and Guidelines on the Right to a Fair Trial*, DOC/OS(XXX)247, principles C(b)(1), K, P(a)(d); IACtHR, *Castañeda Gutman v. Mexico*, 2008, para 100; ECtHR, *Bellet v. France*, 23805/94 (Chamber), 1995, para 34; CAT, *A v. Bosnia and Herzegovina*, 854/2017, para 7.5; CAT, *GC 3*, CAT/C/GC/3, para 5; HRCom, *Gyan Devi Bolakhe v. Nepal*, CCPR/C/123/DR/2658/2015, 2658/2015, 2018, para 7.11.

1175 IAComHR, *Access to Justice*, OEA/Ser.L/V/II.129, 245 ff.; Shelton, *Remedies in International Human Rights Law*, 97 ff. Examples of non-legal impediments for accessing justice can be found in UNDP, *Programming for Justice - Access for All*, 2005, 138 f.; van Rooij/van de Meene, *Access to Justice and Legal Empowerment - Making the Poor Central in Legal Development Co-Operation*, 2008, 10 f.

1176 AComHPR, *Principles and Guidelines on the Right to a Fair Trial*, DOC/OS(XXX)247, principle K; IACtHR, *Saramaka People v. Suriname*, 2007, para 178; IACtHR, *Yakye Axa Indigenous Community v. Paraguay*, 2005, para 63.

Any restrictions on accessibility, be it on the normative or empirical dimension, must be necessary and proportionate for the proper administration of justice or other legitimate aims.[1177]

In the following, these general principles will receive further specification with regard to the most critical aspects of the intake process – outreach (I.) and evidence (II.). The section closes with brief remarks about other potential barriers (III.).

I. Outreach

A lack of information about existing remedies must not impede access to justice.[1178] States cannot rely solely on the initiative of survivors in seeking such information.[1179] Instead, they must actively inform survivors in a way that allows them to realize their right to reparation effectively.[1180] This standard requires information about the possibility to claim reparation and information about how to enter and navigate the process.[1181] As stated above,

1177 IACtHR, *Cantos v. Argentina*, 2002, para 50; ECtHR, *Stubbings and Others v. The United Kingdom*, 22083/93, para 50; HRCom, *General Comment No. 32 - Article 14: Right to Equality Before Courts and Tribunals and to Fair Trial*, CCPR/C/GC/32, 2007, para 18.

1178 ECtHR, *M.S.S. v. Belgium and Greece*, 30696/09 (Grand Chamber), 2011, para 304; ECtHR, *Hirsi Jamaa v. Italy*, 27765/09 (Grand Chamber), 2012, para 204; AComHPR, *Principles and Guidelines on the Right to a Fair Trial*, DOC/OS(XXX)247, principle K(d), P(d); IAComHR, *Reparation Guidelines*, OEA/Ser/L/V/II.131, para 12; HRCom, *Nyaya v. Nepal*, 2556/2015, para 7.9; UNGA, *Basic Principles*, A/RES/60/147, para 11(c), 24; Art. 9(5) Convention on Access to Information, Public Participation in Decision-Making and Access to Justice in Environmental Matters.

1179 IACtHR, *Case of the Ituango Massacres v. Colombia*, 2006, para 340; IACtHR, *Case of the Pueblo Bello Massacre v. Colombia*, 2006, para 209; CAT, *GC 3*, CAT/C/GC/3, para 29; CAT, *Estela Deolinda Yrusta and Alejandra del Valle Yrusta v. Argentina*, CAT/C/65/D/778/2016, 778/2016, 2019, para 7.9.

1180 Cammack, *Reparations in Malawi*, 232; Lira, *The Reparations Policy for Human Rights Violations in Chile*, 61, 73, 84; ICTJ, *Dealing With the 2006 Internal Displacement Crisis in Timor-Leste*, 12; Guillerot, *Reparations in Peru*, 27, 28 f.; ICTJ, *Reparations in Peru*, 9; ILA, *Reparation for Victims of Armed Conflict*, Resolution 1/2014, 2014, principle 5; ECOSOC, *Impunity Principles*, E/CN.4/2005/102/Add.1, principle 33; ECOSOC, *Principles on Housing and Property Restitution for Refugees and Displaced Persons*, E/CN.4/Sub.2/2005/17 Annex, 2005, principle 13.4, 13.8; UNGA, *Basic Principles*, A/RES/60/147, para 12(a), 24; IAComHR, *Reparation Guidelines*, OEA/Ser/L/V/II.131, para 12.

1181 CAT, *GC 3*, CAT/C/GC/3, para 29; CAT, *Yrusta v. Argentina*, 778/2016, para 7.9. The Special Rapporteur on Transitional Justice demands that states inform survivors

to provide truly equal access to justice, states must take due care to reach all survivors, including marginalized ones and survivors in remote places.[1182]

II. Evidence

Evidentiary requirements present an enormous barrier to claim reparation in transitional justice situations. In principle, survivors must demonstrate their eligibility by providing proof that a violation occurred, that the state bears responsibility, and the extent to which they suffered harm because of it. Such evidence is difficult to provide in most transitional justice situations.[1183] In Colombia, the fact alone that 79 % of the land was not registered hindered many survivors of displacement from proving their ownership over land and concurrent right to restitution. To combat such evidentiary problems, most reparation programs ease evidentiary requirements substantially and systematically help with procuring evidence.[1184] When doing so, states need to find a balance. A high evidentiary threshold produces more false negatives. The program could become adversarial, risking revictimizing

of their right to reparation, available programs and registration processes, HRC, *Report on Domestic Reparation Programs*, A/HRC/42/45, para 48, 53. As one example from state practice, Malawi explains survivors their rights, the procedure, how they can make a claim as well as the mandate and goals of the National Compensation Tribunal, Cammack, *Reparations in Malawi*, 232.

1182 CAT, *GC 3*, CAT/C/GC/3, para 32; CAT, *Yrusta v. Argentina*, 778/2016, para 7.9.

1183 Combs, *Deconstructing the Epistemic Challenges to Mass Atrocity Prosecutions*, 2018 Washington Lee L. Rev. 75(1), 223, 243 ff.

1184 ICTJ, *Reparations in Theory and Practice*, 8; Cammack, *Reparations in Malawi*, 228; Cano/Ferreira, *The Reparations Program in Brazil*, 116 ff., 139 f.; Guembe, *The Argentinean Experience*, 26; Houtte et al., *The UNCC*, 343 f., 440; Lira, *The Reparations Policy for Human Rights Violations in Chile*, 69, 81; ICTJ, *Dealing With the 2006 Internal Displacement Crisis in Timor-Leste*, 11; Statute of the Trust Fund for Victims of Hissène Habré's Crimes, art. 20(2); IAComHR, *Reparation Guidelines*, OEA/Ser/L/V/II.131, para 11; ICTJ, *Reparations in Peru*, 9; HRC, *Report on Domestic Reparation Programs*, A/HRC/42/45, para 57. In inter-state cases, the ICJ also eases the standard of proof for reparation in situations of mass violations that cause evidentiary difficulties,ICJ, *Armed Activities Reparations,* para 106, 114, 124. The importance of that fact was iterated, coupled with criticism for the court's still too strict standard, by some of the judges: ICJ, *Armed Activities on the Territory of the Congo (Democratic Republic of the Congo v. Uganda), Reparations – Declaration of Judge Salam,* para 3 ff.; ICJ, *Armed Activities on the Territory of the Congo (Democratic Republic of the Congo v. Uganda), Reparations – Opinion Dissidente de M. le Juge Ad Hoc Daudet,* para 8 ff.

survivors or keeping them from applying.[1185] The controversy between the TFV and the Chamber in the Lubanga case is instructive in that regard, as the TFV argued precisely that too demanding intake standards would discourage survivors from applying or make applying even impossible for them.[1186] If the evidentiary threshold is too low, too many false positives might undermine the program, create tension and frustrate real survivors.[1187]

The right to access to justice prohibits making a remedy ineffective by employing a prohibitive standard of evidence.[1188] It follows that survivors must have a reasonable chance of meeting evidentiary standards under the circumstances they find themselves in. Since different groups of survivors will face different evidentiary obstacles, states cannot employ a one-size-fits-all approach. Some obstacles may be inherent in the type of violation – the erasure of evidence is part of enforced disappearance, for example. The circumstances of the offense might produce others – such as displacement from unregistered land. The state must react differently to these situations and help survivors overcome the concrete barriers they face to provide equal access to justice.

International jurisprudence employs distinct techniques to meet the aforementioned standards. While not necessarily directly applicable to the domestic sphere,[1189] they can provide guidance on what can be necessary to provide equal and effective access to justice. Concerning survivor status, human rights supervisory bodies presume state responsibility if a person suffers harm while under state agents' control.[1190] If a state implements a policy to commit certain violations, circumstantial evidence, indirect evidence, or logical inference can link an instance to that policy, establishing

1185 ICTJ, *Reparations in Theory and Practice*, 8.

1186 See above, ch. 2, D.III.2.b.aa.

1187 Moffett, *Transitional Justice and Reparations*, 398.

1188 ECtHR, *Iovchev v. Bulgaria*, 41211/98 (First Section), 2006, para 146; ECtHR, *Radkov v. Bulgaria (No. 2)*, 18382/05 (Fifth Section), 2011, para 38 f.; FRA, *Handbook on European Law Relating to Access to Justice*, 2016, 122 f. Cf. IACtHR, *Case of the Ituango Massacres v. Colombia*, para 340; IACtHR, *Case of the Pueblo Bello Massacre v. Colombia*, para 209. The ICJ stated in the context of inter-state claims that "a less rigorous standard of proof" is "recognized [...] in the context of [...] compensation affecting large numbers of victims", ICJ, *Armed Activities Reparations*, para 107.

1189 Cf. IACtHR, *Godínez-Cruz v. Honduras (Merits)*, 1989, para 134; ECtHR, *García Ruiz v. Spain*, 30544/96 (Chamber), 1999, para 28.

1190 IACtHR, *Case of the "Street Children" (Villagran-Morales et al.) v. Guatemala (Merits)*, 1999, para 169 f.; ECtHR, *Aksoy v. Turkey*, 21987/93, para 61.

state responsibility.[1191] International bodies presume non-pecuniary harm in cases that almost necessarily produce such harm, e.g., if the survivor suffered a particularly grave human rights violation or lost a close family member.[1192] If the damage's extent is difficult to assess, international bodies often set the amount of reparation in equity.[1193]

Beyond easing standards of proof, the state must also procure evidence itself.[1194] States must investigate credible allegations of human rights violations, collect and secure all available evidence and make the findings available to survivors.[1195] Where evidence is unavailable to survivors or lies within the state's sphere, the state can be obliged to procure it to provide effective access to justice.[1196]

III. Removing Barriers

The obligation to provide access to justice also requires states to remove other disproportionate barriers survivors might face. Time-limits were already considered and will receive more consideration below.[1197] Beyond that, discrimination, harassment, costs, physical remoteness, and many other factors can impede survivors' ability to access reparation programs. As far as

1191 IACtHR, *Bámaca-Velásquez v. Guatemala (Merits)*, para 130.

1192 IACtHR, *Cantoral Benavides v. Peru (Reparations and Costs)*, 2001, para 37; IACtHR, *Case of the "White Van" (Paniagua-Morales et al.) v. Guatemala (Reparations and Costs)*, 2001, para 108. Further practice is cited in Niebergall, *Overcoming Evidentiary Weaknesses in Reparation Claims Programmes*, in: Ferstman et al. (eds.), *Reparations for Victims of Genocide, War Crimes and Crimes Against Humanity - Systems in Place and Systems in the Making*, 2009, 145, 151 ff. The IACtHR further eased the standard of proof where a pattern of a certain violation was established, IACtHR, *Fairén-Garbi and Solís-Corrales v. Honduras (Merits)*, 1989, para 127 ff., 157. For flexibilization of evidentiary standards at the ICC see above, ch. 2, D.

1193 IACtHR, *Case of the "Juvenile Reeducation Institute" v. Paraguay*, 2004, para 288; IACtHR, *Molina-Theissen v. Guatemala*, 2004, para 57.

1194 IAComHR, *Compendium*, OEA/Ser.L/V/II.Doc. 121, para 178

1195 For a comprehensive overview of legal texts and practice see IComJ, *Practitioners' Guide*, 84 ff., 105 ff., 110 ff., 115. See further, HRCom, *Guillermo Ignacio Dermit Barbato et al. v. Uruguay*, 84/1981, para 9.6; ECtHR, *Kaya v. Turkey*, 22729/93 (Chamber), 1998, para 107; ECtHR, *Oğur v. Turkey*, 21594/93 (Chamber), 1999, para 92 f.; IACtHR, *Juan Humberto Sánchez v. Honduras*, 2003, para 186; Pasqualucci, *The Practice and Procedure of the Inter-American Court of Human Rights*, 224 f.

1196 IACtHR, *Velásquez-Rodríguez v. Honduras (Merits)*, para 135; HRCom, *Hiber Conteris v. Uruguay*, A/40/40, 139/1983, 1985, para 7.2.

1197 See above, B.III and below, H.

possible and proportionate, states must overcome those barriers or at least diminish them.[1198] Also, states must give survivors adequate protection to enter the program. Often, survivors continue to live in conflict-affected zones or are subject to threats if they try to present their claim.[1199] While states cannot remove all barriers, they must do everything that can reasonably be expected to ensure survivors a real and practical opportunity to enter the reparation program without discrimination. This standard requires the state to consider the differing needs and vulnerabilities within the survivor population.

E. Content of Reparation Programs

The reader's most pressing question probably does not concern whom to repair but how. How do you adequately repair violations of such gravity and magnitude as required in the transitional situation? Many suggest that this enormous task warrants new concepts. As will be shown below, it is more convincing to keep the standards of chapter one.[1200] Hence, the international law on reparation demands that reparation in transitional justice be comprehensive, complete, and full. While certainly a noble position, it seems impossible to square with reality. The reparation programs chapter two examined had enough difficulties repairing a limited number of survivors, and they did not even come close to providing full reparation. Making them genuinely comprehensive, complete, and in line with the full reparation standard would surely overwhelm their administrative and financial capacities for good.[1201] The problem is even more profound. Comprehensive, complete, and full reparation in transitional justice could not only overwhelm reparation programs but the state as a whole. Full reparation easily results

1198 OHCHR, *Reparation Programmes*, 17; HRCom, *GC 31*, CCPR/C/21/Rev.1/Add.13, para 15; UNGA, *Basic Principles*, A/RES/60/147, para 11(c), 12(b); IAComHR, *Access to Justice*, OEA/Ser.L/V/II.129, para 5, 8, 81 ff.; AComHPR, *Principles and Guidelines on the Right to a Fair Trial*, DOC/OS(XXX)247, principle K(a), (d); UNDP, *Access to Justice*, 138 f.; van Rooij/van de Meene, *Access to Justice and Legal Empowerment*, 10 f.

1199 Illustrative, although in the context of the right to access the then still existing EComHR, ECtHR, *Kurt v. Turkey*, 24276/94, para 160. Of course that obligation can also arise independently based on states' general obligation to respect, protect and ensure human rights, see generally UNGA, *Basic Principles*, A/RES/60/147, para 10.

1200 See below, E.I.

1201 There might be examples in which that is not the case, especially if systematic human rights violations affected a limited subsection of the population only. Canada's residential school system could be a case in point here.

in individual compensation for grave human rights violations surpassing 100.000 USD, not even accounting for additional restitution, rehabilitation, satisfaction, and guarantees of non-repetition. If all survivors of systematic grave human rights violations received such sums while survivors of minor violations also received reparation, the claims could surpass a state's gross domestic product (GDP).[1202] Obviously, reparation should not endanger states' functionality. So how can this mismatch between the possible input and the demanded output be bridged? After arguing that full reparation should remain the standard for transitional justice (I.), the following sections attempt to defuse the situation on three levels: First, they elaborate standards according to which states can finance reparation programs and limit their financial scope (II.). Second, they establish rules governing the internal distribution of limited resources among survivors (III.). Third, they discuss norms on devising adequate reparation measures, which redress the harm suffered with the limited budget available (IV.).

I. Defending Full Reparation

Many scholars argue that full reparation is not suitable for transitional justice.[1203] This claim is more consequential than the argument above that an interpretation of the international law on reparation needs to consider transitional justice's transformative aim.[1204] While the latter leads to a modest adaptation, replacing full reparation would lead to a transitional-justice-specific reparation concept. There is some evidence in practice for this

1202 Roht-Arriaza/Orlovsky, *Reparations and Development*, 173. In the reparation award in the Massacre of Plan de Sanchez Case against Guatemala the IACtHR awarded reparation, worth 7.9 million USD. The massacre was one out of the 626 documented by the TRC. Assuming that 7.9 million USD is the average reparation due, Guatemala would owe almost 5 billion USD to survivors of massacres alone, Sandoval, *Two Steps Forward, One Step Back*, 1194. By the time the judgment was rendered in 2004, this would have amounted to more than a fifth of the country's GDP, https://data.worldbank.org/country/guatemala. Making similar calculations for Peru, de Greiff arrives at a figure worth two thirds of Peru's annual budget, de Greiff, *Justice and Reparations*, 159. For further examples see ILA, *Reparation for Victims of Armed Conflict*, e.g. 321. Of course, states often claim a lack or resources simply to avoid their obligation. This should not serve as a pretext for such claims, HRC, *Report of the Special Rapporteur on Transitional Justice on Reparation*, A/69/518, para 51 ff.

1203 See the sources in this section on transformative reparation.

1204 See above, B.I.

more radical approach.[1205] Yet, it rests on the mistaken assumption that the international law on reparation cannot guide transitional justice reparation efforts since the volatile circumstances and the number of survivors make full reparation impossible.[1206] This view is based on a wrong interpretation of full reparation. The PCIJ stated in the Chorzów Factory Case that reparation must wipe out the consequences of an illicit act *as far as possible.* The principle of full reparation requires optimization, not complete fulfillment at all costs. Accordingly, human rights courts regularly apply the concept of full reparation to situations where it cannot be fulfilled, like torture cases.[1207]

A challenge gaining more traction is that full reparation's conservative character produces unjust results in transitional justice. Full reparation requires putting the survivor in the position that would exist had the violation not occurred. Transitional justice situations usually arise out of unjust circumstances, including structural discrimination, poverty, and insecurity. Since full reparation requires the forward projection of the status quo ante, it likely reproduces these unjust circumstances.[1208]

In response, an alternative vision of reparation in transitional justice promises relief: transformative reparation. Instead of assessing and redressing

---

1205 IACtHR, *Yarce et al v. Colombia*, para 326; IACtHR, *Cotton Field Case*, para 450.; ICC, *Lubanga Reparations Order (Appeals Decision)*, ICC-01/04-01/06-3129, para 17; ICC, *Ntaganda Reparations Order*, ICC-01/04-02/06-2659, para 44, 94 f. An overview over practice and scholarship defending the concept is given by Walker, *Transformative Reparations? A Critical Look at a Current Trend in Thinking About Gender-Just Reparations*, 2015 Intl. J. Transitional Just. 10(1), 108, 112 ff.

1206 Hamber, *The Dilemmas of Reparations - In Search of a Process-Driven Approach*, in: de Feyter et al. (eds.), *Out of the Ashes - Reparation for Victims of Gross and Systematic Human Rights Violations*, 2005, 135, 136 f.; de Greiff, *Justice and Reparations*, 158 ff.

1207 CAT, *GC 3*, CAT/C/GC/3, para 6 ff.

1208 Yepes Uprimny, *Transformative Reparations*, 633 f.; Duggan/Jacobson, *Reparation of Sexual and Reproductive Violence - Moving from Codification to Implementation*, in: Rubio-Marin (ed.), *The Gender of Reparations - Unsettling Sexual Hierarchies While Redressing Human Rights Violations*, 2009, 121, 154; Couillard, *The Nairobi Declaration - Redefining Reparation for Women Victims of Sexual Violence*, 2007 Intl. J. Transitional Just. 1(3), 444, 444, 450 f.; Manjoo, *Introduction - Reflections on the Concept and Implementation of Transformative Reparations*, 2017 Intl. J. Hum. Rts. 21(9), 1193, 1197 ff.; Rubio-Marín/Sandoval, *Engendering the Reparations Jurisprudence of the Inter-American Court of Human Rights - The Promise of the "Cotton Field" Judgment*, 2011 Hum. Rts. Q. 33(4), 1062, 1070; McLeod, *Envisioning Abolition Democracy*, 1646. Most of the cited authors employ a slightly different full reparation standard, requiring the establishment of the situation that existed before the violation occurred. For a repudiation of that standard see above, ch. 1, C. The reproduction of unjust circumstances in the status quo ante will be similar with both approaches.

individual harm, transformative reparation shall change the unjust background conditions that led to the violations. These include structural discrimination, poverty, and others.[1209] While highlighting a critical weakness of full reparation, this exclusive focus on societal transformation carries the danger that individual claims to justice become secondary or disregarded. Survivors have a robust and specific claim against the state based on its wrongdoing. Absorbing those claims in the pursuit of societal transformation would not do justice to the individual violation. As Walker put it: "the resulting 'reparations' [...] may bypass or instrumentalize harmed individuals and groups by treating them as symptoms of a more serious and important justice issue".[1210] In that case, reparation would lose its character as an instrument of individual justice. Experience in transitional justice situations – not least the ones chapter two examined – shows that sidelining individual justice caused survivors frustration and anger, allowed states to evade their reparation obligation, and, ultimately, undermined reparation's legitimacy.[1211] The concept of transformative justice provides little guidance to reign in these concerns. It rarely goes beyond a rough policy proposal. From a legal perspective, it conflates the obligation to repair with other legal obligations, e.g., to progressively realize economic, social, and cultural rights, end discrimination, and fulfill human rights. These obligations have their distinct dogmatics, which are better suited to guide the societal transformation necessary in transitional justice. Their focus on structures rather than individuals better allows them to grasp the specific problems at play. Other transitional justice measures with a stronger focus on society, such as truth commissions or institutional reform, are better placed to achieve that task.[1212]

1209 Yepes Uprimny, *Transformative Reparations*, 637 f.; Duggan/Jacobson, *Reparation of Sexual and Reproductive Violence*, 154; Couillard, *The Nairobi Declaration*, 450 f.; Manjoo, *Introduction*, 1197 ff.; Rubio-Marín/Sandoval, *Engendering the Reparations Jurisprudence of the IACtHR*, 1070.

1210 Walker, *Transformative Reparations?*, 123. A similar argument is forwarded by Moffett, *Reparations for Victims at the International Criminal Court - A New Way Forward?*, 2017 Intl. J. Hum. Rts. 21(9), 1204, 1212 f.

1211 Laplante, *Transitional Justice and Peace Building - Diagnosing and Addressing the Socioeconomic Roots of Violence Through a Human Rights Framework*, 2008 Intl. J. Transitional Just. 2(3), 331, 352; Yepes Uprimny/Saffon, *Reparaciones Transformadoras, Justicia Distributiva y Profundización Democrática*, in: Díaz et al. (eds.), *Reparar en Colombia - Los Dilemas en Contextos de Conflicto, Pobreza y Exclusión*, 2009, 31, 48 ff.

1212 Laplante, *Transitional Justice and Peace Building*, 333.

Notwithstanding transformative reparation's weaknesses, searching for reparation's transformative potential in light of unjust societal circumstances deserves credit and consideration. Fortunately, this is one of the rare situations in which one can have the cake and eat it too – at least partially. Many transformative reparation proponents underestimate both the fruitfulness and adaptability of the full reparation approach in transitional justice situations. Its detailed examination can address concerns without abandoning well-established reparation standards that ensure that individual claims are not sacrificed on the altar of societal transformation.

At the core of the transformative reparation approach lies the interpretation of the right to reparation as requiring the reproduction of unjust circumstances. However, when viewed as part of the human rights system and in light of the object and purpose to realize all human rights, that interpretation of the right to reparation is implausible. Reparation does not override other human rights obligations. The state must fight discrimination, poverty, and structural violence under its obligation to not discriminate, progressively realize economic, social, and cultural rights, and fulfill human rights. It has numerous options to realize those rights aside from reparation, and it continues to have those obligations when devising and implementing reparation programs. The state must take great care that reparation does not cause further human rights violations. Most importantly, it must adhere rigorously to the prohibition of discrimination.[1213] This interplay between the right to reparation and other human rights often requires that reparation actively addresses unjust structures. For example, the Moroccan reparation program disregarded national inheritance law when setting compensation for deceased victims' family members because the law accorded women a smaller share.[1214] Arguably, the obligation not to discriminate forced the Moroccan state to design reparation that way. Admittedly, this falls behind the transformative project. In this scenario, reparation is not intended to overcome societal injustice. It "just" avoids its reproduction. But overcoming societal injustice might very well enter the concept of full reparation. As

1213 IACtHR, *Cotton Field Case*, para 451; Walker, *Transformative Reparations?*, 121 ff. While that sounds like a point too obvious to make, it is highly difficult to create non-discriminatory reparation programs, as a wealth of literature especially from feminist scholarship teaches. See for example Rubio-Marín, *The Gender of Reparations*; Manjoo, *Introduction*, 1194.

1214 Rubio-Marín, *Introduction - A Gender and Reparations Taxonomy*, in: Rubio-Marin (ed.), *The Gender of Reparations - Unsettling Sexual Hierarchies While Redressing Human Rights Violations*, 2009, 1, 17.

mentioned before, teleological considerations require taking the broader transformational aim of transitional justice into account when interpreting the international law on reparation. Beyond that, the distinct nature of harm in transitional justice situations affects the implementation of full reparation in transitional justice. Systematic human rights violations affect whole sectors of society and often society as a whole. As the case studies evinced, systematic violations knit a complicated web, in which individual harm interacts with previous injustices, ongoing discriminatory structures, and the damages other individuals, communities, and society suffered. Most obviously, this is the case for survivors of sexualized violence. Sexualized violence in conflict is often enabled and furthered by previous gender discrimination. Gendered stereotypes, e.g., of unmarriageability or the alleged purity of women, cause or exacerbate the shame, stigma, and ostracism such survivors often experience.[1215] The violation thus causes direct harm and indirect harm through its interactions with discriminatory social dynamics. To thoroughly repair both, working with communities on such discriminatory structures is indispensable. Equal considerations pertain to the reparation of other groups of survivors. Survivors of forced amputation in Sierra Leone suffered exacerbated discrimination and poverty because of their disability.[1216] Remedying their harm also requires ending ableist discriminatory patterns and creating employment opportunities for the disabled.

Thus, a rigorously applied full reparation framework will often require the transformation of previous injustices and discriminatory structures. Still, the two concepts are not the same. The concerns proponents of transformative justice raise enter the full reparation framework only through the backdoor of individual redress. That is fundamentally different than making them the primary objective of reparation. Full reparation does not serve to cure ailments of society. All measures must still be connected to the harm individual survivors suffered. They will fail to address some unjust conditions. Notwithstanding, full reparation can accommodate the transformative logic of reparation in transitional justice the case studies identified.[1217] What falls through the cracks in this approach should not be caught by an excessive account of what reparation can and should do. Instead, one should rely on what is already there: General obligations under international human rights

1215 Duggan/Jacobson, *Reparation of Sexual and Reproductive Violence*, 128 ff. See above, ch. 2, B.II.

1216 See above, ch. 2, B.II.

1217 See above, ch. 2, E.

law and their interaction with reparation, as well as other transitional justice measures, which are better suited to the task.

II. Input: Setting the Financial Scope of the Program

The adherence to the concept of full reparation will firmly put many states in the bind described above. The demands of comprehensive, complete, and full reparation can be so far removed from their financial abilities that finding a normative basis for limiting them is imperative. A normative conflict perspective helps develop such a normative basis: Setting the scope of a reparation program can confront the state with a normative conflict. If they had to spend a large part of their finite budget for reparation, they could encounter difficulties fulfilling other essential functions – healthcare, education, maintaining public order, etc. Since these functions are subject to different human rights and legitimate interests, the state cannot simultaneously fulfill its obligations under the right to reparation and other human rights to the full extend. The following section looks at different strategies to approach this conflict. It first looks at possibilities to increase the size of the pie. A state's budget is finite but not fix. The state can raise resources internally to meet heightened demands (1.) or enlist external support (2.). States can make the conflict less pressing by seeking synergies between reparation and other obligations (3.). While all strategies have their merits, they cannot solve the problem at hand. States cannot simply be obliged to raise the resources necessary. It would often be too much of a burden, and states' economic policy remains their sovereign prerogative. They cannot be allowed to rely on external support to the degree necessary, as that would amount to outsourcing reparation, stripping it of its roots in state responsibility. Seeking synergies cannot solve the problem either, as it also endangers the character of reparation and risks turning it into assistance. Hence, there is no way to avoid the normative conflict between the right to reparation and competing international obligations entirely. Limiting the financial scope of reparation programs remains inevitable. Accordingly, the study will develop a process through which the normative conflict can be solved. It will structure the required balancing act by using Alexy's Weight Formula (4.).[1218] Taken together, these sections will bridge the gap between states' financial capabilities and the exacting demands of full reparation.

1218 See above, B.2.b.

1. Raising Resources

When facing increased demand, states can make policy choices to raise revenue and other resources.[1219] International practice came up with a multitude of options to do so specifically for reparation in transitional justice.[1220]

Economic policy belongs to the core of states' domaine réservé. International law has little to say about how states raise and spend resources. However, save in highly exceptional circumstances, international law does demand that states have the money to discharge their international obligations.[1221] Also, states must seize any reasonable opportunity to avoid normative conflict or make it less pressing.[1222] Since reparation is an international obligation and confronts states with a normative conflict, they must do everything that can be reasonably expected to raise the resources necessary for reparation. Because the choice on how to do that remains states' sovereign prerogative, legal oversight of that matter will and must be limited. The debate about how to assess whether states used their maximum available resources to realize economic, social, and cultural rights can help determine an adequate level of scrutiny. This standard similarly requires states to raise resources for obligations whose complete and immediate fulfillment could overwhelm their capacities. States enjoy a wide margin of appreciation in determining how much resources they raise for that purpose. In addition to looking at the available resources, oversight should concentrate on whether the state's policy choices reflect a sense of importance for the relevant rights.[1223] Thus, states can be obliged to raise resources through means of their choice. However, the

1219 AU, *Transitional Justice Policy,* 2019, para 66(v).

1220 OHCHR, *Reparation Programmes*, 32; HRC, *Report of the Special Rapporteur on Transitional Justice on Reparation*, A/69/518, para 57 f.; AU, *Transitional Justice Policy,* 2019, para 130 ff. In general see Segovia, *Financing Reparations Programs - Reflections From International Experience*, in: de Greiff (ed.), *The Handbook of Reparations,* 2006, 650.

1221 See the short discussion of economic necessity and why it does not apply to most transitional situations, above, ch. 4, A.II.

1222 See above, B.II.2.a.

1223 Alston/Quinn, *The Nature and Scope of States Parties' Obligations Under the International Covenant on Economic, Social and Cultural Rights*, 1987 Hum. Rts. Q. 9(2), 156, 180 f.; Robertson, *Measuring State Compliance With the Obligation to Devote the "Maximum Available Resources" to Realizing Economic, Social, and Cultural Rights*, 1994 Hum. Rts. Q. 16(4), 693, 697 ff. For a similar criterion in the context of reparation in transitional justice, Antkowiak, *Remedial Approaches to Human Rights Violations – The Inter-American Court of Human Rights and Beyond,* 2008 Colum. J. Transntl. L. 46(1), 351, 400 f.

costs of comprehensive, complete, and full reparation can be too great to be within the reach even of ambitious domestic financial policies. The strategy of domestically raising resources alone does not suffice.

2. Enlisting External Support

A strategy often employed to raise resources for reparation is to enlist external support. Many states rely on NGOs, foreign states, international organizations, or other actors to partially fund or administrate their reparation program. Apart from increasing the resources available for reparation, this strategy can also avoid creating double structures and make reparation more effective by entrusting their implementation to actors with experience in that area and sometimes an existing relationship with beneficiaries. At the same time, third-party assistance also risks changing the character of the benefit given. It raises the problem of authorship. A prime example is Sierra Leone. International monetary aid started the entire program. Its implementation relied to more than 50 % on international funds. The first years of the program were funded almost entirely by third actors. International organizations implemented many measures at their costs, and the program co-opted existing NGO-programs, declaring them as reparation without lending decisive support. The extreme example raises the question of whether the state can discharge its obligation to repair without providing the resources for reparation.

a. Funding the Program

The point of departure for answering that question is the definition of reparation as an arithmetic operation rooted in state responsibility, through which *the responsible state* gives the survivor a benefit in acknowledgment of its wrongdoing.[1224] Benefits other entities provide are based on solidarity, not responsibility, and therefore constitute assistance, not reparation.[1225] If

1224 ECtHR, *Scordino v. Italy (No. 1)*, 36813/97 (Grand Chamber), 2006, para 199. See above, Introduction, C.

1225 HRC, *Report of the Special Rapporteur on Transitional Justice*, A/HRC/30/42, para 11. Rombouts et al., in contrast, forward that reparation can be based on solidarity, as from the viewpoint of the survivor, it does not matter, whether adverse effects on their human rights are based on responsibility or, e.g. natural disasters and that it is hence equally compelling morally to repair both kinds of survivors, Rombouts et al., *The Right to Reparation for Victims of Gross and Systematic Human Rights Viola-*

anyone could provide reparation, its secondary purposes – condemnation, retribution, and deterrence – would be ineffective. The message of validity, applicability, enforceability, and importance of human rights would be less credible since the communicating entity is not responsible for violations. The messenger would not be the one who must regain trust. Hence, in principle, the state must provide benefits and acknowledge its responsibility to discharge its obligation to repair. Consequently, if the state merely acts as an interchangeable distributor of external resources, such distribution cannot qualify as reparation.

On the other hand, it would be apposite to the standards established to entirely disallow external contributions to reparation programs. States must raise resources for reparation and use them as effectively as possible to repair survivors.[1226] If external resources were readily available for that purpose, obliging the state to reject them would run counter to those principles. Also, external resources are indispensable for some reparation measures, such as the restitution of objects only available in other countries.

As a result, neither an absolute ban on external resources is justifiable, nor can the responsible state assume a completely interchangeable role as the mere distributor of someone else's funds. In an overall assessment of the respective program, the state's involvement must be so substantial that the benefits it distributes can be qualified as given by the state. The assessment cannot only look at the state's share of the program's costs. Its substantial involvement can also stem from fundraising efforts, planning and implementing the program, or other organizational, operational, strategic, or administrative tasks. This case-by-case assessment applies to the reparation program as a whole and single reparation measures. Each measure must constitute reparation to be a legitimate part of a reparation program. A state cannot offset a minor role in one program part by being more involved in others.

---

tions, 497 f. This, however, does not take into account that states can be obliged to support survivors of, e.g., natural disasters based on their positive human rights obligations. It also seems questionable, whether there really is no difference between survivors of human rights violations based on state responsibility and survivors of natural disasters, as the latter do not comprise a deliberate action on part of the entity responsible. Hence, suffering from such events is even more the result of chance. Where it is not (or not exclusively), for example in case of environmental racism, state responsibility can be established, putting the harm back into the realm of reparation. On environmental racism see Johansen, *Environmental Racism in the United States and Canada – Seeking Justice and Sustainability*, 2020, 1 ff.

1226 See above, E.II.1., 3.

Three scenarios can be distinguished in the application of this standard to the real world. The authorship problem does not arise when the state funds the reparation program with external resources that flow into its general budget.[1227] In that case, the state chooses to allocate resources at its free disposal for reparation, making it a benefit from the state. Authorship becomes questionable if the state relies on external funds, specifically earmarked for the reparation program. Here, the abovementioned case-by-case assessment comes into play. Lastly, states often recover assets from other perpetrators. In Colombia, assets collected from the FARC-EP flowed into the reparation program.[1228] The SLTRC recommended a range of measures to hold non-state actors accountable, e.g., through asset seizure. The originally envisaged reparation program was to include some of these measures.[1229] Fines the ICC orders perpetrators to pay can also flow into reparation efforts.[1230] The Philippines financed part of their reparation program through asset recovery proceedings abroad.[1231] These forms of using other perpetrator's assets to fund the reparation program can take the form of both scenarios discussed above. In principle, another actor's responsibility does not relieve a state from its responsibility for the entire harm sustained because of a violation of international law.[1232] In human rights law, the state is fully responsible for private individuals' acts, if these are attributable or if the state failed to prevent them. The state, therefore, remains accountable to provide full reparation to the survivor even if a private individual contributed to the human rights violation or committed it.[1233] From this perspective, the state cannot rely

1227 See for the example of The Philippines, Carranza, *Plunder and Pain*, 324 f.; Davidson, *Alien Tort Statute Litigation and Transitional Justice - Bringing the Marcos Case Back to the Philippines*, 2017 Intl. J. of Transitional Just. 11(2), 257, 266 ff.

1228 Íñigo Álvarez, *The Obligation to Provide Reparations by Armed Groups - A Norm Under Customary International Law?*, 2020 Netherlands Intl. L. Rev. 67(3), 427, 439 f.

1229 See above, ch. 2, B.IV.2.b. and SLTRC, *Witness to Truth*, vol. 2, para 224 ff.

1230 For details on these examples see above, ch. 2, D.II. and Moffett, *Transitional Justice and Reparations*, 389 f.

1231 Carranza, *Plunder and Pain*, 324.

1232 ILC, *ASR Commentaries*, A/56/10, art. 31, para 12 f.; *D. Earnshaw and Others (Great Britain) v. United States (Zafiro Case)*, R.I.A.A. VI, 1925, 160, 164 f. In case of co-responsibility of a plurality of states, the law is less clear, ILC, *ASR Commentaries*, A/56/10, art. 47 para 4 ff. The ICJ left that question open in ICJ, *Certain Phosphate Lands in Nauru (Nauru v. Australia), Preliminary Objections, Judgment*, I.C.J. Reports 1992, 240, para 48, 56.

1233 IACtHR, *Ximenes-Lopes v. Brazil*, 2006, para 232; The IACtHR and ECtHR award full reparation also for violations of positive obligations, IACtHR, *Case of the Workers of the Fireworks Factory in Santo Antônio de Jesus and Their Families v. Brazil*, 2020,

on perpetrators' assets to provide reparation any more than it can rely on other third parties' assets for that purpose. However, the communicative content of the two scenarios differs. When using perpetrators' assets, the state shows its dedication to enforcing human rights in private relationships. This is essential to achieve the transitional-justice-specific aim of creating generalized horizontal trust.[1234] More generally, retrieving assets from other perpetrators can communicate the validity, applicability, importance, and enforcement of human rights, whereas relying too heavily on other actors risks undermining that message by suggesting that the state seeks to avoid its obligation. Out of this consideration, it seems justified to allow the state to rely to a greater degree on assets recovered from perpetrators than on contributions from third parties.

In each scenario discussed above, it remains essential that the state does not use the reliance on other parties' assets as a pretext to absolve itself from responsibility for the violation. A benefit only constitutes reparation if accompanied by an acknowledgment of wrongdoing – regardless of where the resources come from.

b. Running the Program

Apart from using external funds for the program, states also rely on outside actors to run it. This can produce synergy effects and contribute to the efficient use of limited resources. After all, why should the state set up its own psychological rehabilitation program if an experienced NGO has worked with survivors for years? Accordingly, ample transitional justice state practice and human rights jurisprudence rely on third parties to provide specific reparation measures.[1235] To preserve the reparatory character of the

115 ff., 257 f.; ECtHR, *Berkman v. Russia*, 46712/15 (Third Section), 2020, operative para 7, in which the court awards the 10.000 € claimed by the applicant regardless of the contributions of private actors to the violation. On the normative basis for state responsibility with more details on potential concurrent responsibility and causation see above, Ch. 1 B.III.

1234 See above, ch. 3, C.III.

1235 CEDAW, *V.K. v. Bulgaria*, CEDAW/C/49/D/20/2008, 20/2008, 2011, para 9.16(b)(iii); IACtHR, *Rosendo Cantú et al. v. Mexico*, para 253; ICC, *Information Regarding Collective Reparation*, ICC-01/04-01/06-3273, para 54; Cammack, *Reparations in Malawi*, 229 f.; Guembe, *The Argentinean Experience*, 33; Lira, *The Reparations Policy for Human Rights Violations in Chile*, 68 f.; ICTJ, *Dealing With the 2006 Internal Displacement Crisis in Timor-Leste*, 13; UN Women, *The Conflict did not Bring us*

benefits, the same considerations apply as above. The state must contribute substantially, e.g., by paying for the program's continuation, extension, or making it free for survivors. The state must acknowledge that it supports the implementing partner because of its responsibility for the human rights violation in question. It must ensure that this acknowledgment reaches the survivors who benefit from the measure in question.

Relying on external support can ease the normative conflict by increasing the resources available for reparation and creating synergies with existing programs. The strategy cannot solve the normative conflict between reparation and other interests and obligations, though.

3. Efficiency: Seeking Synergies

Similar problems arise from another strategy states often use to make the normative conflict between the right to reparation and competing claims less pressing. Generally, states are obliged to devise reparation measures as efficiently as possible. That reduces the normative conflict between the right to reparation and other rights and interests because states achieve more reparative effects with the same amount of resources. To accomplish that, states often seek synergies between reparation and assistance. They provide non-excludable goods as collective and service-based reparation from which survivors and the general population profit.[1236] That way, the state can simultaneously fulfill its obligation to repair survivors and its various obligations towards the general population. For example, instead of paying survivors' medical expenses, states can build a hospital, which caters to survivors and the general population. On the downside, the provision of non-excludable goods

---

Flowers - The Need for Comprehensive Reparations for Survivors of Conflict-Related Sexual Violence in Kosovo, 2016, 32; Sharma et al., *From Relief to Redress*, 25, 26; Guillerot, *Reparations in Peru*, 41; Statute of the Trust Fund for Victims of Hissène Habré's Crimes, art. 21(2); ECOSOC, *Pinheiro Principles*, E/CN.4/Sub.2/2005/17 Annex, principle 12.5.

1236 Dixon, *Reparations, Assistance and the Experience of Justice - Lessons From Colombia and the Democratic Republic of the Congo*, 2015 Intl. J. Transitional Just. 10(1), 88, 88 f.; Duthie, *Toward a Development-Sensitive Approach to Transitional Justice*, 299 ff.; Roht-Arriaza/Orlovsky, *Reparations and Development*, 182 ff. See generally on the synergy effects between transitional justice and development, Carranza, *Plunder and Pain*, and the other contributions to the special issue of the journal as well as, Arbour, *Economic and Social Justice for Societies in Transition*; de Greiff/ Duthie (eds.), *Transitional Justice and Development: Making Connections*, 2009.

makes these measures hard to distinguish from assistance.[1237] Blurring the line between reparation and assistance comes with risks. When acting in bad faith, states can "do what [they] should be doing anyway and slap a reparations label on it."[1238] They can seek to avoid their obligation to repair. Colombia did as much when retroactively labeling assistance as reparation.[1239] But even reparation programs enacted in good faith can produce confusion between reparation and assistance. If no clear line divides the two, access of the broader population to reparation measures can delegitimize the program in survivors' eyes.[1240] A clear distinction between reparation and assistance is thus vital to enjoying the benefits of linking the two. Three cumulative criteria serve that purpose. The first two derive from the definition of reparation. Reparation is a benefit given by the responsible state to the survivor in acknowledgment of wrongdoing to remedy the harm caused.[1241] Thus, a benefit a state gives to a survivor can only constitute reparation if it relates to the damage they suffered and is accompanied by an acknowledgment of responsibility.[1242] The state must acknowledge responsibility at the moment it delivers reparation.

1237 OHCHR, *Reparation Programmes*, 26. On the obligation to distinguish, IACtHR, *Case of the Massacres of El Mozote and Nearby Places v. El Salvador*, 2012, para 350.

1238 Roht-Arriaza/Orlovsky, *Reparations and Development*, 192.

1239 See above, ch. 2, C.IV.

1240 All case studies in ch. 2 attest to that fact. The risk is heightened, if perpetrators have access to reparation measures. That was one of the key reasons for the withdrawal of 43 survivors from the Ruto and Sang case before the ICC, ICC, *The Prosecutor v. William Samoei Ruto and Joshua Arap Sang, Common Legal Representative for Victims' Comprehensive Report on the Withdrawal of Victims From the Turbo Area by Letter Dated 5 June 2013*, ICC-01/09-01/11-896-Corr-Red (TC V(A)), 2013, para 12. Generally on the problem in practice see Beristain, *Diálogos Sobre la Reparación – Experiencias en el Sistema Interamericano de Derechos Humanos*, Vol. II, 2008, 508 ff. Of course, in most transitional contexts, no neat line divides survivors and perpetrators, see above, C.II.1.

1241 See above, Introduction, C.

1242 OHCHR, *Reparation Programmes*, 25 f.; HRC, *Report on Domestic Reparation Programs*, A/HRC/42/45, para 30; Rubio-Marín, *The Gender of Reparations - Unsettling Sexual Hierarchies While Redressing Human Rights Violations*, 2009, 109 f.; Yepes Uprimny, *Transformative Reparations of Massive Gross Human Rights Violations - Between Corrective and Distributive Justice*, 2009 Netherlands Q. Hum. Rts. 27(4), 625, 645; HRC, *Report of the Special Rapporteur on Transitional Justice on Reparation*, A/69/518, para 11; Schotsmans, *Victims' Expectations, Needs and Perspectives After Gross and Systematic Human Rights Violations*, 114 f.; ECtHR, *Scordino v. Italy (No. 1)*, 36813/97, para 180; Dixon, *Reparations, Assistance and the Experience of Justice*, 95 ff. While Dixon remarks that recognition can sometimes be harmful to survivors, this conflates different meanings of the term. Public recognition of individuals as survivors can be harmful, e.g. if they are survivors of sexualized violence.

A retroactive declaration cannot magically turn assistance into reparation. It would constitute a bad faith performance of the obligation to repair.[1243]

Third, the relationship between reparation and positive human rights obligations distinguishes reparation from assistance. Reparation is something a *survivor* deserves because of the wrongdoing they suffered. It is unrelated to what that person deserves as a *member of society*, namely the progressive realization of economic, social, and cultural rights and the fulfillment of human rights. If a state owes a benefit under the latter, it cannot be treated as reparation because the survivor would be entitled to it anyway.[1244]

The demands of that requirement vary with the degree of realization of rights in the respective society. In a community where only primary health care is available, specialized services for survivors can be a reparation measure. If a robust health care system exists, progressively realizing the right to health might require that specialized services are available to the population, making them ineligible as a reparation measure. When discharging their positive obligations under human rights law, states must pay special attention to vulnerable and marginalized sectors of the population.[1245] Survivors often belong to these sectors, making it harder for the state to deliver reparation instead of the benefits survivors are entitled to as persons under the state's jurisdiction.

While this sounds clear-cut in theory, it can become muddy in practice. Some reparation measures cannot realistically be provided just to survivors. It would be inhumane and create unbearable community tensions if a health center established to deal with survivors' medical needs refused treatment to anyone else. Especially for collective and service-based reparation, complete exclusivity is simply no option. How then can the distinguishing features

---

However, what is required is not public but personal recognition towards the survivor. Whether it is made public or not is not decisive.

1243 The principle of good faith obliges parties to a treaty to act honestly and fairly, disclose their motives and take into account the fair expectations of the other party and other relevant actors, Kotzur, *Good Faith (Bona Fide)*, in: Wolfrum (ed.), *Max Planck Encyclopedia of International Law,* Online Edition 2009, para 20. Retroactive declarations are a form of evading the obligation to repair and fail to consider the legitimate expectation of survivors that they receive actual benefits as reparation and not only a declaration that what they already have constituted reparation.

1244 Rubio-Marín, *The Gender of Reparations*, 179, 192; Roht-Arriaza/Orlovsky, *Reparations and Development*, 109 f.; HRC, *Report of the Special Rapporteur on Transitional Justice on Reparation*, A/69/518, para 41.

1245 CESCR, *General Comment No. 3 - The Nature of States Parties' Obligations*, E/1991/23, 1990, para 12.

elaborated above be secured? To answer that question, this section needs to delve shortly into the topic of the next one, the design of adequate reparation measures. States use three common strategies to distinguish between reparation and assistance: Prioritization, specialization, and deduction.[1246]

Survivors can receive priority access to services not generally available to the population. If, for example, primary healthcare is not generally accessible, the state can establish health centers first in areas with large survivor populations or implement a referral system specifically for survivors. Specialization refers to the provision of services tailored to the specific harms survivors suffered.[1247] Sierra Leone, for example, provided fistula surgery for survivors of sexualized violence. In the realm of education, it gave courses specifically tailored to the needs of survivors. Lastly, the deduction strategy offers generally available benefits at cheaper rates or free of charge to survivors.

Some authors doubt the validity of the prioritization strategy because the benefit survivors receive is not the measure as such, but receiving it earlier than the general population.[1248] Upon closer inspection, the criticism can be leveled against any of the three strategies, although some authors present the latter two as alternatives to the former. The progressive realization of human rights at one point requires states to provide specialized services to their population and many benefits for free.[1249] Of course, many states in transition are far removed from being obliged to do that. Nevertheless, the time element

1246 Examples for the prioritization strategy are Asamblea Nacional de Nicaragua, Ley de Atención Integral a Víctimas, art. 2; Lira, *The Reparations Policy for Human Rights Violations in Chile*, 69, 70 (also an example for the discount strategy); Presidente de la República de Perú, Decreto Supremo 047-2011-PCM, art. 18(b), 19(d), (e) (also an example for the discount strategy). Examples for the specialization strategy can be found in Guillerot, *Reparations in Peru*, 39 f. (also an example for the discount strategy); General Congress of the United Mexican States, General Victims Act, art. 68(I); Examples for the discount strategy beyond those already mentioned are, Congreso Nacional de Bolivia, Ley 2640, art. 6; Asamblea General de Uruguay, Ley No 18.596, art. 10.

1247 HRC, *Report of the Special Rapporteur on Transitional Justice on Reparation*, A/69/518, para 41 f.; OHCHR, *Reparation Programmes*, 26 f.

1248 HRC, *Report of the Special Rapporteur on Transitional Justice on Reparation*, A/69/518, para 41 f.; OHCHR, *Reparation Programmes*, 26 f.

1249 To give an example, the progressive realization of the right to education requires at some point that primary, secondary and higher education be made free of charge and the right to health requires the availability of specialized services, CESCR, *General Comment No. 22 on the Right to Sexual and Reproductive Health*, E/C.12/GC/22,

provides no principled distinction between the prioritization, specialization, and deduction strategy.

Receiving benefits earlier than the general population can have reparatory value. Since many damages persist or even intensify over time, earlier mitigation measures limit the injury sustained. The reverse situation evinces that: Human rights courts and treaty bodies factor in the time of suffering when determining the amount of damage sustained.[1250] If the time survivors wait for reparation aggravates their harm, receiving a measure alleviating it earlier must be a benefit. Still, if an action was required imminently as a progressive realization of the population's rights, extending it to survivors shortly before does not seem to be of much value. Accordingly, all three strategies' reparative value comes down to how far removed the benefit is from being a positive obligation towards the general population. If the state extends a benefit to survivors five years earlier than it is obliged to provide it to the general population, it has a reparatory function. If it is 20 years, it has a considerable reparatory function. At some point towards the lower end of the scale, where the benefit must be provided imminently to realize the general population's rights, delivering it to survivors shortly beforehand will seize to have a reparatory function at all.

In sum, the three strategies of prioritization, specialization, and deduction can help distinguish between reparation and assistance. To make the distinction as sharp as possible, all three strategies should be employed cumulatively and accompanied by an unequivocal acknowledgment of wrongdoing.

4. Broad Balancing

The standards discerned so far detail the supply-side of reparation in transitional justice: States must raise resources to a certain degree to comply with their obligation to repair, both internally and externally. However, they cannot be obliged to increase resources and are not allowed to rely on external support to the degree necessary to finance comprehensive, complete, and full reparation.[1251] While they can and must seek synergies between reparation

2016, para 12 f.; CESCR, *General Comment No. 13 - Right to Education*, E/C.12/1999/10, 1999, para 6(b)(iii).

1250 IACtHR, *Fernández Ortega et al. v Mexico*, para 293.

1251 This should not detract from the fact that, if political will exists, astonishing sums can be spent on reparation. A striking and shameful example is a large-scale reparation program from Great Britain in the context of outlawing the slave trade –

and the fulfillment of other obligations, they will not be able to evade the normative conflict between the right to reparation and other rights and interests entirely. For that, the conflict is too severe. Instead, the demand-side of reparation in transitional justice warrants attention: Limiting the financial scope of reparation programs becomes inevitable. As mentioned above, a normative conflict perspective justifies doing so. If the aggregated claims to reparation overwhelmed the state's resources, it would have difficulties to fulfill its other essential functions. These functions not only serve legitimate state interests but also meet the human rights of other persons. A normative conflict ensues, which can be resolved with the tools established above, especially balancing.[1252]

---

for slave *owners* for their "lost property". It cost twenty million pounds, which amounted to 40 % of Great Britain's GDP at the time. Today the same share of the GDP would be worth 100 billion pounds. Great Britain paid of the loans needed for the program until 2015, Andrews, *The New Age of Empire*, 56 f.

1252 There is sparse international practice recognizing this conflict and its possible solution through balancing, most importantly the EECC, *Final Award*, para 18 ff., and, with much more caution, ICJ, *Armed Activities Reparations*, para 110, 407. Both bodies ultimately found that they did not need to decide on that issue, because no conflict actually arose in the cases at hand. The ICJ explicitly left the question open, whether this reasoning could require a deduction of the amount of reparation due. The EECC rejected moral damages, also mentioning "Eritrea`s limited economic capacity", EECC, *Final Award*, para 61. The UNSC was also mindful of the "requirements of the people of Iraq, Iraq's payment capacity [and] the needs of the Iraqi economy" when establishing the United Nations Claims Compensation Commission, UNSC, Resolution 687 (1991), S/RES/687 (1991), 1991, para 19. These two mechanisms occupy a unique place in between inter-state post-war reparation mechanisms and those addressed at individuals, which might explain this concern, Günnewig, *Schadensersatz Wegen der Verletzung des Gewaltverbotes als Element Eines Ius Post Bellum*, 2019, 216 ff., 293 ff., 380 f. For an analysis of this practice see Günnewig, *The Duty to Pay Reparations for the Violation of the Prohibition of the Use of Force in International Relations and the Jus Post Bellum*, in: Kreß / Lawless (eds.), *Necessity and Proportionality in International Peace and Security Law*, 2021, 439, 464 ff. For a general discussion see Paparinskis, *A Case Against Crippling Compensation*. For a similar solution concerning reparation for violations of the ius contra bellum see Günnewig, *The Duty to Pay Reparations*, 470 ff. In more detail in German, Günnewig, *Schadensersatz Wegen der Verletzung des Gewaltverbots*, 397 ff. The author finds some basis for the application of balancing in post-war inter-state reparations, see pages 401 ff. Her recourse on May's transitional justice theory to further justify the application could provide an interesting independent theoretical justification for introducing such a principle into the international law on reparation. As May's theory is based on Aristotle's virtue ethic and hence starts from a fundamentally different theoretical basis, the author (regrettably) will not pursue this line of argument fur-

Simply balancing the right to reparation with competing claims does not capture the normative conflict in its full intricacy, though. With an infinite amount of time, the state could fulfill its international obligations while delivering full reparation in a piecemeal fashion with the resources it has left at any given moment. The conflict is thus a tripartite one:

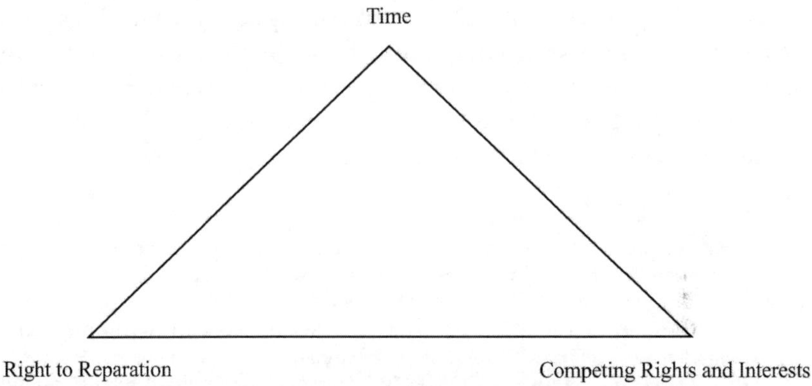

Figure 6: Tripartite Conflict of Reparation in Transitional Justice (created by the author)

In the following, its three elements will be examined in turn, starting with time (a.), continuing with the right to reparation (b.), and finishing with competing rights and interests (c.).

a. Time

Generally, the more time a state has, the more resources its economy generates for reparation. Yet, waiting for reparation further harms survivors. Many types of damage deepen with time, most obviously wounds and chronic diseases. Delayed reparation can also perpetuate survivors' social and economic marginalization.[1253] In the context of individual claims, the rights to an effective remedy and a fair trial oblige states to deliver reparation

ther. While that approach would not explode the limits of the law, it would explode the limits of this book.

1253 Judge Tomka drew further attention to the fact that delayed reparation also causes monetary awards to lose value, ICJ, *Armed Activities Reparations – Declaration of Judge Tomka,* para 10. While the amount of reparation ordered can take account of that fact, the risk is real that it will not. Especially if a reparation program increased

within a reasonable time.[1254] State and international practice show that this requirement also applies to transitional justice.[1255] What is reasonable depends on the legal and factual complexity of the case, its circumstances, authorities' conduct, and the proceedings' importance for survivors.[1256] A systemic backlog in the judicial or administrative system cannot justify delays, as states are responsible for setting up a system that can cope with the pending caseload.[1257] The ECtHR makes a reasonable exception when the backlog is due to a sudden increase in applications, to which the state already reacted with prompt and adequate measures. Among those exceptional situations are political unrest, heightened tension in society, and significant political changes, such as decolonization or the transition to democracy.[1258]

---

reparation amounts over time to balance out inflation, it would probably risk the perception that it treated survivors unequally.

1254 HRC, *Report on Domestic Reparation Programs*, A/HRC/42/45, para 44(a); HRCom, *GC 31*, CCPR/C/21/Rev.1/Add.13, para 19; HRCom, *Sundara Arachchige Lalith Rajapakse v. Sri Lanka*, CCPR/C/87/D/1250/2004, 1250/2004, 2006, para 9.5; CAT, *GC 3*, CAT/C/GC/3, para 39; ECtHR, *De Souza Ribeiro v. France*, 22689/07 (Grand Chamber), 2012, para 81; AComHPR, *GC 4*, para 26, 70; IACtHR, *Case of the Indigenous Communities of the Lhaka Honhat (Our Land) Association v. Argentina*, 2020, para 325; AComHPR, *Principles and Guidelines on the Right to a Fair Trial*, DOC/OS(XXX)247, para 2(i).

1255 Fletcher et al., *Context, Timing and the Dynamics of Transitional Justice – A Historical Perspective*, 2009 Hum. Rts. Q. 31(1), 163, 208 f.; AU, *Transitional Justice Policy*, 2019, para 66(iv); Guembe, *The Argentinean Experience*, 32 f.; Houtte et al., *The UNCC*, 342; ICTJ, *Dealing With the 2006 Internal Displacement Crisis in Timor-Leste*, 8 f.; ECOSOC, *Impunity Principles*, E/CN.4/2005/102/Add.1, principle 32; ECOSOC, *Pinheiro Principles*, E/CN.4/Sub.2/2005/17 Annex, principle 12.1, 12.3; UNGA, *Basic Principles*, A/RES/60/147, para 11(b); General Congress of the United Mexican States, General Victims Act, art. 7(III), 30. On the applicability of the right to a fair trial to the situation at hand see below, F.

1256 ECtHR, *Frydlender v. France*, 30979/96 (Grand Chamber), 2000, para 43; ECtHR, *Nicolae Virgiliu Tănase v. Romania*, 41720/13 (Grand Chamber), 2019, para 209; IACtHR, *Case of the Pueblo Bello Massacre v. Colombia*, para 171; IACtHR, *Radilla-Pacheco v. Mexico*, para 244; IACtHR, *Case of the Indigenous Communities of the Lhaka Honhat (Our Land) Association v. Argentina*, 2020, para 322 ff.; HRCom, *Mariano Pimentel et al. v. The Philippines*, CCPR/C/89/D/1320/2004, 1320/2004, 2007, para 9.2; CERD, *Kamal Quereshi v. Denmark*, CERD/C/66/D/33/2003, 33/2003, 2004, para 6.4; HRCom, *Taito Fa'afete v. New Zealand*, CCPR/C/114/D/1909/2009, 1909/2009, 2015, para 7.3, although the complaint related to criminal proceedings.

1257 ECtHR, *Vocaturo v. Italy*, 11891/85 (Chamber), 1991, para 17.

1258 ECtHR, *Foti and Others v. Italy*, 7604/76 (Chamber), 1982, para 61; ECtHR, *Unión Alimentaria Sanders S.A. v. Spain*, 11681/85 (Chamber), 1989, paras 38 ff.; ECtHR, *Guincho v. Portugal*, 8990/80 (Chamber), 1984, paras 36 ff. Similarly, IACtHR, *Case*

Transferring this jurisprudence to the situation of large-scale administrative reparation programs gives an idea of the time a state can take to deliver reparation. As the case studies showed, the large universe of survivors typically causes a backlog in cases. These cases are often of considerable complexity, including difficulties establishing evidence and a challenging environment for investigations. Uncertain political conditions and heightened tensions can further delay the process. These factors will justify potentially significant delays in comparison to domestic reparation proceedings under normal circumstances. On the other side of the scale, reparation programs usually deal with cases of grave human rights violations, which often leave survivors in a highly vulnerable position. The resulting importance reparation has for survivors makes it incumbent upon the state to speed up the process with all available means – standardized forms and procedures, video-orientation of survivors before entering the program, and assigning the reparation program to specialized agencies and staff are just a few. In sum, the transitional justice situation allows for significant delays in the provision of reparation, as long as the state makes a genuine effort to keep those delays at the minimum level possible.

While the specific amount of time any given proceeding can take cannot be determined in the abstract, the standard discerned here is sufficiently concrete to amend the obligation to provide reparation to an obligation to provide *prompt* reparation. This allows reducing the tripartite conflict to a two-sided one between the aggregated claims to prompt and full reparation and competing rights and interests:

Figure 7: Two-Sided Conflict of Reparation in Transitional Justice (created by the author)

The two-sided conflict can be approached with the methodology to resolve normative conflicts detailed above. For that, it is necessary to define the factors influencing the weight the right to reparation accrues in the balancing exercise.

---

of the Indigenous Communities of the Lhaka Honhat (Our Land) Association v. Argentina, 2020, para 323 ff.; IACtHR, *Garibaldi v. Brasil*, 2009, para 137; IACtHR, *Forneron and Daughter v. Argentina*, 2012, para 74.

b. The Right to Reparation

As a secondary right, the right to reparation does not possess a high abstract weight. It is neither absolute nor does it protect values of supreme importance.[1259] Its concrete importance depends on the degree of interference in any given situation. The further removed the reparation award is from full reparation, the stronger the interference and the heavier the right to reparation's concrete importance. While the concrete importance can only be determined in light of concrete situations, it is generally influenced by the flexibility with which the right to reparation accommodates other rights and interests in its scope of protection. If interpretation already reduces the concept of full reparation on this definitional level, less interference is necessary, and the right to reparation's concrete importance will decline accordingly.

The concept of full reparation provides some openings to consider the context in which it is administered. Reparation must be adequate and proportionate to the gravity of the violation, and the harm suffered.[1260] Under normal circumstances, full reparation fulfills these criteria. If that were true under all circumstances, overarching requirements of adequacy or proportionality would be redundant. Reparation simply had to be equivalent – not proportionate – to the harm suffered. Thus, adequacy and proportionality lessen the strict standards of full reparation in certain contexts.[1261] Given the competing interests in transitional situations, full reparation would place a disproportionate burden on the state. It would be detrimental to the protection of other human rights. Systematic and teleological considerations hence support loosening the strict demands of full reparation in transitional justice to ensure reparation's adequacy and proportionality. Similar considerations pertain to several forms of reparation. Restitution must not constitute a burden out

---

1259 See above, B.II.2.a.

1260 See generally ch. 1, D., as well as UNGA, *Basic Principles*, A/RES/60/147, e.g. para 2(c), 11(b), 15; IAComHR, *Reparation Guidelines*, OEA/Ser/L/V/II.131, para 1; Fletcher et al., *Context, Timing and the Dynamics of Transitional Justice – A Historical Perspective*, 2009 Hum. Rts. Q. 31(1), 163, 208 f.; AU, *Transitional Justice Policy*, 2019, para 66(iv); ECOWAS Court of Justice, *Djot Bayi & 14 Others v. Nigeria and 4 Others*, ECW/CCJ/JUD/01/09, para 45, using the words "just" and "equitable"; Rombouts et al., *The Right to Reparation for Victims of Gross and Systematic Violations of Human Rights*, 452.

1261 Gray, *Remedies*, 891; IACtHR, *Aloeboetoe v. Suriname*, para 49, saying that "in certain cases" the standard may not be appropriate.

of all proportion in comparison with the lower benefit of compensation.[1262] Compensation for non-pecuniary damage is based on equity, considering all the circumstances of the case.[1263] Even compensation for pecuniary damage, costs, and expenses is based on equity if the damage's exact scope is difficult to assess.[1264] The last-mentioned problem is ubiquitous in transitional justice; not only because evidence might be scarce but also because, in uncertain times, some positions such as future earnings evade reliable calculation. Again, it would be inequitable if the demand for compensation would unduly strain the resources available for the rest of society.

All these entry points allow considering the transitional situation's difficult circumstances when assessing the scope of full reparation. However, reducing full reparation on this level has its limits. The transitional situation's constraints typically are so great that the resulting reparation bears little resemblance to full reparation. Interpretation alone cannot justify such an outcome. It cannot negate the right to reparation.[1265] The restrictions transitional justice places on reparation must still be construed as a limitation of the right to reparation. As such, they must be necessary and proportionate, striking a fair balance between the competing positions. The openings the right to reparation's scope of protection offers diminish its concrete importance in that balancing exercise. They do not make balancing unnecessary.

c. Competing Rights and Interests

After having established that the right to reparation can integrate competing claims to a degree in its scope of protection, the other side of the equation warrants attention. Naturally, this section cannot examine all claims potentially competing with reparation. This can only be done in concrete situations. Instead, the following sections will give rough guidance to assessing the weight of groups of claims in the balancing exercise. These groups are positive human rights obligations (aa.), negative human rights obligations (bb.), and state interest (cc.).

1262 ILC, *ASR*, A/56/10, art. 35(b).

1263 See above, ch. 1, C.II.

1264 ECtHR, *Guiso-Gallisay v. Italy*, 58858/00 (Grand Chamber), 2009, para 107; IACtHR, *Myrna Mack Chang v. Guatemala*, para 291; ECtHR, *Andrejeva v. Latvia*, 55707/00 (Grand Chamber), 2009, para 116.

1265 Sands, *Treaty, Custom and the Cross-Fertilization of International Law*, 1998 Yale Hum. Rts. Dev. L. J. 1(1), 85, 102 f.; Pauwelyn, *Conflict of Norms in Public International Law*, 254.

aa. Positive Human Rights Obligations

States often pitch the need for development against extensive reparation programs.[1266] This argument has a legitimate core since the general population has rights to adequate healthcare, life, work, social security, bodily integrity, an adequate standard of living, education, and others. The resources needed for full reparation can seriously stifle progress in all these areas. Positive human rights obligations encapsulate this dimension of the conflict best. These require the state to take positive action to enable persons under its jurisdiction to enjoy their human rights.[1267] They arise both under economic, social, and cultural rights as well as civil and political rights. For both, their abstract weight depends on the rights they are attached to. The weightier the values these rights protect, the higher is the abstract weight of the obligation. Their concrete importance depends on how far the situation at hand falls behind what is legally required.[1268] On the one hand, this depends on the factual situation. The less the enjoyment of human rights is factually possible, the more critical it gets that the state fulfills its positive obligations.[1269] On the other hand, concrete importance depends on the scope of positive obligations. This, in turn, depends on the degree to which the challenges of the transitional situation can influence the scope of protection positive obligations offer. While both civil and political rights and economic, social, and cultural rights are closely connected dogmatically, the methodology for determining this latter point must account for differences in their structure.[1270]

States must employ the maximum amount of available resources to realize economic, social, and cultural rights progressively.[1271] Progressive realization must transpire "as expeditiously and effectively as possible."[1272] When assessing the amount of resources states must invest into progressive realization,

1266 Colvin, *Overview of the Reparations Program in South Africa*, in: de Greiff (ed.), *Handbook of Reparations,* 2006, 176, 186.

1267 Shelton/Gould, *Positive and Negative Obligations*, in: Shelton (ed.), *The Oxford Handbook of International Human Rights Law,* 2013, 562, 562 f.

1268 Above, this has been termed "degree of non-satisfaction", B.II.2.b.

1269 This follows from the discussion of core obligations, above, B.II.2.c and concretely below, E.II.4.c.bb.

1270 cf. Vandenhole, *Conflicting Economic and Social Rights - The Proportionality Plus Test*, in: Brems (ed.), *Conflicts Between Fundamental Rights,* 2008, 559, 588 f.; Eide, *Adequate Standard of Living*, in: Moeckli et al. (eds.), *International Human Rights Law,* 2nd Edition 2014, 195, 212.

1271 Art. 2 (1) ICESCR.

1272 CESCR, *GC 3*, E/1991/23, para 9.

all circumstances need to be considered, including competing demands of international human rights standards.[1273] States enjoy broad discretion in that area. Their choices must be reasonable and reflect the importance and priority of economic, social, and cultural rights.[1274] This high degree of flexibility and the possibility to account for competing demands greatly diminishes the concrete importance of positive obligations under economic, social, and cultural rights. Again though, they cannot be interpreted away.[1275] Fully meeting the demands of the right to reparation cannot require halting progress in realizing economic, social, and cultural rights entirely. A genuine conflict thus still exists and must be resolved by striking a fair balance between progressive realization and reparation.[1276]

Reparation can also affect a state's obligation to fulfill civil and political rights. This obligation entails that the state creates an environment in which individuals can enjoy their rights.[1277] Reparation can infringe this dimension of civil and political rights in two ways. First, the state is obliged to work on infrastructure and other projects to enhance the enjoyment of human rights.[1278] Large-scale reparation programs can divert resources from such projects and slow them down. Second, a state must prevent conflict or other systematic human rights violations as this would strongly impede

1273 CESCR, *Evaluation of the Obligation to Take Steps to the "Maximum Available Resources"*, E/C.12/2007/1, para 8; CESCR, *GC 3*, E/1991/23, para 11; Riedel, *International Covenant on Economic, Social and Cultural Rights (1966)*, in: Wolfrum (ed.), *Max Planck Encyclopedia of Public International Law*, Online Edition 2011, para 8.

1274 Alston/Quinn, *The Nature and Scope of States Parties' Obligations Under the ICESCR*, 180 f.; CESCR, *The Limburg Principles on the Implementation of the International Covenant on Economic Social and Cultural Rights*, E/C.12/2000/13, 2000, para 28.

1275 Sands, *Treaty, Custom and the Cross-Fertilization of International Law*, 102 f.; Pauwelyn, *Conflict of Norms in Public International Law*, 254.

1276 On the necessity to balance the rights of the covenant with state interests, CESCR, *Concluding Observations - Israel*, E/C.12/1/Add.90, 2003, para 31; Generally on positive human rights obligations, ECtHR, *Hatton and Others v. The United Kingdom*, 36022/97, para 98, stating that "the applicable principles are broadly similar. In both contexts regard must be had to the fair balance that has to be struck between the competing interests of the individual and of the community as a whole".

1277 Mégret, *Nature of Obligations*, 103; de Schutter, *International Human Rights Law*, 461; Lavrysen, *Positive Obligations in the Jurisprudence of the Inter-American Court of Human Rights*, 2014 Inter-Am. Eur. Hum. Rts. J. 7, 94, 110; Schabas, *ECHR Commentary*, 90 f.; HRCom, *GC 31*, CCPR/C/21/Rev.1/Add.13, para 7; ECOSOC, *Updated Study on the Right to Food, Submitted by Mr. Asbjorn Eide*, E/CN.4/Sub.2/1999/12, 1999, para 15.

1278 HRCom, *GC 36*, CCPR/C/GC/36, para 26.

the enjoyment of human rights generally.[1279] Reparation can, under certain circumstances, exacerbate tension in the population and thereby enhance the risk that systematic human rights violations resume.[1280]

The abstract and concrete weight of the last-mentioned obligation is exceptionally high, given the grave and multiple dangers conflict poses to the enjoyment of fundamental human rights. This does not translate into a great weight of that obligation in the balancing exercise, though. No straight chain of causation runs from awarding reparation to heightened instability or the resumption of human rights violations. It is never certain whether reparation will exacerbate tension and make the recurrence of systematic human rights violations more likely. Hence, the low or unclear probability with which reparation could lead to these consequences diminishes the weight of that argument accordingly. Besides, the state can mitigate tensions and make resumed conflict less likely.[1281] The obligation's weight should therefore not be overestimated.

The concrete importance of the obligation to enhance the enjoyment of human rights depends on how flexibly its scope of protection accommodates competing claims. The positive obligation to take steps to ensure the full enjoyment of human rights is a due diligence standard. It does not require the state to prevent any infringement of the right concerned but to take reasonable preventive measures.[1282] As the ECtHR detailed:

1279 HRCom, *GC 36*, CCPR/C/GC/36, para 69 f.; HRCom, *General Comment No. 6 - Article 6 (Right to Life)*, HRI/GEN/1/Rev.1, 1982, para 2. Relatedly, the ECtHR considered that the "restoration of peace" is a legitimate aim under the convention, ECtHR, *Sejdić and Finci v. Bosnia and Herzegovina*, 27996/06 (Grand Chamber), 2009, para 45. Of course, one could also categorize this as an issue of the dimension to protect individuals from interference with their rights by third parties or the respect dimension, if there is a danger of renewed systematic human rights violations by state agents. However, on a highly abstract level, the dimension to fulfill captures the holistic work needed to prevent such events from happening. The obligation to respect and protect concern more individualized conduct and thus let broader structural factors of renewed conflict fade from view.

1280 Usually, this will not happen through such a direct causal chain of events that one could classify reparation as the state action that failed to respect human rights. Therefore, on an abstract level, reparation is better conceived as a factor, which caused a worsened human rights situation generally.

1281 Fears of tension were successfully addressed in Timor-Leste by employing mediation teams and because survivors spread the benefits in the community, ICTJ, *Dealing With the 2006 Internal Displacement Crisis in Timor-Leste*, 8 ff.

1282 Shelton/Gould, *Positive and Negative Obligations*, 577.

> *"In determining the scope of a State's positive obligations, regard must be had to the fair balance that has to be struck between the general interest and the interests of the individual, the diversity of situations obtaining in Contracting States and the choices which must be made in terms of priorities and resources. Nor must these obligations be interpreted in such a way as to impose an impossible or disproportionate burden."*[1283]

This context-dependency can account to a degree for the competing demands of the right to reparation and, therefore, somewhat diminishes the concrete importance of positive obligations under civil and political rights. Again, though, competing reparation claims cannot entirely do away with positive obligations under civil and political rights.

bb. Negative Human Rights Obligations

Reparation can also compete with states' negative obligation to respect human rights. In the realm of civil and political rights, reparation can touch upon the obligation to respect by directly interfering with other persons' human rights. Such scenarios are manifold. Consider as an apparent example prosecution as a form of reparation. Their resolution depends on the circumstances. It is impossible to give general guidelines to that effect beyond what was said at the beginning of this chapter. Economic, social, and cultural rights entail two negative obligations. They forbid retrogression in their realization and contain a minimum core of realization, which must not be frustrated.[1284] The abstract weight of those obligations again depends on the abstract weight of the rights in question. Their different structure influences their concrete importance.

Retrogression triggers the presumption that the right concerned is violated. Retrogressive measures can be justified by reference to other rights within the covenant if the state considers all other alternatives against the context of its maximum available resources.[1285] The Committee on Economic, Social

1283 ECtHR, *Ilascu and Others v. Moldova and Russia*, 48787/99 (Grand Chamber), 2004, para 332. Similarly HRCom, *GC 36*, CCPR/C/GC/36, para 21.

1284 CESCR, *GC 3*, E/1991/23, para 9 f.; Saul et al., *The International Covenant on Economic, Social and Cultural Rights - Commentary, Cases and Materials*, 2014, 145 ff.

1285 Such is the standard phrasing by the CESCR. For an enumeration of general comments containing that standard see OHCHR, *Protection of Economic, Social and Cultural Rights in Conflict*, 2015, para 25.

and Cultural Rights (CESCR) noted that it would consider "serious claims on [a state's] limited resources, for example, resulting from [...] recent internal or international armed conflict."[1286] Retrogressive measures can hence be justified with reference to reparation, if necessary and proportionate.[1287] The prohibition's concrete importance in the balancing exercise depends on the severity of retrogression.

The treatment of minimum core obligations under economic, social, and cultural rights is dogmatically less clear. For some rights, the CESCR held that states must fulfill these minimum core obligations immediately and prioritize all available resources for their satisfaction. Whether a state discharged these obligations must be assessed against resource constraints the state faces.[1288] For other rights, the CESCR fleshed out core obligations, for which "a State Party cannot, under any circumstances whatsoever, justify

1286 CESCR, *Evaluation of the Obligation to Take Steps to the "Maximum Available Resources"*, E/C.12/2007/1, para 10.

1287 cf. CESCR, *Letter Dated 16 May 2012 Addressed by the Chairperson of the Committee on Economic, Social and Cultural Rights to States Parties to the International Covenant on Economic, Social and Cultural Rights*, 2012; CESCR, *Concluding Observations on the Fourth Periodic Report of Argentina*, E/C.12/ARG/CO/4, 2018, para 6(e); CESCR, *Concluding Observations on the Fourth Periodic Report of France*, E/C.12/FRA/CO/4, 2016. For further sources of the committee employing that standard see Warwick, *Socio-Economic Rights During Economic Crises - A Changed Approach to Non-Retrogression*, 2016 Intl. Comp. L. Q. 65(1), 249, fn. 58. The author also traces the genesis of the comparatively new standard and offers some critique, 252 ff. The other requirements apart from necessity and porportionality – namely the temporary nature of the measure, non-discrimination and protection of core obligations – are either of no concern for this study or are treated at other points in this chapter. If states limit an economic, social or cultural rights for other reasons than a lack of resources, Art. 4 ICESCR allows them to do so, Saul et al., *The ICESCR*, 257 f. In that case, the restriction must also pursue a legitimate aim, be necessary and proportionate, CESCR, *General Comment No. 21 - Right of Everyone to Take Part in Cultural Life* E/C.12/GC/21, 2009, para 19; Saul et al., *The ICESCR*, 254 ff. The resolution of such conflicts cannot be determined in the abstract, it depends on the factors outlined above, B.II.2, esp. b. Art. 4 ICESCR played a minor role in practice so far since most cases, in which states have to limit economic, social and cultural rights hinge upon the availability of resources, Saul et al., *The ICESCR*, 246 f.

1288 CESCR, *GC 3*, E/1991/23, para 10; CESCR, *Evaluation of the Obligation to Take Steps to the "Maximum Available Resources"*, E/C.12/2007/1, para 6; CESCR, *General Comment No. 19 - The Right to Social Security*, E/C.12/GC/19, 2007, para 60; CESCR, *Limburg Principles*, E/C.12/2000/13, para 72.

its non-compliance."[1289] It is unclear how these two lines of argument relate to each other. Some authors treat the differing standards simply as inconsistencies, heavily criticizing the expanding scope of non-justifiable core obligations.[1290] Mechlem convincingly showed that some nations would be unable to comply with the extensive core obligation catalogs the CESCR drew up especially in its general comments on the right to water and health, should non-compliance truly be unjustifiable. It would also be at odds with the general framework of the International Covenant on Economic, Social and Cultural Rights (ICESCR), its object and purpose, as well as subsequent state practice.[1291] As shown above, it is also theoretically more convincing to perceive core obligations as the result of a proportionality assessment rather than as abstractly defined obligations.[1292] Hence, the core obligations' scope should be identified against the capabilities a state has when directing all available resources to meet them. Falling behind minimum core obligations thus defined is a particularly strong retrogression, which carries such strong concrete importance that it will outweigh almost all competing claims to reparation.[1293]

cc. State Interests

Lastly, large-scale reparation programs can touch any legitimate state interests by diverting resources from them. Among these legitimate interests are upholding the state's internal order and pursuing economic development.[1294] The abstract weight of these interests depends on their importance in the

1289 CESCR, *GC 14*, E/C.12/2000/4, para 47; CESCR, *General Comment No. 15 - The Right to Water,* E/C.12/2002/11, 2003, para 40; CESCR, *The Maastricht Guidelines on Violations of Economic, Social and Cultural Rights,* E/C.12/2000/13, 2000, para 9 f.

1290 Mechlem, *Treaty Bodies and the Interpretation of Human Rights*, 2009 Vand. J. Transnatl. L 42(3), 905, 940 ff.

1291 Mechlem, *Treaty Bodies and the Interpretation of Human Rights*, 943 f.

1292 See above, B.II.2.c.

1293 Should one choose to follow the interpretation of abstract core obligations non-compliance with which cannot be justified, the result would only be a little stronger. The gap between "outweigh almost all competing claims" and "impossible to justify" seems more theoretical than of practical relevance.

1294 Public order is recognized as a legitimate aim for restricting rights in the derogation clauses, namely Art. 4(1) ICCPR, Art. 15 ECHR, Art. 27(1) ACHR. Development needs of the state are recognized in Art. 32(2) ACHR, referring to general welfare for development; Art. 23, 24, 27(2) ACHPR, referring to common interests for development. It was also recognized in IACtHR, *Salvador Chiriboga v. Ecuador*, 2008, para 73.

human rights framework.[1295] The fact that human rights protect the individual against state interests diminishes their abstract weight. There is hence a presumption that human rights take precedence.[1296] Not least because of that, the ECtHR demands that competing positions other than those backed by convention rights must be indisputable imperatives to place a legitimate restriction on individual rights.[1297] This demand is even more robust in the case under consideration because the state assumed the obligation to repair by violating survivors' rights. The state could have avoided the burden of reparation so that easing it for safeguarding state interests requires greater justification than when reparation affects third parties. The concrete importance of state interests depends on the degree to which reparation interferes with them. Again, when it comes to the claim that reparation could put internal order in jeopardy, one must factor in the probability of this event and the possibility to take mitigating measures.[1298]

5. Summary

The resources to be allocated to the reparation program are an outcome of obligations to increase the resources available and distribute them fairly between the competing rights and obligations. The first set of obligations consists of a loose responsibility to raise resources; the duty to seek external support and synergies between reparation and assistance, without diluting reparation's roots in state responsibility. While this makes the normative conflict between prompt reparation and competing obligations less pressing, it is too severe to avoid it entirely. States must balance the aggregate claims to prompt reparation with the positive and negative human rights obligations and state interests with which they conflict. The outcome depends on the abstract weight and concrete importance of the relevant positions and the probability with which they are affected. Naturally, that depends to a large degree on the concrete situation. As far as possible in the abstract, the previous section considered factors that influence the respective positions' weight. It found that the right to reparation does not possess an exceptionally high

1295 See above, B.II.2.b.

1296 Cariolou, *The Search for an Equilibrium by the ECtHR*, 251, 265 f.

1297 ECtHR, *Chassagnou and Others v. France*, 25088/94 (Grand Chamber), 1999, para 113.

1298 For details regarding the concrete weight and the operation of the probability factor in a similar context see above, E.II.4.c.aa.

abstract weight. Its scope of protection can accommodate challenges of the transitional situation, diminishing its concrete importance. The following matrix summarizes decisive factors influencing the weight of other positions in the balancing exercise, using the values of the triadic scale, light, medium, or strong (l, m, s):[1299]

Competing Claim	Abstract Weight	Concrete Importance	Factors Determining Concrete Weight
Positive Human Rights Obligations			
Progressive Realization of Economic, Social, and Cultural Rights	l-s	l-s	- Abstract weight of right(s) realized - Level of realization - Degree of non-satisfaction envisaged - Number of persons affected[1300] - Probability of non-satisfaction
Obligation to Fulfill Civil and Political Rights	l-s	l-s	- Abstract weight of right(s) fulfilled - Degree of fulfillment - Degree of non-satisfaction envisaged - Number of persons affected - Probability of non-satisfaction
Obligation to Prevent Conflict under Civil and Political Rights	s	l-m	- Probability that reparation enhances the risk of resumed conflict

1299 On the triadic scale see above, B.II.2.b.

1300 While the number of persons affected influences the concrete weight of the different rights and interests at play, balancing cannot be reduced to counting the quantity of people affected on each side of the equation. A core function of human rights is to protect minorities, so that giving decisive weight to numbers would undermine one of their fundamental purposes, Çalı, *Balancing Human Rights? Methodological Problems With Weights, Scales and Proportions*, 2007 Hum. Rts. Q. 29(1), 25, 261 ff.; ECtHR, *Hatton and Others v. The United Kingdom - Joint Dissenting Opinion of Judges Costa, Ress, Türmen, Zupančič and Steiner*, 36022/97 (Grand Chamber), 2003, para 14. Hence, it is crucial not to treat balancing as a numbers game. Determining whether an interference with a right is light, medium or strong is at its core a value judgment in light of the object and purpose of the rights in question and the circumstances of the case at hand, Klatt/Meister, *The Constitutional Structure of Proportionality*, 2012, 12, 57.

Competing Claim	Abstract Weight	Concrete Importance	Factors Determining Concrete Weight
Negative Human Rights Obligations			
Prohibition of Retrogression in Realizing Economic, Social, and Cultural Rights	l-s	m-s	- Abstract weight of right(s) whose realization retrogresses - Degree of retrogression - Number of persons affected - Probability of retrogression
Core Obligations under Economic, Social, and Cultural Rights	l-s	s	- Abstract weight of right(s) whose core obligations are concerned - Number of persons - affected - Probability of infringement
Obligation to Respect Civil and Political Rights	l-s	l-s	- Abstract weight of right(s) concerned - Severity of interference - Number of persons affected - Probability of interference
State Interests			
State Interests	l-m	l-s	- Abstract weight of interest(s) - Degree of interference - Probability of interference

Figure 8: Balancing Matrix (created by the author)

Obviously, a matrix covering such diverse and complex situations remains at a high level of abstraction, leaving states a lot of discretion.[1301] Its abstract nature makes the approach prone to abuse. It provides states with the language to justify cuts in reparation demands while not allowing for close scrutiny of those justifications. This makes a caveat all the more important: Any restrictions on the scope of reparation programs must be necessary. States must demonstrate the existence of a normative conflict and the extent to which it justifies diminishing the scope of a reparation program.[1302] They must also attempt everything in their power to avoid normative conflict. They must use their resources as efficiently as possible when providing reparation and design reparation as far as possible in a way that furthers fulfillment of their other obligations instead of conflicting with them.[1303]

1301 See on that also ECtHR, *Pentiacova and Others v. Moldova, Decision on Admissibility*, 14462/02, 2005, 13.

1302 Ducoulombier, *Conflicts Between Fundamental Rights*, 223 f.

1303 On the legal constraints of that strategy see above, E.II.3.

6. Challenges

Challenging the present approach, one could doubt whether the right to reparation is open to balancing at all. After all, the state voluntarily assumed the burden of reparation by choosing to violate human rights. It could act in bad faith if it violated a human right and then claim competing interests to diminish the consequential obligation to award reparation.[1304] This position would make the right to reparation de facto an absolute right, which was shown above to be implausible.[1305] Furthermore, limiting the right to reparation is necessary to safeguard not only state interests but also the rights of others. Denying that possibility would affect not only the responsible state but also third parties. Although somewhat anachronistic, balancing hence better serves the overall goal of protecting all human rights of everyone.

A second challenge could be that balancing merely substitutes one problem with the next. Instead of overwhelming states' resources, the reparation programs' financial scope can be limited so severely that the measures they provide to each survivor become diluted to the degree that reparation becomes meaningless. This challenge will be taken up in the next section, especially when considering the unique role of satisfaction in transitional justice reparation efforts.[1306] But before turning to the output of reparation programs, there is the elephant in the room to address. The reader's main doubt at this point will, in all likelihood, not lie so much with the technical question of whether balancing is permissible in the situation at hand or with a fear of dilution of benefits. Rather, the reader might doubt the author's relationship with reality.

1304 AComHPR, *GC 4*, para 34. The commission holds that states cannot rely on limited resources to evade awarding comprehensive reparation. It leaves room to lower the amount awarded, since comprehensive reparation is a flexible concept. The ECtHR frequently holds that states cannot "cite lack of funds as an excuse for not honouring a judgment debt", ECtHR, *Burdov v. Russia*, 59498/00 (First Section), 2002, para 35; ECtHR, *Sharxhi and Others v. Albania*, 10613/16 (First Section), 2018, para 154. However, it draws this conclusion from Art. 6(1), 13 ECHR, guaranteeing the enforcement of judgments. The line of jurisprudence therefore cannot substantiate the position that the right to reparation cannot be limited. Only under the special circumstance that a judgment ordered the state to pay reparation can it support such a position. Furthermore, it is not a lack of funds as such that provides a justification for limiting the right to reparation, but the existence of legitimate other claims against the state's resources.

1305 See above, B.II.2.a.

1306 See below, E.IV.2.b.

No reality fits in a neat matrix; the particularly complex reality of transitional justice situations even less. Striking a balance by identifying the abstract weight, concrete importance, and probability of interference with all rights and interests reparation programs touch hardly seems to deliver on the author's promise to restore the international law on reparation's guiding function in transitional justice. This doubt cannot be repudiated by further concretizing the matrix or readily admitting that concretizing is feasible only for concrete situations. Instead, expectations towards what the normative conflict approach, and indeed any legal approach, can achieve must be lowered. Law will never provide a formula, which only requires the correct data to deliver the exact amount of resources needed for adequate reparation in transitional justice. For that, the situation is too complex and contingent. Reparation in transitional justice will always result from a political process and be subject to continuing negotiations between the state, survivors, and other actors. In the often dynamic transitional justice situations, reparation programs are constantly renegotiated, reevaluated, and adapted to new developments and information. Law cannot replace that. But the political processes just described often suffer from an equivocation: When debating, which reparation is adequate, the state tends to point to its limited resources, defending reparation's adequacy as the maximum it allegedly was able to administer. Survivors, in turn, criticize reparation as inadequate because it does not serve to overcome their harm. Such an equivocation about what makes reparation adequate is fatal. It renders any debate or negotiation fruitless and frustrates all sides. Law can remedy this situation not by prescribing exact outcomes but by providing the actors involved with a common language and a structured process to justify and criticize reparation efforts. It thereby allows rational debate and fruitful negotiation about the adequacy of reparation in transitional justice. While modest, that – not exact calculation – is what the law on reparation can achieve in transitional justice.

III. Distribution: Breaking Down the Scope of the Program

So far, the analysis treated survivors' claims to reparation as a monolithic aggregate. Once balancing determined the absolute amount of available resources that way, they must be distributed internally among survivors. This distribution equals a zero-sum-game between survivors and hence puts their respective claims to reparation in conflict. The abstract weight of those claims is irrelevant because the conflict exists between different holders of the same right. With the abstract weight the same, each survivor's share should be reduced by the same factor. That way, all claims to reparation would be limited equally, and the result would still reflect the amount of harm suffered.

Alternatively, one could also focus on need, giving a larger share to more indigent or vulnerable survivors. Less affluent survivors rely stronger on reparation to overcome their harm. According to the principle of diminishing marginal utility, the same amount of material benefit has more utility for a poor survivor than for a rich one, all other circumstances being equal.[1307] Still, the object of reparation is not to raise survivors' standard of living. It remedies harm incurred. In many cases, a survivor's poverty will exacerbate the harm suffered from a human rights violation. Losing the only plot of land one relies on for subsistence farming will have much graver consequences than losing part of an agricultural empire. In that case, reparation must account for that exacerbated effect. Nevertheless, its object is then still to remedy harm, not raising the survivor's standard of living. Relying on need, therefore, misconstrues the telos of reparation. The only factor for the just distribution of the available resources among survivors is the seriousness of the harm. In practice, this could mean downscaling measures if their costs and the general burden of providing them would go to the detriment of other survivors. It can consume a disproportionate amount of resources, e.g., to fly survivors out of the country to receive specialized medical treatment. A second-best alternative striking a fairer balance with other needs for reparation might be to mitigate pain and detrimental effects of an ailment until the general health care system is sufficiently developed to provide specialized treatment. Again, it deserves emphasis that states have an obligation to avoid such a conflict as far as possible. Instead of flying in trained psychologists, training could enable laypersons to deliver limited psychological interventions and remit only the gravest cases to the few trained psychologists available in the country.[1308] As in general, the law demands a state's creativity and ingenuity before it can legitimately claim a normative conflict. That will be the subject of the following section.

1307 Sampat Mukherjee et al., *Microeconomics*, 2004, 49 f.

1308 As an example of the feasibility of this approach see the Lubanga-case before the ICC above, ch. 2, D.III.2.b.aa.; Chibanda, *Why I Train Grandmothers to Treat Depression,* TEDWomen2017, 2017.

IV. Output: Devising Adequate Reparation Measures

Obligations to raise resources, use them efficiently, and strike a fair balance between competing demands define reparation programs' input. Internal balancing breaks this number down to how much each survivor is entitled to. That says little about the programs' output. Which concrete reparation measures should the state devise? This section will fill that gap. The starting point is that the international law on reparation demands full reparation for each survivor. After a quick recap of what that entails (1.) the chapter will adapt these demands to the unique transitional situation by according a critical role to satisfaction (2.).

1. Applying Full Reparation in Transitional Justice

As demonstrated, there is no need to change the fundamental rules on reparation in transitional justice.[1309] Survivors must receive restitution, compensation, rehabilitation, satisfaction, and guarantees of non-repetition corresponding to the harm they suffered because of the violation. These measures must serve as far as possible to put them in the position they would be in had the violation not been committed.[1310] It is of little use to specify further in the abstract which reparation measures are adequate for which situation. Devising adequate reparation measures strongly depends on the context. International and national practice abound with examples of adequate measures for different circumstances. Great studies summarize and analyze this question, to which the present one has nothing to add but two general points required by the principle of effectiveness. First, reparation must seek individual effectiveness. To achieve the goal of corrective justice as effectively as possible, reparation must ensure that the individual survivor can overcome their harm as effectively as possible.[1311] The same obligation arises out of the obligation to avoid normative conflict. The more effectively a state uses limited resources to overcome individual harm, the less pressing the normative conflict with competing claims is. The state must thus do more

1309 See above, E.I. The Special Rapporteur on Transitional Justice also demands that the content of reparation programs "must be framed within the principle of 'full reparation'", HRC, *Report on Domestic Reparation Programs*, A/HRC/42/45, para 39.

1310 See above, ch. 1, B., C.

1311 The AU explicitly invokes this principle, AU, *Transitional Justice Policy*, 2019, para 66(iv).

with less. All case studies put this principle into action. For example, most reparation programs coupled individual compensation with seminars on how to best use the money provided, thereby – in theory – enhancing its effect.[1312]

Second, states must look towards general effectiveness, that is, use reparation as effectively as possible to protect human rights through enhancing respect for human rights and establishing general horizontal and vertical trust. The state must tailor the message of validity, applicability, enforceability, and importance of human rights to make state institutions and members of society as trustworthy as possible.[1313] As mentioned above, the obligation to avoid normative conflict also obliges the state, if possible, to design reparation in a way that furthers general interest, decreases tension, and benefits the broader population. Beyond these general considerations, the state still has a significant degree of flexibility in designing reparation measures. There is no single correct solution, and the state is free to choose among measures of equal effectiveness.

These vague clarifications leave untouched a question mark carried over from the previous section. Broadly balancing the aggregated claims to reparation with competing claims might enable the state to award reparation to all survivors and make eligibility restrictions unnecessary. But how can it be prevented that the balancing exercise dilutes the benefits given to each survivor beyond recognition?

2. The Residual Function of Satisfaction

While almost all survivors must be eligible for reparation and receive benefits, not every survivor must "necessarily [receive benefits] at the same level or of the same kind."[1314] Not every survivor must receive costly measures like compensation or go through complex and costly procedures required, e.g., by many restitution cases. Yet, the fundamental problem remains that reducing the material scope of reparation programs while advocating for comprehensive, complete, and full reparation seems to make the dilution of individual reparation measures inevitable. One measure exists, though, which can be rolled out adequately at little cost to a large number of survivors: satisfaction.

1312 See above, ch. 2, B.IV.2.b., c., C.IV.3.b., D.III.3.b.bb.
1313 For this obligation in the context of symbolic reparation see below, E.IV.2.b.
1314 OHCHR, *Reparation Programmes*, 15; HRC, *Report on Domestic Reparation Programs*, A/HRC/42/45, para 45.

a. Defining Satisfaction

As discerned above, international practice rarely defines satisfaction in a way that would allow precise interpretation of its role within a broader framework. Relevant documents, judgments, and other national or international practice usually provide a laundry list of possible measures, including apologies, monuments, commemoration ceremonies, and many others.[1315] Practice gives little indication of what ties these examples together.

As a starting point, chapter one defined satisfaction as a symbolic act to remedy harm that is not financially assessable.[1316] This definition allows two approaches to clarify the role of satisfaction further; one looking at its function, the other at its form.

Functionally, satisfaction addresses harm that is not financially assessable, such as ruptures in a community's social fabric, feelings of humiliation, degradation, etc.[1317] Ideally, it helps survivors lend new meaning to and make sense of their situation,[1318] thereby restoring their dignity, honor, and reputation.[1319] How reparation can achieve these aspiring goals is best explored through its form. All satisfaction measures have in common that any material benefit they might entail is only incidental.[1320] Satisfaction's reparative value lies in its symbolism. At a high level of abstraction, symbols are something that stands in for something else.[1321] Peirce's more detailed

1315 Shelton, *Remedies in International Human Rights Law*, 396, 278; UNGA, *Basic Principles*, A/RES/60/147, para 22(d).

1316 See above, ch. 1, C.III. Shelton, *Remedies in International Human Rights Law*, 383 f.; Odier Contreras-Garduno, *Collective Reparations*, 89.

1317 Non-exhaustive lists of the damages addressed by satisfaction can be found at, Shelton, *Remedies in International Human Rights Law*, 346 f.; Odier Contreras-Garduno, *Collective Reparations*, 89 ff.; McCarthy, *Reparations and Victim Support in the ICC*, 283, 290.

1318 OHCHR, *Reparation Programmes*, 23; Hamber, *Narrowing the Micro and the Macro*, 560, 566.

1319 Wyler/Papaux, *The Different Forms of Reparation - Satisfaction*, 625; ILC, *Second Report on State Responsibility by Special Rapporteur Arangio-Ruiz*, A/CN.4/425, para 13; *Rainbow Warrior Case*, para 122; Ramírez, *La Jurisprudencia de la Corte Interamericana de Derechos Humanos en Materia de Reparaciones*, 80.

1320 Naturally, this distinction is not clear-cut. There will be grey areas, in which a form of reparation will repair both through its material and symbolic value. The individual compensation payment in the Katanga-case at the ICC probably is a case in point. The amount of 250 USD is not so low that it has no material reparatory value whatsoever. Still, the chamber deemed it mostly a symbolic gesture, see above, D.III.b.bb.

1321 Chandler, *Semiotics - The Basics*, 3rd Edition 2017, 2.

semiotic model conceptualizes the sign[1322] as a three-part relationship, consisting of the signifier, the signified, and the interpretant. The signifier is the carrier of a sign's meaning – in the case of a common symbolic reparation measure, e.g., the physical monument. The signified is what the sign stands for – e.g., the validity, applicability, enforceability, and importance of human rights. Through introducing the interpretant, Peirce acknowledges the role of the sign's recipient. The interpretant is the image that any given recipient forms of the sign in their mind. This three-part model gives rise to the process of semiosis: The recipient of a sign perceives its signifier, e.g., the block of stone making up the monument. To understand that the signifier stands in for the signified – e.g., the message of validity, applicability, enforceability, and importance of human rights – the recipient must form an image of that relationship in their mind: the interpretant.[1323] For Peirce, a symbol is a sign for which convention ties the signified to the signifier, e.g., a blindfolded woman holding sword and scale signifying justice. The conventional connection is arbitrary. With that, symbols differ from icons, where the signifier resembles the signified (e.g., iconic illustrations of men and women on toilet doors) and indexes, where the signifier logically connects to the signified (smoke as a sign of fire). Without a natural connection between signifier and signified, interpretation plays a prominent role when decoding a symbol's meaning.[1324] Interpretation relies on the situational context as well as social convention. These limit a sign's potential meanings and can guide the processes of semiosis.[1325] This brief summary of one semiotic approach to symbols cannot do justice to this fascinating theory. But taken together with the functional approach above and the transitional justice theory at the basis of this chapter, it can give an approximate account of what satisfaction is and how it can work in transitional justice.

Peirce teaches that symbols can evoke mental images and thereby communicate with their receivers. For that process to remedy harm, the messages symbols send must have a reparative effect. Thus, if satisfaction shall address moral harm by helping survivors make sense of their situation, restoring their

1322 In semiotics, a symbol often denotes a subform of a sign, although no generally accepted definitions of both terms exist. The understanding of the two terms taken here will be clarified below in this section.

1323 Chandler, *Semiotics*, 29 ff., 35 f.; Manning, *Semiotics and Fieldwork*, 1987, 31 f.; Eco, *A Theory of Semiotics*, 1976, 68.

1324 Chandler, *Semiotics*, 41, 45; Peirce/Hoopes, *Peirce on Signs - Writings on Semiotic*, 1991, 251.

1325 Chandler, *Semiotics*, 178 f., 194.

dignity, honor, and reputation, it must send the corresponding messages. For example, a monument to survivors can communicate that they should take a central place in society instead of suffering marginalization. A commemoration ceremony can lend meaning to violations by communicating that survivors' experiences help society overcome conflict and prevent its recurrence. Simultaneously, symbolic reparation can be particularly well-placed to achieve the transitional-justice-specific aim of reparation. An apology, memorial, or commemoration ceremony has at its core the message that human rights are valid, applicable, enforceable, and important to the state and members of society.

There is no prescribed way of sending these messages. The signifier must connect to its signified in a way that the receivers – survivors and society as a whole – form the corresponding interpretant in their minds. Put less academically: They must receive the intended message. How exactly that can be achieved is a matter of context and cannot be determined in the abstract.

b. Satisfaction's Role in Transitional Justice

No matter what form symbolic reparation takes in the concrete case, it can provide a way out of the dilemma that sticking to full reparation and denying the possibility to exclude survivors from reparation programs caused. Since satisfaction repairs not through material benefits but its symbolic content, it can be administered to many survivors simultaneously. Public apologies, monuments, ceremonies, or other events can reach many survivors in meaningful ways without overburdening the state.[1326] To further ease the financial burden of providing satisfaction, it is essential to recall that both truth and prosecution are forms of symbolic reparation if they deal with the violation suffered by the individual concerned.[1327] Therefore, truth

1326 Antkowiak hints at a similar solution, Antkowiak, *Remedial Approaches*, 399 f.

1327 See above ch. 1, C.III. Hamber, *The Dilemmas of Reparations*, 137 ff. In IACtHR, *Case of the Afro-Descendant Communities Displaced From the Cacarica River Basin (Operation Genesis) v. Colombia*, 2013, the court held that in transitional justice "reparation must be understood in conjunction with other measures of truth and justice (...)", para 470. See further, Lawry-White, *The Reparative Effect of Truth Seeking in Transitional Justice*, 2015 Intl. Comp. L. Q. 64(1), 141, 150 ff. The Special Rapporteur on Transitional Justice excludes other transitional justice mechanisms from the definition of reparation for the reason that they are usually created by other political bodies. It seems to be a practical delimitation rather than one with legal

commissions, prosecutions, and other mechanisms can be considered satisfaction if they relate to the individual survivors' harm.[1328]

An enhanced role of satisfaction runs into a conceptual problem, though. To provide a way out of the dilemma posited above, it must be the sole reparation measure many, if not most, survivors receive. It cannot, however, simply substitute other material forms of reparation. Whereas, e.g., compensation and rehabilitation can address roughly the same harm and are therefore often interchangeable, satisfaction only addresses financially non-assessable harm. Survivors in transitional justice rarely suffered such harm only. Using satisfaction to make truly comprehensive, complete, and full reparation feasible thus requires expanding its role. The principles of effectiveness and adequacy can justify this expansion.

Broad balancing will reduce the amount of material reparation available – be it in the form of compensation, rehabilitation, or other. Since individual reparation awards should be limited by the same factor to break down reparation programs' financial scope, balancing will reduce the claim to material reparation of survivors who have suffered comparatively less harm to close to zero. In those cases, material reparation cannot fulfill its purpose to overcome the harm the individual suffered. Still providing it would be a mere formalism. Even worse, while the minimum amount due would be worthless to individual survivors, in aggregate, it presented a significant sum, which could develop more impact elsewhere. Such an interpretation would hence unnecessarily impair other rights and interests. Its reduced and adverse effects would also undermine the program's legitimacy. Society and survivors would likely not see minimal material reparation as a genuine reparation effort by the state. Under such circumstances, reparation could hardly communicate the validity, applicability, enforceability, and importance of human rights. On the contrary, it might be perceived as mockery. Thus, rigidly sticking to the law's letter would undermine both the individual and transitional-justice-specific reparation goals.

---

significance and can therefore be disregarded in this context, HRC, *Report of the Special Rapporteur on Transitional Justice*, A/HRC/30/42, para 21.

1328 Generally, one can assume that the more personal relevance a mechanism assumes for a survivor, the more satisfaction it provides them. Different factors influence personal relevancy, including the instances the truth commission or prosecution cover, the credibility of the truth uncovered, the individuals prosecuted and the degree of participation of survivors, cf. Lawry-White, *The Reparative Effect of Truth Seeking in Transitional Justice*, 152, 165 ff.

In response, one should raise the threshold of harm above which survivors receive material reparation. If, after the balancing exercise, their claim to reparation is so limited that it could not serve its purposes, they should receive symbolic reparation only. Raising the threshold is not only supported by a sound teleological and systemic interpretation of the right to reparation but also preserves reparation's adequacy. As discussed above, adequacy opens reparation to considerations of context. If the context of reparation changes so that the usual measures fail to further corrective justice, undermine that aim in other cases, and endanger the goals of the transition, they become inadequate.[1329] Besides, social psychology and sociology might support this position, even though due to the author's lack of knowledge in this area, this is advanced as an idea rather than an argument. While details are unsettled, speaking very generally, individuals assess their happiness and feelings of deprivation in relation to others. The reference group(s) with which an individual compares their situation influence their situation assessment.[1330] During systematic human rights violations, the comparison probably yields different results than under "normal" circumstances. It is fair to speculate that a survivor weighs a violation of their right to freedom of expression differently when most people around them lead tranquil lives as opposed to when other people get killed and tortured. If the subjective gravity of harm partially depends on the circumstances, this context-dependency could justify raising the gravity threshold for material reparation in response to systematic human rights violations.

Lastly, the position can also rely on practice. Many states address satisfaction to a broader circle of survivors than those eligible for the reparation programs.[1331] International jurisprudence redeems small quantities of harm,

1329 For similar considerations concerning individual material awards being "disproportionate to what could be achieved", ICC, *Ntaganda Reparations Order*, ICC-01/04-02/06-2659, para 194.

1330 Muffels, *Relative Income and Reference Group Behavior*, in: Michalos (ed.), *Encyclopedia of Quality of Life and Well-Being Research*, 2014, 5446; Frey, *Economics of Happiness*, 2018, 26; Schulze/Krätschmer-Hahn, *Relative Deprivation Theory*, in: Michalos (ed.), *Encyclopedia of Quality of Life and Well-Being Research*, 2014, 5443; Merton, *Contributions to the Theory of Reference Group Behavior*, in: Merton (ed.), *Social Theory and Social Structure*, 1968, 279, 281 ff., 295 f.

1331 Colombia and Sierra Leone are a case in point, see above, ch. 2, B.IV.1.a., C.IV.1. Generally, it is difficult to cite certain instances of state practice as evidence of this approach, since states rarely give detailed reasons, why they choose to implement certain reparation measures over others. Still, many reparation efforts comprise measures of satisfaction directed at much broader survivor populations than those

even if material, through declaratory judgments only.[1332] Such judgments are a form of satisfaction. There is no reason why other forms of satisfaction should not fulfill the same function. On the contrary, the main feature distinguishing declaratory judgments from other forms of satisfaction – namely that such judgments stem from a third party instead of the responsible state – speaks in favor of granting the same function to other satisfaction measures. Measures coming from the responsible state can be more effective in communicating acknowledgment, non-repetition, etc. International jurisprudence, therefore, concords with letting satisfaction suffice to remedy small quantities of harm.[1333] While international bodies hold that other remedies must complement satisfaction, if the violation and harm are severe,[1334] it has been demonstrated above that the principles of effectiveness, systemic integration, adequacy, and – maybe – the context-dependency of the subjective assessment of the gravity of harm dispense with that requirement.

In sum, harm considerably less severe than that suffered by the average survivor population can be redressed exclusively through satisfaction. The exact determination of that relatively loose threshold depends on survivors' harm and the balancing exercise described above. Those survivors can be redressed through satisfaction only, whose claim to material reparation is limited to the degree that it cannot serve reparation's purposes anymore.

3. Summary

The preceding section evinced that while not initially conceived for such situations, the international law on reparation can still guide them when interpreted accordingly. States must still strive towards achieving full reparation with the limited resources the balancing exercise leaves for reparation. They must attempt to erase all harm as far as possible through restitution,

---

covered by the core reparation program. These often consist of apologies and memorialization, e.g. through a national day of victims, see e.g. Shelton, *Remedies in International Human Rights Law*, 383; Burt, *Transitional Justice in the Aftermath of Civil Conflict*, 41 f., 48; ICTJ, *Reparations in Peru*, 8. Likewise, truth commissions often cover a broader range of survivors than the reparation programs proper.

1332 See above, ch. 1, C.II, III.

1333 The IACtHR specifically mentioned that declaratory judgments can constitute "moral satisfaction", placing it in the broader category of satisfaction without distinction, IACtHR, *Victor Neira-Alegría et al. v. Peru (Reparations and Costs)*, para 56.

1334 IACtHR, *Victor Neira-Alegría et al. v. Peru (Reparations and Costs)*, para 56; IComJ, *Practitioners' Guide*, 208.

compensation, rehabilitation, satisfaction, and guarantees of non-repetition. The problem remains that states often will not have the means to provide meaningful material reparation to every survivor. States must limit the financial scope of reparation programs accordingly by balancing the aggregate claims for reparation with competing rights and interests. After distributing the resulting cuts equally among survivors, some who suffered lesser harm inevitably have their claim reduced to close to zero. To still award them minimal material reparation would undermine both purposes of reparation in transitional justice: Minimal material reparation neither furthers corrective justice nor does it contribute to strengthened respect for human rights or the trustworthiness of state institutions and members of society. For that reason, survivors who would not get any meaningful material reparation can be repaired through symbolic means only. That way, they can render meaningful symbolic reparation to a large number of survivors at a relatively small cost and retain material benefits for cases in which they have a reparatory effect.

4. Challenges

Relying mainly on an enhanced role of satisfaction to prevent the dilution of reparation can be challenged in two related ways. First, one could argue that the lofty concept of a raised harm threshold below which symbolic measures suffice to remedy material harm substitutes one arbitrary distinction with the next. Instead of dividing eligible and ineligible survivors, one now distinguishes between survivors that suffered just enough harm to be repaired materially and those that did not suffer quite enough to deserve material reparation – and hence must be satisfied with an apology. Indeed, the concept presented here makes precisely that distinction necessary. To make matters worse, the distinction is similar to the one currently drawn between eligible and ineligible survivors. Usually, only survivors of the supposedly gravest violations are eligible for reparation. Since the amount of harm a violation caused also determines its gravity, the group of ineligible survivors and the proposed group of survivors eligible for symbolic measures only will likely largely overlap in practice. It would also be false to claim that the distinction proposed here will be easier to draw in practice. Given that harm is a vague concept, some cases' categorization as being above or below the threshold will be arbitrary. Again, much must be left to a political process; the law cannot reach the precision one would wish for in such complex circumstances as the transitional situation. It can again provide a language to justify, criticize and challenge certain decisions. But so could the concept currently in use of deeming only survivors of the gravest human rights violations eligible for reparation. So why switch? Even though the two concepts' practical effects might not differ starkly, distinguishing between survivors receiving material reparation or not is anchored more firmly in the international law on reparation. The distinction between the severity of harm suffered is inherent in the international law on reparation. Distinguishing between eligible and ineligible survivors is not. That fact should not only provide lawyers and other firm believers in the intrinsic value of legal reasoning with good reasons to switch to the distinction proposed here. Its compatibility with the international law on reparation also makes for a wholly different message, much more adequate to further the aims of transitional justice. Instead of conditioning human rights enforcement on the availability of resources, awarding all survivors with some form of reparation reinforces the message of validity, applicability, enforceability, and importance of human rights. It can contribute to making state institutions and members of society trustworthy instead of disappointing survivors' normative expectations again.

This hopeful sentiment leads directly to the second challenge: Can it really? Is meager symbolic reparation not bound to disappoint survivors? Not necessarily. The power of symbolic reparation should not be underestimated. If implemented well, they can recognize survivors' suffering, repair social relations and overcome substantial harm. Thereby, they can trigger strong emotions and attain a high significance for survivors and societies as a whole.[1335] This power was summarized nicely by Hamber and Wilson:

> *"[S]ymbolic acts of reparation such as reburials, and material acts of reparation such as payments, serve the same end. Both these forms of reparation can [...] play an important role in processes of opening space for bereavement, addressing trauma and ritualizing symbolic closure. They acknowledge and recognize the individual's suffering and place it within a new officially sanctioned history of trauma. Symbolic representations of the trauma, particularly if the symbols are personalized, can concretize a traumatic event, and help reattribute responsibility. The latter stage is important because labelling responsibility can appropriately redirect blame*

1335 Brown, *Commemoration as Symbolic Reparation - New Narratives or Spaces of Conflict?*, 2013 Hum. Rts. Rev. 14(3), 273, 280 ff.; Greeley et al., *Repairing Symbolic Reparations - Assessing the Effectiveness of Memorialization in the Inter-American System of Human Rights*, 2020 Intl. J. Transitional Just. 14(1), 165. Specifically on memorials, Buckley-Zistel/Schäfer, *Memorials in Transitions - Kollektive Formen des Gedenkens*, in: Mihr et al. (eds.), *Handbuch Transitional Justice*, 2015, 45, 57 ff.

towards perpetrators and relieve the moral ambiguity and guilt survivors often feel."[1336]

The inverse case of inadequate symbolic reparation measures also demonstrates symbolic reparation's power. As mentioned before, the IACtHR caused public outcry and vandalism when it ordered the commemoration of persons killed in a prison riot. It failed to consider that the particular form of commemoration it chose to order communicated that those killed in the riot should be honored on par with the persons they might have killed when fighting for the guerilla Sendero Luminoso.[1337] Symbolic reparation can move people – for better or worse. In addition, it is not one symbolic reparation measure that adequately repairs survivors. An array of different symbolic measures tailored to the context can have the desired effect. Other than distinguishing between eligible and ineligible survivors, repairing some survivors symbolically only thus counts on a firm basis in the international law on reparation. It communicates the validity, applicability, enforceability, and importance of all human rights instead of undermining that message, contributing to the trustworthiness of state institutions and members of society. Most importantly, it can provide meaningful reparation to all survivors instead of denying them their rights.

F. Procedure

With the content of reparation treated at length, the focus can now turn to the procedural site of reparation programs. This area is of lesser normative relevance. The right to an effective remedy as the basis of the right to reparation is an obligation of result. As such, it is more concerned with the outcome of reparation than with the procedure leading up to it. As the principal right addressing procedural issues, the right to a fair trial is not directly applicable to reparation claims against the state. It covers criminal and civil proceedings, not procedures to remedy a violation of a human

1336 Hamber/Wilson, *Symbolic Closure Through Memory, Reparation and Revenge in Post-Conflict Societies*, 2002 J. Hum. Rts. 1(1), 35, 38.

1337 See above, C.II.1. A further negative but highly interesting example of the power of symbolic measures is Anderson's account of how colonial powers sought to redefine the meaning of existing monuments of the culture of colonialized subjects so that they served their ends, Anderson, *Imagined Communities - Reflections on the Origin and Spread of Nationalism*, 2nd Revised Edition 2016, 179 ff.

right.[1338] Nevertheless, the two rights are closely connected: A remedy cannot be effective if it does not comply with fundamental due process rights. These are hence read into the effectiveness criterion of the right to an effective remedy.[1339] Thus, while not requiring such strict procedural safeguards as the right to a fair trial[1340], the right to an effective remedy is not indifferent to procedure. This affects the prioritization of certain survivors in the process (I.), survivor participation (II.) and other due process issues (III.).

I. Prioritization

The caseload administrative reparation programs face warrants a conscious decision on the sequence in which to handle applications. The reparation programs studied in chapter two prioritized vulnerable survivors. Such prioritization can ensure that survivors who can better mitigate delays carry a greater share of the burden of prolonged proceedings. As seen above, the right to an effective remedy, incorporating basic notions of fair trial, demands that reparation proceedings do not become excessively long. While the exceptional circumstances in transitional justice can justify a delay, the state must do everything in its power to make proceedings as expeditious as possible. It must also account for the vulnerabilities of applicants.[1341] Accordingly, the ECtHR held that under conditions of a temporary backlog due to exceptional circumstances, states could prioritize applicants based on their vulnerability and their case's urgency.[1342] In some instances, the IACtHR and ECtHR

1338 Doswald-Beck, *Fair Trial, Right to, International Protection*, in: Wolfrum (ed.), *Max Planck Encyclopedia of Public International Law,* Online Edition 2013, para 1. This already becomes apparent from the French wording of Art. 14 ICCPR, speaking of "droit et obligations de caractère civil" and Art. 6 ECHR. Badawi El-Sheikh, *Preliminary Remarks on the Right to a Fair Trial Under the African Charter on Human and Peoples' Rights*, in: Wolfrum/Weissbrodt (eds.), *The Right to a Fair Trial,* 1997, 327, 331.

1339 HRCom, *Rawle Kennedy v. Trinidad and Tobago*, CCPR/C/74/D/845/1998, 845/1998, 2002, para 7.10, 8; IACtHR, *Velásquez-Rodríguez v. Honduras (Preliminary Objections)*, 1987, para 91; ECtHR, *Scordino v. Italy (No. 1)*, 36813/97, para 195 ff.; HRCom, *Anthony Currie v. Jamaica*, CCPR/C/50/D/377/1989, 377/1989, 1994, para 13.4; IAComHR, *Reparation Guidelines*, OEA/Ser/L/V/II.131, para 9; IAComHR, *Compendium,* OEA/Ser.L/V/II.Doc. 121, para 178; Schmitt, *Access to Justice and International Organizations*, 96 f.

1340 ECtHR, *Geouffre de la Pradelle v. France*, 12964/87 (Chamber), 1992, para 37.

1341 See above, E.II.4.a.

1342 ECtHR, *Zimmermann and Steiner v. Switzerland*, 8737/79 (Chamber), 1983, para 29.

demanded particular attention to especially vulnerable applicants, including their prioritization in proceedings.[1343] This finds support in state practice.[1344] Hence, when vulnerable survivors face excessively long reparation proceedings, the state must prioritize their reparation applications.

II. Participation

Participation of survivors is widely regarded as a hallmark of the quality and legitimacy of a reparation program.[1345] Giving survivors a voice in creating and implementing reparation measures ensures that their needs and views are accounted for. It goes a long way towards making reparation adequate.[1346] Participation also furthers the transitional justice process. When the state engages in a dialogue with survivors on equal footing, it underlines the sincerity of its agenda to ensure that their human rights are valid, applicable, enforceable, and important again. Actively engaging with the recipients of that message will also enhance its effectiveness since the state can ensure that survivors understand the message as intended. Participation can thereby significantly contribute to fostering generalized trust.[1347] Still, while strongly supported by teleological considerations, a right to participation is difficult to establish.

Such a right has a solid legal basis only when it comes to determining eligibility for a reparation program. Since a state entity decides on a claim to

1343 IACtHR, *Furlan and Family v. Argentina*, 2012, para 196; ECtHR, *Codarcea v. Romania*, 31675/04 (Third Section), 2009, para 89; ECtHR, *Mocie v. France*, 46096/99 (Second Section), 2003, para 22.

1344 Cammack, *Reparations in Malawi*, 233; Colvin, *Overview of the Reparations Program in South Africa*, 189; Houtte et al., *The UNCC*, 341 f.; ICTJ, *Transitional Justice in Morocco*, 16; ICTJ, *Reparations in Peru*, 16; Agreement on Accountability and Reconciliation Between the Government of the Republic of Uganda and the Lord's Resistance Army/Movement, 2007 para 9.1.

1345 HRC, *Report of the Special Rapporteur on Transitional Justice on Reparation*, A/69/518, para 74 ff.; OHCHR, *Reparation Programmes*, 15 f.; IACtHR, *Yarce et al v. Colombia*, para 326; AU, *Transitional Justice Policy*, 2019, para 32; ACtHPR, *Comparative Study on the Law and Practice of Reparations for Human Rights Violations*, 2019, 68.

1346 HRC, *Report of the Special Rapporteur on Transitional Justice on Reparation*, A/69/518, para 74 ff.; OHCHR, *Reparation Programmes*, 15 f.; Beristain, *Diálogos Sobre la Reparación – Experiencias en el Sistema Interamericano de Derechos Humanos*, Vol. I, 2008, 441 f.

1347 Wong, *How can Political Trust be Built After Civil Wars?*, 775 f.

reparation during that process, the process must adhere to fundamental due process rights. Among these is the right to be heard, which entails the right to adduce evidence and present one's case.[1348] Denying survivors the right to participate in that phase of the process would not only violate their due process rights it would also render the reparation program ineffective.

Many soft-law documents and some international judgments support a broader right to participation in reparation programs, encompassing involvement in its creation and implementation.[1349] The legal basis of such a right is unclear. It does not arise from the right to take part in public affairs and political decision-making as enshrined in Art. 25 ICCPR. This right does not encompass an individual right to be consulted for specific political questions. Rather, it ensures individuals access to the general public discourse.[1350] Despite the mentioned soft law documents, state practice does not provide much support for such a right either. Many reparation programs offer little opportunity for participation from the outset or cut existing participatory mechanisms at will.[1351]

1348 IACtHR, *Barbani Duarte et al. v. Uruguay*, 2011, para 122; ECtHR, *Perez v. France*, 47287/99 (Grand Chamber), 2004, para 80; ECtHR, *Clinique des Acacias et Autres v. France*, 65399/01 (Third Section), 2005, para 37; AComHPR, *Principles and Guidelines on the Right to a Fair Trial*, DOC/OS(XXX)247, principle A(2)(e).

1349 IACtHR, *Yarce et al v. Colombia*, para 326; IACtHR, *Street Children Case (Merits)*, para 225, 227; ECOSOC, *Impunity Principles*, E/CN.4/2005/102/Add.1, principle 32; AComHPR, *GC 4*, para 18, 70; ECOSOC, *Pinheiro Principles*, E/CN.4/Sub.2/2005/17 Annex, principle 14.1 f.; General Congress of the United Mexican States, General Victims Act, art. 7(XVI).

1350 HRCom, *Marshall v. Canada*, CCPR/C/43/D/205/1986, 205/1986, 1991, para 5.4 ff.; HRCom, *André Brun v. France*, CCPR/C/88/D/1453/2006, 1453/2006, 2006, para 6.4; HRCom, *Nicole Beydon and Others v. France*, CCPR/C/85/D/1400/2005, 1400/2005, 2005 para 4.5.

1351 ICTJ, *Dealing With the 2006 Internal Displacement Crisis in Timor-Leste*, 14 f.; ICTJ, *Transitional Justice in Morocco*, 16 f.; Guillerot, *Reparations in Peru*, 35; ICTJ, *Reparations in Peru*, 12 f., 15; Federal Assembly of the Swiss Confederation, Federal Act on Compulsory Social Measures and Placements Prior to 1981, art. 18(2); Sharma et al., *From Relief to Redress*, 40; Martínez/Gómez, *A Promise to be Fulfilled*, 20, 25 f.; Evans, *The Right to Reparation in International Law for Victims of Armed Conflict*, 156. South Africa explicitly denied a right to participation, Colvin, *Overview of the Reparations Program in South Africa*, 202. The AU's transitional justice policy tellingly refrains from phrasing participation as a right, AU, *Transitional Justice Policy*, 2019, para 32 f. Even the inter-american human rights bodies, generally strong supporters of survivor participation, do not always grant it, Contreras-Garduno, *Collective Reparations, 146 f.;* IACtHR, *Case of the Dismissed Congressional Employees v. Peru, Order of the IACtHR of November 20, 2009*, 2009, para 17, concerning the composition of a commission whose creation the court ordered as reparation. For

It could be argued that providing survivors opportunities to participate in reparation programs is simply necessary to provide adequate reparation. However, as determined in chapter one, whether reparation measures are adequate is not primarily judged against survivors' views but evaluated objectively.[1352] There might be clear-cut situations in which the proper reparation measures are obvious without survivor participation. The mass ouster of public servants after an authoritarian regime came to power might be an example. As long as no complicating factors exist, such cases seem to be repaired adequately by reinstatement and/or compensation for lost earnings. Hence, it cannot abstractly be determined that survivor participation is necessary for the adequacy of reparation. Especially given the discretion states enjoy when devising adequate reparation measures that might not always be the case. The validity of the necessity argument, therefore, depends on the concrete situation and envisaged measure. It only places an obligation on the state to seek survivor participation to the degree necessary to devise adequate reparation measures. It does not necessarily give individual survivors the right to participate.

Regardless of a legal right to participate in reparation programs, it must be stressed that robust survivor participation is a critical strategy to devise good and effective reparation programs. Thus, while not necessarily a legal obligation, states are well-advised to make room for as much survivor participation as possible.[1353]

III. Due Process

The nexus between the right to an effective remedy and the right to a fair trial adds numerous other considerations to reparation programs in transitional justice situations, not all of which can be examined. Applicants' rights to an adversarial process, equality of arms, a reasoned decision, etc., can all become relevant mutatis mutandis for administrative reparation programs.[1354] In

programs granting survivors a right to participation see HRC, *Report of the Special Rapporteur on the Promotion of Truth, Justice, Reparation and Guarantees of Non-Recurrence,* A/HRC/34/62, 2016, para 58.

1352 See above, ch. 1, C.VI.

1353 See in more detail below, Conclusion, F.

1354 Generally on the scope of the right, ECtHR, *Guide on Article 6 of the European Convention on Human Rights*, 2019; Ibáñez Rivas, *Artículo 8*, in: Steiner et al. (eds.), *Convención Americana Sobre Derechos Humanos - Comentario,* 2nd Edition 2019,

general, it can be assumed that these rights can be limited to a much larger degree than under normal circumstances. One must still consider that the right to an effective remedy – as the actual base of administrative reparation programs – is more concerned with outcome than the process. Additionally, the right to an effective remedy can be limited.[1355] Guaranteeing an expeditious remedy, which leads to adequate reparation measures under the challenging circumstances of transitional justice, will require a much greater compromise on the procedural side than usual.

G. Structure

It gradually becomes clear that large-scale reparation programs are a complex endeavor, which requires balancing various factors, considering numerous stakeholders, and catering to a vast universe of survivors. These demanding requirements also affect the structure such reparation schemes must take. The following section examines whether reparation programs must take the form of a special mechanism (I.) and what role the judiciary plays (II.).[1356]

I. An Obligation to Create a Special Mechanism?

The case studies evinced that in transitional justice situations, states resort to special mechanisms to implement reparation – mostly independent administrative programs, whose only purpose is to repair a defined set of survivors. While the right to an effective remedy, on which the right to reparation is based, usually envisages judicial proceedings, it does not preclude administrative forms of providing redress.[1357] This applies especially

256, 268 ff.; On the application of the right to reparation programs, IAComHR, *Reparation Guidelines*, OEA/Ser/L/V/II.131, para 9 f.

1355 See above, B.II.2.a.

1356 I was prompted to think about the following important issues in large part due to the critical comments of my supervisor Claus Kreß during a colloquium, for which I am highly thankful.

1357 ECtHR, *Klass and Others v. Germany*, 5029/71, para 67; CESCR, *General Comment No. 9 - The Domestic Application of the Covenant,* E/C.12/1998/24, 1998, para 9; CESCR, *General Comment No. 16 - The Equal Right of Men and Women to the Enjoyment of all Economic, Social and Cultural Rights (Art. 3 of the Covenant),* E/C.12/2005/4, 2005, para 21. The ICCPR gives priority to judicial remedies, but allows for administrative remedies also, HRCom, *José Vicente and Amado Villafañe Cha-*

to transitional justice situations.[1358] The question is whether states can choose to create special administrative mechanisms to repair survivors in transitional justice or if they are obliged to deploy them.

The previously mentioned character of the right to reparation as an obligation of result speaks against obliging states to deploy special reparation mechanisms. States need to deliver adequate reparation. By which means they do so is their prerogative. Under the unique circumstances of transitional justice, one must doubt, though, whether a regular justice system can deliver adequate reparation. It is reasonable to assume that ordinary administrative procedures or courts are in no position to engage with all the considerations mentioned above satisfactorily – conducting comprehensive outreach, removing barriers to access justice, taking into account evidentiary problems, engaging in broad balancing, etc. Especially broadly balancing a wide array of different interests, many of which concern the state budget, will strain any standard procedure's ability. Beyond remedying the ordinary justice system's factual constraints, special reparation programs have other advantages. Among others, they can be quicker, less adversarial, use resources more effectively, and pose fewer risks for survivors.[1359] They do not disaggregate survivors into individual cases, which can easily let the structural component of systematic human rights violations fade from view. This would inhibit the effective reach of reparation's transitional-justice-specific purpose.[1360] Thus, a procedural obligation to plan and implement a special reparation mechanism will most often be a necessary corollary of the substantive obligation to make adequate reparation. Whether that special mechanism is an administrative reparation program, a special court, or another procedure falls within the state's discretion. Again, the state owes the result of fulfilling the standards of this chapter. As long as the reparation mechanism can do that, its concrete organizational features are of secondary concern.

---

parro and Others v. Colombia, CCPR/C/60/D/612/1995, 612/1995, 1997, para. 5.2; Nowak, *U.N. Covenant on Civil and Political Rights - CCPR Commentary*, 2nd Revised Edition 2005, art. 2(3) para 65; ECtHR, *Ramirez Sanchez v. France*, 59450/00 (Grand Chamber), 2006, para 159, 165; AComHPR, *GC 4*, para 23.

1358 IACtHR, *Operation Genesis v. Colombia*, para 470; ECtHR, *Broniowski v. Poland*, 31443/96 (Grand Chamber), 2004, para 43; AComHPR, *Principles and Guidelines on the Right to a Fair Trial*, DOC/OS(XXX)247, principle P(d); HRC, *Report on Domestic Reparation Programs*, A/HRC/42/45, para 31 ff., providing a list of examples.

1359 de Greiff, *Justice and Reparations*, 160.

1360 de Greiff, *Justice and Reparations*, 458 f.

II. The Role of the Judiciary

The procedural obligation to create a special reparation mechanism does not take the regular judiciary out of the picture entirely. Practice in transitional justice usually follows one of three model relationships between the judiciary and special reparation mechanisms. First, any recourse to courts can be precluded, channeling all reparation efforts through the special mechanism.[1361] Second, seeking primary redress in court can be precluded, but judicial oversight, e.g., of decisions denying eligibility for the reparation program, can be granted.[1362] Third, individual procedures against the state are allowed as primary redress so that courts and the administrative program function in parallel.[1363] The question is whether there are any legal obligations to choose or refrain from choosing any of those relationships (1.). If states grant a role to courts, the further question arises, which standards courts should employ – the transitional-justice-specific standards of this chapter or usual tort standards (2.).

1361 De facto, this was the case in Sierra Leone, see above, ch. 2, B.

1362 Cammack, *Reparations in Malawi*, 221; Asamblea General de Uruguay, Ley No 18.596, art. 22; Guillerot, *Reparations in Peru*, 19 f.; Chile and Argentina can partially serve as an example of this model, Guembe, *The Argentinean Experience*, 31, 40; Lira, *The Reparations Policy for Human Rights Violations in Chile*, 56. For further explanation see the next fn.

1363 Lira, *The Reparations Policy for Human Rights Violations in Chile*, 87 ff.; Guembe, *The Argentinean Experience*, 26. In Argentina as well as in Chile the exclusion of law suits was not complete. In Argentina it depended on the limb of the reparation program and in Chile different courts handled the question differently. Cano/Ferreira, *The Reparations Program in Brazil*, 116; Houtte et al., *The UNCC*, 368; Martínez/Gómez, *A Promise to be Fulfilled*, 30 ff.; UNGA, *Basic Principles*, A/RES/60/147, para 12; IAComHR, *Reparation Guidelines*, OEA/Ser/L/V/II.131, para 5. Since this study deals with state responsibility only, it will not cover civil suits against perpetrators. Generally, the state's responsibility is independent of that from individual perpetrators. Hence, the state owes the full amount of reparation. At the same time, survivors cannot claim more redress than the harm they suffered. Therefore, they should not have a claim against the perpetrator or state, if the other already repaired them. This creates a tension, as a responsible actor might be relieved from their obligation to repair. In practice however, the problem will rarely become salient, as perpetrators usually do not have the means to repair all survivors they owe reparation to. A possible pragmatic solution would be for states to repair survivors and establish mechanisms through which perpetrators contribute to the reparation program. Such a mechanism is proposed by UNGA, *Basic Principles*, A/RES/60/147, para 16.

1. The Relationship Between Special Reparation Mechanisms and the National Judiciary

Generally, states are free to organize their national justice system how they see fit, as long as it provides effective remedies to survivors.[1364] Thus, if each component of the system adheres to the standards elaborated in this chapter, states can let the special mechanism and the ordinary judiciary function parallel, each being a possible primary avenue for redress.[1365] They are also free to condition access to courts on turning to an administrative procedure first, e.g., a reparation program.[1366] If that procedure remedies the harm incurred, any subsequent lawsuit has no merit anymore. States are thus free to reduce the role of courts to that of judicial oversight. International jurisprudence is split on whether the right to an effective remedy requires some sort of judicial oversight at some point or whether a purely administrative procedure – such as an administrative reparation program – can suffice.[1367] Even those bodies that let an administrative procedure

1364 ECtHR, *Silver and Others v. United Kingdom*, 5947/72 (Chamber), 1983, para 113.

1365 This is the model the inter-american human rights system envisages, IACtHR, *Ordenes Guerra y Otros v. Chile*, 2018, para 99 ff.; IAComHR, *Ordenes Guerra and Others v. Chile, Merits Report*, 52/16, 2016, para 96 ff. As said before, courts will most often have difficulties in meeting the standards elaborated in this chapter. It is conceivable though that with the caseload somewhat lifted by a reparation program, they are better placed to apply the standards. Furthermore, states might decide to relegate a specific subset of the survivor population to the courts, whereas other survivors must turn to the special mechanism first. While not using this exact model, Colombia came close to it by relying heavily on courts for land restitution, whereas for other reparation measures, courts played a much more subsidiary role.

1366 See above for the example of Colombia, e.g. ch. 2, C.IV.1.; Cammack, *Reparations in Malawi*, 228. For numerous decision with a bearing on human rights, states set up such proceedings. In the realm of asylum claims the ECtHR considered the judicial review of administrative decisions an effective remedy, ECtHR, *Vilvarajah and Others v. United Kingdom*, 13163/87 (Chamber), 1991, para 125 ff. The IAComHR differs in this respect, arguing that Art. 8(1) and 25(1) ACHR demand the possibility to be heard by a court and have a judicial determination of responsibility, IAComHR, *Ordenes Guerra and Others v. Chile, Merits Report*, 52/16, 2016, para 102. It was argued above, F., why the standards of the right to a fair trial in Art. 8(1) ACHR are not as exacting in the context of reparation proceedings. It is not clear, why there needs to be a judicial establishment of state responsibility, if a state acknowledges responsibility through a reparation program, also for the concrete instance to be repaired, as is necessary for a benefit to constitute reparation, see above Introduction, C. and Ch 4 E.II.3.

1367 Demanding a judicial remedy, IAComHR, *Access to Justice*, OEA/Ser.L/V/II.129, para 16, 164 ff., 190 ff. The IAComHR sees an additional role of the national judiciary to secure reparation from individual perpetrators, IAComHR, *Reparation Guidelines*,

suffice demand a judicial proceeding, however, if it is the only way to safeguard an essential right.[1368] The large caseload in transitional justice situations and the consequential need for categorization, swift proceedings, and standardization produces an inherent risk of wrong decisions, especially concerning atypical cases. The special vulnerability of large parts of the survivor population, the inherent complexity of their cases, scarcity of evidence, and other difficulties accompanying the transitional justice situation make robust procedural guarantees all the more important. Hence, judicial oversight should be considered necessary to guarantee the effectiveness of the remedy provided. State practice supports this view, as states rarely preclude judicial oversight of administrative reparation programs' decisions.[1369] Thus, even according to the less restrictive view, administrative reparation programs must be subject to the possibility of judicial oversight. Taking courts out of the picture entirely is, therefore, no option. Regarding the remaining two models mentioned initially, teleological considerations heavily favor the judicial oversight model over parallelism. Comprehensive administrative reparation programs provide a complete picture of the survivor universe, send a consistent message of validity, applicability, enforceability, and importance of human rights, and reduce overhead costs. Opening the court route as a primary means of redress would severely undercut any reparation program's comprehensiveness and undermine these advantages.

2. Standards for Adjudication

No matter whether as judicial oversight or as parallel primary redress mechanisms, if courts get involved in repairing systematic human rights violations, the question arises, which legislative standards they should

---

OEA/Ser/L/V/II.131, para 5 f.; IACtHR, *García Lucero et al. v. Chile*, para 190 ff.; CAT, *GC 3*, CAT/C/GC/3, para 20, 30; CEDAW, *General Recommendation No. 33 on Women's Access to Justice*, CEDAW/C/GC/33, 2015, para 53. Unclear: UNGA, *Basic Principles*, A/RES/60/147, para 12; AComHPR, *GC 4*, para 23; AComHPR, *Principles and Guidelines on the Right to a Fair Trial*, DOC/OS(XXX)247, principle C(c). Administrative redress is sufficient for HRCom, *GC 31*, CCPR/C/21/Rev.1/Add.13, para 15; CESCR, *GC 9*, E/C.12/1998/24, para 9; ECtHR, *Broniowski v. Poland*, 31443/96, para 43.

1368 ECtHR, *Ramirez Sanchez v. France*, 59450/00 para 165; CESCR, *GC 9*, E/C.12/1998/24, para 9.

1369 Cammack, *Reparations in Malawi*, 224; Colvin, *Overview of the Reparations Program in South Africa*, 124, 129; Guembe, *The Argentinean Experience*, 32, 40, 43; Guillerot, *Reparations in Peru*, 20.

employ. Most courts stick to established principles to determine the amount of reparation due. They treat individual cases before them as normal torts. Consequently, they award much higher material reparation than the parallel special reparation mechanisms. On the international plane, the IACtHR usually follows this example.[1370] Some courts deduct reparation previously awarded by the program from their awards. Others do not take reparation programs into account at all.[1371] These positions result in survivors who go to court receiving multiple amounts of the reparation others receive from the reparation program.

a. Business as Usual: Tort Standards

Malamud-Goti and Grosman justify this result. They argue that it would be unjust if survivors of state violence were foreclosed from the possibility to achieve full reparation, while persons who suffered harm on a different occasion can still claim it.[1372] Yet, as was shown above, lowering the amount of reparation awarded is no choice states can freely embark upon, and courts can refuse to make. It is a matter of resolving a normative conflict that arises in the circumstances of transitional justice. Hence, there is a decisive difference between survivors of systematic human rights violations and "normal" plaintiffs, whose claim does not affect other legal positions to the same degree. The law does not allow courts to treat instances of systematic

1370 See for the example of Guatemala Evans, *The Right to Reparation in International Law for Victims of Armed Conflict*, 160. The IAComHR stated that the state can adopt measures ensuring that the parallel functioning of administrative reparation programs and courts does not overwhelm the national treasury. This could hint at the possibility to oblige courts to take into account amounts received by an administrative program or to use the same standards as administrative programs. Unfortunately, the commission does not clarify, IAComHR, *Ordenes Guerra and Others v. Chile, Merits Report*, 52/16, 2016, para 99; IAComHR, *Principal Guidelines for a Comprehensive Reparation Policy*, OEA/Ser/L/V/II.131, 2008, para 5. The latter option would make courts superfluous though, as survivors had no incentive to turn to the more strenuous procedure.

1371 Cano/Ferreira, *The Reparations Program in Brazil*, 124 f., 129, 146; IACtHR, *Case of the Workers of the Fireworks Factory in Santo Antônio de Jesus and Their Families v. Brazil*, 2020, para 305 itself deemed national reparation awards irrelevant, whereas the commission considered it possible for states to deduct the awards from administrative programs from the reparation it awarded, IAComHR, *Integrantes y Militantes de la Unión Patriótica, Merits Report*, 170/17, 2017, para 1602.

1372 Malamud-Goti/Grosman, *Reparations and Civil Litigation*, 547 ff.

human rights violations as normal torts because they are no normal torts. The contrary approach not only ignores the normative conflict at play but would also yield unfair results. It would necessarily create hierarchies between survivors on other bases than the harm they suffered. Even more than under normal circumstances, access to courts is not evenly distributed in transitional situations. A person's position in society influences how easily they can avail themselves of the protection of courts. Allowing normal tort cases parallel to reparation programs would mainly allow privileged survivors to go to court and receive more reparation than others.[1373] Solving this problem through structural reform of the judicial system[1374] simply substitutes that problem with another: If all survivors had access to courts and received amounts akin to those of "normal torts", the state would be unable to satisfy all claims. This would substitute the competition between survivors with and without access to courts with a competition between survivors with quicker and less quick access to courts. Of course, the state could give survivors incentives to choose the reparation program over judicial proceedings because the former is quicker, provides higher chances of success, etc.[1375] But that would be unjust too. First, the survivors' right to access justice demands that judicial proceedings must not be too burdensome. A too-large disparity between court proceedings and reparation programs is therefore not legally possible. Second, such benefits are only appealing if a survivor cannot offset a court procedure's disadvantages. Given that the survivor population almost always contains highly marginalized, indigent individuals, it seems implausible that the choice between court proceedings and reparation programs is a free one. Again, hierarchies would be created between survivors, not based on their harm, but probably their social position, education, etc.

No matter the proposed fixes, the entire system of allowing tort proceedings parallel to special reparation mechanisms must rely on some survivors being unable to access the former. The approach must therefore rely on unjust

1373 OHCHR, *Reparation Programmes*, 35; de Greiff, *Articulating the Links Between Transitional Justice and Development* 44 f.

1374 This is the response offered to the challenge of unequal access to court by Malamud-Goti/Grosman, *Reparations and Civil Litigation*, 549.

1375 HRC, *Report of the Special Rapporteur on Transitional Justice on Reparation*, A/69/518, para 4. The IAComHR seems to have that solution in mind, hinting at the fact that survivors might deserve more reparation after court proceedings, because they took on a higher risk and burden, IAComHR, *Compendium*, OEA/Ser.L/V/II.Doc. 121, para 177, citing IAComHR, *Integrantes y Militantes de la Unión Patriótica, Merits Report*, 170/17, 2017, para 1601.

and arbitrary hierarchies between survivors. Of course, one could object that this cannot be an argument for giving everyone less. But it is the more just solution to seek a fair balance between all competing claims on the state's resources than to rely on disparities within the survivor community to make reparation possible. Hence, if courts adjudicate reparation claims in transitional situations, they must bow to its factual constraints and refrain from using the ordinary tort approach.[1376]

b. Keeping up With the Times: Transitional Justice Standards

Instead, courts must follow the model created here, removing barriers to access, aggregating all potential claims to reparation the state faces, and balancing them against other claims. There are two problems with that position. First, some of the obligations posited in this chapter only arise because the state must consider all survivors' positions and their aggregate effect. It is not apparent why courts should consider the reparation claims of persons not appearing before them as claimants. Second, even if they had to, they would be unable to do it in most cases. Courts will rarely have the capacity to adjudicate on all obligations posited in this chapter. They often do not have the epistemic abilities to adequately capture barriers to access to justice, to balance all competing positions, etc. When answering these two challenges, three scenarios must be distinguished. In the first, a state already implemented a national mechanism and reduced courts' role to that of judicial oversight. In the second, courts function as a primary avenue of redress parallel to an existent special reparation mechanism. In the third scenario, the state did not take any action, so that courts are the primary and only means of redress.

In the first scenario, neither challenge is that pressing. If an individual appeals the decision of a special reparation mechanism, e.g., because they deem their reparation inadequate, the court can evaluate whether the reparation program adhered to the standards set in this chapter. In this assessment, the court must automatically consider whether the reparation mechanism struck a fair balance between all competing positions. Otherwise, the limitation of the right to reparation of the individual claimant was disproportionate. As

1376 Malawi's National Compensation Tribunal, set up as a special mechanism to deal with the legacy of authoritarianism, recognized the difficulties in following the tort approach when deliberately awarding lower amounts of reparation than was done by ordinary courts earlier, because otherwise the government would run out of funds, Cammack, *Reparations in Malawi*, 236.

the ECtHR held in a case concerning reasonable limitations on compensation for dispossession:

> *"The vast number of persons involved – nearly 80,000 – and the very substantial value of their claims (...) are certainly factors that must be taken into account in ascertaining whether the requisite 'fair balance' was struck."*[1377]

As was argued above, courts must give states deference in these questions.[1378] In this context, the epistemic justification for deference is especially salient, as courts are simply unable to evaluate the state's decision to the last bit. Judicial oversight must only consider whether the state's policy choices are reasonable and whether all other obligations discussed in this chapter were complied with, including, e.g., whether reparation was awarded in a non-discriminatory manner.

In the second and third scenarios, this reasoning provides no basis for applying this chapter's standards to individual court cases. In the third scenario, there is no special mechanism for the court to evaluate. The second scenario does not require the court to do so because it is a primary avenue for redress parallel to the reparation mechanism. In either case, the court must decide independently what constitutes adequate reparation in the single case. This creates the paradoxical situation that each case the court faces does not run into a normative conflict based on limited resources: The state can provide a substantial amount of reparation to any single survivor. But if the court decides each case according to standard tort principles, the state cannot provide a substantial amount of reparation to every single survivor. Deciding cases without regard to their aggregate effect would therefore be unsustainable. It would force the courts to treat later cases differently because, at one point, the resource question would become acute, and the court would impose a disproportionate financial burden on the state. Equality before the law and the principle of legal certainty – both central elements of the rule of law – demand consistency in judicial decisions. They protect legitimate expectations of an applicant that courts follow their previous decisions on similar matters.[1379] While that does not mean that a change in adjudication is impossible, it strongly suggests that courts should not embark upon lines

1377 ECtHR, *Broniowski v. Poland*, 31443/96, para 162.

1378 See above, B.III.

1379 ICJ, *Case Concerning the Continental Shelf (Libyan Arab Jamahiriya / Malta) - Judgment of 3 June 1985*, I.C.J. Reports 1985, 13, para 45; ECtHR, *Nejdet Şahin and Perihan*

of adjudication, which from the outset they cannot sustain for future cases. Otherwise, they foreseeably force themselves to apply the law unequally and inconsistently. Thus, when called upon as a primary avenue of redress, courts must apply all the considerations enumerated so far too. This leads again to the practical challenge that courts are in no position to do so in most transitional justice situations. This challenge is surmountable in the scenario in which a special mechanism exists, and courts function as a primary parallel mechanism for redress. If courts are in no position to adhere to all of this chapter's standards, they can orient themselves at the special mechanism and defer to the state's choices it reflects. Deference provides no solution, though for the scenario in which no special mechanism exists that could provide orientation to courts. However, as determined above, if the ordinary justice system cannot adhere to this chapter's standards, states have the procedural obligation to create a special reparation mechanism that can.[1380] Hence, in that scenario, courts can resort to ordering the state to fulfill this procedural obligation. Such an approach is not alien to international law. Often, especially in case of mass violations, international bodies solely order adequate reparation, leaving the means entirely or partially up to the state.[1381] In some instances of mass violations, international bodies directly ordered a state to set up a reparation procedure specifically for that case.[1382]

III. Summary

In sum, the state must create a special mechanism when necessary to deliver reparation following the standards set in this chapter. Courts must exercise judicial oversight over reparation programs, as summed up by the IACtHR:

Şahin v. Turkey, 13279/05 (Grand Chamber), 2011, para 56 f.; ECtHR, *Siegle v. Romania*, 23456/04 (Third Section), 2013, para 38.

1380 See above, G.I.

1381 Oette, *Bringing Justice to Victims?*, 238.

1382 AComHPR, *African Institute for Human Rights and Development (on Behalf of Sierra Leonean Refugees in Guinea) v. Republic of Guinea*, 249/2002, 2004, para 74; AComHPR, *Zimbabwe Human Rights NGO Forum v. Zimbabwe*, 245/02, 2006, para 215; IACtHR, *Saramaka People v. Suriname*, para 198 ff.; ECtHR, *Kurić and Others v. Slovenia*, 26828/06 (Grand Chamber), 2012, para 412 ff.; CAT, *A v. Bosnia and Herzegovina*, 854/2017, para 9; ACtHPR, *AComHPR v. Republic of Kenya – Judgment on Reparations*, 006/2012, 2022, 8 f.

> *"[...] national mechanisms [...] should be evaluated and encouraged. If these mechanisms do not [. . .] properly repair the human rights violations declared by this Court, recognized in the Convention, the Court, in the exercise of its subsidiary and complimentary [sic] competence, should order the appropriate reparations."*[1383]

Beyond that, the state is not obliged to open courts as a primary means of redress but is free to do so. When called upon, either as an oversight or primary avenue to redress, courts should not treat the case before them as an ordinary tort. The demands of a teleological and systemic interpretation of the right to reparation also bind them. Furthermore, treating such cases as ordinary torts creates arbitrary and, therefore, unjust hierarchies between survivors. Instead, courts must adhere to the standards elaborated in this chapter. If they exercise oversight, they can evaluate the state's reparation program as a limitation on the right to reparation and pay deference towards the state's choices. If they are a primary avenue of redress in parallel to a reparation program, they should orient themselves at its standards. If the state's inactivity results in courts being seized as the only means of redress, they should order the state to fulfill its procedural obligation to provide a special mechanism for redress.

H. The End

All good things must come to an end. This holds for reparation programs and the present study. Honoring that fact, the last remaining question for this chapter is how and when states can end reparation programs, either by excluding further applications (I.) or by shutting programs down entirely (II.).

I. Application Deadlines

Most reparation programs surveyed in chapter two imposed a cut-off date after which survivors could not present their claims to the program anymore.

1383 IACtHR, *Gomes Lund v. Brazil*, para 303. This consideration became especially important in the case of Colombia, IACtHR, *Operation Genesis v. Colombia*, 472 ff.; IACtHR, *Yarce et al v. Colombia*, 328, 340.

This must be distinguished from limiting eligibility because of the time passed since the violation occurred, as discussed above.[1384] Limiting eligibility was based on statutes of limitation. This section concerns time-limits on application to newly created reparation mechanisms, regardless of when the violation occurred. Ample international practice evinces that, in principle, states can impose such time-limits.[1385] These are, however, a limitation on survivors' right to access justice. As such, they must be necessary and proportionate. Imposing time-limits on presenting the initial claim pursues the legitimate aim of facilitating the planning and administration of a reparation program. It ensures that there is a relatively fixed number of survivors to plan for. However, the time-limit must not make survivors' access to the program unrealistic. It must not place unreasonable burdens on them considering their often vulnerable situation. Otherwise, it would be disproportionate.[1386] The aim of gaining security in planning can be reached without having a completely fixed number of survivors to cater to. Small increases will not fundamentally alter the course of the program. For these reasons, time-limits cannot be unreasonably short and must allow for exceptions if survivors had

1384 See above, C.III.

1385 IACtHR, *Velásquez-Rodríguez v. Honduras (Merits)*, para 67; IACtHR, *Case of the Rio Negro Massacre v. Guatemala,* 2012, para 251; IACtHR, *Case of the Mapiripán Massacre v. Colombia,* 2005, para 257; ECtHR, *Guzzardi v. Italy*, 7367/76, para 72; Cammack, *Reparations in Malawi*, 229; Congreso Nacional de Bolivia, Ley 2640, art. 10(f); Congress of the Philippines, Human Rights Victims Reparation and Recognition Act of 2013, sec. 23; Cámara de Diputados de Paraguay, Ley No. 838, art. 1; Federal Assembly of the Swiss Confederation, Reparations Act for Compulsory Social Measures, art. 5; ECOSOC, *Pinheiro Principles*, E/CN.4/Sub.2/2005/17 Annex, principle 13.9. Many states extended the deadlines, introduced exceptions or ultimately abolished them, because not all survivors were able to apply in time: Guembe, *The Argentinean Experience*, 33, 41; Lira, *The Reparations Policy for Human Rights Violations in Chile*, 79, 82. Brazil extended the deadline only for one case due to difficulties in communication, Cano/Ferreira, *The Reparations Program in Brazil*, 115, 126, 134, 141, 146. The UNCC and the reparation program in Northern Ireland had the possibility to consider belated claims, Houtte et al., *The UNCC*, 340; Secretary of State of Northern Ireland, Victims' Payments Regulations 2020, art. 8(2)(b). Morocco did not apply its deadline for unresolved cases of enforced disappearances, ICTJ, *Transitional Justice in Morocco*, 10 f., 16. Peru extended and ultimately abolished its deadline, Burt, *Transitional Justice in the Aftermath of Civil Conflict*, 9; Guillerot, *Reparations in Peru*, 35; ICTJ, *Reparations in Peru*, 17.

1386 HRCom, *Josef Frank Adam v. The Czech Republic*, CCPR/C/57/D/586/1994, 586/1994, 1996, para 11.1; HRCom, *Nyaya v. Nepal*, 2556/2015, para 6.4, 7.9.

good reason not to present their claim before the deadline.[1387] Furthermore, survivors' ability to submit their claims depends on the intake procedure, including the quality of the outreach, the evidentiary requirements the program imposes, and how it erects or removes other barriers to accessing the program. If the state failed to meet the international standards on intake discussed above, it could not profit from these failures.[1388] Thus, if survivors were unable to present their claim within the initial time-limit because of the state's inability to meet its obligations, they must still be allowed to register.

II. End-Dates

The considerations made so far also answer the question whether and when states can shut down reparation programs. Some programs, including the Colombian one, have a fixed end-date.[1389] States can enforce such an end-date if by that time they adequately repaired all survivors. Alas, that is an unlikely scenario. Some damage might require consistent and prolonged attention, potentially for the rest of the respective survivors' lives. Given that not all survivors need such attention and that the costs of reparation programs will decrease over time, such measures might be necessary even after the broad balancing exercise reduced the scope of reparation for each survivor. Such a scenario precludes an end-date affecting all survivors. Similarly, due to the standards elaborated for time-limits on eligibility and claim prescription, survivors might legitimately present claims well after the program's initial conception, to which the state must respond.

Of course, if only a few survivors are left to be repaired, the state can relegate their reparation to the court system or a residual mechanism. Hence, the question is not so much about whether a reparation program can cease to exist at a specific date. The decisive question is whether, after that date, survivors

1387 More generally, the Special Rapporteur on Transitional Justice demands that time frames for registration be flexible, HRC, *Report on Domestic Reparation Programs*, A/HRC/42/45, para 48. The IACtHR considers it possible for new survivors to present themselves after the deadline it established, without elaborating on the circumstances under which such requests would be considered, IACtHR, *Case of the Afro-Descendant Communities Displaced From the Cacarica River Basin (Operation Genesis) v. Colombia*, 2013, para 310 f.;

1388 See above, D. on intake and C.III. on the principle ex iniuria ius non oritur, prohibiting an actor to profit from illegal behavior.

1389 Although the Colombian program had to be prolonged given the severe delays in its implementation, see above, ch. 2, C.IV.5.

remain to be repaired and, if so, whether other mechanisms can discharge all the obligations provided for in this chapter.

I. Summary: A Normative Framework for Reparation in Transitional Justice

How to repair an enormous universe of survivors who suffered grave harm under the difficult circumstances of transitional justice? The international law on reparation can provide normative guidance for that arduous task. Although some departures from its routine operation are warranted, these can be explained and operationalized by applying well-established interpretation techniques.

The present approach started by creating a problem. In summary, with few exceptions, states cannot limit eligibility for reparation programs. The right to reparation arises from every human rights violation suffered by any person, as long as it caused harm. There is no reason why reparation programs should be able to depart from that rule. Therefore, such programs cannot be limited to certain rights or harms only. They cannot exclude certain persons solely on the basis that they are both survivors and perpetrators. And they cannot set arbitrary cut-off dates. Just under very narrow circumstances, which are challenging to meet in transitional justice situations, can states obtain a waiver of the right to reparation from survivors or apply domestic statutes of limitation. Consequently, reparation programs must become fully comprehensive – much more than they are to date.

Making most survivors eligible is not enough to comply with the obligation to provide reparation. Survivors have a right to access justice. They must have the realistic opportunity to obtain redress under the circumstances of the transitional situation. States must, therefore, actively attempt to make the reparation program complete by turning every survivor into a beneficiary. For that, states must conduct outreach campaigns that inform survivors of the reparation program's existence, how to enter it, and navigate the process. They must leave them sufficient time to apply and cannot turn down survivors for delayed applications when they had a good reason for the delay. States must also adjust evidentiary requirements so that survivors can meet them under the challenging circumstances in the transitional society. Lastly, states must remove other barriers to effective access to justice, inter alia, by ensuring physical accessibility and affordability of the reparation program.

And here lies the first problem: Most reparation programs use eligibility and intake as bottlenecks, through which most claims to reparation fail to pass. This currently dominant approach is illegal. Yet, comprehensive, complete, and full reparation inflates reparation programs up to the point at which most of a state's population might be eligible and capable of entering them. The strict stance on these two levers raises a fundamental question: How to pay for and implement reparation on that scale?

One solution could be to abandon the demanding concept of full reparation and adopt a transitional-justice-specific approach, which might allow enough flexibility to focus on less onerous measures. That is not the road the author chose to take. Not only is there no legal basis to deviate from established reparation standards. The most prominent competitor to the concept of full reparation, transformative reparation, risks treating individual claims to justice as secondary to the greater goal of societal transformation. Full reparation, therefore, remains the applicable legal standard, even though the considerations that gave birth to the transformative reparation idea can enrich the concept. With that, a demanding reparation standard meets an unforgiving requirement of total comprehensiveness and completeness. While the state has a loose obligation to raise resources for reparation and can rely to a degree on external support, these strategies cannot prevent reparation programs from becoming too large for the state to handle.[1390] Seeking synergies between reparation and the fulfillment of other obligations can ease the normative conflict. But states cannot use the strategy to strip reparation of its unique character rooted in state responsibility. It, therefore, cannot solve the normative conflict either. Reducing the financial scope of reparation in transitional justice becomes inevitable. Such a reduction can be justified when conceiving the problem as a conflict between all survivors' aggregate rights to prompt reparation and other human rights law obligations and legitimate state interests. In short, if the state fully satisfied all reparation claims, it would have to cut back on many tasks vital to realizing the human rights of all members of society and legitimate state interests. Among those tasks are maintaining and progressively expanding the health care and education system, providing security infrastructure, etc. Instead of fulfilling one position at the expense of the other, the state must strike a fair balance between the aggregate claims to reparation and competing positions, limiting them as necessary and proportionate. By considering the abstract and concrete weight of each position and the probability with which a

1390 Again, one should not underestimate, how much resources can be in play, if political will exists. On the example of Great Britain's extremely costly reparation program for slave *owners*, see above, fn. 1251 and Andrews, *The New Age of Empire*, 56 f.

limitation materializes, one can arrive at a matrix, which indicates the relative weight each position obtains in this balancing exercise. This normative conflict approach allows the state to limit the number of resources needed for reparation as necessary to enable it to cater to other legitimate demands. Unfortunately, the normative conflict approach solves the original problem by creating a bigger one. When states limit the resources available for a truly comprehensive and complete reparation program, the benefits that program provides to each survivor must become diluted up to the point at which they cannot serve as meaningful reparation. According a special role to satisfaction can prevent that from happening. Satisfaction can be provided at a smaller cost to many survivors collectively, e.g., in the form of a public apology, because it repairs not through its material value but symbolic power. While the international law on reparation reserves satisfaction for the reparation of non-material or minor material harm, teleological considerations justify expanding its role in transitional justice. Since all reparation claims must be reduced significantly, those survivors who suffered comparably less harm will end up with claims to material reparation that are next to zero. Awarding such minimal material reparation would neither serve corrective justice nor the transitional-justice-specific aims of reparation. On the contrary, it would undermine them. It better serves the objects and purposes of reparation to repair through purely symbolic measures those survivors who could only demand minimal material reparation after balancing reduced their claim.

Coupling the normative conflict approach and the resulting balancing exercise with an enhanced role of satisfaction allows meaningful reparation to become a reality in transitional justice. The concept offers a more just alternative to treating eligibility and intake as the decisive bottlenecks. The latter differentiate between survivors on the arbitrary basis of their possibility to access justice. In contrast, the present approach differentiates between survivors based on the harm they suffered, as is inherent in the international law on reparation.

It will be beyond any ordinary justice system's ability to meet the obligations elaborated in this chapter in most transitional justice situations. As a consequence, in most transitional situations, states cannot leave reparation to ordinary courts. They must devise a special reparation mechanism, equipped to deal with the challenges of the transitional situation. At the same time, states cannot take courts out of the picture entirely. Judicial oversight is necessary to safeguard the right to reparation under complex transitional circumstances. To provide adequate supervision or redress, courts cannot treat individual cases as ordinary torts but must employ this chapter's standards. They can either evaluate the special mechanism a state created, orient themselves at that mechanism, or oblige the state to create one. All of this must continue until all eligible survivors received adequate reparation.

Of course, as a universal standard, the concept elaborated in this chapter must remain at a high level of abstraction. The notion of normative conflict cannot prescribe an outcome for any particular situation. In reality, reparation programs are contingent on a myriad of factors, not all of which fit neatly into a formula with six variables academics devise in the comfort of their ivory tower. Reparation programs need to be constantly adapted to a rapidly changing environment, changing needs of survivors, unforeseen challenges, shifting political realities, and many other factors. They are not balanced out once to stand the test of time for eternity. The balancing exercise provides a common language through which deviations from the standard of full reparation can be justified and criticized. It thereby allows legal scrutiny and evaluation of state action, which too often is deemed a necessary political decision without alternatives. Facing such a multi-faceted process as reparation in transitional justice, this is probably all lawyers can hope for.

Conclusion – Pushing the Limits of the Law

This study started with a suspicion: Might reparation in transitional justice "explode the limits of the law" – as Hannah Arendt suggested? The first three chapters of this book made abundantly clear that reparation practice in transitional justice deviates significantly from the international law on reparation. Such a disconnect would usually give rise to the simple conclusion that states violate international law – lamentably hardly an occurrence of such rarity that it would be worth deeper inquiry in and of itself. But there are reasons to suspect that blame lies not so much with states but with the law. The international law on reparation, as established in chapter one, seems so far removed from the particular circumstances of transitional justice that it might not be able to provide adequate guidance. However, if the law fails, the consequences could be grave. Survivors could have an even harder time securing justice, which would also impede the transformative aim of transitional justice. For that reason, this study began with a repudiation of Arendt. It started from the thesis that reparation in transitional justice does not explode the limits of the law. It might push the law close to a breaking point, but not beyond it. Did this study manage to corroborate this thesis?

A. A True Observation

The case studies of Sierra Leone, Colombia, and the ICC's Lubanga, Katanga, Al Mahdi, and Ntaganda reparation programs in the DRC and Mali proved the initial observation true. All six programs deviated in significant and similar ways from the international law on reparation. Instead of following its individualistic-conservative approach, Sierra Leone, Colombia and the ICC created special reparation mechanisms, which operated under a collectivistic-transformative logic. These special mechanisms categorized survivors and generalized their harm, which enabled them to cater to thousands, if not millions of survivors. States embarked on significant outreach efforts and removed barriers to access justice. They aimed at more than just restoring survivors to the situation they would be in had the violation not occurred. Instead, they aimed at transforming survivors' lives and positions in society.

B. A Justified Suspicion?

The case studies corroborated the suspicion that the international law on reparation, as it stands, might be inadequate for reparation in transitional justice. States did not deviate from the international law on reparation out of indifference but necessity. They did it to overcome the transitional situation's specific challenges: A large caseload, the need to repair grave harm on a large scale, volatile societal dynamics, pressure on the state's resources, etc. These circumstances made it impossible to carry out thousands if not millions of individual adversarial proceedings, subject to demanding evidentiary requirements. The conservative-individualistic logic of the international law on reparation thus proved difficult to implement in transitional justice. An inquiry into the roles of reparation in transitional justice further deepened the suspicion. Not only does the international law on reparation make it hard to account for the particular exigencies of the transitional justice situation, but it also fails to consider transitional justice's unique purpose. Transitional justice is a transformative project. Apart from providing individual justice under challenging circumstances, it seeks to transform society so that individuals and state institutions respect human rights again. Since the transitional situation is so far removed from that goal, transitional justice operationalizes it by seeking to establish generalized horizontal and vertical trust in that other members of society and state institutions respect human rights again. Reparation contributes to that aim by sending a message to survivors and members of society more generally that members of society and state institutions hold human rights to be valid, applicable to everyday life, enforceable, and important – now and in the future. Reparation thus attains the dual role of fulfilling individual corrective justice and contributing to the goals of the transition. In the form it is applied usually, the international law on reparation does not adequately reflect the latter role.

So, both practical and theoretical reasons support the suspicion that the international law on reparation inadequately reflects the exceptional circumstances of transitional justice. But does that mean that reparation in transitional justice explodes the limits of the international law on reparation?

C. Abandoning the Law?

Justified skepticism could lead to surrender. If the international law on reparation cannot adequately accommodate the challenges of transitional justice, then maybe transitional justice is too complex, contingent, or diverse and escapes regulation by universal international law. Maybe transitional justice must remain a purely political process. That stance comes with significant downsides for survivors, who will often not occupy an essential place in that process. But that only justifies the desirability of regulating reparation in transitional justice through international law. Alas, desirability not always coincides with possibility.

That the desire to regulate reparation in transitional justice lies within the realm of the possible can only be proven by example. Much of this study was dedicated to providing one. The normative framework established to that end in chapter four was off to a rocky start, though; it made it even harder for states to repair survivors in transitional justice. International law prohibits using eligibility and access to the reparation program as bottlenecks, through which most survivors fail to pass. Every survivor has a right to reparation and the right to access proceedings providing it. Reparation programs must therefore become genuinely comprehensive and complete. They must cover all survivors and give them a realistic chance to obtain reparation. To make matters worse, states must still provide full reparation. No transitional-justice-specific approach to reparation is warranted, which might allow states to circumvent their obligation to repair. States cannot seek synergies between reparation and their other obligations to the degree that they confuse reparation with assistance. They cannot rely on external support to the degree that they are outsourcing their obligation to repair. They have to follow through with their reparation programs until every survivor had a chance to apply and receive adequate reparation. In sum, there is no way around the basic premise of the international law on reparation: The responsible state must repair every survivor of a human rights violation by providing restitution, compensation, rehabilitation, satisfaction, and guarantees of non-repetition, which erase the harm caused as far as possible.

At the same time, it would be manifestly unjust to pursue full reparation at all costs. It would overwhelm the state and leave it with little to no resources to fulfill other vital functions.[1391] A way out of this dilemma comes with a normative conflict approach. Since the state cannot fulfill its obligation to repair while fulfilling its other obligations under international law to the full extent, these two sets of obligations conflict. They must be limited so that

---

1391 Again, one should not underestimate, how much resources can be in play, if political will exists. On the example of Great Britain's extremely costly reparation program for slave *owners*, see above, fn. 1251 and Andrews, *The New Age of Empire*, 56 f.

a fair balance is struck between them. This process can be operationalized by weighing the abstract weight of each set of obligations, their concrete importance, and the probability with which interferences materialize. The resulting share of the state's resources available for reparation must be distributed equally between the survivors based on the severity of their harm. Naturally, this process can never result in an exact calculation of the amount of reparation due to each survivor. Reparation in transitional justice will always remain subject to a political process. But the proposed balancing exercise can provide the parties to the process with a common language, through which they can justify, criticize and scrutinize reparation efforts and proposals. Thereby, it can help overcome an equivocation at the heart of many current debates about reparation. Often, the state and survivors have different concepts regarding the adequacy of reparation. While the former argues that it did everything in its power to provide as much reparation as possible, the latter hold that what they received did not suffice to overcome their harm. Frustration, not corrective justice and trust is the main result. A common legal framework determining the adequacy of reparation can bring the parties to the process together and allow, at the very least, for a fruitful negotiation.

Even with this lowered expectation, though, the proposal to balance competing positions only solved the problem that reparation in transitional justice overwhelms the state's resources by creating a new one. If a limited amount of resources is distributed equally between survivors, they only get a fraction of what they are entitled to. Reparation is then so diluted that it becomes meaningless. This problem does not justify deviation from the full reparation concept. Instead, a heavier reliance on symbolic reparation can solve it. Symbolic reparation measures repair not through their material value but their communicative function. Hence, they can be administered to many survivors simultaneously at a limited cost without losing their effectiveness. The international law on reparation only allows repairing survivors with nothing but symbolic means when they suffered financially non-assessable harm or small quantities of financially assessable harm. Unfortunately, that will not be the case in most transitional situations. Teleological interpretation provides a normative justification to expand the scope of symbolic reparation in transitional justice. Once it is necessary to substantially limit the amount of reparation each survivor is entitled to by the same factor, those survivors who suffered comparatively small harm will have their share reduced to close to zero. For those survivors, material reparation can neither fulfill its deontological role to provide corrective justice nor its instrumental role to further respect for human rights and generalized trust. On the contrary, minimal amounts of reparation would be received as a mockery and would undermine reparation's transitional-justice-specific message. This at the cost that fewer resources are available to repair survivors who suffered comparably more harm. Such an interpretation would run counter to the principle of effectiveness. Instead, repairing survivors through symbolic means only, if the limited harm they suffered results in balancing reducing their share of material reparation to close to zero, better serves the aim of corrective justice and the transitional-justice-specific aim of reparation. Since the ordinary judiciary will often be in no position to implement all these obligations adequately, states will often be obliged to create special reparation mechanisms. Courts must exercise oversight over such mechanisms and can also serve as a primary avenue of redress. In any case, they are bound to uphold the normative framework established here and may not treat the cases before them as ordinary torts.

This normative framework shall serve as the example proving that reparation in transitional justice does not explode the limits of the law. As it is usually applied, the international law on reparation does not fit the particular exigencies of transitional justice. However, it can be carefully adapted through interpretation so that it can provide adequate guidance to transitional justice reparation efforts. Whether the normative framework truly fulfills this function must be left for the reader to decide. The author must admit that it remains highly abstract. The guidance it provides in any concrete situation will hence be limited. That, however, is no shortcoming but in keeping with the humble role that the law should play in transitional justice.

D. One More (and Last) Time: The Limits of the Law

Diversity, complexity, and enormous challenges characterize transitional justice situations. Transitional justice measures will, therefore, always be both a legal and a political endeavor. They will always be the result of a political and social process, contingent on the circumstances. They must be constantly revised and adapted to changing contexts, needs, and new information. In such a dynamic situation, the law cannot determine a state's every move. It can provide a minimum standard below which the state must not fall. It can open a space for the processes to flourish by providing a common language in which the actors can negotiate. It can never determine the exact outcome of the process. Truly adequate reparation programs arise from the creativity, ingenuity, and flexibility of the actors devising and implementing them. Law cannot prescribe these qualities. It should therefore be humble, cognizant of what it can achieve and when to make room for more important actors. To put it with the words of Méndez: Law must provide a framework, not a straightjacket.[1392]

E. Overcoming the Blind Spots of Transitional Justice

This limited role is not only adequate for the exceptional circumstances of transitional justice. It also guards against the blind spots and risks of transitional justice practice. As discussed in the introduction, as a transformative project based on human rights, transitional justice is always at risk of becoming part of a new civilizing mission by the Global North. Through its power in international relations and international law, the Global North can hegemonialize standards and condition states' legitimacy on adhering to them. Transitional justice is no exception. Too often, the international community, international "expertise", and international donors drive transitional justice processes. This corrupts transitional justice on the one hand because these actors tend to impose one-size-fits-all-solutions on a great variety of situations. This lack of care for local suitability of transitional justice processes invariably leads to their failure.

On the other hand, this blind spot corrupts transitional justice because it leads to its limited application. Transitional justice processes take place predominantly in the Global South. They treat systematic human rights violations as domestic affairs with little connection to the Global North. As mentioned before, this is not the result of the impeccable legal and moral behavior of the Global North. States in the Global North have their own systematic human rights violations to answer for. They created the deadliest border in the world and discriminate against large parts of their population, to arbitrarily name two.[1393] They were and are involved in systematic human rights violations in the Global South not only as a savior, who provides the resources and "expertise" to overcome the harm that ensued. Often enough, the Global North and the international community contributed to

1392 Méndez, *Peace, Justice and Prevention*, 17.

1393 IOM, *Four Decades of Cross-Mediterranean Undocumented Migration to Europe*, 1; UN, *On the Black Lives Matter Protests and other Mass Demonstrations Against Systemic Racism and Police Brutality – Joint Reflexions by United Nations Senior African Officials*, 2020; Andrews, *The New Age of Empire*, passim.

the structures that gave rise to systematic human rights violations, actively participated in their commission, and profiteered from them. It is thus high time to make transitional justice a genuinely global project; not in the sense that certain actors travel around the world to distribute their wisdom, but in the sense that the distribution of transitional justice efforts should fit the global distribution of systematic human rights violations.

Because legal approaches to transitional justice inherently proceed from a top-down-logic, they exacerbate the risk of hegemonializing certain transitional justice approaches. They are therefore always at risk of reproducing the blind spots and corrupting effects just referred to. For that reason, it serves the adequacy of transitional justice efforts to limit the law's role to provide a framework, which is for the relevant actors to fill.

F. Overcoming the Limits of the Law: Survivor Participation

Under this lens, survivor participation attains a special meaning for reparation in transitional justice.[1394] Admittedly, this study refuted an unconditional norm making survivor participation in reparation programs obligatory. Instead, it took the position that survivor participation is obligatory only insofar as necessary to make reparation adequate. Often, that will be the case. But even where it is not, the fact that survivor participation is not mandatory does not mean that it is not advisable. On the contrary, numerous initiatives founded and led by survivors demonstrate that they often know how to overcome the harm they suffered.[1395] Take, for example, the people of Puerto Berrío, Colombia, who had to live with the fact that the river next to their village washed corpses ashore, which the parties to the conflict threw into the water upstream. They coped with this gruesome reminder of the conflict by reburying the corpses, giving them names, caring for their graves, and asking them favors. With that, they lent new meaning to the situation

1394 Generally on the local dimension of transitional justice and its interactions with other dimensions, McGregor, *International Law as a "Tiered Process" - Transitional Justice at the Local, National and International Level*, in: McEvoy/McGregor (eds.), *Transitional Justice From Below - Grassroots Activism and the Struggle for Change*, 2008, 47. More specifically embedding participation in a wider discourse, Lundy/McGovern, *Transitional Justice From Below*, 123 ff.

1395 McGregor, *International Law as a "Tiered Process"*, 60.

and honored the unknown dead.[1396] Women of the displaced community of Mampuján started to deal with the violations they suffered by weaving quilts, displaying their experiences and hopes. Again, this gave their experiences meaning, helping them to overcome their harm. The group activity brought them together and repaired social relationships in the community.[1397] The Sierra Leonean NGO Fambul Tok assembles communities, which suffered under the conflict at a bonfire to talk about their experiences. It thereby opens a space in which reconciliation becomes possible and often occurs.[1398] Such examples of the resilience, creativity, and ingenuity of survivors abound. States can tap into that invaluable resource by making genuine, meaningful survivor participation possible.

G. *In the end...*

...reparation in transitional justice does not explode the limits of the law. Interpretation can push those limits so that the law provides some guidance to states and societies seeking to repair survivors of systematic human rights violations. Lawyers must remain humble, though. They must be cognizant of the fact that many paths lead to adequate reparation in transitional justice. The law cannot prescribe a single correct one. It can narrow down the range of acceptable paths, among which the society concerned must choose one that fits the situation. To follow the path remains an arduous task, subject to many challenges. Law cannot substitute a lack of will to move forward. Neither can it prescribe the creativity, ingenuity, and flexibility needed to complete the journey. But it can continue to provide limited guidance throughout the journey and help to prevent deviations. In the end, the path will hopefully lead the society concerned to a point at which survivors feel adequately repaired

1396 Abdelrahim, *Puerto Barrío - La Ciudad Donde se Adoptan los Muertos*, El País, 29 September 2012. The artist Juan Manuel Echavarría documented the graves in his thoughtful project "Requiem NN", https://jmechavarria.com/en/work/requiem-nn/.

1397 Ordóñez Narváez, *Los Tejidos de Mampuján - Una Lectura Desde la Reparación Simbólica*, in: Sierra León (ed.), *Reparación Simbólica - Jurisprudencia, Cantos y Tejidos*, 2018, 291, 310 ff., including images of some of the quilts.

1398 Hoffman, *Reconciliation in Sierra Leone - Local Processes Yield Global Lessons*, 2008 Fletcher F. World Aff. 32(2), 129, 132 ff.; Graybill, *Traditional Practices and Reconciliation in Sierra Leone - The Effectiveness of Fambul Tok*, 2010 Conflict Trends 3, 41, 44 ff.; More critically Martin, *Deconstructing the Local in Peacebuilding Practice - Representations and Realities of Fambul Tok in Sierra Leone*, 2020 Third World Q. Online Publication.

and trust that state institutions and their fellow members of society respect human rights again. Law itself cannot bring about that outcome, much less guarantee it. But if cognizant of its limited role, it can help achieve it.

Table of Legislation and Treaties

African Charter on Human and People's Rights, 21 October 1986, 1520 UNTS, 217.

African Union, *Protocol to the African Charter on Human and Peoples' Rights on the Establishment of the African Court on Human and Peoples' Rights*, 25 January 2004.

African Union, *Statute of the Trust Fund for Victims of Hissène Habré's Crimes*, 28-29 January 2018, EX.CL/1040(XXXI) Annex.

Agreement on Accountability and Reconciliation Between the Government of the Republic of Uganda and the Lord's Resistance Army/Movement, 29 June 2007.

American Convention on Human Rights, 17 July 1978, 1144 UNTS, 123.

Asamblea General de Uruguay, *Actuación Ilegítima del Estado Entre el 13 de Junio de 1968 y el 28 de Febrero de 1985 - Reconocimiento y Reparación a las Víctimas*, 19 October 2009.

Asamblea Nacional de Nicaragua, *Ley de Atención Integral a Víctimas*, 31 May 2019, Ley No. 994.

Assembly of States Parties, *Regulations of the Trust Fund for Victims*, 3 December 2005.

Cámara de Diputados de Paraguay, *Ley No. 838 que Indemniza a Victimas de Violaciones de Derechos Humanos Durante la Dictadura de 1954 a 1989*, 12 September 1996.

Congreso de la República de Colombia, *Ley 1448 de 2011 Por la Cual se Dictan Medidas de Atención, Asistencia y Reparación Integral a las Víctimas del Conflicto Armado Interno y se Dictan Otras Disposiciones*, 10 June 2011.

Congreso Nacional de Bolivia, *Ley de Resarcimiento a Víctimas de la Violencia Politica*, 11 March 2004, Ley 2640.

Congress of the Philippines, *Human Rights Victims Reparation and Recognition Act of 2013*, 25 February 2013, Republic Act No. 10368.

Convention Against Torture and Other Cruel, Inhuman or Degrading Treatment or Punishment, 30 October 2001, 1465 UNTS, 85.

Convention for the Protection of Human Rights and Fundamental Freedoms, 3 September 1953, 213 UNTS, 221.

Convention on Access to Information, Public Participation in Decision-Making and Access to Justice in Environmental Matters, 30 October 2001, 2161 UNTS, 447.

Deed of Settlement of the Historical Claims of Ngati Tuwharetoa (Bay of Plenty), 6 June 2003.

European Convention on the Compensation of Victims of Violent Crimes, 1 February 1988, ETS, No. 116.

Federal Assembly of the Swiss Confederation, *Federal Act on Compulsory Social Measures and Placements Prior to 1981*, 30 September 2016.

Final Agreement to End the Armed Conflict and Build a Stable and Lasting Peace, 24 November 2016.

General Congress of the United Mexican States, *General Victims Act*, 30 April 2012.

Indian Residential Schools Settlement Agreement, 8 May 2006.

International Convention for the Protection of All Persons from Enforced Disappearance, 23 December 2010, 2716 UNTS, 3.

International Convention on the Elimination of all Forms of Racial Discrimination, 4 June 1969, 660 UNTS, 195.

International Convention on the Protection of the Rights of All Migrant Workers and Members of Their Families, 17 July 2003, 2220 UNTS, 3.

International Covenant on Civil and Political Rights, 23 March 1976, 999 UNTS, 171.

International Covenant on Economic Social and Cultural Rights, 3 January 1976, 993 UNTS, 3.

International Criminal Court, *Rules of Procedure and Evidence of the International Criminal Court*, 2005.

International Peace Conference, *Convention (IV) Respecting the Laws and Customs of War on Land*, 26 January 1910.

Ministerio de Agricultura y Desarrollo Rural de Colombia, *Decreto 1167 de 2018 por el Cual se Modifica el Artículo 2.15.1.1.16 del Decreto 1071 de 2015, Decreto Único Reglamentario del Sector Administrativo Agropecuario, Pesquero y de Desarrollo Rural, Relacionado con las Zonas Microfocalizadas*, 11 July 2018.

Ministerio de Justicia de Colombia, *Decreto 4800 de 2011 por el Cual se Reglamenta la Ley 1448 de 2011 y se Dictan Otras Disposiciones*, 20 December 2011.

Parliament of Sierra Leone, *Truth and Reconciliation Commission Act 2000*, 2000.

Peace Agreement Between the Government of Sierra Leone and the Revolutionary United Front (Lomé Peace Agreement), 7 July 1999.

Presidente de la República de Colombia, *Decreto 1084 de 2015 por Medio del Cual se Expide el Decreto Único Reglamentario del Sector de Inclusión Social y Reconciliación*, 26 May 2015.

Presidente de la República de Colombia, *Decreto 1290 de 2008 por el Cual se Crea el Programa de Reparación Individual por vía Administrativa Para las Víctimas de los Grupos Armados Organizados al Margen de la Ley*, 22 April 2008.

Presidente de la República de Colombia, *Decreto 4829 de 2011 por el Cual se Reglamenta el Capítulo III del Título IV de la Ley 1448 de 2011 en Relación con la Restitución de Tierras*, 20 December 2011.

Presidente de la República de Perú, *Decreto Supremo 047-2011-PCM*, 24 May 2011.

Protocol Additional to the Geneva Conventions of 12 August 1949, and Relating to the Protocol of Victims of International Armed Conflict (Protocol I), 7 December 1978, 1125 UNTS, 3.

Secretary of State of Northern Ireland, *Victims' Payments Regulations 2020*, 24 February 2020.

Unidad de Restitución de Tierras, *Acuerdo 33 de 2016*, 7 March 2017.

Unidad de Víctimas, *Resolución 00090 de 17 Febrero 2015*, 17 February 2015.

Unidad de Víctimas, *Resolución 00848 de 30 Diciembre 2014*, 30 December 2014.

Unidad de Víctimas, *Resolución 01958 de 6 Junio 2018*, 6 June 2018.
Unidad de Víctimas, *Resolución 03143 de 23 Julio 2018* 23 July 2018.
Vienna Convention on the Law of Treaties, 27 January 1980, 1155 UNTS, 331.

Table of Cases

Affaire Campbell (Royaume-Uni Contre Portugal), R.I.A.A. II, 1145 (10 June 1931).

African Commission on Human and Peoples' Rights, *African Institute for Human Rights and Development (on Behalf of Sierra Leonean Refugees in Guinea) v. Republic of Guinea*, 249/2002 (7 December 2004).

African Commission on Human and Peoples' Rights, *Centre for Minority Rights Development (Kenya) and Minority Rights Group International on Behalf of Endorois Welfare Council v. Kenya*, 276/2003 (4 February 2010).

African Commission on Human and Peoples' Rights, *Commission Nationale des Droits de l'Homme et des Libertés v. Chad*, 74/92 (11 October 1995).

African Commission on Human and Peoples' Rights, *Democratic Republic of Congo v. Burundi, Rwanda, Uganda*, 227/99 (29 May 2003).

African Commission on Human and Peoples' Rights, *Garreth Anver Prince v. South Africa*, 255/02 (7 December 2004).

African Commission on Human and Peoples' Rights, *Groupe de Travail sur les Dossiers Judiciaires Stratégiques v. Democratic Republic of Congo*, 259/2002 (20-24 July 2011).

African Commission on Human and Peoples' Rights, *Malawi African Association and Others v. Mauritania*, 54/91 (11 May 2000).

African Commission on Human and Peoples' Rights, *Noah Kazingachire, John Chitsenga, Elias Chemvura and Batanai Hadzisi (Represented by Zimbabwe Human Rights NGO Forum) v. Zimbabwe*, 295/04 (18 April - 2 May 2012).

African Commission on Human and Peoples' Rights, *Social and Economic Rights Action Center (SERAC) and Center for Economic and Social Rights (CESR) v. Nigeria*, 155/96 (27 October 2001).

African Commission on Human and Peoples' Rights, *Sudan Human Rights Organisation & Centre on Housing Rights and Evictions (COHRE) v. Sudan*, 279/03-296/05 (13-27 May 2009).

African Commission on Human and Peoples' Rights, *Zimbabwe Human Rights NGO Forum v. Zimbabwe*, 245/02 (15 May 2006).

African Commission on Human and Peoples' Rights, *Zimbabwe Lawyers for Human Rights & Associated Newspapers of Zimbabwe v. Republic of Zimbabwe*, 284/03 (3 April 2009).

African Commission on Human and Peoples' Rights, *Zimbabwe Lawyers for Human Rights v. Zimbabwe*, 294/04 (3 April 2009).

African Court on Human and Peoples' Rights, *African Commission on Human and Peoples' Rights v. Republic of Kenya – Judgment on Reparations*, 006/2012 (23 June 2022).

African Court on Human and Peoples' Rights, *Beneficiaries of Late Norbert Zongo v. Burkina Faso (Judgment on Reparations)*, 013/2011 (5 June 2015).

African Court on Human and Peoples' Rights, *Reverend Christopher R. Mtikila v. The United Republic of Tanzania (Ruling on Reparations)*, 011/2011 (13 June 2014).

African Court on Human and Peoples' Rights, *Tanganyika Law Society, the Legal and Human Rights Centre and Reverend Christopher R. Mtikila v. The United Republic of Tanzania*, 009&011/2011 (14 June 2013).

Cayuga Indians (Great Britain) v. United States, R.I.A.A. VI, 173 (22 January 1926).

Committee Against Torture, *E.N. v. Burundi*, CAT/C/56/D/578/2013, 578/2013 (25 November 2015).

Committee Against Torture, *Estela Deolinda Yrusta and Alejandra del Valle Yrusta v. Argentina*, CAT/C/65/D/778/2016, 778/2016 (31 January 2019).

Committee Against Torture, *Hajrizi Dzemajl et al. v. Yugoslavia*, CAT/C/29/D/161/2000, 161/2000 (2 December 2002).

Committee Against Torture, *Saadia Ali v. Tunisia*, CAT/C/41/D/291/2006, 291/2006 (26 November 2008).

Committee Against Torture, *A v. Bosnia and Herzegovina*, CAT/C/67/D/854/2017, 854/2017 (22 August 2019).

Committee on the Elimination of all Forms of Discrimination Against Women, *Inga Abramova v. Belarus*, CEDAW/C/49/D/23/2009, 23/2009 (11-29 July 2011).

Committee on the Elimination of all Forms of Discrimination Against Women, *R.P.B. v. The Philippines*, CEDAW/C/57/D/34/2011, 34/2011 (12 March 2014).

Committee on the Elimination of all Forms of Discrimination Against Women, *V.K. v. Bulgaria*, CEDAW/C/49/D/20/2008, 20/2008 (25 July 2011).

Committee on the Elimination of Racial Discrimination, *Dragan Durmic v. Serbia and Montenegro*, CERD/C/68/D/29/2003, 29/2003 (8 March 2006).

Committee on the Elimination of Racial Discrimination, *Kamal Quereshi v. Denmark*, CERD/C/66/D/33/2003, 33/2003 (10 March 2004).

Committee on the Elimination of Racial Discrimination, *Stephen Hagan v. Australia*, CERD/C/62/D/26/2002, 26/2002 (20 March 2003).

Committee on the Elimination of Racial Discrimination, *V.S. v. Slovakia*, CERD/C/88/D/56/2014, 56/2014 (6 January 2016).

Corte Constitucional de Colombia, *Auto 119 de 2013* (Sala Especial de Seguimiento a la Sentencia T-025 de 2004 y sus Autos de Cumplimiento, 24 June 2013).

Corte Constitucional de Colombia, *C-588 de 2019*, C-588/19 (Sala Plena, 5 December 2019).

Corte Constitucional de Colombia, *Sentencia C-280 de 2013*, C-280/13 (Sala Plena, 15 May 2013).

Corte Constitucional de Colombia, *Sentencia C-330 de 2016*, C-330/16 (Sala Plena, 23 June 2016).

Corte Constitucional de Colombia, *Sentencia C-523 de 2009*, C-523/09 (Sala Plena, 4 August 2009).

Corte Constitucional de Colombia, *Sentencia SU-599 de 2019*, SU-599/19 (Sala Plena, 11 December 2019).

Court of Justice of the Economic Community of West African States, *Djot Bayi & 14 Others v. Nigeria and 4 Others*, ECW/CCJ/JUD/01/09 (28 January 2009).

D. Earnshaw and Others (Great Britain) v. United States (Zafiro Case), R.I.A.A. VI, 160 (30 November 1925).

Ethiopian-Eritrea Claims Commission, *Final Award – Ethiopia's Damages Claims*, RIAA XXVI, 631 (17 August 2009).

European Commission of Human Rights, *Austria v. Italy*, 788/60 (11 January 1961).

European Committee of Social Rights, *Syndicat de Défense des Fonctionnaires v. France (Merits)*, 73/2011 (12 September 2012).

European Court of Human Rights, *Aksoy v. Turkey*, 21987/93 (Chamber, 18 December 1996).

European Court of Human Rights, *Aktas v. Turkey*, 24351/94 (Third Section, 24 April 2003).

European Court of Human Rights, *Al Jedda v. The United Kingdom*, 27021/08 (Grand Chamber, 7 July 2011).

European Court of Human Rights, *Andrejeva v. Latvia*, 55707/00 (Grand Chamber, 18 February 2009).

European Court of Human Rights, *Ashingdane v. The United Kingdom*, 8225/78 (Chamber, 28 May 1985).

European Court of Human Rights, *Bellet v. France*, 23805/94 (Chamber, 4 December 1995).

European Court of Human Rights, *Berkman v. Russia*, 46712/15 (Third Section, 1 December 2020).

European Court of Human Rights, *Big Brother Watch and Others v. The United Kingdom*, 58170/13 (Grand Chamber, 25 May 2021).

European Court of Human Rights, *Broniowski v. Poland*, 31443/96 (Grand Chamber, 22 June 2004).

European Court of Human Rights, *Budayeva and Others v. Russia*, 15339/02 (First Section, 20 March 2008).

European Court of Human Rights, *Burdov v. Russia*, 59498/00 (First Section, 7 May 2002).

European Court of Human Rights, *Cakici v. Turkey*, 23657/94 (Grand Chamber, 8 July 1999).

European Court of Human Rights, *Cardot v. France (Preliminary Objections)*, 11069/84 (Chamber, 19 March 1991).

European Court of Human Rights, *Chassagnou and Others v. France*, 25088/94 (Grand Chamber, 29 April 1999).

European Court of Human Rights, *Clinique des Acacias et Autres v. France*, 65399/01 (Third Section, 13 October 2005).

European Court of Human Rights, *Codarcea v. Romania*, 31675/04 (Third Section, 2 June 2009).

European Court of Human Rights, *Colozza v. Italy*, 9024/80 (Chamber, 12 February 1985).

European Court of Human Rights, *Cyprus v. Turkey*, 25781/94 (Grand Chamber, 12 May 2014).

European Court of Human Rights, *De Souza Ribeiro v. France*, 22689/07 (Grand Chamber, 13 December 2012).

European Court of Human Rights, *Demir and Baykara v. Turkey*, 34503/97 (Grand Chamber, 12 November 2008).

European Court of Human Rights, *Deweer v. Belgium*, 6903/75 (Chamber, 27 February 1980).

European Court of Human Rights, *Eşim v. Turkey*, 59601/09 (Second Section, 17 September 2013).

European Court of Human Rights, *Foti and Others v. Italy*, 7604/76 (Chamber, 10 December 1982).

European Court of Human Rights, *Fretté v. France - Joint Partly Dissenting Opinion of Judge Sir Nicolas Bratza and Judges Fuhrmann and Tulkens*, 36515/97 (Third Section, 26 February 2002).

European Court of Human Rights, *Frydlender v. France*, 30979/96 (Grand Chamber, 27 June 2000).

European Court of Human Rights, *García Ruiz v. Spain*, 30544/96 (Grand Chamber, 21 January 1999).

European Court of Human Rights, *Georgia v. Russia (II)*, 38263/08 (Grand Chamber, 21 January 2021)

European Court of Human Rights, *Georgia v. Russia (II) – Joint partly Dissenting Opinion of Judges Yudkivska, Wojtyczek and Chantura*, 38263/08 (Grand Chamber, 21 January 2021)

European Court of Human Rights, *Geouffre de la Pradelle v. France*, 12964/87 (Chamber, 16 December 1992).

European Court of Human Rights, *Giuliani and Gaggio v. Italy*, 23458/02 (Grand Chamber, 24 March 2011).

European Court of Human Rights, *Golder v. The United Kingdom*, 4451/70 (Plenary, 21 February 1975).

European Court of Human Rights, *Guincho v. Portugal*, 8990/80 (Chamber, 10 July 1984).

European Court of Human Rights, *Guiso-Gallisay v. Italy*, 58858/00 (Grand Chamber, 22 December 2009).

European Court of Human Rights, *Gül v. Turkey*, 22676/93 (Fourth Section,, 14 December 2000).

European Court of Human Rights, *Guzzardi v. Italy*, 7367/76 (Plenary, 6 November 1980).

European Court of Human Rights, *Hassan v. The United Kingdom*, 29750/09 (Grand Chamber, 16 September 2014).

European Court of Human Rights, *Hatton and Others v. The United Kingdom*, 36022/97 (Grand Chamber, 8 July 2003).

European Court of Human Rights, *Hatton and Others v. The United Kingdom - Joint Dissenting Opinion of Judges Costa, Ress, Türmen, Zupančič and Steiner*, 36022/97 (Grand Chamber, 8 July 2003).

European Court of Human Rights, *Hirsi Jamaa v. Italy*, 27765/09 (Grand Chamber, 23 February 2012).

European Court of Human Rights, *Hirst v. United Kingdom (No. 2)*, 74025/01 (Grand Chamber, 8 October 2005).

European Court of Human Rights, *Howald Moor v. Switzerland*, 52067/10 (Second Section, 11 March 2014).

European Court of Human Rights, *Ilascu and Others v. Moldova and Russia*, 48787/99 (Grand Chamber, 8 July 2004).

European Court of Human Rights, *Iovchev v. Bulgaria*, 41211/98 (First Section, 2 February 2006).

European Court of Human Rights, *İpek v. Turkey*, 25760/94 (Second Section, 17 February 2004).

European Court of Human Rights, *Jahn and Others v. Germany*, 46720/99 (Grand Chamber, 30 June 2005).

European Court of Human Rights, *Karatas v. Turkey - Joint Partly Dissenting Opinion of Judges Wildhaber, Pastor Ridruejo, Costa and Baka*, 23168/94 (Grand Chamber, 8 July 1999).

European Court of Human Rights, *Kaya v. Turkey*, 22729/93 (Chamber, 19 February 1998).

European Court of Human Rights, *Klass and Others v. Germany*, 5029/71 (Plenary, 6 September 1978).

European Court of Human Rights, *Kostovska v. the Former Yugoslav Republic of Macedonia*, 44353/02 (Fifth Section, 15 June 2006).

European Court of Human Rights, *Kudla v. Poland*, 30210/96 (Grand Chamber, 26 October 2000).

European Court of Human Rights, *Kurić and Others v. Slovenia*, 26828/06 (Grand Chamber, 26 June 2012).

European Court of Human Rights, *Kurt v. Turkey*, 24276/94 (Chamber, 25 May 1998).

European Court of Human Rights, *Leander v. Sweden*, 9248/81 (Chamber, 26 March 1987).

European Court of Human Rights, *M.S.S. v. Belgium and Greece*, 30696/09 (Grand Chamber, 21 January 2011).

European Court of Human Rights, *Magyar Helsinki Bizottság v. Hungary - Concurring Opinion of Judge Sicilianos, Joined by Judge Raimondi*, 18030/11 (Grand Chamber, 8 November 2016).

European Court of Human Rights, *McCann and Others v. United Kingdom*, 18984/91 (Grand Chamber, 27 September 1995).

European Court of Human Rights, *Mentes and Others v. Turkey*, 23186/94 (Grand Chamber, 24 July 1998).

European Court of Human Rights, *Mocie v. France*, 46096/99 (Second Section, 8 April 2003).

European Court of Human Rights, *Naït-Liman v. Switzerland*, 51357/07 (Grand Chamber, 15 March 2018).

European Court of Human Rights, *N.D. and N.T. v. Spain*, 8675/15 (Grand Chamber, 13 February 2020).

European Court of Human Rights, *Nejdet Şahin and Perihan Şahin v. Turkey*, 13279/05 (Grand Chamber, 20 October 2011).

European Court of Human Rights, *Neumeister v. Austria (Article 50)*, 1936/63 (Chamber, 7 May 1974).

European Court of Human Rights, *Nicolae Virgiliu Tănase v. Romania* 41720/13 (Grand Chamber, 25 June 2019).

European Court of Human Rights, *Öcalan v. Turkey*, 46221/99 (Grand Chamber, 12 May 2005).

European Court of Human Rights, *Oğur v. Turkey*, 21594/93 (Grand Chamber, 20 May 1999).

European Court of Human Rights, *Özel and Others v. Turkey*, 14350/05 (Second Section, 17 November 2015).

European Court of Human Rights, *Papamichalopoulos and Others v. Greece (Article 50)*, 14556/89 (Chamber, 31 October 1995).

European Court of Human Rights, *Pentiakova and Others v. Moldova, Admissibility Decision*, 14462/03 (Fourth Section, 4 January 2005).

European Court of Human Rights, *Perez v. France*, 47287/99 (Grand Chamber, 12 February 2004).

European Court of Human Rights, *Price v. The United Kingdom*, 33394/96 (Third Section, 10 July 2001).

European Court of Human Rights, *Radkov v. Bulgaria (No. 2)*, 18382/05 (Fifth Section, 10 February 2011).

European Court of Human Rights, *Ramirez Sanchez v. France*, 59450/00 (Grand Chamber, 4 July 2006).

European Court of Human Rights, *Saadi v. The United Kingdom*, 13229/03 (Grand Chamber, 29 January 2008).

European Court of Human Rights, *Scordino v. Italy (No. 1)*, 36813/97 (Grand Chamber, 29 March 2006).

European Court of Human Rights, *Sejdić and Finci v. Bosnia and Herzegovina*, 27996/06 (Grand Chamber, 22 December 2009).

European Court of Human Rights, *Sharxhi and Others v. Albania* 10613/16 (First Section, 11 January 2018).

European Court of Human Rights, *Siegle v. Romania*, 23456/04 (Third Section, 16 April 2013).

European Court of Human Rights, *Silver and Others v. United Kingdom*, 5947/72 (Chamber, 25 March 1983).

European Court of Human Rights, *Soering v. The United Kingdom*, 14038/88 (Plenary, 7 July 1989).

European Court of Human Rights, *Stoll v. Switzerland*, 69698/01 (Grand Chamber, 10 December 2007).

European Court of Human Rights, *Stubbings and Others v. The United Kingdom*, 22083/93 (Chamber, 22 October 1996).

European Court of Human Rights, *Sunday Times v. The United Kingdom (Article 50)*, 6538/74 (Plenary, 6 November 1980).

European Court of Human Rights, *Tyrer v. The United Kingdom*, 5856/72 (Chamber, 25 April 1978).

European Court of Human Rights, *Unión Alimentaria Sanders S.A. v. Spain*, 11681/85 (Chamber, 7 July 1989).

European Court of Human Rights, *A. v. The United Kingdom*, 35373/97 (Second Section, 17 December 2002).

European Court of Human Rights, *Varnava and Others v. Turkey*, 16064/90 (Grand Chamber, 18 September 2009).

European Court of Human Rights, *Vilvarajah and Others v. United Kingdom*, 13163/87 (Chamber, 30 October 1991).

European Court of Human Rights, *Vocaturo v. Italy*, 11891/85 (Chamber, 24 May 1991).

European Court of Human Rights, *Z and Others v. The United Kingdom*, 29392/95 (Grand Chamber, 10 May 2001).

European Court of Human Rights, *Zimmermann and Steiner v. Switzerland*, 8737/79 (Chamber, 13 July 1983).

European Court of Justice, *Axel Walz v. Clickair SA*, C-63/09 (6 May 2010).

German Federal Court of Justice, *Kunduz Case*, III ZR 140/15 (6 October 2016).

German Federal Constitutional Court, *Varvarin Case*, 2 BvR 2660/06, 2 BvR 487/07 (13 August 2013).

Human Rights Committee, *André Brun v. France*, CCPR/C/88/D/1453/2006, 1453/2006 (23 November 2006).

Human Rights Committee, *Anthony Currie v. Jamaica*, CCPR/C/50/D/377/1989, 377/1989 (31 March 1994).

Human Rights Committee, *Bakar Japalali and Carmen Baloyo-Japalali v. Philippines*, CCPR/C/125/D/2536/2015, 2536/2015 (30 May 2019).

Human Rights Committee, *Bariza Zaier v. Algeria - Individual Opinion of Gerald L. Neumann (Concurring)*, CCPR/C/112/D/2026/2011, 2026/2011 (15 December 2014).

Human Rights Committee, *Beatriz Weismann Lanza and Alcides Lanza Perdomo v. Uruguay*, CCPR/C/9/D/8/1977, 8/1977 (3 April 1980).

Human Rights Committee, *Devon Simpson v. Jamaica*, CCPR/C/73/D/695/1996, 695/1996 (31 October 2001).

Human Rights Committee, *Fulmati Nyaya v. Nepal*, CCPR/C/125/D/2556/2015, 2556/2015 (11 June 2019).

Human Rights Committee, *Guillermo Ignacio Dermit Barbato et al. v. Uruguay*, CCPR/C/OP/2, 84/1981 (21 October 1982).

Human Rights Committee, *Gyan Devi Bolakhe v. Nepal*, CCPR/C/123/DR/2658/2015, 2658/2015 (4 September 2018).

Human Rights Committee, *H.C.M.A. v. The Netherlands,* CCPR/C/35/D/213/1986, 213/1986 (30 March 1989).

Human Rights Committee, *Hiber Conteris v. Uruguay,* A/40/40, 139/1983 (17 July 1985).

Human Rights Committee, *José Vicente and Amado Villafañe Chaparro and Others v. Colombia,* CCPR/C/60/D/612/1995, 612/1995 (29 July 1997).

Human Rights Committee, *Josef Frank Adam v. The Czech Republic,* CCPR/C/57/D/586/1994, 586/1994 (23 July 1996).

Human Rights Committee, *Mariano Pimentel et al. v. The Philippines,* CCPR/C/89/D/1320/2004, 1320/2004 (19 March 2007).

Human Rights Committee, *Marshall v. Canada,* CCPR/C/43/D/205/1986, 205/1986 (4 November 1991).

Human Rights Committee, *Martínez et al. v. Colombia*, CCPR/C/128/D/3076/2017, 3076/2017 (2 June 2020).

Human Rights Committee, *Mohamed Rabbae, A.B.S. and N.A. v. The Netherlands,* CCPR/C/117/D/2124/2011, 2124/2011 (14 July 2016).

Human Rights Committee, *Nicole Beydon and Others v. France,* CCPR/C/85/D/1400/2005, 1400/2005 (28 November 2005).

Human Rights Committee, *Quinteros v. Uruguay,* CCPR/C/OP/2, 107/1981 (21 July 1983).

Human Rights Committee, *Rawle Kennedy v. Trinidad and Tobago,* CCPR/C/74/D/845/1998, 845/1998 (26 March 2002).

Human Rights Committee, *Rodger Chongwe v. Zambia,* CCPR/C/70/D/821/1998, 821/1998 (16 October - 3 November 2000).

Human Rights Committee, *Roger Judge v. Canada,* CCPR/C/78/D/829/1998, 829/1998 (13 August 2003).

Human Rights Committee, *Sechremelis et al v. Greece,* CCPR/C/100/D/1507/2006/Rev.1, 1507/2006 (7 January 2011).

Human Rights Committee, *Siobhán Whelan v. Ireland,* CCPR/C/119/D/2425/2014, 2425/2014 (11 July 2017).

Human Rights Committee, *Sterling v. Jamaica,* CCPR/C/57/D/598/1994, 598/1994 (22 July 1996).

Human Rights Committee, *Sundara Arachchige Lalith Rajapakse v. Sri Lanka,* CCPR/C/87/D/1250/2004, 1250/2004 (14 July 2006).

Human Rights Committee, *Taito Fa'afete v. New Zealand,* CCPR/C/114/D/1909/2009, 1909/2009 (7 September 2015).

Human Rights Committee, *William Torres Ramirez v. Uruguay,* CCPR/C/10/D/4/1977, 4/1977 (23 July 1980).

Human Rights Committee, *Wilson v. The Philippines,* CCPR/C/79/D/868/1999, 868/1999 (30 October 2003).

Inter-American Commission on Human Rights, *Integrantes y Militantes de la Unión Patriótica v. Colombia, Merits Report,* 170/17 (6 December 2017).

Inter-American Commission on Human Rights, *Maria Laura Ordenes Guerra et al. v. Chile, Merits Report,* 52/16 (30 November 2016).

Inter-American Commission on Human Rights, *Rufino Jorge Almeida v. Argentina, Merits Report,* 147/18 (7 December 2018).

Inter-American Court of Human Rights, *Advisory Opinion on the Compulsory Membership in an Association Prescribed by Law for the Practice of Journalism*, OC-5/85 (13 November 1985).

Inter-American Court of Human Rights, *Advisory Opinion on the Effect of Reservations on the Entry Into Force of the American Convention on Human Rights (Arts. 74 and 75)*, OC-2/82 (24 September 1982).

Inter-American Court of Human Rights, *Advisory Opinion on the Exceptions to the Exhaustion of Domestic Remedies*, OC-11/90 (10 August 1990).

Inter-American Court of Human Rights, *Advisory Opinion on the Right to Information on Consular Assistance in the Framework of the Guarantees of the Due Process of Law*, OC-16/99 (1 October 1999).

Inter-American Court of Human Rights, *Advisory Opnion on the Right to Information on Consular Assistance in the Framework of the Guarantees of the Due Process of Law*, OC-16/99 (1 October 1999).

Inter-American Court of Human Rights, *Aloeboetoe et al. v. Suriname (Reparation and Costs)* (10 September 1993).

Inter-American Court of Human Rights, *Atala Riffo and Daughters v. Chile* (24 February 2012).

Inter-American Court of Human Rights, *Bámaca-Velásquez v. Guatemala (Merits)* (25 November 2000).

Inter-American Court of Human Rights, *Bámaca-Velásquez v. Guatemala (Merits) – Separate Concurring Opinion of Judge Sergio García Ramírez* (25 November 2000).

Inter-American Court of Human Rights, *Case of Bámaca-Velásquez v. Guatemala (Reparations and Costs) – Concurring Opinion of Judge Sergio García Ramírez* (22 February 2002).

Inter-American Court of Human Rights, *Barbani Duarte et al. v. Uruguay* (13 October 2011).

Inter-American Court of Human Rights, *Cantoral Benavides v. Peru (Reparations and Costs)* (3 December 2001).

Inter-American Court of Human Rights, *Cantos v. Argentina* (28 November 2002).

Inter-American Court of Human Rights, *Caracazo v. Venezuela (Reparations and Costs)* (29 August 2002).

Inter-American Court of Human Rights, *Case of Barrios Altos v. Peru (Merits)* (14 March 2001).

Inter-American Court of Human Rights, *Case of the "Juvenile Reeducation Institute" v. Paraguay* (2 September 2004).

Inter-American Court of Human Rights, *Case of the "Mapiripán Massacre" v. Colombia* (15 September 2015).

Inter-American Court of Human Rights, *Case of the Río Negro Massacre v. Guatemala* (4 September 2012).

Inter-American Court of Human Rights, *Case of Ruano Torres et al. v. El Salvador* (5 October 2015).

Inter-American Court of Human Rights, *Case of the "Street Children" (Villagran-Morales et al.) v. Guatemala (Merits)* (19 November 1999).

Inter-American Court of Human Rights, *Case of the "Street Children" (Villagrán-Morales et al.) v. Guatemala (Reparations and Costs)* (26 May 2001).

Inter-American Court of Human Rights, *Case of the "White Van" (Paniagua-Morales et al.) v. Guatemala (Merits)* (8 March 1998).

Inter-American Court of Human Rights, *Case of the "White Van" (Paniagua-Morales et al.) v. Guatemala (Reparations and Costs)* (25 May 2001).

Inter-American Court of Human Rights, *Case of the Afro-Descendant Communities Displaced From the Cacarica River Basin (Operation Genesis) v. Colombia* (20 November 2013).

Inter-American Court of Human Rights, *Case of the Gómez-Paquiyauri Brothers v. Peru* (8 July 2004).

Inter-American Court of Human Rights, *Case of the Indigenous Communities of the Lhaka Honhat (Our Land) Association v. Argentina* (6 February 2020).

Inter-American Court of Human Rights, *Case of the Ituango Massacres v. Colombia* (1 July 2006).

Inter-American Court of Human Rights, *Case of the Massacres of El Mozote and Nearby Places v. El Salvador* (25 October 2012).

Inter-American Court of Human Rights, *Case of the Mayagna (Sumo) Awas Tingni Community v. Nicaragua (Merits, Reparations and Costs)* (31 August 2001).

Inter-American Court of Human Rights, *Case of the Miguel Castro-Castro Prison v. Peru (Merits, Reparations and Costs)* (25 November 2006).

Inter-American Court of Human Rights, *Case of the Pueblo Bello Massacre v. Colombia* (31 January 2006).

Inter-American Court of Human Rights, *Case of the Sawhoyamaxa Indigenous Community v. Paraguay* (29 March 2006).

Inter-American Court of Human Rights, *Case of "The Last Temptation of Christ" (Olmedo-Bustos et al.) v. Chile* (5 February 2001).

Inter-American Court of Human Rights, *Case of the Workers of the Fireworks Factory in Santo Antônio de Jesus and Their Families v. Brazil* (15 July 2020).

Inter-American Court of Human Rights, *Castañeda Gutman v. Mexico* (6 August 2008).

Inter-American Court of Human Rights, *Castillo-Paéz v. Peru* (27 November 1998).

Inter-American Court of Human Rights, *Chaparro Álvarez and Lapo Íñiguez v. Ecuador* (21 November 2007).

Inter-American Court of Human Rights, *Claude-Reyes et al. v. Chile (Merits, Reparations and Costs)* (19 September 2006).

Inter-American Court of Human Rights, *El Amparo v. Venezuela (Reparations and Costs)* (14 September 1996).

Inter-American Court of Human Rights, *Fairén-Garbi and Solís-Corrales v. Honduras (Merits)* (15 March 1989).

Inter-American Court of Human Rights, *Fernández Ortega et al. v Mexico* (30 August 2010).

Inter-American Court of Human Rights, *Fontevecchia y D'Amico v. Argentina* (29 November 2011).

Inter-American Court of Human Rights, *Forneron and Daughter v. Argentina* (27 April 2012).

Inter-American Court of Human Rights, *Furlan and Family v. Argentina* (31 August 2012).

Inter-American Court of Human Rights, *García Lucero et al. v. Chile* (28 August 2013).

Inter-American Court of Human Rights, *Garibaldi v. Brasil* (23 September 2009).

Inter-American Court of Human Rights, *Garrido and Baigorria v. Argentina (Reparations and Costs)* (27 August 1998).

Inter-American Court of Human Rights, *Godínez-Cruz v. Honduras (Merits)* (20 January 1989).

Inter-American Court of Human Rights, *Goiburú et al. v. Paraguay* (22 September 2006).

Inter-American Court of Human Rights, *Gomes Lund et al. ("Guerrilha Do Araguaia") v. Brazil* (24 November 2010).

Inter-American Court of Human Rights, *González et al. ("Cotton Field") v. Mexico* (16 November 2009).

Inter-American Court of Human Rights, *Juan Humberto Sánchez v. Honduras* (7 June 2003).

Inter-American Court of Human Rights, *Judicial Guarantees in States of Emergency (Arts. 27(2), 25 and 8 American Convention on Human Rights)*, OC-9/87 (6 October 1987).

Inter-American Court of Human Rights, *The Kaliña and Lokono Peoples v. Suriname* (25 November 2015).

Inter-American Court of Human Rights, *Kimel v Argentina (Merits, Reparations and Costs)* (2 May 2008).

Inter-American Court of Human Rights, *La Cantuta v. Peru* (29 November 2006).

Inter-American Court of Human Rights, *Loayza-Tamayo v. Peru (Reparations and Costs)* (27 November 1998).

Inter-American Court of Human Rights, *Loayza-Tamayo v. Peru (Reparations and Costs) - Joint Concurring Opinion of Judges A.A. Cançado Trindade and A. Abreu-Burelli* (27 November 1998).

Inter-American Court of Human Rights, *Manuel Cepeda Vargas v. Colombia* (26 May 2010).

Inter-American Court of Human Rights, *Maria Cristina Reveron Trujillo v. Venezuela* (30 June 2009).

Inter-American Court of Human Rights, *Molina-Theissen v. Guatemala* (3 July 2004).

Inter-American Court of Human Rights, *Myrna Mack Chang v. Guatemala* (25 November 2003).

Inter-American Court of Human Rights, *Myrna Mack Chang v. Guatemala - Reasoned Concurring Opinion of Judge Sergio García-Ramírez* (25 November 2003).

Inter-American Court of Human Rights, *Omar Humberto Maldonado Vargas et al. v. Chile* (2 September 2015).

Inter-American Court of Human Rights, *Opinión Consultative Sobre la Denuncia de la Convención Americana Sobre Derechos Humanos y de la Carta de la Organización de los Estados Americanos y sus Efectos Sobre las Obligaciones Estatales en Materia de Derechos Humanos,* OC-26/20 (9 November 2020).

Inter-American Court of Human Rights, *Ordenes Guerra y Otros v. Chile* (29 November 2018).

Inter-American Court of Human Rights, *Perozo et al. v. Venzuela* (28 January 2009).

Inter-American Court of Human Rights, *Radilla-Pacheco v. Mexico* (23 November 2009).

Inter-American Court of Human Rights, *Ríos et al. v. Venezuela* (28 January 2009).

Inter-American Court of Human Rights, *Rodríguez Vera et al. (The Disappeared From the Palace of Justice) v. Colombia* (14 November 2014).

Inter-American Court of Human Rights, *Rosendo Cantú et al. v. Mexico* (31 August 2010).

Inter-American Court of Human Rights, *Salvador Chiriboga v. Ecuador* (6 May 2008).

Inter-American Court of Human Rights, *Saramaka People v. Suriname* (28 November 2007).

Inter-American Court of Human Rights, *Suárez-Rosero v. Ecuador (Reparations and Costs)* (20 January 1999).

Inter-American Court of Human Rights, *Trujillo-Oroza v. Bolivia (Reparations and Costs)* (27 February 2002).

Inter-American Court of Human Rights, *Velásquez-Rodríguez v. Honduras (Compensatory Damages)* (21 July 1989).

Inter-American Court of Human Rights, *Velásquez-Rodríguez v. Honduras (Merits)* (29 July 1988).

Inter-American Court of Human Rights, *Velásquez-Rodríguez v. Honduras (Preliminary Objections)* (26 June 1987).

Inter-American Court of Human Rights, *Velásquez-Rodríguez v. Honduras (Reparations and Costs)* (21 July 1989).

Inter-American Court of Human Rights, *Victor Neira-Alegría et al. v. Peru (Reparations and Costs)* (19 September 1996).

Inter-American Court of Human Rights, *Villamizar Durán y Otros v. Colombia* (20 November 2018).

Inter-American Court of Human Rights, *Ximenes-Lopes v. Brazil* (4 July 2006).

Inter-American Court of Human Rights, *Yakye Axa Indigenous Community v. Paraguay* (17 June 2005).

Inter-American Court of Human Rights, *Yarce et al v. Colombia* (22 November 2016).

Inter-American Court of Human Rights, *Yarce et al. v. Colombia (Interpretation of the Judgment on Preliminary Objections, Merits, Reparations and Costs)* (21 November 2017).

International Center for Settlement of Investment Disputes, *Amco Asia Corporation and Others v. Republic of Indonesia, Award,* ARB/81/1 (20 November 1984).

International Court of Justice, *Advisory Opinion on the Legality of the Threat or use of Nuclear Weapons,* I.C.J. Reports 1996, 226 (8 July 1996).

International Court of Justice, *Ahmadou Sadio Diallo (Republic of Guinea v. Democratic Republic of the Congo), Merits, Judgment,* I.C.J. Reports 2010, 639 (30 November 2010).

International Court of Justice, *Application of the Convention on the Prevention and Punishment of the Crime of Genocide (Bosnia and Herzegovina v. Serbia and Montenegro), Judgment,* I.C.J. Reports 2007, 43 (26 February 2007).

International Court of Justice, *Armed Activities on the Territory of the Congo (Democratic Republic of the Congo v. Uganda), Judgment,* I.C.J. Reports 2005, 168 (19 December 2005).

International Court of Justice, *Armed Activities on the Territory of the Congo (Democratic Republic of the Congo v. Uganda), Reparations,* General List No. 116 (9 February 2022).

International Court of Justice, *Armed Activities on the Territory of the Congo (Democratic Republic of the Congo v. Uganda), Reparations – Declaration of Judge Salam,* General List No. 116 (9 February 2022).

International Court of Justice, *Armed Activities on the Territory of the Congo (Democratic Republic of the Congo v. Uganda), Reparations – Declaration of Judge Tomka,* General List No. 116 (9 February 2022).

International Court of Justice, *Armed Activities on the Territory of the Congo (Democratic Republic of the Congo v. Uganda), Reparations – Separate Opinion of Judge Robinson,* General List No. 116 (9 February 2022).

International Court of Justice, *Armed Activities on the Territory of the Congo (Democratic Republic of the Congo v. Uganda), Reparations – Separate Opinion of Judge Yusuf,* General List No. 116 (9 February 2022).

International Court of Justice, *Armed Activities on the Territory of the Congo (Democratic Republic of the Congo v. Uganda), Reparations – Opinion Dissidente de M. le Juge Ad Hoc Daudet,* General List No. 116 (9 February 2022).

International Court of Justice, *Case Concerning Ahmadou Sadio Diallo (Republic of Guinea v. Democratic Republic of the Congo), Compensation, Judgment,* I.C.J. Reports 2012, 324 (19 June 2012).

International Court of Justice, *Case Concerning Avena and Other Mexican Nationals (Mexico v. United States of America),* I.C.J. Reports 2004, 12 (31 March 2004).

International Court of Justice, *Case Concerning the Continental Shelf (Libyan Arab Jamahiriya / Malta) - Judgment of 3 June 1985,* I.C.J. Reports 1985, 13 (3 June 1985).

International Court of Justice, *Case Concerning the Gabčíkovo-Nagymaros Project (Hungary/Slovakia),* I.C.J. Reports 1997, 7 (25 September 1997).

International Court of Justice, *Case Concerning the Right of Passage Over Indian Territory (Merits),* I.C.J. Reports 1960, 6 (12 April 1960).

International Court of Justice, *Certain Phosphate Lands in Nauru (Nauru v. Australia), Preliminary Objections, Judgment,* I.C.J. Reports 1992, 240 (26 June 1992).

International Court of Justice, *Corfu Channel Case (Merits),* I.C.J. Reports 1949, 4 (9 April 1949).

International Court of Justice, *Dispute Regarding Navigational and Relational Rights (Costa Rica v. Nicaragua),* I.C.J. Reports 2009, 213 (13 July 2009).

International Court of Justice, *Fisheries Case (United Kingdom v. Norway) - Seperate Opinion of Judge Hsu Mo,* I.C.J. Reports 1951, 42 (18 December 1951).

International Court of Justice, *Jurisdictional Immunities of the State (Germany v. Italy: Greece Intervening),* I.C.J. Reports 2012, 99 (3 February 2012).

International Court of Justice, *LaGrand (Germany v. United States of America),* I.C.J. Reports 2001, 466 (27 June 2001).

International Court of Justice, *Legal Consequences of the Construction of a Wall in the Occupied Palestinian Territory (Advisory Opinion),* I.C.J. Reports 2004, 136 (9 July 2004).

International Court of Justice, *Military and Paramilitary Activities in and Against Nicaragua (Nicaragua v. United States of America), Merits,* I.C.J. Reports 1986, 14 (27 June 1986).

International Court of Justice, *North Sea Continental Shelf Case - Dissenting Opinion of Judge Tanaka,* I.C.J. Reports 1969, 172 (20 February 1969).

International Court of Justice, *Reparations for Injuries Suffered in the Service of the United Nations (Advisory Opinion),* I.C.J. Reports 1949, 174 (11 April 1949).

International Court of Justice, *Reservations to the Convention on Genocide - Advisory Opinion,* I.C.J. Reports 1951, 15 (28 May 1951).

International Criminal Court, *The Prosecutor v. Ahmad Al Faqi Al Mahdi, Decision on the Updated Implementation Plan From the Trust Fund for Victims,* ICC-01/12-01/15-324 (Trial Chamber VIII, 4 March 2019).

International Criminal Court, *The Prosecutor v. Ahmad al Faqi al Mahdi, First Transmission and Report on Applications for Reparations,* ICC-01/12-01/15-200 (Registry, 16 December 2016).

International Criminal Court, *The Prosecutor v. Ahmad Al Faqi Al Mahdi, Judgment and Sentence,* ICC-01/12-01/15-171 (Trial Chamber VII, 27 September 2016).

International Criminal Court, *The Prosecutor v. Ahmad Al Faqi Al Mahdi, Lesser Public Redacted Version of "Updated Implementation Plan" Submitted on 2 November 2018 ICC-01/12-01/15-291-Conf-Exp,* ICC-01/12-01/15-291-Red3 (Trust Fund for Victims, 14 October 2019).

International Criminal Court, *The Prosecutor v. Ahmad al Faqi Al Mahdi, Monthly Update Report on the Implementation Plan With Two Confidential Annexes,* ICC-01/12-01/15-283-Red (Trust Fund for Victims, 18 July 2019).

International Criminal Court, *The Prosecutor v. Ahmad Al Faqi Al Mahdi, Public Redacted Judgment on the Appeal of the Victims Against the "Reparations Order",* ICC-01/12-01/15-259-Red2 (Appeals Chamber, 8 March 2018).

International Criminal Court, *The Prosecutor v. Ahmad Al Faqi Al Mahdi, Public Redacted Version of "Decision on Trust Fund for Victims' Draft Implementation Plan for Reparations",* ICC-01/12-01/15-273-Red (Trial Chamber VIII, 12 July 2018).

International Criminal Court, *The Prosecutor v. Ahmad Al Faqi Al Mahdi, Public Redacted Version of "Corrected Version of Draft Implementation Plan for Reparations",* ICC-01/12-01/15-265 (Trust Fund for Victims, 18 May 2018).

International Criminal Court, *The Prosecutor v. Ahmad al Faqi al Mahdi, Public Redacted Version of "Eighteenth Update Report on the Updated Implementation Plan"*, ICC-01/12-01/15-377-Red (Trust Fund for Victims, 29 December 2020).

International Criminal Court, *The Prosecutor v. Ahmad al Faqi al Mahdi, Public Redacted Version of "Eighth Update Report on the Updated Implementation Plan,* ICC-01/12-01/15-331-Red (Trust Fund for Victims, 6 May 2019).

International Criminal Court, *The Prosecutor v. Ahmad al Faqi al Mahdi, Public Redacted Version of "Eleventh Update Report on the Implementation Plan"*, ICC-01/12/01-15-336-Red2 (Trust Fund for Victims, 25 October 2019).

International Criminal Court, *The Prosecutor v. Ahmad al Faqi al Mahdi, Public Redacted Version of "Fourth Monthly Update Report on the Updated Implementation Plan"*, ICC-01/12-01/15-299-Red2 (Trust Fund for Victims, 14 November 2018).

International Criminal Court, *The Prosecutor v. Ahmad Al Faqi Al Mahdi, Public Redacted Version of "Monthly Update Report on the Implementation Plan, Including Notification of the Board of Directors' Decision on the Trial Chamber's Complement Request Pursuant to Regulation 56 of the Regulations of the Trust Fund for Victims"*, ICC-01/12-01/15-277-Red (Trust Fund for Victims, 27 August 2018).

International Criminal Court, *The Prosecutor v. Ahmad al Faqi al Mahdi, Public Redacted Version of "Nineteenth Update Report on the Updated Implementation Plan"*, ICC-01/12-01/15-381-Red (Trust Fund for Victims, 25 February 2021).

International Criminal Court, *The Prosecutor v. Ahmad al Faqi al Mahdi, Public Redacted Version of "Tenth Update Report on the Implementation Plan"*, ICC-01/12/01-15-335-Red2 (Trust Fund for Victims, 4 September 2019).

International Criminal Court, *The Prosecutor v. Ahmad al Faqi al Mahdi, Public Redacted Version of "Third Monthly Update Report on the Updated Implementation Plan"*, ICC-01/12-01/15-288-Red2 (Trust Fund for Victims, 15 October 2018).

International Criminal Court, *The Prosecutor v. Ahmad al Faqi al Mahdi, Public Redacted Version of "Thirteenth Update Report on the Updated Implementation Plan"*, ICC-01/12-01/15-346-Red2 (Trust Fund for Victims, 20 February 2020).

International Criminal Court, *The Prosecutor v. Ahmad al Faqi al Mahdi, Public Redacted Version of "Trust Fund for Victims' Submission of Draft Application Form"*, ICC-01/12-01/15-289-Red (Trust Fund for Victims, 26 October 2018).

International Criminal Court, *The Prosecutor v. Ahmad Al Faqi Al Mahdi, Public Redacted Version of "Trust Fund for Victims' Submission of Draft Application Form"*, ICC-01/12-01/15-289 (Trust Fund for Victims, 30 October 2018).

International Criminal Court, *Ahmad al Faqi al Mahdi, Public Redacted Version of "Twelfth Update Report on the Updated Implementation Plan"*, ICC-01/12-01/15-340-Red (Trust Fund for Victims, 27 December 2019)

International Criminal Court, *The Prosecutor v. Ahmad al Faqi al Mahdi, Public Redacted Version of "Twenty-First Update Report on the Updated Implementation Plan"*, ICC-01/12-01/15-405-Red (Trust Fund for Victims, 31 August 2021).

International Criminal Court, *The Prosecutor v. Ahmad al Faqi al Mahdi, Public Redacted Version of "Twenty-Third Update Report on the Updated Implementation Plan"*, ICC-01/12-01/15-438-Red (Trust Fund for Victims, 25 February 2022).

International Criminal Court, *The Prosecutor v. Ahmad Al Faqi Al Mahdi, Public Redacted Version of "Updated Implementation Plan"*, ICC-01/12-01/15-291 (Trust Fund for Victims, 22 November 2018).

International Criminal Court, *The Prosecutor v. Ahmad Al Faqi Al Mahdi, Reparations Order*, ICC-01/12-01/15-236 (Trial Chamber VII, 17 August 2017).

International Criminal Court, *The Prosecutor v. Ahmad al Faqi al Mahdi, Trust Funds's Submission on the Amendment of the Screening Process,* ICC-01/12-01/15-372 (Trust Fund for Victims, 2 September 2020).

International Criminal Court, *The Prosecutor v. Ahmad al Faqi al Mahdi, "Twentieth Update Report on the Updated Implementation Plan"*, ICC-01/12-01/15-386-Red (Trust Fund for Victim's, 19 May 2021).

International Criminal Court, *The Prosecutor v. Bosco Ntaganda, Annex A to the Public Redacted Version of „Report on Trust Fund's Preparation for Draft Implementation Plan"*, ICC-01/04-02/06-2676-AnxA-Corr-Red (Trust Fund for Victims, 8 June 2021)

International Criminal Court, *The Prosecutor v. Bosco Ntaganda, Decision on the TFV's Second Progress Report on the Implementation of the Initial Draft Implementation Plan*, ICC-01/04-02/06-2730-Conf (Trial Chamber II, 17 December 2021).

International Criminal Court, *The Prosecutor v. Bosco Ntaganda, Decision on the TFV's Fourth Update Report on the Implementation of the Initial Draft Implementation Plan*, ICC-01/04-02/06-2761-Conf (Trial Chamber II, 12 May 2022).

International Criminal Court, *The Prosecutor v. Bosco Ntaganda, Decision on the TFV's Initial Draft Implementation Plan With a Focus on Priority Victims,* ICC-01/04-02/06-2696 (Trial Chamber II, 23 July 2021).

International Criminal Court, *The Prosecutor v. Bosco Ntaganda, Judgment,* ICC-01/04-02/06-2359 (Trial Chamber VI, 8 July 2019).

International Criminal Court, *The Prosecutor v. Bosco Ntaganda, Judgment on the Appeals Against the Decision of Trial Chamber VI of 8 March 2021 Entitled "Reparations Order"*, ICC-01/04-02/06-2782 (Appeals Chamber, 12 September 2022).

International Criminal Court, *The Prosecutor v. Bosco Ntaganda, Public Redacted Version of Decision on the TFV's First Progress Report on the Implementation of the Initial Draft Implementation Plan,* ICC-01-/04-02/06-2718 (Trial Chamber II, 28 October 2021).

International Criminal Court, *The Prosecutor v. Bosco Ntaganda, Public Redacted Version of "Trust Fund's Second Update Report on the Implementation of the Initial Draft Implementation Plan"*, ICC-01/04-02/06-2723-Red (Trust Fund for Victims, 28 December 2021).

International Criminal Court, *The Prosecutor v. Bosco Ntaganda, Public Redacted Version of "Trust Fund First Progress Report on the Implementation of the Initial Draft Implementation Plan"*, ICC-01/04-02/06-2710-Red (Trust Fund for Victims, 23 September 2021).

International Criminal Court, *The Prosecutor v. Bosco Ntaganda, Public Redacted Version of "Trust Fund for Victims' Fourth Update Report on the Implementation of the Initial Draft Implementation Plan"*, ICC-01/04-02/06-2751-Red (Trust Fund for Victims, 24 March 2022).

International Criminal Court, *The Prosecutor v. Bosco Ntaganda, Public Redacted Version of Trust Fund for Victims' Sixth Update Report on the Implementation of the Initial Draft Implementation Plan,* ICC-01/04-02/06-2775-Red (Trust Fund for Victims, 25 July 2022).

International Criminal Court, *The Prosecutor v. Bosco Ntaganda, Public Redacted Version of "Trust Fund for Victims' Third Update Report on the Implementation of the Initial Draft Implementation Plan",* ICC-01/04-02/06-2741-Red (Trust Fund for Victims, 24 March 2022).

International Criminal Court, *The Prosecutor v. Bosco Ntaganda, Sentencing Judgment,* ICC-01/04-02/06-2442 (Trial Chamber VI, 7 November 2019).

International Criminal Court, *The Prosecutor v. Bosco Ntaganda, Trust Fund for Victims' Observations on the Impact of Covid-19 on Operational Capacity,* ICC-01/04-02/06-2517 (Trust Fund for Victims, 21 April 2020).

International Criminal Court, *The Prosecutor v. Germain Katanga, Second Quarterly Update Report,* ICC-01/04-01/07-3865-Red (Trust Fund for Victims, 19 October 2020).

International Criminal Court, *The Prosecutor v. Germain Katanga, Draft Implementation Plan Relevant to Trial Chamber II's Order for Reparations of 24 March 2017,* ICC-01/04-01/07-3751 (Trust Fund for Victims, 25 July 2017).

International Criminal Court, *The Prosecutor v. Germain Katanga, Information Relevant to the Modalities of Implementation of Collective Reparations,* ICC-01/04-01/07-3811 (Trust Fund for Victims, 28 February 2018).

International Criminal Court, *The Prosecutor v. Germain Katanga, Judgment on the Appeals Against the Order of Trial Chamber II of 24 March 2017 Entitled "Order for Reparations Pursuant to Article 75 of the Statute",* ICC-01/04-01/07-3778 (Appeals Chamber, 8 March 2018).

International Criminal Court, *The Prosecutor v. Germain Katanga, Judgment Pursuant to Article 74 of the Statute,* ICC-01/04-01/07-3436 (Trial Chamber II, 7 March 2014).

International Criminal Court, *The Prosecutor v. Germain Katanga, Notification Pursuant to Regulation 56 of the TFV Regulations Regarding the Trust Fund Board of Director's Decision Relevant to Complementing the Payment of the Individual and Collective Reparations Awards as Requested by Trial Chamber II in its 24 March 2017 Order for Reparations,* ICC-01/04-01/07-3740 (Trust Fund for Victims, 17 May 2017).

International Criminal Court, *The Prosecutor v. Germain Katanga, Order for Reparations Pursuant to Article 75 of the Statute,* ICC-01/04-01/07-3728 (Trial Chamber II, 24 March 2017).

International Criminal Court, *The Prosecutor v. Germain Katanga, Public Redacted Version of Decision on the Matter of the Transgenerational Harm Alleged by Some Applicants for Reparations Remanded by the Appeals Chamber in its Judgment of 8 March 2018,* ICC-01/04-01/07-3804-Red (Trial Chamber II, 19 July 2018).

International Criminal Court, *The Prosecutor v. Germain Katanga, Public Redacted Version of the Fifth Quarterly Update Report,* ICC-01/01-04/07-3885-Red (Trust Fund for Victims, 19 July 2021).

International Criminal Court, *The Prosecutor v. Germain Katanga, Report on the Trust Fund's Execution of the Payment of the Individual Reparations Awards*, ICC-01/04-01/07-3772 (Trust Fund for Victims, 4 December 2017).

International Criminal Court, *The Prosecutor v. Germain Katanga, Third Quarterly Update Report*, ICC-01/04-01/07-3870-Red2 (Trust Fund for Victims, 19 January 2021).

International Criminal Court, *The Prosecutor v. Germain Katanga, Transmission de Demandes en Réparation*, ICC-01/04-01/07-3614 (Registry, 12 November 2015).

International Criminal Court, *The Prosecutor v. Germain Katanga, Update Report on the Implementation of the Collective Reparations Awards*, ICC-01/04-01/07-3836-Red (Trust Fund for Victims, 26 July 2019).

International Criminal Court, *The Prosecutor v. Bosco Ntaganda, Joint Response of the Legal Representatives of Victims to the Registry's Observations on Reparations*, ICC-01/04-02/06-2430 (Office of Public Counsel for Victims, 3 October 2019)

International Criminal Court, *The Prosecutor v. Bosco Ntaganda, Reparations Order*, ICC-01/04-02/06-2659 (Trial Chamber VI, 8 March 2021).

International Criminal Court, *The Prosecutor v. Thomas Lubanga Dyilo, Annexe A au Sixième Rapport sur le Progrès de la Mise en Œuvre des Réparations Collectives Conformément aux Ordonnances de la Chambre de Première Instance II des 21 Octobre 2016 (ICC-01/04-01/06-3251) et 6 Avril 2017 (ICC-01/04-01/06-3289) et la Décision du 7 Février 2019 (ICC-01/04-01/06-3440-Red)*, ICC-01/04-01/06-3467-AnxA-Red (Trust Fund for Victims, 14 August 2019).

International Criminal Court, *The Prosecutor v. Thomas Lubanga Dyilo, Decision Approving the Proposals of the Trust Fund for Victims on the Process for Locating New Applicants and Determining Their Eligibility for Reparations*, ICC-01/04-01/06-3440-Red-tENG (Trial Chamber II, 7 February 2019).

International Criminal Court, *The Prosecutor v. Thomas Lubanga Dyilo, Decision Establishing the Principles and Procedures to be Applied to Reparations*, ICC-01/04-01/06-2904 (Trial Chamber I, 7 August 2012).

International Criminal Court, *The Prosecutor v. Thomas Lubanga Dyilo, Décision Faisant Droit à la Requête du Fonds au Profit des Victimes du 21 Septembre 2020 et Approuvant la Mise en Œuvre des Réparations Collectives Prenant la Forme de Prestations de Services*, ICC-01/04-01-06-3495 (Trial Chamber II, 4 March 2021).

International Criminal Court, *The Prosecutor v. Thomas Lubanga Dyilo, Decision on the Submissions by the Legal Representative of Victims V01 in its Response to the Twelfth Report of the Trust Fund for Victims on the Implementation of Collective Reparations*, ICC-01/04-01/06-3508 (Trial Chamber II, 26 March 2021).

International Criminal Court, *The Prosecutor v. Thomas Lubanga Dyilo, Draft Implementation Plan for Collective Reparations to Victims*, ICC-01/04-01/06-3177-AnxA (Trust Fund for Victims, 3 November 2015).

International Criminal Court, *The Prosecutor v. Thomas Lubanga Dyilo, Eighteenth Progress Report on the Implementation of Collective Reparations*, ICC-01/04-01/06-3537-Red (Trust Fund for Victims, 4 August 2022).

International Criminal Court, *The Prosecutor v. Thomas Lubanga Dyilo, Fifteenth Progress Report on the Implementation of Collective Reparations,* ICC-01/04-01/06-3524 (Trust Fund for Victims, 21 October 2021).

International Criminal Court, *The Prosecutor v. Thomas Lubanga Dyilo, Filing on Reparations and Draft Implementation Plan,* ICC-01/04-01/06-3177 (Trust Fund for Victims, 3 November 2015).

International Criminal Court, *The Prosecutor v. Thomas Lubanga Dyilo, First Report to the Trial Chamber on Applications for Reparations,* ICC-01-/04-01/06-2847 (Registry, 28 March 2012).

International Criminal Court, *The Prosecutor v. Thomas Lubanga Dyilo, First Submission of Victim Dossiers,* ICC-01/04-01/06-3208 (Trust Fund for Victims, 31 May 2016).

International Criminal Court, *The Prosecutor v. Thomas Lubanga Dyilo, Fourteenth Progress Report on the Implementation of Collective Reparations,* ICC-01/04-01/06-3519-Red (Trust Fund for Victims, 21 July 2021).

International Criminal Court, *The Prosecutor v. Thomas Lubanga Dyilo, Further Information on the Reparations Proceedings in Compliance With the Trial Chamber's Order of 16 March 2018,* ICC-01/04-01/06-3399-Red (Trial Chamber II, 4 December 2018).

International Criminal Court, *The Prosecutor v. Thomas Lubanga Dyilo, Information Provided Pursuant to Regulation 28 of the Regulations of the Court in Relation to the Trust Fund's "Fifteenth Progress Report on the Implementation of Collective Reparations",* ICC-01/04-01/06-3527 (Trust Fund for Victims, 11 November 2021).

International Criminal Court, *The Prosecutor v. Thomas Lubanga Dyilo, Information Regarding Collective Reparations,* ICC-01/04-01/06-3273 (Trust Fund for Victims, 13 February 2017).

International Criminal Court, *The Prosecutor v. Thomas Lubanga Dyilo, Judgment on the Appeals Against the "Decision Establishing Principles and Procedures to be Applied to Reparations",* ICC-01/04-01/06-3129 (Appeals Chamber, 3 March 2015).

International Criminal Court, *The Prosecutor v. Thomas Lubanga Dyilo, Judgment on the Appeals Against Trial Chamber II's 'Decision Setting the Size of the Reparations Award for Which Thomas Lubanga Dyilo is Liable',* ICC-01/04-01/06-3466-Red (Appeals Chamber, 18 July 2019).

International Criminal Court, *The Prosecutor v. Thomas Lubanga Dyilo, Judgment on the Appeals Against Trial Chamber II's 'Decision Setting the Size of the Reparations Award for Which Thomas Lubanga Dyilo is Liable' - Separate Opinion of Judge Luz del Carmen Ibáñez Carranza,* ICC-01/04-01/06-3466-AnxII (Appeals Chamber, 18 July 2019).

International Criminal Court, *The Prosecutor v. Thomas Lubanga Dyilo, Judgment Pursuant to Article 74 of the Statute,* ICC-01/04-01/06-2842 (Trial Chamber I, 14 March 2012).

International Criminal Court, *The Prosecutor v. Thomas Lubanga Dyilo, Notification d'un Complément Additionnel en Vertu de la Règle 56 du Règlement du Fonds au Profit des Victimes,* ICC-01/04-01/06-3432 (Trial Chamber II, 12 December 2018).

International Criminal Court, *The Prosecutor v. Thomas Lubanga Dyilo, Notification of the Board of Directors' Decision on the Trial Chamber's Supplementary Complement Request Pursuant to Regulation 56 of the Regulation 5 of the Regulations of the Trust Fund for Victims,* ICC-01/04-01/06-3422 (Trial Chamber II, 2 October 2018).

International Criminal Court, *The Prosecutor v. Thomas Lubanga Dyilo, Observations in Relation to the Victim Identification and Screening Process Pursuant to the Trial Chamber's Order of 25 January 2018,* ICC-01/04-01/06-3398 (Trust Fund for Victims, 21 March 2018).

International Criminal Court, *The Prosecutor v. Thomas Lubanga Dyilo, Order Approving the Proposed Programmatic Framework for Collective Service-Based Reparations Submitted by the Trust Fund for Victims,* ICC-01/04-01/06-3289 (Trial Chamber II, 6 April 2017).

International Criminal Court, *The Prosecutor v. Thomas Lubanga Dyilo, Order Approving the Proposed Plan of the Trust Fund for Victims in Relation to Symbolic Collective Reparation,* ICC/01/04-01/06-3251 (Trial Chamber II, 21 October 2016).

International Criminal Court, *The Prosecutor v. Thomas Lubanga Dyilo, Order Instructing the Trust Fund for Victims to Supplement the Draft Implementation Plan,* ICC-01/04-01/06-3198 (Trial Chamber II, 9 February 2016).

International Criminal Court, *The Prosecutor v. Thomas Lubanga Dyilo, Order Relating to the Request of the Office of Public Counsel for Victims of 16 September 2016,* ICC-01/04-01/06-3252 (Trial Chamber II, 21 October 2016).

International Criminal Court, *The Prosecutor v. Thomas Lubanga Dyilo, Public Redacted Version of Filing Regarding Symbolic Collective Reparations,* ICC-01/04-01/06-3223 (Trust Fund for Victims, 19 September 2016).

International Criminal Court, *The Prosecutor v. Thomas Lubanga Dyilo, Redacted Version of "Decision on 'Indirect Victims'",* ICC-01/04-01/06-1813 (Trial Chamber I, 8 April 2009).

International Criminal Court, *The Prosecutor v. Thomas Lubanga Dyilo, Seventeenth Progress Report on the Implementation of Collective Reparations,* ICC-01/04-01/06-3533-Red (Trust Fund for Victims, 4 May 2022)

International Criminal Court, *The Prosecutor v. Thomas Lubanga Dyilo, Sixteenth Progress Report on the Implementation of Collective Reparations,* ICC-01/04-01/06-3530-Red (Trust Fund for Victims, 4 February 2022).

International Criminal Court, *The Prosecutor v. Thomas Lubanga Dyilo, Thirteenth Progress Report on the Implementation of Collective Reparations,* ICC-01/04-01/06-3512-Red (Trust Fund for Victims, 21 April 2021).

International Criminal Court, *The Prosecutor v. William Samoei Ruto and Joshua Arap Sang, Common Legal Representative for Victims' Comprehensive Report on the Withdrawal of Victims From the Turbo Area by Letter Dated 5 June 2013,* ICC-01/09-01/11-896-Corr-Red (Trial Chamber V(A), 5 September 2013).

International Criminal Court, *Situation in the Democratic Republic of the Congo, Decision on the Applications for Participation in the Proceedings of VPRS 1, VPRS 2,VPRS 3,VPRS 4,VPRS 5 and VPRS 6 (Public Redacted Version),* ICC-01/04-101-tEN-Corr (Pre-Trial Chamber I, 19 January 2006).

International Criminal Court, *Situation in the State of Palestine, Decision on the 'Prosecution Request Pursuant to Article 19(3) for a Ruling on the Court's Territorial Jurisdiction in Palestine'*, ICC-01/18-143 (Pre-Trial Chamber I, 5 February 2021).

International Tribunal for the Former Yugoslavia, *Prosecutor v. Duško Tadić, Judgment*, IT-94-1-A (Appeals Chamber, 15 July 1999).

International Criminal Tribunal for Rwanda, *Ferdinan Nahimana, Jean-Bosco Barayagwiza and Hassan Ngeze v. The Prosecutor, Judgment*, ICTR-99-52-A (Appeals Chamber, 28 November 2007).

International Tribunal for the Law of the Sea, *The M/V "Saiga" (No.2) Case (Saint Vincent and the Grenadines v. Guinea)*, ITLOS Reports 1999, 10 (1 July 1999).

Iran-United States Claims Tribunal, *Amoco International Finance Corporation v. Iran*, IRAN-U.S. C.T.R. 15, 189, Case No. 56 (14 July 1987).

Permanent Court of International Justice, *The Factory at Chorzów (Claim for Indemnity) (The Merits)*, P.C.I.J. Series A 17 No. 7 (13 September 1928).

Permanent Court of International Justice, *The Mavrommatis Palestine Concessions Case (Greece v. The United Kingdom)*, P.C.I.J. (ser. B) No. 3, 7 (30 August 1924).

Rainbow Warrior, R.I.A.A. XX, 215 (30 April 1990).

Special Jurisdiction for Peace, *Case 3, Ruling No. 033 of 2021* (12 February 2021).

Tribunal Superior de Medellín, *Olimpo de Jesús Sánchez Caro y Otros, Sentencia* (Sala de Justicia y Paz, 16 December 2015).

United States - German Mixed Claims Commission, *Lusitania Case*, R.I.A.A. VII, 32 (1 November 1923).

United States Court of Appeals, Eleventh Circuit, *Arce v. Garcia* (4 January 2006).

Table of Interviews

Note: The table contains only the interviews cited throughout the book. It does not contain further interviews the author conducted in Sierra Leone, Colombia and at the ICC that do not appear in the citations, but which informed the study.

Langmack, Fin-Jasper, *Group Interview with Efraín Villamíl (Confederación Nacional de Juntas de Acción Communal), Guillermo Cardona Monreno (Confederación Comunal Nacional, Collective Reparation Subject), Jorge Marín Rivela (Survivor, Confederación de Acción Comunal), Jairo Alberto Delgado Beltran (Universidad Pedagógica y Tecnológica de Colombia, Facultad de Derecho), and Gloria Inés González Bravo (Agro Comunal), Bogotá*, 8 October 2018.

Langmack, Fin-Jasper, *Interview with Amadu Bangura (Program Manager Sierra Leone Reparation Program), Freetown*, 8 August 2018.

Langmack, Fin-Jasper, *Interview with Edward Conteh (Survivor, President of Amputees and War-Wounded Association), Freetown*, 17 July 2018.

Langmack, Fin-Jasper, *Interview with Eiah M'Bayoh (Survivor), Grafton*, 26 July 2018.

Langmack, Fin-Jasper, *Interview with John Caulker (President of Fambul Tok), Freetown*, 19 July 2018.

Langmack, Fin-Jasper, *Interview with Lahai Sia-Bintu (Survivor), 26 July 2018, Freetown*, 26 July 2018.

Langmack, Fin-Jasper, *Interview with Osman Kamara (Survivor), Grafton*, 26 July 2018.

Langmack, Fin-Jasper, *Interview with Sanusi Savage (Head of International Organization for Migration Freetown Mission), Freetown*, 11 July 2018.

Langmack, Fin-Jasper, *Interview with Tommy Ibrahim (Director of the Center for Accountability and the Rule of Law), Freetown*, 27 July 2018.

Bibliography

Books

Alto Comisionado Para La Paz / Presidencia De La Republica, *Biblioteca Del Proceso de Paz con las FARC-EP - Tomo VIII*, 2018, Alto Comisionado Para La Paz (Bogotá).

Amerasinghe, Chittharanjan Felix, *Jurisdiction of International Tribunals*, 2003, Brill (The Hague).

Anderson, Benedict, *Imagined Communities - Reflections on the Origin and Spread of Nationalism*, 2nd Revised Edition 2016, Verso (London).

Andrews, Kehinde, *The New Age of Empire - How Racism and Colonialism Still Rule the World*, 2021, Bold Type Books (New York).

Anghie, Antony, *Imperialism, Sovereignty and the Making of International Law*, 2005, Cambridge University Press (Cambridge).

Arendt, Hannah, *Crises of the Republic*, 1972, Harcourt Brace & Company (San Diego).

Arendt, Hannah / Jaspers, Karl / Köhler, Lotte / Saner, Hans, *Hannah Arendt/Karl Jaspers Correspondence, 1926-1969*, 1992, Harcourt Brace Jovanovich (New York).

Aristotle / Rackham, H., *Nicomachean Ethics*, 2014, Harvard University Press (Cambridge).

Assmann, Aleida, *Der Lange Schatten der Vergangenheit – Erinnerungskultur und Geschichtspolitik*, 4th Edition 2021, C.H. Beck (Munich).

Bassiouni, M. Cherif, *Introduction to International Criminal Law*, 2nd Revised Edition 2013, Niijhoff (Leiden).

Beah, Ishmael, *A Long Way Gone - Memoirs of a Boy Soldier*, 2007, Large Print Press (New York).

Benzing, Markus, *Das Beweisrecht vor Internationalen Gerichten und Schiedsgerichten in Zwischenstaatlichen Streitigkeiten*, 2010, Springer (Berlin).

Berghs, Maria, *War and Embodied Memory - Becoming Disabled in Sierra Leone*, 2012, Ashgate Publishing (Abingdon).

Beristain, Carlos Martín, *Dialogos Sobre la Reparación – Experiencias en el Sistema Interamericano de Derechos Humanos*, Volume I, 2008, Instituto Interamericano de Derechos Humanos (San José).

Beristain, Carlos Martín, *Dialogos Sobre la Reparación – Experiencias en el Sistema Interamericano de Derechos Humanos*, Volume II, 2008, Instituto Interamericano de Derechos Humanos (San José).

Berkes, Antal, *International Human Rights Law Beyond State Territorial Control*, 2021, Cambridge University Press (Cambridge).

Bicchieri, Cristina, *The Grammar of Society*, 2006, Cambridge University Press (Cambridge).

Bicchieri, Cristina, *Norms in the Wild*, 2017, Oxford University Press (Oxford).

Biletzki, Anat, *The Philosophy of Human Rights*, 2020, Routledge (New York).

Blumer, Herbert, *Symbolic Interactionism - Perspective and Method*, 1969, Prentice-Hall (Englewood Cliffs).

Blumer, Herbert / Morrione, Thomas J., *George Herbert Mead and Human Conduct*, 2004, AltaMira Press (Walnut Creek).

Brems, Eva, *Human Rights - Universality and Diversity*, 2001, Nijhoff (The Hague).

Brennan, Geoffrey / Eriksson, Lina / Goodin, Robert E. / Southwood, Nicholas, *Explaining Norms*, 2013, Oxford University Press (Oxford).

Casey-Maslen, Stuart / Vestner, Tobias, *A Guide to International Disarmament Law*, 2019, Routledge (New York).

Chandler, Daniel, *Semiotics - The Basics*, 3rd Edition 2017, Routledge (New York).

Charon, Joel M., *Symbolic Interactionism - An Introduction, an Interpretation, an Integration*, 10th Edition 2010, Prentice Hall (Boston).

Coleman, James S., *Foundations of Social Theory*, 1990, Belknap Press of Harvard University Press (Cambridge).

Cook, Alethia H., *Conflict Dynamics - Civil Wars, Armed Actors, and Their Tactics*, 2017, University of Georgia Press (Athens, GA).

Corten, Olivier, *The Vienna Conventions on the Law of Treaties - Vol. I*, 2011, Oxford University Press (Oxford).

Coulter, Chris, *Bush Wives and Girl Soldiers – Women's Lives Through War and Peace in Sierra Leone*, 2009, Cornell University Press (Ithaca).

Crawford, James, *Brownlie's Principles of Public International Law*, 9th Edition 2019, Oxford University Press (Oxford).

Dahrendorf, Ralf, *Homo Sociologicus - Ein Versuch zur Geschichte, Bedeutung und Kritik der Kategorie der sozialen Rolle*, 16. Auflage 2006, Verlag für Sozialwissenschaften (Wiesbaden).

de Greiff, Pablo / Duthie, Roger, *Transitional Justice and Development: Making Connections*, 2009, Social Science Research Council (New York).

de Schutter, Olivier, *International Human Rights Law - Cases, Materials, Commentary*, 2010, Cambridge University Press (Cambridge).

de Vattel, Emer, *The Law of Nations*, 1797, G.G. and J. Robinson (London).

DeJusticia, *La Buena Fe en la Restitución de Tierras - Sistematización de Jurisprudencia*, 2017, DeJusticia (Bogotá).

DeJusticia, *Restitución de Tierras, Política de Vivienda y Proyectos Productivos* 2017, DeJusticia (Bogotá).

del Llano Toro, Federica, *El Desequilibrio Procesal y Probatorio del "Opositor Víctima o Sujeto Vulnerable" en el Proceso de Restitución de Tierras*, 2016, Universidad del Rosario (Bogotá).

Donnelly, Jack / Whelan, Daniel J., *International Human Rights*, 5th Edition 2018, Routledge (New York).

Dwertmann, Eva, *The Reparation System of the International Criminal Court - Its Implementation, Possibilities and Limitations*, 2010, Nijhoff (Leiden).

Echavarria, Josefina A., *In/security in Colombia - Writing Political Identities in the Democratic Security Policy*, 2010, Manchester University Press (Manchester).

Eco, Umberto, *A Theory of Semiotics*, 1976, Indiana University Press (Bloomington).

Edelman, Murray J., *The Symbolic Uses of Politics*, 1964, University of Illinois Press (Urbana).

Elster, Jon, *The Cement of Society*, 1989, Cambridge University Press (Cambridge).

European Union Agency for Fundamental Rights, *Handbook on European Law Relating to Access to Justice*, 2016, European Union (Brussels).

Evans, Christine, *The Right to Reparation in International Law for Victims of Armed Conflict*, 2012, Cambridge University Press (Cambridge).

Fajardo Arturo, Luis / Valoyes Valoyes, Rosa, *Violencia Sexual Como Crimen Internacional Perpetrado por las FARC*, 2015, Universidad Sergio Arboleda (Bogotá).

Frey, B.S., *Economics of Happiness*, 2018, Springer (Cham).

Friedman, Lawrence M., *The Legal System - A Social Science Perspective*, 1975, Russell Sage Foundation (New York).

Fuchs-Kaminski, Denise, *Der Beitrag des Sondergerichtshofs für Sierra Leone zum Völkerstrafrecht*, 2015, Optimus (Göttingen).

Gardiner, Richard K., *Treaty Interpretation*, 2015, Oxford University Press (Oxford).

Griffin, James, *On Human Rights*, 2010, Oxford University Press (Oxford).

Grill, Bartholomäus, *Wir Herrenmenschen - Unser Rassistisches Erbe: Eine Reise in die Deutsche Kolonialgeschichte*, 2019, Siedler (Munich).

Grotius, Hugo / Campbell, A. C., *The Rights of War and Peace - Including the Law of Nature and of Nations*, Autograph Édition de Luxe 1901, M.W. Dunne (Washington).

Günnewig, Elisabeth, *Schadensersatz Wegen der Verletzung des Gewaltverbotes als Element Eines Ius Post Bellum*, 2019, Nomos (Baden-Baden).

Gusfield, Joseph R., *Symbolic Crusade - Status Politics and the American Temperance Movement*, 1963, University of Illinois Press (Urbana).

Habermas, Jürgen, *Between Facts and Norms - Contributions to a Discourse Theory of Law and Democracy*, 1997, Polity Press (Cambridge).

Hartmann, Martin, *Vertrauen - Die Unsichtbare Macht*, 2020, Fischer (Frankfurt am Main).

Hayner, Priscilla B., *Unspeakable Truths - Transitional Justice and the Challenge of Truth Commissions*, 2nd Edition 2011, Routledge (New York).

Hazen, Jennifer M., *What Rebels Want - Resources and Supply Networks in Wartime*, 2013, Cornell University Press (Ithaca).

Hempel, Carl G., *Aspects of Scientific Explanation and Other Essays in the Philosophy of Science*, 1965, Free Press (New York).

Henckaerts, Jean-Marie / Doswald-Beck, Louise, *Customary International Humanitarian Law Volume I - Rules*, 2005, Cambridge University Press (Cambridge).

Henckaerts, Jean-Marie / Doswald-Beck, Louise, *Customary International Humanitarian Law Volume II - Practice Part 2*, 2005, Cambridge University Press (Cambridge).

Herman, Olivia, *Righting Wrongs – Non-State Armed Groups and Reparations for Victims of Armed Conflict, With a Case Study of Colombia,* 2021 (on file with the author).

Honneth, Axel, *The Struggle for Recognition – The Moral Grammar of Social Conflicts,* 1996, MIT Press (Cambridge, Massachusetts).

Hristov, Jasmin, *Paramilitarism and Neoliberalism - Violent Systems of Capital Accumulation in Colombia and Beyond,* 2014, Pluto Press (London).

Humphrey, Michael, *The Politics of Atrocity and Reconciliation - From Terror to Trauma,* 2013, Routledge (London).

Ichim, Octavian, *Just Satisfaction Under the European Convention on Human Rights,* 2014, Cambridge University Press (Cambridge).

Iñigo Álvarez, Laura, *Towards a Regime of Responsibility of Armed Groups in International Human Rights Law,* 2020, Intersentia (Cambridge).

International Commission of Jurists, *The Right to Remedy and Reparation for Gross Human Rights Violations - A Practitioners' Guide,* 2nd Revised Edition 2018, International Commission of Jurists (Geneva).

International Committee of the Red Cross, *Commentary on the Third Geneva Convention,* Online Edition 2020, Cambride University Press (Cambridge), availabe at: https://ihl-databases.icrc.org/ihl/full/GCIII-commentary.

Jaspers, Karl, *The Question of German Guilt,* 1961, Capricorn Books (New York).

Jayawickrama, Nihal, *The Judicial Application of Human Rights Law,* 2nd Edition 2017, Cambridge University Press (Cambridge).

Johansen, Bruce, *Environmental Racism in the United States and Canada – Seeking Justice and Acountability,* 2020, ABC-CLIO (Santa Barbara).

Keen, David, *Conflict and Collusion in Sierra Leone,* 2005, James Currey (Melton).

Klatt, Matthias / Meister, Moritz, *The Constitutional Structure of Proportionality,* 2012, Oxford University Press (Oxford).

Kritz, Nils, *Transitional Justice – How Emerging Democracies Reckon With Former Regimes, Volume 1-3,* 1995, United States Institute for Peace (Washington D.C.).

Kok, Ruth, *Statutory Limitations in International Criminal Law,* 2007, T.M.C. Asser Press (The Hague).

Lauterpacht, Hersch, *The Development of International Law by the International Court,* 1958, Stevens (London).

Legg, Andrew, *The Margin of Appreciation in International Human Rights Law - Deference and Proportionality,* 2012, Oxford University Press (Oxford).

Luhmann, Niklas / Poggi, Gianfranco, *Trust and Power,* 2017, Polity Press (Cambridge).

Luna Escalante, Estefanía, *Tierras Despojadas, ¿Derechos Restituidos? - Encuentros Acerca del Problema de la Tierra en Colombia en un Escenario de "Justicia Transicional",* 2013, Universidad de Antioquia (Medellín).

Magarrell, Lisa / Wesley, Joya, *Learning from Greensboro - Truth and Reconciliation in the United States,* 2008, University of Pennsylvania Press (Philadelphia).

Manning, Peter K., *Semiotics and Fieldwork,* 1987, Sage Publications (Newbury Park).

McCarthy, Conor, *Reparations and Victim Support in the International Criminal Court,* 2012, Cambridge University Press (Cambridge).

Mead, George Herbert / Morris, Charles W. / Huebner, Daniel R. / Joas, Hans, *Mind, Self, and Society*, 2015, University of Chicago Press (Chicago).

Medina Quiroga, Cecilia, *The American Convention on Human Rights - Crucial Rights and Their Theory and Practice*, 2nd Edition 2016, Intersentia (Antwerp).

Merkouris, Panos, *Article 31(3)(c) VCLT and the Principle of Systemic Integration - Normative Shadows in Plato's Cave*, 2015, Brill Nijhoff (Leiden).

Metelits, Claire, *Inside insurgency - Violence, Civilians, and Revolutionary Group Behavior*, 2010, New York University Press (New York).

Migdal, Joel S., *State in Society - Studying how States and Societies Transform and Constitute one Another*, 2001, Cambridge University Press (Cambridge).

Migdal, Joel S., *Strong Societies and Weak States - State-Society Relations and State Capabilities in the Third World*, 1988, Princeton University Press (Princeton, NJ).

Milanovic, Marko, *Extraterritorial Application of Human Rights Treaties - Law, Principles, and Policy*, 2011, Oxford University Press (Oxford).

Miller, Seumas, *The Moral Foundations of Social Institutions - A Philosophical Study*, 2009, Cambridge University Press (Cambridge).

Moffett, Luke, *Justice for Victims Before the International Criminal Court*, 2014, Routledge (Abingdon, Oxon).

Möllers, Christoph, *Die Möglichkeit der Normen*, 2015, Suhrkamp (Berlin).

Müller, Ingo, *Furchtbare Juristen - Die Unbewältigte Vergangenheit der Deutschen Justiz*, 2014, Edition Tiamat (Berlin).

Murphy, Colleen, *The Conceptual Foundations of Transitional Justice*, 2017, Cambridge University Press (Cambridge).

Murray, Daragh, *Human Rights Obligations of Non-State Armed Groups*, 2016, Hart Publishing (Oxford).

Musa, Shavana, *Victim Reparation Under the Ius Post Bellum - An Historical and Normative Perspective*, 2018, Cambridge University Press (Cambridge).

Mutua, Makau, *Human Rights - A Political and Cultural Critique*, 2002, University of Pennsylvania Press (Philadelphia).

Nowak, Manfred, *U.N. Covenant on Civil and Political Rights - CCPR Commentary*, 2nd Revised Edition 2005, N.P. Engel (Kehl).

Nozick, Robert, *Anarchy, State, and Utopia*, 2013, Basic Books (New York).

O'Byrne, Darren, *Human Rights - An Introduction*, 2013, Routledge (London).

Odier Contreras-Garduno, Diana, *Collective Reparations - Tensions and Dilemmas Between Collective Reparations With the Individual Right to Receive Reparations*, 2018, Intersentia (Cambridge).

Orakhelashvili, Alexander, *The Interpretation of Acts and Rules in Public International Law*, 2008, Oxford University Press (Oxford).

Pasqualucci, Jo M., *The Practice and Procedure of the Inter-American Court of Human Rights*, 2nd Edition 2013, Cambridge University Press (Cambridge).

Patton, Michael Quinn, *Qualitative Research and Evaluation Methods*, 2015, Sage (Los Angeles).

Pauwelyn, Joost, *Conflict of Norms in Public International Law - How WTO Law Relates to Other Rules of International Law*, 2003, Cambridge University Press (Cambridge).

Peirce, Charles S. / Hoopes, James, *Peirce on Signs - Writings on Semiotic*, 1991, University of North Carolina Press (Chapel Hill).

Peters, Krijn, *War and the Crisis of Youth in Sierra Leone*, 2011, Cambridge University Press (Cambridge).

Peterson, Martin, *An Introduction to Decision Theory*, 2nd Edition 2017, Cambridge University Press (Cambridge).

Pilloud, Claude / Sandoz, Yves / Swinarski, Christophe / Zimmermann, Bruno / International Committee of the Red Cross, *Commentary on the Additional Protocols of 8 June 1977 to the Geneva Conventions of 12 August 1949*, 1987, International Committee of the Red Cross (Geneva).

Ramírez, Manuel Fernando Quinche / Huertas, Rocío Del Pilar Peña / Hernández, María Mónica Parada / González, Luis Enrique Ruiz / Morales, Ricardo Álvarez, *El Amparo de Tierras - La Acción,el Proceso y el Juez de Restitución*, 2015, Editorial Universidad del Rosario (Bogotá).

Rawls, John, *A Theory of Justice*, Revised Edition 1999, Oxford University Press (Oxford).

Reinhard, Wolfgang, *Die Unterwerfung der Welt - Globalgeschichte der Europäischen Expansion 1415-2015*, Lizenzausgabe für die Bundeszentrale für politische Bildung 2017, C.H. Beck (München).

Reynolds, John, *Empire, Emergency and International Law*, 2017, Cambridge University Press (Cambridge).

Rodenhäuser, Tilman, *Organizing Rebellion - Non-State Armed Groups Under International Humanitarian Law, Human Rights Law, and International Criminal Law,* 2018, Oxford University Press (Oxford).

Rubio-Marín, Ruth, *The Gender of Reparations - Unsettling Sexual Hierarchies While Redressing Human Rights Violations*, 2009, Cambridge University Press (Cambridge).

Safferling, Christoph / Petrossian, Gurgen, *Victims Before the International Criminal Court – Definition, Participation, Reparation,* 2021, Springer (Cham).

Said, Edward, *Colonialism,* 2019, Penguin Books (London).

Sampat Mukherjee / Mallinath Mukherjee / Ghose, Amitava, *Microeconomics*, 2004, Prentice Hall of India (New Delhi).

Sassòli, Marco / Nagler, Patrick, *International Humanitarian Law - Rules, Controversies, and Solutions to Problems Arising in Warfare*, 2019, Edward Elgar Publishing (Cheltenham).

Saul, Ben / Kinley, David H. / Mowbray, Jacqueline, *The International Covenant on Economic, Social and Cultural Rights - Commentary, Cases and Materials*, 2014, Oxford University Press (Oxford).

Schabas, William, *The European Convention on Human Rights - A Commentary*, 2017, Oxford University Press (Oxford).

Schmitt, Pierre, *Access to Justice and International Organizations - The Case of Individual Victims of Human Rights Violations*, 2017, Edward Elgar Publishing (Cheltenham).

Shelton, Dinah, *Remedies in International Human Rights Law*, 3rd Edition 2015, Oxford University Press (Oxford).

Shibutani, Tamotsu, *Society and Personality - An Interactionist Approach to Social Psychology*, 1961, Prentice-Hall (Englewood Cliffs).

Smith, L. T., *Decolonizing Methodologies - Research and Indigenous Peoples*, 1999, Zed Books (London).

Sottiaux, Stefan, *Terrorism and the Limitation of Rights - The ECHR and the US Constitution*, 2008, Hart (Oxford).

Stammler, Philipp, *Der Anspruch von Kriegsopfern auf Schadensersatz*, 2009, Duncker & Humblot (Berlin).

Steinl, Leonie, *Child Soldiers as Agents of War and Peace - A Restorative Transitional Justice Approach to Accountability for Crimes Under International Law*, 2017, T.M.C. Asser Press (The Hague).

Suárez Flórez, Viviana Gisela / Wilches Sierra, Denis Alejandra, *El Movimiento Armado Quintín Lame y su Proceso de Paz - Una Lección de Dignidad y Resistencia*, 2016, Universidad Distrital Francisco José de Caldas (Bogotá).

Terkessidis, Mark, *Wessen Erinnerung Zählt? Koloniales Erbe und Rassismus Heute*, 2019, Hoffmann und Campe (Hamburg).

Unidad de Restitución de Tierras, *Memorias de la Restitución - Lecciones Aprendidas y Metodologias Para Restituir Tierras y Terrotorios en Colombia*, 2018, Unidad de Restitución de Tierras (Bogotá).

Urbina, Francisco J., *A Critique of Proportionality and Balancing*, 2017, Cambridge University Press (Cambridge).

van Rooij, Benjamin / van de Meene, Ineke, *Access to Justice and Legal Empowerment - Making the Poor Central in Legal Development Co-Operation*, 2008, Leiden University Press (Leiden).

Villanueva O'Driscoll, Julia / Loots, Gerrit / Derluyn, Ilse, *Children Disengaged From Armed Groups in Colombia - Integration Processes in Context*, 2013, DeGruyter (London).

Waibel, Michael, *Sovereign Defaults Before International Courts and Tribunals*, 2011, Cambridge University Press (Cambridge).

Walker, Margaret Urban, *Moral Repair - Reconstructing Moral Relations After Wrongdoing*, 2006, Cambridge University Press (Cambridge).

Winter, Stephen, *Transitional Justice in Established Democracies - A Political Theory*, Palgrave Macmillan (Basingstoke).

Young-Bruehl, Elisabeth, *Hannah Arendt - For Love of the World*, 2nd Revised Edition 2004, Yale University Press (New Haven).

Zunino, Marcos, *Justice Framed – A Genealogy of Transitional Justice*, 2019, Cambridge University Press (Cambridge).

Articles and Chapters

Aall, Jorgen, *Waiver of Human Rights - Setting the Scene (Part I/III)*, 2010 Nordic Journal of Human Rights 28(3), 300-370.

Addo, Michael K. / Grief, Nicholas, *Does Article 3 of the European Convention on Human Rights Enshrine Absolute Rights?*, 1998 European Journal of International Law 9(3), 510-524.

Aguirre-Aguirre, Jhon Edier, *Victimario - La Víctima Desconocida del Conflicto Armado Colombiano: Análisis de su Reparación en Torno al Principio de Igualdad*, 2019 Revista Derecho del Estado 43, 291-320.

Alexander, Larry / Moore, Michael, *Deontological Ethics*, in: Edward Zalta (ed.), *Stanford Encyclopedia of Philosophy*, Online Edition 2016, The Metaphysics Research Lab, Stanford University (Stanford).

Alexy, Robert, *Constitutional Rights, Balancing, and Rationality*, 2003 Ratio Juris 16(2), 131-140.

Alexy, Robert, *Die Gewichtsformel*, in: Joachim Jickeli / Peter Kreutz / Dieter Reuter (eds.), *Gedächtnisschrift für Jürgen Sonnenschein*, 2003, De Gruyter (Berlin), 771-792.

Alexy, Robert, *On Balancing and Subsumption - A Structural Comparison*, 2003 Ratio Juris 16(4), 433-449.

Alston, Philip / Quinn, Gerard, *The Nature and Scope of States Parties' Obligations Under the International Covenant on Economic, Social and Cultural Rights*, 1987 Human Rights Quarterly 9(2), 156-229.

Ambach, Philipp, *The International Criminal Court Reparations Scheme – A Yardstick for Hybrid Tribunals?*, in: Gerhard Werle / Andreas Zimmermann (eds.), *The International Criminal Court in Turbulent Times*, 2019, T.M.C. Asser Press (The Hague), 131-144.

Ambos, Kai / Aboueldahab, Susann, *The Colombian Peace Process and the Special Jurisdiction for Peace*, 2018 Diritto Penale Contemporaneo 4, 255-263.

Antkowiak, Thomas, *A Dark Side of Virtue – The Inter-American Court and Reparations for Indigenous People*, 2014 Duke Journal of Comparative and International Law 25(1), 1-80.

Antkowiak, Thomas, *Remedial Approaches to Human Rights Violations – The Inter-American Court of Human Rights and Beyond*, 2008 Columbia Journal of Transnational Law 46(1), 351-419.

Aranguren Romero, Juan Pablo / Cardona Santofimio, Juan Nicolás / Agudelo Hernández, Juan Ángel, *Inhabiting Mourning - Spectral Figures in Cases of Extrajudicial Executions (False Positives) in Colombia*, 2021 Bulletin of Latin American Research 40(1), 6-20.

Arbour, Louise, *Economic and Social Justice for Societies in Transition*, 2007 New York University Journal of International Law and Politics 40(1), 1-28.

Arosemena, Gustavo, *Conflicts of Rights in International Human Rights - A Meta-Rule Analysis*, 2013 Global Constitutionalism 2(1), 6-36.

Arthur, Paige, *How Transitions Reshaped Human Rights - A Conceptual History of Transitional Justice*, 2009 Human Rights Quarterly 31(2), 321-367.

Asiedu, Victor / Berghs, Maria Jeanne, *Limitations of Individualistic Peacebuilding in Postwar Sierra Leone*, 2012 African Conflict & Peacebuilding Review 2(1), 136-151.

Attansio, David L. / Sánchez, Nelson Camilo, *Return Within the Bounds of the Pinheiro Principles - The Colombian Land Restitution Experience*, 2012 Washington University Global Studies Law Review 11(1), 1-54.

Baade, Björnstjern, *Post-Conflict Land Restitution – The German Experience in Relation to Colombian Law 1448 of 2011,* 2021 World Comparative Law 54(1), 3-26.

Badaru, Opeoluwa Adetoro, *Examining the Utility of Third World Approaches to International Law for International Human Rights Law*, 2008 International Community Law Review 10(4), 379-387.

Badawi El-Sheikh, Ibrahim Ali, *Preliminary Remarks on the Right to a Fair Trial Under the African Charter on Human and Peoples' Rights,* in: Rüdiger Wolfrum / David Weissbrodt (eds.), *The Right to a Fair Trial,* 1997, Springer (Berlin), 327-340.

Bahdi, Reem / Kassis, Mudar, *Institutional Trustworthiness, Transformative Judicial Education and Transitional Justice - A Palestinian Experience,* in: Samar El-Masri / Tammy Lambert / Joanna Quinn (eds.), *Transitional Justice in Comparative Perspective,* 2020, Palgrave Macmillan (Cham), 185-216.

Baier, Annette, *Trust and Antitrust,* 1986 Ethics 96(2), 231-260.

Baines, Erin, *Gender Research in Violently Divided Societies - Methods and Ethics of "International" Researchers in Rwanda,* in: Elisabeth Porter (ed.), *Researching Conflict in Africa - Insights and Experiences,* 2005, United Nations University Press (Tokyo), 140-155.

Balta, Alina / Bax, Manon / Letschert, Rianne, *Trial and (Potential) Error - Conflicting Visions on Reparations Within the ICC System,* 2019 International Criminal Justice Review 29(3), 221-248.

Barskanmaz, Cengiz, *Das Kopftuch als das Andere - Eine Notwendige Postkoloniale Kritik des Deutschen Rechtsdiskurses,* in: Berghahn, Sabine/Rostock, Petra (eds.), *Der Stoff aus dem Konflikte Sind – Debatten um das Kopftuch in Deutschland, Österreich und der Schweiz,* 2009, Transcript (Bielefeld), 361-392.

Bassiouni, M. Cherif, *A Functional Approach to General Principles of International Law,* 1989 Michigan Journal of International Law 11(3), 768-818.

Battjes, Hemme, *In Search of a Fair Balance - The Absolute Character of the Prohibition of Refoulement Under Article 3 ECHR Reassessed,* 2009 Leiden Journal of International Law 22(3), 583-621.

Bell, Christine, *The "New Law" of Transitional Justice,* in: Kai Ambos / Judith Large / Marieke Wierda (eds.), *Building a Future on Peace and Justice - Studies on Transitional Justice, Peace and Development,* 2009, Springer (Berlin), 105-126.

Bell, Christine, *Transitional Justice, Interdisciplinarity and the State of the 'Field' or 'Non-Field',* 2009 International Journal of Transitional Justice 3(1), 5-27.

Benvenisti, Eyal, *Occupation, Belligerent,* in: Rüdiger Wolfrum (ed.), *Max Planck Encyclopedia of Public International Law,* Online Edition 2009, Oxford University Press (Oxford).

Berghs, Maria, *Local and Global Phantoms - Reparations National Memory and Sacrifice in Sierra Leone,* in: Patrick Devlieger / Beatriz Miranda-Galarza / Steven Brown / Megan Strickfaden (eds.), *Rethinking Disability - World Perspectives in Culture and Society,* 2016, Garant (Antwerp), 275-291.

Bernal, Carlos / González, Diego / Barraza, María Fernanda / Esguerra, Nicolás / García Jaramillo, Santiago / Benítez, Vicente, *2018 Global Review of Constitutional Law: Colombia,* 2019 International Journal of Constitutional Law 17(2), 671-680.

Besson, Samantha, *Subsidiarity in International Human Rights Law - What is Subsidiary About Human Rights?*, 2016 The American Journal of Jurisprudence 61(1), 69-107.

Betancourt, Theresa S. / Borisova, Ivelina I. / de la Soudière, Marie / Williamson, John, *Sierra Leone's Child Soldiers - War Exposures and Mental Health Problems by Gender*, 2011 Journal of Adolescent Health 49(1), 21-28.

Bianchi, Andrea, *Human Rights and the Magic of Jus Cogens*, 2008 European Journal of International Law 19(3), 491-508.

Bleckmann, Albert, *Zur Feststellung und Auslegung von Völkergewohnheitsrecht*, 1977 Heidelberg Journal of International Law 37, 504-529.

Boehme, Franziska, *Reactive Remembrance - The Political Struggle Over Apologies and Reparations Between Germany and Namibia for the Herero Genocide*, 2020 Journal of Human Rights 19(1), 1-18.

Bong, Shin Hae, *Compensation for Victims of Wartime Atrocities - Recent Developments in Japan's Case Law*, 2005 Journal of International Criminal Justice 3(1), 187-206.

Borer, Tristan Anne, *A Taxonomy of Victims and Perpetrators - Human Rights and Reconciliation in South Africa*, 2003 Human Rights Quarterly 25(4), 1088-1116.

Brems, Eva, *Conflicting Human Rights: An Exploration in the Context of the Right to a Fair Trial in the European Convention for the Protection of Human Rights and Fundamental Freedoms*, 2005 Human Rights Quarterly 27(1), 294-326.

Brodney, Marissa, *Implementing International Criminal Court-Ordered Collective Reparations - Unpacking Present Debates*, 2016 Journal of the Oxford Centre for Socio-Legal Studies 2(1), 1-35.

Broude, Tomer / Shany, Yuval, *The International Law and Policy of Multi-Sourced Equivalent Norms*, in: Tomer Broude / Yuval Shany (eds.), *Multi-Sourced Equivalent Norms in International Law*, 2011, Hart Publishing (Oxford), 1-18.

Brown, Kris, *Commemoration as Symbolic Reparation - New Narratives or Spaces of Conflict?*, 2013 Human Rights Review 14(3), 273-289.

Buckley-Zistel, Susanne / Schäfer, Antonia, *Memorials in Transitions - Kollektive Formen des Gedenkens*, in: Anja Mihr / Gert Pickel / Susanne Pickel (eds.), *Handbuch Transitional Justice*, 2015, Springer VS (Wiesbaden), 45-62.

Buitrago, Francisco, *Armed Actors in the Colombian Conflict*, in: Kees Koonings / Dirk Kruijt (eds.), *Armed Actors - Organised Violence and State Failure in Latin America*, 2004, ZED Books (London), 87-105.

Buti, Antonio, *Reparations, Justice Theories and Stolen Generations*, 2008 University of Western Australia Law Review 34(1), 168-189.

Buyse, Antoine, *Lost and Regained? Restitution as a Remedy for Human Rights Violations in the Context of International Law*, 2008 Heidelberg Journal of International Law 68, 129-153.

Caflisch, Lucius, *Waivers in International and European Human Rights Law*, in: Mahnoush H. Arsanjani / Jacob Cogan / Robert Sloane / Siegfried Wiessner (eds.), *Looking to the Future - Essays on International Law in Honor of W. Michael Reisman*, 2011, Brill Nijhoff (Leiden).

Çalı, Başak, *Balancing Human Rights? Methodological Problems With Weights, Scales and Proportions*, 2007 Human Rights Quarterly 29(1), 251-270.

Çalı, Başak, *Specialized Rules of Treaty Interpretation - Human Rights*, in: Duncan Hollis (ed.), *The Oxford Guide to Treaties*, 2012, Oxford University Press (Oxford), 525-550.

Cammack, Diana, *Reparations in Malawi*, in: Pablo de Greiff (ed.), *Handbook of Reparations*, 2006, Oxford University Press (Oxford), 215-256.

Cannizzaro, Enzo, *Is There an Individual Right to Reparation? Some Thoughts on the ICJ Judgment in the Jurisdictional Immunities Case*, in: Denis Alland / Vincent Chetail / Olivier de Frouville / Jorge Viñuales (eds.), *Unity and Diversity of International Law - Essays in Honour of Professor Pierre-Marie Dupuy*, 2014, Martinus Nijhoff (Leiden), 495-502.

Cano, Ignacio / Ferreira, Patrícia Salvão, *The Reparations Program in Brazil*, in: Pablo de Greiff (ed.), *Handbook of Reparations*, 2006, Oxford University Press (Oxford), 102-153.

Capone, Francesca, *An Appraisal of the Al Mahdi Order on Reparations and its Innovative Elements - Redress for Victims of Crimes Against Cultural Heritage*, 2018 Journal of International Criminal Justice 16(3), 645-661.

Carayon, Gaelle / O'Donohue, Jonathan, *The International Criminal Court's Strategies in Relation to Victims*, 2017 Journal of International Criminal Justice 15(3), 567-592.

Cariolou, Leto, *The Search for an Equilibrium by the European Court of Human Rights*, in: Eva Brems (ed.), *Conflicts Between Fundamental Rights*, 2008, Intersentia (Antwerp), 249-272.

Carozza, Paolo G., *Subsidiarity as a Structural Principle of International Human Rights Law*, 2003 American Journal of International Law 97(1), 38-79.

Carranza, Ruben, *Plunder and Pain - Should Transitional Justice Engage With Corruption and Economic Crimes?*, 2008 International Journal of Transitional Justice 2(3), 310-330.

Carrillo, Arturo, *Justice in Context - The Relevance of Inter-American Human Rights Law and Practice to Repairing the Past*, in: Pablo de Greiff (ed.), *The Handbook of Reparations*, 2006, Oxford University Press (Oxford), 504-538.

Cassar, Alessandra / Grosjean, Pauline / Whitt, Sam, *Legacies of Violence - Trust and Market Development*, 2013 Journal of Economic Growth 18(3), 285-318.

Caswell, Michelle, *Toward a Survivor-Centered Approach to Records Documenting Human Rights Abuse - Lessons From Community Archives*, 2014 Archival Science 14(3), 307-322.

Chappell, Louise, *The Gender Injustice Cascade - 'Transformative' Reparations for Victims of Sexual and Gender-Based Crimes in the Lubanga Case at the International Criminal Court*, 2017 International Journal of Human Rights 21(9), 1223-1242.

Chimni, Bhupinder S., *Third World Approaches to International Law - A Manifesto*, 2006 International Community Law Review 8(1), 3-27.

Ciliberto, Giulia, *A Brand-New Exclusionary Clause to the Prohibition of Collective Expulsion of Aliens - The Applicant's Own Conduct in N.D. and N.T. v Spain*, 2021 Human Rights Law Review 21(1), 203-220.

Clapham, Andrew, *Human Rights Obligations of Non-State Actors in Conflict Situations*, 2006 International Review of the Red Cross 88(863), 491-523.

Clapham, Andrew, *Non-State Actors*, in: Christina Binder / Manfred Nowak / Jane Hofbauer / Philipp Janig (eds.), *Elgar Encyclopedia of Human Rights*, Online Edition 2022, Edward Elgar (Cheltenham).

Clapham, Andrew, *Non-State Actors*, in: Daniel Moeckli / Sangeeta Shah / Sandesh Sivakumaran (eds.), *International Human Rights Law*, 2nd Edition 2014, Oxford University Press (Oxford), 531-549.

Clark, Janine Natalya, *Fieldwork and its Ethical Challenges - Reflections from Research in Bosnia*, 2012 Human Rights Quarterly 34(3), 823-839.

Cohen, Nissim / Arieli, Tamar, *Field Research in Conflict Environments - Methodological Challenges and Snowball Sampling*, 2011 Journal of Peace Research 48(4), 423-435.

Colandrea, Valerio, *On the Power of the European Court of Human Rights to Order Specific Non-Monetary Measures - Some Remarks in Light of the Assanidze, Broniowski and Sejdovic Cases*, 2007 Human Rights Law Review 7(2), 396-411.

Colvin, Christopher, *Overview of the Reparations Program in South Africa*, in: Pablo de Greiff (ed.), *Handbook of Reparations*, 2006, Oxford University Press (Oxford), 176-214.

Combs, Nancy, *Deconstructing the Epistemic Challenges to Mass Atrocity Prosecutions*, 2018 Washington and Lee Law Review 75(1), 223-300.

Contreras, Pablo, *National Discretion and International Deference in the Restriction of Human Rights - A Comparison Between the Jurisprudence of the European and the Inter-American Court of Human Rights*, 2012 Northwestern Journal of International Human Rights 11(1), 28-82.

Contreras-Garduno, Diana / Fraser, Julie, *The Identification of Victims Before the Inter-American Court of Human Rights and the International Criminal Court and its Impact on Participation and Reparation - A Domino Effect*, 2014 Inter-American and European Human Rights Journal 7(1), 174-203.

Correa, Cristián, *Artículo 63*, in: Christian Steiner / Patricia Uribe (eds.), *Convención Americana Sobre Derechos Humanos - Comentario*, 2014, Konrad-Adenauer-Stiftung (Bogotá), 817-888.

Correa, Cristián, *Artículo 63* in: Christian Steiner / Marie-Christine Fuchs / Patricia Uribe (eds.), *Convención Americana Sobre Derechos Humanos - Comentario*, 2nd Edition 2019, Konrad-Adenauer-Stiftung (Bogotá), 1019-1099.

Correa, Cristián, *Operationalising the Right of Victims of War to Reparation*, in: Anne Peters / Christian Marxsen (eds.), *Max Planck Trialogues on the Law of Peace and War - Volume III: Reparations for Victims of Armed Conflict*, 2020, Cambridge University Press (Cambridge).

Couillard, Valérie, *The Nairobi Declaration - Redefining Reparation for Women Victims of Sexual Violence*, 2007 International Journal of Transitional Justice 1(3), 444-453.

Crocker, David A., *Reckoning With Past Wrongs - A Normative Framework*, 2012 Ethics & International Affairs 13, 43-64.

Cruft, Rowan / Liao, Matthew / Renzo, Massimo, *The Philosophical Foundations of Human Rights - An Overview*, in: Rowan Cruft / Matthew Liao / Massimo Renzo (eds.), *Philosophical Foundations of Human Rights*, 2015, Oxford University Press (Oxford), 1-44.

Davidson, Natalie R., *Alien Tort Statute Litigation and Transitional Justice: Bringing the Marcos Case Back to the Philippines*, 2017 International Journal of Transitional Justice 11(2), 257-275.

de Casadevante Romani, Carlos Fernández *International Law of Victims*, 2010 Max Planck Yearbook of United Nations Law 14, 219-272.

de Greiff, Pablo, *Articulating the Links Between Transitional Justice and Development - Justice and Social Integration*, in: Pablo de Greiff / Roger Duthie (eds.), *Transitional Justice and Development - Making Connections*, 2009, Social Science Research Council (New York), 28-75.

de Greiff, Pablo, *DDR and Reparations - Establishing Links Between Peace and Justice Instruments*, in: Kai Ambos / Marieke Wierda (eds.), *Building a Future on Peace and Justice*, 2009, Springer (Berlin), 321-356.

de Greiff, Pablo, *Justice and Reparations*, in: Jon Miller / Rahul Kumar (eds.), *Reparations - Interdisciplinary Inquiries*, 2007, Oxford University Press (Oxford), 153-175.

de Greiff, Pablo, *Justice and Reparations*, in: Pablo de Greiff (ed.), *Handbook of Reparations*, 2006, Oxford University Press (Oxford), 451-478.

de Greiff, Pablo, *A Normative Conception of Transitional Justice*, 2010 Politorbis 50(3), 17-30.

de Greiff, Pablo, *Theorizing Transitional Justice*, in: Melissa Williams / Rosemary Nagy / Jon Elster (eds.), *Transitional Justice*, 2012, New York University Press (New York), 27-51.

de Greiff, Pablo / Wierda, Marieke, *The Trust Fund for Victims of the International Criminal Court – Between Possibilities and Constraints*, in: Koen de Feyter / Stephan Parmentier / Paul Lemmens (eds.), *Out of the Ashes - Reparation for Victims of Gross and Systematic Human Rights Violations*, 2005, Intersentia (Antwerp), 225-244.

de la Hoz del Villar, Katrim / Machado Vásquez, María / Mejía Turizo, Jorge, *El Enfoque de Género Dentro del Sistema Integral de Verdad, Justicia, Reparación y No Repetición*, 2019 Justicia 24(36), 1-16.

de Schutter, Olivier, *Waiver of Rights and State Paternalism Under the European Convention on Human Rights*, 2000 Northern Ireland Legal Quarterly 51(3), 481-508.

de Schutter, Olivier / Tulkens, Françoise, *Rights in Conflict - The European Court of Human Rights as a Pragmatic Institution*, in: Eva Brems (ed.), *Conflicts Between Fundamental Rights*, 2008, Intersentia (Antwerp), 169-216.

de Waardt, Mijke / Weber, Sanne, *Beyond Victims' Mere Presence - An Empirical Analysis of Victim Participation in Transitional Justice in Colombia*, 2019 Journal of Human Rights Practice 11(1), 209-228.

de Wet, Erika, *Jus Cogens and Obligations Erga Omnes*, in: Dinah Shelton (ed.), *The Oxford Handbook of International Human Rights Law*, 2013, Oxford University Press (Oxford), 541-561.

Delagrange, Mikel, *The Path Towards Greater Efficiency and Effectiveness in the Victim Application Processes of the International Criminal Court*, 2018 International Criminal Law Review 18(3), 540-562.

Delgado Mariño, July Paola, *Segundos Ocupantes en el Marco de la Ley 1448 de 2011 - Un Debate Abierto*, in: María del Pilar García Pachón (ed.), *Lecturas Sobre Derecho de Tierras - Tomo II*, 2018, Universidad Externado de Colombia (Bogotá), 193-233.

Denov, Myriam, *Coping With the Trauma of War - Former Child Soldiers in Post-Conflict Sierra Leone*, 2010 International Social Work 53(6), 791-806.

Dickerson, Hollis, *Minimum Standards,* in: Rüdiger Wolfrum (ed.), *Max Planck Encyclopedia of International Law,* Online Edition 2010, Oxford University Press (Oxford).

Dijkstal, Haydee, *Destruction of Cultural heritage Before the ICC – The Influence of Human Rights on Reparations Proceedings for Victims and the Accussed,* 2019 Journal of International Criminal Justice 17(2), 369-390.

Dixon, Peter J., *Reparations, Assistance and the Experience of Justice - Lessons From Colombia and the Democratic Republic of the Congo*, 2015 International Journal of Transitional Justice 10(1), 88-107.

Donat-Catin, David, *Article 75*, in: Kai Ambos (ed.), *Rome Statute of the International Criminal Court - A Commentary*, 4th Edition 2022, C.H. Beck (Munich).

Dörr, Oliver, *Article 31 - General Rule of Interpretation*, in: Oliver Dörr / Kerstin Schmalenbach (eds.), *Vienna Convention on the Law of Treaties - A Commentary*, 2nd Edition 2018, Springer (Berlin), 559-616.

Doswald-Beck, Louise, *Fair Trial, Right to, International Protection*, in: Rüdiger Wolfrum (ed.), *Max Planck Encyclopedia of Public International Law*, Online Edition 2013, Oxford University Press (Oxford).

Dougherty, Beth K., *Searching for Answers - Sierra Leone's Truth and Reconciliation Commission*, 2004 African Studies Quarterly 8(1), 39-56.

du Plessis, Max, *Historical Injustice and International Law - An Exploratory Discussion of Reparation for Slavery*, 2003 Human Rights Quarterly 25(3), 624-659.

Ducoulombier, Peggy, *Conflicts Between Fundamental Rights and the European Court of Human Rights - An Overview*, in: Eva Brems (ed.), *Conflicts Between Fundamental Rights*, 2008, Intersentia (Antwerp), 217-248.

Duggan/Abusharaf, *Reparation of Sexual Violence in Democratic Transitions – The Search for Gender Justice*, in: de Greiff (ed.), The Handbook of Reparations, 2006, Oxford University Press (Oxford), 623-649.

Duggan, Colleen / Jacobson, Ruth, *Reparation of Sexual and Reproductive Violence - Moving from Codification to Implementation*, in: Ruth Rubio-Marin (ed.), *The Gender of Reparations - Unsettling Sexual Hierarchies While Redressing Human Rights Violations*, 2009, Cambridge University Press (Cambridge), 121-161.

Dukalskis, Alexander / Gerschewski, Johannes, *What Autocracies Say (and What Citizens Hear) - Proposing Four Mechanisms of Autocratic Legitimation*, 2017 Contemporary Politics 23(3), 251-268.

Duthie, Roger, *Introduction*, in: Roger Duthie / Paul Seils (eds.), *Justice Mosaics - How Context Shapes Transitional Justice in Fractured Societies*, 2017, International Center for Transitional Justice (New York), 8-39.

Duthie, Roger, *Toward a Development-Sensitive Approach to Transitional Justice*, 2008 International Journal of Transitional Justice 2(3), 292-309.

Dutton, Anne / Ní Aoláin, Fionnuala, *Between Reparations and Repair - Assessing the Work of the ICC Trust Fund for Victims Under its Assistance Mandate*, 2019 Chicago Journal of International Law 19(2), 490-547.

Edel, Mirjam / Josua, Maria, *How Authoritarian Rulers Seek to Legitimize Repression - Framing Mass Killings in Egypt and Uzbekistan*, 2018 Democratization 25(5), 882-900.

Eide, Asbjorn, *Adequate Standard of Living*, in: Daniel Moeckli / Sangeeta Shah / Sandesh Sivakumaran (eds.), *International Human Rights Law*, 2nd Edition 2014, Oxford University Press (Oxford), 195-216.

Eisikovits, Nir, *Transitional Justice*, in: Edward Zalta (ed.), *Stanford Encyclopedia of Philosophy*, Online Edition 2016, The Metaphysics Research Lab, Stanford University (Stanford).

Etinson, Adam, *Human Rights, Claimability and the Uses of Abstraction*, 2013 Utilitas 25(4), 463-486.

Fadil, Nadia, *Asserting State Sovereignty - The Face-Veil Ban in Belgium*, in: Brems, Eva (ed.), *The Experience of Face Veil Wearers in Europe and the Law*, 2014, Cambridge University Press (Cambridge), 251-262.

Falk, Richard, *Reparations, International Law, and Global Justice - A New Frontier*, in: Pablo de Greiff (ed.), *The Handbook of Reparations*, 2006, Oxford University Press (Oxford), 478-503.

Fitzmaurice, *The General Principles of International Law Considered From the Standpoint of the Rule of Law*, 1957 Collected Courses of the Hague Academy of International Law 92, 1-227.

Fitzmaurice, Sir Gerald, *The Law and Procedure of the International Court of Justice 1951-4 - Treaty Interpretation and Other Treaty Points*, 1957 British Year Book of International Law 33, 203-293.

Fitzmaurice, Gerald, *The Law and Procedure of the International Court of Justice - Treaty Interpretation and Certain Other Treaty Points*, 1951 British Year Book of International Law 28, 1-28.

Fletcher, Laurel E. / Weinstein, Harvey M., *Violence and Social Repair - Rethinking the Contribution of Justice to Reconciliation*, 2002 Human Rights Quarterly 24(3), 573-639.

Fletcher Laurel E. / Weinstein, Harvey M. / Rown, Jamie, *Context, Timing and the Dynamics of Transitional Justice – A Historical Perspective*, 2009 Human Rights Quarterly 31(1), 163-220.

Follesdal, Andreas, *Appreciating the Margin of Appreciation*, in: Adam Etinson (ed.), *Human Rights - Moral or Political?*, 2018, Oxford University Press (Oxford), 269-294.

Francioni, Francesco, *The Rights of Access to Justice Under Customary International Law*, in: Francesco Francioni (ed.), *Access to Justice as a Human Right*, 2007, Oxford University Press (Oxford), 1-56.

Frost-Arnold, Karen, *Imposters, Tricksters, and Trustworthiness as an Epistemic Virtue*, 2014 Hypatia 29(4), 790-807.

Furuya, Shuichi, *The Right to Reparation for Victims of Armed Conflict - The Intertwined Development of Substantive and Procedural Aspects*, in: Anne Peters / Christian Marxsen (eds.), *Max Planck Trialogues on the Law of Peace and War - Volume III: Reparations for Victims of Armed Conflict*, 2020, Cambridge University Press (Cambridge), 16-91.

Gaja, Giorgio, *General Principles of Law*, in: Rüdiger Wolfrum (ed.), *Max Planck Encyclopedia of International Law*, Online Edition 2013, Oxford University Press (Oxford).

Gallen, James, *The International Criminal Court - In the Interests of Transitional Justice?*, in: Cheryl Lawther / Luke Moffett / Dov Jacobs (eds.), *Research Handbook on Transitional Justice*, 2017, Edward Elgar (Cheltenham), 305-327.

García-Godos, Jemima / Wiig, Henrik, *Ideals and Realities of Restitution - The Colombian Land Restitution Programme*, 2018 Journal of Human Rights Practice 10(1), 40-57.

Geddes, Barbara, *What do we Know About Democratization After Twenty Years?*, 1999 Annual Review of Political Science 2(1), 115-144.

Geistfeld, Mark, *Placing a Price on Pain and Suffering - A Method for Helping Juries Determine Tort Damages for Nonmonetary Injuries*, 1995 California Law Review 83(3), 773-852.

Gerards, Janneke, *How to Improve the Necessity Test of the European Court of Human Rights*, 2013 International Journal of Constitutional Law 11(2), 466-490.

Gewirth, Alan, *Are There any Absolute Rights?*, 1981 The Philosophical Quarterly 31(122), 1-16.

Gillard, Emanuela-Chiara, *Reparation for Violations of International Humanitarian Law*, 2003 International Review of the Red Cross 85(851), 529-552.

Goldberg, Sanford, *Trust and Reliance*, in: Judith Simon (ed.), *The Routledge Handbook of Trust and Philosophy*, 2020, Routledge (New York), 97-108.

Gordon, Eleanor, *Crimes of the Powerful in Conflict-Affected Environments - False Positives, Transitional Justice and the Prospects for Peace in Colombia*, 2017 State Crime Journal 6(1), 132-155.

Gray, Christine, *Remedies*, in: P. R. Romano Cesare / J. Alter Karen / Avgerou Chrisanthi (eds.), *Oxford Handbook of International Adjudication*, 2013, Oxford University Press (Oxford), 871-896.

Gray, David C., *Extraordinary Justice*, 2010 Alabama Law Review 62, 55-110.

Graybill, Lyn S., *Traditional Practices and Reconciliation in Sierra Leone - The Effectiveness of Fambul Tok*, 2010 Conflict Trends 3, 41-47.

Gready, Paul, *Analysis - Reconceptualising Transitional Justice: Embedded and Distanced Justice*, 2005 Conflict, Security & Development 5(1), 3-21.

Greeley, Robin Adèle / Orwicz, Michael R. / Falconi, José Luis / Reyes, Ana María / Rosenberg, Fernando J. / Laplante, Lisa J., *Repairing Symbolic Reparations - Assessing the Effectiveness of Memorialization in the Inter-American System of Human Rights*, 2020 International Journal of Transitional Justice 14(1), 165-192.

Guembe, María José, *Economic Reparations for Grave Human Rights Violations - The Argentinean Experience*, in: Pablo de Greiff (ed.), *Handbook of Reparations*, 2006, Oxford University Press (Oxford), 21-54.

Günnewig, Elisabeth, *The Duty to Pay Reparations for the Violation of the Prohibition of the Use of Force in International Relations and the Jus Post Bellum*, in: Claus Kreß / Robert Lawless (eds.), *Necessity and Proportionality in International Peace and Security Law*, 2021, Oxford University Press (Oxford), 439-474.

Gusfield, Joseph R., *On Legislating Morals - The Symbolic Process of Designating Deviance*, 1968 California Law Review 56(1), 54-73.

Guzman-Rodriguez, Diana Esther, *Dignity Takings and Dignity Restoration - A Case Study of the Colombian Land Restitution Program*, 2017 Chicago-Kent Law Review 92(3), 871-904.

Haasdijk, Suzan, *The Lack of Uniformity in the Terminology of the International Law of Remedies*, 1992 Leiden Journal of International Law 5(2), 245-263.

Hailbronner, Michaela / Martini, Stefan, *The German Federal Constitutional Court*, in: András Jakab / Arthur Dyevre / Giulio Itzcovich (eds.), *Comparative Constitutional Reasoning*, 2017, Cambridge University Press (Cambridge), 356-393.

Halistoprak, Burak Toygar, *Knowledge Production and its Politicization Within International Relations and Peace Studies*, in: Briony Jones / Ulrike Lühe (eds.), *Knowledge for Peace - Transitional Justice and the Politics of Knowledge in Theory and Practice*, 2021, Edward Elgar (Cheltenham), 21-36.

Hamber, Brandon, *The Dilemmas of Reparations - In Search of a Process-Driven Approach*, in: Koen de Feyter / Stephan Parmentier / Paul Lemmens (eds.), *Out of the Ashes - Reparation for Victims of Gross and Systematic Human Rights Violations*, 2005, Intersentia (Antwerp), 135-150.

Hamber, Brandon, *Narrowing the Micro and Macro - A Psychological Perspective on Reparations in Societies in Transition*, in: Pablo de Greiff (ed.), *The Handbook on Reparations*, 2006, Oxford University Press (Oxford), 560-588.

Hamber, Brandon / Wilson, Richard A., *Symbolic Closure Through Memory, Reparation and Revenge in Post-Conflict Societies*, 2002 Journal of Human Rights 1(1), 35-53.

Hansen, Thomas Obel, *Transitional Justice - Toward a Differentiated Theory*, 2011 Oregon Review of International Law 13(1), 1-54.

Hansen, Thomas Obel, *The Vertical and Horizontal Expansion of Transitional Justice - Explanations and Implications for a Contested Field*, in: Susanne Buckley-Zistel (ed.), *Transitional Justice Theories*, 2014, Routledge (Abingdon), 105-124.

Haraway, *Situated Knowledges – The Science Question in Feminism and the Privilege of Partial Perspective*, 1988 Feminist Studies 14(3), 575-599.

Hardimon, Michael O., *Role Obligations*, 1994 The Journal of Philosophy 91(7), 333-363.

Heffes, Ezequiel / Frenkel, Brian, *The International Responsibility of Non-State Armed Groups – In Search of the Applicable Rules*, 2017 Goettingen Journal of International Law 8(1), 39-72.

Herman, Olivia, *Beyond the State of Play – Establishing a Duty of Non-State Armed Groups to Provide Reparations*, 2021 International Review of the Red Cross 102(915), 1033-1056.

Hessbruegge, Jan Arno, *Justice Delayed, not Denied - Statutory Limitations and Human Rights Crimes*, 2011 Georgetown Journal of International Law 43(4), 335-385.

Hoffman, Danny, *The Meaning of a Militia - Understanding the Civil Defence Forces of Sierra Leone*, 2007 African Affairs 106(425), 639-662.

Hoffman, Elisabeth, *Reconciliation in Sierra Leone - Local Processes Yield Global Lessons*, 2008 Fletcher Forum of World Affairs 32(2), 129-142.

Hoss, Cristina, *Satisfaction*, in: Rüdiger Wolfrum (ed.), *Max Planck Encyclopedia of Public International Law*, Online Edition 2011, Oxford University Press (Oxford).

Houtte, Hans van / Das, Hans / Delmartino, Bart, *The United Nations Compensation Commission*, in: Pablo de Greiff (ed.), *Handbook of Reparations*, 2006, Oxford University Press (Oxford), 321-389.

Huhle, Rainer, *Transitional Justice*, in: Christina Binder / Manfred Nowak / Jane Hofbauer / Philipp Janig (eds.), *Elgar Encyclopedia of Human Rights*, Online Edition 2022, Edward Elgar (Cheltenham).

Hutchison, Marc L. / Johnson, Kristin, *Capacity to Trust? Institutional Capacity, Conflict, and Political Trust in Africa, 2000–2005*, 2011 Journal of Peace Research 48(6), 737-752.

Hutchinson, Sharon, *Uncertain Ethics - Researching Civil War In Sudan*, in: Pottier Johan / Hammond Laura / Cramer Christopher (eds.), *Researching Violence in Africa - Ethical and Methodological Challenges*, 2011, Brill (Leiden), 79-93.

Ibañez, Ana María, *Forced Displacement in Colombia - Magnitude and Causes*, 2009 The Economics of Peace and Security Journal 4(1), 48-54.

Ibañez Rivas, Juana María, *Artículo 25*, in: Christian Steiner / Patricia Uribe (eds.), *Convención Americana Sobre Derechos Humanos - Comentario*, 2014, Konrad-Adenauer-Stiftung (Bogotá), 606-653.

Ibáñez Rivas, Juana María, *Artículo 8*, in: Christian Steiner / Marie-Christine Fuchs / Patricia Uribe (eds.), *Convención Americana Sobre Derechos Humanos - Comentario*, 2nd Edition 2019, Konrad-Adenauer-Stiftung (Bogotá), 256-322.

Íñigo Álvarez, Laura, *The Obligation to Provide Reparations by Armed Groups - A Norm Under Customary International Law?*, 2020 Netherlands International Law Review 67(3), 427-452.

Intemann, Kristen, *25 Years of Feminist Empiricism and Standpoint Theory – Where are we now?*, 2010 Hypatia 25(4), 778-796.

Jackson, Paul, *Reshuffling an old Deck of Cards? The Politics of Local Government Reform in Sierra Leone*, 2007 African Affairs 106(422), 95-111.

Jamar, Astrid, *The Crusade of Transitional Justice - Tracing the Journeys of Hegemonic Claims*, in: The British Academy (ed.), *Violence and Democracy*, 2019, The British Academy (London), 53-59.

Johan, Pottier / Laura, Hammond / Christopher, Cramer, *Navigating the Terrain of Methods and Ethics in Conflict Research*, in: Pottier Johan / Hammond Laura / Cramer Christopher (eds.), *Researching Violence in Africa - Ethical and Methodological Challenges*, 2011, Brill (Leiden), 1-22.

Jones, Karen, *Trust and Terror*, in: Peggy Desautels / Margaret Urban Walker (eds.), *Moral Psychology - Feminist Ethics and Social Theory*, 2004, Rowman and Littlefield Publishers (Lanham), 3-18.

Jones, Karen, *Trustworthiness*, 2012 Ethics 123(1), 61-85.

Jones, Briony / Lühe, Ulrike / Fokou, Gilbert / Logo, Kuyang Harriet / Moro, Leben Nelson / N'Da, Serge-Alain Yao, *Producing Knowledge on and for Transitional Justice - Reflections on a Collaborative Research Project*, in: Briony Jones / Ulrike Lühe (eds.), *Knowledge for Peace - Transitional Justice and the Politics of Knowledge in Theory and Practice*, 2021, Edward Elgar (Cheltenham), 49-73.

Kalshoven, Frits, *State Responsibility for Warlike Acts of the Armed Forces*, 1991 International and Comparative Law Quarterly 40(4), 827-858.

Kämmerer, Jörn Axel, *Colonialism,* in: Rüdiger Wolfrum (ed.), *Max Planck Encyclopedia of Public International Law,* Online Edition 2018, Oxford University Press (Oxford).

Kerbrat, Yann, *Interaction Between the Forms of Reparation,* in: James Crawford / Alain Pellet / Simon Olleson (eds.), *The Law of International Responsibility,* 2010, Oxford University Press (Oxford), 573-588.

Khosla, Madhav, *Proportionality - An Assault on Human Rights? A Reply,* 2010 International Journal of Constitutional Law 8(2), 298-306.

Killander, Magnus, *Interpreting Regional Human Rights Treaties,* 2010 Sur - International Journal on Human Rights 7(13), 145-170.

Kindermann, Harald, *Symbolische Gesetzgebung,* in: Dieter Grimm / Werner Maihofer (eds.), *Gesetzgebungstheorie und Rechtspolitik,* 1988, Springer (Wiesbaden), 222-245.

Kiyani, Asad G., *Avoidance Techniques – Accounting for Canada's Colonial Crimes,* in: Wolfgang Kaleck / Morten Bergsmo / Kyaw Yin Hlaing (eds.), *Colonial Wrongs and Access to International Law,* 2020, Torkel Opsahl Academic Publisher (Brussels), 501-524.

Klatt, Matthias / Meister, Moritz, *Proportionality - A Benefit to Human Rights? Remarks on the I·CON Controversy,* 2012 International Journal of Constitutional Law 10(3), 687-708.

Koji, Teraya, *Emerging Hierarchy in International Human Rights and Beyond - From the Perspective of Non-Derogable Rights,* 2001 European Journal of International Law 12(5), 917-942.

Kotzur, Markus, *Good Faith (Bona Fide),* in: Rüdiger Wolfrum (ed.), *Max Planck Encyclopedia of International Law,* Online Edition 2009, Oxford University Press (Oxford).

Kress, Claus, *Einführung,* in: Urs Kindhäuser / Claus Kreß / Michael Pawlik / Carl-Friedrich Stuckenberg (eds.), *Strafrecht und Gesellschaft – Ein Kritischer Kommentar zum Werk von Günther Jakobs,* 2019, Mohr Siebeck (Tübingen), 1-64.

Kress, Claus, *International Criminal Law,* in: Rüdiger Wolfrum (ed.), *Max Planck Encyclopedia of Public International Law,* Online Edition 2009, Oxford University Press (Oxford).

Kress, Claus / Broomhall, Bruce, *Implementing Cooperation Duties Under the Rome Statute - A Comparative Synthesis,* in: Claus Kress / Bruce Broomhall / Flavia Lattanzi / Valeria Santori (eds.), *The Rome Statute and Domestic Legal Orders - Vol. II: Constitutional Issues, Cooperation and Enforcement,* 2005, Nomos (Baden-Baden), 515-543.

Kress, Claus / Grover, Leena, *International Criminal Law Restraints in Peace Talks to End Armed Conflicts of a Non-International Character,* in: Morten Bergsmo / Pablo Kalmanovitz (eds.), *Law in Peace Negotiations,* 2009, International Peace Research Institute (Oslo), 29-54.

Kretzmer, David, *Emergency, State of,* in: Rüdiger Wolfrum (ed.), *Max Planck Encyclopedia of International Law,* Online Edition 2008, Oxford University Press (Oxford).

Kriebaum, Ursula / Reinisch, August, *Property, Right to, International Protection,* in: Rüdiger Wolfrum (ed.), *Max Planck Encyclopedia of International Law,* Online Edition 2019, Oxford University Press (Oxford).

Laplante, Lisa J., *The Law of Remedies and the Clean Hands Doctrine - Exclusionary Reparation Policies in Peru's Political Transition,* 2009 American University International Law Review 23(1), 51-90.

Laplante, Lisa J., *Transitional Justice and Peace Building - Diagnosing and Addressing the Socioeconomic Roots of Violence Through a Human Rights Framework*, 2008 International Journal of Transitional Justice 2(3), 331-355.

Lavrysen, Laurens, *Positive Obligations in the Jurisprudence of the Inter-American Court of Human Rights*, 2014 Inter-American and European Human Rights Journal 7, 94-115.

Lawry-White, Merryl, *The Reparative Effect of Truth Seeking in Transitional Justice*, 2015 International and Comparative Law Quarterly 64(1), 141-177.

Letsas, George, *The Margin of Appreciation Revisited - A Response to Follesdal*, in: Adam Etinson (ed.), *Human Rights - Moral or Political?*, 2018, Oxford University Press (Oxford), 294-310.

Levi, Margaret / Sacks, Audrey / Tyler, Tom, *Conceptualizing Legitimacy, Measuring Legitimating Beliefs*, 2009 American Behavioral Scientist 53(3), 354-375.

Lewis, Chloé, *Systemic Silencing - Addressing Sexual Violence Against Men and Boys in Armed Conflict and its Aftermath*, in: Gina Heathcote / Dianne Otto (eds.), *Rethinking Peacekeeping, Gender Equality and Collective Security*, 2014, Palgrave Macmillan (London), 203.

Lira, Elizabeth, *The Reparations Policy for Human Rights Violations in Chile*, in: Pablo de Greiff (ed.), *Handbook of Reparations*, 2006, Oxford University Press (Oxford), 55-101.

Lostal, Marina, *Implementing Reparations in the Al Mahdi Case – A Story of Monumental Challenges in Timbuktu*, 2021 Journal of International Criminal Justice 19(4), 831-853.

Lundy, Patricia / McGovern, Mark, *The Role of Community In Participatory Transitional Justice*, in: Kieran McEvoy / Lorna McGregor (eds.), *Transitional Justice From Below - Grassroots Activism and the Struggle for Change*, 2008, Hart Publishing (London), 99-120.

Lykes, Brinton / Mersky, Marcie, *Reparations and Mental Health - Psychosocial Interventions Towards Healing, Human Agency and Rethreading Social Realities*, in: Pablo de Greiff (ed.), *The Handbook of Reparations*, 2006, Oxford University Press (Oxford), 589-622.

Mac-Gregor, Eduardo Ferrer / Möller, Carlos María Pelayo, *Artículo 32*, in: Christian Steiner / Patricia Uribe (eds.), *Convención Americana Sobre Derechos Humanos - Comentario*, 2014, Konrad-Adenauer-Stiftung (Bogotá), 722-733.

Malamud-Goti, Jaime / Grosman, Lucas Sebastián, *Reparations and Civil Litigation - Compensation for Human Rights Violations in Transitional Democracies*, in: Pablo de Greiff (ed.), *The Handbook of Reparations*, 2006, Oxford University Press (Oxford), 539-559.

Manjoo, Rashida, *Introduction - Reflections on the Concept and Implementation of Transformative Reparations*, 2017 International Journal of Human Rights 21(9), 1193-1203.

Marauhn, Thilo / Ruppel, Nadine, *Balancing Conflicting Human Rights - Konrad Hesse's Notion of "Praktische Konkordanz" and the German Federal Constitutional Court*, in: Eva Brems (ed.), *Conflicts Between Fundamental Rights*, 2008, Intersentia (Antwerp), 273-296.

Marboe, Irmgard, *Compensation and Damages in International Law - The Limits of Fair Market Value*, 2006 Journal of World Investment & Trade 7(5), 723-760.

Martin, Laura S., *Deconstructing the Local in Peacebuilding Practice - Representations and Realities of Fambul Tok in Sierra Leone*, 2020 Third World Quarterly, Online Publication.

Mavronicola, Natasa, *What is an 'Absolute Right'? Deciphering Absoluteness in the Context of Article 3 of the European Convention on Human Rights*, 2012 Human Rights Law Review 12(4), 723-758.

Mayer, Robert, *Strategies of Justification in Authoritarian Ideology*, 2001 Journal of Political Ideologies 6(2), 147-168.

Mazzeschi, Riccardo Pisillo, *Reparation Claims by Individuals for State Breaches of Humanitarian Law and Human Rights - An Overview*, 2003 Journal of International Criminal Justice 1(2), 339-347.

McEvoy, Kieran, *Beyond Legalism - Towards a Thicker Understanding of Transitional Justice*, 2007 Journal of Law and Society 34(4), 411-440.

McEvoy, Kieran, *Letting Go of Legalism - Developing a 'Thicker' Version of Transitional Justice*, in: Kieran McEvoy / Lorna McGregor (eds.), *Transitional Justice From Below - Grassroots Activism and the Struggle for Change*, 2008, Hart Publishing (Oxford), 15-46.

McEvoy, Kieran / McConnachie, Kirsten, *Victimology in Transitional Justice - Victimhood, Innocence and Hierarchy*, 2012 European Journal of Criminology 9(5), 527-538.

McGregor, Lorna, *International Law as a "Tiered Process" - Transitional Justice at the Local, National and International Level*, in: Kieran McEvoy / Lorna McGregor (eds.), *Transitional Justice From Below - Grassroots Activism and the Struggle for Change*, 2008, Hart Publishing (London), 47-74.

McIntyre, Juliette, *Declaratory Judgments of the International Court of Justice*, in: Ruth A. Kok / Nikolaos Lavranos (eds.), *Hague Yearbook of International Law*, 2013, Brill (Leiden), 107-157.

McLachlan, Campbell, *The Principle of Systemic Integration and Article 31(3)(C) of the Vienna Convention*, 2005 International and Comparative Law Quarterly 54(2), 279-320.

McLeod, Allegra, *Envisioning Abolition Democracy*, 2019 Harvard Law Review 132, 1613-1649.

McLeod, Carolyn, *Trust*, in: Edward Zalta (ed.), *Stanford Encyclopedia of Philosophy*, Online Edition 2020, The Metaphysics Research Lab, Stanford University (Stanford).

Mechlem, Kerstin, *Treaty Bodies and the Interpretation of Human Rights*, 2009 Vanderbilt Journal of Transnational Law 42(3), 905-947.

Mégret, Frédéric, *The Case for Collective Reparations Before the International Criminal Court*, in: Jo-Anne Wemmers (ed.), *Reparation for Victims of Crimes Against Humanity*, 2014, Routledge (London), 171-189.

Mégret, Frédéric, *Nature of Obligations*, in: Daniel Moeckli / Sangeeta Shah / Sandesh Sivakumaran (eds.), *International Human Rights Law*, 2nd Edition 2014, Oxford University Press (Oxford), 96-118.

Mégret, Frédéric, *Of Shrines, Memorials and Museums - Using the International Criminal Court's Victim Reparation and Assistance Regime to Promote Transitional Justice*, 2010 Buffalo Human Rights Law Review 16, 1-56.

Mégret, Frédéric, *Reparations Before the ICC - The Need for Pragmatism and Creativity*, in: Richard H. Steinberg (ed.), *Contemporary Issues Facing the International Criminal Court*, 2016, Brill (Leiden), 252-263.

Méndez, Juan, *Peace, Justice and Prevention - Dilemmas and False Dilemmas*, in: Mô Bleeker (ed.), *Dealing with the Past and Transitional Justice - Creating Conditions for Peace, Human Rights and the Rule of Law*, 2006, Political Affairs Division IV, Federal Departement of Foreign Affairs (Bern), 15-20.

Méndez, Juan E., *Accountability for Past Abuses*, 1997 Human Rights Quarterly 19(2), 255-282.

Merkouris, Panos, *Interpreting the Customary Rules on Interpretation*, 2017 International Community Law Review 19(1), 126-155.

Meron, Theodor, *On a Hierarchy of International Human Rights*, 1986 American Journal of International Law 80(1), 1-23.

Merton, Robert K., *Contributions to the Theory of Reference Group Behavior*, in: Robert K. Merton (ed.), *Social Theory and Social Structure*, 1968, The Free Press (New York), 279-334.

Meza, Diego Armando Yanez / Escalante, Jessica Tatiana Jimenez, *Transformative Procedural Law in the Reparation of the new Victims of the Armed Conflict in Colombia - Challenges for the State Liability Proceedings*, 2019 Revista Chilena de Derecho 46(1), 129-154.

Michaels, Ralf / Pauwelyn, Joost, *Conflict of Norms or Conflict of Laws - Different Techniques in the Fragmentation of Public International Law*, 2011 Duke Journal of Comparative and International Law 22(3), 349-376.

Mihr, Anja, *An Introduction to Transitional Justice*, in: Olivera Simić (ed.), *An Introduction to Transitional Justice*, 2nd Edition 2020, Routledge (London), 1-28.

Milanovic, Marko, *Norm Conflict in International Law - Whither Human Rights*, 2009 Duke Journal of Comparative & International Law 20(1), 69-131.

Miller, David, *Justice*, in: Edward Zalta (ed.), *Stanford Encyclopedia of Philosophy*, Online Edition 2017, The Metaphysics Research Lab, Stanford University (Stanford).

Miller, Seumas, *Social Institutions*, in: Edward Zalta (ed.), *The Stanford Encyclopedia of Philosophy*, Online Edition 2014, Metaphysics Research Lab, Stanford University (Stanford).

Mock, William B. T., *Pareto Optimality*, in: Deen K. Chatterjee (ed.), *Encyclopedia of Global Justice*, 2011, Springer Netherlands (Dordrecht), 808-809.

Moffett, Luke, *Reparations for "Guilty Victims" - Navigating Complex Identities of Victim-Perpetrators in Reparation Mechanisms* 2016 International Journal of Transitional Justice 10(1), 146-167.

Moffett, Luke, *Reparations for Victims at the International Criminal Court - A New Way Forward?*, 2017 International Journal of Human Rights 21(9), 1204-1222.

Moffett, Luke, *Reparations in Transitional Justice - Justice or Political Compromise?*, 2017 Human Rights and International Legal Discourse 11(1), 59-71.

Moffett, Luke, *Beyond Attribution – Responsibility of Armed Non-State Actors for Reparations in Northern Ireland, Colombia and Uganda*, in: Noemi Gal-Or / Cedric Ryngaert / Math Noortman (eds.), *Responsibilities of the Non-State Actor in Armed Conflict and the Market Place - Theoretical Considerations and Empirical Finding*, 2015, Brill (Leiden), 323,346.

Moffett, Luke, *Transitional Justice and Reparations - Remedying the Past?*, in: Cheryl Lawther / Luke Moffett / Dov Jacobs (eds.), *Research Handbook on Transitional Justice*, 2017, Edward Elgar (Cheltenham), 377-400.

Moraña, Mabel, *El Ojo que Llora - Biopolítica, Nudos de la Memoria y Arte Público en el Perú de Hoy*, 2012 Latinoamérica 54, 183-216.

Moravcsik, Andrew, *Taking Preferences Seriously - A Liberal Theory of International Politics*, 2003 International Organization 51(4), 513-553.

Muffels, Ruud, *Relative Income and Reference Group Behavior*, in: Alex C. Michalos (ed.), *Encyclopedia of Quality of Life and Well-Being Research*, 2014, Springer Netherlands (Dordrecht), 5446-5449.

Muttukumaru, Christopher, *Reparation to Victims*, in: Roy S. K. Lee (ed.), *The International Criminal Court - The Making of the Rome Statute: Issues, Negotiations, Results*, 1999, Kluwer Law International (The Hague), 262-270.

Mutua, Makau, *Savages, Victims, and Saviors - The Metaphor of Human Rights*, 2001 Harvard International Law Journal 42(1), 201-246.

Mutua, Makau, *The Ideology of Human Rights*, 1995 Virginia Journal of International Law 36(3), 589-658.

Mutua, Makau, *What is the Future of Transitional Justice?*, 2015 International Journal of Transitional Justice 9(1), 1-9.

Mutua, Makau / Anghie, Antony, *What Is TWAIL?*, 2000 Proceedings of the Annual Meeting (American Society of International Law) 94, 31-40.

Nagy, Rosemary, *Transitional Justice as Global Project - Critical Reflections*, 2008 Third World Quarterly 29(2), 275-289.

Nelson, Alan, *Explanation and Justification in Political Philosophy*, 1986 Ethics 97(1), 154-176.

Neumann, Gerald, *Subsidiarity*, in: Dinah Shelton (ed.), *The Oxford Handbook of International Human Rights Law*, 2013, Oxford University Press (Oxford), 360-378.

Neuner, Matthias, *The Notion of Continuous or Continuing Crimes in International Criminal Law*, in: Wolfgang Kaleck / Morten Bergsmo / Kyaw Yin Hlaing (eds.), *Colonial Wrongs and Access to International Law*, 2020, Torkel Opsahl Academic Publisher (Brussels), 123-176.

Niebergall, Heike, *Overcoming Evidentiary Weaknesses in Reparation Claims Programmes*, in: Carla Ferstman / Mariana Goetz / Alan Stephens (eds.), *Reparations for Victims of Genocide, War Crimes and Crimes Against Humanity - Systems in Place and Systems in the Making*, 2009, Brill (Leiden), 145-166.

Noack-Lundberg, Kyja, *Impacts of Sexual Violence on Women's Sexual Health*, in: Jane M. Ussher / Joan C. Chrisler / Janette Perz (eds.), *Routledge International Handbook of Women's Sexual and Reproductive Health*, 2019, Routledge (Milton), 468-481.

Noll, Peter, *Symbolische Gesetzgebung*, 1981 Zeitschrift für schweizerisches Recht 100, 347-364.

Nouwen, Sarah M. H., *As You Set Out for Ithaka - Practical, Epistemological, Ethical, and Existential Questions About Socio-Legal Empirical Research in Conflict*, 2014 Leiden Journal of International Law 27(1), 227-260.

Oette, Lutz, *Bringing Justice to Victims? Responses of Regional and International Human Rights Courts and Treaty Bodies to Mass Violations*, in: Carla Ferstman / Mariana Goetz / Alan Stephens (eds.), *Reparations for Victims of Genocide, War Crimes and Crimes Against Humanity - Systems in Place and Systems in the Making*, 2009, Brill (Leiden), 217-242.

Offe, Claus, *How can we Trust our Fellow Citizens?*, in: M.E. Warren (ed.), *Democracy and Trust*, 1999, Cambridge University Press (Cambridge), 42-87.

Ohlin, Jens David, *On the Very Idea of Transitional Justice*, 2007 Whitehead Journal of Diplomacy and International Relations 8, 51-68.

Olaya, Cristian Acosta, *Férrea Pero Consciente - Disciplina y Lazo Identitario en las Organizaciones Clandestinas de las Fuerzas Armadas Revolucionarias de Colombia-Ejército del Pueblo (FARC-EP)*, 2020 Izquierdas 49, 540-553.

Omelicheva, Mariya Y., *Authoritarian Legitimation - Assessing Discourses of Legitimacy in Kazakhstan and Uzbekistan*, 2016 Central Asian Survey 35(4), 481-500.

Onsrud, Mathias / Sjøveian, Solbjørg / Luhiriri, Roger / Mukwege, Dennis, *Sexual Violence-Related Fistulas in the Democratic Republic of Congo*, 2008 International Journal of Gynecology & Obstetrics 103(3), 265-269.

Orakhelashvili, Alexander, *Restrictive Interpretation of Human Rights Treaties in the Recent Jurisprudence of the European Court of Human Rights*, 2003 European Journal of International Law 14(3), 529-568.

Ordóñez Narváez, Valentina, *Los Tejidos de Mampuján - Una Lectura Desde la Reparación Simbólica*, in: Yolanda Sierra León (ed.), *Reparación Simbólica - Jurisprudencia, Cantos y Tejidos*, 2018, Universidad Externado de Colombia (Bogotá), 291-343.

Orford, Anne, *Commissioning the Truth*, 2006 Columbia Journal of Gender and Law 15(3), 851-884.

Ottendörfer, Eva, *Translating Victims' "Right to Reparations" Into Practice - A Framework for Assessing the Implementation of Reparations Programs From a Bottom-Up Perspective*, 2018 Human Rights Quarterly 40(4), 905-931.

Owiso Owiso, *The International Criminal Court and Reparations – Judicial Innovation or Judicialisation of a Political Process?*, 2009 International Criminal Law Review 19, 505-531.

Pachon, Mónica, *Colombia 2008 - Éxitos, Peligros y Desaciertos de la Política de Seguridad Democrática de la Administración Uribe*, 2009 Revista de Ciencia Política (Santiago) 29(2), 327-353.

Paparinskis, Martins, *A Case Against Crippling Compensation in International Law of State Responsibility*, 2020 Modern Law Review 83(6), 1246-1286.

Pasqualucci, Jo M., *Victim Reparations in the Inter-American Human Rights System - A Critical Assessment of Current Practice and Procedure*, 1996 Michigan Journal of International Law 18(1), 1-58.

Pérez-León-Acevedo, Juan-Pablo, *Reparation Principles at the International Criminal Court*, in: Mads Andenas / Malgosia Fitzmaurice / Attila Tanzi / Jan Wouters (eds.), *General Principles and the Coherence of International Law*, 2019, Brill (Leiden), 328-351.

Peté, Stephen / du Plessis, Max, *Reparations for Gross Human Rights Violations in Context*, in: Stephen Peté / Max Du Plessis (eds.), *Repairing the Past? International Perspectives on Reparations for Gross Human Rights Abuses*, 2007, Intersentia (Antwerp), 3-28.

Peters, Anne / Altwicker, Tilmann / Altwicker-Hámori, Szilvia, *Measuring Violations of Human Rights - An Empirical Analysis of Awards in Respect of Non-Pecuniary Damage Under the European Convention on Human Rights*, 2016 Heidelberg Journal of International Law 76(1), 1-51.

Pinzauti, Giulia, *Principle 23*, in: Frank Haldemann / Thomas Unger (eds.), *The United Nations Principles to Combat Impunity - A Commentary*, 2018, Oxford University Press (Oxford), 250-257.

Plant, Marcus L., *Damages for Pain and Suffering Symposium - Personal Injury Litigation*, 1958 Ohio State Law Journal 19(2), 200-211.

Pobije, Erin, *Victims of the Crime of Aggression*, in: Claus Kress / Stefan Barriga (eds.), *The Crime of Aggression – A Commentary*, 2017, Cambridge University Press (Cambridge), 816-860.

Polansky, Ronald M., *Giving Justice its Due*, in: Ronald M. Polansky (ed.), *The Cambridge Companion to Aristotle's Nicomachean Ethics*, 2014, Cambridge University Press (Cambridge), 151-179.

Posner, Eric / Vermeule, Adrian, *Reparations for Slavery and Other Historical Injustices*, 2003 Columbia Law Review 103, 689, 747.

Posner, Eric / Vermeule, Adrian, *Transitional Justice as Ordinary Justice*, 2004 Harvard Law Review 117(3), 761-825.

Rajagopal, Balakrishnan, *Counter-Hegemonic International Law - Rethinking Human Rights and Development as a Third World Strategy*, 2006 Third World Quarterly 27(5), 767-783.

Ramírez, Sergio García, *La Jurisprudencia de la Corte Interamericana de Derechos Humanos en Materia de Reparaciones*, in: Inter-American Court of Human Rights (ed.), *La Corte Interamericana de Derechos Humanos - Un Cuarto de Siglo: 1979-2004*, 2005, Inter-American Court of Human Rights (San José), 1-86.

Riedel, Eibe, *International Covenant on Economic, Social and Cultural Rights (1966)*, in: Rüdiger Wolfrum (ed.), *Max Planck Encyclopedia of Public International Law*, Online Edition 2011, Oxford University Press (Oxford).

Rietiker, Daniel, *The Principle of "Effectiveness" in the Recent Jurisprudence of the European Court of Human Rights - Its Different Dimensions and its Consistency With Public International Law: No Need for the Concept of Treaty Sui Generis*, 2010 Nordic Journal of International Law 79(2), 245-277.

Robertson, Robert E., *Measuring State Compliance With the Obligation to Devote the "Maximum Available Resources" to Realizing Economic, Social, and Cultural Rights*, 1994 Human Rights Quarterly 16(4), 693-714.

Rohlin, Kristina, *The Bias Paradox in Feminist Standpoint Epistemology*, 2006 Episteme 3(1-2), 125-136.

Rohner, Dominic / Thoenig, Mathias / Zilibotti, Fabrizio, *Seeds of Distrust - Conflict in Uganda*, 2013 Journal of Economic Growth 18(3), 217-252.

Roht-Arriaza, Naomi, *Reparations and Economic, Social and Cultural Rights*, in: Dustin N. Sharp (ed.), *Justice and Economic Violence in Transition*, 2014, Springer (New York), 109-138.

Roht-Arriaza, Naomi, *Reparations Decisions and Dilemmas*, 2004 Hastings International and Comparative Law Review 27(2), 157-219.

Roht-Arriaza, Naomi / Orlovsky, Katharine, *A Complementary Relationship - Reparations and Development*, in: Pablo de Greiff / Roger Duthie (eds.), *Transitional Justice and Development - Making Connections*, 2009, Social Science Research Council (New York), 170-213.

Rombouts, Heidy / Sardaro, Pietro / Vandeginste, Stef, *The Right to Reparation for Victims of Gross and Systematic Violations of Human Rights*, in: Koen de Feyter / Stephan Parmentier / Paul Lemmens (eds.), *Out of the Ashes - Reparation for Victims of Gross and Systematic Human Rights Violations*, 2005, Intersentia (Antwerp), 345-504.

Ronzitti, Natalino, *Access to Justice and Compensation for Violations of the Law of War*, in: Francesco Francioni (ed.), *Access to Justice as a Human Right*, 2007, Oxford University Press (Oxford), 95-134.

Rosenfeld, Friedrich, *Collective Reparation for Victims of Armed Conflict*, 2010 Review of the Red Cross 92(879), 731-746.

Ross, Amy, *Impact on Research of Security-Seeking Behaviour*, in: Chandra Lekha Sriram / John C. King / Julie A. Mertus / Olga Martin-Ortega / Johanna Herman (eds.), *Surviving Field Research - Working in Violent and Difficult Situations*, 2009, Routledge (London), 177-188.

Rubio-Marín, Ruth, *Introduction - A Gender and Reparations Taxonomy*, in: Ruth Rubio-Marin (ed.), *The Gender of Reparations - Unsettling Sexual Hierarchies While Redressing Human Rights Violations*, 2009, Cambridge University Press (Cambridge), 1-17.

Rubio-Marín, *The Gender of Reparations in Transitional Societies*, in: Rubio-Marin (ed.), *The Gender of Reparations - Unsettling Sexual Hierarchies While Redressing Human Rights Violations*, 2009, Cambridge University Press (Cambridge), 63-120.

Rubio-Marín, Ruth / de Greiff, Pablo, *Women and Reparations*, 2007 International Journal of Transitional Justice 1(3), 318-337.

Rubio-Marín, Ruth / Sandoval, Clara, *Engendering the Reparations Jurisprudence of the Inter-American Court of Human Rights - The Promise of the "Cotton Field" Judgment*, 2011 Human Rights Quarterly 33(4), 1062-1091.

Rubio-Marín, Ruth / Sandoval, Clara / Díaz, Catalina, *Repairing Family Members - Gross Human Rights Violations and Communities of Harm*, in: Ruth Rubio-Marin (ed.), *The Gender of Reparations - Unsettling Sexual Hierarchies While Redressing Human Rights Violations*, 2009, Cambridge University Press (Cambridge), 215-290.

Russell, Cherry, *Interviewing Vulnerable Old People - Ethical and Methodological Implications of Imagining our Subjects*, 1999 Journal of Aging Studies 13(4), 403-417.

Ryngaert, Cedric, *State Responsibility, Necessity and Human Rights*, 2010 Netherlands Yearbook of International Law 41, 79-98.

Sabogal Urrego, Ricardo, *Los Mecanismos de la Acción de Restitución de Tierras - Garantías Para las Víctimas y la Reconciliación*, in: María del Pilar García Pachón (ed.), *Lecturas Sobre Derecho de Tierras - Tomo II*, 2018, Universidad Externado de Colombia (Bogotá), 167-192.

Sandoval, Clara, *Two Steps Forward, One Step Back - Reflections on the Jurisprudential Turn of the Inter-American Court of Human Rights on Domestic Reparation Programmes*, 2018 International Journal of Human Rights 22(9), 1192-1208.

Sandoval, Clara / Moffett, Luke, *Tilting at Windmills – Reparations and the International Criminal Court*, 2021 Leiden Journal of International Law 34, 749-769.

Sands, Philippe, *Treaty, Custom and the Cross-Fertilization of International Law*, 1998 Yale Human Rights and Development Law Journal 1(1), 85-105.

Schabas, William, *Conjoined Twins of Transitional Justice - The Sierra Leone Truth and Reconciliation Commission and the Special Court*, 2004 Journal of International Criminal Justice 2(4), 1082-1099.

Schabas, William, *Reparation Practices in Sierra Leone and the Truth and Reconciliation Commission*, in: Koen de Feyter / Stephan Parmentier / Paul Lemmens (eds.), *Out of the Ashes - Reparation for Victims of Gross and Systematic Human Rights Violations*, 2005, Intersentia (Antwerp), 289-308.

Schaffner, Kenneth F., *Approaches to Reduction*, 1967 Philosophy of Science 34(2), 137-147.

Schanke, Elise, *Housing and Reintegration of Amputees and War-Wounded in Sierra Leone*, 2004 Forced Migration 21, 60.

Schieder, Siegfried, *Neuer Liberalismus*, in: Siegfried Schieder / Manuela Spindler (eds.), *Theorien der Internationalen Beziehungen*, 2010, Verlag Barbara Budrich (Opladen), 187-222.

Schlütter, Birgit, *Aspects of Human Rights Interpretation by the UN Treaty Bodies*, in: Geir Ulfstein / Helen Keller (eds.), *UN Human Rights Treaty Bodies - Law and Legitimacy*, 2012, Cambridge University Press (Cambridge), 261-319.

Schönsteiner, Judith, *Dissuasive Measures and the Society as a Whole - A Working Theory of Reparations in the Inter-American Court of Human Rights*, 2007 American University International Law Review 23(1), 127-164.

Schotsmans, Martin, *Victims' Expectations, Needs and Perspectives After Gross and Systematic Human Rights Violations*, in: Koen de Feyter / Stephan Parmentier / Paul Lemmens (eds.), *Out of the Ashes - Reparation for Victims of Gross and Systematic Human Rights Violations*, 2005, Intersentia (Antwerp), 105-134.

Schulze, Michaela / Krätschmer-Hahn, Rabea, *Relative Deprivation Theory*, in: Alex C. Michalos (ed.), *Encyclopedia of Quality of Life and Well-Being Research*, 2014, Springer Netherlands (Dordrecht), 5443-5445.

Segovia, Alexander, *Financing Reparations Programs - Reflections From International Experience*, in: Pablo de Greiff (ed.), *The Handbook of Reparations*, 2006, Oxford University Press (Oxford), 650-675.

Seibert-Fohr, Anja, *Transitional Justice in Post-Conflict Situations*, in: Rüdiger Wolfrum (ed.), *Max Planck Encyclopedia of Public International Law*, Online Edition 2015, Oxford University Press (Oxford).

Sellers, Jefferey, *State-Society Relations*, in: Mark Bevir (ed.), *The SAGE Handbook of Governance*, 2011, SAGE Publications (London), 124-141.

Sharp, Dustin N., *Addressing Dilemmas of the Global and the Local in Transitional Justice*, 2014 Emory International Law Review 29(1), 71-118.

Sharp, Dustin N., *Emancipating Transitional Justice From the Bonds of the Paradigmatic Transition*, 2015 International Journal of Transitional Justice 9(1), 150-169.

Shelton, Dinah, *Human Rights, Remedies*, in: Rüdiger Wolfrum (ed.), *Max Planck Encyclopedia of Public International Law*, Online Edition 2006, Oxford University Press (Oxford).

Shelton, Dinah, *Normative Hierarchy in International Law*, 2006 American Journal of International Law 100(2), 291-323.

Shelton, Dinah, *Reparations*, in: Rüdiger Wolfrum (ed.), *Max Planck Encyclopedia of Public International Law*, Online Edition 2009, (Oxford).

Shelton, Dinah / Gould, Ariel, *Positive and Negative Obligations*, in: Dinah Shelton (ed.), *The Oxford Handbook of International Human Rights Law*, 2013, Oxford University Press (Oxford), 562-583.

Slyomovics, Susan, *Reparations in Morocco - The Symbolic Dirham*, in: Barbara Rose Johnston / Susan Slyomovics (eds.), *Waging War, Making Peace - Reparations and Human Rights*, 2009, Left Coast Press (Walnut Creek), 95-114.

Sorensen, Roy, *Vagueness*, in: Edward Zalta (ed.), *The Stanford Encyclopedia of Philosophy*, Online Edition 2018, Metaphysics Research Lab, Stanford University (Stanford).

Spielmann, Dean, *Allowing the Right Margin - The European Court of Human Rights and The National Margin of Appreciation Doctrine: Waiver or Subsidiarity of European Review?*, 2017 Cambridge Yearbook of European Legal Studies 14, 381-418.

Sriram, Chandra Lekha, *Beyond Transitional Justice - Peace, Governance, and Rule of Law*, 2017 International Studies Review 19(1), 53-69.

Stahn, Carsten, *Reparative Justice After the Lubanga Appeal Judgment - New Prospects for Expressivism and Participatory Justice or 'Juridified Victimhood' by Other Means?*, 2015 Journal of International Criminal Justice 13(4), 801-814.

Stoetzler, Marcel/Yuval-Davis, Nira, *Standpoint Theory, Situated Knowledge and the Situation Imagination,* 2002 Feminist Theory 3(3), 315-333.

Sullivan, Ann, *The Politics of Reconciliation in New Zealand*, 2016 Political Science 68(2), 124-142.

Sullivan, Scott M., *Changing the Premise of International Legal Remedies - The Unfounded Adoption of Assurances and Guarantees of Non-Repetition*, 2002 UCLA Journal of International Law and Foreign Affairs 7, 265-302.

Sultana, Farhana, *Reflexivity, Positionality and Participatory Ethics - Negotiating Fieldwork Dilemmas in International Research*, 2007 ACME: An International Journal for Critical Geographies 6(3), 374-385.

Sunstein, Cass, *On the Expressive Function of Law*, 1996 University of Pennsylvania Law Review 144(5), 2021-2053.

Sveaass, Nora / Lavik, Nils Johan, *Psychological Aspects of Human Rights Violations - The Importance of Justice and Reconciliation*, 2000 Nordic Journal of International Law 69(1), 35-52.

Teitel, Ruti, *Transitional Justice Genealogy*, 2003 Harvard Human Rights Journal 16, 69-94.

Theurer, Karina / Kaleck, Wolfgang, *Dekolonialisierung des Rechts - Ambivalenzen und Potenzial*, in: Karina Theurer / Wolfgang Kaleck (eds.), *Dekoloniale Rechtskritik und Rechtspraxis*, 2020, Nomos (Baden-Baden), 11-58.

Thornhill, Chris / Miron, Ronny, *Karl Jaspers*, in: Edward Zalta (ed.), *The Stanford Encyclopedia of Philosophy*, 2020, The Metaphysics Research Lab (Stanford).

Tigroudja, Hélène, *La Satisfaction et les Garanties de Non-Repetition de l'Illicite*, in: Société de Législation Comparée - Unité Mixte de Recherche de Droit Comparé de Paris (ed.), *Réparer les Violations Graves et Massives des Droits de l'Homme - La Cour Interaméricaine, Pionnière et Modèle?*, 2010, Unité Mixte de Recherche de Droit Comparé de Paris (Paris), 69-90.

Tomuschat, Christian, *Reparation for Victims of Grave Human Rights Abuses*, 2002 Tulane Journal of International and Comparative Law 10, 157-184.

Tomuschat, Christian, *Reparation in Favour of Individual Victims of Gross Violations of Human Rights and International Humanitarian Law*, in: Marcelo Kohen (ed.), *Promoting Justice, Human Rights and Conflict Resolution Through International Law - Liber Amicorum Lucius Caflisch*, 2006, Nijhoff (Leiden), 569-590.

Torpey, John, *Victims and Citizens – The Discourse of Reparation(s) at the Dawn of the New Millenium*, in: Koen de Feyter / Stephan Parmentier / Paul Lemmens (eds.), *Out of the Ashes - Reparation for Victims of Gross and Systematic Human Rights Violations*, 2005, Intersentia (Antwerp), 35-52.

Ukoha, Ukiwo, *Hidden Agendas In Conflict Research - Informants' Interests And Research Objectivity In The Niger Delta*, in: Pottier Johan / Hammond Laura / Cramer Christopher (eds.), *Researching Violence in Africa - Ethical and Methodological Challenges*, 2011, Brill (Leiden), 137-153.

van Boven, Theo, *Categories of Rights*, in: Daniel Moeckli / Sangeeta Shah / Sandesh Sivakumaran (eds.), *International Human Rights Law*, 2nd Edition 2014, Oxford University Press (Oxford), 143-156.

van Boven, Theo, *Victim's Rights to a Remedy and Reparation - The United Nations Principles and Guidelines*, in: Carla Ferstman / Mariana Goetz (eds.), *Reparations for Victims of Genocide War Crimes and Crimes Against Humanity - Systems in Place and Systems in the Making*, 2nd Edition 2020, Nijhoff (Leiden), 15-37.

van den Herik, Larissa, *Addressing "Colonial Crimes" Through Reparations? Adjudicating Dutch Atrocities Committed in Indonesia*, 2012 Journal of International Criminal Justice 10(3), 693-705.

van der Meerwe, Hugo / Moyo, Annah, *Transitional Justice for Colonial Era Abuses and Legacies - African versus European Policy Priorities*, in: Wolfgang Kaleck / Morten Bergsmo / Kyaw Yin Hlaing (eds.), *Colonial Wrongs and Access to International Law*, 2020, Torkel Opsahl Academic Publisher (Brussels), 41-68.

van den Wyngaert, Christine, *Victims Before International Criminal Courts - Some Views and Concerns of an ICC Trial Judge*, 2011 Case Western Reserve Journal of International Law 44(1 and 2), 475-496.

van der Schyff, Gerhard, *Cutting to the Core of Conflicting Rights - The Question of Inalienable Cores in Comparative Perspective*, in: Eva Brems (ed.), *Conflicts Between Fundamental Rights*, 2008, Intersentia (Antwerp), 131-148.

Vandenhole, Wouter, *Conflicting Economic and Social Rights - The Proportionality Plus Test*, in: Eva Brems (ed.), *Conflicts Between Fundamental Rights*, 2008, Intersentia (Antwerp), 559-589.

Vargas Valencia, Fernando, *Antecedentes Normativos y Jurisprudenciales Sobre Justicia Restaurativa en Colombia - A Propósito de la Reparación de Víctimas en el Acuerdo Final de Paz*, in: María del Pilar García Pachón (ed.), *Lecturas Sobre Derecho de Tierras - Tomo II*, 2018, Universidad Externado de Colombia (Bogotá), 135-166.

Viane, Lieslotte / Brems, Eva, *Transitional Justice and Cultural Contexts - Learning from the Universality Debate*, 2010 Netherlands Quarterly of Human Rights 28(2), 199-224.

Vinjamuri, Leslie / Snyder, Jack, *Law and Politics in Transitional Justice*, 2015 Annual Review of Political Science 18, 303-327.

von Arnauld, Andreas, *How to Illegalize Past Injustice – Reinterpreting the Rules of Intertemporality,* 2021 European Journal of International Law 32(2), 401-432.

von Haldenwang, Christian, *The Relevance of Legitimation – A new Framework for Analysis*, 2017 Contemporary Politics 23(3), 269-286.

von Soest, Christian / Grauvogel, Julia, *Identity, Procedures and Performance - How Authoritarian Regimes Legitimize Their Rule*, 2017 Contemporary Politics 23(3), 287-305.

Vrielink, Jogchum, *Symptomatic Symbolism - Banning the Face Veil 'as a Symbol'*, in: Brems, Eva (ed.), *The Experience of Face Veil Wearers in Europe and the Law,* 2014, Cambridge University Press (Cambridge),184-193.

Waldorf, Lars, *Institutional Gardening in Unsettled Times - Transitional Justice and Institutional Contexts*, in: Roger Duthie / Paul Seils (eds.), *Justice Mosaics - How Context Shapes Transitional Justice in Fractured Societies*, 2017, International Center for Transitional Justice (New York), 40-83.

Waldron, Jeremy, *Rights in Conflict*, 1989 Ethics 99(3), 503-519.

Walker, Margaret Urban, *Transformative Reparations? A Critical Look at a Current Trend in Thinking About Gender-Just Reparations,* 2015 International Journal of Transitional Justice 10(1), 108-125.

Warwick, Ben T. C., *Socio-Economic Rights During Economic Crises - A Changed Approach to Non-Retrogression*, 2016 International and Comparative Law Quarterly 65(1), 249-265.

Weakliem, David, *Public Opinion, Political Attitudes and Ideology*, in: Thomas Janoski / Robert Alford / Alexander Hicks / Mildred Schwartz (eds.), *The Handbook of Political Sociology - States, Civil Societies and Globalization*, 2005, Cambridge University Press (Cambridge), 227-246.

Weber, Sanne, *Trapped Between Promise and Reality in Colombia's Victims' Law - Reflections on Reparations, Development and Social Justice*, 2020 Bulletin of Latin American Research 39(1), 5-21.

Weiffen, Brigitte, *Transitional Justice - Eine Konzeptionelle Auseinandersetzung*, in: Anja Mihr / Gert Pickel / Susanne Pickel (eds.), *Handbuch Transitional Justice*, 2015, Springer (Wiesbaden), 1-21.

Weinrib, Ernest Joseph, *Corrective Justice in a Nutshell*, 2002 University of Toronto Law Journal 52(1), 349-356.

Weinrib, Ernest Joseph, *The Gains and Losses of Corrective Justice*, 1994 Duke Law Journal 44(2), 277-297.

Wenzel, Nicola, *Human Rights, Treaties, Extraterritorial Application and Effects*, in: Rüdiger Wolfrum (ed.), *Max Planck Encyclopedia of International Law*, Online Edition 2008, Oxford University Press (Oxford).

Williams, Sarah / Opdam, Jasmine, *The Unrealised Potential for Transformative Reparations for Sexual and Gender-Based Violence in Sierra Leone*, 2017 International Journal of Human Rights 21(9), 1281-1301.

Winter, Stephen, *Towards a Unified Theory of Transitional Justice*, 2013 International Journal of Transitional Justice 7(2), 224-244.

Wittich, Stephan, *Compensation*, in: Rüdiger Wolfrum (ed.) *Max Planck Encyclopedia of Public International Law*, Online Edition 2008, Oxford University Press (Oxford).

Wittich, Stephan, *Non-Material Damage and Monetary Reparation in International Law*, 2005 Finnish Yearbook of International Law, 321-368.

Wong, Pui-Hang, *How can Political Trust be Built After Civil Wars? Evidence From Post-Conflict Sierra Leone*, 2016 Journal of Peace Research 53(6), 772-785.

Wood, Michael, *The Rights of Victims to Reparation - The Importance of Clear Thinking*, 2018 Heidelberg Journal of International Law 78(3), 541-543.

Woodward, James, *Explanation in Social Theory - Comments on Alan Nelson*, 1986 Ethics 97(1), 187-195

Wouters, Jan / Verhoeven, Sten, *Prescription*, in: Rüdiger Wolfrum (ed.), *Max Planck Encyclopedia of International Law*, Online Edition 2008, Oxford University Press (Oxford).

Wühler, Norbert, *Reparations and Legal Succession – What Happens When the Victims Are Gone?*, 2018 Heidelberg Journal of International Law 78(3), 597-602.

Wyler, Eric / Papaux, Alain, *The Different Forms of Reparation - Satisfaction*, in: James Crawford / Alain Pellet / Simon Olleson (eds.), *The Law of International Responsibility*, 2010, Oxford University Press (Oxford), 623-637.

Yepes Uprimny, Rodrigo / Saffon, Maria Paula, *Reparaciones Transformadoras, Justicia Distributiva y Profundización Democrática*, in: Catalina Díaz / Nelson Camilo Sánchez / Rodrigo Uprimny (eds.), *Reparar en Colombia - Los Dilemas en Contextos de Conflicto, Pobreza y Exclusión*, 2009, DeJusticia (Bogotá), 31-70.

Yepes Uprimny, Rodrigo, *Transformative Reparations of Massive Gross Human Rights Violations - Between Corrective and Distributive Justice*, 2009 Netherlands Quarterly of Human Rights 27(4), 625-648.

Zahar, Marie-Joelle, *Fieldwork, Objectivity, and the Academic Enterprise*, in: Chandra Lekha Sriram / John C. King / Julie A. Mertus / Olga Martin-Ortega / Johanna Herman (eds.), *Surviving Field Research - Working in Violent and Difficult Situations*, 2009, Routledge (London), 191-212.

Zalaquett, Jose, *Balancing Ethical Imperatives and Political Constraints - The Dilemma of new Democracies Confronting Past Human Rights Violations*, 1992 Hastings Law Journal 43(6), 1425-1438.

United Nations Documents

Commission on Human Rights, *Situation of Human Rights in Afghanistan*, E/CN.4/1998/70, 21 April 1998.

Commission on Human Rights, *Study Concerning the Right to Restitution, Compensation and Rehabilitation for Victims of Gross Violations of Human Rights and Fundamental Freedoms – Final Report Submitted by Mr. Theo van Boven, Special Rapporteur*, E/CN.4/Sub.2/1993/8, 2 July 1993.

Committee Against Torture, *General Comment No. 3 of the Committee Against Torture - Implementation of Article 14 by States Parties*, CAT/C/GC/3, 19 November 2012.

Committee on Economic, Social and Cultural Rights, *Concluding Observations - Israel*, E/C.12/1/Add.90, 26 June 2003.

Committee on Economic, Social and Cultural Rights, *Concluding Observations on the Fourth Periodic Report of Argentina*, E/C.12/ARG/CO/4, 1 November 2018.

Committee on Economic, Social and Cultural Rights, *Concluding Observations on the Fourth Periodic Report of France*, E/C.12/FRA/CO/4, 13 July 2016.

Committee on Economic, Social and Cultural Rights, *An Evaluation of the Obligation to Take Steps to the "Maximum of Available Resources" Under an Optional Protocol to the Covenant*, E/C.12/2007/1, 10 May 2007.

Committee on Economic, Social and Cultural Rights, *General Comment No. 3 - The Nature of States Parties' Obligations*, E/1991/23, 14 December 1990.

Committee on Economic, Social and Cultural Rights, *General Comment No. 9 - The Domestic Application of the Covenant*, E/C.12/1998/24, 3 December 1998.

Committee on Economic, Social and Cultural Rights, *General Comment No. 13 - Right to Education*, E/C.12/1999/10, 8 December 1999.

Committee on Economic, Social and Cultural Rights, *General Comment No. 14 - The Right to the Highest Attainable Standard of Health*, E/C.12/2000/4, 11 August 2000.

Committee on Economic, Social and Cultural Rights, *General Comment No. 15 - The Right to Water*, E/C.12/2002/11, 20 January 2003.

Committee on Economic, Social and Cultural Rights, *General Comment No. 16 - The Equal Right of Men and Women to the Enjoyment of all Economic, Social and Cultural Rights (Art. 3 of the Covenant)*, E/C.12/2005/4, 11 August 2005.

Committee on Economic, Social and Cultural Rights, *General Comment No. 19 - The Right to Social Security*, E/C.12/GC/19, 23 November 2007.

Committee on Economic, Social and Cultural Rights, *General Comment No. 21 - Right of Everyone to Take Part in Cultural Life* E/C.12/GC/21, 21 December 2009.

Committee on Economic, Social and Cultural Rights, *General Comment No. 22 on the Right to Sexual and Reproductive Health*, E/C.12/GC/22, 2 May 2016.

Committee on Economic, Social and Cultural Rights, *Letter Dated 16 May 2012 Addressed by the Chairperson of the Committee on Economic, Social and Cultural Rights to States Parties to the International Covenant on Economic, Social and Cultural Rights*, 16 May 2012, available at: https://static.uni-graz.at/fileadmin/grazprocess/Letter_May2012.pdf.

Committee on Economic, Social and Cultural Rights, *The Limburg Principles on the Implementation of the International Covenant on Economic Social and Cultural Rights*, E/C.12/2000/13, Reissued Version, 2 October 2000.

Committee on Economic, Social and Cultural Rights, *The Maastricht Guidelines on Violations of Economic, Social and Cultural Rights*, E/C.12/2000/13, Reissued Version, 2 October 2000.

Committee on the Elimination of All Forms of Discrimination Against Women, *Consideration of Sixth Periodic Reports of States Parties - Sierra Leone*, CEDAW/C/SLE/6, 1 November 2012.

Committee on the Elimination of all Forms of Discrimination Against Women, *General Recommendation No. 28 on the Core Obligations of States Parties Under Article 2 of the Convention on the Elimination of All Forms of Discrimination Against Women*, CEDAW/C/GC/28, 16 December 2010.

CEDAW, *General Recommendation No. 30 on Women in Conflict Prevention, Conflict and Post-Conflict Situations*, CEDAW/C/GC/30, 18 October 2013.

Committee on the Elimination of all Forms of Discrimination Against Women, *General Recommendation No. 33 on Women's Access to Justice*, CEDAW/C/GC/33, 23 July 2015.

Committee on the Elimination of All Forms of Discrimination Against Women, *List of Issues and Questions in Relation to the Sixth Periodic Report of Sierra Leone - Replies of Sierra Leone*, CEDAW/C/SLE/Q/6/Add.1, 22 January 2014.

Committee on the Rights of the Child, *General Comment No. 5 - General Measures of Implementation of the Convention on the Rights of the Child*, CRC/GC/2003/5, 27 November 2003.

Economic and Social Council, *Principles on Housing and Property Restitution for Refugees and Displaced Persons*, E/CN.4/Sub.2/2005/17 Annex, 28 June 2005.

Economic and Social Council, *The Right to Redtitution, Compensation and Rehabilitation for Victims of Gross Violations of Human Rights and Fundamental Freedoms – Final Report of Special Rapporteur, Mr. M. Cherif Bassiouni, Submitted in Accordance With Commission Resolution 1999/33*, E/CN.4/2000/62, 18 January 2000.

Economic and Social Council, *Updated Set of Principles for the Protection and Promotion of Human Rights Through Action to Combat Impunity*, E/CN.4/2005/102/Add.1, 8 February 2005.

Economic and Social Council, *Updated Study on the Right to Food, Submitted by Mr. Asbjorn Eide*, E/CN.4/Sub.2/1999/12, 28 June 1999.

Human Rights Committee, *Concluding Observations of the Human Rights Committee - Central African Republic*, CCPR/C/CAF/CO/2, 25 July 2006.

Human Rights Committee, *Concluding Observations on the Initial Report of Sierra Leone*, CCPR/C/SLE/CO/1, 17 April 2014.

Human Rights Committee, *General Comment No. 6 - Article 6 (Right to Life)*, HRI/GEN/1/Rev.1, 30 April 1982.

Human Rights Committee, *General Comment No. 25 - Article 25 (Participation in Public Affairs and the Right to Vote)*, CCPR/C/21/Rev.1/Add.7, 12 July 1996.

Human Rights Committee, *General Comment No. 27 - Article 12 (Freedom of Movement)*, CCPR/C/21/Rev.1/Add.9, 2 November 1999.

Human Rights Committee, *General Comment No. 29 - Article 4: Derogations During a State of Emergency*, CCPR/C/21/Rev.1/Add.11, 31 August 2001.

Human Rights Committee, *General Comment No. 31 - The Nature of the General Legal Obligation Imposed on States Parties to the Covenant*, CCPR/C/21/Rev.1/Add.13, 26 May 2004.

Human Rights Committee, *General Comment No. 32 - Article 14: Right to Equality Before Courts and Tribunals and to Fair Trial*, CCPR/C/GC/32 (23 August 2007).

Human Rights Committee, *General Comment No. 34 - Article 19: Freedoms of Opinion and Expression*, CCPR/C/GC/34, 12 September 2011.

Human Rights Committee, *General Comment No. 36 on the Right to Life*, CCPR/C/GC/36, 30 October 2018.

Human Rights Committee, *Guidelines on Measures of Reparation Under the Optional Protocol to the International Covenant on Civil and Political Rights*, CCPR/C/158, 30 November 2016.

Human Rights Committee, *Report on Follow-Up to the Concluding Observations of the Human Rights Committee*, CCPR/C/119/2, 18 May 2017.

Human Rights Council, *Annual Report of the United Nations High Commissioner for Human Rights on the Situation of Human Rights in Colombia*, A/HRC/37/3/Add.3, 2 March 2018.

Human Rights Council, *Human Rights and Transitional Justice*, A/HRC/RES/21/15, 11 October 2012.

Human Rights Council, *Human Rights, Democracy and the Rule of Law*, A/HRC/RES/19/36, 19 April 2012.

Human Rights Council, *Report of the Special Rapporteur on Extrajudicial, Summary or Arbitrary Executions, Philip Alston - Mission to Colombia*, A/HRC/14/24/Add.2, 31 March 2010.

Human Rights Council, *Report of the Special Rapporteur on the Promotion of Truth, Justice, Reparation and Guarantees of Non-Recurrence*, A/HRC/34/62, 27 December 2016.

Human Rights Council, *Report of the Special Rapporteur on the Promotion of Truth, Justice, Reparation and Guarantees of Non-Recurrence*, A/HRC/42/45, 11 July 2019.

Human Rights Council, *Report of the Special Rapporteur on the Promotion of Truth, Justice, Reparation and Guarantees of Non-Recurrence, Pablo de Greiff*, A/69/518, 14 October 2014.

Human Rights Council, *Report of the Special Rapporteur on the Promotion of Truth, Justice, Reparation and Guarantees of Non-Recurrence, Pablo de Greiff*, A/HRC/30/42, 7 September 2015.

Human Rights Council, *Report of the Special Rapporteur on Violence Against Women, its Causes and Consequences, Rashida Manjoo*, A/HRC/14/22, 28 May 2014.

Human Rights Council, *Report of the Working Group of Experts on People of African Descent on its Mission to Germany*, A/HRC/36/60/Add.2, 15 August 2017.

Human Rights Council, *Situation of Human Rights in Libya, Including the Implementation of Technical Assistance and Capacity-Building and Efforts to Prevent and Ensure Accountability for Violations and Abuses of Human Rights*, A/HRC/40/46, 4 February 2019.

Human Rights Council, *Statement by Professor Philip Alston, UN Special Rapporteur on Extrajudicial Executions - Mission to Colombia 8-18 June 2009*, 19 June 2009, available at: https://reliefweb.int/report/colombia/statement-professor-philip-alston-un-special-rapporteur-extrajudicial-executions.

Human Rights Council, *Statement on the Protests Against Systemic Racism in the United States*, 5 June 2020, available at: https://www.ohchr.org/en/NewsEvents/Pages/DisplayNews.aspx?NewsID=25927&LangID=E.

International Commission of Inquiry on Darfur, *Report of the International Commission of Inquiry on Darfur to the United Nations Secretary-General – Pursuant to Security Council Resolution 1564 of 18 September 2004*, 25 January 2005.

International Law Commission, *Articles on State Responsibility*, A/56/10, 9 August 2001.

International Law Commission, *Draft Articles on Responsibility of States for Internationally Wrongful Acts - With Commentaries*, A/56/10, 9 August 2001.

International Law Commission, *Draft Articles on the Responsibility of International Organizations*, A/66/10, 2011.

International Law Commission, *Draft Conclusions on Identification of Customary International Law - With Commentaries*, A/73/10, 6 August 2018.

International Law Commission, *Fragmentation of International Law - Difficulties Arising From the Diversification and Expansion of International Law*, A/CN.4/L.682, 13 April 2006.

International Law Commission, *Report of the International Law Commissions - Fifty-Seventh Session (2 May - 3 June and 11 July - 5 August 2005)*, A/60/10, 2005.

International Law Commission, *Second Report on State Responsibility, by Mr. Gaetano Arangio-Ruiz, Special Rapporteur*, A/CN.4/425, 9 and 22 June 1989.

International Law Commission, *Third Report on State Responsibility by Mr. James Crawford, Special Rapporteur*, A/CN.4/507, 4 August 2000.

International Law Commission, *Third Report on State Responsibility, by Mr. Roberto Ago, Special Rapporteur*, A/CN.4/246, 18 May 1971.

Multi-Partner Trust Fund, *Enhancing Social Protection and Rehabilitation fo War Victims Through Reparations, Project Document*, May 2013, available at: http://mptf.undp.org/factsheet/project/00086861.

Multi-Partner Trust Fund, *Updated Consolidated Report on Projects Implemented Under the Sierra Leone Multi-Donor Trust Fund*, 27 May 2015, available at: http://mptf.undp.org/document/download/14591.

Office of the United Nations High Commissioner for Human Rights, Preliminary Observations from the Official Visit to Bosnia and Herzegovina by the Special Rapporteur on the Promotion of Truth, Justice, Reparation and Guarantees of Non-Recurrence, Mr. Fabián Salvioli (2-10 December 2021), 10 December 2021, available at: https://www.ohchr.org/EN/NewsEvents/Pages/DisplayNews.aspx?NewsID=27946&LangID=E.

Office of the United Nations High Commissioner for Human Rights, *Protection of Economic, Social and Cultural Rights in Conflict*, 2015, available at: https://www.ohchr.org/Documents/Issues/ESCR/E-2015-59.pdf.

Office of the United Nations High Commissioner for Human Rights, *Rule of Law Tools for Post-Conflict States - Reparation Programs*, available at: https://www.ohchr.org/Documents/Publications/ReparationsProgrammes.pdf.

Office of the United Nations High Commissioner for Human Rights, *Study on the Right to Truth*, E/CN.4/2006/91, 8 February 2006.

Peace Building Fund, *Final Programme Narrative Report*, PBF/SLE/A-4, 28 February 2010.

Peace Building Fund, *NaCSA/IOM Reparations Project Proposal*, PBF/SLE/A-4, 5 March 2008.

Secretary General of the United Nations, *Guidance Note of the Secretary-General on the United Nations Approach to Transitional Justice*, March 2010, available at: https://www.un.org/ruleoflaw/files/TJ_Guidance_Note_March_2010FINAL.pdf.

Secretary General of the United Nations, *The Rule of Law and Transitional Justice in Conflict and Post-Conflict Societies - Report of the Secretary-General*, S/2004/616, 23 August 2004.

United Nations, *On the Black Lives Matter Protests and other Mass Demonstrations against Systemic Racism and Police Brutality – Joint Reflexions by United Nations Senior African Officials*, 14 June 2020, available at: https://news.un.org/en/story/2020/06/1066242.

United Nations Development Program, *Evaluation of UNDP Assistance to Conflict-Affected Countries - Case Study Sierra Leone*, 2006, available at: http://web.undp.org/evaluation/documents/thematic/conflict/SierraLeone.pdf.

United Nations Development Program, *Programming for Justice - Access for All*, 2005, available at: https://www.asia-pacific.undp.org/content/rbap/en/home/library/democratic_governance/programming-for-justice.html.

United Nations Division for the Advancement of Women, *Good practices in Combating and Eliminating Violence Against Women - Report of the Expert Group Meeting*, 2005, available at: https://www.un.org/womenwatch/daw/egm/vaw-gp-2005/docs/FINALREPORT.goodpractices.pdf.

United Nations General Assembly, *Adverse Consequences for the Enjoyment of Human Rights of Political, Military, Economic and Other Forms of Assistance Given to Colonial and Racist Regimes in Southern Africa*, A/RES/33/23, 29 November 1978.

United Nations General Assembly, *Basic Principles and Guidelines on the Right to a Remedy and Reparation for Victims of Gross Violations of International Human Rights Law and Serious Violations of International Humanitarian Law*, A/RES/60/147, 16 December 2005.

United Nations General Assembly, *Contemporary Forms of Racism, Racial Discrimination, Xenophobia and Racial Intolerance - Note by the Secretary-General*, A/74/321, 21 August 2019.

United Nations General Assembly, *Declaration of Basic Principles of Justice for Victims of Crime and Abuse of Power*, A/RES/40/34, 29 November 1985.

United Nations General Assembly, *Declaration on the Protection of All Persons From Enforced Disappearance*, A/RES/47/133, 18 December 1992.

United Nations General Assembly, *Measures to Combat Contemporary Forms of Racism and Racial Discrimination, Xenophobia and Related Intolerance*, A/RES/56/267, 15 May 2002.

United Nations General Assembly, *The Situation in Bosnia and Herzegovina*, A/RES/46/242, 25 August 1992.

United Nations General Assembly, *Situation of Human Rights in Afghanistan*, A/RES/51/108, 12 December 1997.

United Nations General Assembly, *Situation of Human Rights in Afghanistan*, A/RES/53/165, 25 February 1999.

United Nations General Assembly, *Situation of Human Rights in the Republic of Bosnia and Herzegovina, the Republic of Croatia and the Federal Republic of Yugoslavia (Serbia and Montenegro)*, A/RES/49/196, 23 December 1994.

United Nations General Assembly, *Situation of Human Rights in the Territory of the Former Yugoslavia*, A/RES/47/147, 18 December 1992.

United Nations General Assembly, *Situation of Human Rights in the Territory of the Former Yugoslavia - Violations of Human Rights in the Republic of Bosnia and Herzegovina, the Republic of Coratia and the Federal Republic of Yugoslavia (Serbia and Montenegro)*, A/RES/48/153, 20 December 1993.

United Nations High Commissioner for Refugees, *Global Focus Colombia*, 2020, available at: http://reporting.unhcr.org/node/2542?y=2018 - year.

United Nations High Commissioner for Refugees, *Sexual and Gender-Based Violence against Refugees, Returnees and Internally Displaced Persons - Guidelines for Prevention and Response*, May 2003, available at: https://cms.emergency.unhcr.org/documents/11982/51689/UNHCR%2C+Sexual+and+Gender-Based+Violence+against+Refugees%2C+Returnees+and+Internally+Displaced+Persons.+Guidelines+for+Prevention+and+Response%2C+2003/9591f62d-4f6a-4faf-8c03-df0d6bacf871.

United Nations Security Council, *Fifth Report of the Secretary-General on the United Nations Observer Mission in Sierra Leone*, S/1999/237, 4 March 1999.

United Nations Security Council, *Report of the Secretary-General on the Protection of Civilians in Armed Conflict*, S/2009/277, 29 May 2009.

United Nations Security Council, *Resolution 687 (1991)*, S/RES/687 (1991), 8 April 1991.

United Nations Security Council, *Resolution 827 (1993)*, S/RES/827 (1993), 25 May 1993.

United Nations Security Council, *United Nations Verification Mission in Colombia - Report of the Secretary-General*, S/2019/780, 1 October 2019.

United Nations Women, *The Conflict did not Bring us Flowers - The Need for Comprehensive Reparations for Survivors of Conflict-Related Sexual Violence in Kosovo*, July 2016, available at: https://www.unwomen.org/en/digital-library/publications/2016/8/the-conflict-did-not-bring-us-flowers.

Working Group on Enforced or Involuntary Disappearances, *General Comment on Women Affected by Enforced Disappearances*, A/HRC/WGEID/98/2, 14 February 2013.

Other Documents of International Mechanisms

African Commission on Human and Peoples' Rights, *General Comment No. 3 on the African Charter on Human and Peoples' Rights - The Right to Life (Article 4)*, 4-18 November 2015.

African Commission on Human and Peoples' Rights, *General Comment No. 4 on the African Charter on Human and Peoples' Rights - The Right to Redress for Victims of Torture and Other Cruel, Inhuman or Degrading Punishment or Treatment (Article 5)*, 23 February - 4 March 2017.

African Commission on Human and Peoples' Rights, *Principles and Guidelines on the Right to a Fair Trial and Legal Assistance in Africa*, DOC/OS(XXX)247, 2003.

African Commission on Human and Peoples' Rights, *Study on Transitional Justice in Africa*, 2019.

African Court on Human and Peoples' Rights, *Comparative Study on the Law and Practice of Reparations for Human Rights Violations*, 2019

Assembly of States Parties, *Independent Expert Review of the International Criminal Court and the Rome Statute System – Final Report*, 30 September 2020.

European Court of Human Rights, *Guide on Article 6 of the European Convention on Human Rights*, Updated Version, 31 August 2019.

European Court of Human Rights, *Practice Directions - Just Satisfaction Claims*, 28 March 2007, available at: https://www.echr.coe.int/Documents/PD_satisfaction_claims_FRA.pdf.

Inter-American Commission on Human Rights, *Access to Justice as a Guarantee of Economic, Social, and Cultural Rights - A Review of the Standards Adopted by the Inter-American System of Human Rights*, OEA/Ser.L/V/II.129, 7 September 2007.

Inter-American Commission on Human Rights, *Annual Report of the Inter-American Commission on Human Rights 2012*, 6 June 2013.

Inter-American Commission on Human Rights, *Principal Guidelines for a Comprehensive Reparation Policy*, OEA/Ser/L/V/II.131, 19 February 2008.

Inter-American Commission on Human Rights, *Truth, Justice and Reparation in Transitional Context – Inter-American Standards*, OEA/Ser.L/V/II.Doc 121, 12 April 2021.

Inter-American Court of Human Rights, *Annual Report 2011*, 30 December 2011.

International Criminal Court, *Launch of the Information Campaign on the Opening of the Trial of Thomas Lubanga Dyilo in Ituri*, available at: https://www.icc-cpi.int/pages/item.aspx?name=launch+of+the+information+campaign+on+the+opening+of+the+trial+of+thomas+lu.

International Criminal Court, *Opening of the Trial in the Case of Germain Katanga and Mathieu Ngudjolo Chui on 24 November, 2009*, 20 November 2009, available at: https://www.icc-cpi.int/pages/item.aspx?name=PR477.

International Criminal Court, *The Role of the ICC in the Transitional Justice Process in Colombia - Speech by James Stewart, Deputy Prosecutor of the International Criminal Court*, 30-31 May 2018, available at: https://www.icc-cpi.int/iccdocs/otp/201805SpeechDP.pdf.

Miscellaneous

Abdelrahim, Jaled, *Puerto Barrío - La Ciudad Donde se Adoptan los Muertos,* El País, 29 September 2012, available at: https://blogs.elpais.com/kilometro-sur/2012/09/puerto-berr%C3%ADo-la-ciudad-donde-se-adoptan-los-muertos.html.

African Union, *Transitional Justice Policy,*February 2019, available at: https://au.int/sites/default/files/documents/36541-doc-au_tj_policy_eng_web.pdf.

Ammann, Odile, *On the Interpretability of Customary International Law – A Response to Nina Mileva and Marina Fortuna,* Opinio Juris, 7 October 2019, available at: http://opiniojuris.org/2019/10/07/on-the-interpretability-of-customary-international-law-a-response-to-nina-mileva-and-marina-fortuna/.

Ambos, Kai, *Another Challenge for Colombia's Transitional Justice Process - Aggravated Differential Treatment between Armed Forces and FARC*, EJIL:Talk!, 19 October 2018, available at: https://www.ejiltalk.org/another-challenge-for-colombias-transitional-justice-process-aggravated-differential-treatment-between-armed-forces-and-farc/.

Ambos, Kai, *Transitional Justice Without Truth?*, EJIL:Talk!, 27 August 2018, available at: https://www.ejiltalk.org/transitional-justice-without-truth/.

Amnesty International, *Living Insecurity - How Germany is Failing Victims of Racist Violence,* June 2016, available at: https://www.amnesty.org/download/Documents/EUR2341122016ENGLISH.PDF.

Amnesty International, *Sierra Leone - Getting Reparations Right for Survivors of Sexual Violence*, AFR 51/005/2007, 16 October 2007, available at: https://www.amnesty.org/en/documents/AFR51/005/2007/en/.

Apoyo a Víctimas de Violencia Socio-Político Pro Recuperación Emocional, *Aspectos Psicosociales de la Reparación Integral*, 2006, available at: http://corporacionavre.org/wp-content/uploads/2015/03/psicosocial1.pdf.

Baier, Annette, *Trust - The Tanner Lectures on Human Values*, available at: https://tannerlectures.utah.edu/_documents/a-to-z/b/baier92.pdf.

Berghs, Maria / Conteh, Edward, *'Mi At Don Poil' - A Report on Reparations in Sierra Leone for Amputee and War-Wounded People*, 2014, available at: https://www.researchgate.net/publication/263931738_'Mi_At_Don_Poil'_A_Report_on_Reparations_in_Sierra_Leone_for_Amputee_and_War-_Wounded_People.

Bermúdez Liévano, Andrés, *More Time to Redress Colombia's Victims - The Question is How*, JusticeInfo.net, 24 October 2019, available at: https://www.justiceinfo.net/en/reparations/42712-more-time-to-redress-colombia-victims-question-is-how.html.

Bermúdez Liévano, Andrés, *Will Colombia's FARC be Allowed to Clear Mines to Repair Their Victims?*, Justiceinfo.net, 2 March 2020, available at: https://www.justiceinfo.net/en/43929-will-colombia-farc-be-allowed-to-clear-mines-to-repair-their-victims.html.

Bradley, Sean / Maughan, Philippe / Fusato, Massimo, *Sierra Leone - Disarmament, Demobilization and Reintegration (DDR)*, 2002 World Bank Africa Region Findings & Good Practice Infobriefs No. 81.

Burt, Jo-Marie, *Transitional Justice in the Aftermath of Civil Conflict - Lessons from Peru, Guatemala and El Salvador*, 2018, available at: http://www.dplf.org/sites/default/files/pictures/transitional_justice_final.pdf.

CARICOM Reparations Commission, *10-Point Reparation Plan*, available at: https://caricomreparations.org/caricom/caricoms-10-point-reparation-plan/.

Casa de la Mujer, *Primera Encuesta de Prevalencia - Violencia Sexual en Contra de las Mujeres en el Contexto del Conflicto Armado Colombiano 2001-2009*, 2011, available at: https://reliefweb.int/sites/reliefweb.int/files/resources/2011-03-23-Report-Espanol.pdf.

Centre on Housing Rights and Evictions, *Housing Rights in West Africa - Report of Four Fact-Finding Missions*, 2004, available at: https://www.humanitarianlibrary.org/sites/default/files/2013/08/COHRE_HousingRightsInWestAfricaDraft.pdf.

Centro de Investigación y Educación Popular, Programa Para la Paz, *Reparación Psicosocial*, 2011, available at: http://datoscolombianuncamas.org/images/abook_file/reparacion psicosocial.pdf.

Centro Nacional de Memoria Histórica, *¡Basta Ya! Colombia - Memorias de Guerra y Dignindad*, 2014, available at: http://centrodememoriahistorica.gov.co/descargas/informes2013/bastaYa/basta-ya-colombia-memorias-de-guerra-y-dignidad-2016.pdf.

Centro Nacional de Memoria Histórica, *Entre la Incertidumbre y el Dolor - Impactos Psicosociales de la Desaparición Forzada*, 2014, available at: http://www.centrodememoriahistorica.gov.co/descargas/informes2014/desaparicion-forzada/Tomo-III.pdf.

Centro Nacional de Memoria Histórica, *La Guerra Inscrita en el Cuerpo*, 2017, available at: http://www.centrodememoriahistorica.gov.co/descargas/informes-accesibles/guerra-inscrita-en-el-cuerpo_accesible.pdf.

Centro Nacional de Memoria Histórica, *Una Nación Desplazada - Informe Nacional del Desplazamiento Forzado en Colombia*, 2015, available at: http://www.centrodememoriahistorica.gov.co/descargas/informes2015/nacion-desplazada/una-nacion-desplazada.pdf.

Colectivo de Abogados "José Alvear Restrepo" et al., *Organizaciones y Víctimas Exigimos Mayor Compromiso del Congreso con el Acuerdo de Paz*, 23 May 2017, available at: https://www.colectivodeabogados.org/?Organizaciones-y-victimas-exigimos-mayor-compromiso-del-Congreso-con-la.

Comisión Colombiana de Juristas, *Radiografía de la Restitución de Tierras en Colombia - Informe Presentado Ante la Comisión Interamericana de Derechos Humanos por Incumplimiento de Reparación a las Víctimas Despojadas de Tierras en Colombia*, 2019, available at: https://www.coljuristas.org/documentos/tmp/Radiografia_de_la_restitucion_de_tierras_en_Colombia_2019.pdf.

Comisión Colombiana de Juristas et al., *Panorama de Violaciones al Derecho a la Vida, Libertad e Integridad de Líderes Sociales y Defensores de Derechos Humanos en 2016 y Primer Semestre de 2017*, October 2017, available at: http://www.coljuristas.org/documentos/libros_e_informes/panorama_de_violaciones_a_lideres_y_defensores_2016-2017.pdf.

Comisión para el Esclarecimieto de la Verdad, la Convivencia y la No Repetición, *Hay Futuro si hay Verdad*, 2022, available at: https://www.comisiondelaverdad.co/hay-futuro-si-hay-verdad.

Comisión de Seguimiento y Monitoreo a la Implementación de la Ley 1448 de 2011, *Cuarto Informe al Congreso de la República Sobre la Implementación de la Ley de Víctimas y Restitución de Tierras*, August 2017, available at: https://www.contraloria.gov.co/contraloria/talento-humano?p_p_id=101&p_p_lifecycle=0&p_p_state=maximized&p_p_mode=view&_101_struts_action=%2Fasset_publisher%2Fview_content&_101_assetEntryId=790533&_101_type=document&inheritRedirect=false.

Comisión de Seguimiento y Monitoreo a la Implementación de la Ley 1448 de 2011, *Quinto Informe de Seguimiento al Congreso de la República 2017-2018*, 17 August 2018, available at: https://www.procuraduria.gov.co/portal/media/file/180822-quinto-informe-ley-victimas.pdf.

Comisión de Seguimiento y Monitoreo a la Implementación de la Ley 1448 de 2011, *Segundo Informe de Seguimiento y Monitoreo a la Implementación de la Ley de Víctimas y Restitución de Tierras 2012-2013*, August 2013, available at: https://www.contraloria.gov.co/documents/20181/462047/Informe+final+Victimas+2013-segundo+informe.pdf/480618da-b3da-4284-90d7-77ef5d442720?version=1.0.

Comisión de Seguimiento y Monitoreo a la Implementación de la Ley 1448 de 2011, *Sexto Informe de Seguimiento al Congreso de la República 2018-2019*, 16 August 2019, available at: https://www.procuraduria.gov.co/portal/media/file/sexto_informe_seguimiento_congreso_ republica_2018_2019.pdf.

Comisión Histórica del Conflicto y sus Víctimas, *Contribución al Entendimiento del Conflicto Armado en Colombia*, February 2015, available at: http://www.humanas.unal.edu.co/observapazyconflicto/files/5714/6911/9376/Version_final_informes_CHCV.pdf.

Consejo Nacional de Política Económica y Social República de Colombia, *Política Para la Adopción e Implementación de un Catastro Multipropósito Rural-Urbano (CONPES 3859)*, 13 June 2016, available at: https://colaboracion.dnp.gov.co/CDT/Conpes/Económicos/3859.pdf.

Consultoria Para los Derechos Humanos y el Desplazamiento / United States Agency for International Development, *13 Propuestas Para la Adecuación Participativa de la Normativa Sobre Víctimas al Acuerdo Final de Paz Entre las FARC-EP y el Gobierno de Colombia - Aportes Para la Implementación del Subpunto 5.1.3.7*, 2017, available at: https://www.codhes.org/~codhes/images/TRECE_propuestas.pdf.

Correa, Cristián, *Inter-American Court's Dangerous Precedent in Limiting Insurgents' Right to Reparations*, JusticeInfo.net, 2 September 2015, available at: https://www.justiceinfo.net/en/tribunals/1862-inter-american-court-s-dangerous-precedent-in-limiting-insurgents-right-to-reparations.html.

Corte Constitucional Amplió la Vigencia de la Ley de Víctimas, El Espectador, 5 December 2019, available at: https://www.elespectador.com/noticias/judicial/corte-constitucional-amplio-la-vigencia-de-la-ley-de-victimas-articulo-894429.

Council of Europe, *Eradicating Impunity for Serious Human Rights Violations - Guidelines Adopted by the Committee of Ministers on 30 March 2011 at the 1110th Meeting of the Ministers' Deputies*, H/Inf (2011) 7, 30 March 2011.

Council of the European Union, *Council Conclusions on EU's Support to Transitional Justice*, 13576/15 Annex, 16 November 2015.

Council of the European Union, *The EU's Policy Framework on Support to Transitional Justice*, 13576/15 Annex to Annex, 16 November 2015.

de Luca, Giacomo / Verpoorten, Marijke, *From Vice to Virtue? Civil War and Social Capital in Uganda - LICOS Discussion Paper Series 298/2011*, 2011, Leuven University (Leuven).

de Vos, Dieneke, *Colombia's Constitutional Court Issues Landmark Decision Recognising Victims of Reproductive Violence in Conflict*, IntLawGrrls, 11 January 2020, available at: https://ilg2.org/2020/01/11/colombias-constitutional-court-issues-landmark-decision-recognising-victims-of-reproductive-violence-in-conflict/.

DeJusticia, *Coadyuvancia a Solicitud de Suspensión Provisional de los Efectos del Decreto 1167 de 2018, por el Cual se Modifica el Artículo 2.15.1.1.16 del Decreto 1071 de 2015*, 19 November 2018, available at: https://www.dejusticia.org/wp-content/uploads/2018/11/Coadyuvancia-a-solicitud-de-suspensión-provisional-de-los-efectos-del-Decreto-1167-de-2018.pdf.

Denov, Myriam, *Child Soldiers in Sierra Leone - Experiences, Implications and Strategies for Rehabilitation and Community Reintegration*, August 2005, available at: http://www.operationspaix.net/DATA/DOCUMENT/5552~v~Child_Soldiers_in_Sierra_Leone__Experiences_Implications_and_Strategies_for_Rehabilitation_and_Community_Reintegration.pdf.

Duffy, Helen, *Articles on Responsibility of States for Internationally Wrongful Acts and Human Rights Practice*, EJIL:Talk!, 5 August 2021, available at: https://www.ejiltalk.org/articles-on-responsibility-of-states-for-internationally-wrongful-acts-and-human-rights-practice/.

Duffy, Helen, *Georgia v. Russia – Jurisdiction, Chaos and Conflict at the European Court of Human Rights*, JustSecurity, 2 February 2021, available at: https://www.justsecurity.org/74465/georgia-v-russia-jurisdiction-chaos-and-conflict-at-the-european-court-of-human-rights/.

El-Zein, Jamal / Langmack, Fin-Jasper, *Conceptualizing Guarantees of Non-Repetition - Chances and Risks for Human Rights Jurisprudence*, Conference Paper Presented at: AHRI Conference 2018 (Edinburgh), on file with the author.

Forensic Architecture, *Pushbacks in Melilla – ND and NT v. Spain*, 15 June 2020, available at: https://forensic-architecture.org/investigation/pushbacks-in-melilla-nd-and-nt-vs-spain.

Government of Sierra Leone, *White Paper on the Truth and Reconciliation Report*, 29 June 2005, available at: https://witness.typepad.com/gillian_in_salone/files/whitepaper2.pdf.

Guillerot, Julie, *Reparations in Peru - 15 Years of Delivering Redress*, September 2019, available at: https://reparations.qub.ac.uk/report-reparations-in-peru-15-years-of-delivering-redress/.

HOPE - Sierra Leone, *Report of Symbolic Reparations (Memorials and Reburials) - Bomaru, Kailahun District, 21st - 23rd March 2009*, 2009, available at: https://www.iofc.org/sites/default/files/media/document/sy/symbolic_reparations_bomaru_21-23_march_2009_with_corrections_22_jan_2010_1.pdf.

Humala Sobre Chavín de Huántar - No voy a Dar ni un Sol a los Terroristas, RPP Noticias, 26 June 2015, available at: https://rpp.pe/politica/actualidad/humala-sobre-chavin-de-huantar-no-voy-a-dar-ni-un-sol-a-los-terroristas-noticia-811351.

Human Rights Center at the University of California, Berkeley, School of Law, *The Victims' Court? A Study of 622 Victim Participants at the International Criminal Court*, 2015, available at: https://www.law.berkeley.edu/wp-content/uploads/2015/04/VP_report_2015_final_full2.pdf.

Human Rights Watch, *African Union - No Reparations for Ex-Chad President's Victims*, 26 January 2021, available at: https://www.hrw.org/news/2021/01/26/african-union-no-reparations-ex-chad-presidents-victims.

Human Rights Watch, *"We'll Kill You if You Cry" - Sexual Violence in the Sierra Leone Conflict*, January 2003, available at: https://www.hrw.org/report/2003/01/16/well-kill-you-if-you-cry/sexual-violence-sierra-leone-conflict.

Integrated Regional Information Network News, *Lack of Aid Funds for Amputees, Rape Survivors, War Widows*, 23 February 2009, available at: http://www.irinnews.org/report/83100/sierra-leone-lack-aid-funds-amputees-rape-survivors-war-widows.

Internal Displacement Monitoring Centre, *Global Report on Internal Displacement*, 2020, available at: https://www.internal-displacement.org/global-report/grid2020/.

International Center for Transitional Justice, *Dealing With the 2006 Internal Displacement Crisis in Timor-Leste - Between Reparations and Humanitarian Policymaking*, 8 July 2012, available at: https://www.ictj.org/publication/dealing-2006-internal-displacement-crisis-timor-leste-between-reparations-and.

International Center for Transitional Justice, *Estudio Sobre la Implementación del Programa de Reparación Individual en Colombia*, 2015, available at: https://www.ictj.org/sites/default/files/ICTJ-COL-Estudio-reparacion-individual-2015.pdf.

International Center for Transitional Justice, *From Principles to Practice - Challenges of Implementing Reparations for Massive Violations in Colombia*, 19 October 2015, available at: https://www.ictj.org/sites/default/files/ICTJ_Report_ColombiaReparationsChallenges_2015.pdf.

International Center for Transitional Justice, *An Overview of Conflict in Colombia*, 2009, available at: https://www.ictj.org/sites/default/files/ICTJ-Colombia-Conflict-Facts-2009-English.pdf.

International Center for Transitional Justice, *Reparations in Peru - From Recommendations to Implementation*, 26 June 2013, available at: https://www.ictj.org/publication/reparations-peru-recommendations-implementation.

International Center for Transitional Justice, *Reparations in Theory and Practice*, 2007, available at: https://www.ictj.org/sites/default/files/ICTJ-Global-Reparations-Practice-2007-English.pdf.

International Center for Transitional Justice, *Report and Proposals for the Implementation of Reparations in Sierra Leone*, 1 December 2009, available at: https://www.ictj.org/publication/report-and-proposals-implementation-reparations-sierra-leone.

International Center for Transitional Justice, *Transitional Justice and DDR - The Case of Sierra Leone*, June 2009, available at: https://www.ictj.org/sites/default/files/ICTJ-DDR-Sierra-Leone-CaseStudy-2009-English.pdf.

International Center for Transitional Justice, *Transitional Justice in Morocco - A Progress Report*, 1 November 2005, available at: https://www.ictj.org/publication/transitional-justice-morocco-progress-report.

International Center for Transitional Justice, *What is Transitional Justice?*, 2009, available at: https://www.ictj.org/sites/default/files/ICTJ-Global-Transitional-Justice-2009-English.pdf.

International Law Association, *The Hague Conference (2010) - Reparation for Victims of Armed Conflict*, 2010 Conference Reports, 291-345.

International Law Association, *Reparation for Victims of Armed Conflict*, Resolution 1/2014, 7-11 April 2014.

International Organisation for Migration, *Four Decades of Cross-Mediterranean Undocumented Migration to Europe - A Review of the Evidence*, 2017, available at: https://publications.iom.int/books/four-decades-cross-mediterranean-undocumented-migration-europe-review-evidence.

International Organization for Migration, *What Hope of Reparations for Sierra Leone's War Victims?*, 17 November 2009, available at: https://www.iom.int/migrant-stories/what-hope-reparations-sierra-leones-war-victims.

KROC Institute for International Peace Studies, *Tercer Informe Sobre el Estado de Implementación del Acuerdo de Paz de Colombia*, available at: https://kroc.nd.edu/assets/321729/190523_informe_3_final_final.pdf.

Langmack, Fin-Jasper, *Reforming Land Restitution – A Concerted Effort to Derail Colombia's Transitional Justice System?*, EJIL:Talk!, 2 November 2018, available at: https://www.ejiltalk.org/reforming-land-restitution-a-concerted-effort-to-derail-colombias-transitional-justice-system/.

Levy, Shoshana, *Can Colombia's Special Jurisdiction for Peace be Considered Slow? A Preliminary Comparative Study of Trials of International Crimes,* Justice in Conflict 2021, available at: https://justiceinconflict.org/2021/03/03/can-colombias-special-jurisdiction-for-peace-be-considered-slow-a-preliminary-comparative-study-of-trials-for-international-crimes/.

Marc, Alexandre / Willman, Alys / Aslam, Ghazia / Rebosio, Michelle / Balasuriya, Kanishka, *Societal Dynamics and Fragility - Engaging Societies in Responding to Fragile Situations*, 2013, available at: https://issuu.com/world.bank.publications/docs/9780821396568/1?e=1107022/2829928.

Markard, Nora, *A Hole of Unclear Dimensions – Reading ND and NT v. Spain*, EU Immigration and Asylum Law and Policy, 1 April 2020, available at: http://eumigrationlawblog.eu/a-hole-of-unclear-dimensions-reading-nd-and-nt-v-spain/.

Martínez, Denis / Gómez, Luisa, *A Promise to be Fulfilled - Reparations for Victims of the Armed Conflict in Guatemala*, August 2019, available at: https://reparations.qub.ac.uk/assets/uploads/Guatemalan-Report-ENG-LR.pdf.

Mauritius Truth and Justice Commission, *Report of the Truth and Justice Commission Volume 1*, November 2011, available at: https://www.usip.org/sites/default/files/ROL/TJC_Vol1.pdf

Mazurana, Dyan / Carlson, Khristopher, *From Combat to Community - Women and Girls of Sierra Leone*, 2004, available at: https://www.peacewomen.org/assets/file/Resources/NGO/PartPPGIssueDisp_CombatToCommunty_WomenWagePeace_2004.pdf.

McVeigh, Karen, *2017 was the Deadliest Year on Record for Colombian Human Rights Defenders,* The Guardian, 1 May 2018, available at: https://www.theguardian.com/global-development/2018/may/01/2017-deadliest-year-on-record-colombian-human-rights-defenders.

Merriam-Webster, *They - Pronoun,* Online Edition 2021, available at: https://www.merriam-webster.com/dictionary/they.

Merriam-Webster, *Words We're Watching - Singular "They"*, available at: https://www.merriam-webster.com/words-at-play/singular-nonbinary-they.

Ministerio del Interior de Colombia, *El Enfoque Diferencial y Étnico en la Política Pública de Víctimas del Conflicto Armado*, 2015, available at: https://gapv.mininterior.gov.co/sites/default/files/cartilla_enfoque_diferencial_fin_1.pdf.

Moffett, Luke, *Reparations at the ICC - Can it Really Serve as a Model?*, 19 July 2019, available at: https://www.justiceinfo.net/en/justiceinfo-comment-and-debate/opinion/41949-reparations-at-the-icc-can-it-really-serve-as-a-model.html.

Moffett, Luke, *Reparations in Transitional Justice - Justice or Political Compromise?*, 2019 Queen's University Research Paper 2019-07.

Mollay, Sean/Bell, Christine/Welikala, Asanga/Houlihan, Erin, *Emergency Law Responses and Conflict-Affected States in Transition*, Verfassungsblog, 13 March 2021, available at: https://verfassungsblog.de/emergency-law-responses-and-conflict-affected-states-in-transition/.

Montes Alba, Andrés, *El Reclamo de las Víctimas al Gobierno por Demoras en las Indemnizaciones,* El Espectador, 21 February 2018, available at: https://www.elespectador.com/noticias/nacional/el-reclamo-de-las-victimas-al-gobierno-por-demoras-en-las-indemnizaciones-articulo-740308.

Nairobi Declaration on Women's and Girls' Right to a Remedy and Reparation, 2007, available at: https://www.fidh.org/IMG/pdf/NAIROBI_DECLARATIONeng.pdf.

National African American Reparations Commission, *Preliminary Reparations Program – A Document for Review, Revision and Adoption as a Platform to Guide the Struggle for Reprations for People of African Descent in the U.S.,* 18 September 2015, available at: https://ibw21.org/docs/naarc/NAARC_Preliminary_Reparations_Program.pdf.

National Commission for Social Action, *Annual Report 2014*, 2014, available at: http://www.nacsa.gov.sl/documents/NaCSA-Annual-Report-2014.pdf.

National Commission for Social Action, *Annual Report 2015*, 2015, available at: http://www.nacsa.gov.sl/documents/NaCSA-Annual-Report-2015.pdf.

National Commission for Social Action, *NaCSA Pays 2,250 Female War Victims Nationwide*, 7 October 2019, available at: http://www.nacsa.gov.sl/news/nacsa-pays-2250-female-war-victims-nationwide.html.

National Commission for Social Action, *Sierra Leone Reparations Programme Newsletter*, October 2016, available at: http://www.nacsa.gov.sl/documents/Reparations-Newsletter-1st-Edition.pdf.

National Commission for Social Action, *Statistical Overview of Administered Reparations*, on file with the author.

Oficina de Promoción Social, *Programa de Atención Psicosocial y Salud Integral a Víctimas del Conflicto Armado - Documento Marco*, 2017, available at: https://www.minsalud.gov.co/sites/rid/Lists/BibliotecaDigital/RIDE/DE/PS/Documento-Marco-papsivi-2017.pdf.

Oficina de Promoción Social, *Programa de Atención Psicosocial y Salud Integral a Víctimas en el Marco de la Ley 1448 de 2011 - Versión 2 Justada*, 2012, available at: https://www.minsalud.gov.co/Documentos y Publicaciones/PAPSIVI VERSION PRELIMINAR 25 Febrero 2013.doc.

Ottendörfer, Eva, *The Fortunate Ones and the Ones Still Waiting - Reparations for War Victims in Sierra Leone*, 2014, available at: https://www.hsfk.de/fileadmin/HSFK/hsfk_downloads/prif129.pdf.

Pellet, Alain, *"Human Rightism" and International Law - Gilberto Amado Memorial Lecture*, 2000, available at: http://pellet.actu.com/wp-content/uploads/2016/02/PELLET-2000-Human-rightism-and-international-law-G.-Amado.pdf.

Peruvian Truth and Reconciliation Commission, *Final Report*, 2003, available at: https://www.cverdad.org.pe/ingles/ifinal/index.php

Physicians for Human Rights, *War-Related Sexual Violence in Sierra Leone - A Population-Based Assessment*, 2002, available at: https://phr.org/wp-content/uploads/2002/06/sierra-leone-sexual-violence-2002.pdf.

Preparatory Committee, *Article 66 - Reparations to Victims: Rolling Text*, UD/A/AC-249/1998/WG-4/IP, 21 March 1998.

Preparatory Committee, *Report of the Preparatory Committee on the Establishment of an International Criminal Court*, A/Conf.183/2/Add.1, 14 April 1998.

President Koroma Apologizes to Sierra Leonean Women, Sierra Express Media, 29 March 2010, available at: http://sierraexpressmedia.com/?p=6911.

Procuraduría General de la Nación, *Primer Informe al Congreso Sobre el Estado de Avance de la Implementación del Acuerdo de Paz 2016 - 2019* August 2019, available at: https://www.procuraduria.gov.co/portal/media/file/Primer informe al Congreso sobre el estado de avance de la Implementación%20del%20Acuerdo%20de%20Paz%202016%20-%202019.pdf.

Programa por la Paz, *La Viga en el Ojo*, 2003, available at: https://issuu.com/cinepppp/docs/propaz_costosdelaguerra.

Raimondo, Giulia, *N.D. and N.T. v Spain - A Slippery Slope for the Protection of Irregular Migrants*, Border Criminologies, 20 April 2020, available at: https://www.law.ox.ac.uk/research-subject-groups/centre-criminology/centreborder-criminologies/blog/2020/04/nd-and-nt-v-spain.

Redress, *Rehabilitation as a Form of Reparation Under International Law*, December 2009, available at: https://redress.org/wp-content/uploads/2018/01/The-right-to-rehabilitation.pdf.

Rivera, Juan Camilo, *Opinión - ¿Pueden los/las ex FARC ser Considerados Víctimas?*, 2020 ICON-S Colombia, available at: https://www.eafit.edu.co/escuelas/derecho/iconscolombia/Paginas/opinion-pueden-los-las-ex-farc-ser-considerados-victimas.aspx.

Sanchez, Camilo / Rudling, Adriana, *Reparations in Colombia - Where to? Mapping the Colombian Landscape of Reparations for Victims of the Internal Armed Conflict*, February 2019, available at: https://reparations.qub.ac.uk/assets/uploads/ColombiaReparationsPolicyReportFORAPPROVAL-SP-HR-NoCrops.pdf.

Secretaría Técnica del Componente de Verificación Internacional / Centro de Investigación y Educación Popular / Programa por la Paz / Centro de Recursos para el Análisis de Conflictos, *Cuarto Informe de Verificación de la Implementación del Acuerdo Final de Paz en Colombia Para los Verificadores Internacionales Felipe González y José Mujica*, 29 November 2019, available at: https://www.cinep.org.co/Home2/component/k2/647-cuarto-informe-de-verificacion-de-la-implementacion-del-acuerdo-final-de-paz-en-colombia-para-los-verificadores-internacionales.html.

Secretaría Técnica del Componente de Verificación Internacional / Centro de Investigación y Educación Popular, Programa por la Paz / Centro de Recursos para el Análisis de Conflictos, *Primer Informe de Verificación del Primer Año de Implementación del Acuerdo Final de Paz en Colombia Para los Verificadores Internacionales Felipe González y José Mujica*, February 2018, available at: https://www.cinep.org.co/images/csivi/Primer-Informe-STCVI---Febrero-2018.pdf.

Secretaría Técnica del Componente de Verificación Internacional / Centro de Investigación y Educación Popular, Programa por la Paz / Centro de Recursos para el Análisis de Conflictos, *Quinto Informe de Verificación de la Implementación del Acuerdo Final de Paz en Colombia Para los Verificadores Internacionales Felipe González y José Mujica*, 4 March 2019, available at: https://www.cinep.org.co/Home2/component/k2/670-quinto-informe-de-verificacion-de-la-implementacion-del-acuerdo-final-de-paz-en-colombia-para-los-verificadores-internacionales.html.

Secretaría Técnica del Componente de Verificación Internacional / Centro de Investigación y Educación Popular, Programa por la Paz / Centro de Recursos para el Análisis de Conflictos, *Segundo Informe de Verificación de la Implementación del Acuerdo Final de Paz en Colombia Para los Verificadores Internacionales Felipe González y José Mujica* May 2018, available at: https://www.cinep.org.co/publicaciones/es/producto/segundo-informe-de-verificacion-de-la-implementacion-del-acuerdo-final-de-paz-en-colombia-para-los-verificadores-internacionales-felipe-gonzalez-y-jose-mujica-a-f-6-3-2/.

Secretaría Técnica del Componente de Verificación Internacional / Centro de Investigación y Educación Popular, Programa por la Paz / Centro de Recursos para el Análisis de Conflictos, *Sexto Informe de Verificación de la Implementación del Acuerdo Final de Paz en Colombia Para los Verificadores Internacionales Felipe González y José Mujica*, 19 June 2019, available at: https://www.cinep.org.co/Home2/component/k2/704-sexto-informe-de-verificacion-de-la-implementacion-del-acuerdo-final-de-paz-en-colombia-para-los-verificadores-internacionales.html.

Secretaría Técnica del Componente de Verificación Internacional / Centro de Investigación y Educación Popular, Programa por la Paz / Centro de Recursos para el Análisis de Conflictos, *Tercer Informe de Verificación del Primer Año de Implementación del Acuerdo Final de Paz en Colombia Para los Verificadores Internacionales Felipe González y José Mujica* August 2018, available at: https://www.cinep.org.co/Home2/component/k2/624-tercer-informe-de-verificacion-de-la-implementacion-del-acuerdo-final-de-paz-en-colombia-para-los-verificadores-internacionales.html.

Sharma, Govinda / Gallen, James / Moffett, Luke / Pokharel, Laxmi, *From Relief to Redress - Reparations in Post-Conflict Nepal*, October 2019, available at: https://reparations.qub.ac.uk/assets/uploads/QUB-Nepal_Report_ENG_DP.pdf.

Sierra Leone Truth and Reconciliation Commission, *Witness to Truth - Final Report of the Truth and Reconciliation Commission*, 5 October 2004, available at: http://www.sierraleonetrc.org/index.php/view-the-final-report/table-of-contents.

Sikkink, Kathryn / Pham, Phuong / Johnson, Douglas / Dixon, Peter / Marchesi, Bridget / Vinck, Patrick, *Evaluation of Integral Reparations Measures in Colombia - Executive Summary*, 2015, available at: https://pdf.usaid.gov/pdf_docs/PA00KSXQ.pdf.

Subcomité Técnico de Medidas de Satisfacción, *Guía de Medidas de Satisfacción*, available at: https://gapv.mininterior.gov.co/sites/default/files/guia_de_medidas_de_satisfaccion.pdf.

The Siracusa Principles on the Limitation and Derogation Provisions in the International Covenant on Civil and Political Rights, 1985 Human Rights Quarterly 7(1), 3-14.

Truth and Reconciliation Commission of Canada, *Honouring the Truth, Reconciling the Future - Summary of the Final Report of the Truth and Reconciliation Commission of Canada*, available at: http://nctr.ca/assets/reports/Final Reports/Executive_Summary_English_Web.pdf.

Unidad Administrativa Especial de Gestión de Restitución de Tierras Despojadas, *RUPTA - Registro Único de Predios y Territorios Abandonados*, November 2017, available at: https://www.restituciondetierras.gov.co/documents/10184/34449/CARTILLA+RUPTA.pdf/5208e6c9-ce38-4fae-b47a-2142ae428954.

Unidad de Restitución de Tierras, *ABC Para Jueces en Materia de Restitución de Tierras*, 2012, available at: https://www.restituciondetierras.gov.co/documents/10184/227457/ABC.pdf/96b6eb53-16c4-42bc-8a0f-8be383c05c58.

Unidad de Restitución de Tierras, *Programa Proyectos Productivos Para Población Beneficiaria de Restitución de Tierras*, available at: https://www.restituciondetierras.gov.co/documents/10184/34449/Programa+de+Proyectos+Productivos+para+población+beneficiaria+de+Restitución+de+Tierras/50743dd5-75ab-472c-8ff6-ce710755bf95.

Unidad de Víctimas, *ABC del Modelo de Operación con Enfoque Diferencial y de Género*, 27 February 2017, available at: https://www.unidadvictimas.gov.co/sites/default/files/documentosbiblioteca/abcinstrumentalizacionmodeloconenfoquediferencialydegenero.pdf.

Unidad de Víctimas, *Boletín Fichas Estadísticas Nacional*, 2020, available at: http://fichaestrategica.unidadvictimas.gov.co/.

Unidad de Víctimas, *Elementos Para la Incorporación del Enfoque Psicosocial en la Atención, Asistencia y Reparación a las Víctimas*, 2014, available at: https://issuu.com/tayis/docs/elementos_para_la_incorporaci__n_de.

Unidad de Víctimas, *Guía Operativa Para la Implementación de Acciones de Enfoque Diferencial y de Género en los Procesos de Asistencia y Reparación a las Víctimas*, 27 February 2017, available at: https://www.unidadvictimas.gov.co/sites/default/files/documentosbiblioteca/guiaoperativaparalaimplementaciondeaccionesdeenfoquediferencialydegeneroenlaatencionyreparacionalasv.pdf.

Unidad de Víctimas, *Manual de Criterios de Valoración V2*, 2017, available at: https://www.unidadvictimas.gov.co/es/manual-criterios-de-valoracion-v2/37950.

Unidad de Víctimas, *Modelo de Reparación Colectiva*, 2018, available at: https://www.unidadvictimas.gov.co/es/modelo-de-reparacion-colectiva/43808.

Unidad de Víctimas, *Proceso de Acompañamiento al Retorno, Reubicación o Integración Local*, 2015, available at: https://www.unidadvictimas.gov.co/es/prevención-y-atención-de-emergencias/proceso-de-acompañamiento-al-retorno-reubicación-o-integración.

Unidad de Víctimas, *Retornos y Reubicaciones - Hacia la Reparación Integral a Víctimas del Desplazamiento Forzado*, 2015, available at: https://www.unidadvictimas.gov.co/es/escuela-de-reparaciones/retornos-y-reubicaciones-hacia-la-reparación-integral-las-v%C3%ADctimas-del.

van Boven, Theo, *The United Nations Basic Principles and Guidelines on the Right to a Remedy and Reparation for Victims of Gross Violations of International Human Rights Law and Serious Violations of Intenrational Humanitarian Law*, United Nations Audiovisual Library, 2010, available at: https://legal.un.org/avl/pdf/ha/ga_60-147/ga_60-147_e.pdf.

Washington Office on Latin America, *Colombia - Don't Call it a Model*, 2010, available at: https://www.wola.org/2010/07/colombia-dont-call-it-a-model/.

Wilson, *FARC During the Peace Process*, Perry Center Occasional Paper, November 2020, available at: https://www.williamjperrycenter.org/sites/default/files/publication_associated_files/FARC%20During%20the%20Peace%20Process%20.pdf.

Zweites Deutsches Fernsehen, *Günter Gaus "Zur Person" - Interview With Hannah Arendt*, 28 October 1964, available at: https://www.youtube.com/watch?v=dsoImQfVsO4.